RE-MEMBER

SERIES ON TRANSITIONAL JUSTICE

The Series on *Transitional Justice* offers a platform for high-quality research within the rapidly growing field of transitional justice. The research is, of necessity inter-disciplinary in nature, drawing from disciplines such as law, political science, history, sociology, criminology, anthropology and psychology, as well as from various specialised fields of study such as human rights, victimology and peace studies. Furthermore, the research is international in outlook, drawing on the knowledge and experience of academics and other specialists in many different regions of the world.

The series is aimed at a variety of audiences who are either working or interested in fields such as crime and justice; human rights; humanitarian law and human security; conflict resolution and peace building. These audiences include academics, researchers, students, policy makers, practitioners, non-governmental organisations and the media.

All books published within the series are subject to a double-blind peer review by recognised authorities in the field.

Published titles within the series:

1. Stephen Peté and Max Du Plessis, *Repairing the Past? International Perspectives on Reparations for Gross Human Rights Abuses* (2007), 978-90-5095-492-1
2. Laura Stovel, *Long Road Home, Building Reconciliation and Trust in Post-War Sierra Leone* (2010), 978-94-000-0028-5
3. Andy Aitchison, *Making the Transition. International Intervention, State-Building and Criminal Justice Reform in Bosnia and Herzegovina* (2011), 978-94-000-0140-4
4. Stef Vandeginste, *Stones left unturned. Law and Transitional Justice in Burundi* (2010), 978-94-000-0115-2
5. Antoine Buyse (ed.), *Margins of Conflict. The ECHR and Transitions to and from Armed Conflict* (2011), 978-94-000-0157-2
6. Gaby Oré Aguilar and Felipe Gómez Isa (eds.), *Rethinking Transitions. Equality and Social Justice in Societies Emerging from Conflict* (2011), 978-1-78068-003-3
7. Richard Zajac Sannerholm, *Rule of Law after War. Ideologies, Norms and Methods* (2012), 978-1-78068-008-8
8. Nicola Palmer, Phil Clark and Danielle Granville (chief editors), *Critical Perspectives in Transitional Justice* (2011), 978-1-78068-035-4
9. Edda Kristjánsdóttir, André Nollkaemper and Cedric Ryngaert (eds.), *International Law in Domestic Courts: Rule of Law Reform in Post-conflict States* (2012), 978-1-78068-041-5
10. Bas van Stokkom, Neelke Doorn and Paul van Tongeren (eds.), *Public Forgiveness in Post-Conflict Contexts* (2012), 978-1-78068-044-6

Series on Transitional Justice, Volume 11

RE-MEMBER

Rehabilitation, Reintegration and Reconciliation of War-Affected Children

Edited by

Ilse DERLUYN, Cindy MELS,
Stephan PARMENTIER and
Wouter VANDENHOLE

intersentia

Cambridge – Antwerp – Portland

Intersentia Publishing Ltd.
Trinity House | Cambridge Business Park | Cowley Road
Cambridge | CB4 0WZ | United Kingdom
Tel.: +44 1223 393 753 | Email: mail@intersentia.co.uk

Distribution for the UK:
Hart Publishing Ltd.
16C Worcester Place
Oxford OX1 2JW
UK
Tel.: +44 1865 517 530
Email: mail@hartpub.co.uk

Distribution for the USA and Canada:
International Specialized Book Services
920 NE 58th Ave. Suite 300
Portland, OR 97213
USA
Tel.: +1 800 944 6190 (toll free)
Email: info@isbs.com

Distribution for Austria:
Neuer Wissenschaftlicher Verlag
Argentinierstraße 42/6
1040 Wien
Austria
Tel.: +43 1 535 61 03 24
Email: office@nwv.at

Distribution for other countries:
Intersentia Publishing nv
Groenstraat 31
2640 Mortsel
Belgium
Tel.: +32 3 680 15 50
Email: mail@intersentia.be

Re-Member. Rehabilitation, Reintegration and Reconciliation of War-Affected Children
Ilse Derluyn, Cindy Mels, Stephan Parmentier and Wouter Vandenhole (eds.)

Artwork on cover: Author Jan Jordaan, title 'Hurt', medium Linocut, 1999. From the *Universal Declaration of Human Rights – International Print Portfolio, Article 5*, published by Art for Humanity, South Africa, 1999

GPRC
Guaranteed
Peer Reviewed
Content

ISBN 978-94-000-0027-8
NUR 828

British Library Cataloguing in Publication Data. A catalogue record for this book is available from the British Library.

PREFACE

Radhika Coomaraswamy
Special Representative of the United Nations Secretary-General for Children and Armed Conflict

I am pleased to write this preface on the occasion of the publication of the proceedings coming out of the international conference on 'Rehabilitation and Reintegration of War-Affected Children', held in Brussels, Belgium, in October 2009.

CHILD SOLDIERS

One important category of children in armed conflict are the many thousands of child soldiers who are recruited and trained to play an important role in the violence. In relation to this category of children, it is worthwhile to draw attention to two major aspects, i.e. the reintegration of these children and the accountability of those who recruit them.

The reintegration of child soldiers has been a complex issue which has tested even the best programmes on the ground. The Paris Principles of 2007 give us the best guidance, as they contain key insights that need implementation and relate to social and economic rights of children, as well as their rehabilitation and reintegration. Three overarching guidelines configure the entire reintegration effort. Firstly, children must be heard and be enabled to participate in all decisions affecting them, so as to ensure that these decisions are taken in their best interest. Some children for example may think that they are wasting their time at school while they want to learn practical skills. Secondly, non-discrimination is an absolute must in any reintegration programme. It is important that former child soldiers do not receive a preferential treatment over those who have not been associated with armed groups. Also, particular attention should be given to girls, so as to ensure that they are involved in the reintegration effort and to see to it that their specific needs are being met. Thirdly, the capacity of reintegration programmes and the actors involved should be strengthened in order to ensure their self-sustainability. This is particularly important when it comes to schools and hospitals.

Apart from these overarching guidelines, the same Paris Principles also contain four operational principles that must be implemented to strengthen the effectiveness of the programmes geared at reintegrating child soldiers into society. First of all, the programmes must not be implemented in a generalistic and abstract manner but in a context-specific way that allows the particular circumstances of the children to be taken into account. Furthermore, programmes should not be individualistic only but also be family-focused since strengthening family ties reduces the risk of re-recruitment of children and is beneficial to their development in general. However, programmes aimed at the family require longer term support, and local ownership of the programmes. This brings us to the third operational principle, being the engagement of the local community. This does not only reinforce the sustainability of the programmes, but also allows other children in the community to benefit from any reintegration programme. Finally, the training for livelihood and skills should take an important place in any reintegration and rehabilitation programme. In this respect, it is important to further build upon the skills that the children have already acquired.

However, it is crystal clear that tackling the issue of child recruitment can not only be done by focusing on the victim. The other side, namely the accountability for those who recruit children must be paid attention to. In this respect, the efforts made by the International Criminal Court in recent years to bring to trial child recruiters already make a difference on the ground. Moreover, prosecutions at the national level should also constitute an integral part of strengthening the accountability of war criminals.

A more difficult issue is whether children who have perpetrated crimes should be prosecuted for their actions. Here, the Paris Principles are quite clear, stating that these children should not be prosecuted or punished but their crimes should be addressed through programmes of alternative justice, restorative justice, or truth and reconciliation processes which at the same time guarantee their legal protection as minors.

CHILDREN AND ARMED CONFLICT IN GENERAL

Since assuming the function of Special Representative of the Secretary-General for Children and Armed Conflict in April 2006, my office has sought to develop a strong partnership with the academic community with the broad objective of facilitating research to fill the critical gaps in knowledge that hamper advocacy and programmatic responses for children that are relevant to the needs of child protection practitioners on the ground; I therefore welcome the remarks of all the academics in this volume along with their activist partners who have done excellent and groundbreaking research on the important topic of the reintegration of children associated with armed groups. Drawing from extensive field experience and the work of activists and UN colleagues, the research gives us the state of the art knowledge in this field.

It will be equally important that the results of this conference be widely disseminated to all stakeholders involved, not the least to the children affected by armed conflict themselves.

FOREWORD

A Children's Rights Approach to Recovery and Reintegration: An Agenda for Action

Jaap E. Doek
Former chairperson of the Committee on the Rights of the Child

This book is a most welcome contribution to the growing body of multidisciplinary scholarship on children's rights. By focusing on recovery, reconciliation and reintegration, it expands the scope of much of the literature on children in armed conflict from the recruitment and participation of child soldiers to the broader questions of rebuilding societies and healing and reintegrating children who have been affected by armed conflict.

I will use the opportunity given to me to write a foreword to set an agenda for action at the international level that may facilitate reconciliation, recovery and reintegration. I will insist in particular on the need for prevention; universal ratification of the Optional Protocol to the Convention on the Rights of the Child on the Involvement of Children in Armed Conflict (OPAC); the adoption of the Paris Principles and Guidelines by the UN General Assembly; and the establishment of a fund for the recovery and reintegration of children affected by armed conflict (CAACs). But first, by way of preliminary question, I will examine whether the recovery and reintegration of CAACs is a matter of human rights or international humanitarian law. Before I present my agenda for action, I will introduce a children's rights approach, in which I will try to identify the specific rights of war-affected children and the related obligations of states and others.

1. REHABILITATION AND REINTEGRATION OF WAR-AFFECTED CHILDREN: A HUMAN RIGHTS MATTER (?)

1.1. INTERNATIONAL HUMANITARIAN LAW

International instruments of humanitarian law are important for the protection of children affected by war, notably the Geneva Convention relative to Protection of Civilian Persons in Time of War (1949).[1] They contain various provisions for the protection of children under the age of 15, i.e. parties to a conflict have to take measures necessary to ensure that children under fifteen who are orphaned or are separated from their families as a result of the war are not left to their own resources and that their maintenance and education are facilitated in all circumstances. Furthermore, parties to the conflict must endeavour to arrange for all children under twelve to be identified by the wearing of identity discs or by some other means (Art. 24). The Convention also contains provisions for the protection of children in occupied territories, on the internment of children and on their right to education (Arts. 50, 82 and 94).

Protocol I to the Geneva Convention (1977) provides for the special protection of children in Article 77 with the well-known rule that children under 15 years shall not be recruited or participate in hostilities. These rules were also included in Article 38 CRC, despite many efforts in the open-ended working group on the drafting of the CRC to set a higher standard for recruitment and involvement in hostilities.[2] Article 4, para. 3 of Protocol II to the Geneva Convention (1977) requires that children shall be provided with the care and aid they need and in particular shall receive education, while steps shall be taken to facilitate reunification with their families. It furthermore allows for the removal of children, with consent of their parents or other responsible persons, to safer areas.[3]

So international humanitarian law, in particular the Geneva Conventions of 1949 and Protocols I and II of 1977, is relevant, although the provisions focus more on protection as such than on recovery and reintegration. This should be understood in light of the fact that these instruments focus on the protection of

---

1 The Geneva Convention is applicable to all cases of declared war or of any other armed conflict between two or more states (Art. 2) and its application shall cease (in principle) on the general close of military operations (Art. 6). Protocol I supplements all four Geneva Conventions and deals with (among others) the protection and treatment of wounded, sick and shipwrecked persons, with missing and dead persons and with the status of combatants and prisoners of war and measures in favour of women and children. Protocol II applies to all armed conflicts not covered by Protocol I (Art. 1) and which take place in the territory of the contracting State Party between its armed forces and dissident armed forces or other organised armed groups.

2 S. Detrick, *The UN Convention on the Rights of the Child. A Guide to the "Travaux Préparatoires"*, Martinus Nijhoff, Dordrecht/Boston/London, 1992; L.J. Le Blanc, *The Convention on the Rights of the Child. United Nations Lawmaking on Human Rights*, University of Nebraska Press, Lincoln, 1995; UNOHCHR, *Legislative History of the Convention on the Rights of the Child*, United Nations, New York/Geneva, 2007 (UN doc. HR/PUB/07/1).

3 D. Fleck (ed.), *The Handbook of Humanitarian Law in Armed Conflicts*, Oxford University Press, Oxford, 1995; C. Hamilton and T. Abu El-Haj, 'Armed Conflict: The Protection of Children under International Law', (1997) 5 *The International Journal of Children's Rights* 1–46.

civilians *during* wars or armed conflicts. It is also self-evident that the process of recovery and social reintegration should not be put on hold until the war is over. Already during the period of armed conflict efforts in that regard should be made and these efforts need to be supported by the full implementation of the provisions of humanitarian law for the protection of children. This is confirmed by the reference to the obligations of States Parties under international humanitarian law in both Article 38 CRC and Article 22 ACRWC, i.e. to ensure the care and protection of children affected by armed conflicts in accordance with international humanitarian law.

1.2. THE PARIS COMMITMENTS AND PRINCIPLES AND GUIDELINES

Two of the leading documents on the recovery and reintegration of children affected by armed conflict are the *Paris Commitments to protect children from unlawful recruitment or use by armed forces or armed groups* and the *Principles and Guidelines on children associated with armed forces or armed groups*, adopted in February 2007 by a group of states at a conference in Paris. A discussion of these important documents, currently endorsed by 100 states, goes beyond the scope of a foreword (see Nylund's chapter), but I was and still am surprised that the time and energy invested was not used (perhaps with some extra effort) to have the Principles and Guidelines adopted by the UN General Assembly. UN Guidelines have a higher status and are morally stronger than a document adopted at a conference and endorsed by less than half of the UN member states.[4]

Remarkably, the Paris Commitments make only a very limited reference to the CRC, except for a call to ratify the CRC and OPAC as a matter of priority.[5] In §17 for instance, the endorsing states commit themselves to ensuring that any programmes or actions to prevent the recruitment and use of children and to support unlawfully recruited or used children are based on humanitarian law. In §19 on funding child protection, no reference is made to the CRC either.

The Paris Principles and Guidelines do recognize as overarching principles among others the four principles of the CRC: non-discrimination (Art. 2), the best interests of the child as a primary consideration (Art. 3), the right to life, survival and development (Art. 6) and the right of the child to respect for her/his

4 It is even more puzzling that they are not UN guidelines given the very clear and consistent commitment of the Security Council to preventing and reducing the recruitment and involvement of children in armed conflicts; see Resolutions 1261 (1999), 1314 (2000), 1379 (2001), 1460 (2003), 1539 (2004) and 1612 (2005).

5 As mentioned in the preamble. It is only in the paragraphs on child perpetrators of (serious) war crimes that treatment is required in line with the CRC (§12).

views and participation (Art. 12). The chapter on release and integration does not, however, make specific reference to the rights of the child as enshrined in the CRC. It leaves us with the question whether the recovery and reintegration of war-affected children must be considered as a matter of humanitarian law or as a matter of human rights.

1.3. REHABILITATION AND REINTEGRATION: A HUMAN RIGHTS IMPERATIVE

The question whether human rights law is relevant to rehabilitation and reintegration is inter alia triggered by the fact that Article 38, §4 CRC refers to an obligation under international humanitarian law and by the discussion of the status of the OPAC, Article 6 of which deals among others with measures to be taken to provide children recruited for or used in hostilities with all appropriate assistance for full recovery and social reintegration. There are three possible categorisations of the OPAC: as a human rights instrument, as part of international humanitarian law, or as a hybrid instrument straddling the divide between human rights and international humanitarian law (IHL).

Bennoune has compiled and analysed the arguments and consequences of each of the three options.[6] With reference to the drafting history and the text of the OPAC, the jurisprudence of the CRC Committee and the views of NGOs and experts, she came to the conclusion that the OPAC is a human rights instrument. To consider OPAC as an IHL instrument would limit its application to situations of armed conflict and undermine the protection of children and their human rights, or at least some of them, which call for the protection of the individual at all times, in war and peace alike. The option to treat the OPAC as a hybrid instrument could allow for innovative human rights interpretations while still recognizing the important connections to and bases in IHL. But the downside is that doing so muddles the waters and thereby possibly gives rise to a lot of confusion. Augmenting Bennoune's well-founded conclusion, I'd like to add the following specifically in relation to the matter of rehabilitation and reintegration: even if one limits the scope of the OPAC to situations of armed conflict, we should emphasise that the protection provided under the CRC applies to all children at all times, in war and peace alike. Thus, and regardless of one's opinion on the status of the OPAC, the rehabilitation and reintegration of war-affected children is a human rights imperative.

---

6 K. Bennoune, *Memorandum on The Nature and Sphere of Application of the Optional Protocol to the Convention on the Rights of the Child on the Involvement of Children in Armed Conflict prepared for the Coalition to Stop the Use of Child Soldiers* (May 2009, on file with the author).

2. THE INTERNATIONAL LEGAL FRAMEWORK: GENERAL OBSERVATIONS

The major international human rights instruments that provide the legal framework for the rehabilitation and reintegration of war-affected children are the CRC and its OPAC, and for African countries additionally the ACRWC.[7] Discussion of the legal framework requires a kind of definition of rehabilitation and reintegration. To avoid the battle with words which usually accompanies efforts to define a concept, let me just make some 'defining' remarks:

a. the CRC Committee does not like the word 'rehabilitation' because of its possible connotation with disabilities. Therefore – and in line with the text of Article 6 OPAC and the CRC[8] – I will use the term 'recovery' instead of 'rehabilitation';
b. recovery measures focus on repairing as good as possible the physical and psychological trauma that the child has suffered from participating in armed conflict or as a witness of the effects of hostilities;
c. measures of social reintegration include efforts to reunite the child with her/his family and community of origin as much as possible, and to support the child in developing her/his personality and talents to their fullest potential, notably through education/vocational training and in finding healthy and secure employment or work. In short: all efforts to support the child in her/his full and harmonious development while assuming a constructive role in society;
d. for children recruited or used in armed conflicts, the recovery and integration process starts with demobilisation or other forms of release from the armed forces/groups concerned (including disarmament, where applicable). I will not deal with these measures and only note that Article 6 OPAC requires States Parties to take all feasible measures to ensure that children within their jurisdiction who have been recruited and used in hostilities are demobilised or otherwise released from service. The CRC and the ACRWC do not contain specific provisions in that regard.

In what follows, I will make some general observations on the rights-based approach, followed by a discussion of some specific problems: the criminal responsibility of children, children with disabilities, and displacement.

---

7 The SAARC Convention on Regional Arrangements for the Promotion of Child Welfare in South Asia (Kathmandu, 2002) does not contain specific provisions relating to children affected by war.

8 The term 'rehabilitation' only appears in Art. 23 (on children with disabilities) and Art. 24 CRC (rehabilitation). Art. 39 uses the terms 'recovery' and 'social reintegration' in relation to child victims of, *inter alia*, abuse, exploitation, cruel or inhuman treatment and armed conflict.

2.1. OPTIONAL PROTOCOL ON THE INVOLVEMENT OF CHILDREN IN ARMED CONFLICT (OPAC)

Given its specific nature, we will first look at the Optional Protocol on the Involvement of Children in Armed Conflict for provisions on the recovery and reintegration of child victims of war. Adopted by the UN General Assembly in Resolution A/RES/54/263 of 25 May 2000, this Protocol requires States parties to take all feasible measures to ensure that children (persons under the age of 18) do not take a direct part in hostilities (Art. 1). Furthermore, the OPAC prohibits the compulsory recruitment of children into armed forces (Art. 2) and armed groups (Art. 4). It also requires States parties to the OPAC to set a minimum age at least at 16 for voluntary recruitment, while ensuring that this recruitment is genuinely voluntary and with the informed consent of the child and her/his parents or legal guardians.

This Optional Protocol is an amendment to Article 38 CRC, which sets the minimum age for recruitment and direct participation in hostilities at the age of fifteen. In this regard it should be noted that the African Charter on the Rights and Welfare of the Child (ACRWC) has set the age at 18, requiring States Parties to this Charter to ensure that no child shall take a direct part in hostilities and to refrain in particular from recruiting any child (art. 22 ACRWC). This standard is also known as the 'straight 18 standard'.

The attention given in this Protocol to recovery and reintegration is very limited. Article 6, §3 OPAC contains the following provision:

> States Parties shall take all feasible measures to ensure that persons within its jurisdiction recruited or used in hostilities contrary to the present Protocol are demobilized or otherwise released from service. States Parties shall, when necessary, accord such persons all appropriate assistance for their physical and psychological recovery and their social reintegration.

This provision limits the obligation of the state to the provision of assistance for the recovery and social reintegration of children *recruited or used in hostilities*. It does not cover all other children who are victims of war. This is certainly disappointing, but can simply be explained by the fact that the focus of this Optional Protocol is on the recruitment and involvement of children in armed conflict. Furthermore, Article 6 OPAC does not specify the nature, the timing, the duration or the setting of this assistance. This is therefore a missed opportunity to provide for specific principles and rules for the recovery and social reintegration of *all* war-affected children, including the role of parents and the community. The OPAC (Art. 6) does not make a specific reference to international humanitarian law when requiring States Parties to provide assistance for the recovery and social reintegration of war-affected children.

Important is Article 7 OPAC, requiring States Parties to cooperate in the implementation of the OPAC, with special attention to preventing the violation of the OPAC's rules and to recovery and social reintegration, which are again limited to the category of children mentioned above.[9] Article 6, §2 OPAC contains a provision that is often overlooked: rich States Parties shall provide (technical and/or financial) assistance via multilateral, bilateral or other programmes or 'inter alia through a voluntary fund (...)'.

The Optional Protocol is an annex to the CRC, and has to be interpreted in connection with and/or in the context of the CRC. This approach is confirmed in the preamble to the OPAC, stating inter alia that the States Parties are to bear in mind 'that... observance of applicable human rights instruments [is] indispensable for the full protection of children, in particular during armed conflicts and foreign occupation'. States also reaffirm 'that the rights of children require special protection' and call for 'continuous improvement of the situation of children without distinction, as well as for their development and education in conditions of peace and security'.

From these statements it is clear that the protection of war-affected children should not only be based on provisions in the OPAC, but should be governed by all the rights enshrined in the CRC and when applicable (also) those in the ACRWC, e.g. all States Parties to the CRC that have also ratified the OPAC are bound by the obligation to implement that Convention fully. In other words: the CRC is the legal framework for the recovery and social reintegration of all war-affected children and requires a comprehensive and holistic child rights-based approach. This is (at least implicitly) confirmed by the reporting rule that, after a separate initial report on the implementation of this Protocol, any further information shall be included in the regular reports on the implementation of the CRC as a whole (Art. 8, §2 OPAC). Reporting under the OPAC thus becomes an integral part of the overall process of implementing the CRC. The provisions of the OPAC are meant to amend, strengthen or specify provisions in the CRC.

2.2. THE CONVENTION ON THE RIGHTS OF THE CHILD

The key building bloc of the legal framework is Article 2 CRC: States Parties shall respect and *ensure* the rights enshrined in the CRC to each child within their

9 For unknown reasons, Art. 7 OPAC uses the term 'rehabilitation' whereas Art. 6 talks about 'recovery'.

jurisdiction without discrimination of any kind. It means that all children affected by armed conflict, and not only those who are/have been recruited or used in hostilities (via Demobilisation, Disarmament and Reintegration (DDR) programmes) are entitled to the maximum enjoyment of their rights under the CRC. Article 3 ACRWC contains a similar provision stating that every child shall be entitled to the enjoyment of the rights and freedoms recognized and guaranteed in the Charter.

These provisions are not only a solid legal foundation for recovery and integration programmes as an obligation of the State, but also are binding guidance for the content and the implementation of these programmes. This is particularly important given the fact that the OPAC limits the obligations of States Parties to the provision of 'all appropriate assistance' (see Art. 6, §3 OPAC and earlier remarks in this regard). It means inter alia that recovery and reintegration programmes for all war-affected children, both in their development and implementation, should respect and implement all the rights of the child enshrined in the CRC. For practical reasons I will limit myself to highlighting the importance of some of these rights.

First and given the CRC Committee's emphasis on the obligation to take general measures of implementation (see General Comment No. 5), programmes for the recovery and social reintegration of children affected by armed conflict should as much as possible be an integral part of a comprehensive, well coordinated and adequately resourced national policy for the implementation of children's rights. This will avoid these programmes becoming narrowly focused on immediate, short-term responses to the trauma children have suffered as a result of their experiences during armed conflict and also promote benefits for the children from, for example, long-term health, education and social policies. They have, like all other children in the country, the right to the highest attainable standard of health and this requires access to all available health care services (Art. 24 CRC). They must be provided with free and compulsory primary education and secondary education and vocational training, either for free or with financial assistance in case of need (Art. 28 CRC). Furthermore, they have the right to a standard of living adequate for their physical, mental, spiritual, moral and social development (Art. 27 CRC). These and other rights in the CRC, such as the right to protection from all forms of violence and exploitation (Arts. 19, 32–36 CRC), but also the right to rest, leisure and to engage in play, recreational and cultural activities, apply to all children, including children affected by armed conflict. It is important to underscore this in order to ensure that these children are not provided only with short-term support for their recovery and reintegration. This recovery requires full and ongoing respect for and implementation of their rights.

I would like to emphasise the following:

- All children affected by armed conflict should be provided with meaningful opportunities to express their views and to participate actively in the preparation and implementation of the programmes, while ensuring that their views are given due weight (Art. 12);[10]
- The primary responsibility of parents for the upbringing of their children, including the responsibility to secure the conditions of living necessary for the child's development (Arts. 18 and 27 CRC), implies that they should be actively involved as much as possible in the recovery and reintegration of their children. In this regard, it is important to note that States Parties must respect the rights of parents and, where applicable, of members of the extended family and the community, to provide the child, in accordance with her or his evolving capacities, appropriate direction and guidance in the exercise by the child of the rights recognized in the CRC (Art. 5). This obligation indicates that not only the parents but also the extended family and the community should play a role in the recovery and reintegration process.
- States Parties have the obligation to provide parents with support and assistance in the performance of their child-rearing responsibilities, inter alia by establishing institutions, facilities and services for the care of children (Art. 18) and by providing, in case of need, material assistance and support programmes, particularly with regard to nutrition, clothing and housing (Art. 27).

These provisions of the CRC indicate clearly that recovery and reintegration programmes require the involvement not only of the children themselves but also of their parents, extended family and community, and of the government to undertake measures to the maximum extent of its available resources (Art. 4). This means that the state must provide as much human and financial resource as possible for the implementation of the programmes and should seek international support and cooperation. As the CRC Committee stated in General Comment no. 5: 'Whatever their economic circumstances, States are required to undertake all possible measures towards the realization of the rights of the child, paying special attention to the most disadvantaged groups.'

The ACRWC contains similar provisions in Article 14 (on health care), Article 11 (on education), Article 20 (on assuring an adequate standard of living) and Articles 15, 27–29 (on exploitation). Finally, in the provisions specific to armed conflict, both the CRC and the ACRWC (Art. 38 and Art. 22 respectively)

---

10 With regard to the interpretation and implementation of Art. 12 CRC, see General Comment No. 12 of the CRC Committee: *The Right of the Child to be Heard*, UN Doc. CRC/C/GC/12 of 1 July 2009.

require States Parties to take all feasible measures in accordance with their obligations under international humanitarian law to ensure the protection and care of children who are affected by armed conflict.[11]

Let me summarise my general observations. The CRC is *the* best international legal framework for the recovery and social reintegration of *all* war-affected children, because it is applicable to *all* children in a war-affected country without discrimination of any kind. It will therefore contribute to an all-inclusive policy of care and protection covering all children and tailored to their specific needs. The CRC also provides the specific rights to, for example, health care, education, adequate living conditions that are critical elements of an effective long-term process of recovery and social reintegration. The ACRWC confirms this approach with some important additions (e.g. on the elimination of harmful traditional practices).

The assistance to recovery and social reintegration that States Parties to OPAC must provide is limited to children recruited or used in armed conflict. This is disappointing, but can simply be explained by the fact that the OPAC's focus is on the recruitment and involvement of children in armed conflict, and more specifically on setting specific age limits in that regard. Unfortunately, this focus has resulted in a missed opportunity to provide for much more specific principles/rules for various aspects of transitional justice and in particular for the recovery and social reintegration of *all* war-effected children (including the role and responsibilities of parents and communities). The one specific opportunity provided by the OPAC, i.e. an international voluntary fund, has been neglected.

Finally, an important complement to the CRC as *the* international legal framework is international humanitarian law. IHL contains various provisions with a focus on the protection and care of children during 'officially' declared wars or other armed conflict. However, IHL does not define a child as a person under 18, but limits it specific attention for children to those under the age of fifteen.

3. SOME SPECIAL PROBLEMS

The efforts to assist war-affected children with their full recovery and social reintegration face many problems and challenges. While this is not the place to discuss these problems and challenges in detail, from a rights perspective there is reason to draw attention to some of these problems.

---

11 It should be noted that Art. 22 ACRWC contains also the very general clause that States Parties shall undertake to respect and ensure respect for rules of international humanitarian law applicable in armed conflicts which affect the child.

3.1. CRIMINAL RESPONSIBILITY OF CAACs

One of the problems with the recovery and social reintegration of war-affected children is the fact that some of them have committed very serious crimes which can qualify as crimes against humanity and/or war crimes. The Rome Statute clearly states that the International Criminal Court has no jurisdiction regarding such crimes if committed by a person below the age of 18. So it is left to the national authorities to decide how to treat children who allegedly committed very serious (war) crimes. These may be dealt with through a Truth and Reconciliation Commission or under the rules of the criminal code.

It is in my opinion not a contribution to full recovery and social reintegration just to ignore the (suspected) commission of crimes or, even worse, to treat it as a taboo issue (don't ask, don't tell). It is in line with respect for the child as a rights-holder also to hold him/her responsible for the serious violations of the rights of others he/she may have committed. The full implementation of rules for juvenile justice in the CRC (Arts. 37 and 40) and the related international standards (Beijing and Havana Rules) provides for such accountability with the clearly stated commitment to treat the child in a manner consistent with the promotion of the child's sense of dignity and worth and with the aim of promoting the child's reintegration and the child's assuming a constructive role in society.

In line with Article 40, §3, b CRC, measures should be taken to deal with children accused of having infringed the penal law without resorting to judicial proceedings. In other words, when appropriate not penal sanctions but alternative measures should be applied. First and foremost, juvenile justice for these children should be restorative justice that reconciles the child with her/his family and community with a view to her/his social reintegration. The CRC Committee is of the opinion that alternative measures such as restorative justice should not be limited to minor offences.[12] As was stated in the Lima Declaration (2009) on Restorative Juvenile Justice:

> Experience shows that restorative juvenile justice can also play an important role in addressing serious crimes. For example, in many armed conflicts children are used as child soldiers and forced to commit unspeakable crimes targeting especially their own family members, their neighbours and their community. Restorative justice is very often the only way of bringing reconciliation to victims and offenders alike in a war-torn society where victims of offences suffer as do child offenders, having been forced to commit offences. Without such reconciliation the reintegration of child

---

12 For more information on the interpretation and implementation of the CRC in this regard, see General Comment No 10 of the CRC Committee on *Children's Rights in Juvenile Justice*, UN doc. CRC/C/GC/10 of 9 February 2007.

soldiers in their communities is not possible, much to the detriment of the then ostracised child as well as the community bereft of workforce and under threat of criminal behaviour of the excluded child.[13]

3.2. CHILDREN WITH DISABILITIES

Amongst the very visible effects of war are the children with disabilities resulting from intentional amputations or explosions of landmines and other devices/ weapons. Unfortunately, the end of war does not put an end to the risk of children being disabled by landmine explosions. Many international efforts have been and are being undertaken to prevent and address the problems of Anti-Personnel Landmines (e.g. the Ottawa Convention 1997 and the Guidelines for Landmine and Unexploded Ordnance Awareness Education).

Special attention should also be given to the rights of children with disabilities in the context of recovery and reintegration programmes. Awareness raising and education on the dangers of landmines and other unexploded devices are important, but strong, systematic and ongoing efforts have to be made to ensure that children with disabilities enjoy a full and decent life in conditions which ensure dignity, promote self-reliance and facilitate the child's active participation in the community (Art. 23 CRC and Art. 7 Convention on the Rights of Persons with Disabilities – CRPD, 2006). It requires not only well-trained people to treat the disabilities, but also ongoing support for the families of these children (e.g. the growing bodies and bones of these children will require on average a new prosthesis every six months). Prevention of discrimination and access to regular, or if necessary special, education are other issues that require special attention. These and other measures which have to be taken by the State as much as possible with the involvement of the children themselves and with the support of NGOs and other sections of civil society are elaborated in the CRC Committee's General Comment no. 9 on the rights of children with disabilities. It is clear from Article 23 and other provisions in the CRC and from the CRPD that the protection and realisation of the rights of children with disabilities must be an integral part of the legal framework for recovery and social reintegration programmes.[14]

---

13 The Lima Declaration (2009) on Restorative Juvenile Justice was adopted at the First International Conference on Restorative Juvenile Justice, held in Lima (Peru) on 2–7 November 2009. See also ECOSOC Resolution 2002/12 Basic Principles on the use of restorative justice programmes in criminal matters.

14 See also *The Paris Principles and Guidelines on children associated with armed forces or armed groups*, §§7.50 – 7.53 (Paris, February 2007).

3.3. DISPLACED CHILDREN

Many millions of children are displaced (internally or across borders) by armed conflict and are the most frequent victims of violence, disease, malnutrition and death. They often become separated from their parents and families and are thereby exposed to far greater danger and exploitation. For instance, adolescents are especially vulnerable to forced recruitment, abduction, trafficking and sexual exploitation. These children have the right to receive special protection and humanitarian assistance in the enjoyment of their rights under the CRC. Efforts have to be made to trace the parents or other family members in order to obtain information necessary for the child's reunification with her or his family. If parents or family cannot be found, the child must be provided the same protection as any other child permanently or temporarily deprived of her or his family environment for any reason (Arts. 22 and 20 CRC).

Displaced children have the same rights as other children to food, health care and education, as well as the right to preserve their identity and cultural, linguistic and inheritance rights. It should be noted that governments are responsible for the welfare of Internally Displaced Persons (IDPs), including children. Unfortunately, governments are often unable or unwilling to provide these children with the assistance and protection they are entitled to. Many IDP children live in refugee camps. Although intended as temporary refuge, they often become shelters where entire generations of children grow up. Ongoing efforts are needed for their safe return to their families and communities, but at the same time measures have to be taken to improve living conditions in the camps.

4. AN AGENDA FOR ACTION

4.1. PREVENTION

It may be considered too idealistic or even naïve, but we should continue to undertake efforts, and strengthen them where possible, to prevent children from becoming war-affected and therefore in need of rehabilitation and reintegration. We may never succeed in having a war-free world, but we must try to establish an effective worldwide prohibition on the recruitment of children and on their active involvement in armed conflict, and undertake all other available measures to prevent children from becoming victims of armed conflict. It goes well beyond the scope of this foreword to discuss in detail the many political, social, economic and other measures necessary to prevent armed conflict. I will limit myself to some observations on the measures that can and must be taken to stop the recruitment or enlistment of children in armed forces or groups and/or their active participation to hostilities.

To prevent children from becoming victims of armed conflict as a result of their recruitment and/or direct participation in armed forces or groups, the following actions should be taken:

- Maximum efforts to achieve the universal ratification of the Optional Protocol to the CRC on the Involvement of Children in Armed Conflict in order to establish a global and legally binding commitment to stopping the recruitment of children and/or their active involvement in armed conflicts, not only as combatants but in any other role. The OPAC entered in to force on 12 February 2002 and so far it has been ratified by 143 states, including the US, which has not yet ratified the CRC. More than 50 percent of the African states (32 out of 53) have ratified or acceded to the OPAC. In addition, so far 45 African states have ratified the ACRWC. If the remaining eight States ratify this Charter, all African states will be bound by the 'straight 18 standard'. I am pleased to see that upon my suggestion, the Special Representative of the Secretary General on children and armed conflict now conducts a global campaign ('Zero under Eighteen') for the universal ratification of the OPAC by 12 February 2012.
- Within the framework of the implementation of the OPAC, all states should establish a minimum age of 18 for both compulsory recruitment and voluntary enlistment in armed forces and for their involvement in armed conflict. These standards should also be applicable to armed groups – this is in fact already the case.[15] It should be noted that almost all African states that have ratified the OPAC have the minimum age for voluntary recruitment set at 18 years.[16]
- All States Parties to the OPAC should explicitly criminalise the violation of these standards and establish extra-territorial, preferably universal jurisdiction. In its Concluding Observations on the initial reports of States Parties, the CRC Committee systematically makes recommendations to that effect. The International Criminal Court only deals with the crimes of recruiting and using children below the age of 15 years in armed conflict. But if all States party to the OPAC take the measures suggested and effectively implement them, it will result in clear global standards with the message that no one who violates them will escape justice.[17] This would make a crucial

15 Art. 4 OPAC already sets these standards: 'Armed groups that are distinct from the armed forces of a State should not, under any circumstances, recruit or use in hostilities persons under the age of 18 years'. And: 'States Parties shall take all feasible measures to prevent such recruitment and use (...)'.

16 Only Cape Verde has a minimum age of 17 for voluntary recruitment while Egypt has set this age at 16 and at 18 for conscription.

17 Art. 6 OPAC requires States Parties to take all necessary legislative, administrative and other measures to ensure effective implementation and enforcement of the provisions of OPAC in their jurisdiction. But it does not specify the nature of these measures and is in that regard much weaker than the Optional Protocol on the sale of children, child prostitution and child

contribution – in addition to other measures – to a reduction in the number of children who are seriously affected by armed conflict.

4.2. ESTABLISHMENT OF A VOLUNTARY FUND

The establishment of an international voluntary fund has so far been neglected. Its feasibility should be actively explored in order to provide children, their parents and communities with the extra support they may need and with compensation for the violations of their rights.

I am not aware of any of the main players in this field (Special Representative of the UN Secretary General on Children and Armed Conflict, the Coalition to Stop the Use of Child Soldiers, UNICEF etc.) taking concerted or targeted actions to establish such a fund. This is most regrettable because such a voluntary fund could be used for:

- community support with a view to creating the necessary conditions for recovery and social reintegration of *all* war-affected children, e.g. by improving health care and education;
- individual support for war-affected children, in particular children mentally and/or physically disabled as a result of armed conflict. This support should provide for ongoing assistance and guidance for children with disabilities and could, where appropriate, provide financial compensation for the harm done to a child, a family or a community.

I would like to refer to the marginal impact of repeated expressions of concern about the impunity of the people responsible for the very serious crimes committed during armed conflict. Given this reality and in light of the right of everyone to an effective remedy for acts violating her or his fundamental rights (Art. 8 UDHR; Art. 2 ICCPR), would it not be a simple matter of justice to have an international fund that can provide at least some remedies?

---

pornography. This OP contains provisions on the criminality of specified acts (Art. 3), on the establishment of extraterritorial jurisdiction (Art. 4) and on extradition (Art. 5).

CONTENTS

PART I
SETTING THE SCENE: THREE DISCIPLINARY PERSPECTIVES

INTRODUCTION

Children Affected by Armed Conflict at the Intersection of Three Fields of Study

Cindy Mels, Ilse Derluyn, Stephan Parmentier and Wouter Vandenhole

1. GENERAL BACKGROUND

The recruitment of child soldiers has been hitting the headlines in politics and the media for many years. However, many commentators seem to forget that a much broader circle of children is affected by armed conflicts in general. While there are no reliable estimates of the number of children currently living in war-affected areas worldwide, UNICEF (2006) reports that conflicts in the decade to 2006 killed more than two million children and left another six million injured or permanently disabled, twenty million homeless, and over one million separated from their parents.[1] Countless others have been orphaned, raped or forced to witness acts of violence.[2] It is estimated that during war, 5 per cent of child deaths result from direct violence and 95 per cent from malnutrition, illness or infection.[3] Even when children are not directly affected by exposure to violence or disease, their lives may be changed by the burden of displacement, the loss of caregivers, socio-economic hardship, the destruction of infrastructure, crops and livestock, etc.[4] In consequence, the many challenges in dealing with children affected by armed conflict extend far beyond the issue of the recruitment and subsequent demobilisation of child soldiers to include also questions concerning the rehabilitation/recovery, reintegration and reconciliation – not necessary in that order – of all youths.

1 Unicef, *State of the world's children*, Unicef, New York, 2006.

2 G. Machel, *The Impact of War on Children*, Hurst & Company, London, 2001.

3 R. Albertyn, S. Bickler, A. van As, A.J. Millar and H. Rode, 'The Effects of War on Children in Africa', (2003) 19 4 *Pediatric Surgery International* 227–232.

4 T. Betancourt and K. Khan, 'The Mental Health of Children Affected by Armed Conflict: Protective Processes and Pathways to Resilience', (2008) 20 3 *International Review of Psychiatry*, 317–328.

It is striking that, in general terms, academic work has taken a rather narrow view of these issues as well. International law has focused on a number of very specific issues, such as age limits for the recruitment of children in children's rights law, and the punishment of recruiters of children in international criminal law. The discipline of psychology has put its emphasis on the effects of traumatic exposure on individuals and their recovery therefrom, although it has been looking for a more psychosocial perspective, trying to incorporate the broader war-affected context. Finally, studies in the field of transitional justice have paid remarkably little attention until recently to the role of children in transitional justice mechanisms, both as victims and as offenders.

These approaches stand in stark contrast to the complex reality of armed conflict and the involvement of children therein. Current armed conflicts are characterised by a mixture of political, economic, military and social forces in competition for power and scarce resources, and civilians are increasingly being targeted in a violent manner.[5] The resulting exposure to traumatic events, human rights violations and flight experiences poses an important threat to the physical and emotional well-being of the civilian population, with a particularly high risk for children and youngsters.[6] The associated development of emotional problems in children not only affects their functional status, it can also cause feelings of hatred and negative attitudes towards reconciliation, undermining peacebuilding and rehabilitation efforts.[7] On the other hand, in contemporary political conflict the sequence of events is hardly predictable and instability and hardship often linger on.[8] Despite formal peacebuilding efforts (*e.g.* the organisation of national elections, international peace treaties, etc.), upsurges of violence may cause new displacement, loss and scarcity, repeatedly alternating crisis with recovery, as such actions seldom tackle the root causes of contemporary conflict or what

5 J. Goodhand, and D. Hulme, 'From Wars to Complex Political Emergencies: Understanding Conflict and Peace Building in the New World Disorder' (1999) 20 1 *Third World Quarterly* 13–26.

6 J. Barenbaum, V. Ruchkin and M. Schwab-Stone, 'The psychosocial aspects of children exposed to war: practice and policy initiatives' (2004) 45 1 *Journal of Child Psychology & Psychiatry* 41–62; I. Derluyn, E. Broekaert, G. Schuyten and E. De Temmerman, 'Post-Traumatic Stress in Former Ugandan Child Soldiers', (2004) 363 5 *Lancet* 861–863; Machel, *supra* note 2.

7 C. Bayer, F. Klasen and H. Adam, 'Association of Trauma and PTSD Symptoms with Openness to Reconciliation and Feelings of Revenge among Former Ugandan and Congolese Child Soldiers', (2007) 298(5) *Journal of the American Medical Association* 555–559; P. Pham, H. Weinstein and T. Longman, 'Trauma and PTSD Symptoms in Rwanda: Implications for Attitudes toward Justice and Reconciliation', (2004) 294 5 *Journal of the American Medical Association* 602–612.

8 M. Van Ommeren, S. Saxena and B. Saraceno, 'Mental and social health during and after acute emergencies: emerging consensus?', (2005) 83 *Bulletin of the World Health Organization* 71–76; Goodhand & Hulme, *supra* note 5.

sustains it.[9] In the long term, many indirect effects of prolonged violence – e.g., poverty, the destruction of infrastructure and the economy, displacement, insecurity, etc. – persist. As a result, the impact of war and violence extends well beyond the period of crisis or active warfare, and also affects several areas of child and adolescent functioning, such as physical health, emotional well-being, education, moral development, etc.[10]

Furthermore, contemporary warfare is marked by a fuzzy distinction between perpetrators and victims: children are forcibly recruited as child soldiers and participate in armed conflict, and the frequently ethnic nature of these conflicts turns every civilian into a potential victim or a perpetrator ready to defend his group's interests.[11] Such practices not only increase the risk of psychological damage,[12] but pose particular challenges to the processes of peacebuilding and transitional justice.

The complex nature of contemporary conflict and its direct and indirect consequences call for comprehensive approaches to post-war interventions. Operationally speaking, we argue that such alternatives should strive for a sustainable integration of humanitarian 'crisis' intervention on the one hand and long-term development ('development cooperation') on the other, traditionally two separated phases in aid responses to crisis, each with their own goals, methods and funding.[13] Academically speaking, we think that the fields of psychosocial assistance and transitional justice are likely to contribute usefully to a multidisciplinary, comprehensive approach, as they take into account the broader context of social, political and economic destabilisation caused by conflict.[14] And children's rights, as codified in the 1989 Convention on the Rights

---

9 S. Autesserre, 'Hobbes and the Congo: Frames, Local Violence, and International Intervention', (2009) 63 2 *International Organization* 249–280; T. O'Dempsey and B. Munslow, 'Globalisation, Complex Humanitarian Emergencies and Health', (2006) 100 5 *Annals of Tropical Medicine & Parasitology* 501–515; C. Steenkamp, 'The Legacy of War: Conceptualizing a "Culture of Violence" to Explain Violence after Peace Accords', (2005) 94 379 *The Round Table* 253–267.

10 C. Mels, I. Derluyn, E. Broekaert and Y. Rosseel, 'The Psychological Impact of Forced Displacement and Related Risk Factors on Eastern Congolese Adolescents Affected by War', (2010) 51 10 *Child Psychology & Psychiatry* 1096–1104; K. Miller, P. Omidian, A. Rasmussen, A. Yaqubi and H. Daudzai, 'Daily Stressors, War Experiences, and Mental Health in Afghanistan', (2008) 45 4 *Transcultural Psychiatry* 611–638; W. Moss, M. Ramakrishnan, D. Storms, A. Henderson Siegle, W. Weis, I. Lejnev and L. Muhe, 'Child Health in Complex Emergencies', (2006) 84 1 *Bulletin of the World Health Organisation* 58–64.

11 Barenbaum et al., *supra* note 6; Goodhand & Hume, *supra* note 5.

12 Bayer et al., *supra* note 7; Derluyn et al., *supra* note 6.

13 M. Van Rooyen, S. Hansh, D. Curtis and G. Burnham, 'Emerging issues and future needs in humanitarian assistance', (2001) 16 4 *Prehospital & Disaster Medicine* 216–222.

14 K. Miller and M. Rasco, 'An Ecological Framework for Addressing the Mental Health Needs of Refugee Communities', in K. Miller and L. Rasco (eds.), *The Mental Health of*

of the Child (CRC) and the 2000 Optional Protocol on the Involvement of Children in Armed Conflict (OPAC), offer a normative framework for this multidisciplinary endeavour and should also be open to challenge and improvement.

These important developments were deemed by the editors of this book to constitute sufficient reasons to organise an international conference of academics, policy-makers and practitioners. They all gathered on 21–22 October 2009 at the Royal Academy for Science and the Arts in Brussels under the general theme 'Rehabilitation and Reintegration of War-Affected Children' and discussed the many aspects of this topic. All keynote lectures, as well as a selection of papers presented at the conference, have been brought together in this book. Its aim is to contribute to a multidisciplinary and comprehensive approach to the rehabilitation, reintegration and reconciliation of children affected by armed conflict. In line with this approach, the structure of the book has not been guided by disciplinary perspectives, nor by a regional focus. Instead, after an introductory piece on each of the three main disciplinary perspectives (part I), chapters are ordered in accordance with the perspective from which they are written: some contributions build on previous experiences with practices and approaches, inducing a range of 'lessons learnt' (part II), while others explore resources for psychosocial wellbeing – on both the individual and the community levels – through empirical research (part III). A final part offers a wide range of critical reflections on disciplinary assumptions or biases, approaches and missing themes. Together, the three main perspectives and the various contributions of this book constitute an interesting exchange of ideas and practices with the broad aim of understanding the rehabilitation, reintegration and reconciliation of war-affected children and of exploring how they can again become members of their communities and societies, how they can 're-member'.

2. INTRODUCING THIS BOOK

In line with the concept explained above, this collection of essays is composed of four main parts.

2.1. The first part sets the scene by offering three disciplinary perspectives, i.e. international human rights law, psychology and transitional justice.

Bo Viktor Nylund provides a mainly legal analysis of the current status of international law relevant to the recovery and reintegration of children affected

Refugees. Ecological Approaches to Healing and Adaptation, Lawrence Erlbaum Associates, New Jersey, 2004, 1–64.

by armed conflict. Nylund points out that while the CRC has a general focus on recovery and reintegration, it is only children recruited or used by armed forces or groups who benefit from specific protection for recovery and reintegration. Other groups of children do not benefit from the same level of protection. The focus on children and armed conflict within the Security Council therefore has added value, the more so since its focus has been extended recently beyond child recruitment. Peace agreements have generally had a very ad hoc focus on children, and most frequently focus on the recovery and reintegration needs of children recruited or used.

Mike Wessells offers a psychological perspective on the psychosocial well-being of war-affected children and advocates a community resilience approach. His paper starts from some central criticisms on the current approaches to the psychosocial well-being of war-affected children and adolescents, both when investigating their well-being and when searching for possibilities to support them. Based on these criticisms, a different approach is put forward, emphasising the necessity to start from a 'holistic' perspective, both on the well-being of war-affected children and on the support that needs to be constructed for them. The author describes the advantages of a 'community resilience approach', the way in which 'community resilience' can be conceptualised, the preventive capacities of 'resilient communities' regarding the psychosocial well-being of children, and the possibilities 'resilient communities' can create for working towards reconciliation.

Jeremy Sarkin's chapter introduces a transitional justice perspective. Transitioning societies face huge challenges as they confront potential tensions between peace and justice. Individual and collective needs must be balanced against the political realities faced by a new government, which has in all likelihood inherited a fragile state and limited political power. In addition, post-atrocity policies often carry the dual aims of preventing future human rights violations and repairing the damage caused by past abuse. Sarkin makes a distinctive contribution to transitional justice studies by exploring the needs of child victims of war. Secondly, he argues that the reintegration and rehabilitation of children need to be linked specifically to processes of reconciliation. In his view, transitional justice mechanisms and tools have the ability to make a substantial impact on children who have suffered abuse during conflict. Thirdly, Sarkin explores the relationship between reintegration and rehabilitation ('the psychological') and reconciliation ('the political'). In his view, victims, and children themselves, may want and also need 'justice' to achieve authentic reintegration and reconciliation. In the transitional justice context reintegration and rehabilitation cannot proceed without a focus on reconciliation as a way of establishing or recovering the dignity and humanity of people rooted in human rights and their acceptance by individuals and society.

2.2. Part II analyses past experiences in the fields of international law, transitional justice and psychosocial interventions across a variety of settings and populations affected by war. The authors in this part evaluate past and current practices, programmes and approaches, reflect on lessons learnt, and present recommendations and alternatives for the future. Covering a broad diversity of perspectives and geographical regions, the assorted contributions illustrate some persistent issues. Each chapter presents a particular outlook on the way forward, aiming to inspire professionals and theorists in a refreshing manner.

Javier Ciurlizza addresses the relative absence of children as relevant actors in transitional justice policies – despite their involvement in armed conflict as both victims and perpetrators of violence – and argues for their inclusion in transitional justice processes. As an impetus, lessons can be drawn from past experiences, in particular by documenting the role of children in previous truth commissions. The author therefore provides a systematic analysis of the position of children in truth commissions arising out of four different scenarios of political transition in Latin America, i.e. Argentina, Colombia, Guatemala and Peru. By comparing the main findings of truth-seeking and truth-telling mechanisms in these countries, as well as their recommendations concerning the involvement of children, he offers important reflections on the way forward.

Adding experiences from a thoroughly different context, ***Pietro Sullo*** addresses the importance of child-focused transitional justice approaches in post-genocide Rwanda. He outlines the sophisticated transitional justice policies that followed the Rwandan genocide, which mainly relied on a retributive justice approach that included an international *ad hoc* tribunal, national courts and community-based jurisdictions. He also sketches the national policies for children and the associated recent legislation on the rights of the child. Using this framework, the author evaluates Rwanda's experiences with its community-based *gacaca* courts, analysing to what extent they are child-focused and offer minors opportunities to participate. In line with the general call for culture-sensitive methods involving traditional and/or informal justice systems, Sullo's analysis of this Rwandan grassroots approach to post-violence reconstruction offers important insights to guide further child-friendly transitional justice practices.

Building further on the Rwandan case, but from a psychosocial perspective, ***Kirrily Pells*** analyses and compares three programmes aimed at children in the aftermath of the genocide. She describes in detail some recurring aspects of service provision in the programmes under analysis, and uncovers the similarities and particularities of their goals, approaches and methods. Additionally, these programmes' perceived strengths and weaknesses are evaluated by the youth participating in them through focus group discussions and individual interviews. The author compares how several aspects of service provision throughout these programmes were experienced by their beneficiaries, and reflects on their implications for family and community functioning. In doing so, she uncovers and illustrates a mismatch between child, family and community needs on the one hand, and service provision on the other. This divergence not only limits the long-term sustainability of programmes in society, it also risks creating new sources of tension within the community. In conclusion, the author presents ideas on participation and rights engagement as a possible way forward.

The power of the concepts 'participation' and 'community' in psychosocial assistance is elaborated further by ***Jessica Muir and Elhum Shakerifar*** from a very different context. The authors address the needs of refugee children fleeing from violent conflict and separated from their families during exile. They outline the functioning of 'Dost', a programme embedded in a community centre in the United Kingdom that provides psychosocial assistance to young separated refugees through education, play and youth work, advice and advocacy. The strength of this project lies in the particular holistic framework it engages in. Its individual casework provides practical help and advocacy, activating young people's resilience. Simultaneously, it aims at working through past trauma and current insecurities through a reliable relationship with the caseworker. A second pillar for the promotion of rehabilitation and recovery is the stability and continuity offered by the community, providing a sense of 'home' and unconditional belonging. Additionally, the community is fostered as a network of support, helping young people to build systematic resilience.

Directing our focus towards the phenomenon of child soldiering, ***Lucia Withers'*** chapter outlines key developments in international efforts to end the recruitment and use of children in armed conflict. It highlights some of the challenges involved in the release and reintegration of children associated with armed forces and groups, noting that child soldiering remains widespread for several reasons, despite the significant attention devoted to the issue. The author argues that while disarmament, demobilisation and reintegration (DDR) programmes and funding for them are generally short term, successful reintegration is a long-term exercise which needs to be linked to longer-term recovery and reconstruction programmes. The root causes of recruitment in each given context must also be addressed and a greater emphasis placed on prevention in order to break cycles of recruitment and re-recruitment. This not only requires a focus on the individual child and his or her specific needs, but should also encompass a broader approach that works towards changing the environment to which children are being returned, both at the family and community level and in society.

Martien Schotsmans uses the case of Sierra Leone to illuminate the issue of the abduction of children and youths in conflict, and the failure of reintegration and rehabilitation years after its official ending. Based on recent field research, the chapter analyses the reasons for unsuccessful intervention and the challenges remaining. It addresses the relationship between reintegration and transitional justice processes on the one hand, and the traditional values of justice and reconciliation and the broader societal environment on the other. Even though children have not been prosecuted in this particular case, the author raises the question whether there is a need for more accountability of youths with respect to the communities where they committed crimes. Equally, the communities' responsibility for the alienation of and discrimination against these youths – distinguished as one of the causes of the conflict – is acknowledged. Other issues addressed are the fear of revenge or rejection, the generation conflict and secret society practices, illustrating how cultural issues challenge DDR and transitional justice.

The chapter by ***Ann Lorschiedter and Femke Bannink-Mbazzi*** focuses on children and youth affected by war in Northern Uganda. By means of a historical overview of the background of the conflict, the authors first analyse the phenomenon of child soldiering, then widen the focus to all war-affected youth. Subsequent peacebuilding and psychosocial rehabilitation responses are critically reviewed, and the limitations of conventional approaches towards the study of the subject are addressed. Building on their critique, the authors present an alternative approach implemented in Northern Uganda. Entailing a combination of vocational skills training for youth, training for teachers and income-generating activities, the programme illustrates how opportunities can be created for all Northern Ugandan children and youth.

The following chapter opens up the perspective of large-scale political relations in the Horn of Africa, and Eritrea in particular. ***Daniel Mekonnen*** first analyses the protracted history of human rights violations in that country, proceeding from the advent of Italian colonialism in 1890 up to the current totalitarianism of the People's Front for Democracy and Justice (PFDJ), the only 'legitimate' political party, which has ruled the country since its independence in 1991. The author argues that Eritrea currently represents one of the most militarised societies in the world and that this context has grave consequences for children's rights. Despite severe restrictions on access for independent observers, the government has been known for its enlistment by force of thousands of underage children into the regular army, even as late as 2009. This is clearly contrary to Eritrea's international obligations emanating from international treaties and customary international law, and also entails grave legal implications for the Eritrean government and the individual criminal responsibility of some senior government officials. Mekonnen argues that pressure from inside the country and from the international community is needed in order to move the Eritrean government in a different direction and thus allow the development of future transitional justice options for Eritrea.

As a concluding reflection on policy and practice concerning war-affected children, the last chapter looks back to the more distant past. By means of a historical overview, ***Frank Caestecker*** illustrates how children have been a debatable privileged category for child protection initiatives during armed conflict throughout the 20th century. He describes three cases in which European children were singled out for organised displacement and refugee protection between 1936 and 1945: Basque children during the Spanish civil war, German-Jewish children persecuted by the Nazis in the late 1930s and children in France in the early 1940s. Outlining the rationale used for these interventions, their concrete implementations and long-term consequences, the author illustrates that humanitarian policy and intervention is highly politicised. He points out how the interests of the children were not always a priority in rescue operations, and how the most vulnerable children were excluded, in consequence of the political interests involved.

2.3. Part III contains the results of empirical research – involving several methods and populations around the world – with the aim of uncovering the main resources for the psychosocial well-being of children affected by armed conflict, whether formal or informal, individual or communal. The scientific evidence presented here holds important implications for practice and for future programmes of a psychosocial nature.

The study by ***Sofie Vindevogel, Kathleen Coppens, Ilse Derluyn, Gerrit Loots and Eric Broekaert*** analyses the role and potential value of reception centres for the psychosocial rehabilitation and reintegration of former child soldiers in Northern Uganda from different social ecological levels, taking substantive quantitative data as its starting point. Vindevogel compares data capturing the profile of a group of former child soldiers attending a reception centre with that of former child soldiers in the community, the latter a sample consisting of both self-demobilised children and those previously assisted by a reception centre. Additionally, the inclusion of social indicators in the second sample's assessment allows the effects of formalised support offered by reception centres during the reintegration phase to be compared with non-formal resources available in the community. While the analyses are merely indicative, they raise questions about the exclusiveness of reception centres and stimulate reflection on its limitations and possible implications.

In a second contribution, ***Kathleen Coppens, Sofie Vindevogel, Ilse Derluyn, Gerrit Loots and Eric Broekaert*** bring out the voices of staff members of rehabilitation centres for child soldiers in Northern Uganda, their working methods and experiences. Despite the large number of reintegration programmes running in this area, little is known about how psychosocial support is implemented concretely, nor about the problems that local practitioners may encounter in this area. These data, gathered through interviews with staff and management members of seven rehabilitation centres and through document analysis, generate a useful inventory of psychosocial support activities organised by rehabilitation centres in Northern Uganda. Furthermore, the authors develop critical reflections on rehabilitation centres' work, and formulate some recommendations on potential options for supporting former child soldiers in Northern Uganda and beyond.

Situated in Northern Uganda, the focus of ***Sarah Kamya and Charles Bwana***'s study is on revealing the specific situation of girl child soldiers returning from captivity. In their paper they articulate an account of these girls' experiences during abduction, during reception and upon return into the family and community, captured through in-depth interviews. Poverty, stigmatisation and the lack of identity for their children emerge as main issues of concern for these young mothers upon reintegration. These accounts are augmented by the perspectives of practitioners, parents/guardians and government officials on the achievements of current programmes, and the many remaining challenges they consider that they face. Building on both viewpoints, the authors discuss the lessons learnt from the reintegration and rehabilitation of girl mothers in Northern Uganda, and advocate the establishment of comprehensive strategies in the community, going well beyond micro-level perspectives.

Mulanda Juma addresses the specific challenges in supporting the substantial, yet often forgotten group of self-demobilised former child soldiers. These children, who do not receive support from the national government or international organisations, are often assisted by local community organisations. Building on her own experiences and observations in the field and those of local NGOs, the author provides an overview of the practices occurring within such local community organisations aimed at facilitating the psychosocial reintegration of demobilised children in the Kivu regions of the eastern Democratic Republic of Congo (DRC). From this, she extracts strategies used by local organisations and families to help self-demobilised children, challenges encountered and lessons learnt. The author concludes that despite their potential, communities are often unable to tap effectively into locally available resources to address former child combatants' reintegration needs properly. She argues that to be effective, capacity building is essential and more participation by local actors is needed, with the support of the government and international organisations.

Despite the broadly recognised psychosocial needs in war-affected populations, conflict settings are often characterised by the lack of organised mental health services. Nonetheless, several systems of psychosocial support, both formal and informal, function within resource-poor conflict societies, which in turn can serve as a basis for creating and sustaining the most appropriate services. This is the rationale behind the study of ***Theresa Betancourt, Sandra Zaeh, A'Nova Ettien and Laura Khan*** in Sierra Leone, which assesses the needs of its war-affected youths, the formal and non-formal systems of mental health care and psychosocial support that address these needs, and what kinds of services must be further developed and implemented to provide higher quality and sustainable care. Betancourt and colleagues investigate this by combining qualitative data obtained from war-affected youths, caregivers and community members with data from key informants in mental health services in Sierra Leone. They identify reasons for the continuing inadequacy of the mental health services in Sierra Leone, as well as the ways in which current untapped strengths and resources for resilience in war-affected families and communities might contribute to a more effective and inclusive approach to mental health in the future. The authors argue that it is critical that humanitarian relief models are able to recognise local resources and capacity, and to transition them into more sustainable forms of support for war-affected youth over time.

By means of a literature review of the mental health and psychosocial needs of war-affected children and programming responses in Northern Uganda, ***James Okello, Ilse Derluyn, Seggane Musisi and Eric Broekaert*** address the (mis-) match between these children's needs and programming responses. They focus attention on the diverse needs found in these children, and argue that different settings, in particular communities and schools, appear to be an essential resource for war-affected children's psychosocial well-being. However, current programming responses reveal several important gaps, including limited attention to the diversity of children's needs and living contexts.

2.4. The last part of this collection, called 'Looking back, reaching forward', engages in some critical reflections on the foundations of policies and practices that deal with the reintegration, rehabilitation and reconciliation of children affected by armed conflict. Its goal is to deconstruct and even rethink some of the taken-for-granted strategies and interventions and to explore some ways to move forward in this field.

Vanessa Pupavac, in a more theoretical piece, critically wonders why global policy-makers have turned therapeutic programmes that were previously considered a luxury into a humanitarian priority for war-affected populations. Indeed, providing psychosocial programmes to war-affected populations is not a self-evident communal priority given so many other urgent basic needs. She confronts contemporary policies, which presume that therapeutic governance of disasters and war-affected 'corrosive' communities are required, with earlier sociological accounts of the presumed spontaneous creation of 'therapeutic communities'. The chapter further considers the limitations of psychosocial approaches in addressing the future development of war-affected children. For Pupavac, the question of what children are being integrated into is a crucial one: are they being reintegrated into conditions in which they can thrive or can they merely hope to survive? She argues that the loss of a wider global social and political purpose, i.e. the sense of meaninglessness that today especially pervades Western societies, hampers the potential for reintegrating children. The author concludes that psychosocial rehabilitation programmes will run the risk of rehabilitating children into ongoing international social inequalities unless they are accompanied by alternative progressive political and social visions.

The chapter by ***Cindy Mels, Ilse Derluyn, Eric Broekaert and Koen Vlassenroot*** examines how contemporary international disaster approaches construct war-affected children. The authors consider the limitations of psychosocial approaches in addressing the future development of war-affected children and posit the importance of knowing into which reality children are being integrated. The paper considers how social pessimism and disorientation with the decline of progressive politics has led to a preoccupation with children, but also how the contemporary crisis of meaning, following Bracken, inhibits the ability to reintegrate children. Because children literally embody future society, it goes without saying that an age anxious about the future should be anxious about children's development, and especially the recovery of children who have been affected by war. Reality is different, however, as the authors demonstrate on the basis of their empirical study in eastern Congo. The psychosocial models of cycles of trauma and violence reflect social pessimism about the potential for social transformation and the transcendence of the past. Other eras were more optimistic about the spontaneous recovery of children without professional intervention when society believed it was forging a better world for children in peace.

Maria Luisa Bartolomei, for her part, focuses on girls and young women who are involved in armed conflicts and organised armed violence in Latin America and the specific demobilisation, reintegration and rehabilitation needs of boys and girls in those armed groups. Her contribution stems from the sociology of law and from gender studies and looks at the interrelation between gender, age, class and ethnicity. Although many children are involved in wars today, she argues that it is equally important to account for those children who are also involved in organised armed violence. The objective is to understand the true nature of the problem of how armed children and young people are affected socially, economically and politically in the Latin American region as a whole. The chapter addresses the two specific cases of Colombia and El Salvador and takes into consideration the role played by various national and international NGOs.

Finally, ***Yannick Weyns***, in his critical piece, starts from the fact that children's rights are taken as an overarching guideline and that reintegration programmes purport their full implementation. In South Kivu children's rights are also widely seen as 'best practices' in programmes aimed at the reintegration of children associated with armed forces and groups. The author acknowledges that a major success of the rights-based approach has been to redefine children affected by armed conflict in a new inclusive way, i.e. by going beyond soldiering and also taking girls into account, but also points at some 'structural silences' in the discourse on children's rights. One of them relates to the fact that the concepts and categories of children's rights have to be situated in their genealogy and context, and may not necessarily be transposed without further ado to every situation in the world. Drawing on narratives of spirit possession amongst former *mayi-mayi* and of children struggling to come to terms with their guilt in South Kivu, DRC, he illustrates how the cultural elements and the reality of child soldiers as perpetrators are systematically undervalued. Cultural causes and ramifications, the loss of identity and feelings of guilt are difficult to file under a specific children's right that is infringed, nor is it possible to identify a specific duty-bearer. However, the author argues that these cultural dimensions need to be part and parcel of real reintegration efforts and that a children's rights-based approach is able to incorporate these dimensions, including in South Kivu.

3. LESSONS LEARNT AND CHALLENGES FACED

The above paragraphs testify to the richness of ideas and debates that surround the topic of children affected by armed conflict. In this volume we have tried to approach this topic from three different angles and have concluded that there is a need to pay more attention to each other's approaches. The introductory legal part, for example, identifies two major gaps in law, namely to understand how processes of transitional justice may contribute to the recovery and reintegration of children affected by armed conflict, and to look at the role that children can play in their own recovery and reintegration. In the psychosocial approach, community programmes and community resilience take centre stage, as they are considered to have a strong potential for reconciliation. And the transitional justice chapter provides the confluence of the psychosocial and the political aspects and raises the question to what extent can international human rights law be enforced effectively during war and violent conflict.

In the following pages we wish to explore what can be learnt from the preceding book chapters for each of the three fields under review – children's rights law, psychosocial perspectives and transitional justice – and what some of the most salient challenges are for each field.

3.1. CHALLENGES FOR CHILDREN'S RIGHTS

It is clear that the situations of children affected by armed conflict produce many challenges for the field of children's rights law, both legal and non-legal. A recent special issue of *Human Rights & International Legal Discourse* has fleshed out some salient legal issues.[15]

3.1.1. Beyond Child Soldiers, Beyond Age Limits

Children's rights were quite comprehensively codified in a legally binding way in the CRC, which was adopted in 1989. With regard to armed conflict, this treaty was complemented in 2000 by a subsequent mini-treaty, the OPAC.

It is noteworthy that children's rights law, and other legal sub-disciplines such as international criminal law, international humanitarian law and international labour law, all seem to focus on child soldiers as their primary concern, rather than on children affected by war in general. Indeed, most of the discussions have focused on the recruitment and participation of children in armed conflict and on the age limit to be applied (with the debate being geared towards the adoption of a 'straight 18' approach).[16] Whereas the CRC defines a child as every person under the age of eighteen, the age limit used in Article 38 CRC is fifteen years. In the OPAC, the age limit was raised to eighteen, with the exception of voluntary recruitment.

Nonetheless, some attention has been paid to children affected by armed conflict other than those who were recruited for armed struggle. First of all, in Article 38 §4 CRC in particular States commit themselves to taking 'all feasible measures to ensure protection and care of children who are affected by an armed conflict', '[i]n accordance with their obligations under international humanitarian law to protect the civilian population in armed conflicts'. Article 39 CRC provides that States need to take 'all appropriate measures to promote physical and psychological recovery and social reintegration of a child victim' of, *inter alia*,

15 W. Vandenhole, S. Parmentier and I. Derluyn (eds.), 'Special Issue: International Law on Children and Armed Conflict', (2011) 5 *Human Rights & International Legal Discourse*.

16 See *e.g.* A. Sheppard, 'Child Soldiers: Is the Optional Protocol Evidence of an Emerging "Straight-18" Consensus?', (2000) 8 *International Journal of Children's Rights* 37–70.

armed conflicts. It adds: 'Such recovery and reintegration shall take place in an environment which fosters the health, self-respect and dignity of the child.' The OPAC devotes some attention to physical and psychological recovery and social reintegration, but only in the context of the demobilisation of child soldiers (Article 6 §3).

Furthermore, the Principles and Guidelines on children associated with armed forces or armed groups (the 'Paris Principles'), adopted in 2007, pay much more attention to recovery and reintegration. The Paris Principles, which constitute an update of the 1997 Cape Town Principles, were adopted in February 2007 in Paris by a broad range of States, and have since been endorsed by 100 States (as of 27 September 2011). In the Paris Principles, 'reintegration' is mentioned eighty-eight times, 'recovery' three times, and 'rehabilitation' only twice. It should be noted of course that these Principles do not focus exclusively on children who have been associated with armed forces or armed groups. Under the overarching general principle of non-discrimination, it is said that measures to secure the reintegration of children into civilian life should 'not stigmatise or make any negative distinction between children who have been recruited or used and those who have not [...]' (§3.3). The same paragraph warns that it is 'detrimental to all conflict-affected children if other vulnerable children who have not been associated with armed forces or armed groups are placed at a disadvantage vis-à-vis those who have been so associated'. Among the operational overarching principles it is emphasised that funding should be made available for activities in communities 'benefiting a wide range of conflict-affected children' and that reintegration activities should 'avoid maintaining distinctions between children formerly associated with an armed force or armed group and other children in the communities to which they reintegrate' (§3.24). Section 7 on release and reintegration explicitly and repeatedly emphasises the need to pay attention as well to other war-affected children and families (§7.3; 7.30) and warns that inappropriate material assistance to children who have been associated with an armed force or armed group may impede reintegration, 'particularly if it is perceived to be rewarding children who have committed acts harmful to their community' (§7.33). Reintegration is often mentioned in combination with release and protection, or in the context of formal disarmament, demobilisation and reintegration processes (DDR). The Paris Commitments, yet another initiative to protect children from unlawful recruitment and use by armed forces and groups, tend to refer to children affected by armed conflict rather than to child soldiers.

To conclude, while the Paris Principles may be criticised for not referring more explicitly to the children's rights legal framework (see Doek's foreword), the latter can clearly learn from the Principles as far as the scope of children is concerned, as well the relationship to the reintegration of children.

3.1.2. *Clarifying Concepts*

The CRC and the OPAC mainly refer to (physical and psychological) 'recovery' and social reintegration; Article 7 OPAC mentions 'rehabilitation' and 'social reintegration'. These notions are not necessarily legal ones, which may explain why there is often uncertainty about their meaning and scope when they appear in legal texts.

Neither recovery nor rehabilitation has been defined in the Paris Principles, but recovery has been associated with physical and psychosocial aspects at the level of individuals (§7.6.4), while rehabilitation has been considered as a social issue (§3.6). Child reintegration is defined in the Paris Principles as

> the process through which children transition into civil society and enter meaningful roles and identities as civilians who are accepted by their families and communities in a context of local and national reconciliation. Sustainable reintegration is achieved when the political, legal, economic and social conditions needed for children to maintain life, livelihood and dignity have been secured. This process aims to ensure that children can access their rights, including formal and non-formal education, family unity, dignified livelihoods and safety from harm.
> (Paris Principles, 2007, §2.8).

Further on, the text clarifies that reintegration is a long-term process requiring a long-term commitment and funding, that reintegration programmes should be flexible and enabling, and that these programmes should 'link at the earliest possible stage with other development programs and actors to build the local and national capacity necessary to provide longer-term support to these children and their communities' (§3.25).

Although the notion of reintegration may not have a strictly defined meaning in law, it does not seem to be contested. In the context of juvenile justice, reintegration is understood to be based on a rejection of 'the assumption that the difficulties which children face are necessarily individual' and it has been said to consider the social environment of the child.[17] Rehabilitation, on the other hand, is a concept that may raise more opposition in certain contexts. In the 2005 *Basic*

---

17 G. Van Bueren, *Article 40: Child Criminal Justice*, in A. Alen, J. Vande Lanotte, E. Verhellen, F. Ang, E. Berghmans and M. Verheyde (eds.), *A Commentary on the United Nations Convention on the Rights of the Child*, Martinus Nijhoff, Leiden/Boston, 2006, 12. On the other hand, Article 14 §4 of the International Covenant on Civil and Political Rights, which was adopted in 1966, refers to rehabilitation.

Principles and Guidelines on the Right to a Remedy and Reparation for Victims of Gross Violations of International Human Rights Law and Serious Violations of International Humanitarian Law (often referred to as the *van Boven/Bassiouni Principles*), rehabilitation is explicitly mentioned as a form of reparation for victims of gross violations of international human rights law and serious violations of international humanitarian law, alongside restitution, compensation, satisfaction and guarantees of non-repetition.[18] Reintegration is said to 'include medical and psychological care as well as legal and social services'.[19] So despite not being clearly defined, it seems to have a positive connotation in international human rights law, i.e. it constitutes a form of reparation. In a juvenile justice context, however, rehabilitation seems to have acquired a negative connotation, as it tends to be associated with an undesirable form of social control. The concept of rehabilitation is said also to imply that the responsibility for offences 'lies solely with an individual who can be removed from society for treatment and once restored, released'.[20]

In sum, the question of children and armed conflict reveals the lack of a uniform and broadly shared understanding in children's rights law of such key concepts as rehabilitation and reintegration. Reintegration seems to be preferred over rehabilitation in a juvenile justice approach. The notion of recovery seems most underdeveloped from a legal point of view. In a psychosocial approach, both concepts seem to be imbued with a positive meaning, which could be introduced in children's rights approaches too.

3.1.3. Hard Questions

The study of children affected by armed conflict touches on some of the hard questions of children's rights, i.e. questions that prove difficult if not impossible to answer but that linger on as cross-cutting tensions or paradoxes in the field of children's rights.

A first question pertains to age limits. The general definition of the child in Article 1 CRC refers to the age of eighteen, but there are some exceptions to this general age limit. In fact, since no political compromise could be found on the minimum age of criminal responsibility, Article 40 CRC does not contain any

---

18 On the issue of reparations, see *inter alia* K. De Feyter, S. Parmentier, M. Bossuyt and P. Lemmens (eds.), *Out of the Ashes. Reparation for Victims of Gross and Systematic Human Rights Violations*, Intersentia, Antwerp/Oxford, 2005; P. De Greiff (ed.), *The Handbook of Reparations*, Oxford, Oxford University Press, 2006.

19 UN doc. A/60/147 of 16 December 2005, §21.

20 G. Van Bueren, *supra* note 17, at 12.

age limit at all.[21] With regard to the recruitment or direct participation of children in hostilities, the age limit was lowered to fifteen (Article 38 CRC).[22] While the child liberationists have argued that age should not matter when it comes to human rights, others have submitted that the age differentiation needs to be assessed against the principles of non-discrimination law.[23] It remains a matter of debate whether it is more useful to have abstract age limits, which have the advantage of legal certainty but are not specified, or whether it is better to assess in each individual case the maturity of the child concerned, which allows for an individual approach but may be very subjective. And if an abstract age limit is preferred, the question remains which age(s) is/are relevant from a children's rights perspective. The age limits incorporated into the CRC and other instruments tend to be the result of a political compromise, not of an assessment of scientific evidence that these are the right ages to go by.

A second tension exists between protection (or what Breen has called 'paternalism') and autonomy. That tension is not a legal one, but goes back to the underlying notion of childhood. These two schools of thought or perspectives on childhood (protection or autonomy) have also informed the CRC. On the one hand, there is the view that children need special protection and priority care. That was the almost exclusive theme of the 1924 and 1959 Declarations, which should of course be understood in light of the two World Wars.[24] This protectionist view has been referred to as the biomedical model of childhood: 'children as passive victims who are psychologically scarred and vulnerable'.[25] On the other hand, there are proponents of recognising children as autonomous individuals and 'fully-fledged beneficiaries of human rights'.[26] In non-legal terms reference is made to 'children's agency, resilience and coping mechanisms'.[27] Following Eide, it may be argued that a balance has been struck between these two schools: 'The CRC sees the child as an initially highly vulnerable person in need of protection, nurturing and care who under parental guidance gradually prepares for an independent life in a social setting of rights

21 Meanwhile, the Committee on the Rights of the Child suggested the age of twelve in its 2007 general comment on juvenile justice: see UN doc. CRC/C/GC/10 of 25 April 2007, §32.

22 In the OPAC, the age was raised to 18, except for voluntary recruitment.

23 C. Breen, *Age Discrimination and Children's Rights. Ensuring Equality and Acknowledging Difference*, Martinus Nijhoff, Leiden/Boston, 2006.

24 P. Cantwell, 'The Origins, Development and Significance of the United Nations Convention on the Rights of the Child', in S. Detrick, *The United Nations Convention on the Rights of the Child: A Guide to the "Travaux Préparatoires"*, Martinus Nijhoff, Dordrecht/Boston/London, 1992, 19, at 19.

25 R. Hinton, 'Children's Participation and Good Governance: Limitations of the Theoretical Literature', (2008) 16 *International Journal of Children's* Rights 285, at 288.

26 Cantwell, *supra* note 24, at 27.

27 Hinton, *supra* note 25, at 288.

and duties when reaching eighteen'.[28] That balance does not solve all questions, though, for it is unclear to what extent the recognition of autonomy also implies by necessity the responsibility – including the criminal responsibility – of the child concerned. The general attitude towards children affected by armed conflict, and child soldiers in particular, seems to be one of protection and priority care. If their agency and autonomy were to be emphasised – assuming that both notions can more or less be considered as synonymous – would that imply that they are to be held (criminally) responsible for their acts? Or alternatively, if one does not want to hold them criminally responsible – as appears to be the general consensus – is one then forced to downplay their autonomy and to stress their vulnerability and need for protection? This question is also at the core of discussion on juvenile justice and the minimum age of criminal responsibility. An emphasis on the autonomy of the child in the context of armed conflict and juvenile justice risks having individuating and decontextualising effects. While this tension has been flagged on various occasions, proposed answers tend to remain rather vague, e.g. that accountability does not always imply criminal responsibility.[29] Here, inspiration from other forms of accountability outside of the criminal paradigm may be found in the transitional justice literature.

A third fundamental question has to do with the effects of singling out children who have been recruited or used by armed forces or groups as beneficiaries of reintegration programmes. The same question could be asked about girls. While not drawing attention to specific categories of affected children, focusing on them only on the basis of their particular vulnerability may lead to stigmatisation or further victimisation, in particular also in the communities into which they are reintegrated. Psychosocial approaches seem to try and combine an inclusive approach with attention to special needs.

Fourthly, in instances of child exploitation, children's rights law tends to pay more attention to what adults do to children, and therefore to the need for prosecution and punishment of the perpetrators, than to what children experience and the role that they can and should play in their own recovery and reintegration. This may explain why the provisions on children and armed

---

28 A. Eide, *Article 27: the Right to an Adequate Standard of Living*, in A. Alen, J. Vande Lanotte, E. Verhellen, F. Ang, E. Berghmans and M. Verheyde (eds.), *A Commentary on the United Nations Convention on the Rights of the Child*, Martinus Nijhoff, Leiden/Boston, 2006, 3.

29 K. Arts, 'General Introduction: A Child Right-Based Approach to International Criminal Responsibility', in K. Arts and V. Popovski (eds.), *International Criminal Accountability and the Rights of Children*, Hague Academic Press, The Hague, 2006, 3, at 13–14; M. Happold, 'The Age of Criminal Responsibility for International Crimes under International Law', in K. Arts and V. Popovski (eds.), *International Criminal Accountability and the Rights of Children*, Hague Academic Press, The Hague, 2006, 69, at 83–84.

conflict mainly focus on the recruitment of children. In this case, a victim-oriented perspective on children could usefully be borrowed from other disciplines such as victimology.

Finally, some salient structural silences have been pointed out in children's rights law. Children's rights and their concepts and categories are not just objectively given, they are necessarily social constructs through their genealogy and the context in which they are applied. Children's rights are not merely an instrument, they actively define and structure how we perceive reality and act upon it. Given the influence of children's rights in the assessment, the programming and the evaluation of reintegration programmes, they risk becoming a self-referential closed regime. The question therefore arises how the fulfilment of children's rights has an impact on the degree of reintegration of a child. This question is pertinent because in particular culture and the views of the child soldier perpetrator tend to be systematically undervalued (see Weyns's chapter in this book).

3.2. CHALLENGES FOR PSYCHOSOCIAL APPROACHES

Let us then turn to some of the challenges that the many situations of children in armed conflict pose for psychosocial approaches.

3.2.1. Consolidating Psychosocial Intervention

It can be argued that the 'psychosocial' focus emerging from this book clearly illustrates that a new consensus has been reached. While past discussions of interventions addressing the psychological consequences of war often revolved around paradigmatic issues (e.g., psychiatric versus psychosocial, individual versus community), all contributions to this volume place a strong emphasis on the cultural and social context in which interventions take place, often explicitly using a social ecology model for analysis and intervention. Moreover, with the endorsement of the Interagency Standard Committee's Guidelines on Mental Health and Psychosocial Support in Emergency Settings, launched in 2007, it is now generally acknowledged that individualised and specialised psychiatric interventions should be integrated into an overall multi-layered approach, taking into account the resources and needs of the broader community affected by war.[30]

30 Interagency Standard Committee, *IASC Guidelines on mental health and psychosocial support in emergency settings*, Geneva, IASC, 2007.

Nonetheless, recognition of the breadth of the issues related to child mental health in war-affected societies sensibly complicates this field of intervention. The recognition that interventions should be contextually adequate eradicates the possibility of a universalised 'one-size-fits-all' approach and complicates the transferability of lessons learnt from one setting to another. While the purpose of 'guidelines' is to offer direction and to inspire, they are often misunderstood as 'directives' without capturing their core meaning. As a consequence, a main challenge for the field of psychosocial interventions in the coming years lies in the consolidation of critical analyses and creative thinking as an integral part of psychosocial programming, despite restrained budgets, time frames and political constraints. Moreover, such analyses should be inspired and supported by long-term perspectives and multi-sectoral approaches, as well as by the local community and the 'targeted groups' themselves.

3.2.2. Holistic and Long-Term Consensus, Yet Special Group Targeting and Short-Term Funding

Remarkably, while there appears to be consensus on the need for a holistic, non-targeted approach as the basis for psychosocial intervention in war-affected areas, many authors contributing to this volume have nonetheless singled out some specific groups. As a matter of fact, the editors of this volume encountered a similar dynamic during the preparations for the conference at the origins of the book: while the conference and the call for papers were explicitly organised around war-affected children, the majority of the papers that were psychosocially oriented focused primarily on former child soldiers, as did the media reporting on the conference. This seems illustrative of a wider trend that puts child soldiers on the centre stage to the detriment of broader concerns around war-affected children in general.

These findings may also relate to the current policies of NGOs, governments and other funding agencies as they generally focus on a 'categorical' approach, and thereby often target 'most vulnerable' groups, such as child soldiers. This happens at the expense of the non-categorical but 'holistic' approach that many actors working in the field are advocating. This continuing tension between policy-driven directions and the concrete reality on the ground (where the long-lasting and deeply rooted negative consequences of categorical approaches to intervention can be seen) makes the case for intensive cooperation and networking between all actors working in a specific context. This far-reaching collaboration is needed to ensure that a holistic, all-encompassing approach may arise, both for the groups targeted and for the interventions used. It is also of importance to avoid too many overlaps between the range of interventions.

Secondly, an overall theme running through several chapters in this volume, particularly those analysing post-conflict settings, is the important gap between the conflict and the post-conflict phase. The latter phase tends to witness an overall withdrawal of the support and interventions offered by international organisations. However, there is convincing evidence that societies and their populations still have important needs, even when the conflict has come to an end. These needs are rarely addressed, or only to a limited extent, as many (international) agencies and organisations decrease their interventions in post-conflict areas due to diminishing funding. This gap between crisis intervention and long-term development cooperation is not only a huge challenge for the populations involved but may also constitute an important risk of resurgent violent conflict.[31] Further analysis from the fields of post-conflict and transitional justice will be needed to underpin these intuitions.

3.2.3. Community-Based Buzz

Reflecting a recently prevailing trend in humanitarian psychosocial assistance, all contributing authors generally advocate a community-based approach. In recent years 'community-based' has evolved into a popular and broadly used term in research and interventions in war-affected communities, thereby unfortunately obscuring its meaning.

From an academic perspective, community-based refers to 'efforts to work in collaboration or partnership with communities and/or settings to address local concerns and hopes for improvement'.[32] It implies that local influences are included throughout the intervention process, ranging from problem definitions to subsequent planning, programming and implementation.[33] As such, community-based approaches are closely related to the concepts of participation, capacity building and cultural sensitivity. Within a humanitarian framework, the community-based approach aims to establish that (1) those affected by an emergency will be better protected; (2) their capacity to identify, develop and sustain solutions will be strengthened; and (3) humanitarian resources will be used more effectively.[34] Humanitarian actors are seen as facilitators in this process, supporting the community in presenting their needs, priorities and problem definitions, and in formulating and implementing sustainable culturally

31 Van Rooyen et al., *supra* note 13.

32 E. Tricket, 'Multilevel Community-based Culturally Situated Interventions and Community Impact: an Ecological Perspective', (2009) 43 *American Journal of Community Psychology* 257–266.

33 B. Israel, A. Schultz, E. Parker and A. Becker, 'Review of Community-based Research: Assessing Partnership Approaches to Improve Public Health', (1998) 19 *Annual Review of Public Health* 173–202.

34 UNHCR, *A community-based approach in UNHCR operations*, Geneva, UNHCR, 2008.

and socially appropriate responses, building on local strengths and resources. However, it seems that not all authors or organisations claiming to work according to a community-based approach actually involve local community members in such an extensive way. In his review of community-based interventions in public health, McLeroy and his colleagues distinguished four categories of applications given to the concept:[35]

(1) community as setting, i.e. the geographical location in which interventions are implemented;
(2) community as target, referring to the goal of creating healthy community environments;
(3) community as resource: external agents address a predetermined problem by involving community members and using community resources and assets; and
(4) community as agent: working with naturally occurring units of solution within the community to address their problems.

In order to avoid the hollowing of a community-based approach in war-affected settings, the challenge for the coming years in our view lies in clarifying its content and strengthening its leading principles. As a promising new concept, its efficacy and usefulness should be valued according to genuine implementations of its principal ideas, and not on mediocre imitations applying its name.

Apart from definitions as core issues, the following challenges equally arise with reference to community-based work in war-affected populations: what or who is considered a 'community', and what is to be done when community-based practices collide with a rights-based approach? Firstly, what looks like a group sharing certain cultural or social features with a collective identity and common goals may in fact be a heterogeneously compounded collection of people divided by social class, ethnicity, political engagement, language etc. Communities are defined by whom they exclude, just as much as by whom they include.[36] Working with communities thus requires a critical awareness of who is included for partnership (and who is not), and how this confines the identification of local needs, resources and solutions. Secondly, while a community-based approach tends to be considered as a way of guaranteeing the right to participation that derives from a human rights framework, the responsibility to respect individual human rights may not always coincide with certain community practices, convictions and priorities. In fact, the emphasis on individual (and, according to some, mostly western) human rights may become particularly evident when

35 K. McLeroy, B. Norton, M. Kegler, J. Burdine and C. Sumaya, 'Community-based Interventions', (2003) 93 4 *American Journal of Public Health* 529–533.

36 Ibid.

addressing certain loaded issues, such as sexual or gender-based violence and youth participation in atrocities.

3.2.4. Limited Evidence Base

Finally, those book chapters that address the diverse areas of psychosocial interventions in conflict and post-conflict settings clearly show that in psychology and psychiatry the existence of an 'evidence base' to support the efficacy of a certain intervention has become the new standard for programming. Consequently, the lack of hard data regarding the outcomes following interventions in war-affected populations has often been addressed as a substantial limitation to psychosocial programming in such emergency settings. However, together with the difficulties of conducting research in conflict settings, several large methodological constraints hamper this type of assessment, resulting in a limited evidence base in respect of psychosocial support interventions for children and adolescents in (post-)conflict settings. Moreover, the important role of context (cultural, social, material) also in research areas should not be forgotten, questioning clearly the possible transferability of evidence on intervention efficacy gathered in one specific setting or group to other contexts or groups. This again urges continuing challenging adaptation of all interventions to the changing needs of the communities concerned.

3.3. CHALLENGES FOR TRANSITIONAL JUSTICE

Finally we take a closer look at the challenges posed by children in armed conflict for the field of transitional justice.

3.3.1. Children as Victims of Armed Conflict

Most contributions to this volume accept that children are heavily affected by armed conflict, because they are in a vulnerable position and therefore not able to cope adequately with the violence experienced and its consequences. The same ideas permeate the growing literature on transitional justice, in which children are predominantly conceived of as victims of armed conflict. Yet, it should also be stressed that the field of transitional justice, both in theory and in practice, has paid extremely limited attention to children as independent persons distinct from their parents, their guardians or other adults. Only in very recent years have we witnessed some publications with a more explicit focus on children within the context of transitional justice.[37] This assessment is even more

---

37 See in particular S. Parmar, M.J. Roseman, S. Siegrist and T. Sowa (eds.), *Children and Transitional Justice – Truth-Telling, Accountability and Reconciliation*, UNICEF, 2010; Unicef

noteworthy because Aptel and Ladisch argue that as of 2010 'over 1 billion children worldwide lived in countries or territories affected by armed conflict, and over one-quarter of them were under the age of five'.[38] Based on various estimates, they think that children and youth under the age of nineteen years constitute over 42 per cent of people living in countries affected by conflict, i.e. 4 out of every 10 persons. These realities are in line with a broad concept of transitional justice that focuses not only on the 'political transitions' and the new elites that take the place of old regimes, but first and foremost on tackling the legacies of 'large scale abuses of human rights' irrespective of the exact political context they have arisen in. The latter concept was formulated in the 2004 report of the Secretary General of the United Nations, who broadly defined transitional justice as 'the full range of processes and mechanisms associated with a society's attempts to come to terms with a legacy of large-scale past abuses, in order to ensure accountability, serve justice and achieve reconciliation'.[39]

The figures also constitute clear forms of mass victimisation, which in the words of Fattah refers to 'victimization directed at, or affecting, not only individuals but also whole groups. In some cases the groups are very diffuse, the members have nothing or not much in common, and the group is not targeted as a specific entity. More often, however, the acts of victimization are directed against a special population.'[40] Within the concept of mass victimisation, the transitional justice literature also offers three important distinctions to denote the many faces of victimhood.[41] The first is between individual victims and collective victims, the latter being the result of violent actions directed at a specific population (e.g. ethnic, ideological or religious group) and at society at large. Another distinction is between direct victims, who have suffered direct effects such as killing, abuse, detention, etc, and indirect victims. The latter category can be defined narrowly to include only the direct victims' family members, who experience hardship and pain as a result of the crimes committed, or more

---

Innocenti Research Centre and International Center For Transitional Justice, *Children and Truth Commissions*, UNICEF Innocenti Research Centre/ICTJ, Florence/New York, 2010; C. Aptel and S. Ladisch, *Through a New Lens: a Child-Sensitive Approach to Transitional Justice*, New York, International Center for Transitional Justice, 2011 (also available at www.ictj.org).

38 Aptel and Ladisch, *supra* note 37, at 5. These figures are based on the Institute of Heidelberg's *Conflict Barometer 2010* and the United Nations Population Division's *World Population Prospects* for 2010.

39 United Nations Security Council, *The rule of law and transitional justice in conflict and post-conflict societies*, Report of the Secretary-General to the Security Council, 23 August 2004, S/2004/616, 4.

40 E. Fattah, *Understanding Criminal Victimization*, Prentice Hall Inc, Scarborough CA, 1991, 412.

41 L. Huyse, 'Victims', in D. Bloomfield, T. Barnes and L. Huyse (eds.), *Reconciliation after Violent Conflict. A Handbook*, International Idea, Stockholm, 2003, 54–56 (also available from www.idea.int).

widely to encompass persons who have been traumatised as a result of having witnessed the crimes being committed, such as neighbours, friends and bystanders. The third distinction is based on the time dimension and relates to first-generation and second-generation victims. According to Huyse, violent conflicts can produce a new generation of young people who are traumatised in various ways, and this may be a source of new conflict in the future.[42] It is clear that children who are affected by armed conflict can be victims of many sorts, i.e. they can be victims of both the first and the second generation, they can be direct and indirect victims alike, and they can be part of individual and of collective victimhood. All three distinctions are not only relevant to understanding the relationship between the harm done and the person(s) affected, but they also constitute important criteria for identifying who can participate in transitional justice mechanisms that are set up to deal with the past and to construct a new future.

While children's rights law focuses squarely on the rights of children and a psychosocial approach looks predominantly at the needs of children, it can be argued that the perspective of transitional justice is mostly concerned with the opportunities to provide such rights and satisfy such needs for the population of affected children, and with the obstacles facing such provision. The chapters in the present volume clearly demonstrate that the many mechanisms of transitional justice developed over the last twenty years may have paid some attention to children as victims of human rights violations and international crimes, but that they have hardly focused on the roles that children could play within such mechanisms. The examples of truth commissions where children have testified about their experiences and have been able to express their expectations for the future can be counted on the fingers of one hand:[43] by way of example, the Sierra Leone Truth and Reconciliation Commission established a protocol with child protection agencies in the country to allow children to participate in the proceedings as witnesses; and in Liberia a memorandum of understanding between the truth commission and the National Child Protection Network listed some strategies for the protection of children who participated in the commission's hearings. The same can be said of courts and tribunals in criminal prosecutions or civil proceedings, both in terms of the limited participation of children as well as of the need to take special measures to protect them when they are included. One area of transitional justice that has arguably affected children the most is the systems and procedures for reparations set up in many jurisdictions.[44] Following the Van Boven/Bassiouni Principles listed above, the right to reparation for victims of serious human rights violations is not limited

42 Ibid., at 56.
43 Unicef, *supra* note 37, at xi-xii.
44 Along the same lines, Aptel and Ladisch, *supra* note 37, at 26 ff.

to monetary compensation but also includes restitution of property, rehabilitation measures, satisfaction and symbolic measures, as well as guarantees of non-repetition in the future of the past violations. Several chapters in this volume indicate that children are particularly affected by the rehabilitation measures that aim to reintegrate and resocialise them into regular society after the violent conflict has come to an end. Some authors also suggest that children are no longer exclusively seen as passive subjects who can benefit from certain services and privileges, but that they can also be conceived of as active actors who possess interesting ideas and can make proposals about their own future. To take these into account when designing rehabilitation and reintegration programmes is far from an easy task, but very much in line with a 'process-oriented approach' to reparations.[45] A recent report argues that much more work needs to be done to reform institutions in such a way that they create child-focused and child-friendly environments away from hostilities and conflict.[46] The above lines thus make clear that the large numbers of children affected by armed conflict pose huge challenges for transitional justice mechanisms, both in focusing on child victims of conflict and in allowing children to participate in the proceedings of such mechanisms.

3.2.2. What About Perpetrators of Serious Crimes?

The field of transitional justice is not only concerned with the consequences of atrocities for victims but also aims at establishing the accountability of the perpetrators of serious crimes and human rights violations. Even more, in the early years when transitional justice emerged as a new and encompassing concept criminal prosecutions were strongly advocated as a moral need for society and as a legal duty of the new regime.[47] Next to criminal procedures at the national level, the last twenty years have seen the establishment of a number of important international ad hoc tribunals (such as for the former Yugoslavia – ICTY, and for Rwanda – ICTR) and the new and permanent International Criminal Court (ICC). All testify to the importance of calling to account the instigators of armed conflict and the perpetrators of specific crimes, and to punish them for breaking the rules of war and peace. Although a systematic comparison of international criminal cases goes beyond the scope of this introductory chapter, it seems clear

45 H. Rombouts and S. Parmentier, 'The International Criminal Court and its Trust Fund are Coming of Age: Towards a Process Approach for the Reparation of Victims', Special Issue on Victim Reparation and the International Criminal Court, edited by J.-A. Wemmers, (2009) 16(2) *International Review of Victimology*, 149–182.

46 Unicef, *supra* note 37, at xiii.

47 See *inter alia* D. Orentlicher, 'Settling Accounts: the Duty to Prosecute Human Rights Violations of a Prior Regime', (1991) *Yale Law Journal* 100, 2537–2615; N. Kritz (ed.), *Transitional Justice: How Emerging Democracies Reckon with Former Regimes*, 3 vols, US Institute of Peace, Washington D.C., 1995.

that the vast majority of allegations and criminal charges leading to the arrest and conviction of offenders has related to crimes committed against adults. One notable exception is of course the recruitment and use of children in violent hostilities, which is the particular problem of child soldiers used either as assistants in warfare or for sexual exploitation. The first case at the ICC, still pending at the moment, was opened in 2006 against the former leader of the Union of Congolese Patriots, Thomas Lubanga Dyilo, charging him with the war crime of recruiting and using children in hostilities in an illegal way.[48] On the basis of their fieldwork in the eastern part of the DRC, Aptel and Ladisch argue that this case did not always meet with great enthusiasm from the local population, nor did it immediately lead to the demobilisation of children from non-state armed groups.[49]

The cases of child soldiering of course raise another and very particular issue, namely that these children cannot only be regarded as victims of armed conflict, but are also perpetrators of serious crimes. Often forced by militia leaders to kill or torture members of their community or even their family, the children find themselves trapped in the military logic and find it difficult to return to their communities. These situations are very good examples of the so-called 'role reversals' that are well known in transitional justice, as well as in criminology and victimology, namely when victims become offenders and vice versa.[50] As indicated above, international children's law prohibits the recruitment and use of child soldiers under the age of fifteen (in the CRC) and even under eighteen (OPAC), but reality shows that this practice continues to occur on a large scale.[51] At the same time, child soldiers cannot be held criminally responsible for their criminal acts under the age of fifteen, which raises serious problems in terms of accountability, one of the key values of transitional justice. It also creates the need to develop other than purely criminal or judicial forms of accountability for child soldiers in order for them to assume responsibility for their cruel deeds and hence to become members of society and the community again.

Despite the many procedural particularities of the different international tribunals, they seem to share one common thread, namely a limited space for the victims of the crimes at stake. This is particularly true for the two *ad hoc* tribunals, which neither allow the participation of victims during the proceedings

---

48 Prosecutor v. Lubanga Dyilo, Case No. ICC-01/04–01/06 (see website of the ICC: www.icc-cpi.int).

49 Aptel and Ladisch, *supra* note 37, at 22–24.

50 See ***e.g.*** M. Mamdani, *When Victims Become Killers: Colonialism, Nativism, and the Genocide in Rwanda*, Princeton University Press, Princeton, 2001.

51 W. Vandenhole, S. Parmentier and I. Derluyn, 'International Law on Children and Armed Conflict: the Interface between Various Normative Frameworks', (2011) 5 *Special Issue of Human Rights and International Legal Discourse* 2, at 5-9.

except as witnesses, nor foresee any possibility for reparation awards. Arguably, these lacunae have been amended in the Rome Statute of 1998 establishing the ICC, which does allow the participation of victims during the investigation and the trial proceedings (Articles 19 and 68), as well as the possibility of receiving reparations by court order (Article 75).[52] The limited experience of the ICC thus far suggests that many victims do indeed participate in the proceedings and have officially registered to be eligible for reparation orders. Moreover, the novel model of the Trust Fund for Victims (TFV) provides services to victims of the whole situation at stake before the Court, but outside any court proceedings. Recent information discloses that the TFV has started to invest a fair amount of resources in the demobilisation of child soldiers, the education and skills development of all children affected by war, and material help to parents, mostly in the DRC and Uganda.[53]

3.2.3. The Political Context of Armed Conflict

A last aspect of the context of transitional justice relates to the nature of the violent conflicts themselves. While transitional justice and post-conflict justice are often used interchangeably, they are not identical, as the latter concept – according to Bassiouni – refers to two related meanings, one being 'retributive and restorative justice with respect to human depredations that occur during violent conflicts' (in other words, mostly dealing with the past), the other being 'restoring and enhancing justice systems which have failed or become weakened as a result of internal conflicts' (in other words, geared towards the future).[54] Whatever the broad meaning of post-conflict, it is clear that the violent conflict should have come to an end before any initiatives towards justice can be undertaken. However, this is often a serious problem as some violent conflicts are still ongoing, e.g. in Colombia, and in some cases the conflict that seems to have come to an end tends to flare up at regular intervals, e.g. in the DRC. For children who are affected by such conflicts, and have the need and the right to be assisted, this distinction is not purely semantic but entails real-life consequences, as it is far more difficult to help them and render services while violence is still ongoing. This dilemma again constitutes a major challenge for transitional justice, namely to assess at what point some kind of assistance can be organised for the most vulnerable victims.

---

52 S. Sacouto and K. Cleary, 'Victims' Participation in the Investigations of the International Criminal Court', (2008) 17 *Transnational Law and Contemporary Problems* 73–105; see also C. Stahn, H. Olasolo and K. Gibson, 'Participation of Victims in Pre-Trial Proceedings of the ICC', (2006) 4 *Journal of International Criminal Justice* 219.

53 See www.trustfundforvictims.org (last consulted on 25 September 2011).

54 C. Bassiouni (ed.), *Post-Conflict Justice*, Transnational Publishers, Ardsley, 2002, xv.

Finally, it is also important to point towards the other end of the spectrum. It should be clear that the coined expression 'to prevent is better than to cure' also extends to violent conflicts and to giving attention to the place of children therein. Whatever legal rights are conferred upon children, whatever psychosocial programmes are deployed for the benefit of children, whatever forms of accountability are established to protect children, violent conflicts always tend to create many obstacles to their implementation and realisation. Some call it reconciliation, while others call it peacebuilding, but in many cases they mean the same.[55] The *credo* of peacebuilders is that every dollar or euro spent on post-factum remedies could be better spent on preventive actions, and in a much cheaper way. A great deal of research clearly demonstrates that populations of war-affected areas realise quite well the importance of doing justice in order to build peace, and highly value both types of effort as a way of preventing violent conflict in the longer run.[56] In this sense, it is argued here that to make children affected by armed conflict again full members of their own society and community, it is important to offer them adequate services of rehabilitation, reintegration and reconciliation.

4. ACKNOWLEDGEMENTS

This introduction would not be complete without some sincere words of thanks to the institutions and the persons who have supported us in staging the international conference of October 2009 and the subsequent book project. First of all, we wish to acknowledge the important and indispensable funding from the Flemish Interuniversity Council (VLIR), the UNICEF Chair in Children's Rights at the University of Antwerp, the Flemish Fund for Scientific Research (FWO Vlaanderen) and the Royal Academy for Science and the Arts in Brussels. Each has, in its own way, contributed significant resources to enable the conference to be organised, invite a wide range of experts from Europe and beyond, and thus provide the substantive material contained in this volume. Moreover, the conference organisers and editors of this book like to express their warm gratitude to the other members of the Organising Committee: Terry Amssoms, Julie Ryngaert and Yannick Weyns (University of Antwerp), Kathleen Coppens (Free University of Brussels), Sofie Vindevogel (Ghent University), Monica Aciru (Catholic University of Leuven), Jean-Luc Onckelinx (United Nations Regional Information Centre, Brussels) and Sylvie Fouet (UNICEF Belgium, Brussels). Without their voluntary and intense commitment for more

---

55 Bloomfield et al., *supra* note 41.

56 L. Reychler and T. Paffenholz (eds.), *Peace Building. A Field Guide*, Lynne Rienner Publishers, London, 2001; L. Reychler and J.M. Kalere, *R. D. Congo. Pays de l'avenir. Construisons ensemble une paix durable. Livre Ouvert*, ed. CPRS, Leuven, 2010.

than a year, very few of the original ambitions of this project would have been realised. The quality of the book manuscript was tremendously improved through the thorough language check and copy editing skills of, amongst others, Zoltan Honfi. Our thanks also go the general editors of the Series on Transitional Justice who expressed their keen interest to include this volume as part of their series, and to Elmar Weitekamp (University of Tuebingen) in particular for having organised the complex review process in good standing. Finally, this book would not have seen the light of day without the unwavering support of Kris Moeremans and Tom Scheirs from Intersentia Publishers (Cambridge/Antwerp/Portland).

The editors sincerely hope that this volume, which covers many different issues concerning children in situations of armed conflict, finds its way to the community of scholars, policy-makers and practitioners who deal with this complex phenomenon on a daily basis, and to the media and other agents who report on these issues. May the insights shared in this book also become available to the target group, the children themselves all over the world, and may they be beneficial to them in order to improve their living conditions in the short and the long term.

PART I

SETTING THE SCENE: THREE DISCIPLINARY PERSPECTIVES

INTERNATIONAL LEGAL PROTECTION FOR THE RECOVERY AND REINTEGRATION OF WAR-AFFECTED CHILDREN

Bo Viktor Nylund

1. INTRODUCTION

Throughout history, children have suffered disproportionately in armed conflicts. However, recent trends towards civil war and internal conflict rather than armed conflict between organised state armed forces seem to have put the civilian population in increasingly dire situations. In recent decades issues such as the flow of small arms, the proliferation of armed groups and the use of indiscriminate weapons have all led to increased vulnerability for children.[1] Obviously, modern communications technology has also increased global awareness regarding issues affecting children in armed conflict.

In considering the needs for recovery and reintegration of war-affected children, there are distinct groups and needs that can be identified: the larger group of war-affected children in general, and those with specific protection concerns. When researching the impact of today's conflicts on children, a number of issues come up. The first very visible and tangible impact is that on infrastructure and services that provide for the basic necessities to ensure the right to life and development for children. This includes access to water, food, health and education. But children are also affected emotionally and sometimes psychologically, which needs to be considered not only in the immediate response to humanitarian crises but also in their long-term development. Specific protection issues that may have arisen due to the conflict include family separation, child recruitment, trafficking, abduction and gender-based violence, to mention but a few. Some of these are international crimes, where children are victims and also witnesses and perpetrators of crimes. It is in relation to these issues that

1 Office of the Special Representative of the Secretary-General for Children and Armed Conflict and UNICEF, *Machel Study 10-Year Strategic Review, Children and Conflict in a Changing World*, 2009.

transitional justice questions become particularly relevant, as does the extent to which current normative frameworks have been able to grapple with them.[2]

The purpose of this chapter is to analyse the international legal framework applicable to recovery and reintegration for war-affected children, and to identify some of the gaps and current issues in this regard. I will be looking at a post-conflict scenario, hence mostly considering situations where international humanitarian law has ceased to apply and as such the Convention on the Rights of the Child (CRC) and its Optional Protocol on the Involvement of Children in Armed Conflict (OP-CAAC)[3] are the key reference documents. This does not mean to say that international humanitarian law would never be applicable in the contexts within which recovery and reintegration work is being done, but it is outside the scope of this particular chapter. The focus on children and armed conflict within the Security Council will also be reviewed, as well as peace agreements to date and how these have or have not focused on the recovery and reintegration of war-affected children.

2. BROAD PROTECTION FOR RECOVERY AND REINTEGRATION OF WAR-AFFECTED CHILDREN IN INTERNATIONAL LAW

The CRC is unique not only because it has received nearly universal ratification (only Somalia and the United States have not ratified the Convention), but also because it applies throughout the peace – conflict – post-conflict – peace spectrum. The CRC, contrary to some other human rights instruments, does not have a derogation clause that would allow States to identify rights that can be derogated from in an armed conflict or other emergency situations.

The CRC is also unusual in that it specifically refers to international humanitarian law in its Article 38, and it also has several other articles that are particularly relevant to armed conflict situations, although not necessarily exclusively so. In other words, more so than other human rights instruments is this Convention conflict-sensitive; it has looked to address at least some of the key issues facing children in armed conflict. The CRC is the only human rights law instrument that makes reference to international humanitarian law, although it is still very much focused on the obligations of States Parties (not extending to warring parties or armed groups in the way that international humanitarian law

---

2 *Report of the Secretary-General on Children and Armed Conflict*, UN doc. A/63/785-S/2009/158.

3 *Convention on the Rights of the Child*, UN doc. A/RES/44/25 (12 December 1989), entry into force 2 September 1990. *The Optional Protocol on the Involvement of Children in Armed Conflict*, UN doc. A/RES/54/263 (25 May 2000), entry into force 12 February 2002. As of 21 November 2011 there are 143 State Parties to this Protocol.

does), even if it could be argued that at least some of the provisions might be applicable to non-state actors as well.[4]

The most frequently relevant Article in the CRC when discussing the recovery and reintegration needs of war-affected children is Article 39. During the drafting of the CRC, the Norwegian delegation presented an idea which had never been recognised in international law before, the end result for which reads:

> States Parties shall take all appropriate measures to promote physical and psychological recovery and social reintegration of a child victim of: any form of neglect, exploitation, or abuse; torture or any other form of cruel, inhuman or degrading treatment or punishment; or armed conflicts. Such recovery and reintegration shall take place in an environment which fosters the health, self-respect and dignity of the child.[5]

Some of the early drafts had stronger legal obligations than the version finally adopted.[6] Delegations also had different views about the words recovery and reintegration, as in different languages these words meant different things. The original text had only used the expression "rehabilitation", and in the end the agreement was to include "recovery" to reflect the differing views. The Canadian delegation, however, wanted the records to reflect that it would have preferred only the word "reintegration".[7] This type of controversy would clearly have arisen from concerns that children who have fled from their place or country of origin would have a right to recovery anywhere, not only in their original place.

As far as "social reintegration" is concerned, this aim cannot be achieved unless action for recovery is taken at the same time. In other words, you cannot have one without the other. Social reintegration speaks to action on behalf of the family and the community, allowing the child to be reintegrated in a society that is familiar to him or her.

In this context it is also interesting to note that the language relevant to "armed conflicts" as triggering the need for special consideration was not

---

4 The Optional Protocol on the Involvement of Children in Armed Conflict goes in a different direction as it also establishes obligations for non-state actors. The CRC itself also speaks of the responsibility of the family, and hence is somewhat different from other human rights instruments. For a more in-depth study of the human rights obligations of non-state actors, see A. Clapham, 'Human Rights Obligations of Non-State Actors in Conflict Situations', (2007) 88 863 *International Review of the Red Cross*, at 502.

5 There are no reservations to Article 39.

6 During the considerations of the 1988 Working Group, the words "legal, administrative and other measures" were exchanged for "all measures", and in the 1989 Working Group the words "appropriate" was inserted between "all" and "measures" so as not to put an unduly strong obligation on the State. See *Considerations of the 1988 Working Group*, UN doc. E/CN.4/1988/28, at 17–18 (10th Session), UN doc. E/CN.4/1988/WG.1/WP.1/Rev.2, at 23 for the work of the 1988 Working Group, and UN doc. E/CN.4/1989/48, at 93–94 for the 1989 Working Group. The word "appropriate" was inserted as a result of a suggestion made by the US Government, which was supported by the representative of the Federal Republic of Germany and Norway.

7 *Considerations of the 1988 Working Group*, UN doc. E/CN.4/1988/28, at 17.

included until proposed in the 1989 Working Group.[8] In the deliberations the representative of Norway argued that the Article then would cover an aspect of armed conflict, which the Convention would otherwise have left uncovered.

Looking more closely at the provisions of Article 39, it is first necessary to note that it has two main parts, the first regarding recovery and reintegration, and the second regarding the type of environment in which activities to that end should take place.

Physical recovery would cover the essential rights of a child to food, water, health and sanitation.[9] "Psychological" may include services that restore normalcy, such as education and psycho-social support activities through recreation and play. But it may also include specific protection issues, which will be dealt with in more detail below.[10]

The second sentence of Article 39 reads as follows: "Such recovery and reintegration shall take place in an environment which fosters the health, self-respect and dignity of the child." This obligation can be read together with other principles found in the Convention, such as taking into account the best interests of the child and ensuring non-discrimination in undertaking activities for recovery and reintegration.[11] Non-discrimination would also apply to gender and to providing specific services for girls that cater to their needs.

Important in the context of recovery and reintegration is the provision in the Convention for taking into account the evolving capacities of the child, and the provision related to assuring that "the child who is capable of forming his or her own views" is able to do so with due weight given "in accordance with the age and maturity of the child".[12] So, for instance, the Committee on the Rights of the Child has considered "that recognizing the right of the child to express views and to participate in various activities, according to her/his evolving capacities, is beneficial for the child, for the family, for the community, the school, the State, for democracy".[13] This shows how the legal foundations of the Convention are important in the context of transitional justice, where children have traditionally not played a role, be they criminal proceedings, truth commissions, peace processes or other transitional justice mechanisms.

---

8 *Considerations of the 1989 Working Group*, UN doc. E/CN.4/1989/WG.1/WP.57. This proposal was submitted by a drafting group consisting of Argentina.

9 *Consideration of Reports Submitted by States Parties under Article 44 of the Convention, Concluding Observations: Sri Lanka*, UN doc. CRC/C/15/Add.207 (2 July 2003), §174.

10 In reviewing the report of Liberia the Committee speaks of those who have been directly or indirectly affected by the traumatic experiences of the war. *Consideration of Reports Submitted by States Parties under Article 44 of the Convention, Concluding Observations: Liberia*, UN doc. CRC/C/15/Add.236 (1 July 2004), §59.

11 R. Hodgkin and P. Newell, *Implementation Handbook for the Convention on the Rights of the Child*, UNICEF, 2008, 591.

12 Article 12 of the CRC.

13 Committee on the Rights of the Child, *Report on the forty-third session*, September 2006, Day of General Discussion. The concept of evolving capacities comes from article 5 and 14 of the Convention and is strongly related to the age and maturity of the child.

In international criminal proceedings, while children generally cannot be prosecuted under such schemes, it has been recognised that children can be witnesses in relation to crimes against children, or as also recognised by the Convention, children's issues can be presented by their representatives as long as they are taken into account appropriately.[14] The appearance of child witnesses in international criminal proceedings started in the Special Court for Sierra Leone, and the standards and practice developed there informed the way that the International Criminal Court has now begun to practice including children in the proceedings. Such standards and practice include the hiring of specialized staff, assessing and addressing any particular vulnerabilities of children who are coming forward as witnesses, providing counselling to the child before, during and after the testimony, as well as follow-up and referrals as appropriate to safeguard the return and continued well-being of the child.[15]

In this context it can be noted how children's participation has been promoted in truth commissions as particularly appropriate because of the non-judicial and consultative nature of such fora.[16] To be successful, the messages developed by truth commissions also need to be communicated back to children in order to make their participation meaningful.[17] Children can also become active in peace processes and while the proceedings where peace agreements are being negotiated may not lend themselves towards child participation, it will enhance the sustainability of those processes to listen to children's voices. These issues need to be further explored and comprehensively addressed by child protection agencies. The Convention on the Rights of the Child provides the basis for allowing the child to play a role in his/her own reintegration, including through transitional justice processes.

The provision focusing on the environment in Article 39 is to set a framework for a certain level of quality of the action.[18] It should therefore place an obligation on the state and the international community to strive towards establishing a

14 For instance, in the *Lubanga* case the Special Representative of the Secretary-General provided an amicus brief and appeared as a witness before the International Criminal Court on the issue of how children are conscripted or enlisted into armed groups in light of the crime of child recruitment as listed in the Rome Statute. See *The Prosecutor V. Thomas Lubanga Dyilo, Written Submission of the United Nations Special Representative of the Secretary-General on Children and Armed Conflict, Submitted in Application of Rule 103 of the Rules of Procedure and Evidence* (18 March 2008), and *Press Statement of the Special Representative on Children and Armed Conflict: International Criminal Court – UN Official testifies on the Lubanga case*, The Hague/New York, 6 January 2010.

15 See A. Michels, *Psychosocial Support for Children: Protecting the rights of child victims and witnesses in transitional justice processes*, Innocenti Working Paper No. 2010–14, Florence, UNICEF Innocenti Research Centre, which builds on the experiences gained from both international tribunals as well as truth commissions.

16 UNICEF and International Center for Transitional Justice, *Children and Truth Commissions*, 2010.

17 *Truth and Reconciliation Commission Report for the Children of Sierra Leone*, Child-Friendly Version, Graphic Communications Group Limited, Accra, Ghana, 2004.

18 *Considerations of the 1988 Working Group*, UN doc. E/CN.4/1988/28, at 17.

sound environment to deal appropriately with a broad range of children's recovery and reintegration needs.

3. SPECIFIC PROTECTION FOR RECOVERY AND REINTEGRATION IN INTERNATIONAL LAW: CHILD RECRUITMENT

While the legal obligation in Article 39 is rather vague, it does provide for a basic level of protection on behalf of war-affected children's need for recovery and reintegration support. It can also be used in conjunction with other provisions in the Convention in order to strengthen the provisions of Article 39, especially when considering specific protection issues such as survivors of torture, refugee children, children separated from their families, or survivors of gender-based violence, but also with respect, for instance, to taking into account provisions that promote child participation.[19] The Committee on the Rights of the Child has also encouraged system-building through, for instance, undertaking studies and training service providers.[20] It is difficult to care for such children individually unless there are some systems that can cater for a large number of children. For instance, establishing a strong juvenile justice system in a war-affected country can serve children who have been prosecuted for participating in the conflict, or girls who are survivors of gender-based violence.[21]

In terms of specific provisions for the recovery and reintegration of war-affected children, the OP-CAAC covers these issues for children who have been recruited or used by armed forces or groups in article 6 (3):

> States Parties shall take all feasible measures to ensure that persons within their jurisdiction recruited or used in hostilities contrary to the present Protocol are demobilized or otherwise released from service. States Parties shall, when necessary, accord to such persons all appropriate assistance for their physical and psychological recovery and their social reintegration.

---

19 Hodgkin and Newell, *supra* note 11 at 589.

20 *Consideration of Reports Submitted by States Parties under Article 44 of the Convention, Concluding Observations: Croatia*, UN doc. CRC/C/15/Add.243 (3 November 2004), §65.

21 The 2009 report of the Secretary-General calls upon national and international actors to support and expand programmes to ensure that children who are victims of violations have access to appropriate services and response. *Report of the Secretary-General on Children and Armed Conflict*, UN doc. A/63/785-S/2009/158 (26 March 2009), §174. For instance, UNICEF's Board approved policies addressing the recovery and reintegration for children who have been released from armed groups and forces. See *Core Commitments for Children in Emergencies*, UNICEF 2005, and *UNICEF Child Protection Strategy*, E/ICEF/2008/5/Rev.1 (20 May 2008).

Article 7 provides additional focus on cooperation among States Parties in rehabilitation and social reintegration, technical cooperation and financial assistance "in consultation with the States Parties concerned and the relevant international organizations".

The drafting history of this provision makes interesting reading. At its first session, the Working Group drafting the OP-CAAC considered that it was necessary to have some text in addition to what had been proposed by the Committee on the Rights of the Child, and "some members of the working group felt that new articles were needed to address issues such as the physical and psychological reintegration of child victims of armed conflicts".[22] The representative of Cuba proposed language to cover "rehabilitation and reintegration", specifying that it would guarantee medical care and adequate nutrition.[23]

However, at the second session of the working group, when the provision was being considered, this was changed into a preambular paragraph, providing a much less structured focus. This paragraph was proposed by the delegations of Australia and Cameroon, and was placed before the original seventh preambular paragraph: "Convinced of the need to strengthen international cooperation regarding the physical and psychosocial rehabilitation and social reintegration of children who are victims of armed conflicts."[24]

The matter was then left aside for the subsequent working groups, and it was not until the sixth and final session that a more serious discussion on the topic was held, when "several delegations supported the idea of including in the optional protocol a separate provision on cooperation in implementing the protocol, including through international assistance for the rehabilitation and social reintegration of child soldiers".[25]

Canada and Norway put forward a proposal which took the language on recovery and reintegration back into the operative paragraphs; however, the *travaux préparatoires* do not shed any light on what happened in the negotiation process between the proposed version and that which was adopted, which completely reflects the language of the CRC itself.[26] Nor is further clarity provided in terms of what might be meant by these words in a legal sense, although further obligations are placed on the action of releasing the children, and also the provision of an interesting aspect in Article 7(1) that prohibits any

[22] *Report of the Working Group on a Draft Optional Protocol to the Convention on the Rights of the Child on Involvement of Children in Armed Conflicts*, UN doc. E/CN.4/1995/96 (10 February 1995), §29.

[23] Ibid., §147.

[24] *Report of the Working Group on a Draft Optional Protocol to the Convention on the Rights of the Child on Involvement of Children in Armed Conflicts on Its Second Session*, UN doc. E/CN.4/1996/102 (21 March 1996), §§89, 128–130.

[25] *Report of the Working Group on a Draft Optional Protocol to the Convention on the Rights of the Child on Involvement of Children in Armed Conflicts on Its Sixth Session*, UN doc. E/CN.4/2000/74 (27 March 2000), §44.

[26] Ibid., §46.

negative acts that may hinder recovery and reintegration, and also binds States to consult "relevant international organisations".

The Committee on the Rights of the Child, in reviewing progress of States Parties to the OP-CAAC, has paid particular attention to "information on the measures adopted [...] with a view to ensuring that the rights and best interests of children who have been the victims of the practices prohibited under the Optional Protocol are fully recognized".[27] In submitting their reports, States are requested to "indicate what measures are taken to ensure legal, psychological and other training for those who work with victims". Reports should also "describe existing public and private demobilization programmes that provide child victims of recruitment with assistance in social reintegration, paying special attention to family reunification, and physical and psychological recovery".[28] The Committee has also requested States to report on "existing remedies and reparations that may be sought by child victims of recruitment and in particular on the role of the State in enforcing such measures". It is interesting to note that little emphasis is placed on the extent to which consultation has been undertaken with relevant international organisations, although there is a request for information as to whether the State Party has cooperated with the Office of the Special Representative of the Secretary-General for Children and Armed Conflict.[29] This is a shortcoming in dealing, for instance, with former child recruits who have been prosecuted under domestic jurisdictions, wherein Governments should be encouraged to seek the advice of child protection agencies on how to deal with such matters in a child-friendly way.

In reviewing State Party reports, the Committee has also looked at the question of assistance for physical and psychological recovery. In reviewing the report of Chile,

> the Committee welcomes the information that the State Party has implemented a resettlement programme as a tool to ensure protection for Colombian refugees, as well as its commitment to receive Palestinian refugees coming from Iraq, including children affected by armed conflict. It also notes with appreciation the projects aiming at the regularization of all children entering into the State party's territory, irrespective of the migratory status of their parents, in order to guarantee access to education and health to them on an equal footing as Chilean nationals. However, the Committee notes that no specific measures have been taken to identify children who may have been recruited or used in hostilities abroad and that no specific programmes are available for their recovery and reintegration.[30]

---

27 *Revised Guidelines Regarding Initial Reports to Be Submitted by States Parties under Article 8, Paragraph 1, of the Optional Protocol to the Convention on the Rights of the Child on Involvement of Children in Armed Conflict*, UN doc. CRC/C/OPAC/2 (19 October 2007), §27.

28 Ibid., §29.

29 Ibid., §35.

30 *Consideration of Reports Submitted by States Parties under Article 8 of the Optional Protocol to the Convention on the Rights of the Child on the Involvement of Children in Armed*

It should be noted that very few countries where child recruitment has been a great problem have reported to the Committee to date.[31] Uganda is, however, one example where the issue was considered:

> The Committee, while noting the valuable reintegration efforts undertaken by NGOs to provide physical and psychological recovery for demobilised children, is concerned that such efforts are primarily short-term and are hampered by the lack of adequate resources and State party support. The Committee also notes with concern that demobilised children may be recruited into the armed forces, in particular when the reconciliation process with kin and local community lacks assistance. The Committee is concerned that customary reconciliation practices may re-victimise children who have been recruited or used in hostilities, especially girls who have suffered sexual violence. The Committee recommends that the State party strengthen long-term efforts to provide reintegration measures in order to provide all children who have been recruited or used in hostilities with immediate and child and gender-sensitive multidisciplinary assistance for their physical and psychological recovery, in accordance with article 6, paragraph 3, of the Optional Protocol. The State party is recommended to significantly increase its support for reintegration and recovery measures, ensure that they are accessible in affected regions and develop such programmes in consultation with concerned communities.[32]

Such advice provided by the Committee to the Government in its Concluding Observations is useful for follow-up advocacy by child protection agencies.

In dealing with donor governments, the Committee has also commended State Parties for providing support to reintegration programmes.[33] Similar to the Chilean case, the Committee, in reviewing the report of Sweden, promoted the establishment of services for children who may come from other countries: "The State party should ensure that all unaccompanied asylum-seeking children have access to adequate services, including social and health services and

---

Conflict, Concluding Observations: Chile, UN doc. CRC/C/OPAC/CHL/CO/1 (13 February 2008), §21.

31 While 141 States had ratified the Optional Protocol by 12 May 2011, some 90 of those States have accepted the "straight 18" standard, which is optional for voluntary recruitment under the Optional Protocol. Only about one third of the states that have ratified the Optional Protocol have yet had their implementation deliberated before the Committee on the Rights of the Child. See also Committee on the Rights of the Child, *Revised Guidelines Regarding Initial Reports to Be Submitted by States Parties under Article 8, Paragraph 1, of the Optional Protocol to the Convention on the Rights of the Child on Involvement of Children in Armed Conflict*, UN doc. CRC/C/OPAC/2 (19 October 2007).

32 *Consideration of Reports Submitted by States Parties under Article 8 of the Optional Protocol to the Convention on the Rights of the Child on the Involvement of Children in Armed Conflict, Concluding Observations: Uganda*, UN doc. CRC/C/OPAC/UGA/CO/1 (17 October 2008), §§30 and 31.

33 Sweden is one such example: *Consideration of Reports Submitted by States Parties under Article 8 of the Optional Protocol to the Convention on the Rights of the Child on the Involvement of Children in Armed Conflict, Concluding Observations: Sweden*, UN Doc. CRC/C/OPAC/SWE/CO/1 (6 July 2007), §5.

accommodation, irrespective of the municipality in which they are accommodated." The Committee urged "that asylum-seeking children who have been involved in armed conflict receive all appropriate assistance for their physical and psychological recovery and social reintegration".[34]

In the case of the Philippines, the Committee recommended that: "[t]he State party ensure that special and adequate attention is paid to children who have been recruited or used in hostilities when entering into negotiation and talks with armed groups, especially in the area of prevention, physical and psychological recovery and social reintegration."[35] It is noteworthy that recently the Moro Islamic Liberation Front (MILF) and UNICEF signed an Action Plan focusing among other issues on the recovery and reintegration of children recruited or used by the MILF.[36]

The fact that States, in line with Article 4(2), "shall take all feasible measures to prevent such recruitment and use, including the adoption of legal measures necessary to prohibit and criminalize such practices" provides a kind of safeguard as far as transitional justice measures are concerned under local jurisdictions or universal jurisdiction. However, pieces of implementing legislation are still few and far between, and when developed there are often shortcomings.[37] Hence, this is an area still calling for major advocacy and support to Governments to start drafting such laws, as they are not just a legislative act but provide an opportunity to raise awareness and address issues of accountability in the long term. Such legislation not only needs to criminalise the recruitment or use of children, but also to address the question of universal jurisdiction, the criminal responsibility of children themselves, and the recovery and reintegration needs of former child soldiers.

It is also important to note that in negotiating the release of children many armed groups make the release conditional because as they claim, and often rightly so, the children have ended up with the armed group because of a lack of services available in the communities, for instance, the lack of education. This again reemphasises the point that reintegration does not work without recovery. Effective political advocacy for upholding the legal standards against the recruitment of children are, for instance, difficult to maintain unless solid recovery and reintegration programmes are in place.

---

34 Ibid., §§24 and 25.

35 *Consideration of Reports Submitted by States Parties under Article 8 of the Optional Protocol to the Convention on the Rights of the Child on the Involvement of Children in Armed Conflict, Concluding Observations: The Philippines*, UN doc. CRC/C/OPAC/PHL/CO/1 (15 July 2008), §21.

36 *Action Plan between the Moro Islamic Liberation Front (MILF) and the United Nations in the Philippines regarding the Issue of Recruitment and Use of Child Soldiers in the Armed Conflict in Mindanao*, 1 August 2009.

37 Coalition to Stop the Use of Child Soldiers, *Child Soldier Global Report*, 2008, 22.

The words "social reintegration" acquires a very specific meaning in the context of dealing with children who have been associated with armed groups and forces. Returning such children to their home communities may sometimes require specific awareness-raising or trust-building activities, as they may have carried out crimes against their own communities, as is also recognised by the Paris Principles and Guidelines on Children Associated with Armed Forces or Armed Groups.[38] Generally, in language relevant to children recruited or used by armed forces and groups there is reference to "release and reintegration" as one coherent whole. The release process is part of and adds value to the reintegration process if done correctly.

The Paris Principles put specific emphasis on what is called the "inclusive approach to reintegration", in other words making sure that children associated with armed forces or groups are not given services that are not available to other children and families in the same community, thereby further stigmatising these children. Links through social welfare programmes are also important to ensuring that children and families are linked up with various services that may anyway be available in their community (income generation, vocational training, etc.).

Some very difficult but important issues come up in relation to the recovery and reintegration of children who have been recruited or used by armed groups or forces in situations where such children are being prosecuted for international crimes. In fact, the question of legal responsibility may arise in considering amnesties or pardons in the context of developing peace agreements. Generally, child protection actors agree that children should be considered primarily as victims, in line with international juvenile justice standards within a framework of restorative justice and social rehabilitation.[39] In other words, in domestic jurisdictions there is generally no problem with prosecuting children as long as appropriate child-friendly procedures apply. It is also generally agreed that in international jurisdictions children should not be prosecuted, as they are not among those who bear the greatest responsibility for the crimes committed.[40] It becomes tricky in situations where there are no guarantees of child-friendly procedures, and child protection agencies need to make sure that children are channelled through a restorative justice process so as not to remain in jail for

---

38 *The Paris Commitments and Principles to Protect Children from Unlawful Recruitment or Use by Armed Forces or Armed Groups*, www.unicef.org/protection/files/ParisCommitments120207english.pdf, 2007.

39 See *Report of the Secretary-General on Children and Armed Conflict*, UN doc. A/63/785-S/2009/158 (26 March 2009), §171.

40 The Rome Statute does not have jurisdiction over persons under the age of 18, and in the Sierra Leone Special Court children were never prosecuted, although the Court had the mandate to do so. See also No Peace Without Justice and UNICEF Innocenti Research Centre, *International Criminal Justice and Children*, September 2002, 33.

years to come. In such situations it may be necessary to advocate for some type of amnesty or pardon in line with the best interests of the child.[41]

In reviewing the vast range of work under international law, child recruitment is receiving the most attention in terms of specific protection for recovery and reintegration. Other protection issues do not benefit from these kinds of provision, although as we will see from the process in the Security Council below, gender-based violence may be the next area to develop such standards and programmatic response in greater detail. Article 39 of the CRC, in connection with other articles of the Convention, can as mentioned above also be used for other issues, but this would obviously not provide for the same specificity and strength of legal argument.

4. ADDRESSING ACCOUNTABILITY FOR RECOVERY AND REINTEGRATION: THE INVOLVEMENT OF THE SECURITY COUNCIL

The Security Council's engagement on issues related to children affected by armed conflict can arguably be seen as a natural component of its mandated function "to save succeeding generations from the scourge of war", lending itself towards the recovery and reintegration needs of children. The purpose here is not to undertake a detailed review of the monitoring and reporting mechanism created by the Security Council, but to look at this mechanism from the perspective of establishing a framework for the recovery and reintegration of war-affected children.

In 1998, the Security Council for the first time organised a thematic debate on children and armed conflict, which resulted in a Presidential Statement which set out a kind of mission statement: "The Security Council expresses its intention to pay serious attention to the situation of children affected by armed conflicts."[42] Since 1999 the Security Council has adopted seven resolutions on children and armed conflict, each developing further the mechanism for addressing issues relevant to children and armed conflict.

One aspect that is of relevance to recovery and reintegration efforts is that the resolutions have continued to highlight the importance of incorporating child protection within peacekeeping missions, including an emphasis on supporting programmes for recovery and reintegration. In 1999, the Security Council adopted two country-specific resolutions highlighting not only the plight of children in Sierra Leone and the Democratic Republic of Congo, but also the

41 This was, for instance, the situation following the capture of some 99 children in Sudan following the attack by the Justice and Equality Movement on Omdurman. Republican Decree No 276 for the year 2008 allowed for a presidential pardon so the children could be channelled back to their families and communities.

42 *Statement by the President of the Security Council*, UN doc. SC/PRST/1998/18.

need to engage particular child rights and protection expertise in support of the respective Special Representatives.[43] This was to become standard practice in the years to come when establishing new UN peace mission mandates or when reviewing existing mandates. Country-specific resolutions, as far as children are concerned, focus on several distinct issues: they emphasise the impact of armed conflict on children; they highlight specific issues related to child recruitment and the Disarmement, Demobilisation and Reintegration (DDR) processes; and they include child protection aspects in peacekeeping mandates and provide for the deployment of child protection advisors.[44]

It was in its 2001 resolution that the Security Council for the first time noted activities relevant to monitoring and reporting, requesting the Secretary-General to "[c]ontinue and intensify, on a case by case basis, monitoring and reporting activities by peacekeeping and peace-building support operations on the situation of children in armed conflict".[45] This was the beginning of what was to become the systematic involvement of the Security Council in issues relevant to children and armed conflict, and the development of a system for monitoring and reporting grave violations of children's rights linked to responses assisting the recovery and reintegration of conflict-affected children. In his report the following year, the Secretary-General for the first time included the so-called name and shame list in an annex to the report, which listed "parties to armed conflict who recruit or use children" as requested by the Council in resolution 1379.[46]

In 2003, the "era of application", as called for by Secretary-General Kofi Annan, was endorsed by the Security Council, and in resolution 1460 he was asked to report on increasingly concrete measures for stopping the recruitment and use of children in armed conflict.[47] Resolution 1460 also referred to action

43 See *Democratic Republic of Congo*, UN doc. S/RES/1279 (30 November 1999), §5(e). The resolution asked the Special Representative "[t]o maintain liaison with all parties to the Ceasefire Agreement to facilitate the delivery of humanitarian assistance to displaced persons, refugees, children, and other affected persons, and assist in the protection of human rights, including the rights of children." The resolution for Sierra Leone was rather more detailed. The Security Council emphasized "that the plight of children is among the most pressing challenges facing Sierra Leone, welcomes the continued commitment of the Government of Sierra Leone to work with the United Nations Children's Fund, the Office of the Special Representative of the Secretary-General for Children and Armed Conflict and other international agencies to give particular attention to the long-term rehabilitation of child combatants in Sierra Leone, and reiterates its encouragement of those involved to address the special needs of all children affected by the conflict." Sierra Leone, UN doc. S/RES/1270 (22 October 1999), §18.

44 The recent resolution on Chad is a good example; see Security Council Resolution S/RES/1861 (2009).

45 Resolution on *Children and Armed Conflict*, UN doc. S/RES/1379 (20 November 2001), §10(c).

46 *Report of the Secretary-General on Children and Armed Conflict*, UN doc. S/2002/1299 (26 November 2002). UN doc. S/RES/1379 (§16) included a request for this list.

47 *Resolution on Children and Armed Conflict*, UN doc. S/RES/1460 (30 January 2003), §16(c).

plans, ensuring that the work on monitoring and reporting would not become an end in itself.[48]

The 2004 resolution in turn requested the Secretary-General to "[d]evise [...] an action plan for a systematic and comprehensive monitoring and reporting mechanism".[49] This development culminated in the system that was developed subsequent to the 2005 report of the Secretary-General, and the adoption of Security Council resolution 1612 in 2005 focusing on countries listed in the annexes to the Secretary-General's report. It was also through resolution 1612 that the Security Council decided to establish a working group "consisting of all members of the Council to review the reports of the mechanism",[50] which has now become the key mechanism through which the Security Council remains seized of the issue of children and armed conflict.[51]

In resolution 1612 the Security Council acknowledges that the process "has generated progress, resulting in the release and reintegration of children into their families and communities". The resolution also highlights the importance of implementing action plans and "stresses that effective disarmament, demobilization and reintegration programmes for children, building on best practices identified by UNICEF and other relevant child protection actors, are crucial for the well-being of all children who [...] have been recruited or used by armed forces and groups [...], and urges national Governments and donors to ensure that these community-based programmes receive timely, sustained and adequate resources and funding".[52]

The situations listed in the annexes of the Secretary-General's annual report also benefit from annual country-specific reports. Based on information emanating from the monitoring and reporting mechanism, these report on grave child rights violations that have occurred and if possible the party responsible. The country reports also highlight what actions have been undertaken to address and respond to these violations. This has given rise to detailed reviews of different country situations and recommendations have been provided to the respective countries for follow-up and action. It is important to note that both lack of access and the volatile security situation on the ground in many countries often affect the ability to develop recovery and reintegration programmes.

The importance of linking the monitoring and reporting activities to concrete action cannot be emphasised strongly enough.[53] It is important that operational

---

48 Ibid., §4.

49 *Resolution on Children and Armed Conflict*, UN doc. S/RES/1539 (22 April 2004), §2.

50 *Resolution on Children and Armed Conflict*, UN doc. S/RES/1612 (26 July 2005), §8.

51 Six violations are being monitored through this mechanism, namely killing or maiming of children; recruiting or using child soldiers; attacks against schools or hospitals; rape or other grave sexual violence against children; abduction of children; denial of humanitarian access for children.

52 *Resolution on Children and Armed Conflict*, UN doc. S/RES/1882 (4 August 2009), §13.

53 See also *Report of the Secretary-General on Children and Armed Conflict*, UN doc. A/63/785-S/2009/158 (26 March 2009), where "measures to achieve sustainable reintegration of children

agencies on the ground, such as UNICEF, UNHCR and OHCHR, stick to their mandated approaches in delivering humanitarian action or human rights activities relevant to children and civilian populations in need. The monitoring and reporting work can inform their activities on the ground, but they have a most important role in enhancing the opportunities for advocacy with warring parties.

The risk otherwise is that their work in light of the mandate received through the Secretary-General to implement Security Council resolution 1612 becomes politicised and seen mainly through the lens of the political processes before the Council. The monitoring and reporting is not an end in itself; it must lead to advocacy and action on the ground. As far as the Security Council framework helps advance the agenda for recovery and reintegration it is useful, but when not, other work should go ahead. It is therefore important that while such operational agencies contribute towards the body of information at the global level, at the same time they do so only to the extent that is useful to their operational goals.

The information collected becomes the basis of analysis and advocacy at different levels, with the most important opportunity arising at the country level. As the information is passed by the Secretary-General to the Security Council, this can trigger both action and a response at the very highest level.[54] However, at the country level the information gives the Country Taskforce and child protection agencies a concrete and informed foundation on which to engage with the parties to the conflict.

As first called for by Security Council resolution 1460 and reiterated in 1539 and 1612, a commitment should be translated into an action plan to end the recruitment and use of children by the armed forces and groups involved. An action plan is a concrete and time-bound commitment to halt all new recruitment of children and to separate and release all children associated with the group or force. It is normally developed jointly by the Country Taskforce and the armed force or group and outlines commitments and the operational steps to ensure the release of all children, including programmatic reintegration activities to assist the children in making the transition from military to civilian life.

The importance of an action plan is related to the fact that it constitutes a concrete tool whereby the Country Taskforce and the SCWG can monitor the progress of implementation in releasing children, thus enabling them to hold the signatory to the plan accountable for its commitments though continuous dialogue and engagement. To date, almost 20 action plans and deeds of commitment have been signed with a number of armed forces and groups. It is

---

affected by conflict" is identified as an "emerging concern".

54 K. Barnett and A. Jefferys, *Full of Promise: How the UN's Monitoring and Reporting Mechanism Can Better Protect Children*, Humanitarian Practice Network Paper, Number 62, September 2008.

not the purpose here to go into detail on each of the plans, but to highlight through a couple of examples their relevance to recovery and reintegration.

The lengthy negotiations for the release of children in Nepal followed the successful peace process in 2006 that led to the conclusion of the Comprehensive Peace Agreement between the Government of Nepal and the Communist Party of Nepal (Maoist), and perhaps gives an example of a mechanism that took time to become successful. Only at the end of 2009 was the United Nations successful in securing the release of children, many of whom by then had become adults. While the development of an action plan was successful in the end, this shows how political these processes can become, leading to a host of other child protection concerns as a result.[55] At the time of writing the recovery and the reintegration programmes on behalf of some 3,000 Nepalese children have started.

The case of Sudan illustrates well how the engagement of the Security Council with the issue of children and armed conflict can be used as a platform for advocacy. Following the publication of the Secretary-General's second Annual Report on Children and Armed Conflict in Sudan, a joint UN-Government Committee was established to initiate dialogue on the reported violations. This represents a significant step forward in terms of engagement of the Government. Moreover, following the signing of an action plan with the Sudan Liberation Army/Movement (SLA/M) in 2007 on the release of children associated with its armed group, additional groups came forward expressing their interest in dialogue and in signing similar action plans, leading to the signature of an Action Plan by the Government of Southern Sudan in 2009.[56] Despite these political developments and successes in establishing appropriate frameworks for action, the actual numbers of released children remain small.[57]

The format and key principles of an action plan have yet to be standardised across countries with established monitoring and reporting mechanisms, as well as what type of response measures will be included, as currently they do not follow a unified approach. While this may not be a problem per se, it could be exploited by some parties to conflict. The monitoring and reporting mechanism has only been fully operational in a small number of countries since 2005, and the above examples have many problems in terms of implementation and making the action plans a reality for children on the ground. There is a risk that parties

55 *Action Plan between the Government of Nepal, the Unified Communist Party of Nepal – Maoist, and the United Nations in Nepal Regarding the Discharge of Disqualified Maoist Army Personnel and Related Tasks*, 16 December 2009. Child protection issues that arose in the meantime include keeping children together with adults, limited freedom of movement, and the right to recovery and reintegration not being fulfilled.

56 *Action Plan between the Sudan People's Liberation Army (SPLA) and the United Nations Regarding Children Associated with the SPLA in Southern Sudan*, 20 November 2009.

57 *Report of the Secretary-General on Children and Armed Conflict in Sudan*, UN doc. S/2009/84 (10 February 2009), §§51 and 52.

to conflict will seek to develop such plans just to be seen as collaborating and in order to gain status internationally. The short time frame has made it difficult to assess the extent of the direct impact of the work on children's lives on the ground. Whereas children have been released in some of the countries under consideration, reports of new recruitment cases and other grave child rights violations continue to be documented. Nonetheless notable progress has been achieved in raising the profile of the monitoring and reporting work and thereby the plight of children affected by armed conflict, and strong political commitment has resulted in frameworks for addressing these issues.

One major shortcoming to date has been that formally the action plans have only included child recruitment (although some of them have gone further) and not all six violations that are covered under the monitoring and reporting mechanism.[58] With resolution 1882, this is now expanded to include also "patterns of killing and maiming of children and/or rape and other sexual violence against children, in situations of armed conflict".[59] This means that it will be necessary to consider action plans for the recovery and reintegration of children who are survivors of sexual violence, and some kind of support to children who are maimed due to the conflict, or support to families of children who have been killed. In fact, it would be useful to include all six violations as part of action plans, although it will still take time to get political agreement in this regard.

5. THE USE OF PEACE AGREEMENTS TO ADDRESS RECOVERY AND REINTEGRATION FOR WAR-AFFECTED CHILDREN

The peace process is part of an effort to promote recovery and reintegration following an armed conflict. In the interest of space I will not deal here with the legal nature of peace agreements; suffice it to say that they are not strictly speaking international treaties nor are they domestic law, but many features of peace agreements create legally binding obligations on the parties who have signed up to them.

A serious effort to include children's issues specifically in peace agreements started only in the late 1990s. To what extent the peace agreements as such have been successful is not part of the scope of this work; rather, I will concentrate on the legal implications, as well as to some extent the implications for programmes

58 See footnote 51.

59 *Resolution on Children and Armed Conflict*, UN doc. S/RES/1882 (4 August 2009), §3.

related to the recovery and reintegration of children, which to varying degrees highlight successes.[60]

The early examples in pre-Machel study days refer to the conclusion of the Washington Agreement in 1994 relevant to the situation in Bosnia and Herzegovina, relating to which there was a reference to the CRC, and the situation in Chiapas, relating to which there was language concerning survival rights and basic services and the right to education (language and traditional clothing).[61] As early as 1976, the Tripoli Agreement (Philippines) referred to the right to education as a specific issue relevant to children. In Guatemala, there was a provision for special attention being provided to children in the peace agreement, which stated: "[t]he programme [of overall reconstruction] shall treat former combatants, women, young people and disabled persons as sectors requiring specific priority attention."[62]

While there have also been a number of general references to children in peace agreements, child recruitment is the most common feature. The other issues included in peace agreements seem to be raised in a very ad hoc manner.

Children are seen as a vulnerable group requiring special attention (Liberia, Burundi); a couple of agreements include provisions for tracing and family reunification (Sudan-Uganda Agreement, Sudan CPA and Darfur Peace Agreement). Protection from violence in IDP camps, protection against sexual and gender-based violence, and the establishment of specialised police units for women and children are all mentioned in the Darfur Peace Agreement. There is reference to investment in boarding schools to benefit the children of nomadic families (Eastern Sudan Peace Agreement), which could potentially even lead to the institutionalisation of children who would be better off with their families. The rights to health and education are also mentioned in a couple of agreements (Sierra Leone and Burundi).[63] Protection of returnee children, property rights

---

60 The question of how to make peace agreements more successful is dealt with in detail in the *Report of the Secretary-General: In Larger Freedom: Towards Development, Security and Human Rights for All*, UN doc. A/59/2005.

61 *Washington Agreement Signed by Bosnian Prime Minister Haris Silajdzic; Croatian Foreign Minister Mate Granic; Bosnian Croat Representative Kresimir Zubak: Confederation Agreement between the Bosnian Government and Bosnian Croats* (1 March 1994), www.usip.org/library/pa/bosnia/washagree_03011994_toc.html. *Actions and Measures for Chiapas Joint Commitments and Proposals from the State and Federal Governments and the Ezln* (16 February 1996), www.usip.org/library/pa/chiapas/agreement_960216.html.

62 *The Final Agreement on the Implementation of the 1976 Tripoli Agreement between the Government of the Republic of the Philippines (GRP) and the Moro National Liberation Front (MNLF) with the Participation of the Organization of Islamic Conference Ministerial Committee of Six and the Secretary General of the Organization of Islamic Conference* (2 September 1996), www.usip.org/library/pa/philippines/tripoli_12231976.html.

63 It is also worth noting that the Convention on the Rights of the Child makes reference to "peace" in Article 29(1(d)) in relation to education, in that the State has an obligation in regard to "the preparation of the child for responsible life in ... peace". The issue of education in peace agreements has been extensively dealt with in INTERNATIONAL SAVE THE CHILDREN

and psychosocial support for children are elements of the Burundi peace agreement.[64]

Since 1996, out of 10 peace agreements that had some mention of children's issues, five have made specific reference to some kind of recovery and reintegration. The table below allows for a comparative analysis of the provisions that have been included:

Agreement	**Provisions relevant to recovery and reintegration**
Liberia, 2003[65]	"accord special attention to the issue of child combatants. b. It shall, accordingly, mobilize resources with the assistance of the International Community, especially in cooperation with the Office of the U.N. Special Representative for Children in Armed Conflict, UNICEF, the African Committee of Experts on the Rights and Welfare of the Child and other relevant agencies, to address their special demobilization and re-integration needs."
Nepal, 2006[66]	"not to conscript or use children who are aged 18 or below in the armed force. Children thus affected shall be rescued immediately and appropriate assistance as may be needed shall be provided for their rehabilitation."
Sierra Leone, 1999[67]	"The Government shall accord particular attention to the issue of child soldiers. It shall, accordingly, mobilize resources, both within the country and from the International Community, and especially through the Office of the UN Special Representative for Children in Armed Conflict, UNICEF and other agencies, to address the special needs of these children in the existing disarmament, demobilization and reintegration processes."

ALLIANCE, *Where Peace Begins: Education's Role in Conflict Prevention and Peacebuilding*, 2008.

64 *Arusha Peace and Reconciliation Agreement for Burundi*, 28 August 2000, www.usip.org/library/pa/burundi/pa_burundi_08282000_toc.html.

65 *Comprehensive Peace Agreement between the Government of Liberia and the Liberians United for Reconciliation and Democracy (LURD) and the Movement for Democracy in Liberia (MODEL) and Political Parties*, 18 August 2003, www.usip.org/library/pa/liberia/liberia_08182003_cpa.html, article XXXI on Vulnerable Groups.

66 *Unofficial Translation of the Comprehensive Peace Agreement Concluded between the Government of Nepal and the Communist Party of Nepal (Maoist)*, 21 November 2006, article 7.6.1.

67 *The Government of the Republic of Sierra Leone and the Revolutionary United Front of Sierra Leone (RUF/SL)*, 7 July 1999, www.usip.org/library/pa/sl/sierra_leone_07071999_toc.html, article XXX on Child Combatants.

68 *Agreement on Permanent Ceasefire and Security Arrangements Implementation Modalities During the Pre-Interim and the Interim Periods between the Government of the Sudan (GoS) and the Sudan People's Liberation Movement/Sudan People's Liberation Army (SPLM/SPLA)*, 31 December 2004, www.usip.org/library/pa/sudan/pa_sudan.html, articles 24.9–24.11.

Agreement	Provisions relevant to recovery and reintegration
Sudan, Comprehensive Peace Agreement, 2005[68]	"recruitment of child soldiers" a ceasefire violation. Among guiding principles: "The demobilization of all child soldiers within six months of the signature of the Comprehensive Peace Agreement." "UNICEF, ICRC and other international organisations are called upon to assist in the child component of the DDR in the Sudan."
Sudan, Darfur Peace Agreement, 2006[69]	"The Parties shall release all boys and girls associated with armed forces and groups. UNICEF, UNHCR, and the ICRC shall be called upon to assist in the identification, removal, family unification and reintegration of children associated with armed forces and groups." "UNICEF and other child protection organizations shall be called upon to support and assist in the identification, removal, family reunification and reintegration of children associated with armed forces and armed groups."

The focus on children's issues in peace agreements is an important advocacy opportunity. Once the parties to a conflict are aware of the legal obligations, they may recognise the need to put in place programmes for the recovery and reintegration of children. This is critically important for the successful reintegration of children, as international law does not deal with practical matters related to what good reintegration programmes should look like.[70]

A good example of recognition for the need of a programme for the release and reintegration of children is the Sudan Comprehensive Peace Agreement (CPA). The civil war in Southern Sudan began in 1983 and raged for more than 20 years, ending with the adoption of the CPA.[71] The CPA covers the southern third of Sudan's territory and includes agreements on the sharing of political power and national resources between two governments within one country. All groups had to align themselves either with the Government or the Sudan People's Liberation Movement/Army (SPLM/A) following the signing of the Comprehensive Peace Agreement. This seems to have more or less worked, although it took some time for some groups.

The CPA included substantive provisions concerning children, including a general reference to the CRC and a provision on the general rights of children. It also had specific provisions relating to the release of child soldiers within six months of the signature of the agreement. A specific provision was also made for children separated from their families in order to cater for the tracing of their

69 *Darfur Peace Agreement*, 5 May 2006, www.unmis.org/english/dpa.htm, article 275.

70 A. Ayissi, *Protecting Children in Armed Conflict: From Commitment to Compliance, Disarmament Forum*, no. 3 (2002) at 5.

71 *Agreement on Permanent Ceasefire and Security Arrangements Implementation Modalities During the Pre-Interim and the Interim Periods between the Government of the Sudan (Gos) and the Sudan People's Liberation Movement/Sudan People's Liberation Army (SPLM/SPLA).'*

families and family reunification. UNICEF and the ICRC were called upon to assist in the child component of DDR in Sudan.

The CPA was the backbone for child release and reintegration in the areas covered by the CPA. In this context, it was consistently referred to by both the Government of Southern Sudan and the Government of National Unity.[72] There were areas in which it was not clear how child DDR would be implemented, especially in the three Areas between the North and the South, nor was it implemented within the required timeframe, but without any doubt the CPA was the "body of law" that was referred to for the specific provisions. It was also complemented by an Interim Constitution, which had the bearing of prime law in the national legal system and provided backing for the CPA.[73]

The Darfur Peace Agreement (DPA), which was adopted in May 2006, is the most comprehensive of all agreements in dealing with children's issues. The agreement included provisions related to identification, removal, family unification and reintegration of children associated with armed forces and groups. It also included provisions relating to sexual and gender-based violence, as well as special protection measures for women and children in the camps, including services provided by police specific to women and children.[74]

The gender aspect is an important one. International law concerning the recruitment and use of children in armed forces and groups is not gender sensitive. However, peace agreements can add that element, as was done in the Darfur Peace Agreement. Paragraph 275 of the Darfur Agreement states:

> The Parties shall release all boys and girls associated with armed forces and groups. UNICEF, UNHCR, and the ICRC shall be called upon to assist in the identification, removal, family unification and reintegration of children associated with armed forces and groups.

Gender sensitivity is important in this context, as is the definition of who is a child soldier, because girls easily become excluded if they are not specifically highlighted. Sometimes, girls carry guns just like boys and are easily recognised as "child soldiers", but sometimes they are involved as cooks or used for the purposes of forced sex. In the release process girls have been often excluded from reintegration programmes either because they were not armed and not considered "child soldiers" or because no one thought to include them. Obviously, the DPA did not hold up peace in Darfur, but it nevertheless provided, and

---

72 See for instance UNICEF, *Assessment of Unicef Supported Programmes for Reintegration of Children Formerly Associated with Armed Groups and Forces in Sudan*, 2008.

73 *Agreement on Permanent Ceasefire and Security Arrangements Implementation Modalities During the Pre-Interim and the Interim Periods between the Government of the Sudan (Gos) and the Sudan People's Liberation Movement/Sudan People's Liberation Army (SPLM/SPLA).*

74 *Darfur Peace Agreement,* Articles 3, 17, 21, 22, 25, 26, 27 and 29 all have relevance to children.

continues to provide to date, a forum for discussion to try and address the situation of children.[75]

As we have seen from the above, peace agreements can also add detail and allow for contextual interpretation, which will enhance the legal standard in a given situation. However, there is still room for making the child dimensions of peace agreements more comprehensive, considering the vast recovery and reintegration needs that exist and go beyond the needs of children who have been recruited or used by armed groups and forces.

6. CONCLUSIONS

As we have seen from the above analysis there are some provisions at the international level for the recovery and reintegration of war-affected children, but still many gaps. Comprehensive frameworks are in place only for children who have been recruited or used by armed groups or forces, and there is much room for developing further and more specific standards in other areas as well.

Some of the focus on recovery and reintegration may not need to be specific to children, but the arguments found in international law are compelling, and can be used more proactively in advocacy at the international and national levels in order to bring the same focus found in the CRC and the OP-CAAC into other initiatives as well. Such normative standards do not have to come in the form of treaties, but can also be included in peace agreements, action plans and other forms of agreement that provide for practical approaches to addressing the recovery and reintegration needs of children.

Generally, the area of transitional justice and children, and how it relates to their successful recovery and reintegration, is underexplored, with many issues remaining difficult because they have still not been considered so as to reach agreement on some of the approaches. While there is no "one size fits all" solution, it would be useful to study further the linkages between transitional justice and the psycho-social well-being of children, in other words, how different procedures may or may not feed into the recovery process for a child.

In all of this it would be important to bring in the children and young people more proactively, exploring how they can participate in the recovery of their own society and how they can influence the peace or transitional justice process.

[75] *The Action Plan between the Sudan Liberation Movement/Army (SLM/A) and the United Nations Children's Fund regarding Children associated with the SLM/A*, 11 June 2007 is an example of such an undertaking. The SLM/A is a signatory to the Darfur Peace Agreement, and in the Action Plan the Agreement is consistently referred to. The Sudan Tribune reported that 36 children were released on 27 July 2009.

PSYCHOSOCIAL WELL-BEING AND THE INTEGRATION OF WAR-AFFECTED CHILDREN: TOWARD A COMMUNITY RESILIENCE APPROACH

Michael WESSELLS

Armed conflict inflicts a heavy burden of suffering on children[1], who are defined under international law as people under 18 years of age. Typically, children comprise approximately half the population of war-torn countries, the physical infrastructure and social fabric of which are ravaged by conflict. The effects on children and their societies are likely to be systemic and long-lasting.

The horrors of war are most conspicuous not in statistics but in the voices of young people. Speaking in November 2009 about the Israeli military attacks a year earlier, a 14-year-old Palestinian woman from Gaza told me "I was so frightened and overwhelmed I just wished I was dead and could die right at that moment…". It is well documented that such experiences leave in their wake psychological problems such as depression, post-traumatic stress disorder (PTSD), anxiety, and other mental health problems.[2] These problems are

1 G. MACHEL, *The impact of war on children*, David Philip, Cape Town, 2001; UNICEF, *Machel Study 10-year Strategic Review: Children and Conflict in a Changing World*, New York, 2009.

2 R. APFEL and B. SIMON (eds.), *Minefields in their hearts*, Yale University Press, New Haven, 1996; T. BETANCOURT and T. WILLIAMS, 'Building an evidence base on mental health interventions for children affected by armed conflict', (2008) 6 1 *Intervention,* 39–56; P. BOLTON, J. BASS, T. BETANCOURT, L. SPEELMAN et al., 'Interventions for depression symptoms among adolescent survivors of war and displacement in northern Uganda: A randomized control trial', (2007) 298 5 *JAMA*, 519–527; Y. DANIELI, N. RODLEY and L. WEISAETH (eds.), *International responses to traumatic stress*, Amityville, NY Baywood, 1996; I. DERLUYN, E. BROEKAERT, G. SCHUYTEN and E. DE TEMMERMAN, 'Post-traumatic stress in former Ugandan child soldiers', (2004) 363 *The Lancet*, 861–863; A. DYREGOV, R. GJESTAD and M. RAUNDALEN, 'Children exposed to warfare', (2002) 15 *Journal of Traumatic Stress,* 59–68; L. JONES, 'Responding to the needs of children in crisis', (2008) 20 3 *International Review of Psychiatry,* 291–303; R. MOLLICA, C. POLE, L. SON et al., 'Effects of war trauma on Cambodian refugee adolescents' functional health and mental health status', (1997) 36 *Journal of the American Academy of child and Adolescent Psychiatry,* 1098–1106; W. YULE, R. STUVLAND, F. BAINGANA and P. SMITH, 'Children in armed conflict', in B. GREEN et al. (eds.), *Trauma interventions in war and peace,* Kluwer, New York, 2003, 217–242.

compounded by the structural violence – particularly the deep poverty – that robs people of their dignity, makes it difficult to meet basic needs and imposes untold suffering.

The promotion of the psychosocial well-being of children who live in zones of armed conflict and in post-conflict settings ought to be a high priority for the international humanitarian community. Damage to rising generations undermines social capital, impedes development and productivity as measured in Disability Adjusted Life Years[3] and constitutes an assault on the human spirit. Unfortunately, humanitarian efforts to enable children's psychosocial well-being in war zones have themselves been problematic.

In many war-torn countries, both the conceptual frameworks that guide intervention and the interventions themselves have been divided into two poles.[4] At one pole have been specialised, clinical approaches that emphasise the importance of clinical problems and of intervention by professionals such as psychiatrists and trauma counsellors. At the other pole have been holistic, community-based approaches that emphasise attention to non-clinical issues such as family separation, stigmatisation and loss of hope and emphasise the importance of psychosocial support organised by groups of affected people, governments and non-specialists. This polarisation has made it difficult to construct a comprehensive conceptualisation of how children have been affected by war as well as the comprehensive support that is badly needed.

In addition, most psychosocial interventions on behalf of war-affected children have focused narrowly on deficits.[5] Although attention to deficits is necessary, a deficits overemphasis can create a misleading picture of war-affected children as hapless victims. In fact, children are active makers of meaning who seek to make sense out of what happens in their lives, and in war zones they attempt to actively engage and cope with the myriad life adversities they face.[6] In addition, significant numbers of war-affected children exhibit remarkable

---

3 D. Chisholm, S. Saxena and M. Van Ommeren, *Dollars, DALYs and decisions: Economic aspects of the mental health system*, WHO, Geneva, 2006.

4 Betancourt et al., *supra* note 2; M. Wessells and M. Van Ommeren, 'Developing inter-agency guidelines on mental health and psychological support in emergency settings', (2008) 6 3/4 *Intervention*, 199–218.

5 B. Barber, 'Glimpsing the complexity of youth and political violence', in B. Barber (ed.), *Adolescents and war: How youth deal with political violence*, Oxford University Press, New York, 2009, 3–32; M. Wessells, *Child soldiers: From violence to protection*, Harvard University Press, Cambridge, 2006.

6 Barber, ibid.; N. Boothby, A. Strang and M. Wessells (eds.), A *world turned upside down: Social ecological approaches to children in war zones*', Kumarian, Westport, 2006; L. Jones, 'Adolescent understandings of political violence and psychological well-being', (2002) 55 *Social Science and Medicine*, 1351–1371; G. Straker, *Faces in the revolution*, David Philip, Cape Town, 1992; M. Wessells and K. Kostelny, 'Youth soldiering: An integrated framework for understanding psychosocial impact', in B. Barber (ed.), *Adolescents and war: How youth deal with political violence*, Oxford University Press, New York, 2009, 105–122.

resilience, though they still need support.[7] This resilience is due in part to war-affected children's assets – cognitive and social competencies, coping strategies, and an array of supports from family, peers, religious leaders and others – which they use to support their own well-being.

At the same time, there has been too strong a focus on individual well-being. Although this tendency is understandable in light of the emphasis of Western psychology on the individual, it is a poor fit with the low- and middle-income countries that are home to most contemporary armed conflicts. Affected people often understand the effects of war through a collectivist lens that emphasises not individual problems but the collective problems associated with the destruction of homes, schools, health posts and community spaces. In rural Angola, a 14-year-old boy who had formerly been a soldier and who showed signs of PTSD such as repeated nightmares said: "The reason I cannot sleep at night is that the spirit of the man I killed comes to me and asks 'Why did you do this to me?'" Both he and his community viewed his spiritual affliction not as an individual affliction but a collective problem since an angry spirit was believed to have great power to harm the community by causing crop failure, illness and other problems.[8] In many other situations, too, the wounds of war are viewed primarily in collective terms, as acute anguish often comes from children's inability to support their families or from threats of ongoing insecurity that blunt the hopes of all young people.[9] The fact that this spiritual problem of the Angolan young man sits outside the scope of the conceptual frameworks of Western psychologists indicates the importance of listening to young people. Sadly, one of the greatest gaps in psychosocial assistance is the listening gap, as too few humanitarian workers devote sufficient attention to trying to understand how local people themselves view their problems. This example also illustrates that war-affected children who live in rural areas of sub-Saharan Africa tend to understand the effects of armed conflict in spiritual terms.[10] The greatest distress arose not from an individual problem but from the rupture of the harmony between the living community and the world of the ancestors. In the view of this young person and the members of his

---

7 Wessells, *supra* note 5; N. Boothby, J. Crawford and J. Halperin, 'Mozambican child soldier life outcome study: Lessons learned on rehabilitation and reintegration efforts', (2006) 1 1 *Global Public Health*, 87–107.

8 M. Wessells and C. Monteiro, 'Psychosocial interventions and post-war reconstruction in Angola: Interweaving Western and traditional approaches', in D. Christie, R.V. Wagner and D. Winter (eds.), *Peace, conflict, and violence: Peace psychology for the 21st century*, Upper Saddle River, Prentice-Hall, 2001, 262–275; M. Wessells and C. Monteiro, 'Healing the wounds following protracted conflict in Angola: A community-based approach to assisting war-affected children', in U.P. Gielen, J. Fish and J.G. Draguns (eds.), *Handbook of culture, therapy, and healing*, Mahwah, Erlbaum, 2004, 321–341.

9 J. Boyden and S. Gibbs, *Children and war*, United Nations, Geneva, 1997; J. Boyden and G. Mann, 'Children's risk, resilience, and coping in extreme situations', in M. Ungar (ed.), *Handbook for working with children and youth: Pathways to resilience across cultures and contexts*, Thousand Oaks, Sage, 2005.

10 A. Honwana, *Child soldiers in Africa*, University of Pennsylvania Press, Philadelphia, 2006.

community, what was needed was the conduct of a spiritual cleansing ritual that would clean him of his spiritual impurities, honour the ancestors and restore the balance between the living community and the ancestors.

This chapter outlines a more comprehensive conceptualisation of impact and a suitably holistic intervention strategy that takes into account children's capacities for coping and the resilience associated with social assets. The first section sketches a holistic framework for conceptualising the psychosocial well-being of war-affected children. The second part then explores how to develop comprehensive psychosocial support for children affected by war. Bringing forward insights and lessons learned from the field, it suggests the importance of taking a resilience approach that organises holistic, community-based support and builds upon the existing assets and strengths that affected populations have. Recognising the importance of avoiding the pendulum effect wherein psychosocial interventions have alternately underemphasised or overemphasised resilience, the chapter concludes with reflections on Do No Harm issues that arise in applying a resilience approach.

1. A HOLISTIC CONCEPTUALISATION OF IMPACT

Analyses of the impact of war on children have sometimes erred by conceptualising war-affected children as a homogeneous category. In reality, it is highly diverse and includes children who are affected at different levels and in different ways by a wide array of risk factors. As outlined below, the primary implication is that a comprehensive approach to psychosocial support should include different kinds of intervention.

1.1. DIVERSITY

An essential step toward effective practice is to step behind the term "war-affected children" and appreciate the diverse psychosocial issues that can be obscured by that term. In conflict zones, children are subjected to a wide array of protection risks that threaten their well-being. These include family separation, displacement, loss of home and property, recruitment, deprivation of education, gender-based violence, stigma associated with disability, HIV and AIDS, trafficking and dangerous labour, among many others. Each of these risks can affect psychosocial well-being in distinctive ways, and they create the need for very different kinds of support. For a separated child, the key immediate intervention needed is family tracing and unification, whereas for a girl who has been raped a different constellation of interventions – health, legal, psychosocial, etc. – is needed. Also, children are often affected by multiple risks, cautioning against intervention strategies that have too singular a focus.

Issues of age, gender and social class also make it difficult to speak of war-affected children as if they were a homogeneous category. Very young children have special vulnerabilities, yet are invisible in most war contexts. Youth, such as teenagers and young adults, also have specific vulnerabilities since they are prime targets for recruitment. Lacking adequate education and employment opportunities, youth in post-conflict settings are often idle, alienated and at risk of crime and drug use. Girls are often at increased risk because of their marginal status in patriarchal societies and their susceptibility to forms of gender-based violence such as sexual violence and forced early marriage. Among the most vulnerable children, however, are those from lower socio-economic classes whose poverty had created significant risks even before the conflict but who suffer disproportionately during and after the conflict.

Psychosocial impacts of war also vary according to other factors such as the "dose" or levels of exposure to violence, pre-existing vulnerabilities such as mental health problems, and the amount and quality of current support. In addition, the impacts of war depend not only on past violence but on current living conditions.

1.2. EVERYDAY DISTRESS

Although external psychologists and psychiatrists often focus on the prevalence of PTSD and related disorders, war-affected children frequently say that their greatest sources of distress are not the residues of past violence but everyday problems related to their current situation.[11] For example, following the conflict in East Timor children often identified their biggest worries as not having adequate shelter or enough food. In many post-conflict zones, food insecurity propels children into living on the streets, where they are at increased risk of abuse and exploitation.

Among the greatest sources of distress is ongoing insecurity, which undermines healing and well-being. Post-conflict zones may be as dangerous as active war zones since they are saturated with violence associated with crime, banditry and the breakdown of law and order. Also, severe poverty creates enormous stresses at household level and frequently leads to increased family violence, which strongly affects children in war zones.[12] In the camps for

---

11 Barber, *supra* note 5; Wessells and Kostelny, *supra* note 6; B. Barber, 'Political violence, social integration, and youth functioning: Palestinian youth from the Intifada', (2001) 29 3 *Journal of Community Psychology*, 259–280; M. Eggerman and C. Panter-Brick, 'Suffering, hope, and entrapment: Resilience and cultural values in Afghanistan', (2001) 71 1 *Social Science and Medicine*, 71–83; K. Miller and P. Omidian, 'Daily stressors, war experiences, and mental health in Afghanistan', (2008) 45 *Transcultural Psychiatry*, 611–638.

12 J. Annan and M. Brier, 'The risk of return: Intimate partner violence in Northern Uganda's armed conflict', (2009) 70 *Social Science and Medicine*, 152–159; J. Garbarino and K. Kostelny, 'The effects of political violence on Palestinian children's behavioral problems',

displaced people in northern Uganda, rape and gender-based violence were a major source of insecurity that had a powerful impact on women. In 2005, women in several camps told me that their lives were so bad because of poverty and gender-based violence that they wished their lives would end soon.

However, it is not always survival or security needs that cause the greatest distress in war-affected children. Following a spate of brutal wars, children and youth in West Africa frequently reported that lack of education was their greatest worry.[13] For many children, the loss of home and parental income compels a painful decision to drop out of school in order to work to help support their family. In Burundi, widespread unemployment and poverty have created a crisis of hope[14] and have made it very difficult for youth to assume the roles that are normally expected of young men. Having a positive role is an essential part of finding meaning in difficult circumstances, and the inability to fulfil desired and expected roles causes anguish and humiliation.

It is important to keep in mind that everyday sources of distress are grounded in structural violence, which is arguably the greatest source of psychological harm from a long-term perspective. For example, in the West Bank profound distress arises from the structural violence of the Occupation, which occasions everyday problems such as the frustration, humiliation and domination experienced at checkpoints. In post-conflict zones such as Guatemala, significant numbers of people are affected by ongoing discrimination, which squashes dignity and hope while killing people slowly. In conceptualising the impact of armed conflict, then, it is essential to focus not only on particular episodes of violence but also on the wider systems of oppression and social injustice in which they are rooted.[15]

1.3. IMPLICATIONS FOR PRACTICE

These points about the multiplicity of sources of distress and the impacts on war-affected children indicate the necessity of taking a holistic approach to psychosocial support for such children. A holistic approach entails multi-sectoral work in areas such as income generation, education (non-formal and formal) and child protection as well as in methods that Western-trained psychologists are

(1996) 67 *Child Development*, 33–45; V. Khamis, 'Child psychological maltreatment in Palestinian families', (2001) 24 8 *Child Abuse and Neglect*, 1047–1059.

13 J. Lowicki, *Youth speak out*, Women's Commission for Refugee Women and Children, New York, 2005.

14 P. Uvin, *Life after violence: A people's story*, Penguin, New York, 2008.

15 Christie et al., *supra* note 8.

more likely to be familiar with.[16] To take a holistic approach requires "getting outside the box" of mainstream psychology.

Taking a holistic approach also entails analysis of the social ecologies in which children develop[17] and the strengthening of support at different levels – individual, household, community and societal. For example, if a formerly recruited girl who had been sexually violated were returning to her village, individual support might include individual emotional processing, vocational skills training and income generation, and the conduct of a cleansing ritual by a traditional healer to rid the girl of spiritual impurities. Family support might include steps such as family trading and reunification and mediation to help handle non-violently the conflicts that frequently arise following life in the bush. Community support might include access to education and efforts to reduce stigma by increasing awareness of how the girls had suffered and encouraging the social integration of the girls and their children. At the societal level, advocacy efforts might be needed to enable older girls' access to education and also to end discrimination against girls and support a wider women's rights agenda.

The diversity of the sources of distress and impacts on children cautions against one-size-fits-all approaches. In post-conflict zones, many children may be supported by organising access to education, either through schools or through non-formal venues such as child-friendly spaces.[18] However, there will be other children, such as separated children or survivors of sexual violence, who need specific support tailored to their particular situation and needs. Thus, different layers of psychosocial support are needed in order to develop a comprehensive approach.

A convenient way of representing this idea is in the form of an intervention pyramid having four layers.[19] The base of the pyramid consists of steps to provide security and meet basic needs. When these needs are met, the majority of children will recover without specialised assistance by virtue of receiving non-formal support from family, friends, teachers, religious leaders and others. The

---

16 Wessells, *supra* note 5; Wessells and Kostelny, *supra* note 6; J. Annan, C. Blattman and R. Horton, *The state of youth and youth protection in northern Uganda: Findings from the Survey for War Affected Youth*, UNICEF, Kampala, 2006; M. McCallin, 'Community involvement in the social reintegration of child soldiers', in P. Bracken and C. Petty (eds.), *Rethinking the trauma of war*, Free Association, London, 1998, 60–75.

17 Boothby et al., *supra* note 6; U. Bronfenbrenner, *The ecology of human development*, Harvard University, Cambridge Press, 1979; A. Dawes and D. Donald, 'Improving children's chances: Developmental theory and effective interventions in community contexts', in D. Donald, A. Dawes and J. Louw (eds.), *Addressing childhood diversity,* David Philip, Cape Town, 2000, 1–25.

18 K. Kostelny and M. Wessells, 'The protection and psychosocial well-being of young children following armed conflict: Outcome research on child centered spaces in northern Uganda', (2008) 3 2 *The Journal of Developmental Processes,* 13–25.

19 Inter-Agency Standing Committee, *IASC Guidelines on Mental Health and Psychosocial Support in Emergency Settings*, IASC, Geneva, 2007.

second layer includes family and community support such as tracing and reunification for separated children and access to education for children who had previously lacked it. The third layer consists of focused, nonprofessional support such as peer support groups or income generating activities for survivors of sexual violence. The top layer includes the specialised support from psychiatrists, psychologists and traditional healers that is needed by severely affected children who are unable to function well. Although severely affected children are typically a small minority, they are an important group because they may include thousands of people, and the failure to support them can lead to much suffering and social disruption.

As this pyramid indicates, the psychosocial support system for war-affected children should be just as systematic as are the risks that harm children's well-being in war zones. To build this systematic support requires the work of many different agencies – typically international NGOs, UN agencies and government ministries – and of civil society actors at different levels. In order for this system to work, however, there must be effective coordination and referral mechanisms across different layers. As called for in the *IASC Guidelines on Mental Health and Psychosocial Support in Emergency Settings*, coordination is the joint responsibility of the Health Cluster and the Protection Cluster. In practice, however, effective coordination is one of the greatest of all humanitarian challenges.

An important implication of the multi-layered system of supports is that the majority of war-affected children will recover with the help of indigenous support. In other words, self-help within groups of affected people is a core part of psychosocial support for war-affected children.[20] This fundamental point is at the heart of a community resilience approach to psychosocial support.

2. A COMMUNITY RESILIENCE APPROACH

Numerous considerations argue in favour of taking a resilience approach rather than the deficits approach that is used widely by outside agencies. For one thing, a community resilience approach puts the emphasis on what people naturally do to enable children's psychosocial well-being. This emphasis is a useful antidote to the tendency of many humanitarian agencies to rush in, plant their flag, and build new support initiatives without taking stock of what support is already there. Ideally, it leads practitioners to ask first what people are doing to support each other and to build on this existing support. This approach is highly respectful, and it identifies the assets and resources that affected people have. A key lesson learned from programming in many countries is that psychosocial programmes are more likely to yield sustainable psychosocial support to the extent that they mobilise and build on existing resources and assets. In many

20 Ibid.

conflict situations, the external support established by humanitarian agencies collapses at the end of the funding period. Such unsustainable approaches are not only wasteful but are incapable of providing the long-term psychosocial support that war-affected children need and are entitled to.

In addition, a community resilience approach promotes the sense of empowerment and agency that are at the heart of effective programming. Resilience approaches promote empowerment and a sense of control in that they highlight and build upon what people already do to support each other. By virtue of their orientation, they encourage self-help and steps by children, families and communities to promote each other's well-being. Evidence from many emergencies, including conflict situations, indicates that the reestablishment of a sense of control and hope is a fundamental promoter of psychosocial well-being.[21] In contrast, deficits approaches tacitly portray war-affected children as victims, which is hardly an empowering view. Many deficits approaches worsen this problem by speaking of survivors as traumatised, thereby pathologising normal reactions to extreme events.[22] Further, the use of labels such as "mass trauma" carries the risk of reducing to medical terms problems that have deep roots in socio-historical, political and economic conditions.[23]

A community resilience approach also helps to circumvent the problems associated with an excessive focus on individual issues. If, as suggested earlier, some of the main psychosocial impacts on children are communal, it makes sense to develop support strategies that have a communal focus. Further, taking a community approach makes it possible to support many different war-affected children, thereby bypassing the problems of jealousy and social division that occur when aid is targeted only on particular individuals or groups.

Last but not least, a community resilience approach offers opportunities to support war-affected children on a wide scale. Following armed conflict, large numbers of children need psychosocial support, yet individually focused approaches make it difficult to support children on the scale that is needed. These potential benefits, however, are likely to be realised in practice only if they are backed by a coherent conceptualisation of the nature of community resilience, including its dynamic and transformative aspects.

---

21 S. Hobfoll et al., 'Five essential elements of immediate and mid-term mass trauma intervention: Empirical evidence', (2007) 70 4 *Psychiatry*, 283–315.

22 Bracken, *supra* note 16.

23 R. Punamaki, 'Political violence and mental health', (1989) 17 *International Journal of Mental Health*, 3–15; D. Summerfield, 'A critique of seven assumptions behind psychological trauma programmes in war-affected areas', (1999) 48 *Social Science and Medicine*, 1449–1462.

2.1. CONCEPTUALISING COMMUNITY RESILIENCE

Among humanitarian workers, resilience is often thought of as people's ability to "bounce back" following a setback. Although this metaphor has its merits, it suffers from being too static. To speak of bouncing back implies that following difficulties, including extreme challenges, people return to something like their previous state, when in fact people may be transformed by their experiences. In fact, there is evidence from areas such as post-traumatic growth that over time, people may not only recover but also become stronger. At community level, it would be unwise to suggest that returning to the pre-war conditions is a positive outcome, particularly since the pre-war conditions contained the seeds of war.

The metaphor of bouncing back also implies that resilience is a quality or characteristic that one either has or does not have. In children, however, a more dynamic conceptualisation is needed, as a child who seems resilient at one moment can become overwhelmed moments later if the calamities of war intrude. One useful way of thinking about how this shift can occur is in terms of the balance between risk and protective factors such as quality family care and positive strategies of coping and adaptation.[24] When protective factors outweigh risk factors, children are resilient and cope relatively well with the adversities they face. But when the risk factors outweigh the protective factors, children are not resilient and are likely to suffer negative developmental outcomes. Research indicates that an accumulation of risk factors produces exponential increases in the likelihood of negative outcomes for children.[25] These dynamic aspects of resilience are best captured by conceptualising resilience as a process rather than as a static quality. Masten and colleagues[26] defined resilience as "the processes of, capacity for, or patterns of positive adaptation during or following exposure to adverse experiences that have the potential to disrupt or destroy the successful functioning or development of the person".[27] This definition not only reflects the dynamic aspects of resilience but also underscores the importance of capacities for positive adaptation. These capacities may include specific coping skills, wider cognitive or emotional competencies, or strategies for adaptation.

---

24 M. Rutter, 'Protective factors in children's response to stress and disadvantage', in M. Kint and J. Rolf (eds.), *Primary prevention of psychopathology, Vol. 3. Social competence in children,* University Press of New England, Hanover, 1979, 49–74; M. Rutter, 'Resilience in the face of adversity', (1985) 147 *British Journal of Psychiatry,* 598–611.

25 Rutter, ibid.; Garbarino, *supra* note 12.

26 A. Masten, 'Ordinary magic: Resilience processes in development', (2001) 56 3 *American Psychologist,* 227–238; A. Masten, K. Best and N. Garmezy, 'Resilience and development: Contributions from the study of children who overcome adversity', (1990) 2 *Development and Psychopathology,* 425–424.

27 A. Masten and J. Obradovic, 'Disaster preparation and recovery: Lessons from research on resilience in human development', (2008) 13 1, Art. 9., *Ecology and society,* see online: http:www.ecologyandsociety.org/vol13/iss1/art9/.

Because there is no widely accepted definition of community resilience, a useful first step is to build on the above definition, which had been developed in regard to individuals. Extending this definition, community resilience may be defined as the community-level processes of and capacities for positive adaptation during or following exposure to adverse circumstances. This definition does not assume that communities are essentially like individuals. In fact, communities may have emergent properties and have very different processes for positive adaptation than individuals do. For example, in Afghanistan there are collective norms of *zakat* wherein people give food and other necessities to needy people. In addition, the way in which communities decide how to adapt to a crisis is very different from the way in which individuals take such decisions. Group decisions are inherently more complex and involve diverse actors (e.g., government leaders, traditional leaders, elders, respected young people, etc.) who have different levels of power, status and influence.

A conceptual cornerstone of a community resilience approach is that a community is not an island but is embedded in a larger social system with which it continually interacts. This systems approach is necessary for capturing the transactional, relational nature of child development.[28] Similarly, community development has transactional, relational qualities since the quality of community support for war-affected children depends on the interactions between the community and the wider system. If, for example, a particular community aided girls by enabling them to earn an income from selling particular items, this activity would be supported by connecting the girls with markets beyond the community. In terms of programming, it calls attention to the importance of building effective linkages between the community and sources of support for children at higher levels (e.g. district, provincial, societal). It also highlights the need to couple community-level work with efforts to support children at a wider level. An ecological systems orientation, then, is an essential part of a community resilience approach.

Of necessity, this conceptualisation of community resilience in terms of dynamic process, capacities, and adaptation with transformation is preliminary. It is too early to carve one's understanding of community resilience in stone. What makes communities resilient and how resilient communities function may be quite different in a rural setting than in the complex urban settings that are home to a rapidly increasing percentage of the global population. Significant variation may also occur due to differences of culture, social norms, community structure and leadership, and the wealth and resource base of the context. At this juncture, it is useful to avoid taking a highly formulaic approach and to adopt instead the position that "we don't know what we don't know". A useful first step is to identify exemplars of a community resilience approach that simultaneously

[28] Ibid.

illustrate aspects of community resilience and illuminate the role that external agencies can play in supporting it.

2.2. PREVENTION

Among the key things that resilient communities do is to prevent harm to children by helping to create a protective environment that minimises risks and strengthens protective factors. An example from Afghanistan[29] illustrates how outside facilitation can be useful in enabling communities to develop a more protective environment.

In north-eastern Afghanistan, in the period 2003–2006 following the defeat of the Taliban, worsening economic conditions led families to marry their daughters at progressively younger ages in order to obtain the bride price. Girls as young as 11 years of age were being married to 55-year-old men, leading to reproductive health problems and abuse. So upsetting was this practice that young girls in Badakshan province committed suicide by throwing themselves off a bridge. Although young girls in the region needed psychosocial support, the highest priority was to prevent the forced early marriages.

To prevent this problem, community members who were part of the local child protection committee that had been formed with the assistance of ChildFund/Afghanistan decided that the local imams were in the best position to help. Community members and Afghan staff of ChildFund visited the local imam and explained how the practice was harming the girls and pointed out that marrying girls at such young ages was not a tradition. All the imams demonstrated concern for the girls' well-being, and some noted that nothing in sharia law compelled such early marriage. In over half the communities, the imam agreed to try to help the community end the harmful practice.

Working in a collective manner, the imams convened a community discussion in which they pointed out the harm caused to the girls and stated that marrying off such young girls had no basis in Islamic law or tradition. Because of the respect accorded to the imams, this message changed local attitudes toward the practice and created an atmosphere in which older men and others could suggest an alternative. In most cases, the communities took a decision to return to the more customary Afghan practice of girls marrying at 14–15 years of age. Viewed through the lens of the UN Convention on the Rights of the Child, this was an imperfect solution. Although no rigorous evaluation was conducted, trusted sources within the communities and the NGO indicated that girls' well-being increased and the spate of young female suicides ended.

This example illustrates well how resilient communities are able to change themselves in order to address the adversities that harm community members. It

---

29 Kostelny, *supra* note 6.

also shows how community assets and community agency play a key role in enabling community resilience. The success of this effort owed much to the influence of the imams, who are key community resources in a fervent Islamic society such as Afghanistan. Other important assets were the child protection committee workers' understandings of how community change occurs. This understanding, coupled with the informal networks that led to the imam's door, were instrumental in achieving positive outcomes for girls. Looking earlier in the causal chain, these outcomes relied on the efforts of empowered community members. It is unlikely that change on such a sensitive issue could have been achieved by didactic approaches in which outsiders attempt to raise awareness of child rights and point out the harm being done.[30]

2.3. COMMUNITY RECONCILIATION

In post-conflict situations, a significant priority is the disarmament, demobilisation and reintegration (DDR) of formerly recruited children. The reintegration of formerly recruited children is a high priority because most of the children suffered as a result of their recruitment. In fact, their right to psychosocial support is guaranteed under the UN Convention on the Rights of the Child (Article 39). Without reintegration support from their families and communities, there is a risk that formerly recruited children will turn to crime and banditry or become mercenaries and continue ongoing cycles of violence.[31] Current evidence indicates that outside support may not be essential in all situations, as many formerly recruited children return home on their own and do as well as many children who went through formal DDR programmes.[32] This indicates that families and communities already have significant assets to aid reintegration.[33]

In some contexts, however, the return of formerly recruited children to their communities poses special challenges that warrant outside intervention and support. Following the brutal war in Sierra Leone, for example, formerly recruited children frequently returned to villages they had attacked when they had been part of the rebel group, the Revolutionary United Front (RUF). In this context, there was a risk of reprisal attacks against and rejection of the formerly recruited children. The risk of hostilities also increased due to the fact that after the war, the same villages that received returning former RUF members also

---

30 M. Wessells, *What are we learning about protecting children in the community? An inter-agency review of the evidence on community-based child protection mechanisms in humanitarian and development settings: Executive summary*, Save the Children UK, London, November 2009.

31 Wessells, *supra* note 5.

32 Annan et al., *supra* note 16.

33 Wessells, *supra* note 5.

received youth who had formerly fought with the Civilian Defence Forces (CDF), which villages had organised to protect themselves from the RUF. The return of former combatants who had fought each other posed significant needs for community reconciliation and non-violent conflict resolution.[34] To make matters yet worse, the official DDR programme in Sierra Leone committed the classic error of giving benefits such as clothing and seeds and tools to former soldiers while denying these benefits to the youth in the communities who had been attacked and who may have been worse off than the soldiers had been. The resulting jealousies and social divisions made work on community reconciliation a necessity.

To address these problems, ChildFund Sierra Leone took a community resilience approach in the Northern province (2002–2004) that mobilised people around addressing the significant needs of war-affected children, built on cultural assets, and promoted reconciliation and reintegration. Initially, meetings among groups of villages were convened with the purpose of identifying common, unmet needs of children. Commonly identified needs were for civic works projects such as schools, health posts and roads that connected the village with large markets in other places. The aim was to use these civic works as common ground for building partnership between the villages and stimulating the desire for cooperative action, which is one of the best means of reducing inter-group conflict.[35] This was part of a broader strategy of reconciliation wherein formerly recruited youth would cooperate with youth who had not been recruited in the construction of the identified facilities. A key part of the plan was to transform the identity, acceptability and status of the formerly recruited youth by having them engage in actions that benefitted the entire community, thereby enabling community members to see them in a different light and to feel that a measure of restorative justice had been achieved.

As the community discussions proceeded, simultaneous efforts were made to activate traditional mechanisms of reconciliation that had been disrupted by the conflict and mass displacement. ChildFund facilitators from Sierra Leone encouraged reflection on how all people, including formerly recruited children, had suffered. This was important in developing empathy, which helped to weaken images of the young people as attackers who had not suffered. Also, the facilitators asked the community members which methods of resolving conflict had been helpful in the past and whether they wanted to activate them in the current setting. This lead to excited discussion of methods such as proverbs, song, dance, dialogue and other means, and also to collective decisions to

34 M. Wessells and D. Jonah, 'Recruitment and reintegration of former youth soldiers in Sierra Leone: Challenges of reconciliation and post-accord peace building', in S. McEvoy-Levy (ed.), *Troublemakers or Peacemakers? Youth and post-accord peace building*, University of Notre Dame Press, Notre Dame, Indiana, 2006, 27–47.

35 M. Sherif, O. Harvey, B. White, W. Hood and C. Sherif, *Intergroup Cooperation and Competition: The Robbers Cave Experiment*, University Book Exchange, Norman, 1961.

reactivate traditional methods that had proven useful previously. During these discussions, an important dialogue of unity evolved in which people proclaimed "we are all Sierra Leoneons", thereby helping to quiet the fears and sense of difference that had helped to animate the war.

After this groundwork had been established, work teams consisting of even numbers of youth who had or had not been formerly recruited were formed, and the teams built the facilities that their communities had selected. Overall, 53 civic works projects were completed. For their work, the youth received a small compensation (53,000 leones, approximately US$ 27 at the time), which was essential in keeping the participants from returning to the bush. Subsequently, they received vocational counselling, vocational training and small loans for earning an income in selected occupations such as carpentry and metal work.

This process aided community reconciliation by reducing tensions between formerly opposed or fearful groups. The humanising influence of the process was visible in participants' statements that they no longer feared those on the other side but viewed them as human beings. Community members began to see the formerly recruited youth not as predators or trouble-makers but as citizens of the community who could contribute to the collective good in peaceful ways. More broadly, the process enabled villages that had been set apart by war to cooperate and engage in the collaborative dialogue and decision making that is a central part of community resilience.

The process also helped to bring the community into the wider peace process. Before the project had begun, elders had described the peace process as a distant process that was organised by politicians but that had little to do with life in the community. Through these activities, however, communities came to realise that peace at the grassroots level is important, and they empowered themselves to do their part in the wider peace process. To be sure, the external agency played a valuable role in facilitating the change, but once the process had begun, the community took charge of it, directed it, and felt ownership of it. Research in numerous domains has shown that a sense of community ownership is of fundamental importance in producing effective, sustainable outcomes on behalf of war-affected children.[36]

3. DO NO HARM

Although a community resilience approach has many advantages, there are many complexities associated with it. All psychosocial interventions, including those guided by a community resilience approach, have unintended

[36] Wessells, *supra* note 30.

consequences, and some of these cause harm.[37] Through critical reflection, one can identify various Do No Harm issues that arise in using community resilience approaches (as well as other approaches) and move into a position to prevent them. This section identifies five such issues (this is by no means an exhaustive list) and their implications for practitioners and policy makers.

3.1. MINIMISING THE NEED FOR SUPPORT

A potential risk in taking a community resilience approach is that the emphasis on resilience will downplay or minimise the need for support. The field of psychosocial support has had a pendulum effect wherein resilience is alternately overemphasised or underemphasised. Too often, discussions of resilience create the impression that everyone is fine and there is no need for psychosocial support. This impression can lead to failures to provide needed psychosocial support for children who have been severely affected. In addition, political leaders may and actually have used resilience metaphors to deny affected people needed but costly support.

To say that children and communities exhibit resilience does not imply that they have no need for support. The harsh reality of war zones is that all children, families and communities need support of different kinds, such as material, social, economic and spiritual support. Dynamic resilience models embody the principle that resilience changes over time, depending on the balance of risk and protective factors. In light of the dizzying pace of change in conflict and post-conflict zones, practitioners and policy makers should always work to organise support for the most severely affected people. Also they should recognise the ongoing need to strengthen the protective factors and to minimise the risk factors in the community systems that can either nourish or impede the well-being of children and families.

3.2. COMPLEXITIES OF "COMMUNITY" AND POWER DYNAMICS

The term "community resilience" can be problematic unless it is informed by careful analysis of the complexities associated with groups of affected people in war zones. To begin with, there may be no recognisable community since armed conflicts devastate social cohesion and pit people against each other in a struggle

---

37 M. Wessels, 'Do No Harm: Challenges in organizing psychosocial support to displaced people in emergency settings', (2008) 25 1 *Refuge*, 6-14.
M. Wessels, 'Do No Harm: Toward contextually appropriate psychosocial support in international emergencies', (2009) 64 8 *American Psychologist*, 842-854.

for basic necessities. Moreover, there may be little sense of community among displaced people who are thrown together by circumstances but who come from different regions and have important differences of ethnicity, language and religious orientation, among others. In urban areas that are home to a rapidly increasing percentage of the world's population, it can be difficult to identify communities. These problems do not warrant rejection of a community resilience approach but point to the necessity of tailoring the approach to fit the local context. The complexities of war zones defy simplistic, one-size-fits-all approaches that mistakenly imply that an approach that worked in one context can be taken off the shelf and applied in other situations with equally positive results.

Furthermore, narratives about community resilience are less than helpful if they obscure the complex power dynamics amongst groups of affected people. Although the term "community" may evoke rosy images of unity and mutual support, a community may be run by a chief and a small elite group who make the decisions and privilege particular people or groups while marginalising others. In many contexts, the poorest of the poor and members of groups that had long been subject to discrimination are excluded from community decision making and activities. In extremely patriarchal societies, women are frequently excluded from or marginalised in community decision making, which is viewed as the province of men. To avoid these problems, practitioners should build into community resilience approaches a strong emphasis on process, dynamic change over time, and transformation for social justice and full inclusion. From a policy standpoint, this is a necessity for insuring that the rights and dignity of all people are respected.

3.3. ROMANTICISED VIEWS OF CULTURE

Because community resilience approaches build on local assets and strengths, overzealous practitioners may tacitly or explicitly condone all cultural practices. Local culture, however, may contain not only helpful practices but also harmful practices such as forced early marriage, female genital mutilation/cutting, and accusations of child witchcraft. For practitioners who work within a human rights idiom, human rights standards, including the best interests of the child principle, should be used as a guide to what constitutes appropriate or harmful practices and to avoid supporting harmful practices.

An important, if often overlooked, feature of culture is that it is fluid and dynamic. This fundamental insight undermines ill-conceived attempts to either romanticise or demonise local culture. Because cultural practices evolve over time, a practice such as parents giving their daughter's hand in marriage could (with the girl's consent) support children's well-being at one time, whereas it may subsequently morph into a form that is harmful. Yet it is equally important to recognise that harmful cultural practices are not ossified by tradition and impervious to change. Particularly in a globalised environment, different traditions and cultures come into contact, and local people frequently choose to intermix ideas and practices from different cultures. Over time, harmful practices can change through a slow process that is guided by local actors.[38]

3.4. SHORT-TERM APPROACHES

One of the greatest challenges to community resilience approaches is the tendency of many donors to provide short-term funding, typically for periods of only one year. By definition, community resilience approaches require a slower, longer-term orientation that builds community ownership and centres around community mobilisation and empowerment. In addition, community resilience requires having sustainable psychosocial support because the adverse effects of armed conflict do not end in a year but persist over long periods of time.[39] The need for sustainable support contrasts starkly with the tendency for outside agencies to create external support initiatives that collapse after the funding period has ended. To address this problem, donors should provide multi-year funding. Also, right from the start of a humanitarian crisis practitioners should work in a manner that builds community ownership and sustainability.

3.5. WEAK EVIDENCE BASE

The field of psychosocial support for war-affected children lacks a strong foundation of evidence regarding which interventions work and produce sustainable outcomes.[40] The weak evidence base makes it difficult to be fully accountable to people in need since it leaves practitioners unable to say with certainty that their approaches are effective, or more effective than other approaches that might have been used. The weak evidence base also helps to create an "anything goes" atmosphere in which practitioners try out different approaches, including inappropriate ones that cause unintended harm.[41]

The need for a stronger evidence base is nowhere more apparent than in regard to community resilience approaches. To date, outcome studies that have

---

38 G. Mackie and J. Le Jeune, *Social dynamics of abandonment of harmful practices: A new look at the theory*, Innocenti Research Centre, Florence, 2009.

39 Betancourt et al., *supra* note 2; Boothby et al., *supra* note 6; D. Silove, Z. Steel and A. Bauman, 'Mass psychological trauma and PTSD: Epidemic or cultural illusion?', in J.P. Wilson and C.S. Tang (eds.), *Cross-cultural assessment of psychological trauma and PTSD*, Springer, New York, 2007, 319–336.

40 Betancourt, ibid.; Wessells et al., *supra* note 37.

41 Wessells, *supra* note 37.

used measures of deficits significantly outnumber studies that have used measures of assets, coping, adaptation and resilience.[42] Equally important, the field of psychosocial support continues to emphasise measures of individual well-being. Few culturally validated measures are available currently of community and family well-being.

To address this gap, donors should give additional funding for the systematic evaluation of programmes, including the use of more holistic, collective measures of resilience and well-being. Practitioners should on a regular basis conduct systematic evaluations of programmes in order to collect information that can be used to strengthen practice. Collectively, these and other steps will help the still young field of psychosocial support to mature and to achieve its fullest potential for supporting war-affected children, families and communities in their hour of greatest need.

42 B. Barber and J. Schluterman, 'An overview of the empirical literature on adolescents and political violence', in B. Barber (ed.), *Adolescents and war: How youth deal with political violence,* Oxford University Press, New York, 2009, 35–61.

INTEGRATING TRANSITIONAL JUSTICE AND DISARMAMENT, DEMOBILISATION AND REINTEGRATION

The Need to Achieve Rehabilitation, Reintegration and Reconciliation for Child Soldiers and Child Victims of Enforced Disappearances

Jeremy SARKIN

1. INTRODUCTION

An estimated 2 million children died as a result of armed conflict between 1994 and 2004.[1] During this period about 6 million children were disabled or injured.[2] Since the 1990s thousands of children have suffered the fate of enforced disappearance. At the same time there are an estimated 300,000 child soldiers[3] in about 21 conflicts around the world.[4] These numbers include forced, conscripted, and voluntary children from state as well as non-state actors.[5] The problem is thought to be worst in Africa and Asia, but there are also instances in Europe and the Americas.[6] In Colombia, for example, there are an estimated 14,000 children under thez age of ten involved in armed conflicts,

1 A. DAVIDSON, 'Child Soldiers: No Longer a Minor Incident', (2004) 12 *Willamette Journal of International Law and Dispute Resolution* at 144.

2 Ibid.

3 See further Coalition to Stop the Use of Child Soldiers, *Child Soldiers Global Report*, 2008.

4 A. SHEPPARD, 'Child Soldiers: Is the Optional Protocol Evidence of an Emerging "Straight-18" Consensus?', (2000) 12 *The International Journal of Children's Right*, 37–70.

5 A. DAVIDSON, *supra* note 1 at 141.

6 W. SENEVIRATNE, 'International Legal Standards Applicable to Child Soldiers', (2003) 39 *Sri Lanka Journal of International Law* at 39.

in Uganda 20,000 children[7] and an estimated 70,000 in Burma.[8] Up to 200,000 children were left orphaned during the civil war in Mozambique.[9] About 1 million Angolan children lost one parent in the war in that country and almost 300,000 lost both parents.[10] Thus, the situation of children after war, and other types of conflict, is severe and in need of ongoing attention,[11] especially as far as the needs of the child victim is concerned.[12]

Besides the effect that conflict has on children, who are mostly merely bystanders, but dramatically affected, often as a result of the conflict, children are at times forced to commit human rights violations, including murder, amputations, rapes[13] and other forms of sexual violence[14] during hostilities.[15] This is done intentionally to make the abducted child feel stigmatised and less likely to try to run away and return home.[16] Stigmatising children may also be a problem after their return home, and thus steps ought to be taken to prevent this, and deal with it where it has occurred.[17]

This chapter explores the needs of child victims. It explores specifically their needs for reintegration and rehabilitation linked to processes of reconciliation. It does not focus, however, on dealing with children or others as perpetrators of

---

7 L. Dowdney, *Returning Home – Children's Perspectives on Reintegration – A Case Study of Children Abducted by the Lord's Resistance Army in Teso, Eastern Uganda,* Coalition to Stop the Use of Child Soldiers, February 2008 at www.child-soldiers.org/document/get?id=1299.

8 A. Davidson, *supra* note 1 at 142.
On more recent developments concerning children in Burma, see HREIB, *Forgotten Future: Children and Armed Conflict in Burma,* Human Rights Education in Burma, 18 March 2009 at http://hreib.com/statements-/54-forgotten-future-children-affected-by-armed-conflict-in-burma.html.

9 K. Maier, *War, Famine and the Reform Process in Mozambique,* Human Rights Watch, U.S., 1992.
See further N. Boothby, J. Crawford and J. Halrepin, 'Mozambique Child Soldier Life Outcome Study: Lessons Learned in Rehabilitation and Reintegration Efforts', (2006) *Better Care Network.*

10 *Angola: IRIN Focus on Children of War,* IRIN Humanitarian News and Analysis, 14 June 2001 at www.irinnews.org/Report.aspx?ReportID=22192.

11 Machel, *10-Year Strategic Review, Children and Conflict in a Changing World,* Part 2 of A/62/228, OSRSG/CAAC and UNICEF, 2007. See earlier G. Machel, *Impact of Armed Conflict upon Children,* Report of the Expert of the Secretary-General, Ms Graca Machel – This seminal report documents the plight of the world's war-affected children, exposing the United Nations.

12 J. Sarkin and E. Daly, *Reconciliation in Divided Societies: Finding Common Ground,* University of Pennsylvania Press, Philadelphia, 2007, at 65–67.

13 A. Davidson, *supra* note 1 at 141–142.

14 See further, *Taking the Next Step: Strengthening the Security Council's Response to Sexual Violence and Attacks on Education in Armed Conflict,* Human Rights Watch, 20 April 2009 at www.hrw.org/en/news/2009/04/20/taking-next-step.

15 B. Fonseka, 'The Protection of Child Soldiers in International Law', (2001) 2 *Asia-Pacific Journal on Human Rights and the Law,* 69–89.

16 See *Facts about Child Soldiers,* Human Rights Watch, 3 December 2008, www.hrw.org/en/news/2008/12/03/facts-about-child-soldiers.

17 J. Macveigh, S. Maguire and J. Wedge, *Stolen Futures: The Reintegration of Children Affected by Armed Conflict,* Save the Children, London, 2007.

violence. Obviously, dealing with perpetrators, including those who are children, and finding ways of ending the use of child soldiers, reducing enforced disappearances and other violations against children or those that affect children, are vital.

This chapter therefore focuses on children as victims and how to they ought to be dealt with in the aftermath of conflict. It argues that reintegration and rehabilitation for children need to be linked specifically to processes of reconciliation. It is further argued that such processes must occur at various levels, including the inter-personal, between individuals, between groups and at the national level. All these processes will impact on and make more effective the process of reintegration and rehabilitation, not only for individual children but for children in general. It will also have dramatic and positive effects on society at large.

The chapter therefore firstly focuses on what has been occurring with regard to children that have been affected by enforced disappearances, both as direct and indirect victims, so as to lay out the circumstances that exist around the world. The chapter then explores what processes can be followed to achieve reconciliation for these types of children and what could assist them in their process of being reintegrated and rehabilitated.

2. HOW WAR AFFECTS CHILDREN

It is not surprising that the most vulnerable group affected by war has been children.[18] This accords with the accepted situation that woman, children, the elderly and people with disabilities are traditionally the most vulnerable to human rights violations.[19] Where, however, the child is a girl child[20] her vulnerability is even greater because of both her age and her gender. According to Coomaraswamy female children are "particularly vulnerable in situations of armed conflict. The girl child is often forced to play multiple roles in the conflict

18 See on vulnerable groups J. Sarkin, A. Cook, 'Who is Indigenous?: Indigenous Rights Globally, in Africa and among the San in Botswana' (2010) 18 *Tulane Journal of International and Comparative Law*, 1–38; J. Sarkin and M. Koenig, 'Ending Caste Discrimination in India: Human Rights and the Responsibility to Protect at the Domestic and International Levels', (2010) 41 3 *George Washington International Law Review*, 541–576.

19 UN Human Rights Council, Report of the Working Group on Enforced or Involuntary Disappearances, *Promotion and Protection of All Human Rights, Civil, Political, Economic, Social and Cultural Rights, Including the Right to Development*, Annex 1, General A/HRC/10/9, 6 February 2009.

20 See for example V. Beth, *Reaching the Girls: Study on Girls' Association with Armed Forces and Groups in the DRC*, Save the Children UK and the NGO Group (CARE, IFESH and IRC), November 2004.

including sex slave, mother, domestic aide and combatant, often simultaneously."[21]

A number of characteristics make children particularly attractive and vulnerable to those looking to build their armed forces. For example, children tend to be more obedient and are not mature enough to protest against unreasonable or particularly dangerous orders.[22] A reason for the existence of child soldiers is the widespread availability of small arms, without which children probably could not participate in killing.[23] The demographics of many countries that experience child soldiering see a high proportion of young people.[24] The social realities of poverty,[25] migration, ethnic tension and discrimination also leave children more vulnerable to becoming involved in armed conflict.[26]

Children are, however, also targeted for a range of other reasons, including their race, ethnicity or some other minority status. Thus, the ethnicity of the victim is often motivation for an enforced disappearance. For example, in Guatemala in the 1980s a majority of children subjected to enforced disappearance were of Mayan origin.[27] These children were targeted because of their ethnicity: to take these children would "eliminate" the next generation of indigenous peoples, peoples who were deemed a threat to the regime.[28] The issue of enforced disappearance and children will be investigated further in this paper.

Children bear the brunt of war and conflict-induced trauma in a range of ways that impact on their civil, political and socio-economic rights, as well as a range of other rights. They are damaged by conflict in ways that have many long-term negative impacts. They suffer the economic, social, sociological, political, psychological and other consequences of these circumstances.[29] They are specifically affected by war in a variety of ways. At worst, they are made to participate in acts of war or are victims (particularly sexual victims) of the lawlessness that pervades war-torn areas. They are at times directly victimised by

---

21 R. Coomaraswamy, *UN Doc. Statement at the Paris International Conference Free Children from War*, 5 February 2007.

22 B. Fonseka, *supra* note 15, 69–89.

23 S.L. Wells, 'Crimes Against Child Soldiers in Armed Conflict Situations: Application and Limits of International Humanitarian Law', (2004) 12 *Tulane Journal of International and Comparative Law*, 287–306.

24 K. Vandergrift, 'Challenges in Implementing and Enforcing Children's Rights', (2004) 37 *Cornell International Law Journal* 584.

25 On socio-economic deprivation and political instability as causes, see A. Twum-danso, *Africa's Young Soldiers: The Co-option of Childhood Institute for Security Studies Monograph 82*, April 2003.

26 V. Druba, 'The Problem of Child Soldiers', (2002) 48 3/4 *International Review of Education* at 271–277.

27 T. Scovazzi and G. Citroni, *The Struggle Against Enforced Disappearance and the 2007 United Nations Convention*, Leiden/Boston, Martinus Nijhoff, 2007, 18.

28 Ibid. at 18–19.

29 See Y. Kemper, *Youth in War to Peace Transitions: Approaches of International Organizations*, Berghof Research Centre for Constructive Conflict Management, Paper No. 10.

war if they become orphans, or victims of direct violence – from sexual violence, or from the famine, disease, poverty and displacement that so often accompanies wars. Witnessing horrific scenes, including the deaths of siblings and parents, will also have continuing psychological repercussions. Even children who are not the direct victims of warfare[30] are often war's secondary victims because the adult role models that children need are themselves wounded. Children living near traumatised adults have to deal with rage, alcoholism, polarised and unpredictable behaviours and other kinds of social dysfunction. Children who grow up near traumatised adults are often the secondary victims; they are the victim's victims.[31]

Beyond the impact on each child, there is considerable physical and psychological damage to the community.[32] Former child soldiers return to their communities as victims as well as perpetrators; their families and communities must wrestle with the fact that while the children are victims of war, they have also committed atrocious crimes.[33]

3. DEVELOPMENTS TO DEAL WITH ACTS PERPETRATED AGAINST CHILDREN DURING CONFLICT

Much has been done over the last two decades to deal with the needs of children at the level of international law. Between 1989, with the development of the Convention on the Rights of the Child,[34] and 2009, there have been over twelve International Conventions, Resolutions, Statutes and Protocols, including most recently the 2005 and 2009 UN Security Council Resolutions on Children in Armed Conflict.

The 2000 Optional Protocol to the Convention on the Rights of the Child on the involvement of children in armed conflict had by October 2009 been ratified by 130 States. There is a clause in the Optional Protocol which calls for the "rehabilitation and social reintegration of persons who are victims of acts contrary to this Protocol, including through technical cooperation and financial assistance".[35] This is, however, the only such reference in an instrument that is

30 On whether child soldiers are perpetrators or victims, see *Child Soldiers: Criminals or victims?* AI Index: IOR 50/02/00, Amnesty International.

31 See further for example D. Bar-on, 'Children of Perpetrators of the Holocaust. Working Through One's Own Moral Self', (1990) 53 3 *Psychiatry Interpersonal and Biological Processes* at 229.

32 W. Seneviratne, *supra* note 6 at 40.

33 A. Davidson, *supra* note 1 at 154.

34 See I. Cohn and G. S. Goodwin-gill, *Child Soldiers: The Role of Children in Armed Conflict*, Oxford University Press, Oxford, 1994.

35 *Optional Protocol to the Convention on the Rights of the Child on the Involvement of Children in Armed Conflict*, Article 7. Compare Nylund's chapter at 41-42.

directly focused on the specific needs of victims. The rest of the Protocol focuses on steps that States must take to prevent the use of child soldiers.

Thus, much has been done to establish norms prohibiting the use of child soldiers. Security Council Resolution 1261 (1999) emphasised the responsibilities of States to end impunity and to prosecute those responsible for war crimes and other egregious crimes perpetrated against children and encouraged cooperation, the consideration of best practices and the necessity of developing clear action plans against those who violate international obligations.[36] UN Security Council Resolution 1539 (2004)[37] created a mechanism for monitoring[38] violations by all parties with regard to the involvement of children in armed conflict as well as the broader impact of armed conflict on children.[39] In addition, it established a special Working Group comprised of all 15 members of the Security Council to supervise the implementation of these measures and ongoing monitoring.[40] It has been functioning for a number of years and has issued 20 sets of conclusions on 11 countries, while the monitoring and reporting mechanism has been active in 13 countries.[41]

It is gratifying that the six previous Security Council Resolutions on Children in Armed Conflict (1261, 1314, 1379, 1460, 1539, and 1612)[42] were followed up with a new resolution in August 2009 (resolution 1882 on children and armed conflict). This resolution mandates the UN Secretary-General to expand the "list of shame" beyond the recruitment and use of child soldiers[43] so as now also to include the names of those responsible for killing and maiming children as well as those who commit grave sexual violence against children during war.

---

36 *UN Security Council Resolution*, UN Doc. 1999/1261.

37 Other UN Security Council Resolutions on Children and Armed Conflict are UN Doc. 2003/1460, 2004/1539, 2005/1612.

38 *Getting It Done and Doing It Right – A Global Study on the United Nations-led Monitoring & Reporting Mechanism on Children and Armed Conflict*, Watchlist on Children in Armed Conflict, September 2008 at www.watchlist.org/reports/pdf/global-v8-web.pdf.

39 *UN Security Council Resolution on Children and Armed Conflict*, UN Doc. 2004/1539. See also K. Barnett and A. Jeffrys, 'Full of Promise: How the UN's Monitoring and Reporting Mechanism can better protect Children', (2008) 62 *Humanitarian Practice Network*.

40 *UN Security Council Resolution*, UN Doc. 2005/8460; HR/4864.

41 *Taking the Next Step: Strengthening the Security Council's Response to Sexual Violence and Attacks on Education in Armed Conflict*, *supra* note 14.

42 See further G. McHugh, 'Strengthening Protection of Children Through Accountability: The role of the UN Security Council in holding to account persistent violators of children's rights and protections in situations of armed conflict', (2009) 3 *Conflict Dynamics International*.

43 On the legal issues, see N. Arzoumanian and F. Pizzutelli, 'Victims and perpetrators: Issues of Responsibility Relating to the Problem of Child Soldiers in Africa', (2003) 12 *International Review of the Red Cross* 827, at 852. M. du Plessis, 'Children Under International Criminal Law' (2004) 13 2 *African Security Review*.

4. DEVELOPMENTS ON THE USE OF CHILD SOLDIERS

A number of other useful developments have intensified the fight against the recruitment and use of child soldiers. One of these was the landmark ruling on 1 June 2004 of the Appeals Chamber of the Sierra Leone Special Court, which ruled that the recruitment of child combatants is a crime under international law.[44] Another positive development is the fact that the International Criminal Court is prosecuting a number of cases, including Thomas Lubanga Dyilo from the Democratic Republic of the Congo (DRC), for recruiting child soldiers.[45]

A bold and symbolically important step, in the domestic context, is the enactment by the USA of the Child Soldiers Accountability Act of 2008, which makes it a federal offence for citizens and non-citizens to recruit or use child soldiers who are under the age of 15. This has been followed up with the Child Soldier Prevention Act of 2009, which limits training, financing and other military assistance by the USA for states that have child soldiers in either state or state-supported forces.

Also to be welcomed is the recent UN Peacekeeping Child Protection Policy, which responds to Security Council resolutions 1612 and 1882 by increasing the mainstreaming of child protection across the UN.

It is therefore encouraging to see the steps taken around the world to address the issue of child soldiers, and particularly to end impunity for the use of child soldiers.

While the last several years have seen improvements in monitoring, prosecution and deterrence,[46] insufficient attention has been paid to the needs of children as victims, either as child soldiers or as victims of the broader conflict. The resolution mechanisms to deal with children as victims and provide them with assistance after conflict are limited. In practice, this has been a major omission in the area. While it is very useful that much progress has been made in the fight against the use of child soldiers, more ought to be done at the level of both policy and practice to deal with the consequences of the use of children during war, and the effects of war on children. In this regard Cohn has noted that the needs of children are generally not taken into account in peace-making and peace processes. She has argued that this

---

44 Press Release of the Special Court, dated 01/07/2004, on Special Court website at www.sc-sl.org/Press/pressrelease-060104. See S.H. Bald, 'Searching for a Lost Childhood: Will the Special Court of Sierra Leone Find Justice for its Children?', (2002) 18 2 *American University International Law Review*, 537–583.

45 On prosecuting children see C. Reis, 'Trying the Future, Avenging the Past: The Implications of Prosecuting Children for Participation in Internal Armed Conflict', (1996–1997) 28 3 *Columbia Human Rights Law Review*, 629–656.

46 R. Coomaraswamy, *supra* note 21.

therefore ensured the marginalisation of issues such as the reintegration and rehabilitation of children after war and conflict.[47] This was noted also in part in the finding by the Special Representative of the Secretary-General for Children and Armed Conflict, Mr Olara A. Otunnu, who declared a need for an "Era of Application" in his Report to the Commission on Human Rights in 2003. He noted that the challenge was, and remains, to implement "international norms and standards for the protection of children affected by armed conflict".[48]

Greater effort should now be devoted to prevention, demobilisation/reintegration and other steps to develop a human rights culture in countries. Steps ought to be taken to promote and protect democracy, human rights, the rule of law and good governance and to advance reconciliation. More ought to be done to assist individuals, especially children, to deal with the legacy of war and conflict after the conflict has ended.

5. CHILDREN AS DIRECT AND INDIRECT VICTIMS OF ENFORCED DISAPPEARANCES

An enforced disappearance is defined as the "arrest, detention, abduction or any other form of deprivation of liberty by the agents of the State or by persons… acting with the authorization, support or acquiescence of the State".[49] It is further characterised by the State's "refusal to acknowledge the deprivation of liberty or by concealment of the fate or whereabouts of the disappeared person",[50] thus placing the person subjected to the enforced disappearance "outside the protection of the law".[51]

While enforced disappearances as a phenomenon has its roots in Latin America, it is now international in scope. In fact enforced disappearance is a global phenomenon affecting almost all countries. However, Latin America is particularly well known for enforced disappearances.

This act is perpetrated to spread general fear, terror, intimidation and uncertainty throughout the society in question.[52] It is a way to coerce the citizens of a State and to deter those who may be inclined to speak out against, or criticise,

---

47 I. Cohn, 'Protection of Children in Peacemaking and Peacekeeping Processes', (1999) 12 *Harvard Human Rights Journal*, 129–195.

48 O. Otunna, *Economic and Social Council, Rights of the Child: Annual Report of the Special Representative of the Secretary-General for Children and Armed Conflict*, UN Doc. E/CN.4/203/77, 3 March 2003, www.child-soldiers.org/childsoldiers/committeeontherightsofthechild.

49 *International Convention for the Protection of All Persons from Enforced Disappearance*, part I/Art 2.

50 Ibid.

51 Ibid.

52 A. Davidson, *supra* note 8.

those in power. It is a form of social repression, as fear of the unknown will surely deter any person from even thinking something that could make them visible to those who may accuse them of being critical of the regime in power.

While it is difficult to assess how many people have been disappeared, the numbers total into the hundreds of thousands.[53] The UN Working Group on Enforced or Involuntary Disappearances has alone been seized of 53,337 cases between 1980 and 2010. While enforced disappearances occur everywhere, it is more likely to occur in states where there is conflict, especially where military or paramilitary groups operate, and where there are political, cultural, ethnic or other types of tension.

Children are sometimes the targets of enforced disappearance as they are especially vulnerable to it. Fortunately, in the past most direct enforced disappearances of children, it seems, did not result in the child's death, which is the fate of many adults that are subjected to this type of crime.[54] More research is needed on these issues.

Victims of enforced disappearances, including children, are subjected to interrogation, torture, and other cruel, inhumane and severe conditions.[55] Victims may be kept naked and subjected to further atrocities, such as rape.[56] A victim may also be forced to witness or participate in the torture of other victims held captive at that location by the perpetrators. Domestic and international laws must therefore pay close attention to their protection, regardless of whether the child is a direct or indirect target of the crime.

The practice of enforced disappearance has devastating effects on the children of a victim.[57] For a child who witnesses an abduction, it will leave a lasting and traumatic impression, one that will certainly haunt the child for many years, if not always. In addition to the deep emotional and developmental impacts a child will certainly feel as a result of the enforced disappearance of a parent, the child will also probably suffer a financial impact. The parents or guardians of the child are likely to be the financial supporters of the family and with their disappearance the family is often left without a means of support.

Usefully, the Inter-American Commission has stated that children "have a fundamental right to their identity as persons and to know that identity. They also have the right to recover the memory of their natural parents and to know that those parents never abandoned them. They have the right to be in contact with their natural family so that they can nurture and provide continuity to that

---

53 See Scovazzi and Citroni, *supra* note 27 at 2.

54 Inter-American Court of Human Rights, *A Report of the Inter-American Commission on Human Rights 1987–1988*, OEA/Ser.L/V/II.74, 16 September 1988 at 8.

55 Ibid.

56 Ibid.

57 See similarly E. Montgomery and E. Krogh, 'Children of Torture Victims – Reactions and Coping', (1992) 16 6 *Child Abuse and Neglect*, 797–805.

memory of affection."[58] "The desperate, frantic search by grandparents, and in some cases by parents of children who have disappeared, sums up the pain and anxiety that is experienced when people are faced with the fact that somewhere, alongside unknown people, a child is growing up without any connection with his or her family, people, or in some extreme cases, country."[59]

Argentina's Dirty War is probably the most well-known example of the emotional, social and ravaging violation through enforced disappearances by a government. Hundreds of children were stolen during the period of military rule in Argentina from 1976 to 1983 and about 9,000 to 30,000 young adults and adolescents were forcibly taken from their homes by Argentine military personnel and killed. Hundreds of children were born in captivity to mothers who were kidnapped and kept alive for the sole purpose of giving birth to children who were then taken away from them and given either to military officials and their families or put up for adoption.

The National Commission on the Disappeared (CONADEP), formed in 1983 by President Raul Alfonsin to investigate cases of enforced disappearances and other human rights violations during Argentina's dirty war, described in detail the torture and murder of the disappeared persons, including hundreds of children. The report of the Commission provided a separate discussion of "children and pregnant women who disappeared" in its chapter on victims.[60] Over 11 per cent of the disappearances were of minors from new-borns to youth up to the age of twenty.[61] Most significantly, the report identified 8,960 missing persons and was crucial in helping the victims to discover the truth about the atrocities committed.[62] As a result of CONADEP's findings, a number of officials were tried for their crimes.[63]

Many cases that came to court saw a judge order genetic testing of the child, the adoptive parents and the claiming relatives. By 1995, as a result of a genetic bank, 220 missing children were claimed and identified.[64] In 1999 Congress passed a law creating a "Historical Reparation Fund for the Location and Restitution of Children Kidnapped or Born in Captivity". Under this law, the

58 Scovazzi and Citroni, *supra* note 27.

59 N. Mas, *A. Children and pregnant women who disappeared,* The Victims, Part II, http://web.archive.org/web/20031014132004/nuncamas.org/english/library/nevagain/nevagain_ 213.htm.

60 N. Mas, *(Never Again): A Report by Argentina's National Commission on Disappeared People,* (English Translation), 1986 at 286–320.

61 N. Mas, *Victims,* Part II http://web.archive.org/web/20040630181805/nuncamas.org/english/library/nevagain/nevagain_210.htm.

62 See CONADEP, *Recommendation of the National Commission,* National Commission on the Disappeared at www.yendor.com/vanished/recommendations.html (last visited 4 April 2009).

63 *In re Extradition of Suarez Mason,* 694, F. Supper at 676 and 683.

64 V.B. Penchaszadeh, 'Genetic Identification of Children of the Disappeared in Argentina', (1997) 52 1 *Journal of the American Medical Women's Association.*

Mothers of Plaza de Mayo will receive about $25,000 a month for two years to assist their efforts to search for their disappeared children.[65]

In Guatemala, out of the 45,000 enforced disappearances that occurred from 1979 to 1986, 4,950 involved children.[66] Children would be captured either individually or with their parents. They would be taken from their homes as a means of punishing relatives who might have opposed the government.[67] Initially the children would be killed and buried to hide the evidence but later they were illegally adopted, both domestically and internationally.[68] The Guatemalan Truth Commission[69] did not interview children of victims of enforced disappearances or adults who were children at the time of the disappearances.[70] It was the case of *Villagran Morales v. Guatemala*[71] that brought the torture, ill treatment, detention and murder of Guatemalan street children by the Guatemalan National Police before the Inter-American Court of Human Rights for the first time.

During El Salvador's twelve-year civil war, numerous human rights violations occurred,[72] including the enforced disappearances of over 2,000 children.[73] The El Salvador Truth Commission,[74] although acknowledging that children were victims of enforced disappearances, made no recommendations focusing on children.[75]

---

65 G. Lois and M. Lacabe, *In search of vindication: Reparations for Human Rights Violations in Argentina*, Paper presented at the Hague Appeal For Peace Conference in May 1999, www.derechos.org/koaga/vii/lois.html.

66 Scovazzi and Citroni, *supra* note 27.

67 UN Human Rights Council, *supra* note 19.

68 Ibid.

69 See *Guatemalan Truth Commission Report*, http://shr.aaas.org/guatemala/ceh/report/english/toc.html.

70 Ibid.

71 Judgment of 19 November 1999, *(Villagrán-Morales et al.) v. Guatemala*, case of the 'Street Children', Section 178.

72 See *United States Department of State Country Profile: El Salvador* at www.state.gov/r/pa/ei/bgn/2033.htm.

73 See *Amnesty Rips Salvadoran Government Over 'Disappeared Children'* at http://us.oneworld.net/places/el-salvador/-/article/amnesty-rips-salvadoran-government-over-disappeared-children.

74 See also United States Institute Of Peace, *Truth Commissions Digital Collection: Reports: El Salvador:* 'The Commission was not able to verify the existence of general directives from the FMLN leadership to its constituent organizations authorizing enforced disappearances. It did receive complaints of some 300 cases of disappearance, which occurred mainly in areas where FMLN exercised greater military control. It was not possible to establish the existence of any pattern from an analysis of these complaints. Nevertheless, links were observed between disappearances, forcible recruitment by FMLN and cases of extrajudicial execution by FMLN members of individuals labeled spies or traitors.', www.usip.org/library/tc/doc/reports/el_salvador/tc_es_03151993_casesA.html.

75 See *Informe de la Comisión de la Verdad para El Salvador, De la Locura a la Esperanza* (Report of the Commission on the Truth for El Salvador, From Madness to Hope: The Twelve-Year War in El Salvador), UN SCOR, 48th yr., Annexes, UN Doc. S/25500, 1993.

However, as a result of the case *Serrano-Cruz Sisters v. El Salvador*,[76] a genetic bank was created so that victims and their relatives could re-establish family ties and identify missing children. The Inter-American Court of Human Rights required El Salvador to "adopt all necessary measures to create a system of genetic information that allows genetic data that can contribute to determining and clarifying the relationships and identification of the disappeared children and their next of kin to be obtained and conserved".[77]

These examples show that much has occurred to deal with children. Much has been done to deal with the perpetrators of crimes against children at international level but that has not always translated into steps to tackle the problems domestically. The fact that so many child soldiers still exist, and so many other human rights violations continue to be perpetrated, means that states need to take more specific steps to deal with the issue. It is, however, with children, and their needs as victims, that much more work is needed. As can be seen above, there have been good efforts by a range of states and institutions to address the needs of child victims. Certainly, the establishment of the ICC Trust Fund for victims might be helpful if sufficient funding reaches many victims. But many more resources are needed, as well as greater political will, to achieve practical effects for child victims in many places around the world where war and conflict have occurred, and continue to occur.

6. RESOURCES AND MECHANISMS TO ADDRESS THE PROBLEMS OF WAR-AFFECTED CHILDREN

While much research has been done on the effects of war on children, there are often insufficient resources available to assist children, especially in the places where the majority of wars are occurring – in the global south. Often disarmament, demobilisation and reintegration strategies (DDR) focus on adult soldiers at the expense of children. There is often one programme for all those in need of DDR. This can be problematic. Children's needs are different in this context from those of adults.[78]

There is a need to focus on these issues in the day-to-day situations of a number of countries, which are often deemed transitional.[79] This is the case because these societies usually have the fewest resources, the least number of the

76 *Serrano-Cruz Sisters v. El Salvador* 2005, Inter American Court of Human Rights.

77 Ibid.

78 G. Narayan, *Children Affected by Armed Conflict: Programming Framework Canadian International Development Agency*, CIDA/2002.

79 K. Hill and K. H. Langholtz, 'Rehabilitation Programs for African Child Soldiers', (2003) 15 3 *Peace Review* 279, at 287.

professionals required to make the necessary interventions and often the least political will to rehabilitate and reintegrate children after war or conflict.

Transitional justice mechanisms and tools have the ability to make substantial progress with and impacts on children that have suffered abuse during conflict. However, until now using transitional justice mechanisms and tools for the rehabilitation and reintegration of war-affected children has not been widespread. Some Truth and Reconciliation Commissions (TRCs) have played a part in this regard. TRCs, or other similar processes, are vital to gaining information and allowing victims to testify as to their experiences. This will be explored below.

TRCs allow an accurate historical record to be produced of what occurred during the conflict and what caused it, as well as preventing denial by those who perpetrated human rights abuses.[80] This in and of itself is useful for society as a whole, but very useful for individual victims who can benefit from the cathartic effects of the process.[81] It can also sometimes be used to bring perpetrators to justice.[82]

However, Truth (and Reconciliation) Commissions often fail to focus on the needs of children sufficiently. Some TRCs have focused on the needs of children, including the South African Commission.[83] The SATRC held a number of hearings to understand the effects of apartheid on the children of South Africa. The East Timor Commission for Reception, Truth and Reconciliation was given powers to "take special measures" in hearings involving the testimonies of special groups of victims, including women and children.[84]

Critically, TRCs can assist individuals, including children, in reconnecting with their communities, particularly if they have components that are deliberately designed to assist in this psychological phase. Alternatively, and possibly in conjunction, informal mechanisms may also be effective.[85] Post-conflict healing methods and processes may provide survivors with access to each other, so that they can talk among themselves and provide support for each other. This may promote personal reconciliation because there may be many stories that victims are willing to tell each other but might not be willing to share with the nation or

80 H. Sensibaugh, 'Why Reconciliation is Possible in Iraq', (2008) 23 *Fletcher Journal of Human Security*, 5–35.

81 See generally R. Beneduce, 'Contested Memories: Peace building and Community Rehabilitation after Violence and Mass Crimes A Medico-Anthropological Approach', in B. Pouligny, S. Chesterman and A. Schnabel. (eds.), *After Mass Crime: Rebuilding States and Communities*, United Nations University Press, Tokyo, 2007.

82 See *Amnesty International Truth Commissions*, www.amnesty.org/en/international-justice/issues/truth-commissions.

83 J. Sarkin, *Carrots and Sticks: The TRC and the South American Amnesty Process*, Intersentia, Antwerp, 2004.

84 Ibid. ss. 16.1–16.4. See further J. Sarkin, 'Achieving Reconciliation in Divided Societies: Comparing the Approaches in Timor-Leste, South Africa and Rwanda' (2008) 3 2 *Yale Journal of International Affairs*, 11–28.

85 Ibid.

the world. These kinds of process may achieve just as much cathartic effect, and maybe as much healing. TRCs should therefore make more direct efforts to address the needs of children, especially in societies where they have been child soldiers or borne the brunt of the abuses perpetrated in that state.

7. ACHIEVING REHABILITATION, REINTEGRATION AND RECONCILIATION FOR WAR-AFFECTED CHILDREN

Post-conflict societies often focus on disarmament, demobilisation and reintegration as strategies after conflict. In this context I want to focus on their connection to reconciliation.[86] This connection was recognised by the Paris Principles and Guidelines on Children Associated with Armed Forces or Armed Groups (drawn up in 2007),[87] which found that reintegration is:

> the process by which children transition into civil society and enter meaningful roles and identities as civilians who are accepted by their families and communities in a context of local and national reconciliation. Sustainable reintegration is achieved when the political, legal, economic and social conditions needed for children to maintain life, livelihood and dignity have been secured.[88] This process aims to ensure that children can access their rights, including formal and non-formal education, family unity, dignified livelihoods and safety from harm.[89]

Certainly, demobilisation and reintegration require education,[90] the re-establishment of family ties and the development of a post-war identity.[91] All of these issues are also reconciliation strategies. As with reconciliation, it takes time for true reintegration and rehabilitation to occur. It takes time for children to heal from their experiences, for communities to welcome them back and for

86 See also Savage, Tyrone and Z. Sonkosi, 'Ritual, Reparation and Reintegration: The Challenge of Reconciliation in Post-Conflict African Societies', in E. Doxtader and C. Villa-Vicencio (eds.), *To Repair the Irreparable: Reparation and Reconstruction in South Africa*, David Philip, Cape Town, 2004.

87 These principles updated the *Cape Town Principles and Best Practices on the Recruitment of Children into the Armed Forces and on Demobilization and Social Reintegration of Child Soldiers in Africa*, 1997, www.unicef.org/emerg/files/Cape_Town_Principles(1).pdf.

88 Kemper, *supra* note 29.

89 UNICEF, *Paris Principles,* www.un.org/children/conflict/english/parisprinciples.html.

90 S. Nicolai and C. Triplehorn, 'The role of Education in protecting Children in Conflict', (2003) 3 *Humanitarian Practice Network,* at 24. See also G. Menon and A. Arganese, *Role of Education and the Demobilization of Child Soldiers – Aspects of an Appropriate Education Program,* Issue Paper Number 2, USAID, http://pdf.usaIbid.gov/pdf_docs/PNADI663.pdf.

91 Seneviratne, *supra* note 6 at 40.

children to transition to a "normal life".[92] Planning needs to begin early and be wide-ranging.[93]

Without doubt there is often tension around issues of truth, justice, peace, reconciliation, and rehabilitation and reintegration, as well as others, as the community, victims and children themselves may want, and need, "justice" to achieve authentic reintegration and reconciliation.[94] Ann Davison notes that "to provide some sort of respite from grief for the victims and the local community, and to aid in the assimilation of these children back into society, there may need to be criminal responsibility for these acts".[95] This could include a range of actions, from trials and convictions to traditional healing, forgiveness and reconciliation processes.[96] The discussion of child soldiers being convicted for crimes they committed, even if conscripted illegally and forced to commit the crimes, is clearly a complex one and will need to be part of a reintegration approach, while also impinging on questions around reconciliation.

In the transitional justice context, therefore, reintegration and rehabilitation must also mean a focus on reconciliation as a means of establishing or recovering the dignity and humanity of a person, rooted in human rights, and the acceptance of this by the individual and society.[97] When each individual's dignity is accepted by all others, reconciliation has begun. Reconciliation's source is in the dignity of each human being, and its manifestation is in repaired relationships. This is perhaps the most common, generally accepted interpretation of reconciliation. It is often viewed as the coming together, the antithesis of falling or growing apart. Reconciliation has a normative – almost a moral – aspect as well. It is the coming together (or re-coming together) of things that *should* be together. Unlike its less common relative, conciliation, *re*conciliation is a coming together of things that once were united but have been torn asunder – a return to or re-creation of the status quo ante.

Reconciliation thus implies the repairing of a relationship, whether real or imagined. It is about the return (or creation) of normalcy. Thus, it has great appeal in societies whose pre-eminent challenge is how to be normal again after a particularly devastating event such as genocide or war. How do people who were once neighbours live together again after one has murdered the other's family? How does a teacher teach when everyone in the class has witnessed unspeakable horrors? How does a child learn after her parents have been killed and her

92 Ibid.

93 *The Paris Commitments to protect Children from unlawful Recruitment or use by Armed Forces or Armed Groups*, France Diplomatie, §19.

94 Davidson, *supra* note 1 at 154.

95 Ibid.

96 Vandergrift, *supra* note 24 at 550.

97 See J. Sarkin and H. Sensibaugh, 'How Historical Events and Relationships Shape Current Attempts at Reconciliation in Iraq', (2009) 26 4 *Wisconsin International Law Journal* 1033–1077.

brothers and sisters brutally treated? Survivors of violence require two related but distinct kinds of healing.[98] The simplest level may be cognitive: they need to understand what happened to them. Although they experienced a personal trauma, their experience was in the context of larger political violence which many victims do not fully comprehend. This is especially true where the victims are children or are chosen randomly or where they are used as pawns by political forces. For instance, in Australia many aboriginals did not understand that their personal experience of being taken away from their families was part of Australia's policy of purging itself of the aborigines.[99] Cognitive healing is also important where the perpetrators maintained secrecy about the fate of victims. In Latin America, a principal form of violence was to cause people to "disappear" and the fate of many remains unknown to this day.[100] Hamber and Wilson describe this as an "ontological uncertainty among survivors and a psychological experience of what Freud termed the *uncanny*".[101] This phenomenon, they argue, is common among survivors who must mourn without a corpse. The uncanny feeds on uncertainty (Is he/she alive? Is he/she dead?). Both the survivor and the dead inhabit a symbolically social space. "Both are part of society but removed from society."[102] Cognitive healing entails obtaining information about the political context in which the individual crimes occurred and specific details about the fate of individual victims. This can have major benefits for the healing process of the individual because it removes the haunting doubt and sense of isolation that often accompanies ongoing psychological stress. Cognitive healing alleviates the burden of feeling that one has to bear the brunt of the violation on one's own.

The more complex kind of healing is psychological. Survivors of trauma and other types of political violence suffer from a huge range of psychological maladies. These may include fears that manifest themselves in nightmares, hyper-arousal, and mood swings that oscillate between controlling and withdrawal; disconnection from society at large and from formerly close friends and family in particular; and feelings of worthlessness and insignificance. Often these are direct results of deliberate efforts by torturers and other perpetrators of

---

98 J Herman, *Trauma and Recovery*, Basic Books, New York, 1992, 37.

99 See further R.P. Hill, 'Blackfellas and Whitefellas: Aboriginal Land Rights, The Mabo Decision, and the Meaning of Land', (1995) 17 *Human Rights Quarterly* at 303.

100 See for example CONADEP, N. Mas, *The Report of the Argentine National Commission on the Disappeared*, New York, 1986. S. Farrar and C. Grossman, 'Disappearances in Honduras. The Need for Direct Victim Representation in Human Rights Litigation', (1995) 15 3 *Hastings International and Comparative Law Review*, at 363; M. Popkin and N. Roht-Arriaza, 'Truth as Justice: Investigatory Commissions in Latin America', (1995) 20 *Law and Social Inquiry* 1–79; N. Roht-arriaza, 'Truth Commissions and Amnesties in Latin America: The Second Generation', (1999) 92 *Contemporary International Law Issues* at 313.

101 B. Hamber and R. Wilson, *A Symbolic Closure through Memory, Reparation and Revenge in Post-Conflict Societies Human Rights*, Working Papers, Number 5, 24 April 2000, www.du.edu/humanrights/workingpapers/index.html.

102 Ibid.

abuse to dehumanise people, to weaken their personality and to diminish their sense of dignity. This lack of self-esteem in the aftermath of trauma is likely to have material consequences for the survivor, who may be less able to function productively in a job or in a social setting or even in the day-to-day obligations of caring for a family. Survivors are also often confused by the conflicting desires to simultaneously forget the trauma and hold onto it. Holding on may seem counterintuitive, but many survivors need to retain the reality of the trauma sometimes just long enough to make sense of it, but sometimes longer because it has become a part of their self-identity.

The themes of cognitive and psychological healing permeate the psychological literature of trauma studies, although relatively little attention has been paid to the overlap between personal healing and political reconciliation. Maria Ericson identifies a number of psychological issues that arise in conflict situations. The first is experiences of trauma and bereavement, which, among other things, destroys the victim's fundamental assumptions about the safety of the whole world, the positive value of the self and the meaning of the order of creation. In the case of internal conflicts, deep animosity and distrust emerges. In such cases, collective trauma and bereavement accumulate. Furthermore, experiences of separation and inequalities become a reality as parties to the conflict compete for political or economic dominance. In order to address all these, she proposes various interventions to ensure that healing takes place. Those aimed at alleviating trauma include:

1. The establishment of safety, including bodily integrity, basic health needs, safe living conditions, financial security, mobility, a plan for self-protection, safe and reliable relationships, and social support.
2. Remembrance and mourning, telling the story of one's trauma.
3. Reconnection with ordinary life. This includes taking steps towards empowerment to protect oneself against future danger, as well as engagement with particular individuals and pursuing justice in the form of holding perpetrators accountable. It also includes recognising the gender dimension in the process of mourning.[103]

These issues are dealt with in more depth below.

While these interventions are designed to help individuals heal, they also help to promote social reconciliation, which Ericson defines as "the establishment of a positive and sustainable peace between people involved in armed conflict".[104] Psychologist Judith Herman has likewise focused on these three same stages of

103 CONADEP, Mas, *supra* note 100.

104 M. Ericson, *Reconciliation and the search for a shared moral Landscape: An exploration based upon a study of Northern Ireland and South Africa*, Frankfurt, Peter Lang, 2001, 86–96.

safety, remembrance and mourning, and reconnection, although her work focuses on trauma outside of the political context.[105] The confluence of the psychological and the political is clear: aspects of political reconciliation permeate virtually all three stages of psychological healing. It may be useful, then, to understand individual reconciliation in terms of these stages, laid across a political landscape.

8. SAFETY

Firstly, safety has to be created. Governments can help establish and promote safety in a number of ways. One is to allay fears publicly through public announcements and formal campaigns that deter would-be violators. Obviously, public statements need to be backed up by concrete action. These forms of action will depend on the nature of the trauma from which individuals in the country are recovering. The provision of basic needs is another aspect of physical safety. The government must ensure, at the very least, that basic needs, such as food, water, shelter, sanitation, medical care and counselling, are being met. As Graeme Simpson has noted, "[w]e can rebuild the social fabric and negotiate political settlements; but unless we meet people's economic needs, those agreements are worth very little".[106] Just as a newly democratic government's provision of services and goods can promote reconciliation, failing to do so may significantly impede it. In addition to the physical harms that directly result from hunger, exhaustion and disease, many individuals may feel further depressed both by their inability to provide for themselves and their families and by their own lack of energy. Such depression in turn increases the risk of behaviour that is destructive to the self and to others, including violence and substance abuse.

9. MOURNING AND REMEMBRANCE

The second stage towards healing is mourning and remembrance. Nations in transition are only now beginning to understand the importance of dealing with the past. By contrast, the vast majority (if not the entirety) of psychological literature has insisted for a century that remembering the past is a necessary precondition for healing. The extreme pain, helplessness, vulnerability and sense of betrayal that characterise trauma are so inconsistent with the experiences and

105 Herman, *supra* note 98 at 156–157. Another book that describes a process of healing is M. Walzer, *On Toleration*, Yale University Press, New Haven, 1997. Walzer describes five separate stages of toleration, from the 'resigned acceptance of difference for the sake of peace' to 'the enthusiastic endorsement of difference'.

106 G. Simpson, 'Reconstruction and Reconciliation: Emerging from transition', (1997) 7 4 *Development in Practice*, 475–478.

values that develop over a lifetime that the event stands apart and disconnected from the trajectory of the person's life. Going back to the point of rupture, this time from a position of strength and safety, is necessary to give continuity to a person's life story.[107] In this light, recovery itself is the process of reconciling the trauma with the rest of the person's life. Perhaps we should not say "I've reconciled myself to this trauma" so much as "I've reconciled this trauma to myself". The goal is to create a whole self that incorporates the traumatic event.

Meaning or healing or restorative truth may be the most challenging if only because it cannot be readily ascertained from a single source. This dialectic element needs to be developed over time, by a constellation of perspectives. This is perhaps what reconciliation commissions or ministries can do best. Only a significant policy initiative is capable of gathering all the other elements and putting them together in a way that gives meaning to the events for the survivor and for the society as a whole. A commission can provide the response to the witness that he needs in order to give his words meaning and can create the space in which other citizens understand and continue to learn from the events. Such a process encourages the society as a whole to listen, absorb and begin the healing process that leads to reconciliation. A faulty process that opens up the wounds without providing the support necessary for reconciliation will lead only to renewed hostility. On the other hand, having no process at all may lead to social fragmentation, because the pain and anger may never find an outlet and may therefore ferment until they erupt. Thus, careful planning and preparation is crucial to ensuring that the process achieves its aims and objectives.

Some basic principles should be heeded if the programme is to be effective. First, survivors must be allowed to talk only on their own terms. No programme that *requires* survivors to tell their stories can be therapeutic. They must be allowed to talk whenever they want, if at all. And they must be allowed to tell their story *how*ever they want – including whatever details seem important to them and leaving out details as they choose. Encouraging, coaxing or guiding is useful, though insisting or directing or making the process mandatory is not.

Second, there must be room for emotional release and understanding. Survivors should be asked how they felt, what they saw, what hurt, and what they wanted. They should be allowed to tell their story entirely from their own point of view, without regard for the perspective of the perpetrators. Police station recounting of rape events often presents the archetypal counter-example, where the talking may be forced and is more likely to be psychologically destructive than constructive for the victim unless the listener is particularly sympathetic and the survivor's emotional state and privacy are respected. In most situations, however, telling the story of the rape repeats the trauma because it reinforces the

---

107 The idea of continuity is also suggested in HERMAN, *supra* note 98 at 176, quoting Y. DANIELI, speaking of "the importance of reclaiming the patient's earlier history in order to re-create the flow of the patient's life and restore a sense of continuity with the past".

power dynamic of the rape itself: the victim is required to tell the story as the police want to hear it, not as the victim experienced it. Training is especially important here for investigators, statement-takers and counsellors.

Third, there must be a response to the recounting. A survivor cannot be expected to tell this painful story into a black hole. Those who hear and bear witness to the story must be prepared to enhance, or at least not detract from, the survivor's continuing need for safety and vindication. This may include helping the survivor to see some meaning in the trauma, perhaps by placing the trauma in the larger context of the political strife or even by helping the victim to understand the motivations of the perpetrators.

This is a particularly tricky area, both in individual therapy and in national reconciliation. In both cases, the audiences – the ones who receive the information and respond to it – have to decide where to place themselves on the continuum from complete neutrality to vindication of the survivor's experience. In the context of gross human rights abuses, the moral quandary is minimal: there is no justification for human rights abuses and adamant condemnation of such behaviour is necessary not only to vindicate and support the survivor but also to promote the other goals of national reconciliation, including establishing respect for the rule of law and promoting a culture of respect for human rights. The nation must, in the words of Judith Herman, "affirm a position of moral solidarity with the survivor".[108] On the other hand, a public entity condemning the actions of its constituent members puts itself in a political quandary: to do so without any concern at all for their reaction is to court revenge[109] and possibly to retard the cause of reconciliation. South Africa, for instance, tried to hold the balance between solidarity with the victims and condemnation of the perpetrators in part by having the TRC examine, without condoning, the actions and motivations of the perpetrators.[110] In this way, personal and national narratives were developed in tandem.

10. RECONNECTION

The third stage of the healing process is reconnection. The conventional wisdom is that individual reconciliation requires a reconnection between the survivor and the perpetrator. In this view, healing is contingent on the propensity of the

108 Herman, *supra* note 98 at 178.

109 See S.H. Kim and R.H. Smith, 'Revenge and Conflict Escalation', (1993) 9 1 *Negotiation Journal* 37–43. See also J. Malamud-Goti, 'Dignity, Vengeance, and Fostering Democracy', (1998) 29 3 *Inter-American Law Review* 417–50.

110 This balance was not always satisfactorily maintained: some argue that the process was less victim-friendly than it ought to have been, and often perpetrator-focused. See *TRC Report,* Vol. 5, Chapter 7.

perpetrator to show remorse or seek forgiveness.[111] This view, however, is increasingly being challenged, both by survivors and by the psychologists who study them. Albie Sachs argues that reconciliation does not require each victim to forgive each perpetrator, nor perpetrators to apologise[112] nor the parties to embrace. That is asking too much, he says, and it is inappropriate. Sachs emphasises the cognitive aspect of healing, entailing "some kind of basically shared understanding of the terrible things that were done, and who did them. Reconciliation also involves an understanding of how it happened and what the context was."[113]

While the survivor needs to let go of the perpetrator, recovery is marked by the extent to which she reconnects with her social milieu.[114] This is especially true for survivors from certain cultures that highly value the community. In too many instances, a survivor is shunned not despite her ordeal but because of it. This is particularly true with rape victims, but it might be true in many other instances as well. A torture victim who provided information to his captors might be ostracised upon his release if his information in fact did or was perceived to have resulted in harm to others. A child who was impressed into military service might be alienated when he tries to return home. Thus, the victim's natural inclination to withdraw is compounded by the community's inclination to ostracise. Most successful therapy addresses this need. Indeed, most traditional village-based rituals recognised the importance of reintegration, and new therapeutic models of treatment are beginning to emphasise this as well.

11. COUNSELLING AND THERAPY

Models that are developed for adults should recognise the distinct needs of children. While story-telling remains an important aspect of child therapy, art,

---

111 See T. Klosterman, 'The Feasibility and Propriety of a Truth Commission in Cambodia: Too Little? Too Late?', (1998) 15 *Arizona Journal of International and Comparative Law* 833, at 838.

112 The issue of apology is a major issue around the world and is often perceived by states as the prelude to them having to pay reparations. See J. Sarkin, 'Holding Multinational Corporations Accountable For Human Rights And Humanitarian Law Violations Committed During Colonialism And Apartheid: An Evaluation Of The Prospects Of Such Cases In Light Of The Herero Of Namibia's Genocide Case And South African Apartheid Cases Being Brought In The United States Under The Alien Torts Claims Act', in E. Brems and P. Van der Heede (eds.) *Bedrijven en Mensenrechten,* Maklu, Antwerp, 2003.
N. Tavuchis, *Mea Culpa: A Sociology of Apology and Reconciliation*, Stanford University Press, Stanford, 1991.

113 A. Sachs, 'His Name was Henry', in W. James and L. Van de Vijver (eds.), *After the TRC – Reflections On Truth And Reconciliation In South Africa,* Ohio University Press, Athens, 2001, 97.

114 See G.I. Chufrin and H.H. Saunders, 'A Public Peace Process', (1993) 9 3 *Negotiation Journal*, 155–177 and R. Kraybill, 'The Cycle of Reconciliation', (1995) 14 3 *Conciliation Quarterly* 7–8.

drama and other forms of expression may be more useful outlets for their stories. In addition, and particularly for younger children, non-verbal therapeutic models such as play or touching and hugging may be effective. Although or perhaps *because* the child population is least able to demand the services it needs or to develop them on their own, NGOs and governments must pay special attention to the extreme needs and vulnerabilities of this group.[115]

The East Timor reconciliation programme included art as therapy for people who are survivors of torture. The art allows participants "creative ways to express both their pain and their hopes for the future".[116] In Bosnia, music has been used as therapy and as recreation, especially to help children.[117] Other programmes are aimed directly at helping children's psychological needs. One of these is the Centre for Peacemaking and Community Development (CPCD), which opened a children's rehabilitation centre in May 1997 on the edge of Grozny, Chechnya.[118]

Camps for young people in war-torn societies have also become quite popular in recent years. These types of camp bear a remarkable similarity to one another, though their locations are as varied as their constituencies. They are designed to encourage youngsters to follow the path of peace rather than of war when they go back home by introducing them to members of the "other" group, and by helping them to understand their own feelings of pain and anger that result from the conflict.

Seeds of Peace includes activities such as rock-climbing that force bonds between Israeli and Palestinian youngsters.[119] In this way, the youngsters come to individualise the conflict – the war is no longer between Israel and the Palestinian authority, but rather between her family and my family. These programmes also include several hours each day of guided discussion in which participants talk about how they feel about the conflicts that may define their lives. Another purpose is educational: to teach tomorrow's leaders about the possibility of peace and the tools that are necessary to achieve that peace.[120] This

---

[115] On the role NGOs can play see T. PORTER, 'The Hardest Call: Why Save the Children Withdrew from Darfur', (2005) 30 6 *Humanitarian Exchange Magazine* and D. SBARDELLA, 'Community-Based Child Protection in The Gaza Strip', (2009) 44 9 *Humanitarian Exchange Magazine*. See also *The Power of Partnership: Guiding Principles for Partnerships to End Violations Against Children during Armed Conflict*, July 2006 and *Violations Against Children in Armed Conflicts: An Action Plan for Monitoring, Reporting and Response*, October 2004, Watchlist on Children and Armed Conflict.

[116] CAVR, *Healing Workshop for Survivors of Serious Human Rights Abuses*, organized by the CAVR and held on 23–27 June 2003 in Dili, www.easttimor-reconciliation.org.

[117] See, for instance, the Pavarotti Music Centre, operating in Mostar under the aegis of the NGO War Child.

[118] C. HUNTER, 'Reconstruction and reconciliation work in Chechnya', *Committee for Conflict Transformation Support Newsletter*, www.c-r.org/ccts/ccts6/hunter6.htm.

[119] For a useful study on the area see R. TERRIS and V. INOUE-TERRIS, 'A Case Study of Third World Jurisprudence – Palestine: Conflict Resolution and Customary Law in a Neo-patrimonial Society' (2002) 20 *Berkeley Journal of International Law* 462.

[120] See further J.P. LEDERACH, *Preparing for Peace: Conflict Transformation Across Cultures*, Syracuse University Press, Syracuse, NY, 1995 and J.P. LEDERACH, *Building Peace: Sustainable*

idea has also taken root in Uganda, where a group runs youth camps whose aim is to teach young people basic "Skills and Tools for Reconciliation and Non-violence and to promote and manage Peace Work in the participants' countries and elsewhere". The camp includes traditional camp activities such as campfires, games and sports, but also intellectual components, such as learning about the international and regional dimensions of conflict and conflict-management skills, and personal development components that expose youths to aspects of diverse cultures and provide them with opportunities to reflect on and discuss matters relating to difference, conflict and peace.[121] The camp also includes leadership skills to increase the likelihood that youths who are fortunate enough to experience the camp will expose others to these ideas.

Recovery is finding a way to integrate the trauma into the rest of the person's experience. Without this recovery or reconciliation, the two realities of the survivor's life lie in tension with one another – the trauma narrative in which evil prevails over good and in which the survivor deserves the punishment, and the healing narrative, in which friends and family can be trusted and evil is punished. A new reality needs to be constructed that reflects the principal values of the survivor, but that can accommodate the traumatic event. The question in this model, then, is not whether to deal with the past, but how.

12. CONCLUSION

Transitioning societies face monumental challenges as they confront possible tensions between peace and justice. Individual and collective needs must be balanced against the political realities faced by a new government, which in all likelihood inherited a fragile state and limited political power. In addition, post-atrocity policies often carry the dual aims of preventing future human rights violations and repairing the damage caused by the past abuse.

Post-conflict states have several options through which they may address these issues. For example, comprehensive accounts of the past are often sought as a useful tool to aid societies in their transition from oppression to peace. However, atoning for the past is often seen as running counter to the aims of national reconciliation, unity and institutional reconstruction. Accordingly, post-conflict governments often choose policies based upon the contexts of their transitions, taking into account the seriousness of the crimes committed as well

---

Reconciliation in Divided Societies, United States Institute of Peace Press, Washington, D.C., 1997.

121 See further H. Asseffa, *Peace and Reconciliation as a Paradigm: A philosophy of peace and its implications on conflict, governance and economic growth in Africa*, Nairobi Peace Initiative, NPI Monograph Series, 1993.

as the resources available.[122] In so doing, they face choices including the prudence of adopting amnesty,[123] criminal trials or truth commissions.

While reconciliation takes place at different levels within a nation, personal, inter-personal, collective and national given that individuals are the building blocks of society, population-wide trauma can hinder national reconstruction at every level. Thus, post-trauma national health[124] is contingent upon broad individual healing. Nevertheless, reconciliation is a long-term process aimed at addressing these formidable obstacles. As such, it requires measured programmes and processes.

This chapter has therefore focused on children as victims and the need to deal with them and their needs. This is because children's needs, as a vulnerable group, are not always given sufficient attention after war or conflict. For a variety of reasons, including the fact that they are not a lobby group with resources, children's needs are given rhetorical attention, but little in the way of resource attention. This is especially so where society is short of resources, which is often the case in these situations.[125]

For children to be rehabilitated and reintegrated back into their societies after war or conflict takes much effort and many resources. It is necessary to provide security, education and training, health, access to housing, food, and a range of social services. Specific trauma counselling may be necessary but is often unavailable. The ability for the children and their families to be economically integrated is also a key requirement.[126]

However, that is only one dimension of what needs to occur as a range of transitional justice issues need to be tackled, including prosecution,[127] truth recovery and reparations.[128] Reconciliation also needs to occur at different

---

122 J. Sarkin and E. Daly, 'Too many questions, too few answers: Reconciliation in transitional societies', (2004) 35 3 *Columbia Human Rights Law Review* 101–168.

123 See J. Sarkin, 'An Evaluation of the South African Amnesty Process', in A. Chapman and H. van der Merwe (eds.), *Truth and Reconciliation: Did the TRC Deliver*, University of Pennsylvania Press, Philadelphia, 2008, 93–115.

124 A. Zwi and N. Grove, Researching With Children in Conflict-Affected Settings, (2006) 34 7 *Humanitarian Exchange Magazine*.

125 J. Sarkin, 'A Study of the Effect on Corporal Punishment of the South African Transitional Constitution and Bill of Rights', (1995) 9 *International Journal of Children's Rights* at 369.

126 Y. Kemper, *supra* note 29. See also *International Labor Organization 2007 (December) Prevention of Child Recruitment and Reintegration of Children Associated with Armed Forces and Groups – Strategic Framework for Addressing the Economic Gap.*

127 See further J. Sarkin, 'Atrocity, Punishment and International Law' (2008) 30 4 *Human Rights Quarterly* 1028–1042.

128 See further J. Sarkin, 'Reparations for Gross Human Rights Violations in Africa: The Great Lakes', in S. Pete and M. du Plessis, *Repairing the Past – International Perspectives on Reparations for Gross Human Rights Abuses*, Intersentia, Antwerp, 2007, 199–231; J. Sarkin and C. Fowler, 'Reparations for Historical Human Rights Violations: The International and Historical Dimensions of the Alien Torts Claims Act Genocide Case of the Herero of Namibia', (2008) 9 *Human Rights Review* 331–360; J. Sarkin, *Colonial Genocide and Reparations Claims in the 21st Century: The Socio-Legal Context of Claims under International*

levels.[129] Collaboration at local, regional and international levels is often necessary to achieve reintegration and reconciliation. The question is whether there is the political will necessary to implement measures to protect and reintegrate children after armed conflict.[130] Political support from all parties to the conflict is necessary.

States should also go beyond simply ratifying international instruments concerning children by giving specific and direct effect to the Child Rights Convention as well as the Optional Protocol in their laws and in the situation on the ground. For this to occur, and for the effects to be felt, will take sustained effort by States and others and many resources. Solutions must also address the underlying causes of the conflict and tackle such problems such as poverty, access to resources, discrimination and inequality, as well as a range of other issues.

Law by the Herero against Germany for Genocide in Namibia, Praeger Security International, Westport, 2009, 23–228.

129 See J. Sarkin, 'Achieving Reconciliation in Divided Societies: Comparing the Approaches in Timor-Leste, South Africa and Rwanda' (2008) 3 2 *Yale Journal of International Affairs* 11–28; J. Sarkin and G. Dalco, 'Promoting Human Rights and Achieving Reconciliation at the International Level' (2006) 1, Part 1 *Law, Democracy and Development* at 69–99 and Part 2 at 49–69.

130 W. Seneviratne and P.W. Singer, 'Talk is Cheap: Getting Serious about Preventing Child Soldiers', (2004) *Cornell International Law Journal* 37.

PART II

LESSONS LEARNT FROM CURRENT PRACTICES AND APPROACHES

AND THE CHILDREN LEARNED NOT TO CRY

Stories About Children and Transitional Justice in Latin America

Javier Ciurlizza

1. INTRODUCTION

Latin America has been the region of the world in which Transitional Justice has had the earliest and largest case studies. Not only because the term was coined in the middle of the first wave of political transitions in the region – the Southern Cone experience, but also because during the last 30 years countries and societies have tried different approaches to addressing a past of violence and, at the same time, to testing the strength of their own democracy and institutions. Although there is sufficient empirical evidence about the terrible impact of violence on children, they have not been a relevant actor in the definition of transitional justice policies, both from the perspective of victimhood and from the horrible consequences of being involved in the conflict. However, children have been severely affected by the violent practices of dictators, merciless guerrilla leaders, the leniency of states and by abusive armies. They have been told, again and again, that they must learn not to cry.

The importance of furthering efforts to support children's involvement in transitional justice processes was identified during an expert discussion on Transitional Justice and Children convened by the UNICEF Innocenti Research Centre (IRC) in November 2005. As an outcome of the meeting it was proposed that research on children and truth commissions be undertaken, identifying good practices and lessons learned, and recommending strategies to improve and facilitate children's participation in future truth commissions. UNICEF and the International Center for Transitional Justice (ICTJ) initiated a process of documentation on the role of children in truth commissions. Different documents can be consulted to expand on this general approach.[1]

This chapter will analyse the ways in which truth commissions in Latin America have tackled the issue of children, taking into account the quite different scenarios of political "transitions", from the classic transit from a dictatorship to a democracy to the application of transitional justice measures to an ongoing conflict situation. It will review the main findings of these truth-seeking and truth-telling mechanisms in Argentina, Guatemala, Peru and Colombia, with some references to other Latin American countries. It will also analyse the recommendations, if any, that truth commissions in these countries elaborated regarding children.

This chapter addresses the question why children are virtually ignored in truth-seeking and truth-telling mechanisms in Latin America, and how this situation affects the legitimacy and efficiency of transitional justice processes in the region.

We will refer to other transitional justice mechanisms (*inter alia*, reparations, prosecution and institutional reform) but will not go into a deep consideration of their complex ramifications, both because this would need more space than is available for this chapter, but also because the empirical data are much more difficult to gather. Truth commission reports are at least written and available.

This is not an attempt to build a theory on children and transitional justice in Latin America, but only a first approach to the connections of truth-telling mechanisms and a significant dimension of human rights violations. This issue is still waiting to be addressed seriously by academia and practitioners in the transitional justice field.

---

1 UNICEF INNOCENTI RESEARCH CENTRE, Expert Paper Series on Children and Transitional Justice at www.unicef-irc.org. The topics under consideration include: *Basic Assumptions Concerning Children and Transitional Justice; Children and Accountability for Grave Crimes: Emerging International Practice and Standards; Children and Criminal Responsibility: the International Legal Framework; Children and Torture: Legal Framework and Medical and Psychological Impacts; Protection Measures and Psychosocial Support for Child Witnesses; Children and Reparations; Children and Transitional Justice in Colombia and Peru; Genetic Tracing, Disappeared Children and Justice; Children and the South African Truth and Reconciliation Commission; Child and Adolescent Participation and Agency in the Sierra Leone Truth and Reconciliation Commission; Children's Involvement in the CAVR in Timor-Leste; Child and Adolescent Participation in the Liberian Truth and Reconciliation Commission; Restorative Justice After Mass Violence: Opportunities and Risks for Children and Youth; Community and Family Responses to Youth Formerly Associated with Armed Forces and Armed Groups; Accountability for Sexual and Gender-based Crimes within the LRA; Traditional Mechanisms for Accountability: Mato Oput and Children in Northern Uganda; Children, Education and Reconciliation; Truth Commissions and National Curriculum: the Recordandonos Resource in Peru; Children and Economic Opportunities and Reform in Transitional Justice Contexts.*

2. TRANSITIONAL JUSTICE

Transitional justice is a field much more developed in practical than in theoretical bases. In fact, theory has been created *ex post* national and regional experiences. Political scientists created terms and concepts to understand the meaning of political transitions in Europe during the 1970s, and the arrangements developed, for example, in Spain, tended to be extrapolated to other realities, like the analysis of pacts and agreements in Argentina and Chile between 1983 and 1989.

The origins of the field, as depicted by Paige Arthur, can be associated with the emergence of the term. Although many of the questions incorporated into the current transitional justice perspective appeared immediately after the Second World War, and even before, the term was only used for the first time in 1992 and two years later the literatures on human rights and political transformation added it as one of the major challenges for countries which pass from authoritarian regimes to emergent democracies.[2] Considerations about human rights standards and the links between peace and justice were submitted to the Security Council with a view to ask the UN Secretary General for a special report on "societies in transition" and mechanisms for tackling impunity. This report appeared in 2004 and has been recently reviewed.[3]

Being an underdeveloped field in theory and concept brings at least two substantial consequences: (a) there is no convincing definition of transitional justice that can cover the multiple possibilities of results and processes; and (b) an understanding that perhaps it is a good idea to leave transitional justice as an open definition precisely because it is not encapsulated into a single dimension.

However, the better and more useful definitions of transitional justice refer precisely to the adjectival aspects of the field. They help us to understand in which ways transitional justice is relevant to producing a useful description of a political process. At the same time, this is not a definition that can be circumscribed into a specific social science or descriptive category. Transitional justice is inextricably linked with normative categories and values. Indeed, the vast majority of practitioners in the field come from law or, more precisely, from international human rights law or international humanitarian law.

---

2 P. Arthur, 'How Transitions Reshapes Human Rights: a conceptual history of transitional justice', (2009) 31 *Human Rights Quarterly* at 323. According to Arthur, the first usage of the term "transitional justice" came in a *Boston Herald* article describing a conference in Salzburg named "Justice in times of transition" (1992). In 1995, Neil Kritz published its fourth volume *Transitional Justice: how democracies reckon with former regimes.* This had a tremendous impact on new organisations (including the International Center for Transitional Justice, founded in 2001) and uniform references to the mechanisms adopted by countries to "deal" with a past of abuses.

3 UN Secretary General, *The rule of law and transitional justice in conflict and post-conflict societies*, UN document, 23 August 2004 (S/2004/616).

In this sense, Gonzalez talks about three simultaneous dimensions of transitional justice, or three different but concurrent perspectives from which an observer or practitioner can apply categories and concepts. Transitional justice talks about norms, about principles and about power.[4] The International Center for Transitional Justice uses the term "arrangements" to better describe it not as a static concept but as a fluid process of definitions, applications, and ulterior definitions.[5] Roht-Arriaza points out the two different meanings of transitional justice, which can be broadly or narrowly defined. A narrow view can be criticised, she says, *for ignoring root causes and privileging civil and political rights over economic, social and cultural rights.* By doing so, following this argument, transitional justice would particularly marginalise the needs of segregated populations, such as children.[6]

Summing up, and with the caution that this is not – regrettably – a general concept that the reader can apply to everything, we can use the term "transitional justice" to refer to the sort of arrangements created in order to provide solutions for problems which emerge in political transitions, and that refer to rights, values, laws and power equilibriums. To be a little more precise, what we understand as transitional justice is *the substantial link between the rights of the victims of atrocities in massive wars or conflicts and the political arrangements or agreements which underlie the transformation of politics in a particular context.*[7] This open definition helps us to understand better that transitional justice does not refer solely to the techniques of conflict resolution, peacebuilding or the power sharing that is needed when and where a conflict is coming to an end, or the sort of pre- and post-transitional situations when and where an authoritarian regime ceases to exist and is replaced by a democracy. These problems are of course pertinent to understanding the kinds of mechanism that can be created to address the legacy of that war or the inheritance of that dictatorship. But transitional justice is not well suited for producing sustainable proposals for political arrangements, as such.

---

4 E. Gonzalez, 'The Peruvian Truth and Reconciliation Commission and the Challenge of Impunity', in N. Roht-Arriaza and J. Mariezcurrena (eds.), *Transitional Justice in the Twenty-First Century: Beyond Truth versus Justice*, Cambridge University Press, Cambridge, 2006, 70–93.

5 International Center For Transitional Justice, *What is transitional justice?*, at www.ictj.org/en/tj.

6 N. Roth-Arriaza and J. Mariezcurrena, *supra* note 4.

7 The definition provided by the report of the UN Secretary General to the Security Council is frequently used, which says that: "full range of processes and mechanisms associated with a society's attempts to come to terms with a legacy of large-scale past abuses in order to ensure accountability, service justice and achieve reconciliation. These may include both judicial and non-judicial mechanisms with differing levels of international involvement (and none at all) and individual prosecutions, reparations, truth-seeking, institutional reform, vetting and dismissals, or a combination thereof."

At the same time, transitional justice tends to direct its conceptual and operational focus to the rights of the victims. It is not, in this sense, a neutral science that can consider the victims only, at best, as part of the elements of a political arrangement (as happened in Spain when the interests of victims were silenced very effectively and then the "model" was and is still sold as a world example, particularly in Latin America). However, although transitional justice worries about due respect for the human rights of the victims, it is not a discipline in which "rights" are the only consideration to be taken into account in considering the institutional options to be pursued. Human rights activists and victims' organisations tend to view transitional justice with mistrust, as happens with policy makers. The former associate the term with amnesties, pardons and all sort of arrangements in which accountability can be sacrificed for the sake of peace and stability. The latter complain on the prosecutorial side of transitional justice and prefer to isolate the term "reconciliation" from any other demands, or to use (erroneously) the term "restorative" as opposed to any pretention of criminal justice for perpetrators.

There is a close connection between transitional justice and human rights. However, the advantage of the former is that it takes from the latter a set of principles and tries to elaborate policy proposals that can help societies to address a violent past, to promote reparations, and to prosecute those who are responsible for mass crimes. The problem is that, in doing this, transitional justice may refer to certain agreements and arrangements in order to tackle confronted obstacles, apparent or real.

3. TRANSITIONAL JUSTICE AND CHILDREN

As happened over many years with international human rights law and, more generally, with legal systems in many parts of the world, children have been hidden behind a curtain of paternalistic views about their role in political arrangements. In fact, children are simply deemed irrelevant in most of the literature, which deals with transitions as political processes. It is only in Africa that children have become a sensitive issue, mostly because of their massive participation in armed conflicts and the cases built around the crime of recruitment in connection with the jurisdiction of the International Criminal Court.

If we consider transitional justice as a set of arrangements that looks to protect and promote human rights, then we can conceptually make the direct link between the rights of children and truth, justice, reparations and guarantees of non-repetition. In fact, the impulse has come from international humanitarian law and, more recently, international human rights law to create a discourse about the role of children in armed conflict and the absolute rights that have to be protected from the effects of violence. The universal shift during the 1980s from children as an "object of protection" to children as a "subject of rights" has also helped to transform institutional systems into more proactive measures, and has had practical consequences for the criminal law dimensions of children's rights.

However, the insertion of children issues into transitional justice mechanisms is slow and halting. We simply do not know how to produce effective recommendations for tackling the right of a child to know the truth about massive crimes which have affected him or her personally or his or her family. We do not know how to incorporate children into a truth-telling process in which we can give them a voice without destroying the safety net that is represented by anonymity, particularly for sexual offences. We have been quite useless in trying to provide specific reparations for children without reverting – once again – into a paternalistic view of children that have to be protected. We have very few ideas about the participation of children in prosecutorial efforts, or how to treat children as witnesses. Legal systems are clumsy at dealing with perpetrators under 18, and most of our efforts have failed because our legal systems tend to criminalise the "anti-social" conduct of minors. Finally, we have not been capable of incorporating a transitional justice perspective into the public and social policies designed to protect children in the context of guarantees of non-repetition.

There are too few examples of mechanisms in which children have participated fully and satisfactorily and too few examples of mechanisms in which the needs, aspirations and specificities of children and how their rights might be exercised have been built in from the start. The recommendations found in the literature are still vague and general (articulation, more consultation, more investigation, ...).[8] This happens simultaneously with the increasing sophistication of transitional justice measures implemented to create and conduct truth commissions, reparations systems, different options for prosecution, and a series of advanced institutional reforms and guarantees of non-repetition. This paradox needs to be addressed urgently.

Latin America has not been an exception to this regrettable deficit of transitional justice theory regarding children.

---

8 A. Smith, 'Basic Assumptions of Transitional Justice and Children', in UNICEF Innocenti Research Centre (IRC), *Expert Paper Series on Children and Transitional Justice*, November 2005.

4. MODELLING TRANSITIONAL JUSTICE IN LATIN AMERICA

To create categories or "models" of transitional justice is always dangerous, even in a region that appears to be homogeneous in terms of politics and culture. However, in order to provide a systematic analysis of children and transitional justice issues and links in the region, we can refer to four different levels or groups of experiences, and we have chosen one of each to review the connections between truth commissions and children.[9]

- Early transitions from dictatorship to democracy (Argentina, Chile, Uruguay, Paraguay, Brazil).
- Peace processes and peacebuilding after armed conflict (Guatemala, El Salvador, Nicaragua).
- Complex transitions from authoritarian regimes to weak democracies (Peru, Ecuador, Paraguay, Honduras)
- Ongoing conflicts and transitional justice mechanisms (Colombia).

Politics is more complex than any other category and Latin America is an example that confirms this principle. It was understood that the "transitions" in the Southern Cone and Central America were short periods of arrangements in which "normality" would emerge as a logical consequence of political agreements. Politicians in charge of these processes (for good or evil reasons) had the experience of elite arrangements that could provide *sound* solutions for conflicts. At the end, this had been the *business* in civil wars and armed conflicts in Latin America for the last 80 years of its history.

However, societies and institutions had become more complex than the dream of "bipartisanship" that had made things "easier" at the moment of peace and transformation. Substantial changes in civil society, the emergence of a vigorous human rights movement and the internationalisation of values (such as democracy, with the corresponding doses of popular participation) made it impossible to secure short-term solutions for the political dilemmas in Latin America. This is why transitions, which were envisioned and designed with a short-term strategy in the minds of policy makers, have had setbacks or spectacular developments even 30 years after the crimes were committed.

Economic and institutional crises have opened new spaces of confrontation for transitional justice in Latin America. Liberalisation processes, generalised in the

9 Some other countries can be placed into one or more of these categories, although they do have a substantial transitional agenda and pending issues to be addressed. Mexico, for example, passed through a process that resembles the Peruvian experience (the PRI regime defeated and an electoral reform to open the country for political participation), and certain parts of its territory can be considered as more in a process of peace building (Guerrero and Chiapas) and even in an ongoing conflict situation (Ciudad Juarez).

continent during the 1990s, helped in some places to reopen the debate about the crimes of the past, but at the same time created a trend of economically liberal and politically conservative leaders (Menem in Argentina and Fujimori in Peru). A certain stability in the democratic regimes (broken in Honduras in 2009) and moderate economic growth have helped to re-establish the middle sectors in society and to achieve a relative reduction in the high indicators of poverty, but the evolution is highly uneven.

5. CHILD INVOLVEMENT IN TRANSITIONAL JUSTICE IN LATIN AMERICA

5.1. CHILDREN AND TRUTH-TELLING MECHANISMS

With the exception of Colombia, the other countries had the common feature of official mechanisms of truth-seeking and truth-telling, which were associated with a wider strategy to deal with a past situation of human rights violations. It is always difficult to include Colombia in comparative analysis, but this chapter will try to do so.

Transitional justice mechanisms are not absent from the Colombian process, including truth-telling and truth-seeking mechanisms. Due to the demobilisation of paramilitaries, during the last four years important information has been gathered in "free versions" given by former members of these illegal organisations. No matter how many lies and misinformation are included in these statements, the process has allowed certain facts to be established (for example, the identification of mass graves in many parts of the territory) that would have not been possible to obtain otherwise.

Besides, there is an ongoing effort through an official truth-telling procedure under the National Commission of Reparation and Reconciliation, namely the Working Group on Historical Memory, an independent group of well respected academics which has released two reports on specific cases. Even the Supreme Court of Justice created a Truth Commission in 2005, which published its final report at the end of 2009, to investigate a particular event that happened in 1985. Moreover, dozens of unofficial initiatives on truth-seeking are spreading in different parts of the country.

We can, therefore, apply to Colombia certain questions about the treatment of children in truth-seeking and truth-telling efforts. These questions are:

- How are children treated as victims in the official reports?
- Are there any recommendations about children in these reports?

- How is the quality of the data of the truth-telling mechanism in relation to children?
- Is there any policy regarding the disarmament, demobilisation and reinsertion of child combatants?

We will look into these questions into each country, seeking common patterns and, if feasible, to make some general remarks.

5.2. THE "*NUNCA MÁS*" FOR CHILDREN IN ARGENTINA[10]

Transitional justice in Argentina suffered a series of sudden movements between 1983, when democracy was restored after seven years of military dictatorship, and 2003, when Nestor Kirchner assumed the presidency and the impunity laws were finally repealed. Transitional mechanisms were immediately established when the military left power and adopted through the National Commission for the Disappeared (CONADEP), as well as through public trials in which members of the military juntas were swiftly convicted and sentenced, some of them to life imprisonment. The dirty war organised by the military had left at least 25,000 disappeared. However, by 1986 President Alfonsín had ceded to the pressures of the economic meltdown and the military and had paved the way for impunity.

The result was the *due obedience* and the *full stop* laws, which precluded any possibility of continuing with the trials of the perpetrators. The administration of Carlos Menem completed the impunity circle, granting pardons to the few that remained in prison. Reparations were granted for the relatives of the disappeared, but Menem firmly opposed to any kind of prosecution. Another economic crisis in 1999 averted any serious attempt to review the impunity laws as other more compelling social problems focused the attention of society and the media. However, the defeat of Menem in the 2003 election paved the way for the revision of the human rights policy. The Supreme Court and the Legislature repealed the impunity laws and hundreds of cases were reopened. Nearly 1,400 members of the armed forces and security corps have been prosecuted, although only 58 have so far been convicted.[11]

---

10 For further reading on transitional justice in Argentina, we recommend: C. Acuña, 'Transitional Justice in Argentina and Chile: A Never-Ending Story?', in J. Elster, (ed.), *Retribution and Repatriation in the Transition to Democracy*, New York, Cambridge University Press, 2006, 206–238; P. Valdez, 'El pasado, un tema central del presente. La búsqueda de verdad y justicia como construcción de una lógica democratica', en IDEA International, *Verdad, Justicia Y Reparación: Desafios Para La Convivencia Social*, San José de Costa Rica, Instituto Interamericano de Derechos Humanos, 2005.

11 Centro de Estudios Legales y Sociales, *Crímenes del terrorismo de estado*, at www.cels.org.ar/wpblogs/.

Human rights violations in Argentina resulted mainly as a direct consequence of actions organised by the military dictatorship. The report *Nunca Más,* published at the end of 1984, made known 8,961 cases, which have since been complemented with new information.

Of the disappeared reported in *Nunca Más,* 1.5 percent were children under 15 years old, but more than 10 percent were between 15 and 20 years old. Three percent were pregnant women, most of whom gave birth while being held in clandestine centres. The commission concentrated on 172 children who were abducted and removed from their biological families. This case remains open and recently new DNA tests proved the extraction of children, born to be sold or given in illegal adoption. Another 250 teenagers (between 13 and 18 years old) were also part of the long list of the disappeared.

Different groups have made the issue of abducted children a central issue for campaigning and advocacy. Specific actions have included identification efforts by, for example, *Abuelas de la Plaza de Mayo.* However, the findings of the CONADEP were general and preliminary and additional investigations have filled in the picture. The military in power in Argentina between 1976 and 1983 implemented a complex policy of abduction of recently born children as part of a brutal strategy of thievery and blackmail.[12]

The report described the clandestine operations developed when children were in the targeted family. In many cases, this resulted in direct abduction for ultimate adoption by some repressor. In other cases, the children witnessed the torture inflicted on their parents or were themselves tortured. Many of them are part of the long list of the disappeared that can be seen in the memorial of Rio de la Plata.[13]

Recommendations from CONADEP were also very general and it was assumed that the prosecutions to follow would be able to establish further measures regarding truth, justice and reparations. However, the magnitude of the tragedy led the Commission, headed by the writer Ernesto Sábato, to propose the enactment of laws needed for the children and relatives to receive "economic assistance", scholarships and work positions. This was a quite preliminary phrasing of the concept of reparations.[14]

---

12 Comision Nacional De Estudio Sobre Personas Desaparecidas, *Nunca Mas*, at www.desaparecidos.org/arg/conadep/.

13 Ibid.

14 Ibid.

5.3. THE ONGOING DRAMA OF CHILDREN IN COLOMBIA[15]

Colombia suffers from the longest active armed conflict in the world, started at least as far back as 1964, although there is a debate about the connection between violence and politics in Colombian history and some trace the beginnings of the current violence to 1948 or even earlier. There is no clear indicator about how many deaths and disappearances have happened during the conflict. The levels of violence have decreased during the last 8 years, but vast portions of Colombian territory are still war zones. A process of demobilising the paramilitary organisations started in 2004 and a system of "peace and justice" governs the submission of more than 3,000 former members of the paramilitary to justice. Although the results are meagre, the information obtained has been important for opening criminal investigations in some cases, but impunity remains the rule for many crimes.

To talk about a transitional justice process in Colombia is obviously problematic. Peace and conflict resolution (or humanitarian concerns) should be the priority for the Colombians and the international community. In fact, the release of hostages, the displaced people (8 percent of the total population, according to official figures) and the mine zones are daily concerns in the country. However, the failure to achieve an agreement with the guerrillas (both FARC and ELN) and the military success of the Uribe administration have opened another front: negotiation with the paramilitaries, which many saw as the reinsertion of former allies into the Colombian armed forces. Truth-seeking mechanisms, reparations for victims and a certain dose of justice are spreading all over the country not only, and not mainly, from the top but also from the victims' organisations and amongst civil society.

Participation of children in the armed conflict in Colombia has been historically widespread and systematic. The guerrillas have declared that, formally, they do not recruit children under 15, but their practice says otherwise. The statements of leaders of these organisations have recently revealed the participation of children in armed organisations. Forced recruitment by the army, although attenuated in recent times and subjected to more control, is still pervasive in some areas.

15 For basic elements of the complex Colombian transitional justice process, please read: L. Laplante and K. Theidon, *Transitional justice in times of conflict: Colombia's ley de justicia y paz*, at http://students.law.umich.edu/mjil/article-pdfs/v28n1-laplante-theidon.pdf; C. Diaz, *Bid for justice and peace*, in conference papers of Peace and Justice conference, International Center for Transitional Justice, Nuremberg, 2008, at www.humansecuritygateway.com/documents/PJC_Colombia_bidforjusticeandpeace.pdf; J. Ciurlizza, 'Peace in Colombia from the perspective of transitional justice', in *Fundacion Ideas para la Paz and Wilson International Center for Scholars, Cuadernos del conflict – Peace initiatives and Colombia's armed conflict.*

Some international and local NGOs provide different estimates of how many children have been involved in the conflict recently. According to Human Rights Watch, the figure was more than 11,000 by 2002.[16] The Office of the High Commissioner for Human Rights estimated in the same year that the figure was about 14,000 and the Ombudsman Office said on its annual report that they were nearly 6,000.[17] This is linked to the general difficulties in Colombia of finding reliable figures on victims.

In 2005, specific legislation was passed (Peace and Justice) in order to provide a procedure for the demobilisation of paramilitaries throughout the country.[18] In the first 6 months of the process, the heads of paramilitary fronts included only 185 children to be demobilised. More than 300 children have been given in custody to the state welfare institution. Strong evidence suggests that these groups routinely used children but their leaders have denied this policy in their "free versions" given to local prosecutors.

A revealing report that appeared in November 2008 in a local journal stated that one paramilitary group released 80 children directly to their families, when the conversations with the government were starting. The reason for the bosses keeping this practice out of sight was precisely the harsh penalties associated with this crime and the eventual jurisdiction of the International Criminal Court.

Between 1999 and 2006, the amazing figure of 2,916 children appear to have been demobilised, or have deserted, from armed illegal organisations, most of them from the guerrillas.[19] In many cases, the guerrillas use children extensively in information missions, but in some they have participated directly in combat. The decision announced by the Directorate of FARC in 1998, that recruitment would "only" start with children older than 15 years old, was directly linked with the negotiations opened in San Vicente del Caguán, forming part of the preconditions

16 Human Rights Watch, *Aprenderás a no llorar, Reclutamiento forzado de menores de edad en Colombia*, HRW Report, 2003.

17 Defensoria del Pueblo, according to E. Yarce, See at www.bibliotecapiloto.gov.co/bib_autor/noticias/colombia/enero/10a_31.htm.

18 Law 975 was reviewed by the Constitutional Court, which provided that it was necessary to protect and promote the rights of the victims and, to do this, it was indispensable to advance a full investigation into the crimes and that the benefits to be given had to be heavily conditioned upon reliable information given by the demobilised and their contribution towards full reparation and restitution. After 5 years, there have been no convictions and the Supreme Court has criticised the investigations and recommended that a full truth commission should be implemented.

19 Coalico, Coalition Against the Participation of Children in the Armed Conflict of Colombia In 2006, an information system on children and youth was implemented in Colombia. According to the data collected by different institutions, 2,212 children of school age were reported as combatants of armed organisations in a six-year period.

for a humanitarian agreement. At the Rome Conference in the same year, where the definition of crimes was discussed, ICRC delegates provided advice to the guerrillas to bring their regulations up to the minimum standards of international humanitarian law.

The history, however, is somewhat different. FARC was a movement associated with rural guerrillas, in which family and communal relations were important. Children were associated with the group from a very early age. Hundreds of children have been enrolled into their ranks. Hundreds died in combat and from disease in the harsh conditions of the jungle and the hiding places of their fronts. Something similar happened with the other guerrilla movements, although not on the scale of FARC. In fact, the participation of children in M-19 was rare, given its more urban character.

Another element to be considered is forced recruitment. The army has been accused of recruiting minors for many years. As in other cases (Guatemala and Peru), the 18-years-old mark seems to have been only a token reference in military conscription practice in Colombia. This has changed in recent years, but some dispute the statement of the Uribe administration, according to which it has forbidden the recruitment of under-18s since at least 2002.

The ongoing conflict in Colombia does not at present allow the establishment of a fully-fledged truth-seeking mechanism. Information on human rights violations is scarce and scattered. However, important information systems have been developed for displaced people since 1997. This phenomenon affects at least 2.8 million Colombians and the indicators developed by the government, in accordance with a mandate established by the Constitutional Court, reveal that more than 600,000 children were directly affected by the displacement process.[20]

5.4. GUATEMALA: COMBATANTS BEFORE, "*MARITOS*" TODAY[21]

The Civil War in Guatemala left more than 200,000 dead and disappeared in a long and cruel armed conflict that lasted 36 years and had its peak between 1982

---

20 In judgment T-025 the Constitutional Court declared a "state of affairs unconstitutional", referring to the situation of displaced people in Colombia. It ordered the government to develop effective public policies for this population and to report periodically to the Court its advancement according to specific indicators. The Constitutional Court has been a central vehicle of human rights protection in the country, developing concepts such as "constitutional bloc" to understand the interconnection between national and international law when regulating human rights.

21 For further reading on the transitional justice process in Guatemala, I recommend: H. Mack, 'Guatemala, La Reconciliación en Guatemala: un proceso ausente', en IDEA International,

and 1984, a period in which a 'genocide' against the Maya population was perpetrated.[22] Political agreements between the guerrilla front and the government, with the active participation of the United States and the United Nations, paved the way for the cessation of hostilities, but only 8 years later was it possible to approve constitutional and legal reforms that led to the creation of a truth commission (*Comisión de Esclarecimiento Histórico*), which documented the tragedy of the forcible displacement of more than 1.5 million of persons. The economic crisis and the constraints of the new democratic government impeded the establishment of a prosecutorial authority which could follow up the direct finding of the truth commission (preceded by a similar effort made by the Catholic Church), and the lack of independence of judges and prosecutors hampered the efforts to bring perpetrators to justice.

Guatemala suffered the consequences of an extended network of drug trafficking and organised delinquency, particularly affecting the young in gangs organised in major cities of the United States (maras). These gangs are integrated with Mexican cartels that dominate the drug business and other illegal activities. Some members of these new illegal organisations are former members of the armed forces and the guerrilla groups. Guatemala is now the third most violent Latin American country, according to the Global Peace Index.[23]

The United Nations agreed with the government of Guatemala to create a Special Commission Against Impunity (CICIG) which, in principle, does not deal with the crimes of the past, but which supports the efforts of public prosecutors and the police in dealing with organised crime. This new attempt to tackle impunity and organised crime is closely linked with the mostly unresolved cases from the civil war. Democracy in this country is on the verge of collapse.

The peace agreements reached between the guerrilla groups (*Unión Revolucionaria Nacional Guatemalteca*) and the government preceded the establishment of two major efforts at truth-seeking and truth-telling. The first was led by the Catholic Church (*Memory Reconstruction of Guatemala – REHMI*) and headed by Bishop Gerardi (killed in 1998). The second was an official truth commission (*Comisión de Esclarecimiento Histórico*). Both mechanisms shocked the country and the international community through their findings, revealing the cruelty of the military repression during the war, including an accusation of genocide against the Maya population.

Verdad, justicia y reparación: desafíos para la convivencia social, San José de Costa Rica, Instituto Interamericano de Derechos Humanos, 2005.

22 For the full report, see: http://shr.aaas.org/guatemala/ceh.

23 Global Peace Index at www.visionofhumanity.org/images/content/GPI-2009/2009-GPI-ResultsReport-20090526.pdf.

As has been noted before in this chapter, the population of Guatemala is predominantly young. Indeed, children represent almost a third of the total population and 45 percent of the rural population. It is easy to understand how deep the effect of the war was on children, particularly the rural and the poor. They were forcibly recruited on a massive scale by the army and the guerrilla groups and killed, tortured and disappeared routinely.

Both truth-seeking mechanisms report extensively on the crimes committed by children, but stopped short of describing (at least with same accuracy) the implications of the war for children. The Rehmi project concentrated on emblematic cases in which children were substantially victimised by the armed contenders, but particularly by the army.

5.5. THE PERUVIAN TRC AND THE ELUSIVE ISSUE OF CHILDREN[24]

Peru's transitional justice is a very peculiar combination of a collapsed authoritarian regime (Fujimori) and the slow termination of an internal armed conflict. In fact, the 69,000 dead and disappeared reported by the Truth and Reconciliation Commission occurred mainly between 1980 and 1992, while the 1990s was a decade of widespread corruption and a *counter-subversive state without subversion*.[25] The transition itself was short in formal terms (9 months of provisional administration), but the legacy of that transition is still ongoing and uncertain in the country.

Subversive organisations in Peru collapsed very quickly between 1992 and 1995. However, they did not disappear and evolved (particularly Shining Path) into small groups located in the coca crop areas of the country, located in two valleys. One of these groups has reappeared recently, killing police officers and military personnel as well as threatening local authorities. The ghost of violence is still a matter of concern for Peruvians and explains how Fujimori, recently sentenced to 25 years for murder, is still popular and "Fujimorism" an electoral option.

Collective reparations have been implemented and prosecutions taken against 160 military and police officers. There are more than 1,800 persons in prison for crimes associated with subversion and terrorism. However, the findings of the

24 For further reading: L. Magarrell and L. Filippini (ed)., *El legado de la verdad: la justicia penal en la transición peruana*, Perú, Centro Internacional para la Justicia Transicional; Idehpucp, Instituto de Democracia y Derechos Humanos, Pontificia Universidad Católica del Perú, 2006.

25 This is the title of the chapter of the Peruvian TRC report, which talks about the Fujimori administration. See: www.cverdad.org.pe.

Truth Commission were harshly criticised by many as exaggerations and the refusal of Peruvian elites to recognise the cruelty of the conflict tell a lot about the lack of basic understanding of what kind of democracy Peru has to build.

Violence in Peru, as reported by the Truth and Reconciliation Commission, started in May 1980, when a group named "Shining Path" initiated its self-proclaimed "popular war" to replace the "bourgeois state" with the "republic of new democracy". However, violent circumstances were not strange for this Andean country, as the high levels of poverty that affected its rural population, particularly the children, can test place civil order under strain.

Nevertheless, the 15 years of extreme violence unleashed first in the Andes, and then on the rest of the country, was the most brutal and bloody process Peru had experienced during its turbulent history (which included one major international war). The TRC report revealed that at least 69,000 persons had been killed or disappeared during the conflict, and that 3 in 4 of the victims were of indigenous origin. Violence severely affected the poor and had dramatic effects in the destruction of peasant communities, ethnic groups of the central jungle and women and children. The first conclusion of the report was that there was the need for a national sense of "shame" as Peruvians in the cities, particularly in Lima, had ignored the tragedy of their countrymen and that discrimination and racism had aggravated the effects of this war.

According to the TRC's figures, 12.5 percent of the victims were children under 18. However, certain forms of violence affected children with particular severity. More than 35 percent of those forcibly recruited, both by the subversive organisations and the army, were children and 25 percent of cases of sexual assault and rape were minors.[26]

In particular, minors were subjected to illegal detention by the security forces during the 1980s and in 1992, a law enacted by Fujimori reduced the minimum age for criminal responsibility for terrorism from 18 to 15 years. More than 209 children were sentenced to prison and even to life imprisonment during the next three years, before the law was finally repealed after protests and campaigns by human rights organisations. Conditions of detention for these children were miserable and restrictions severe. In some forced transfers, some children were tortured and beaten by the police.

As in Argentina, many children disappeared together with their families. The Ombudsman Office keeps records of 46 children of under 5 years old who were abducted by the security forces, particularly between 1983 and 1984 in the region of Ayacucho. However, there has been no further investigation or search for their whereabouts.

---

26 Truth and Reconciliation Commission, *Final report* at 586.

The attitude of the army in the regions controlled by the subversives was of a profound lack of trust in and criminalisation of peasant communities. In a congressional hearing, an army lieutenant declared that even the elderly and the children had to be eliminated, as they were potential terrorists.[27] Sexual violence was used against many children, even under 10 years old, as a method of direct punishment or to intimidate their families. In the public hearings conducted by the TRC, horrendous stories were heard about this practice in certain military barracks.

The participation of children in the war was active, not only through forced recruitment but also as part of the deliberate strategies of certain actors. A UN report published in 1995 estimated that more than 4,000 children were active members of civil defence committees, organisations that derived from the "*rondas campesinas*" (traditional self-defence structures), but which were put under military control after 1991.[28] Little is known about the demobilisation of these children after the end of the war, but many of them are still involved in illegal activities in the coca crop valleys.

Shining Path was responsible for more than 50 percent of the murders of children during the war (43 percent of the total deaths and disappearances are charged to them). Forced recruitment and sexual violence were also frequent crimes committed by the subversives.

The participation of children in the war was an official policy of Shining Path, even as "students" or "apprentices". An official statement of this group said in 1988: "*... make the children participate in the war. They can perform different tasks and through them, they will understand the need to transform the world, changing ideology and adopting the proletariat's.*[29]

Small children under 11 years old were named the *red pioneers* and entrusted with tasks of surveillance and support. Once the children turned 12, they were taught how to use a gun and to fabricate explosives. Some of them were used as "bomb children", forced to carry dynamite to military objectives. On several occasions, the children died before reaching the target. Shining Path had a criminal and deliberate policy of brainwashing children, starting at 4 or 5 years

---

27 Congreso De La Republica, *Comisión Investigadora de los Hechos de Accomarca*, *Testimony of Lieutenant Telmo Hurtado: "La mayoría es gente que actúa en contra de nosotros, por la ideología que lleva ya es muy difícil de volverlos a captar [...] como le dije, yo he tomado la determinación de eliminarlos."*

28 Office of the Special Representative of the Secretary General for Children and Armed Conflict.

29 Truth and Reconciliation Commission, *Final report* at 613: "*... hay que hacer que nos niños participen en la Guerra. Ellos pueden asumir tareas diversas y, a través de esas actividades, entenderán la necesidad de transformar el mundo, cambiando de ideología y adoptando la del proletariado".*

old, extracting them from their families and convincing them that the "party" was the only family they needed.

Although to a lesser degree, MRTA also recruited children, as was evident during the hostage-taking operation in the Japanese Embassy in 1997, in which half of the members of the group were between 16 and 18 years old. All of them died after the military operation.

Sequels of the war on children have been evaluated only in segmented portions of the Peruvian territory. Reparations have been, until now, only of a collective character, which impedes making visible the tragic consequences that war had for thousands of children in the country. There have been no specific programmes targeted at child combatants and the TRC report was not precise in its recommendations on this issue.

The methodology of the Peruvian TRC included testimony-taking and public hearings, amongst other research mechanisms. A team of more than 350 interviewers and 4,000 volunteers went into the country to collect information. However, there was no specific strategy for children.

5.6. DEMOGRAPHICS AND CRIMINALITY

The countries we analyse have been affected over the last 30 years by a general process called "demographic transition",[30] in which most are moderating their population growth, although not at the levels of the "ageing" process in Europe. Of the countries to be analysed, in Guatemala at least 50 percent of the population is under 15 years old, while Colombia and Peru have rates of around 35 percent and Argentina less than 25 percent.

Since 1968, Colombia has been leading the number of homicides per 100,000 people. In the last Human Development Report, Colombia has a rate of 62.7, compared with a rate of 25.5 for Guatemala and 9.5 and 5.5 for Argentina and Peru respectively. However, the situation in Guatemala is worsening quickly, while the murder rate in Colombia remains at least stable. The killing rate in Guatemala has doubled in the last three years.[31]

The figure is more serious for Guatemala if we analyse the mortality rate for children under 5. The average for Latin America is 22 deaths per 100,000 inhabitants, but in Guatemala 39 children die of different causes before reaching

---

30 Comision Economica para America Latina, 'Estadísticas demográficas de Celade', at www.eclac.org/Celade/SitDem/DE_SitDemTransDemDoc00e.html.

31 United Nations Development Program, *Human Development Report 2009*, http://hdrstats.undp.org/indicators/263.html.

5 years old, while in Colombia and Peru the rate is about 20.[32] The data is also worrisome regarding the proportion of children between 5 and 15 years old who are working. Although the average for Latin America is 11, in Guatemala more than 30 children out of 1,000 are working, and most of them in poor conditions.

We have not found data on the participation of children in illegal activities in Latin America, but we can reasonably argue that at least in Colombia, Guatemala and Peru, most of the children that are reported to be working in the rural areas are linked with different types of abuse or illegal activity. They are known as *raspachines* in Colombia, *pájaros fruteros* in Peru and *maritos* in Guatemala. Most of the children who are currently in these borderline sectors are extremely vulnerable to illegal organisations.

Demography will certainly influence the composition of urban societies and middle and upper classes in Latin America. However, the rural and poor population does not seem to be affected by this trend. High birth rates (clearly evident in the rural populations of Guatemala and Peru, for example) will continue to affect vast sectors, precisely those most affected by war and human rights violations. In this context, the invisibility of affected children will continue to be a major problem for the articulation of significant public policies, as the Latin American elites will not need to consider this population as a central problem, either in economic or political terms.

6. CONCLUSION

We said at the beginning of this essay that transitional justice mechanisms, at least in Latin America, have not been able either to include children as a fundamental actor in the processes or as a substantial topic which can illustrate specific recommendations, for example in truth commission reports. To be fair, we have to add that there is little communication and dialogue between the field of children's rights and the discipline of transitional justice.

The four cases analysed here have a common element regarding their treatment of children issues: they are a partial component of a larger tragedy. Violations of children's rights are depicted not as systematic patterns of aggression but as a logical consequence of systematic and generalised patterns of human rights violations. The kidnapping of children in Argentina was a consequence of the enforced disappearance of their parents; while the forced recruitment of minors by armed actors in Peru was a sequel to internal displacement and subsequent

32 Fondo de las Naciones Unidas para la Infancia, *Estado Mundial de la Infancia, Salud materna y neonatal*, 2009.

abandonment by their relatives. This follows the patterns of a traditional approach to children rights: they have to be built and understood as small dimensions of adult rights and, therefore, they must be protected.

Transitional justice faces the challenge of moving towards a better understanding of children as the subject of specific rights during and after dictatorship or conflict and also as actors of their own destiny and fate. There are sufficient elements in the cases analysed to establish firmly certain roots of massive violations affecting children. They are particularly useful for armed groups or state terror because they are profitable (forced labour and adoption, for example), efficient in war (to plant bombs or to spy, for example) and highly productive (producing weapons or providing information, for example). We cannot simply say that children are affected in war and dictatorship because adults, particularly their relatives, are also affected. On many occasions, targeted children are deliberately chosen to be victims.

We need to go deeper into certain aspects of research about the consequences for children of violence on political grounds. With the notable exception of Argentina, research on the psychosocial dimension of mass crimes committed against children is scarce in Latin America. The long-term effects of forced recruitment are not addressed by well-funded state programmes. Community initiatives, although important, are insufficient in large-scale contexts. More field research is needed, such as the projects developed in African countries. The existing analysis is mostly of a legal nature. This is a direct consequence of decisions taken by courts in recent years, particularly in Colombia and Peru.

Educational tools are usually identified as the best way to measure whether a truth commission is correctly addressing issues relevant for children. This implies changes in curricula, the incorporation of truth and reconciliation as educational concepts and transformation of the roles of teachers and students.

Research is less developed regarding the ethnic variables and strong differences in the role of children in indigenous communities. This was made evident in the TRCs in Guatemala and Peru, although the consequences are not clear in terms of education and reconciliation with particular indigenous communities (for example, Maya Kem in Guatemala). Prosecutions for crimes committed against children must be a particular imperative according to international and national law. Although there is no agreement about permitting amnesties for certain crimes committed during armed conflict, in the inter-American system the general trend is towards considering pardon mechanisms inadmissible when there are serious violations of international law.

To prosecute children under 18 who have participated in serious crimes is a matter of contention, particularly for those who were between 15 and 18 when the crime occurred. The general recommendation is to reinforce the juvenile criminal system or to apply restorative justice measures, but it is not clear which rules should apply in particularly serious cases.

Truth-seeking mechanisms have not incorporated deliberate strategies for identifying children as a particularly vulnerable sector of crimes. When some of them have done so (particularly in Argentina and Peru), the conclusions are mostly of a legal nature, without assessing the consequences. The recommendations of truth commissions include particular suggestions for children, but they are too general and do not allow the articulation of practical measures to ensure the non-repetition of patterns of violence against children.

The participation of children in truth-seeking mechanism has been virtually non-existent. Children have not been allowed to give public testimony and information about them comes generally from relatives and friends. On the few occasions in which children have been allowed to talk directly (in certain regions of Guatemala and in the outreach strategy of the Peruvian TRC), the impact has been important.

We can conclude that there is an urgent need to assess the particular effect of transitional measures on children, and to produce particular strategies (and even specific mechanisms) to address the deficit of truth, justice and reparation for certain violations, such as forced labour (and participation in war is a kind of labour in this context).

WHEN HURBINEK SURVIVES*

Transitional Justice and Children's Rights: Lessons Learnt from Rwanda

Pietro SULLO**

1. INTRODUCTION: AN OVERVIEW OF TRANSITIONAL JUSTICE AND CHILDREN

Despite the large-scale victimisation of children[1] and youth in conflict and post-conflict settings, transitional justice mechanisms have traditionally paid little attention to their needs.[2] Even though some truth commissions have focused and shed light on abuses committed against children (for instance, the Sierra

* See P. LEVI, *La tregua*, Einaudi, Torino, 1963, 27–29, English text edition, *The Reawakening*, Touchstone Publisher, New York, 1995, 25–26: 'He looked about three years old, no one knew anything of him, he could not speak and he had no name; that curious name, Hurbinek, had been given to him by us, perhaps Hurbinek was a nobody, a child of death, a child of by one of the women who had interpreted with those syllables one of the inarticulate sounds that the baby let out now and again. He was paralysed from the waist down, with atrophied legs, thin as sticks; but his eyes, lost in his triangular and wasted face, flashed terribly alive, full of demand, assertion, of the will to break loose, to shatter the tomb of his dumbness. The speech he lacked, which no one had bothered to teach him, the need of speech charged his stare with explosive urgency: it was a stare both savage and human, even mature, a judgement, which none of us could support, so heavy was it with force and anguish...
During the night we listened carefully: ... from Hurbinek's corner there occasionally came a sound, a word. It was not, admittedly, always exactly the same word, but it was certainly an articulated word; or better, several slightly different articulated words, experimental variations on a theme, on a root, perhaps on a name. Hurbinek, who was three years old and perhaps had been born in Auschwitz and had never seen a tree; Hurbinek, who had fought like a man, to the last breath, to gain his entry into the world of men, from which a bestial power had excluded him; Hurbinek, the nameless, tiny forearm – even his – bore the tattoo of Auschwitz; Hurbinek died in the first days of March 1945, free but not redeemed. Nothing remains of him: he bears witness through these words of mine'.

** The author thanks Professor Stephan Parmentier, K.U.Leuven, Avocats Sans Frontières, permanent mission in Rwanda and Clémentine Uwamuguha for the support provided.

1 For the purpose of this paper 'child' is every individual below the age of 18, in line with article 1 of the 1989 Convention on the Rights of the Child.

2 See on this point S. SIEGRIST, 'Child Rights and Transitional Justice', in S. PARMAR, M.J. ROSEMAN, S. SIEGRIST and T. SOWA (eds.), *Children and Transitional Justice. Truth-Telling, Accountability and Reconciliation*, Harvard University Press, Cambridge, 2010, pp. 2–3.

Leone Truth and Reconciliation Commission), these violations have usually been framed as an outcome of violence largely experienced and perpetrated by adults. The pioneering research activity conducted by Graça Machel on the 'Impact of armed conflict on children' has spread awareness on the fact that 'war violates every right of the child' and pawed the way to a child-sensitive approach to post-conflict issues.[3] The work carried out by the South African Truth and Reconciliation Commission (TRC) has had valuable reverberations also in this regard, pointing out the position of children as a direct target of discriminatory apartheid policies and stressing the consequent necessity to deal with this legacy. Even though the Human Rights Violations Committee[4] of the TRC did not directly involve children in its hearings, owing to concerns regarding their safety and the possibility of a retraumatisation of the young victims, it has triggered a major debate on the way, and extent to which, transitional justice mechanisms should take into account children's experiences in order to address their needs. Moreover, truth commissions may be able to offer children a forum in which they can actively participate in and contribute towards formulating transitional justice strategies. This opportunity, however, raises at the same time several doubts as to how to identify what transitional justice practices are best suited to participation by children. Further questions to be answered concern the potential risks of children's involvement in truth-seeking mechanisms as well as the protection measures that need to be adopted, the suitability of forms of accountability for youth previously involved in violence and the most opportune reintegration and rehabilitation measures. This represents an underexplored research field, which needs new contributions aimed at answering the abovementioned questions. Challenges regarding the linkage and involvement of children in transitional justice can also be seen as opportunities not to be missed. Involving minors in criminal trials' hearings, for instance, is a great as well as ambitious opportunity, as they, being both witnesses and victims, need special protection and proper psychological support. On the other hand, children involved in conflicts as perpetrators must be considered at the same time as victims, which requires particular attention when specific accountability

---

3 See *Impact of armed conflict on children*, A/51/306 26 August 1996; see also *Machel Study 10-Year Strategic Review Children and Conflict in a Changing World*, April 2009, co-published by the Office of the Special Representative of the Secretary-General for Children and Armed Conflict United Nations New York, USA, para. 30: 'War violates every right of a child – the right to life, the right to be with family and community, the right to health, the right to the development of the personality and the right to be nurtured and protected. Many of today's conflicts last the length of a "childhood", meaning that from birth to early adulthood, children will experience multiple and accumulative assaults. Disrupting the social networks and primary relationships that support children's physical, emotional, moral, cognitive and social development in this way, and for this duration, can have profound physical and psychological implications'.

4 The South African TRC was articulated in a threefold structure comprising the Human Rights Violations Committee, the Amnesty Committee and the Reparation Committee.

measures are conceived and subsequently adopted. The relationship between disarmament, demobilisation and reintegration (DDR) programmes for children and transitional justice strategies represents another crucial sector, the complexity of which will be to some extent addressed in respect of the Rwandan case in the following paragraphs. Finally, reparations programmes should also be shaped and implemented in a child-friendly manner in order to distinguish and highlight the specific needs to be satisfied when the victims of violence are minors. Some transitional justice experiments carried out by the Sierra Leone Truth and Reconciliation Commission and the adoption of traditional justice mechanisms, such as *Mato-Oput* in Uganda (see further), can provide a useful framework for identifying best practices, mistakes and lessons learnt for the elaboration of further child-friendly strategies for the future.

This chapter is the result of a review of the main literature on the topic as well as of three months of field research carried out in Rwanda between July and October 2009. I spent these months monitoring the hearings of *Inkiko Gacaca,*[5] the main transitional justice (and supposedly reconciliation) mechanism developed in Rwanda to address the legacy of the 1994 genocide, as well as interviewing researchers, civil society representatives, NGO staff and, most importantly, ordinary Rwandans (many of them children during the genocide) on the role played by children in both the 1994 slaughters and the reconstruction process following the mass violence.

This chapter focuses on the victimisation of children during and after the 1994 Rwandan genocide, as well as on the transitional justice approach implemented in order to deal with its legacy. Post-genocide Rwanda has been chosen as a case study for several reasons, as I will argue in more detail below. It is at the same time a key test for transitional justice in general terms as well as a challenge regarding the integration and rehabilitation of violence-affected children. Moreover, I argue that children's involvement in shaping transitional justice strategies, as well as their participation in its mechanisms, can be properly adopted as a litmus test for both the success of post-conflict reconstruction and the reconciliation process, especially in countries such as Rwanda, where more than 50 per cent of the population are aged under 15. Redressing children's wounds and traumas should in fact be a crucial objective in the reconstruction and reconciliation agenda of the Rwandan government. The thousands of minors affected by the 1994 genocide are currently the protagonists of the rebuilding process of the country. Disregarding their needs might consequently undermine

---

5 The term *Gacaca* literally means in *Kinyarwanda* 'little lawn', or 'little grass', and evokes the space where Rwandan communities used to settle disputes in precolonial times. Inspired to some extent by this tradition, a few years after the genocide the Rwandan government established *Inkiko Gacaca* (*Gacaca* tribunals), community-based jurisdictions aimed at trying those individuals charged with genocide.

the capacity of the backbone of the young Rwandan society to look constructively at the future. Consistently with these basic assumptions, the main research question of this chapter will be the following: how has the legacy of the genocide for children been dealt with in Rwanda? Did the transitional justice strategies employed take into account child-friendly best practices? Has the fragile setting provided by the genocide been the premise for new violations of children's rights or has the Rwandan government committed itself to abiding by the internationally agreed standards set out in the Convention on the Rights of the Child (CRC)? Rwandan post-genocide transitional justice policies will be assessed against international instruments establishing and granting children's rights, transitional justice best practice concerning minors as well as against the framework provided by the *Key Principles for Children and Transitional Justice: Involvement of Children and Consideration of Children's Rights in Truth, Justice and Reconciliation Processes.*[6] This document in particular acknowledges the proactive driving role which children can play when involved in post-conflict settings where specific transitional justice mechanisms are needed by highlighting that

> Children have an important role to play in transitional justice processes because they are victims and witnesses of crimes committed, and may also be recruted and used in hostilities. In addition, as family members and citizens of their communities, children are key partners in reconciliation and peace-building processes [...] Common minimum standards on children and transitional justice should be developed, drawing on good practices and lessons learned, and based on the Convention on the Rights of the Child (CRC) and other international and regional standards and treaties.[7]

2. CHILDREN AND CRIMINAL JUSTICE: A LEGAL FRAMEWORK

The Committee on the Rights of the Child, the body set up for monitoring the implementation of the CRC, has repeatedly pointed out that most of the violations suffered by children are concentrated in the field of juvenile justice. Two third of the states parties that have submitted reports to the Committee are responsible for such violations.[8] Article 6.5 ICCPR prohibits the death penalty

---

6 This document is the outcome of the Children and Transitional Justice Conference, organized in 2009 by the UNICEF Innocenti Research Centre and the Human Rights Programme at Harvard Law School, see Parmar et al., *supra* note 4, available at www.unicef-irc.org/publications/pdf/tj_publication_eng.pdf.

7 Ibid., Preamble, 404–405.

8 See on this point Innocenti Digest, *Juvenile Justice*, UNICEF, International Child Development Centre, Florence, 1999.

for individuals who committed a crime when younger than 18. Similarly, article 14.4 of ICCPR, which includes fair trial standards, states that '[i]n the case of juvenile persons, the procedure shall be such as will take account of their age and the desirability of promoting their rehabilitation'. The most relevant norms of international law protecting children in conflict with the law are entrenched in the CRC (in particular articles 37 and 40), as well as in soft law instruments such as the 1985 United Nations Standard Minimum Rules for the Administration of Juvenile Justice (the so-called Beijing Rules), the 1990 United Nations Rules for the Protection of Juveniles Deprived of their Liberty (JDLs) and the United Nations Guidelines for the Prevention of Juvenile Delinquency (the Riyadh Guidelines). Article 37 of the CRC in particular affirms that '[n] either capital punishment nor life imprisonment without possibility of release shall be imposed for offences committed by persons below eighteen years of age', as well as that '[t]he arrest, detention or imprisonment of a child (...) shall be used only as a measure of last resort and for the shortest appropriate period of time'. At the same time, article 40 establishes the principle according to which juvenile justice should be aimed at 'promoting the child's reintegration and the child's assuming a constructive role in society'. Moreover, article 40 promotes 'measures for dealing with such children (those accused of, or recognised as having infringed the penal law) without resorting to judicial proceedings'.[9] This principle is also enforced by the Beijing Rules, which introduce the notion of 'diversion' (Rule 11): '[c]onsideration shall be given, wherever appropriate, to dealing with juvenile offenders without resorting to formal trial by the competent authority'. The Riyadh Guidelines, finally, frame the lack of compliance of the conduct of minors with social and legal norms within the process of growth and maturation of the child, pointing out that usually misbehaviours are inclined to disappear.[10] Even though the CRC urges states to promote the creation of 'laws, procedures, authorities and institutions specifically applicable to children', currently there is no binding rule obliging the adherents to establish separate and specialised justice systems devoted to minors. There is a trend in international and domestic law discouraging the adoption of measures imposing on children restriction of liberty in both the pre-trial and sentencing phases. It is important, however, to stress that alternative systems can be subject to experimentation, 'providing that human rights and legal safeguards are fully respected' (Art. 40.3.b). The family group conferencing developed in South Africa has paved the way for other systems relying on pre-colonial models, which are currently in the spotlight. Needless to say, even from a perspective

---

9 This rationale is shared also by Rule 5 of the Beijing Rules, which affirms that 'the juvenile justice system shall emphasize the well-being of the juvenile', while at the same time it proclaims the principle of proportionality.

10 See in particular Rule 5.e.

acknowledging the phenomenon of legal pluralism, the need for them to abide by minimum fair trial standards must be satisfied.[11]

Despite the proliferation of international hard and soft law instruments providing a detailed body of norms regarding minors in conflict with the law, the minimum age of criminal responsibility is not universally established and it varies significantly from country to country. The CRC in fact limits itself to urging states to establish 'a minimum age below which children shall be presumed not to have the capacity to infringe the penal law'.[12] Similarly, no international standards exist for children living in detention facilities with their mothers.[13] These rules have been conceived with regard to ordinary contexts where juvenile crime, even though acknowledged as a crucial problem to be paid the highest attention, does not reach the peaks contemplated in phases of large-scale human rights violations. The latter is the context in which transitional justice policies need to be elaborated.

3. CHILDREN AND TRANSITIONAL JUSTICE: A LOOK AT BEST PRACTICE

The abovementioned *Key Principles for Children and Transitional Justice* includes 'Principles for Child Protection and Participation in Transitional Justice',[14] which, even though not binding on states, provide an interesting and updated set of guidelines. These Principles underscore in particular that:

- The best interests of the child should guide transitional justice processes.
- Children must be treated with dignity and respect.
- Transitional justice mechanisms – including when designing and implementing policies and child-friendly procedures – should ensure the protection of children against violence and promote their physical and psychological well-being.
- Protection of the identity of the child and the child's privacy must be guaranteed at all times.
- Children have the right to participate in decisions affecting their lives. The participation of children should be voluntary, with the informed consent of the child and parent or guardian. The decision not to participate can also be a form of participation.

11 Innocenti Digest, *supra* note 8, 12.

12 See article 40.3.a. of the CRC. The Beijing Rules establish that 'the beginning of that age shall not be fixed at too low an age level, bearing in mind the facts of emotional, mental and intellectual maturity' (Rule 4.1). On this point see Innocenti Digest, *supra* note 10, 4–5.

13 Ibid., 14. As a consequence of the genocide this issue also assumes crucial importance in Rwanda, where children are allowed to remain with their mothers in prison until they are three years old.

14 *Key Principles for Children and Transitional Justice, supra* note 8, 406–407.

- Policies and procedures to protect the rights of children involved in transitional justice processes should include a specific focus on adolescents and should be consistent with the evolving capacities of the child.
- A gender-sensitive approach to participation in transitional justice processes should include a focus on the protection of the rights of girls and should address their specific needs and experiences.
- Participation should be non-discriminatory and should include, as appropriate, diverse ethnic, racial, religious and other groups, and take into consideration the specific needs of children with disabilities.
- Transitional justice processes should facilitate the realization of children's civil, political, economic, social and cultural rights. A human rights-based approach to transitional justice processes should be holistic and sustainable, addressing the root causes of armed and political violence, and strengthening the protective environment for children in their families and communities.

The *Key Principles for Children and Transitional Justice* also develop 'Specific Principles and Programmatic Recommendations' concerning judicial mechanisms, truth-commissions and truth-seeking mechanisms, outreach and consultation, local, traditional and restorative justice processes, reparations for children, and institutional reform. As to the issue of accountability, proper accountability mechanisms are required for those who commit crimes against children and in particular suggest that no amnesty should be granted to those individuals responsible for gross violations of human rights against minors, especially in the case of genocide, war crimes and crimes against humanity. The *Key Principles for Children and Transitional Justice* point out an emerging consensus that 'children associated with armed forces or armed groups who may have been involved in the commision of crimes under international law shall be considered primarily as victims, not only as perpetrators'.[15] Explicitly referring to article 12 of the CRC, the Principles refer to the children's right to participate in judicial proceedings affecting them, which should adopt child-sensitive legal procedures.[16]

Very interestingly, because directly relevant to Rwandan post-genocide justice policy, the *Key Principles for Children and Transitional Justice* also mention local, traditional and restorative justice processes as transitional justice tools. This mirrors the growing attention paid by scholars and transitional justice practitioners to culture-sensitive approaches based on traditional and/or informal justice systems, as stressed in 2004 by the United Nations Secretary-General in his report entitled *The rule of law and transitional justice in conflict and post-conflict societies*.[17] After recognising that '[l]ocal, traditional and

15 Ibid., 408.
16 Ibid., 409.
17 Report of the Secretary-General, UN Doc. S/204/616.

restorative justice processes can contribute to accountability',[18] the *Key Principles for Children and Transitional Justice* call for more research effort to be focused on understanding these processes and their potential, as well as their shortcomings. They also stress the crucial role of traditional leaders, teachers and, more generally, those adults who form 'an effective safety net' for children.[19]

As to the outreach and consultations, the *Key Principles for Children and Transitional Justice* urge caution regarding the actual involvement of children in a transitional justice process, insisting that they need to be adequately informed of their rights.[20] They encourage institutional reform[21] aimed at redressing children's missed opportunities, caused by the conflict, in education, access to health care, justice and economic development. In this context reparations, the most victim-focused transitional justice instrument,[22] are given particular attention.[23]

The *Key Principles for Children and Transitional Justice* also encourage educational system reform and in particular the elaboration of a curriculum establishing a link with truth commissions '[i]n order to ensure that human rights, citizenship, life skills and the history of the conflict are included'.[24] Interestingly for the purpose of this chapter, the *Children and Transitional Justice Key Principles Document* urges judicial reform aimed at reshaping judicial systems in a gender- and child-sensitive manner.

Finally, it is worth to glance at the UN Secretary-General's famous 2004 report on *Rule of Law and Transitional Justice in Conflict and Post-conflict Societies*. By paying attention to traditional and informal justice systems as transitional justice mechanisms, the Secretary-General's report has officially opened the floor to debate on the adoption of such tools in conflict and post-conflict settings. According to some scholars, traditional and informal justice systems embody the potential to play a culture-sensitive role in fragile contexts where formal justice systems, often inherited from a recent colonial past,[25] are perceived as

---

18 *Key Principles for Children and Transitional Justice*, *supra* note 6, 412.

19 Ibid., 414.

20 Ibid., 411–412.

21 Ibid., 415–417.

22 See P. de Greiff, *The handbook of reparations*, Oxford University Press, Oxford, 2006.

23 *Key Principles for Children and Transitional Justice*, *supra* note 6, 414–415.

24 Ibid., 417.

25 Mahmood Mamdani very sharply underscores the ambiguous role that Western law and the rule of law principle had during and after the colonisation era. See on this point *When Victims Become Killers: Colonialism, Nativism, and the Genocide in Rwanda*, Princeton University Press, Princeton, 2002, 24: 'From the outset, modern Western colonialism presented itself as a civilizing project. In Kipling's well-known phrase, colonialism was "the white man's burden". (...) The architecture of the modern state was inscribed in modern law, Western law. And rule of law was in turn central to the construction of civilized society.

foreign and are largely distrusted. *Bashingantahe*[26] in Burundi, *Mato-Oput*[27] in Uganda, *Gacaca*[28] in Rwanda, to consider only the African continent, are increasingly in researchers' and transitional justice practitioners' spotlights. It remains, however, to address a fundamental issue concerning their compatibility with international human rights standards and a strategy through which they could be revisited in order to abide by the international legal framework. More research is needed on traditional and informal justice systems' suitability as a child-friendly transitional justice mechanism. This chapter aims at contributing in this direction through an assessment of Rwanda's *gacaca* courts.

4. CHILDREN AND GENOCIDE

Genocidal policies have not spared the lives of innocent children, victimised on a large scale during the Armenian and Khmer Rouge genocides as well as in European concentration camps during the Second World War.

According to article 2 of the 1948 Genocide Convention the *actus reus*, or material element of the crime, consists of certain acts that are carefully listed, which, to be punishable, need to be committed with the moral element of the crime of genocide, the so-called *mens rea*, the 'intent to destroy, in whole or in part, a national, ethnical, racial, or religious group'. The list includes two criminal conducts regarding children in particular: '[i]mposing measures intended to prevent birth within the group' (paragraph d) and '[f]orcibly transferring children of the group to another group' (paragraph e). Even though the Convention does not clarify what is meant by children,[29] paragraphs (d) and (e) of article II are particularly important in relation to the genocidal practices committed against them. As to the former, Adolph Eichmann, for instance, was tried in Israel because he was charged with 'devising measures intended to

Wherever in the non-Western world the white man carved out colonies, the civilization project was marked by a turn-key import: Western law. At its outset, the Western colonial project was no less than to wipe clean the civilization slate so as to introduce Western norms through Western law; modernization would have to be Westernization.'

26 L. Huyse and M. Salter (eds.), *Traditional Justice and Reconciliation after Violent Conflict. Learning from African Experiences*, International Institute for Democracy and Electoral Assistance, Stockholm, 2008.

27 Ibid.

28 In my opinion the current Rwandan *Inkiko Gacaca* are, due to their highly formalised structure, neither traditional nor informal jurisdictions, even though they are rooted in precolonial Rwandan customary law.

29 Most of the countries refer to article 1 CRC, defining a child as anyone under eighteen years of age.

prevent child bearing among the Jews'.[30] Moreover, in *Akayesu*,[31] the Trial Chamber of the International Criminal Tribunal for Rwanda (ICTR) affirmed that rape might be subsumed within paragraph (d) of article II of the Convention.

Paragraph (e), article II of the Genocide Convention, was added 'almost as an afterthought, with little substantive debate or consideration'.[32] This was due to the fact that during the Convention's drafting some states' delegates tried to challenge the idea that genocide might be committed by the transfer of children and asked for historical examples of genocide perpetrated through the forcible transfer of children. In particular, Platon Morozov, Russian representative, held that 'no one had been able to quote any historical case of the destruction of a group through the transfer of children'.[33] In 1997 in fact the Australian Human Rights and Equal Opportunities Commission documented and condemned the practice of forcible transfer of aboriginal children perpetrated by Australian governments as it violated article II (e) of the Genocide Convention.'[34] Moreover, as authoritatively established by the ICTR in *Akayesu* (and despite the fact that the Genocide Convention always requires a result when dealing with the material element of the crime of genocide, i.e. in the case of paragraph (e) the actual transfer of the children), threats of transfer are punishable under the Convention.[35] This was confirmed by the Preparatory Commission for the International Criminal Court when drafting the Elements of Crimes, whose coordinators' discussion paper stated that the term 'forcible' is 'not restricted to direct acts of physical force and may include, but is not necessarily restricted to, threats or intimidations'.[36]

---

30 *A-G Israel v. Eichmann*, note 59, para. 199.

31 *Prosecutor v. Akayesu*, Case No. ICTR-96-4-T, Judgment, 2 September 1998, paragraph 507.

32 W.A. Schabas, *Genocide in International Law*, Cambridge University Press, Cambridge, 2000, 175: 'The provision is enigmatic, because the drafters clearly rejected the concept of cultural genocide. The International Law Commission treated paragraph (e) as "biological genocide". But the idea for such a provision originated in the Secretariat draft, which quite logically proposed that "forcible transfer of children to another human group" be considered as an act of cultural genocide.'

33 UN Doc. E/AC.6/SR.82.

34 Australian Human Rights and Equal Opportunities Commission, *Bringing Them Home, Report of the National Inquiry into the Separation of Aboriginal and Torres Strait Islander Children from Their Families*, 270–275.

35 *Prosecutor v. Akayesu*, Case No. ICTR-96-4-T, Judgment, 2 September 1998, paragraph 505: 'As in the case of measures intended to prevent births, the objective is not only to sanction a direct act of forcible physical transfer, but also to sanction acts of threats or trauma which would lead to the forcible transfer of children from one group to another.'

36 UN Doc. PCNICC/1999/WGEC/RT.3.

4.1. THE RWANDAN GENOCIDE: CHALLENGES FOR TRANSITIONAL JUSTICE

The term genocide appeared for the first time in a UN Security Council document in Resolution 925, adopted on 8 June 1994 with respect to the Rwandan crisis.[37] Exploring the historical roots and the sequence of events of the Rwandan genocide[38] is beyond the scope of this chapter, which limits itself to underscoring some features of the 1994 cycle of violence, as well as its linkage with and challenges for transitional justice strategies. This research focuses on transitional justice and children in the wake of the Rwandan genocide for several reasons. First, Rwanda is a key test for transitional justice mechanisms because of the unprecedented peaks of violence and brutality reached in 1994, which was marked by a high degree of popular involvement. Secondly, given the geographical and economic constraints that oblige victims and perpetrators to live side by side, Rwanda must necessarily address the legacy of the past by tackling pressing issues such as developing reintegration and rehabilitation strategies for all the stakeholders involved in the genocide, and particularly for children. Thirdly, despite its lack of resources and low rank in the human development index, Rwanda is the first country in the history of human kind uncompromisingly willing to prosecute all its citizens involved in the genocide by respecting the principle of 'duty to prosecute'. To this aim, three different judicial bodies have been established: the UN ICTR was set up in November 1994, the Rwandan national courts were given jurisdiction to prosecute genocide perpetrators in 1996, and *gacaca* courts, legislation on which was adopted from 2000 onwards. With the institution of the *gacaca* courts, three different jurisdictional layers were set up to deal with the legacy of the genocide, launching an unprecedented experiment that transformed Rwanda in a sort of 'juridical laboratory'.[39] Finally, Rwanda's experiment in adopting a local justice approach within a transitional justice framework turned out to be the most ambitious ever, with nearly 1.5 million individuals tried by *gacaca*, which have been considered as a possible model for future transitional justice efforts.

---

37 Schabas, *supra* note 32, 155.

38 Some of the most authoritative scholars include A. Des Forges, *Leave None to Tell the Story*, Human Rights Watch, New York, 1999; Mamdani, *supra* note 27; P. Uvin, *Aiding Violence: The Development Enterprise in Rwanda*, Kumarian, West Hartford, 1998; E. Stover and H.M. Weinstein (eds.), *My Neighbor, My Enemy*, Cambridge University Press, Cambridge, 2004.

39 L. Waldorf, 'Mass Justice for Mass Atrocities: Rethinking Transitional Justice as Local Justice', (2006) 79 1 *Temple Law Review*, 1–87.

4.2. CHILDREN AS A TARGET OF THE RWANDAN GENOCIDE

The Rwandan genocide of 1994 violated children's rights on a tremendous scale. According to governmental data, the massacres claimed the lives of 1,074,017 Rwandans, 50.1 per cent of them less than 18 years old.[40] Children were a direct target of the genocidal violence and were often forced to experience, commit and witness every kind of abuse. They were not only tortured, raped and killed, but also forced to commit the most heinous crimes, being victimised twice, as a direct target of the violence and as forced perpetrators. Beside children who were direct victims of the violence, today Rwanda has to heal traumatised children survivors and to assist 400,000 orphans, 10 per cent of Rwandan children, and the children of those adults jailed because they played the role of perpetrators during the genocide. Additional care is moreover required for street children, who are often the target of exploitation by adults. It also has to find proper accountability measures for children involved in the violence. All this represents a daunting challenge for what is an economically very undeveloped country.

The hundreds of thousands of children suddenly orphaned and forced to earn a living on their own are one of the most bitter legacies of the genocide, which suddenly eliminated the traditional structures charged with child protection based on the extended family and public care. According to international observers, at least 400,000 Rwandan children experienced the loss of parental or any other form of care at a certain point of their lives.[41] Some 300,000 children live in child-headed households, surviving on five dollars a month.[42] This generation of children, representing a vulnerable group, has been targeted by every form of violence and exploitation. The phenomenon has also involved unaccompanied mothers, i.e. girls who gave birth, sometimes as a consequence of rape, during displacement in refugee camps, whose number peaked in 1996.[43] Consistent with articles 20 and 22 of the CRC, Rwanda's government promoted a policy labelled 'one child one family', aimed at tracing original families for

---

40 Republic of Rwanda, Ministry of Local Government, Information and Social Affairs, *National Policy for Orphans and Other Vulnerable Children*, Kigali, 2003, 1.

41 UN Agencies in Rwanda, *Common Country Assessment 1999–2000*, Paper 11, *Child Protection*, 6; Women's Commission for Refugee Women and Children, *Rwanda's Women and Children: The long road to Reconciliation*, New York, 1997; Republic of Rwanda, Ministry of Local Government, Information and Social Affairs, *National Policy for Orphans and Other Vulnerable Children*, Kigali, 2003, 8.

42 UN Agencies in Rwanda, *supra* note 41, 6. See also World Vision, UNICEF, *Qualitative Needs Assessment of Child-Headed Households in Rwanda*, Kigali, 1998, which calls for more research in order to confirm the figures given.

43 UN Integrated Regional Information Networks (IRIN), *Great Lakes: Special Feature-Unaccompanied Children*, July 1997, para. 3. See also *Rwanda. The Preventible Genocide, The Report of the International Panel of Eminent Personalities to Investigate the 1994 Genocide in Rwanda and the Surrounding Events*, 1999, 141–156.

reunification and where that was not possible, providing foster families.[44] Many children were, however, placed in orphanages, the condition of which was not always acceptable,[45] according to aid workers. Other children were informally adopted by relatives or strangers, which made it very difficult to trace them. Some of those children who found shelter abroad were adopted by European families, sometimes triggering a dispute with Rwanda's government when it asked them to return back. Around 30,000 minors have found foster families in eastern Congo, where living conditions are particularly challenging. Altogether, by 1999 relief agencies had placed more than 62,000 children in families out of the 122,000 who were unaccompanied.[46] But paradoxically the genocide is still able to orphan children decades after its end, as Rwanda's youth currently loses those parents who were intentionally infected with HIV as a killing strategy during the 1994 massacres. Children are also deprived of needed parental care every time an adult is involved in a genocide trial as an accused, which happens very often due to the inflexible policy of full accountability pursued by the government,[47] especially through *gacaca* courts. Nothing better than this actual threat of unexpected lost of parental care epitomises the current presence of the genocide in Rwandan children's daily lives.

4.3. ARBITRARY ARREST AND DETENTION OF CHILDREN AS GENOCIDE PERPETRATORS

Because of their age and immaturity, children were susceptible to genocide propaganda, acting not only as killers but also committing the whole range of crimes connected with the genocide. They often followed the examples of their parents and relatives, while at other times they acted to save themselves or their loved ones. These children have to be seen as victims of the genocide too; they need trauma healing and deserve proper reintegration and rehabilitation measures.

No fewer than 5,000 children, many of whom display marks of severe trauma,[48] have been arrested because of suspected involvement in the genocide in Rwanda. Sometimes children worked as informers for both killers and victims.[49] The

44 *Regulations for Orphans and Separated Children's Centres*, Government of Rwanda, Kigali, 1994; Republic of Rwanda, Ministry of Local Government, Information and Social Affairs, *supra* note 41, 14.

45 See Human Rights Watch, *Lasting Wounds: Consequences of Genocide and War for Rwanda's Children*, April 2003, 29.

46 Ibid., 29.

47 Republic of Rwanda, Ministry of Local Government, Information and Social Affairs, *supra* note 41, 22.

48 See Human Rights Watch, *supra* note 45, 10.

49 Ibid., 10.

Rwandan government has recognised this situation and has promised to regularise it. Detainees without regular arrest warrants and case files have sometimes spent more than five or six years in prison and lockups before being processed. Often violence has been exerted in order to compel prisoners to confess their alleged crimes. This practice targeted male and female adults indiscriminately, as well as children and other vulnerable groups.[50] Large-scale arrests of adults and children followed the repatriation from Zaire after the closure of the refugee camps in 1996. Arbitrary arrests of children continued in some areas of the country years after the genocide and the ensuing emergency phase was ended.[51]

The youngest genocide suspect arrested in Rwanda was seven years old during the genocide. Children under 14, the youngest age of criminal responsibility in Rwanda, cannot be put into pretrial detention, as they are supposed to join rehabilitation programmes in order to be reintegrated into society. Hundreds of them were transferred after arrest to the Gitagata education centre, the conditions of which were described by UNICEF staff in 2000 as 'abominable'.[52] Some were sent to solidarity camps before being reintegrated into their families. When in December 2000 500 minors were released, not much attention was paid to the fact that 400 children under 14 at the time of genocide were still being detained.[53]

4.4. CHILD SOLDIERS

Children recruited into militia groups, the most sadly famous of which were the *Impuzamugambi* ('those with a single purpose'), affiliated with the *Coalition pour la Défense de la Républic,* and the *Interahamwe* ('those who work together'), which represented the youth wing of Habyarimana's political party, the *Mouvement républicain national pour la démocratie et le développement*, actively participated in the genocide.

Children known as *kadogo* (in Swahili: little one) were also employed by the Rwandan Patriotic Front (RPF) to overthrow Habyarimana's dictatorship and to stop the genocidal regime, taking a direct part in the fighting. Many children were demobilised from the RPF without benefiting from any integration programme, which means that they were not able to receive primary education. This happened because, according to Kees Kingma, 'the child soldiers did not

50 Ibid. This practice has been widely reported by international organisations and NGOs.
51 Ibid.
52 Ibid., 20.
53 Avocats Sans Frontières, *Justice Pour Tous au Rwanda*, 19.

pass through a demobilization camp, and were in fact not formally demobilized'.[54] Rwanda's demobilisation and reintegration efforts recognised two other groups of combatant children, those who fought in the ranks of the Army for the Liberation of Rwanda (ALIR), led by officials faithful to the genocidal government in the Democratic Republic of the Congo, and those from other rebel groups in DRC.

The Rwandan government set up a Demobilisation and Reintegration Commission (RDRC), which has demobilised around 54,000 combatants since 1995; it includes a child protection unit. In 2004 the RDRC initiated a project for child soldiers and adopted the Cape Town Principles.[55] It implemented two DDR phases lasting respectively from 1997 to 2001 and from 2002 to 2007, during which it demobilised 563 child soldiers from various armed groups active in DRC. Only two of them were girls; as argued by the Head of the RDRC's child protection unit, Alex Rusagara, girls have proven to be keen on self-demobilisation since '[a]ccording to the Rwandan culture, girls are not very willing to come forward (for demobilization) because the general thinking is that they have been raped or (had sexual relations)'.[56] Before demobilising, child ex-combatants are supposed to attend a three-month rehabilitation programme. Save the Children, however, reported that children used to spend a much longer time in rehabilitation centres because the sensitisation campaign targeting the families and children's communities often failed to meet its objectives. When they demobilise, ex child soldiers receive health care for one year and a basic kit including blankets, mosquito nets, shoes and school uniforms, but no money.[57] The evaluation undertaken by UNICEF of the reintegration policy implemented in Rwanda was generally positive.[58] Finally, it is worth emphasising that cases of forced recruitment of minors into the Local Defence Force were occasionally reported in the aftermath of the genocide and later.[59]

5. CHILDREN AND POST-GENOCIDE JUSTICE

In Rwanda the age of criminal responsibility is fixed at 14 years, below which individuals cannot be held accountable. The government's list of the main perpetrators to be brought to justice includes about 2,000 names; only 1 per cent

---

54 K. Kingma, *The Rwanda Demobilization and Reintegration Program: Evaluation Report Prepared for the United Nations Development Program*, Kigali, 2001, 11.

55 The Cape Town Principles were adopted in 1997. More details can be found in Nylund's chapter in this book.

56 Waldorf, *supra* note 39, 13.

57 Ibid.

58 Ibid.

59 Human Rights Watch, *supra* note 45, 12–13.

of these individuals were minors during the genocide. The ICTR, despite the lack of a provision granting immunity to minors in its statute, decided not to try minors responsible for the Rwandan genocide, while the ICC, by virtue of article 26 of the Rome Statute, is not allowed to try minors. Rwanda is the first country to prosecute children for genocide. This is a quite questionable choice, as it is very difficult to demonstrate that a child had the *mens rea*, i.e. the 'intent to destroy, in whole or in part, a national, ethnical, racial, or religious group', necessary in order to commit genocide.

A study by Save the Children USA in 1995 found that according to most Rwandans, the death penalty was the right punishment for children involved in the genocide.[60] Most of the minors[61] arrested for genocide-related crimes have experienced the shortcomings of the Rwandan justice system: arbitrary arrests, appalling detention conditions and unfair and delayed trials. Some of them have been tried for alleged genocide crimes even though they were younger than 14 when the genocide was perpetrated: this is partially due to the fact that birth records have sometimes been destroyed. Moreover, they have not been separated from adults in prisons and lockups and have been imprisoned for years without a regular case file. According to UNICEF in 2002, 4,000 minors arrested in the aftermath of the genocide were then still awaiting trial.[62]

5.1. ORDINARY COURTS

Pursuant to Rwanda's 1996 Organic Law 8/1996,[63] individuals accused of genocide were categorised in four groups with decreasing criminal responsibility: 1) masterminds, planners and perpetrators of sexual torture; 2) killers and their accomplices; 3) those responsible for serious attacks without causing death; 4) property offenders. This categorisation is crucial to understanding post-genocide justice in Rwanda, as it has also been adopted, currently with some modifications, by *gacaca* legislation. Those included in the first category, until 2007 when it was abolished, risked the death penalty if adults at the time of the crime, while if minors they were susceptible to a sentence of up to 20 years.

The 1996 law introduced benches comprising magistrates for minors (art. 19 Organic Law 8/1996), which were, however, abolished by the subsequent *gacaca*

60 Ibid.

61 I use the term minor to indicate those children who were under the age of 18 when they were involved in genocide even if older than 18 at the time of the trial.

62 Human Rights Watch, *supra* note 45.

63 Organic Law 8/96 on the organisation of prosecution for offences constituting the crime of genocide or crimes against humanity committed since 1 October 1990.

legislation, as well as a guilty-plea procedure[64] unknown in Rwanda's legal system. The aim of this provision was to encourage spontaneous confessions by perpetrators, in order to overcome one of the main potential prosecutorial obstacles, a lack of evidence in many genocide-related cases. Confessing perpetrators must give details of the offences committed, including the names of victims and accomplices, and offer an apology; in exchange for this they receive a considerable reduction of sentence. Those whose names are published in the government's list of the most serious perpetrators and classed as category one offenders, however, lose the possibility of benefitting from the plea-bargaining procedure. The 1996 genocide law does not embody a specific focus on children, nor does it provide special child-friendly procedures. Minors between 14 and 18 years are entitled to a punishment reduction, while those younger than 14 are held not to be criminally responsible and to deserve rehabilitation. Neither the death penalty nor life imprisonment is provided for minors, the harshest punishment being a twenty-year sentence. Normally they receive half of the sentence envisaged for adults and the Penal Code provides for mitigating circumstances to be considered by the judges.[65] Minors prosecuted are supposed to be tried separately from adults, but several cases of group trials of those pleading guilty have been reported.[66] Article 36 of Organic Law 8/96 grants those accused the right to a defence counsel of their choice, but not at the expense of the state, not even for minors. This provision amounts to a violation of both article 14 (3) (d) of the ICCPR, which envisages free legal aid when the interest of justice so requires, and article 40 of the CRC, which grants children the right to legal assistance in the preparation of their defence.

According to the NGO Avocats Sans Frontières,[67] minors at the time of the genocide in Rwanda were tried at a pace three times slower than adults. The government, in other words, has not made trials of minors supposedly involved in the genocide a priority: while representing around 3.5 per cent of the prison population, in 2000 minors made up only 1.2 per cent of individuals brought to trial.[68] Children's rights guaranteed by the Universal Declaration, the ICCPR and the CRC have also reportedly been disregarded, particularly as to the due process guarantees embodied in article 37 of the latter. In Rwandan judicial practice defendants, adult as well as minor, are allowed access to a defence lawyer only after a trial has been commenced. As abuse of pre-trial detention was widely

---

64 The right to participate in the procedure, which cannot be denied, may be exercised at any time before the criminal file is brought to the attention of the President of the competent tribunal. This right can only be exercised once and the confession can be withdrawn.

65 See articles 73, 77, 82 and 83 of Rwanda's Penal Code.

66 Human Rights Watch, *supra* note 45, 15.

67 Avocats Sans Frontières, *supra* note 53, 19. Among NGOs, Avocats Sans Frontières in particular has provided legal representation and training in juvenile justice, significantly contributing to setting up the first Rwandan Bar in 1997.

68 Ibid., 19.

and indiscriminately practised and documented in the aftermath of the genocide, it translated into a *de facto* deprivation of access to a legal counsel and into a consequent violation of pre-trial rights. Minors were also jailed and prosecuted together with adults.

Through a joint project the Ministry of Justice and UNICEF have tried to confront the problems surrounding juvenile justice by providing legal assistance to minors accused of genocide. The project was, however, caught between financial and organisational constraints, unfolded in an environment sometimes hostile to all individuals accused of genocide[69] and has not reached the totality of needy children.[70] The needs of children in conflict with the law were in theory prioritised in the 2003 national policy for orphans and other vulnerable children. The latter envisaged the establishment of pilot models for alternatives to imprisonment, a special police unit for the protection of children and the prevention of infractions, and a chamber for minors in courts to ensure judicial and social support for children charged with criminal offences.[71] The abovementioned plan has unfortunately not yet been implemented.

5.2. *GACACA* COURTS

Stuck with the backlog faced by the ordinary courts and with a prison population burning 2 per cent of the gross national product, Rwanda decided to embark on the most ambitious transitional justice experiment ever, by setting up thousands of community-based *gacaca*[72] courts distributed in every administrative unit of the country. The *gacaca* tribunals have manifold stated objectives: to speed up genocide-related trials, to reconstruct the truth concerning the genocide while providing Rwandans with a sharable historical record and to strengthen the process of national reconciliation. In the *gacaca* legislation the only reference to children concerns those who were minors at the time of the offence committed as they are entitled to a penalty reduction. As participation in the hearings is limited to Rwandans aged at least 18, children are not allowed to take part in the *gacaca* trials either as witnesses or as victims, but only as perpetrators if older than 14. Such a policy, consistent with the post-genocide justice approach practised in

69 Ibid., 16.

70 Ibid.

71 Republic of Rwanda, Ministry of Local Government, Information and Social Affairs, *supra* note 41, 17.

72 Article 143 of the Rwandan constitution introduced the *gacaca* as 'specialised' courts, clearly stressing that 'no special courts shall be created'. Article 152 explains their jurisdiction, which is the same as the national court on genocide and crimes against humanity except for those crimes falling within the jurisdiction of other tribunals. Key features of *Inkiko gacaca* are the capillary distribution along Rwanda's administrative structure, popularly elected lay judges, the mandatory participation of all citizens aged at least 18, the absence of a defence lawyer and the extreme flexibility of the procedures adopted.

Rwanda, which was based from the outset on retribution, is, however, questionable in light of best practice involving children in transitional justice.

The election of magistrates started in October 2001, when 250,000 lay judges were elected by the Rwandan people to cover about 11,000 courts. They went through very brief training sessions of around 36 hours per judge.[73] The qualifications required to become *inynamungayo* are simple: Rwandan nationality, at least 21 years of age, absence of criminal charges and being acknowledged by the community as a wise and tolerant person. These requirements represent the only guarantee of a fair trial for the defendants, since the system does not allow the accused to have a defence lawyer and lacks clear evidential mechanisms.[74] In every Rwandan basic administrative unit, the cell, a *gacaca* tribunal is set up and mandated to collect evidence for charging or discharging the defendants. Along with the judges' bench, the local community of the cell or sector, consisting in the totality of the adult population that acts as the *gacaca* assembly, plays a crucial role. The local community acts as both public prosecutor and defence lawyer, providing the population with a unique forum for discussing the events surrounding the genocide. The capillary territorial distribution of *gacaca* tribunals and the large-scale involvement of the population mark an attempt to redistribute responsibility for dealing with the Rwandan past. While the criminal process limits the participation of common people – and is diminished in its familiarity and common understanding due to its high level of formalisation – the *gacaca* procedure tries to attract the highest possible number of Rwandans.[75] The *gacaca* pilot phase was launched in June 2002, covering about ten per cent of the country. In order to address the problems encountered during the pilot phase, the government amended the law in June 2004.[76] The cells are responsible for collecting information on the

73 D. Hayle, *Rwanda's Experiment in People's Courts (gacaca) and the Tragedy of Unexamined Humanitarianism: A Normative/Ethical Perspective*, University of Antwerp, Institute of Development Policy and Management, 2008, 18–31.

74 Ibid.

75 Pursuant to Organic Law 40/2000, the first organic law establishing *gacaca*, the courts were organised according to a pyramidal hierarchy, consisting of cells (9,500), followed by sectors (1,550), districts (106) and provinces (12). The ultimate control of legitimacy was exercised by a special chamber of Rwanda's Supreme Court. Once a sentence was issued it could be appealed before the *gacaca* court in the next higher position within the pyramid. The cell is the basic unit of Rwandan administration and is very close to the population, which constitutes the cell assembly that is called to elect the members of the judging *Siége*. This initially comprised 19 members, but was then progressively reduced to the current seven. Some members of this *Siége* comprised the general assembly of the superior *gacaca*, the sector *gacaca*. The mechanism kept working in this fashion until it found exhaustion in the provincial *gacaca*, currently abolished, which had appeal jurisdiction over the lower *gacaca*.

76 Organic Law 16/2004 of 19 June 2004, Establishing the Organisation, Competence and Functioning of Gacaca Courts Charged With Prosecuting and Trying the Perpetrators of the Crime of Genocide and Other Crimes against Humanity Committed between October 1, 1990 and December 31, 1994.

genocide and the population is invited to take part in this process. The *Siége* collects the information and records it on a *Cahier d'Activité*. Another important task at cell level is the classification of those accused in the abovementioned categories of perpetrator.

Gacaca legislation allows for plea bargaining and penalty reduction, with sentences served partially in carrying out community services, the *Travaux d'Intérêt Général* (TIG), which are aimed at the reintegration of convicted individuals. A crucial role in this procedure is assigned to the confession before the local assembly, which functions at the same time to speed up the trials and as a reconciliation device. It must be read publicly, embody a formal apology to the victims and their families, and be approved by the assembly. Once it is approved, the confessor receives a reduced punishment.

Gacaca relied initially on the categorisation of perpetrators into different groups according to the gravity of the crimes committed, as established by Organic Law 8/1996. The categorisation criteria have been subject to several amendments and currently accused individuals are divided into three groups. According to the law currently in force the cells have jurisdiction over property-related crimes falling within category three, while the sectors deal with second and first category crimes. In fact the 2004 law merged categories two and three into a single category two. It also reduced the number of courts and judges. Pursuant to the current legislation the harshest sentence that *gacaca* can issue is life imprisonment in solitary confinement, a punishment often considered to be a form of torture.[77] Further legislative amendments have also allowed *gacaca* courts to try perpetrators allegedly falling within category one (originally subject only to ordinary courts), responsible for the most heinous crimes such as genocide planning and rape. Consequently, *gacaca* have jurisdiction over sexual crimes committed against women and girls, a very sensitive issue to be tackled only with due care and competence. In order to grant victims the expected privacy, an 'in camera' procedure has been established in which women[78] testify in closed session without an audience before a *gacaca* judge they trust or before a police officer. This formula has been criticised by women's associations, as it violates the privacy of the victims: especially in rural areas, where people know

---

[77] In December 2008 Rwanda prohibited life imprisonment in solitary confinement for detainees transferred from the ICTR. The penalty is, however, in force for individuals tried and convicted in Rwanda of genocide. The penalty's rationale is questioned by human rights activists, who consider it a form of torture. Human Rights Watch, *Rwanda: End Lifetime Solitary Confinement*, 29 January 2009, available at www.unhcr.org/refworld/docid/498703b81a.html.

[78] Women and girls were not the only victims of sexual abuses during the genocide and my over-simplification is due to the fact that they represent the overwhelming majority of the victims of such crimes.

each other, it is very easy to identify women who benefit from this procedure and consequently those who have been raped.

Inkiko Gacaca have deeply divided scholars and human rights supporters, often being depicted as the cradle of the best and of the worst for post-genocide Rwanda. Numerous aspects of the *gacaca* system have been criticised,[79] and it is often regarded by scholars as a mechanism for the government to gain legitimacy and as a way of freezing the truth regarding the genocide that will never help Rwandans to achieve national reconciliation, which might be better pursued through political efforts and rather than retributive justice.[80]

From the perspective of children's rights, *gacaca* courts do not respect fair trial standards. On paper, they provide Rwandans with an unprecedented discussion forum in which all victims, perpetrators, bystanders, adults and children during the genocide can express their feelings and opinions and contribute to truth, justice and reconciliation. No country in transition from genocide has dared so much in terms of a grass-roots approach to its violent past. The opportunity for those victimised when they were children to participate in asking questions and testifying in *gacaca* hearings is an important instrument for recovering the truth about what occurred in 1994. This is crucially important, for instance, to all those victims who want to know the fate and whereabouts of their relatives. To see the punishment of perpetrators can also contribute to reinforcing social trust and may help victims in overcoming their trauma. This ideal frame needs, however, to be set in its own context, Rwanda's daily life and judicial practice. Much of the success of the *gacaca* process depends on the communities where it is implemented, with the risk of potentially different outcomes.[81] Relevant aspects of *gacaca* legislation with respect to children concern, for instance, the lack of child-friendly procedures, the disregard for reparations programmes as well as limits in addressing sexual violence. As to the first point, it is clear that minors at the time of the crime are treated by *gacaca* law by the same yardstick as adults, except for the penalties. In other words, the best interests of the child were not considered a parameter when the *gacaca* law was drafted. It is worth emphasising that within the jurisdiction of *gacaca* courts fall – and are consequently punished – crimes that do not normally constitute genocide, for instance property crimes. *Gacaca* judges are not asked to prove the criminal intent to commit genocide 'beyond any reasonable doubt' and this translates into the possibility that children may be convicted of ordinary crimes as *génocidaires*.

79 Waldorf, *supra* note 39, 17–18.

80 Ibid.

81 See P. Clark, 'The Rules (and politics) of Engagement: The Gacaca Courts and Post-Genocide Justice, Healing and Reconciliation in Rwanda', in P. Clark and Z.D. Kaufman (eds.), *After Genocide. Transitional Justice, Post-conflict Reconstruction and Reconciliation in Rwanda and Beyond,* Columbia University Press, New York, 2009.

Cases of minors tried as adults have also been reported, as well as cases of children tried despite being below the minimum age for criminal responsibility. Moreover, trauma-healing experts affirm that the procedure before *gacaca*, where outbursts of sorrow and rage are understandably admissible, can be highly risky for traumatised victims. Hence *gacaca per se* do not embody any particular healing potential for children.[82] During interviews with members of an association of orphaned children, it also emerged that their testimonies were often underestimated during *gacaca,* as adults did not rely on their credibility.[83] One of the members of the Dukundane Family, an association of orphans of the genocide, stated:

> In my understanding, *Gacaca* jurisdiction is a system set by the government to speed up cases of those criminals but it provides also justice that heals. That is true but there are some issues that I do not agree with *Gacaca* system: how come they compel a person to confess and plead guilty so that his/her punishment could be reduced? There are also other issues of *Gacaca* that give me headache, when a killer narrates all the evil things he committed, for example, he/she hacked a person, another confesses that after raping a woman he killed her by introducing a big sharpened stick (locally known as "*igisongo*") into her sex, and another admits to have killed a person by an old hoe (locally known as "*agafuni*"), and they say all of this in front of the relatives and friends of the diseased victims by smiling as if they are happy. There are other people who do not consider confession seriously and others when they are accused, they prefer to confess crimes committed by their family members.[84]

This passage also clarifies in part the attitude and the disappointment of child survivors towards transitional justice policies in Rwanda, as they are put in the general category of survivors (*rescapés*) and their specific needs as children are not addressed. They also criticise *gacaca* because of the possibility of a reduced penalty for the perpetrators.[85] The TIG have disappointed survivors' associations, as the work carried out by the *genocidaires* is not aimed at benefiting victims in particular, but all Rwandans.[86] Threats against survivors' children as a consequence of the *gacaca* process have also been reported.[87] What represents the most serious shortcoming of the *gacaca* and transitional justice project in Rwanda is, however, the lack of a reparation programme. Children, as

---

82 Interview with Professor Simon Gasibirege, Kigali, 26 September 2009, on file with author.

83 Interview with the Dukundane Family, 29 October 2009, on file with author.

84 See on this point C. Mutegarugori and Dukundane Family, *Ishavu ry'Abato. Ubuhamya kuri Jenocide yakorewe abatutsi mu Rwanda*, Kigali, 2009, 147 (translation by Clémentine Uwamuguha).

85 Ibid.

86 Ibid.

87 Immigration and Refugee Board of Canada, *Rwanda: Whether children of witnesses who appear before the gacaca courts are subject to threats or mistreatment from defendants who come into contact with witnesses in order to pressure these witnesses*, 21 November 2006, RWA101908.FE, available at www.unhcr.org/refworld/docid/47d6547523.html.

a vulnerable group, are among the first victims of such a choice. More than a decade after the 1996 law envisaging the Compensation Fund for Victims of the Genocide and Crimes against Humanity, the Fund has yet to be established. The Fund was meant to compensate genocide victims in the frequent instances when convicted perpetrators were insolvent. A further 2002 project, defining victims very broadly without requiring any actual injury, has also failed to address the issue of reparations. Disappointment was triggered by the government's decision to provide reparations for demobilised soldiers, who were seen by victims as perpetrators, leaving victims on their own.[88] *Gacaca* are able to provide some actual or symbolic reparations, such as property restitution or apology statements by the perpetrators, but a fund for victims with a special focus on children is acutely needed. Finally, *gacaca* do not embody a gender perspective for addressing the issue of woman and girl victims of rape.

6. CONCLUSION

The reverberations of the Rwandan genocide are still acutely felt in Rwandans' daily lives as well as in the Great Lakes region, the stabilisation of which represents a key issue in the peace process of the African continent. The genocide was also the premise for the installation of a cycle of long-term systematic violence against children, which needs to be urgently addressed if it is not to compromise the transitional justice agenda of Rwanda.

The post-genocide government has promoted specific domestic policies, laws and targeted action plans in order to comply with international and regional standards protecting the rights of children, but the latter are not always coherently implemented. When evaluating Rwanda's transitional justice efforts it must be borne in mind that the legacy of the genocide for the juvenile justice system in particular would represent a daunting challenge for any judicial model on earth. Rwanda's transitional justice and reconciliation strategies have not adopted a specific focus on children, despite the large-scale victimisation they suffered during and in the aftermath of the genocide.

The transitional justice strategies Rwanda has set in motion are undoubtedly marked by a retributive logic, aimed at uncompromisingly pursuing a policy of full criminal accountability for all those involved in genocide-related crimes, no matter whether adults or children. On the one hand, this has meant a lack of attention to the needs of child victims of the genocide, who have been deprived of both the expected reparation programmes as well as suitable healing plans. On the other, children accused of genocide-related crimes have not benefited

---

88 Waldorf, *supra* note 39, 17–18.

from any of the child-sensitive opportunities provided by international hard and soft law instruments. The 'leading principles of a comprehensive policy for juvenile justice' have been disregarded when implementing transitional justice strategies in Rwanda.[89] The principle of the best interests of the child, for instance, means that 'the traditional objectives of criminal justice, such as repression/retribution, must give way to rehabilitation and restorative justice objectives in dealing with child offenders',[90] which is contradicted by the strict policy of prosecution of genocide-related crimes in Rwanda. Similarly, children in conflict with the law have been discriminated against with respect to adults, while their right to be heard has not been taken into account. Nor has the voice of children been paid due attention when shaping transitional justice policies or during *gacaca* hearings, where they are permitted to play a role only in the capacity of accused person.

While recognising the context and constraints in which Rwanda is forced to act, a passive acceptance of the *status quo* would translate into a catch-22 hampering the reconstruction of the social fabric. To be effective the reconciliation process, one of the stated and emphasised goals of the post-genocide political leadership, needs to encompass precise child-centred healing and reparation strategies. Reconciliation in fact cannot be considered a by-product of other processes and cannot be expected as a spontaneous outcome of a policy of full accountability based on criminal justice. The special protection due to children under the juvenile justice system has been completely disregarded in post-genocide Rwanda, in particular by the *gacaca* system. In part these pitfalls are due to the internal tension between the goals *inkiko gacaca* are intended to achieve, since it is very difficult to achieve simultaneously objectives such as truth, justice and reconciliation through a single mechanism. Moreover, traditional *gacaca* as constituted in pre-colonial times did not envisage the participation of children. Finally, it is questionable whether the use of a (to some extent) traditional and inclusion-oriented justice system can be effective when the available social capital has been torn apart so severely by colonisation and by the genocide.

Focusing on child-oriented transitional justice strategies in a country as young as Rwanda is not only a policy option, it is also a necessity where most of the population is aged under 15. To conclude that transitional justice in Rwanda can correctly be represented as a missed opportunity for children may seem to be technically correct when adopting the point of view of human rights instruments and of lists of best practices. Things are, however, much more nuanced if we consider the challenges posed by the genocide. It is time to draw upon the lessons to be learnt from Rwanda and further develop child-centred transitional justice

---

89 Ibid.

90 Ibid.

approaches enabling minors to be not only objects of protection and redress, but subjects of rights. Children's points of view on conflicts are a valuable instrument for their resolution. If transitional justice has by its very definition a transformative[91] capacity, if it embodies the potential to be simultaneously backwards and forwards looking, past and future oriented, we have to open its gates to the contribution of children.

91 W. Lambourne, 'Transitional Justice and Peacebuilding after Mass Violence', (2009) 3 *The International Journal of Transitional Justice*, 28–48.

"WE HAVE LIFE WITHOUT LIVING"

Addressing the Legacies of Genocide for Rwanda's Children and Youth

Kirrily Pells

1. INTRODUCTION

The 1994 Rwandan genocide is a stark illustration of the changing nature of conflict in the late twentieth century and the increasingly different and new ways in which children are involved, as captured in Graça Machel's seminal 1996 study for the United Nations on the *Impact of Armed Conflict on Children.* For instance, human rights reports documented the active participation of children and youth in devising survival strategies, committing murder, raping women and girls, stealing, burning and destroying houses, and acting as informants.[1] Subsequently, it has been estimated that ten percent of children have lost one or both parents, 110,000 orphans are living in child-headed households (CHH), 7,000 children live on the streets and 19,000 children aged 0–14 years are infected by HIV/AIDS.[2] The shattering of social relations has destroyed traditional protective structures, meaning children are left inadequately supported in their daily struggle for survival, compounded by the emotional distress caused by loss or imprisonment of loved ones.[3]

1 African Rights, *Rwanda – not so innocent: when women become killers,* African Rights, London, 1995; Human Rights Watch, *Leave none to tell the story: genocide in Rwanda,* Human Rights Watch, New York, 1999, at www.hrw.org/reports/1999/rwanda/ (accessed 20/09/04).

2 Human Rights Watch, *Lasting wounds: consequences of genocide and war,* Human Rights Watch, New York, 2009, at www.hrw.org/reports/2003/rwanda0403/ (accessed 01/09/04); UNICEF, *Rwanda: statistics,* 2009, at www.unicef.org/infobycountry/rwanda_statistics.html (accessed 13/09/09).

3 The genocide resulted in 20,000 children born of rape (Torgovnik, 2009) and an estimated 227,500 child-headed houses due to parental imprisonment, death in the massacres or as a consequence of the transmission of HIV/AIDS to around 350,000 women raped during the genocide. However, exact numbers are disputed, see HRW, 1996: 'Problems documenting gender-based crimes.'

Traditionally, the predominant response within academia, policy briefings and the media in interpreting the impact of such 'extraordinary' events is to approach individuals, both adults and children, as being traumatized and so in need of psychological assistance.[4] In the case of children, this understanding is applied in conjunction with stage development theories[5] which argue that conflict influences long-term psychological, social and emotional development owing to the trauma left in its wake.[6] The inherent vulnerability of children, according to this paradigm, therefore necessitates urgent psychological intervention in order to facilitate 'normal' growth and development and to prevent the intergenerational transmission of trauma.[7]

Rwanda is a vivid example of all these phenomena – the changing nature of conflict, the capturing of its impact upon children in psychological terms – and so has acted as a testing ground for approaches ranging from the biomedical to psychosocial, Christian-orientated and rights-based initiatives. Reflective of these different approaches and drawing on the priorities identified by children and young people during four periods of participatory action research in Rwanda, conducted between 2006 and 2009, the chapter explores the work of three programmes: firstly, CARE Rwanda's Nkundabana Initiative for Psychosocial Support (NIPS); secondly, Save the Children UK's child protection programme; and finally, the childcare and development programme of the Rwandan organization 'Abana', in conjunction with its counselling and evangelism mission.[8] The programmes were evaluated by participants and triangulated with the perspectives of staff to assess the efficacy of the different strategies used in addressing the priorities of children and young people. The lessons learnt here are particularly pertinent given the ongoing regional

---

4 A. Dyregrov, L. Gupta, R. Gjestad and M. Raundalen, 'Children exposed to warfare: a longitudinal study', (2002) 15 1 *Journal of Traumatic Stress*, 59–68; A. Marsella, M. Freidman, E. Gerrity and R. Scurfield (eds.), *Ethno cultural aspects of posttraumatic stress disorder*, American Psychological Association, Washington, D.C., 1996.

5 E. Erikson, *Childhood and society*, Pelican, London, 1965; J. Piaget, 'The stages of the intellectual development of the child', (1962) 26 *Bulletin of the Menninger Clinic*, 120–128.

6 G. Machel, *Impact of armed conflict on children*, New York, 1996, UN Document A/51/306, at 175, www.unicef.org/graca/a51-306_en.pdf, (accessed 20/09/04).

7 M. Allwood, D. Bell-dolan, and S. Husain, 'Children's trauma and adjustment reactions to violent and nonviolent war experiences', (2002) 41 4 *Journal Of The American Academy Of Child And Adolescent Psychiatry*, 450–457; R. Punamäki, 'The uninvited guest of war enters childhood: developmental and personality aspects of war and military violence', (2002) 8 *Traumatology*, 45–63.

8 Abana is a pseudonym for the Rwandan organization studied and is the Kinyarwanda word for children. I decided to anonymise the NGO in order to protect the identity of participants. The much larger scale of the international organisations discussed here and their respective programmes afford participants greater protection, and the evaluation reports on which the case studies draw are publically available. See Thurman, Pells and Ntaganira (2006) and Save the Children UK (2009).

instability in northern Uganda and the Democratic Republic of the Congo and the need for context-specific approaches.

Based on these findings, the chapter builds on existing critiques of the dominance of a narrowly-constructed psychological model for addressing the lives of children and young people affected by conflict. Instead, taking an interdisciplinary approach, the chapter proposes a holistic and contextually grounded paradigm of the everyday experience, which recognizes that children and young people respond to the changing dynamics and forms of post-conflict everyday life whilst also being actively engaged in its creation. It argues that rights-based approaches offer great potential in addressing issues faced by children and young people, yet can be strengthened by drawing upon insights gained from other approaches in order to become more effective and relevant to daily life.

2. "*IHAHAMUKA*": BREATHLESS WITH FEAR

The experiences of children during and after the 1994 Rwandan genocide have been interpreted and understood, in the main, in psychological terms. A Harvard study typifies this genre by stating 'that the entire Rwandan population is in a state of psychological shock and social withdrawal' with 'potentially dire implications for the country's economic and political future'.[9] Although not exclusively used with reference to the young, this trauma-orientated approach based upon estimates of those traumatised or suffering from PTSD has dominated existing research involving Rwandan children.[10]

This psychological focus dominated interventions. Indicative of this approach is the Trauma Recovery Program (TRP) operated by UNICEF in Rwanda, with the assistance of the Ministries of Rehabilitation and Health, between October

---

9 Harvard School Of Public Health, *Harvard study reports major mental health crisis in Rwanda*, 16 December 1996, at www.hsph.harvard.edu/press/releases/press12161996.html (accessed 13/09/04).

10 N.W. Boris, L. Brown, T. Thurman et al., 'Depressive symptoms in youth heads of household in Rwanda: correlates and implications for intervention', (2008) 162 9 *Archives of Pediatric and Adolescent Medicine*, 836–843; P. Bolton, R. Neugebauer and L. Ndogoni, 'Prevalence of depression in rural Rwanda based on symptom and functional criteria', (2002) 190 9 *Journal of Nervous Mental Disease*, 631–637; A. Dyregrov, L. Gupta, R. Gjestad and E. Mukanoheli, 'Trauma exposure and psychological reactions to genocide among Rwandan children', (2000) 13 1 *Journal of Traumatic Stress*, 3–21; I. Palmer, 'Psychosocial costs of war in Rwanda', (2002) 8 *Advances in Psychiatric Treatment*, 17–25; P. Pham, H. Weinstein and T. Longman, 'Trauma and PTSD symptoms in Rwanda: implications for attitudes toward justice and reconciliation', (2004) 292 *Journal of the American Medical Association*, 602–612; L. Wulsin and A. Hagengimana, 'PTSD in survivors of Rwanda's 1994 war', (1998) 15 4 *Psychiatric Times*, at www.psychiatrictimes.com/p980412.html (accessed 22/07/04).

1994 and November 1997.[11] A multiwave empirical study was conducted using the Impact of Events Scale (IES) and a Grief Reaction Inventory to assess the magnitude and nature of exposure to the events of the genocide.[12] It recorded that two thirds of children reported that they sometimes or often feel so sad that they can hardly cope with life, and sixty-four per cent thought that life was not worth living.[13] Upon the basis of this information a National Trauma Centre (NTC) was established in Kigali to provide clinical services, collect data, provide outreach support and trauma education in the communities and train counsellors. Yet the Evaluators of the TRP stressed its failure to extend assessment beyond PTSD symptoms or explore resiliency, arguing that 'from an intervention point of view we cannot erase the traumatic exposures'.[14] Following the handover of the NTC to the Rwandan Department of Health in 1997, it became unsustainable. Funding was not available and it was not used by the majority of the population.[15]

This over-reliance on narrowly conceived psychological interventions was criticised by Machel, who criticized the lack of integration of local knowledge and understandings of child development and healing into programmes and argued that 'institutionalizing children and identifying them as traumatized can impose an inherent stigma and contribute to isolation and withdrawal'.[16] Indeed the word 'trauma' did not exist in Kinyarwanda until the numerous NGOs intervening in this field created the phrase *Ihahamuka,* meaning literally 'breathless with fear'.[17] Thus this chapter does not deny the existence of trauma but questions its framing according to a Western biomedical model and the proposition that this is a universally valid paradigm that encompasses the totality

---

11 Dyregrov et al., ibid.

12 The Impact of Events Scale and the Grief Inventory are assessment tools which through psychiatric interviews, questionnaires and rating scales seek to quantify symptoms and generate an overall score to measure the severity of an individual's response to a specific event.

13 L. Gupta, *Follow-up survey of Rwandan children's reactions to war related violence from the 1994 genocide.* UNICEF Evaluation Division, 1998, 12–13, at www.unicef.org/evaldatabase/RWA_98-800.pdf (accessed 08/08/04).

14 J. Søren, R. Neugerbauer, T. Marner, S. George, L. Ndahiro and E. Rurangwa, *Rwandan children and their families: understanding, prevention and healing of traumatisation*, European University Centre for Mental Health and Human Rights, Copenhagen and New York, 1997, at 5, www.unicef.org/evaldatabase/RWA_1997_002_Part1.pdf, www.unicef.org/evaldatabase/RWA_1997_002_Part2.pdf, www.unicef.org/evaldatabase/RWA_1997_002_Part3.pdf, www.unicef.org/evaldatabase/RWA_1997_002_Part4.pdf (accessed 22/07/04).

15 L. Levers, L. Lopez, D. Kamanzi, D. Mukamana, K. Pells and D. Bhusumane, 'Addressing urgent community mental health needs in Rwanda: culturally sensitive training interventions', (2006) 16 *Journal of Psychology in Africa*, 261–272.

16 Machel, *supra* note 6, 177–178.

17 Wulsin and Hagengimana, *supra* note 11.

of experience and alone charts the way ahead for addressing the situations faced by children affected by conflict.[18]

3. "ACTS OF THE EVERYDAY"[19]

Despite the dominance of the biomedical model, it has become increasingly contested both within and outside the discipline of psychology. Interestingly, this critique is emanating largely from practitioners who have been or who are engaged in war-torn contexts.[20] Patrick Bracken, for example, describes trauma as a 'psychological corset' which attempts to fit all experiences into one universal concept.[21] Instead, these practitioners argue that biomedical and cognitive approaches to trauma are only one way of perceiving the situation of children in the aftermath of conflict and are far less relevant when considering that the meanings given to the symptoms are shaped by a host of other factors, including history, culture, religion, politics and personal life experiences.[22] Contrary to assumptions of vulnerability and passivity inherent within the trauma paradigm, research conducted by Lynne Jones in Bosnia has demonstrated that children are in the main resilient and capable of navigating highly complex situations. She concluded that the lasting well-being of the children did not correlate solely with the amount or length of violence to which the children had been exposed, or with ratings on PTSD scales. Instead, what mattered was 'how personally disruptive the event had been: What had happened to their family and friends and the landscape in which they lived?'.[23] Therefore, interpreting the responses of children to conflict solely through the diagnostic criteria for PTSD fails to

---

18 J. Breslau, 'Cultures of trauma: anthropological views of posttraumatic stress disorder in international health', 113 28 *Culture, Medicine and Psychiatry*; L. Jones, *Then they started shooting, Growing up in wartime Bosnia,* Harvard University Press, Cambridge, 2004, 201–202.

19 C. Nordstrom and A. Robben (eds.), *Fieldwork under fire: contemporary studies of violence and survival,* University of California Press, Berkeley, 1995, at 7.

20 P. Bracken, *Trauma. Culture, meaning and philosophy,* Whirr Publishers Ltd., London, 2002; J. Boyden, *Social healing in war-affected and displaced children*, 2001, at www.asylumsupport.info/publications/rsc/healing.htm (accessed 20/09/04); J. Boyden and J. De Berry (eds.), *Children and youth on the front line. Ethnography, armed conflict and displacement,* Berghahn Books, New York/Oxford, 2004; Jones *supra* note 19; L. Dowdney (ed.), *Trauma, resilience and cultural healing: how do we move forward?,* The Coalition Against Child Soldiers, London, 2007, at www.child-soldiers.org/psychosocial/Trauma,Resilience_and_Cultural_Healing_2007.pdf (accessed 29/03/07); N. Boothby, A. Strang and M. Wessells (eds.), *A world turned upside down: social ecological approaches to children in war zone,* Kumarian Press, Bloomfield, 2006; D. Summerfield, 'A critique of seven assumptions behind the psychological trauma programmes in war-affected areas', (1999) 48 *Social Sciences and Medicine,* 1449–1462, at http://earlybird.qeh.ox.ac.uk/rfgexp/rsp_tre/student/natconf/toc.htm (accessed 12/07/04).

21 Bracken, ibid., at 80.

22 Bracken, ibid.; Summerfield, *supra* note 21; Jones *supra* note 19.

23 Jones, ibid., at 245.

capture what is prioritised by children as problematic in their lives and which factors adversely affect their well-being.

Similarly, focus group discussions conducted with Rwandan children and young people affirmed the importance of the everyday. Whilst the genocide and/or poverty provided a backdrop to all that happens within daily life, in the narratives of the young people these factors permeate the everyday in the form of economic and social problems. The most prominent of the concerns raised by children and young people were social relationships and the community, economic livelihoods and education, a sense of belonging and meaning in life and accessing rights. The loss or absence of parents to provide love, care and advice seems to be the single biggest factor in making their daily life a struggle. This does not necessarily mean that the young people are not coping, but it does emphasise that the post-genocide situation has brought on new responsibilities for these young people, such as caring for siblings, being exposed to the dangers of abuse and exploitation, dealing with stigma because of poverty, parental illness and/or the involvement of family members in the genocide and above all, overcoming isolation from the larger community. When faced with all these problems the young people concluded that their daily struggle to survive stems from their orphaned status: 'you think I have these problems because I don't have parents'. The reminder that their parents are dead subsequently leads them think about the genocide: 'If the genocide had not taken place my parents and the others would be there' (female, focus group participant, 2006). Thus the participants in my focus groups presented the legacies of the genocide – namely their parents' deaths – as more problematic than 'traumatic memory' concerning the events of the genocide. For example, one girl, who heads a household of eight siblings and other relatives, summarised her situation thus: 'we've got used to the genocide, it's daily life that is the problem' (female, interview, 2006). She has come to terms with the death of her parents; she now struggles to provide for her family.[24]

Consequently, with these priorities in mind, this chapter builds upon anthropological and sociological discussions of the everyday, developed in the work of anthropologists.[25] The focus shifts from the conflict zone and intrapsychic functioning to the realm of everyday life, its structures, processes, practices and happenings. Drawing upon Das et al., this chapter argues that the 'struggle to survive' occurs within the 'context of a damaged social fabric' and thus the importance of an understanding of 'the everyday' must be privileged

24 K. Pells, 'We've got used to the genocide; it's daily life that's the problem', (2009) 21 3 *Peace Review*, 339–346.

25 V. Das, A. Kleinman, M. Ramphele and P. Reynolds (eds.), *Violence and subjectivity*, Oxford University Press, Oxford, 2000 and Das et al., *Remaking a world: violence, social suffering, and recover*, Oxford University Press, Oxford, 2001.

over the construction of 'traumatic memory'.[26] Recognising that increasingly there is no clear divide between the 'conflict' and 'post-conflict' phases, as violence continues albeit in more indirect ways, the everyday is not only a site of destruction but also one of creation. The everyday redirects attention to events in the present and the future, which are often as difficult and challenging as those in the past. Rebuilding a life in the present is equally, if not more important for restoring individual and communal agency, so aiding the transformation of lives and relationships and 'the creation of a new normality'.[27] Thus I argue that the paradigm of the everyday, with its social, economic, cultural and political spheres of daily life, facilitates a holistic and contextually grounded analysis of the situations of children and young people post-conflict. The challenges remain: how best to engage practically with this paradigm to facilitate the transformation of lives, relationships and environments in the aftermath of conflict and also how best to facilitate the agency of children and young people, to build on their capacities. It is necessary therefore to turn to a comparison of different programming approaches in order to offer some initial responses to the questions posed.

4. PROGRAMMING APPROACHES WITH CHILDREN AND YOUNG PEOPLE IN RWANDA

The following three case study programmes were selected as they seek to address the priority areas identified by the children and young people in focus group discussions of everyday life: social relationships, livelihoods and education, accessing rights and full participation within daily life.

CARE Rwanda's NIPS project is a community-based approach for supporting children and youth living in child/youth-headed households (C/YHH) or in families affected/infected with HIV/AIDS. The criteria for participation is that at the time of selection youth are 21 years or younger and are the head of their household. Youth are then eligible to participate until the head of household reaches 24 years of age. Community members, including children and the local authorities, help CARE staff to identify those who fit the above criteria and children verify that the identified youth are amongst those living in the most vulnerable circumstances, often adding names of those who have been excluded. The project relies primarily on community volunteers called Nkundabana, who provide guidance and care for children living without adult support. Children and youth nominate persons whom they trust and with a good reputation in the

26 Das et al., ibid., *Violence and subjectivity*, 10–11; Das et al., ibid., *Remaking a world: violence, social suffering, and recover*, at 4.

27 Das et al., ibid., *Violence and subjectivity*, at 27.

community as Nkundabana and the community is asked to confirm these selections. CARE presents the NIPS model as an attempt to provide a foundation for economic and livelihood security and act as a basis from which advocacy and child protection functions can be initiated.[28]

The overreaching objective of Save the Children's (SC) child protection programme is to build new, and strengthen existing, community, local and national child protection systems and to improve the capacity of government at these levels to deliver co-ordinated, participatory planning and resource mobilisation for children living in vulnerable circumstances. As part of this programme a set of training, mobilisation and public awareness materials on child rights and protection was developed in conjunction with the Ministry in charge of Family and Gender Promotion (MIGEPROF). During the course of the programme four structures (Children's Forums, Child Protection Committees, Nkundabana and Children's Corners) have been established for the realisation of children's rights and child protection.[29] Together these form the Child Protection Networks (CPNs) at each administrative level (village, cell and sector). The project has been coordinated at district level by the Child Rights Coordination Group and by Project Management Committee (PMCs) operating at sector level.[30]

Abana is a Christian evangelical organisation that aims to address the spiritual, psychological and physical needs of orphans and widows of the genocide. Abana works through establishing communities of survivors who come together to worship, to support one another and to organise community-based development activities. Abana provides individual counselling and group support through fellowship meetings and child/youth camps, where activities include testimonies, biblical teaching, life skills and having fun and playing games. In addition, the childcare and development programme encompasses a sponsorship scheme for children between 2 and 13 years old, providing for education fees, materials and transport, and assistance with healthcare costs and shelter.

CARE and SC are rights-based organisations, albeit with slightly different emphases. SC draws directly upon the UN Convention on the Rights of the Child (CRC) and is seeking to entrench Article 12, the right to participation, as the cornerstone of its programming approach. In contrast, CARE interprets a

---

28 The evaluation of NIPS draws upon data gathered as part of the end of project evaluation conducted with Thurman and Ntaganira, in addition to my own fieldwork, 2006.

29 The role of the Nkundabana within SC's programme is much less comprehensive than the Nkundabana within NIPS, being fewer in number and involving visits to CHH and advocacy on their behalf to the CPNs.

30 In addition to my own fieldwork, the evaluation of SC's child protection programme draws upon a participatory evaluation of lessons learnt and best practices, which I conducted with SC, see Save the Children UK, 2009.

rights-based approach more broadly, to include concepts from livelihoods analysis, humanitarian relief and development work, which were historically undertaken by the organisation. In the case of CARE's NIPS programme evaluated here, rights-based principles are combined with psychosocial language and concepts of vulnerability and resilience. Abana offers a complete contrast by framing all activities with reference to biblical teaching and is deeply rooted in an evangelical interpretation of Christian doctrine.

In returning to the four spheres of the everyday, this section evaluates the strengths and weaknesses of the different case studies in addressing children and young people's priorities by analysing qualitative data gathered using mixed participatory methods within focus group discussions and individual interviews with participants.

4.1. THE SOCIAL SPHERE: MAKING, BREAKING AND TRANSFORMING RELATIONSHIPS

Within the discussions of everyday life the loss of parents, whether to the genocide, HIV/AIDS or prison, was presented by children as a critical factor inhibiting the realisation of rights and creating social isolation. Responding to this need, across the case study programmes a mixture of relationships are formed, in terms of both whom they are between and the basis on which they are founded. With regard the latter, three processes are at work: the building of new supportive relations, the breaking of old exploitative relations and the transforming of existing relationships. In terms of whom the relationships are between three types can be identified: amongst child and youth participants, between participants and adults and between participants and the wider community. Within the programmes the emphasis on these different types and processes varies, which, as will become apparent, is linked in part to the programmatic approach taken by the NGO.

Firstly, all three programmes bring youth together, whether in associations (CARE), forums (SC) or supportive communities (Abana). Despite the different purposes of these groups, the resultant benefits identified by youth were broadly the same: meeting with others in similar situations, sharing experiences and problems and having fun. For participants, building relationships with their peers directly targets one of their biggest challenges, social isolation, and so was felt to be one of the most successful aspects of all the programmes. This response was more pronounced amongst participants from Abana and CARE, the majority of whom experienced rejection and dehumanisation during the genocide and continue to be stigmatised and marginalised from the wider community due to being orphans and/or heads of household.

Notwithstanding these overall similarities, the divergent purposes of the groups yielded further differing areas of positive change. The major functional difference in this area of relationship building amongst youth is the linking of the social and economic spheres in the programme run by CARE through the associational model, in contrast to the more didactic function of SC's Children's Forums and the supportive religious communities of Abana. For participants, the associations fulfil a dual purpose. The youth form new supportive relationships not only to combat isolation but also to gain economic and social protection through peer education, vocational skills and tools (e.g., sewing machine, agricultural equipment). This enables participants to escape exploitative relations such as child labour or sexual abuse and so generates hope for the future.[31]

In contrast, the functions of the Children's Forums and Abana are largely focused on sensitisation, either on issues of rights or on Christian teaching. Although both have developed economic functions, these are not currently a central feature of the programme. Participants in both programmes valued the knowledge gained, felt that it was relevant to their lives, noted that it had contributed to a shift in behaviour and enabled some to break out of exploitative relations. For example, the Children's Forums in each sector meet monthly with the Child Protection Committees to analyse problems in the community, devise solutions and strategies for advocacy and to inform authorities about individual cases of abuse or out-of-school youth.

However, both programmes generated a similar frustration among participants with the emphasis being placed on knowledge rather than a resource gap. This reflects the assumption too often made by NGOs that children and young people do not have knowledge, whether that be of rights, sexual health, the importance of education or other relevant areas. Yet many children and young people amongst whom I researched were articulate in the language of rights. Instead, the chasm lies in the arena of implementation. The growth of sensitisation programmes globally have been critiqued for their failure to deal with the root causes of rights violations.[32] It should therefore be questioned whether

---

31 As recognised by children and young people, these 'exploitative' relationships are frequently essential to survival and not totally detrimental, as in the case of labour, for example, from which children gain money upon which their household depends. However, focus group participants perceived these relationships in the main in a negative light, given the lack of dignity shown and ill-treatment received.

32 K.E. Cheney, *Pillars of the nation: child citizens and Ugandan national development*, University of Chicago Press, Chicago, 2007, 64–66; R. Evans, 'The two faces of empowerment in conflict', (2008) 3 1 *Research in Comparative and International Education*, 50–64; S. Shepler, 'The rites of the child: global discourses of youth and reintegrating child soldiers in Sierra Leone', (2005) 4 2 *International Journal of Human Rights*, at 200; S.C. White, 'Children's rights and the imagination of community in Bangladesh', (2007) 14 *Childhood*, at 510.

sensitisation programmes are in themselves enough to break exploitative relations between children and adults and to transform relations in the community.

The second type of relationship being formed through the programmes is between children and adults. The adults are staff members of the NGOs and/or those selected from the community for involvement in the programme. As with relationship building amongst youth, despite the different approaches used the benefits identified by youth in having contact with supportive adults are similar: the youth feel listened to, that they have value, are less isolated and unsupported, and become more positive about the future. Likewise, on closer investigation, despite the apparently similar responses from participants different factors emerge as significant in assisting relationship building with adults. A series of instructive contrasts can be drawn between CARE's NIPS programme and the other case studies. It is not only the breadth of roles fulfilled by the Nkundabana but also the basis on which these relationships are founded that help to explain the effusive responses coming from NIPS participants. The Nkundabana simultaneously address a number of priority areas for youth that cross-cut the spheres of the everyday: support in accessing healthcare, education and vocational training opportunities, advocating for rights and providing emotional support and guidance. Moreover, the Nkundabana are based in the community and so on hand to address issues, whereas Abana and SC all have staff and volunteers working in the community, there is not the same scheme of one adult allocated to a few households which they visit regularly. The lower ratio of staff/ volunteers to participants partially explains the frustrations of not being listened to or having the same level of adult contact. It also strengthens documentation of the difference brought about by the presence of a supportive caregiver for children living in vulnerable circumstances globally, especially in the context of the HIV/AIDS epidemic.[33]

However, the presence of supportive adults in the community does not alone explain the positive responses of NIPS participants. Equally important as the type of relationship being formed is the process underpinning it. CARE staff ask children and young people to compile a list of qualities which should be possessed by Nkundabana and also people whom they already trust in the community. Community members are asked to verify these choices. Youth write

33 G. Foster, C. Makufa, R. Drew, S. Kambeu and K. Saurombe, 'Supporting children in need through a community-based orphan visiting programme', (1996) 4 8, *AIDS Care*, 389–403; L. Richter, G. Foster and L. Sherr, *Where the heart is: meeting the psychosocial needs of young children in the context of HIV/AIDS*, Bernard van Leer Foundation, The Hague, 2006, at www.bernardvanleer.org/publication_store/publication_store_publications/where_the_heart_is_meeting_the_psychosocial_needs_of_young_children_in_the_context_of_hivaids/file (accessed 13/07/06).

a contract for their Nkundabana stating the responsibilities of both parties. If the Nkundabana do not fulfil these responsibilities then they can be and have been asked to step down by the children. During the rollout of the Nkundabana model in another region of Rwanda this selection process was side-stepped to save time and instead CARE staff allocated Nkundabana to participants. This was unsuccessful as the Nkundabana and youth did not bond and so the decision was taken to restart the programme from scratch to enable the youth to select their own Nkundabana (staff, interview, 2007). Children cannot be expected to bond with just anyone, especially given the high levels of distrust prevalent in Rwandan society in general and especially amongst survivors.

The NIPS model is an interesting combination of the more contractual nature of a rights bearer/holder relationship with a personalised aspect introduced through the selection process as participants select their own Nkundabana. The rights or contractual dimension to the relationship between Nkundabana and participants creates a level of accountability, developing the relationship between adults and children into partnerships in order to realise rights, such as tackling issues around land. This is confirmed further by the evolution of the Child Protection Networks established by SC. At the outset the emphasis was placed on training children, while the adults raised concerns over not understanding procedures and the nature of their roles and responsibilities. In the early stages therefore the children felt less supported in their activities. This highlights a problem frequently encountered in NGO programming with children, where too much emphasis is placed on children as agents of change without enough support. Moreover, rights language can strain existing relationships as children try and claim rights that parents are unable to fulfil due to poverty, resulting in a potential backlash against the children raising issues of abuse.[34] As will be discussed more fully in the political section, relationships are conceived by youth as partnerships and this should inform understandings of empowerment and participation, with children and adults working together rather than separately.

Within the social sphere, the largest divergence amongst the programmes comes in the third area of relationship-building, between participants and the community, with each approach bringing benefits and drawbacks for participants. Abana focuses on the creation of Christian communities, bringing together orphans and widows to support one another. This is the most socially exclusive of the three approaches, establishing 'parallel communities' rather than working in existing communities. The priority is to create a safe space where survivors can be with others who can understand what they have been through and where they can be listened to and valued, all aspects highlighted by child and youth participants as being important. However, for Abana participants the

---

[34] Cheney, *supra* note 32, 64–66.

lack of interaction with the wider community was not raised as directly problematic, unlike frequent references to the difficulties of having to live alongside perpetrators. This suggests that participants are not receiving the skills that they need for their everyday lives.

In comparison, within NIPS and through SC's CPNs the emphasis is on transforming community relations through formalising existing support networks and including adults in the programme who already have an interest in the well-being of children and youth. As noted previously children cannot be expected to transform communities on their own and change cannot occur in a vacuum. The transformatory approaches of CARE and SC have produced a number of important outcomes for both participants and the wider community. Firstly, through engaging the wider community there is a better understanding of what the programmes are about and their rationale, which in turn facilitates implementation. In the case of NIPS the wider community is actively engaged through the identification of youth, verification of Nkundabana and community fun days. Community members stated that NIPS has facilitated their understanding of the problems facing participants and their responsibilities towards them. Likewise, participants in SC's Child Protection Committees commented on how the programme had shifted attitudes:

> Before Save the Children's training our parents' committee was only concerned with children in school, not those children out of school or those who drop out. We did not have access to information about how to help those children. Now we are working to reintegrate these children at school (Child Protection Committee member, focus group, 2007).

Secondly, engagement with the programmes has led community members to reconsider their discriminatory attitudes, generating behavioural change. Through the programme's activities, everyday encounters are created, potentially leading to reconciliation, or at least a better understanding of the situation of others. Both programmes include children from different backgrounds, survivors, those with parents in prison and in the case of SC, children living with their parents. Rather than through an artificial forum such as a reconciliation 'club', through concrete activities like income-generation associations or child protection initiatives located in the everyday, communities are being brought together through a common purpose. This supports findings from other post-conflict contexts, where ex-combatants and civilians come together to rebuild community buildings, so grounding more abstract concepts of peace and reconciliation in daily life.[35]

The first and second points have translated into a third: community-initiated support to assist children living in vulnerable circumstances, such as through the construction of housing, provision of food and taking sick children to hospital. This increases the chances of the programme becoming sustainable in the long term.[36] Similarly, SC's protection programme focuses on transforming community relationships and breaking exploitation through calling duty-bearers to account and also creating new means of protection. This collaborative approach builds mutual trust between children, communities and local authorities, which is vital in a post-conflict context where distrust is prevalent. Children feel that they are listened to and valued by the authorities, who respond to their requests for assistance in intervening in cases of abuse or resistance from community members and in providing material resources for the most vulnerable. In return, local authorities see children as partners in development initiatives through providing information and ideas and organising income-generation activities, so contributing to poverty reduction at the micro-level.

Despite these clear successes, the interventions of CARE and SC have caused new friction within the communities. With both these cases there is still not enough knowledge in the communities of the purposes of the programmes, which in a society permeated by suspicion leads to resistance. This can also be attributed to jealousy and resentment at what participants receive (in the case of CARE) and for both programmes due to opposition to children and youth raising rights issues. Ironically, interventions designed to break exploitative relations can result in children being further isolated, as they are removed from labour networks for instance[37] or become seen as 'CARE's children'.[38] There is the danger therefore that interventions such as these have the opposite effect to what is intended. Rather than community members learning of their responsibilities towards children and taking action for the realisation of rights, some members see the care and protection of children as being the responsibility of NGOs. It has been reported, although not verified, that programmes focusing on children who head households lead to parents 'abandoning' their children in

---

35 M. G. Wessells and D. Jonah, 'Reintegration of former youth soldiers in Sierra Leone: challenges of reconciliation and post-accord peacebuilding', in S. Mcevoy-Levy (ed.), *Troublemakers or peacemakers? Youth and post-accord peace building*, University of Notre Dame Press, South Bend, Indiana, 2005, 40–41.

36 Unaids, Unicef and Usaid, *Children on the brink 2004, a joint report on new orphan estimates and a framework for action*, 2004, 38–39, at http://synkronweb.aidsalliance.org/graphics/OVCY/documents/0000008e00.pdf (accessed 21/06/06).

37 Cheney, *supra* note 35, at 44.

38 White, *supra* note 33, at 518.

the hope they will become incorporated into a NGO programme and be better provided for. This phenomenon has been observed by Luzze[39] in a study of a Ugandan World Vision programme targeting children heading households, which had weakened community support for orphans and discouraged fostering, as participants in the programme were better off than their neighbours.

In summary, the centrality of relationships – making, breaking and transforming – within the case study programmes mirrors their importance in the everyday lives of children and young people. Whether in building relations amongst youth through communities, associations or forums, or between children and adults acting in a supportive or mentoring capacity, the programmes bring an immediate impact on the lives of participants. Supportive relationships are important to children worldwide, but here they take on added significance when parents are dead or absent and children and youth find themselves isolated and stigmatised. In immediate terms therefore, the specific programme approach does not have a bearing on the outcomes for participants, as the benefits identified were largely similar. Instead, it is in the longer term that different outcomes can be projected, notably the sustainability of transformed relationships and escape from old exploitative relations. In this area, approach is significant and occurs particularly in the domain of transforming community relations, determining whether the organisation is looking outwards by working with children within the context of their communities (CARE and SC) or inwards through the creation of new supportive communities (Abana). Thus where a rights-based approach adds value is through bringing a transformative dimension to relationships with the community. Participants find that through their relationships with Nkundabana or Child Protection Committees, their relations with the community at large are being transformed in a positive direction. Strengthening relations in the community has the best hope for sustained support and begins the long process of reconciliation.

However, the rights-based programmes face the practical difficulty of identifying the duty-bearers to call to account as immediate caregivers given that parents are frequently absent in this context, the reason for organisations such as Abana forming their own supportive communities. Yet the gap identified is not predominately one of knowledge, namely what children need to ensure their physical and psychological well-being, but rather one of resources and children having that first close supportive relationship in place through which other rights can be accessed, as demonstrated by NIPS, which is based in the

---

39 F. Luzze, *Survival in child-headed households: a study on the impact of World Vision support on coping strategies in child-headed households in Kakuuto County, Rakai District, Uganda*, 2002, unpublished.

community and upon community relations. The attention of the rights-based approach to process is key as here participants select the Nkundabana and their choices are validated by the community, so enabling the development of trust and partnerships between children, adults, the wider community and CARE. Rights therefore need to be embedded in social relations, both to be realised and to negate adverse consequences of interventions such as resentment and jealousy, a challenge faced particularly within the economic sphere by the introduction of resources.

4.2. THE ECONOMIC SPHERE: LIVING NOW, BUILDING FOR THE FUTURE

Along with relationships, at the top of children and young people's priorities is education, which is seen in the long term as a means of getting a job in order to provide for themselves and their families. Further economic concerns include shelter, healthcare and land, the lack of which creates vulnerability to exploitation, reinforces stigma and acts as a 'constant reminder' of the past. Each of the three case studies aimed at strengthening the ability of all or some participants to access educational and livelihood opportunities through a mixture of distribution of materials, provision of skills training and advocacy. As with relationship building the manner in which this is done is associated with the approach taken by the NGO leading to a number of different intended and unintended outcomes, both positive and negative.

Emerging from participants' responses, what is crucial is not only what resources are provided but also to whom, upon what criteria and by what means. Through its sponsorship programme for children aged between 2 and 13 years old Abana provides direct assistance with education fees, materials and transport, and assistance with healthcare costs and shelter. CARE groups participants together in associations, through which materials for income generation, assistance with shelter, healthcare and education-related costs are provided. Although the Children's Forums have elaborated their own income-generation and resource distribution schemes, this was an initiative of participants rather than constituting a core activity planned by SC. Instead, the focus is on strengthening community-based organisations' advocacy to local authorities for greater economic support for child protection activities.

Across the programmes those who receive any materials or training are extremely grateful. The resources provided address the priority areas in the everyday identified by children and young people, namely education, livelihood, health and shelter. However, within the programmes the order of what is funded does not always match the order preferred by participants. For instance, the poor quality of the shelters inhabited by children heading households was a primary concern of NIPS participants, yet housing materials were only provided to a very few. This demonstrates that what an NGO and what programme participants deem as priorities may vary and in particular greater attention needs to be devoted to the hidden barriers to educational and livelihood opportunities provided by NGO programmes, such as poor health and care for younger siblings.

Turning to the issue of for whom the resources are provided, it is instructive to look at the differences within and across the programmes between those who receive and those who do not. For example, NIPS participants resented the fact that some participants had received a new shelter or were given health insurance and others had not, and did not understand the selection criteria. In contrast, the rationale behind distributing radios to girls only was understood by participants and so accepted: 'Even though they gave radios to girls alone, they explained to us that they are more at risk to have problems than boys especially when they come from neighbours where they go to listen to radio at night because they can be attacked and raped' (male, focus group, 2006). Participants are aware of the constraints facing NGOs – 'NIPS cannot solve everything' (male, focus group, 2006) – but get frustrated when they do not understand the criteria used to determine the allocation of resources. Recognising that NGOs do not have limitless funds, are faced with overwhelming numbers of those in need and so must prioritise areas of intervention and recipients, the key issue therefore is how the resources are distributed, who decides and upon what criteria.

Likewise, NIPS demonstrates the importance of involving community members in decisions regarding the provision and allocation of resources to reduce negative sentiments. Participants, Nkundabana and community members all noted that the provision of material goods invoked jealousy within the wider community. This echoes findings from other areas affected by HIV/AIDS, which suggests that if the community is involved and has a stake in the programme then participants are less likely to become a target for reprisals or further stigmatisation.[40] However, this is not only a matter of understanding, as some community members understood the justification of resource distribution but emphasised their own poverty. Equally, whilst CARE is attempting to build community structures of support for youth by distributing resources through the Nkundabana, they or their own children are frequently also in need of similar resources and there is a danger of volunteers burning out in caring for both their own families and the households they support. This suggests that whilst involving the community in the distribution of resources aids the

40 Foster et al., *supra* note 34, at 399; C. Grainger, D. Webb and L. Elliott, 'Children affected by HIV/AIDS: rights and responses in the developing world', (2001) *Working Paper* 23, Save the Children UK, London, 2001, at 42.

strengthening of participation, in impoverished communities care must be taken not to elevate youth above the standard of living of their neighbours.[41] An important lesson is flexibility. NGOs should continuously assess the living conditions of their participants and monitor the emerging vulnerability of others within their community.

In the economic sphere, it is Save the Children which has the most distinctive approach in attempting to strengthen communities to participate in local development planning and governance, rather than direct material assistance, so implementing the most 'traditional' rights-based approach. Training given to the Children's Forums and Child Protection Committees has resulted in advocacy efforts translating into local authorities distributing resources, such as materials for housing and schooling, and bringing structural change through the introduction of a child rights programming line in Gicumbi District's budget. This resulted in the amount of money available for addressing the situation of children living in vulnerable circumstances being quadrupled from 6 to 42 million Rwandan Francs (7, 289 to 51, 023 Euros). This programme demonstrates both the advantages and disadvantages of an approach centred on advocacy. By not directly distributing resources, SC does not create the same tensions found in the other three case studies, although as an INGO there remains an expectation amongst community members that materials will be handed out.[42] At the same time, participation in the Forums and Committees takes adults and children away from income-generating activities and thus precludes the most impoverished from participating. Participation is not cost-free and the danger with a rights-based approach aimed at long-term structural change is neglect of a present in which people are struggling to survive, so creating a barrier to participation in training initiatives.

Significantly, it is this area that saw the greatest level of innovation by Forum members, who invested their own money in small income-generating activities to provide materials and uniforms to children otherwise unable to attend schools. The knowledge gained was spread amongst the Forums by peer training. On a personal level this demonstrates the commitment of participants to the programme, but in addition the difference brought by a small amount of resources can bring a lot of change. As noted in the previous section, resources are needed alongside training in order that children can escape from exploitative relationships and to break the cycle between poverty and violence.

---

41 Foster, ibid.; M.G. Wessells, 'A living wage. The importance of livelihood in reintegrating former child soldiers', in Boothby et al., *supra* note 20.

42 SC has provided office materials to sector authorities to facilitate the monitoring and evaluation of children's rights in the community and the development of action plans. One motorcycle was delivered to each sector in order that officials could travel to investigate cases of abuse and coordinate the CPNs.

For example, youth, Nkundabana and community members all commented on the reduction in criminal behaviour and prostitution amongst NIPS participants. This echoes findings from other post-conflict contexts where a lack of training with job opportunities at the end has led young people to rejoin fighting forces or engage in criminal activities.[43] Given the instability caused by armed factions operating in the Great Lakes area, lessons should be learnt from the child 'regional warriors' of Western Africa, who went from one conflict to another due to a lack of other livelihood opportunities.[44] For example, Forum members discussed children crossing the Rwandan border to look for work.

In summary, the case studies demonstrate that the economic sphere requires a series of delicate balances to be struck: between enabling children to access education and vocational opportunities and ensuring that they can provide for themselves and their families in the short term; between facilitating long-term structural change and not neglecting the urgency of immediate needs; between addressing the situation of those living in the most vulnerable circumstances and not creating jealousy and resentment within the community; between securing donor requirements and securing funding while allowing for flexibility in programme direction and development; and finally between ensuring that resources reach those in greatest need and by handing over control to communities riddled with different agendas and affiliations.

In making these decisions the case studies demonstrate that it is not so much what resources are provided (as these are broadly similar across the programmes) but how they are distributed which makes the difference and in particular the need for greater clarity over 'vulnerability' criteria.[45] Whilst one of the greatest strengths of a rights-based approach is its focus on the long term, this is also potentially its greatest weakness as it may lead to neglect of the present. Here the 'mixed' approach of CARE is beneficial as to ensure long-term change through education and training, participants need food and materials in order to attend. Rights-based programming can also learn from other approaches, with measures such as the income-generating schemes of the Children's Forums, which are

43 Human Rights Watch, *Youth, poverty and blood: the lethal legacy of West Africa's regional warriors,* Human Rights Watch, New York, 2005, at www.hrw.org/reports/2005/westafrica 0405/ (accessed 04/05/05); Wessells, *supra* note 41.

44 Human Rights Watch, ibid.

45 This point is reinforced by a recent MIGEPROF/UNICEF study, which concluded that NGO interventions are still supply- rather than demand-driven and fail to recognise that problems are not necessarily unique to orphans but are the result of poverty (2008). On the other hand, the report is still based on criteria of vulnerability, estimating that 83.3 per cent of Rwandan children are orphans or vulnerable children. With such a high figure, the practical utility as well as the assumptions implicit in the term should be questioned.

designed to fit around studying. Moreover, there is a need for a broader understanding of rights education. Training in child rights and child rights programming should be accompanied by life skills training in activities such as income generation and provision of information on where to access support such as health insurance and micro-credit. Rights cannot be realised by training alone and income generation is vital in a resource-constrained environment to facilitating children's access to rights, such as education through having money for school materials. Finally, relationships and resources need to be considered simultaneously. Here the associational and community-managed savings model employed by CARE works well.[46] Relationships can be stressed by the introduction of resources but they are also a means of mitigating tension through participatory decision-making and clear channels of communication. Together, they enable children and young people to live in the present but build for the future.

4.3. THE CULTURAL SPHERE: MEANING MAKING AND CULTURAL SCRIPTING

Based upon the focus group discussions with children and young people, it emerged that creating a sense of meaning and purpose in life is critical for a positive outlook on the future and to generate resilience. This sense of meaning and purpose can derive from social relationships and be enhanced by educational and livelihood opportunities, but exists also in the symbolic sphere, through understanding and interpreting experience. Within this cultural realm individual and collective experience interact, forming part of the process of the creation of self, society and the everyday. NGOs are actors too in this process of world building through the concepts and language used to frame their programmes and the action undertaken in implementation. This section considers the role played by NGOs in the interpretation of individual and collective experience and the contexts in which the programmes create space for participants to make sense of their worlds and whether children can influence these debates.

In the first instance the different programme approaches act as a prism through which the NGO (re)constructs the problems faced by the children and young people and offers a range of possible solutions. As noted previously each

---

46 This supports findings from elsewhere. Wessells describes 'solidarity groups' established with former child soldiers in Sierra Leone, who received a loan to start a small business following training. The repayment of the loans was 99 per cent and Wessells argues that 'the combination of mentoring by older artisans, business training, and continuing staff support, along with the young people's determination to earn a living, probably contributed to the high repayment rates': Wessells *supra* note 41.

organisation uses a differing range of concepts to devise its programmes but Abana addresses the issues of past experience and meaning-making most directly of all the programmes. Abana focuses upon helping children and young people find meaning and purpose in their lives through the Christian faith, supported by Abana communities and a Christian approach to counselling. Counselling and giving testimony are intertwined at Abana as meaning is given to experience through the Christian faith and those who have been 'healed' are then instructed to reach out to others in similar circumstances. This reflects Seale's conception of 'resurrective narrative' as a means by which individuals make meaning within their daily lives and strengthen their membership of a particular community at times when social bonds are or have been under threat of destruction. The testimonies from Abana youth illustrate this process at work. By including their personal narratives within the 'grand cultural script' of salvation, many young people have found a sense of meaning and purpose in their lives through membership of a Christian community. Many participants felt that giving testimony during worship enabled them to feel less alone, to talk about what they had been through and have hope for the future: 'My future becomes very nice because I hope in my God because I can't find anything without God. It is God who gives me all the things I want and is my safeguard. Therefore I hope and believe' (female, focus group discussion, 2007). As demonstrated by research from other conflict/post-conflict situations, religiously derived meaning can strengthen the ability of young people to make sense of their worlds and cope with hardship.[47]

Conversely, other participants questioned the emphasis on counselling, stressed the need for words to be accompanied by actions and the difficulty of giving testimony. Some young people frame their narratives according to Abana's message of survival for a purpose, but those who do not are reinterpreted: 'It was not another orphan who directed you to Abana but God' (worship leader, 2007). Arguably therefore meaning is imposed and agency undermined, both in terms of meaning-making and in living, as everything in life is down to the will of God. This has the potential to encourage passivity: 'I want to learn to drive and become a taxi driver but God has the last say' (male, interview, 2007).

In synthesising a trauma model with Christian teaching, is Abana developing an approach more applicable to the Rwandan context, given the religiosity of Rwandan society? On the one hand, similar criticisms can be raised as those directed against the trauma mode, namely the professionalisation of everyday experience and the question of who has the authority to give meaning to experience, albeit here individual experience is being reinterpreted according to

---

47 M. Wessells and A. Strang, 'Religion as resource and risk. The double-edged sword for children in situations of armed conflict', in Boothby et al., *supra* note 20, at 208.

a soteriological as opposed to a psychological discourse. On the other hand, does this matter when the vast majority of Abana youth find this approach helpful and do not offer these objections? As an outsider raising these objections am I doing the very thing I am criticising, imposing my interpretation of the situation? However, it should be borne in mind that in a large way this approach is self-selecting as youth who do not find it helpful might not stay and there may be others who feel obliged to stay in the hope of material assistance for their families.

Moreover, what can and should be questioned are the longer-term consequences, not just individually in terms of retraumatisation but collectively in terms of the foundation on which these communities are being built. Manifestly this basis is an evangelical interpretation of the Christian faith and doctrine, but the language and teaching being used essentialises the difference between 'God with us' and the 'Devil with them'. The implied message is that one should stay away from others not like oneself as 'the Devil is still around' and 'has many swords… to hurt us' (worship leader, 2007). On the one hand it could be argued that the projection of blame for the genocide onto the Devil could facilitate reconciliation by placing blame or responsibility on an exterior force, but on the other it is inferred in the teachings that individuals succumbed to the Devil and continue to do so. Thus the militant language used can be seen as reinforcing divisions within society, isolating Abana communities from the world around and as with a biomedical trauma model, failing to deal with the root causes of conflict.[48]

The rights-based programmes of CARE and SC deal with the legacies of the genocide, but do not directly address meaning-making. NIPS has a counselling component, but the emphasis is placed on increasing the economic productivity of participants to contribute 'positively to peace and reconciliation for the future of their country'. In approaching trauma as being located in the present, CARE reflects the majority of children and young people's priorities and the importance of 'concrete' reconciliatory activities.[49] In the case of SC, the child rights toolkit does not include any discussion of the genocide. Yet in a context where the teaching of history is prohibited the task of addressing the past, albeit indirectly, has fallen to human rights education, which has come to the fore with a multiplicity of training materials and children's rights forums and clubs aimed at sensitising the population. The problems associated with sensitisation activities have already been touched upon, in placing an emphasis on a knowledge rather than a resource gap. In addition, sensitisation programmes have the tendency to propose a predetermined solution, thus operating as a reframing process, not unlike the language and processes of trauma healing and testimony just

48 Wessells and Strang, ibid. 217.

49 Wessells and Jonah, *supra* note 36, at 40–41.

critiqued. Sarah White[50] in Bangladesh and Susan Shepler[51] in Sierra Leone observe this phenomenon where sensitisation is 'proposed as the solution to almost every problem in society'. The decontextualisation of human rights education from the surroundings in which it is operating, especially in terms of history, the socio-cultural environment and an engagement with politics and issues of power, obscures rather than illuminates the root causes of rights violations.

However, it is argued here that it is not rights language per se that is problematic but rather that a greater understanding is needed of how rights language is being operationalised and the purposes to which it is being put, in particular its engagement with power and the interaction between local, national and international levels. Within my focus group sessions children did not use the language of participation directly, in terms of wanting 'to participate'. Instead, emerging from the discussions were two distinct forms of participatory practice. The first I have called 'performed participation'.[52] This is drawn from children's portrayal of participation as an activity extraordinary to their daily lives, often taking the form of consultation and involving the language of listening and being heard: '[t]here were workers who came and asked us if we had mosquito nets, if we had a radio, if we ate meat…' (female, focus group, 2006). The majority of young people were in agreement that this was a one-off event, rarely followed up: 'they come, talk with us, leave, then we never hear from them again' (female, focus group 2006). This lack of follow-up, or being really heard, has promoted a level of scepticism amongst the young about the motives of those using the language of rights and participation. 'Are the UN people here to help or for business?', asked one focus group participant (male, 2006). It also ignores many children's desire to have a greater say in the running of programmes and to build collaborative relationships with NGOs. 'People should come to ask for our opinions. NGOs which assist children can come to consult us, we are ready to give our contribution of ideas', stated one girl (2006), a sentiment echoed across the focus groups. This demonstrates that the use of rights discourses is not enough to bring changes and unless it is accompanied by action then it is liable to fall victim to disillusionment as it is disconnected from the daily realities faced by children and young people. Likewise, amongst Ugandan children Cheney observed 'deep personal commitments to national development but also the paradox of powerlessness that many children experience on a daily basis'.[53]

---

50 White, *supra* note 32, at 510.

51 Shepler, *supra* note 32, 197–211.

52 K. Pells, '"No one ever listens to us": challenging obstacles to the participation of children and young people in Rwanda', in B. Percy-Smith and N. Thomas (eds.), *A handbook of children's participation: perspectives from theory and practice*. Routledge, London, 2009, 196–203.

53 Cheney, *supra* note 32, at 3.

A similar picture emerges in Rwanda with rural children especially feeling left behind in the process of development: 'we can't enter Vision 2020 because of the life we are living today' (male, focus group, 2007).[54]

Throughout this section the importance to children and young people of creating a sense of meaning and purpose in life has been reiterated. The case studies demonstrate that this can be achieved through a range of means, from counselling and religion, to securing livelihoods and rights. Despite the different conceptual foundations between the programmes, it has been suggested that the ways in which these are operationalised are similar, aiming to fit personal narratives and experiences within wider narratives of salvation or rights as the solution to all ills. In the case of rights, the discrepancy between its rhetorical usage and local lived realities may account for the disillusionment expressed. This does not mean that rights are not meaningful concepts for children and young people, as evidence from the Children's Forums, for example, illustrates children employing rights language to further their claims. Instead, disillusionment occurs within the operationalisation phase, either through a narrow interpretation of what constitutes children's rights programming (often focusing on sensitisation, for example) or unrealistic claims of what rights are able to achieve. In so doing there is a danger that organisations risk undermining the very principles of human rights which they are promoting. This results in 'performed participation' which fails to take account of the socio-cultural and politico-economic context in which these organisations are intervening. In order to prevent decontextualisation and disillusionment therefore, organisations need to be less focused on rights evangelisation and better educated themselves on how these principles play out in practice, and give greater consideration to the scope given to children and young people for influencing these processes, matters to which we now turn.

4.4. THE POLITICAL SPHERE: "PERFORMED" OR "LIVED" PARTICIPATION

Within discussions of everyday life, for children and young people participation was defined in terms of decision-making and control (or the lack thereof) over their daily lives. In response, this section explores two key areas. Firstly, how much scope for participation is contained within the case study programme activities and how transferable are the actions and skills learnt into the daily lives

[54] Vision 2020 is a strategy of the Rwandan government which sets out the key priorities and indicators for the development of the country, to be achieved by 2020 (MINECOFIN, 2000); *Rwanda vision 2020*, Kigali, at www.enterprise-development.org/download.aspx?id=548 (accessed 23/01/09).

of participants? Secondly, the location in which the participatory activities/ programmes are occurring is considered. In contrast to the 'performed participation' discussed in the previous section, the need for 'lived participation', rooted in the structures and activities of daily life is advocated as enhancing accountability.

Beginning with participation and transferable skills, who are the participants and what form participation takes need to be taken into account. Each case study has a target group, determined at the outset. Abana works with children and youth orphaned by the genocide and members are also those willing to testify to the Christian mission of the organisation in front of the Abana community. CARE and SC set the parameters of the target group (child/youth-headed households in the case of the former, specific administrative sectors in the case of the latter) but allow scope for peer and community identification or election of specific participants. This raises a number of issues with the selection processes.

With the exception of SC, the organisations intervened with specific 'categories' of children. The National Policy for Orphans and Vulnerable Children (OVC) provides the policy backdrop to this approach. Despite stressing the 'multiple causes and effects of vulnerability' and its cross-cutting nature, the Policy sets out fifteen categories of 'vulnerable children'.[55] However, as argued by children both within and outside NGO programmes these categories are not monolithic, mutually exclusive or hierarchical, i.e. the assumption that orphans will be living in the most vulnerable circumstances. For example, NIPS focus group participants stressed that inclusion in the programme should not be restricted to child-headed households or even orphans and they felt that the age criterion of 21 was too restrictive. While research participants recognised the vulnerability of orphans' circumstances, they emphasised the equivalent vulnerability of other youth in the community, highlighting in particular children who are disabled, residing with HIV-positive parents or living in extreme poverty even if both parents are alive.

In addition, labelling can lead to stigmatisation, especially where a child has been orphaned due to HIV/AIDS. As observed elsewhere, within Rwanda 'OVCs' has become a shorthand for referring to those children living in vulnerable circumstances.[56] By referring to children as 'vulnerable', it reinforces the notion of victimhood and locates the source of the vulnerability within the child rather than the environment, suggesting that the child rather than the environment

---

55 Minaloc (2004), *National policy for orphans and vulnerable children*, at www.youthpolicy.com/Policies/Rwanda_National_Policy_for_OVCY.cfm (accessed 21/06/06).

56 Unaids, Unicef and Usaid, *supra* note 37, at 8.

should be the object of transformation, and so failing to address the root causes of poverty.

Furthermore, by introducing categorisation into an already divided society there is the danger of creating new forms of segregation. Whereas poverty is a common denominator, intervening with one category, such as genocide orphans, exacerbates tensions and undermines the daily realities experienced by many youth: 'we are all orphans together and face the same problems' (female, focus group discussion, 2006). Other children referred to themselves as being in 'the wrong group' for receiving support. This reflects White and Choudhury's observations in Bangladesh on how children involved in NGO programmes could become exclusionary towards others and seen as the responsibility of the intervening agency.[57] The social section above discussed how the potential for such phenomena occurring can be reduced if the entire community is involved and seen to benefit, as is largely the case with the NIPS programme. Moreover, it underscores the importance of transparency in the selection process.

Inclusion in a programme does not equate to participation, not just in terms of whether a participatory approach to programming is used, but also whether there are hidden barriers both within the programme and in daily life that prevent meaningful engagement. This may impact disproportionately on some children as opposed to others. Within NIPS, those responsible for caring for siblings could not always partake in the livelihood skills training, for example. A rights-based analysis should take account of these factors also. Likewise, the Children's Forums are not truly representative of all children living in the community as their members are all in school. It is recognised that children who are responsible for households or engaged in labour have less time to join meetings and that the Forums appear to be doing a good job in seeking out vulnerable children in the communities, soliciting their ideas, recording their needs and informing them of their rights. However, it would increase the representative nature of the Forums if more out-of-school youth were actually members. It would build the capacity of these children to advocate directly for their rights rather than through others, and so build the skills and capacities of these youth.

This raises the questions of what constitutes 'participation'. What are the participation activities within the programme? Do they act as an end in themselves or are they part of the overall programming process? Within Abana, children 'participate' in the activities of the community but are not involved in

---

57 S.C. White and S.A. Choudhury, 'The politics of child participation in international development: the dilemma of agency', (2007) 19 4, *The European Journal of Development Research*, at 542.

decision-making regarding the organisation. Both CARE and SC state that participation is at the core of their work with children, who are involved in the direction and development of the programme. Participation is argued to have been mainstreamed throughout operations, although in reality this has only occurred from the implementation phase.

NIPS participants contribute to the programme's direction through sharing their concerns and priorities with CARE staff and Nkundabana and by attending Advisory Committee meetings. Embedded within the programme is a participatory monitoring tool where activities are held every four months to evaluate the existing project and propose future directions. CARE then responds to the children on how their opinions and suggestions have been taken into account. Children are also able to raise their own self-identified issues. However, involving participants further in decision-making and the design of programme activities could alleviate current frustrations regarding unmet expectations. The majority of youth reported that they wished their Nkundabana listened more to their ideas, suggesting that more opportunities for youth engagement are needed. As noted above, participants were only involved from the implementation stage, which may account for the lack of clarity among youth concerning the programme's aim, objectives and resources available, creating misconceptions and unrealistic expectations. Likewise, participants do not always understand why resources are at times allocated to some and not others. Instead, determining programme priorities with youth and being open about programme and resource limitations would promote more realistic expectations and improve satisfaction. This suggests also that youth need more opportunities to voice their ideas and concerns than are currently available in order that NIPS becomes more responsive to the needs and capacities of participants.

Local ownership also stems from creating channels of accountability at the community level whereby children are central actors in their own development. In this area SC has been very successful. Through the advocacy efforts of the Children's Forums, members have secured basic material assistance, such as school materials for the poorest children in their communities, access to essential services and notably the reintegration of out-of-school youth. This enables children to illustrate to local authorities in a practical way their capacity to engage on local issues, which is an effective way of convincing local authorities to open up space for children's participation in decision-making processes. This is demonstrated by the process whereby at each administrative level the authorities are consulting children on who are those living in the most vulnerable circumstances in the community, what their needs are and what support the forums need in facilitating the rights realisation of these children. These suggestions have been encompassed in sector and district development plans and in an increased budget for these purposes. These findings confirm the importance of collaboration between children, communities and organisations working for child protection and government structures at each administrative level, which is increasingly documented as best practice.[58]

Greater support therefore needs to be given to the work of participants in devising and implementing strategies and in particular in dealing with the resistance that they have often encountered. This is also an ethical consideration. It is not always advisable for children to secure the protection and fulfilment of rights on their own. This highlights the second key area: where is participation occurring? Whilst there is an ever-burgeoning literature on the merits of participation,[59] this has focused more on the 'whos' and 'hows' of participation rather than the 'wheres'. The importance of the spatial dimension of power and participation is advocated by Kesby who, drawing upon Foucault's conception of power, argues that for empowerment and participation 'the discourses and practices that constitute its effects will be embedded in and constitutive of, particular material sites and spaces' which 'must be repetitively performed in order to stabilise these effects'.[60] He notes that whilst forums, for example, provide a space for reflection on the everyday, enabling participants to discuss controversial issues and 'rehearse performances for alternative realities', at the same time they are 'shaped by their imminent return to the power soaked public and domestic spaces of the everyday.'[61]There is a danger of participatory discourses ending up being a 'performance', as critiqued in the previous section. 'Performed participation' is not totally without value, as it provides a platform for children's ideas and opinions and can be a tool for exploring issues, but the level of sustainability and long-term change achieved by this type of participation can be questioned. In a performance the audience does not have to respond or follow up on what has been witnessed. 'Performed participation' is thus largely tokenistic and replicates the disempowerment and power imbalances experienced by children in daily life, resulting in the disillusionment with rights and participation seen in the last section.

In order to transform everyday life, participation and empowerment must be embedded here. In contrast with 'performed participation' I propose 'lived participation', which is conceptualised as a means of accessing other rights, as

58 UNAIDS, UNICEF and USAID, *supra* note 37, at 39; FOSTER et al., *supra* note 34, 401–402.

59 UNAIDS et al., ibid.; G. LANSDOWN, *Promoting children's participation in democratic decision-making*, UNICEF Innocenti Insight, Florence, 2001, at www.iicrd.org/cap/files/insight6_0.pdf (accessed 09/06/06).

60 M. KESBY, Re-theorising empowerment-through-participation as a performance in space: beyond tyranny to transformation, (2005) 30 4 *Signs: Journal of Women in Culture and Society*, 2037–2065.

61 Ibid.

part of an ongoing series of supportive relationships, implemented through the structures and activities of daily life, in the context of enabling those who have been marginalised to achieve an oft-repeated desire of becoming 'like the other children'. Participation is thus rooted in everyday life, such as the regular meetings between local authorities and children participating in NIPS and the Forums, rather than being one-off events that are not followed up.

In conclusion, discussing meaningful participation brings together all four spheres of the everyday. Participation covers a multitude of practices and so must not be supported uncritically, which in so doing often results in it becoming a substitute for action. For young people meaningful participation is that which restores or gives new agency previously inhibited by conflict and its aftermath, which manifests as control and direction over their lives that strengthens resiliency and so generates 'hope for the future'. Children desire greater scope for participation within their daily lives. Participation is viewed as a tool for accessing other rights and not an end in itself. The most successful context for this to occur is in building protective and reciprocal relationships in the community through 'lived participation'. Participatory practice cannot be imposed from the top downwards, or else is met with resistance from the community. Nor is successful programming focused on children in isolation but in their everyday environments and relationships. Moreover, NGOs need to make further efforts to internalise participatory practice, including considering hidden barriers to participation, as well as externally within their own operations to involve communities in decisions over resources and programme direction. This requires a series of shifts in current programming, away from interventions based on 'categories' and participatory activities and towards locally derived understandings of the intersecting barriers to engaging in participatory processes in the everyday and exploring the spatial dimension to rights and participation.

5. CONCLUSION: REHUMANISING RIGHTS

The title of this chapter, "we have life without living", is taken from a Rwandan young person's description of their daily life. Through focus group discussions of daily life emerged the priorities of relationships, education and livelihoods, meaning-making and belonging, control and direction over one's life. Each of these areas is a struggle; however, contrary to the trauma paradigm these children and young people are not passive but actively finding ways to address the problems faced. Instead, the paradigm of the everyday redirects attention to events in the present and the future, which are often as difficult and challenging as those in the past. Moreover, the everyday, with its social, economic, cultural and political spheres of daily life, facilitates a holistic and contextually grounded analysis of the situations of children and young people in post-conflict environments. In questioning how best to engage practically with this paradigm to facilitate the transformation of lives, relationships and environments in the aftermath of conflict, the three case studies explored offer important lessons learnt.

Firstly, rights-based approaches can engage with everyday realities experienced by children and young people, but for participants a meaningful engagement is not exclusive to rights-based approaches and particularly in the areas of building relationships, processes of meaning-making and ensuring 'lived participation' there are lessons to be learnt. Moreover, just because an approach is labelled as 'rights-based' does not mean that it will engage meaningfully with the everyday. In part this is due to the broad number of positions encompassed within rights-based programming, but also to the frequently wide discrepancy between theory and practice. An additional problem faced with rights-based approaches where the rights-holders (children) call the duty-bearers (adults) to account is that in this environment it is not always readily apparent who are the duty-bearers. This highlights the danger within children's rights programming of focusing on children in isolation when in fact children are embedded in a web of social relations and their socio-economic circumstances are tied up with those of other community members.[62] This suggests that rights-based approaches need to be more cognisant not only of the indivisibility of rights but also of the interdependence of rights claims between children and adults in order to deal with the root causes of violations.

Secondly, there is a danger that in applying a rights-holder and duty-bearer analysis, with its emphasis upon equality, accountability and transparency, the more 'human' dimensions to the relationship, such as love, affection and care, may be overlooked. This is an issue prioritised by children, who often cite the 'right to love' (technically not within the CRC), but one often neglected in bigger NGO programmes (with the exception of the mentoring side to NIPS through which CARE is building upon the emphasis within psychosocial programming on close, supportive relationships). In comparison, these 'human' aspects are given greater scope within the non-rights-based programme of Abana. Here, therefore, rights-based approaches have something to learn from other methods of engaging with the everyday through 'rehumanising' rights in terms of

62 E. Burman, *Developments: child, image, nation,* Routledge, Hove/New York, 2008, at 1; J. Hart, 'Children's participation and international development: attending to the political', (2008) 16 3 *International Journal of Children's Rights,* 410–411; S. Moses, 'Children and participation in South Africa: an overview', (2008) 16 2 *International Journal of Children's Rights,* 330–331.

everyday social relationships, creating greater relevance to the lives of children and young people.

The focus upon relationship building and the breaking of exploitative relations is one, if not the principal, success of Abana and CARE's programmes in the eyes of participants and matches children and young peoples' prioritisation of relationships within daily life. Whilst this demonstrates that the success of relationship building is not linked solely to rights-based approaches, from the case studies it is apparent that a rights-based approach can bring value in introducing an outward rather than inward gaze, towards involving a wider section of the community. CARE involves the wider community in the programming process, unlike Abana, which establishes separate communities and thus potentially reinforces existing social divisions.

Thirdly, it is important not to go to the other extreme and focus on social relationships to the neglect of resources and livelihoods. All the case studies demonstrate the intertwined nature of resources and relationships. Children and young people who were not in receipt of material assistance within certain Abana communities were far less optimistic than their peers in communities where this was provided. Equally, lack of material resources prevented participation by the poorest children in the Children's Forums. This highlights the need for a greater linkage to be made between rights as relationships and access to resources through using rights to generate structural reform. In the case of NIPS, participants were able to access resources through their relationships with the Nkundabana.

However, resources are not just a constructive factor in relationship building but can be detrimental in terms of creating new sources of tension within the community. NIPS participants reported jealousy from the wider community, which destroyed existing relationships or served to prevent new ones being forged. This tension can also occur within a programme, as illustrated by Abana and CARE, where some participants receive materials and others do not. This necessitates greater attention to rights as process: who decides who receives what, when and how? As suggested by NIPS, when a right-based approach is employed and communities are involved in this decision-making process then tensions are reduced and greater sustainability and local ownership generated.

This stems in part from the fourth lesson learnt, namely the significance of the centrality of accountability and transparency to rights-based approaches. Accountability is another area in which rights-based approaches are argued to make a significant contribution.[63] SC is the most typical of a rights-based approach in this sense in focusing upon the facilitation of processes where children and community members can call the local authorities to account for fulfilling children's rights. Likewise, through the local advisory committees NIPS participants interact with the local authorities. However, NIPS has two innovative accountability components: the contractual nature of the relationship between Nkundabana and participants and the participatory monitoring tool which creates a direct channel of communication between CARE staff and participants.

This suggests that the level of accountability is in part dependent upon the mainstreaming of participatory practices throughout the programme. Whilst rights-based approaches do have the potential to build on children's capacity for problem solving and process of world building, such as the income-generating activities of the Children's Forums, conversely in both programmes 'participation' was only introduced at the implementation stage, limiting the scope for participants to control the direction of the programme. Thus while the levels of responsiveness to participants and of participation are higher in programmes using rights-based language, there still remains a large gap between the rhetoric around accountability and participation and the reality, which creates cynicism and disillusionment.

In conclusion therefore, rights can and do engage with the everyday but need to become more effective in order to retain their relevance and deal with specific situations which arise in the aftermath of conflict. This requires a more expansive understanding of rights, not necessarily in terms of content but rather in operationalisation, in building relationships and in the processes underpinning programming, with particular attention to 'lived' as opposed to 'performed' participation. Rights cannot capture all that children and young people need, such as love, affection and a sense of meaning. Here, rights-based approaches can be 'rehumanised' by drawing on these strengths in other programming approaches. This is essential in order to respond better to the everyday priorities of children and young people affected by conflict, so transforming these 'lives without living'.

---

[63] P. Gready, 'Rights-based approaches to development: what is the value-added?', (2008) 18 6 *Development in Practice*, 741–742.

REHABILITATING SEPARATED CHILDREN THROUGH HOLISTIC, COMMUNITY-BASED MODELS

Jessica Muir and Elhum Shakerifar

1. INTRODUCTION

Since the year 2000 more than 15,000 separated children[1] have entered the UK seeking asylum.[2] Many of these children and young people have fled war, enduring traumatic events and losses. Once in the UK, they face secondary stresses such as navigating welfare and legal systems that are often incoherent, inconsistent and unsettling. As a result, the already complex process of rehabilitation in exile is made even more difficult.

In response to the issues that young separated refugees[3] face, Dost, meaning *friend*, was set up nine years ago. Dost is based within the communal space of the Trinity Centre, a community centre and independent charity in East London; it is used by individuals of all ages and backgrounds for education, recreational purposes and support services. Within this community setting Dost aims to provide psychosocial assistance to vulnerable children, including young refugees separated from their families and fleeing violent conflict. A holistic approach is necessary as the needs of separated children, like those of all children, are multiple and interdependent. To this end, Dost provides education, play and youth work, and advice and advocacy (casework).

1 'Unaccompanied children' are children under 18 years of age who 'are separated from both parents and are not being cared for by an adult who, by law or custom has responsibility to do so' (UNHCR, 1994). However, recent trends have highlighted that not all children are unaccompanied as defined above and that children living with extended family members or other adults may face similar risks to those encountered by unaccompanied children. Subsequently, UNHCR encourages the usage of the term 'separated children' to draw attention to the potential protection needs of this group (UNHCR, 2001, 2004).

2 National Register for Unaccompanied Children, www.nruc.gov.uk.

3 In this paper we use 'separated children' and 'young separated refugees' interchangeably to refer to children seeking asylum as well as those that have been granted limited leave to remain under the UN Convention Relating to the Status of Refugees (1951) and/or The Human Rights Act (1988).

The first section of this paper will investigate in depth how Dost's flexible casework model therapeutically benefits young separated refugees who are new to the UK. A central aim is to elucidate the subtle multiplicity of factors needed to aid the psychological recovery and social rehabilitation of war-affected children. The paper will go on to explore how the wider framework of Dost and the Trinity Centre strengthens the casework model's ability to provide psychosocial support. Dost's other integral services of education and play offer young separated refugees the opportunity to access community and natural healing processes. Moreover, the relationship that children and young people are able to build within the Trinity Centre's space, as well as the intergenerational interaction that can take place within the community context, is fundamental to social rehabilitation processes.

This paper makes use of anecdotal evidence accrued over the past three years working with war-affected children separated from their families. Quotes from young people are from semi-structured interviews conducted for the purposes of an ongoing piece of research relating to belonging and community. In order to protect the identities of children and young people referred to in this paper, all names and identifying elements have been changed.

2. DOST'S CASEWORK MODEL

> *'The chance events that cleave us together or apart, what a complex trace they leave: so personal as to be almost incommunicable, so fugitive as to be almost irrecoverable. Yet seeing through a glass, however darkly, is to be less blind.'*
>
> Vikram Seth, *Two Lives*, 2005

2.1. THE PRESENT: DEALING WITH SECONDARY STRESSES FIRST

War-affected children that come to the UK seeking refuge are considered bureaucratically as asylum-seeking or refugee children. As children, their need for protection is acknowledged according to the 1989 United Nations Convention on the Rights of the Child (UNCRC), which was ratified in part by the UK in 1991 and fully in September 2008 (before which time separated children were considered as asylum seekers first, children second). The UNCRC also informs the Children's Act of 2004, the UK's legislation regarding the care and protection of children in the UK. Most war-affected children that Dost works with are separated children subject to immigration control. This term 'separated children' recognises 'that children separated from their parents suffer physically, socially and psychologically as a result of being deprived of the care and protection of parents or other primary carer(s)'.[4] These children and young people are entitled to support from local authority social services departments under the provisions of the Children's Act of 1989. As such, separated children are supplied with a package of state care, including housing (ranging from foster care for under 16s to semi-independent accommodation for over 16s), medical help, a social worker and a weekly stipend.

Dost's casework model provides advice and advocacy to young separated refugees on any of the problems that they may be facing. Generally, young refugees need support with the asylum process, with accessing appropriate welfare services and with assuring their mental wellbeing. Dost's caseworkers are trained to hold in mind the broad range of young separated refugees' experiences, to look beyond labels and problems and see young people with individual histories and layers of experience. Furthermore, the support that the Dost casework model offers is long term and consistent so that the young refugees accessing it have a steady and reliable point of contact.

All young separated refugees accessing Dost's casework model have experienced traumatic events and losses. Traumatic experiences can be defined in many ways but are broadly acknowledged to have an 'essentially overwhelming impact on the mind, emotions and soul, after which the sufferer often feels that he or she will never be the same again'.[5] Yet, when beginning casework with young separated refugees, we find that the 'emotional wounds' created by trauma are rarely the focus of initial work.[6] Instead, for practical and therapeutic reasons the focus remains strongly on the present and the problems it presents. Indeed, the stresses that separated children encounter in exile are numerous. Separated from their family and the social fabric that grounded and guided them, they must learn to cope with complex feelings of isolation as they adjust to a completely new environment alone. In addition to this, many young people find that their most basic needs are unmet: they often do not have adequate legal representation, safe appropriate housing, regular contact with their social worker, sufficient funds for food and travel or their legal entitlement to aftercare services. It is therefore understandable that their primary focus is gaining the practical help that they require to begin resettling.

---

4 H. Crawley, G. Bruce, J. Coker, N. Finch, S. Rowlands, S. Shutter and A. Stanley, *Working with children and young people subject to immigration control. Guidelines for best practice*, Immigration Law Practitioners Association, London, 2004, at 5.

5 M. Lanyado, 'The treatment of traumatisation in children', in A. Horne and M. Lanyado (eds.), *Child and adolescent psychotherapy: psychoanalytic approaches,* Routledge, Cornwall, 2008, 275–91.

6 Ibid.

Dost caseworkers aim to help young people with these problems through advice and advocacy work. This can be seen in the case of sixteen-year-old Abdul from Somalia. Abdul was referred to Dost by a therapist from a local Child and Adolescent Mental Health Service. He explained that Abdul needed practical assistance with a number of issues and had therefore been unable to engage in the therapeutic process. It became clear to the caseworker when she began work with Abdul that he had fallen through a number of gaps in his statutory care package. Firstly, despite being a young separated refugee he was living alone in noisy bed and breakfast accommodation that had inadequate cooking facilities and a lack of privacy. As a result, he was eating cheap take-away food every day. Abdul was also being looked after under Section 17 of the Children Act 1989, which meant that he was not entitled to his rights, such as aftercare services, a named social worker or funds for everyday education and travel costs. Furthermore, he did not have a solicitor to present his asylum case to the UK immigration department (the Home Office).

Abdul's caseworker tackled these problems with him step by step over a period of three months. Firstly, she advocated on his behalf for appropriate accommodation and a move from Section 17 of the Children Act to Section 20, which would legally ensure that his rights were being met. When this advocacy work was ignored she referred him to a specialist community care solicitor, who used legal channels to ensure that Abdul received new accommodation and a fuller package of care under Section 20 of the Children Act 1989. Abdul's caseworker also referred him to an immigration solicitor at a firm with an excellent reputation. Throughout this work she kept in regular contact with Abdul and accompanied him to appointments.

The psychological benefits of such practical help at this stage are multifaceted. Many studies show that 'secondary stresses, which occur in exile, can have as much of an impact, if not more, than the original traumatic events in the refugee's country of origin'.[7] Therefore assisting young separated refugees with some of the problems that they are facing during resettlement can help to reduce the risk of damaging psychological effects caused by trauma being worsened rather than healed. Furthermore, casework has the ability to activate war-affected children and young people's inner resilience, which can aid the process of psychological recovery. Advocacy work gives young refugees choices and shows what actions can be taken to break the existential barriers that prevent their most tangible needs being met. As Melzak notes, 'after prolonged periods of helplessness and powerlessness, being enabled to make real choices that affect

[7] M. Stedman, *Social and political considerations in working with refugees*, Medical Foundation for the care of victims of torture, 1999, at 5, see at www.torturecare.org.uk/resources/publications/2146.

the present and future' can foster resilience.[8] When one casework client was asked in a Social Service meeting what his caseworker did for him, he replied: 'She gives me courage – makes me brave'.

Another important therapeutic element that casework can potentially promote is an increased sense of security through a reliable relationship. According to Bowlby, secure attachments remain crucial for mental well-being throughout our lives.[9] Separated children have had their lives shattered in myriad ways due to conflict and can suffer further instability during so-called periods of resettlement. For example, one Iraqi client named Hamid had been kidnapped, witnessed the execution of colleagues and found his father's mutilated dead body lying outside his home. He then had to flee to the UK without his family. Once in the UK, Hamid's life felt fragmented for various reasons. He was relocated to an area miles from his Social Services borough and found it difficult to contact his social worker when facing problems; moreover, most of the time he did not know who his social worker was because she/he changed so frequently. He also felt as though he was living in a legally induced state of limbo because he had not received a decision from the Home Office on his asylum case. However, the fact that Hamid had one caseworker with whom he could easily meet on a regular basis to address all the issues that he was facing fostered a layer of continuity and attachment in what was an otherwise uncertain context.

Indeed, the relationship a young separated refugee builds with their caseworker can also give them a sense of mental containment that aids psychological recovery. William Bion developed Melanie Klein's theory that people communicate on an unconscious level and project emotions that make them uncomfortable, which are then felt by the one onto which those feelings were projected.[10] Thus, by listening closely and acknowledging the anxieties that the young person is experiencing, caseworkers can facilitate this process of containment. For instance, during meetings with young people it is often noticeable from observing their initially tense then gradually relaxing body language how discussing the secondary stresses that they are facing can calm them. Caseworkers usually find that during this initial period of work, when young people are discussing their anxieties, they prefer to keep the past and the traumatic events that occurred firmly out of focus. Instead, discussions of pain usually centre on the physical anxiety caused by practical problems or psychosomatic complaints such as chest pains and non-specific body pain. Young people may even appear to be in a numb dissociative state, as 'the repertoire of

---

8 S. Melzak, 'Psychotherapeutic work with child and adolescent refugees from political violence', in *supra* note 5.

9 J. Bowlby, *A secure base*, Routledge, London, 2008, 137–138.

10 M. Waddell, *Inside lives, psychoanalysis and the growth of the personality*, Karnac, London, 2002, at 30.

their feeling, perceiving and functioning becomes restricted' or partly 'frozen'.[11] However, this can be an important stage in the process of self-healing for war-affected children and young people as 'temporary withdrawal can provide unique vantage points from where to review and reassess their lives, their present and future; it may also assist them by allowing them to digest the impact of their losses, by creating a respectful stance to mourn the dead, by enabling them to regroup and redirect their energy more appropriately'.[12] Caseworkers at Dost have learnt from experience that at this stage young people are usually not ready to discuss their mental health or mental health treatment. What appears to be more important is having someone to assist them with their practical problems, a dependable person who acknowledges their resilience and is willing to help hold their anxiety. This can give war-affected children and young people the mental space they need to begin self-healing.

2.2. THE PAST: BUILDING STORIES ON SECURE FOUNDATIONS

The foundations that have been built during the initial stages of casework often become a base for further work that focuses more on internal and past worlds. As this section will explore, such work can play an important part in the psychological recovery of young separated refugees. A key component to this work is the fact that young people have had time to withdraw mentally and quietly 're-story and restore themselves' without premature therapeutic intervention.[13] Trust is another essential component to this work and grows when young people can see that their caseworker is reliable and understanding of their problems and anxieties.

In time, young people often share stories with their caseworker about their lives before departure. They feel enabled to move beyond the 'thin narratives of victimhood' and restricted, linear explanations of why they sought asylum that starting life in the UK forces them to repeat.[14] Instead, on the way to appointments or during meetings with their caseworker young people may mention their families, their favourite foods, music they like, landscapes they miss. Stories appear naturally and subtly; when one young person discovered his caseworker was from Scotland he keenly told her about the beautiful mountains

---

11 R.K. Papadopoulos, 'Refugees, home and trauma', in Papadopoulos (ed.), *Therapeutic care for refugees*, Karnac, London, 2005, at 32.

12 Ibid., at 33.

13 Ibid., at 34.

14 R. Kohli, 'The sound of silence: listening to what unaccompanied children say and do not say', (2006) 36 5 *British Journal of Social Work*, at 6, http://bjsw.oxford journals.org/cgi/content/full/36/5/707?login_referer=http%3a%2F.

in his own home country and how he walked and climbed them regularly. These 'thicker' stories are important to the process of psychological recovery because they can help separated children reconstruct positive aspects of their lives and home countries.[15] For example, in one meeting an Iraqi young person, who usually appears very serious, laughingly recounted how at school he had been 'a joker' and regularly played practical jokes on his teachers and classmates. This illustrates how sharing these stories can also be an opportunity for young people to feel more 'whole' to someone and present different sides of their personalities that have been subjugated in exile.

However, it is not just positive stories of the past that appear but also stories of traumatic events and mental pain. The components of trust and time often encourage young people to widen the explanatory narratives around their feelings of anxiety and psychosomatic complaints, so that past and inner factors emerge. For example, one young person from Afghanistan who regularly complained to his caseworker of not being able to sleep at night gradually began to connect his sleeplessness with deep-rooted feelings of anxiety that he had felt in Afghanistan. He discussed with his caseworker how more and more young boys had been 'disappearing' from his village and it was not safe for anyone to venture out the house on their own, so much so that eventually he could not even go to school. This anxiety and fear had been compounded by his father's disappearance, his dangerous journey to the UK as well as feelings of isolation in his new school. These conversations helped him to connect the past with the present and enabled him to see that his chronic sleeplessness was not extraordinary, but an ordinary reaction to extraordinary circumstances.

Moreover, discussions of trauma between young separated refugees and their caseworkers can provide another layer of mental containment, as the conversations and silences they share help to hold and process feelings of sadness. This is particularly pertinent once significant pieces of casework have been resolved or decisions on their immigration status have been made, for it is often at this point that many young refugees appear to be left with a mental space into which grief is poured as present worries are reduced. One Iraqi young person, who had visited his local doctor on a number of occasions because he was convinced there was something physically wrong with him, began to explain that he could not concentrate in college and that his chest hurt because he could not stop thinking about his sister and mother in Iraq. He went on to say that he remembered things – his friend, a good boy who had been killed, a neighbour who had been killed – and then began to cry, eventually laying his head on the table and sobbing. The caseworker listened and her ability to witness rather than avoid his grief, in this and future discussions, provided essential therapeutic

---

15 Ibid.

support. As Melzak notes, a key factor in the psychological recovery of war-affected children is 'being enabled to reflect on one's experiences, past and present, both the "difficult to understand" and the truly overwhelming experiences'.[16]

It is important to note that at this stage caseworkers, where appropriate, make referrals on young people's behalf so that they can receive more specialist therapeutic support. The overwhelming inner pain that some young people feel can result in self-harming, substance abuse or even suicidal thoughts. In cases like this, external help from mental health professionals is often required and caseworkers make referrals for help immediately. Such cases clearly illustrate how war-affected children and young people psychologically benefit from having a reliable figure in their life with whom they can share their stories of pain and who can explain what support is available to them and how to access it. Isolated young refugees are at risk of suffering alone with no knowledge of or access to the support that is available to them. Many young people do not have the inner resources that they need to face the emotional impact of trauma without professional help. This could be because of a history of psychological vulnerability due to other traumatic experiences, the sheer scale of their trauma or unsupportive past relationships.[17] One young person had been sexually abused by her uncle before fleeing from her war-torn home country, which was the prime focus of her rehabilitation process rather than her experiences of war. Another young person had had a difficult relationship with both his father and mother, which was the focus of many conversations with his caseworker. In fact the difficult relationship with his parents seemed to be at the root of his internal destabilisation as opposed to the external traumatic events that one might suspect without knowing his history.

2.3. CASEWORK IN DOST'S CONTEXT

As the project of a community-based NGO, Dost caseworkers work in tandem with statutory services and liaise closely with statutory professionals that may be in separated children's networks (including social workers, therapists, doctors, solicitors, foster carers, teachers etc.). Over the past nine years, Dost has developed and maintained good relations with professionals and institutions involved in the cases of young refugees, including Social Services teams, Child and Adolescent Mental Health Services (CAMHS), solicitors, and local schools and colleges. This high level of collaboration enables work in the best interests of

16 Melzak, *supra* note 8.

17 D. Summerfield, 'War and mental health: a brief overview', (2000) 321 7255 *British Medical Journal*, at 232.

the child. Maintaining these links is fundamental to Dost as a small project that delivers high-risk work, as it ensures a large and supportive framework.

In order to manage risk, Dost is supported by CAMHS, which facilitates a monthly staff support group and case consultation meeting, enabling Dost to assist young people with complex needs. Caseworkers also have individual clinical consultations with a therapist from the Institute of Family Therapy. These meetings are in addition to the monthly supervision meetings for each member of staff and the weekly team meetings where all new referrals are discussed. Referrals to Dost are made from statutory bodies (including social services, child and family consultation services and schools), as well as from other NGOs (such as the Helen Bamber Foundation, Shelter, the Refugee Council and the Children's Society). Additionally, many young people make self-referrals or peer-referrals to Dost. Dost accepts 95 per cent of referrals, who are encouraged to engage with all three areas of education, play and advice and advocacy.

2.4. THE FUTURE: CIRCULAR ROUTES FORWARD

Casework normally comes to a close once young people feel more able to face their past and manage the tangible problems that may be part of the present. It is around this point that young people are ready to step into the future with increased confidence. Caseworkers aim to tighten the network of statutory agencies around young separated refugees so that they have greater support in the future. Initial steps in the casework process, such as ensuring that young separated refugees are placed under section 20 of the Children's Act and therefore more likely to have regular contact with their social worker, can do this. It is also important to ensure that young separated refugees who are living in foster placements feel happy and comfortable with the families that they are living with. However, for various reasons young people still often return to their caseworker at future stages for further support. Some young people do so because they feel at ease discussing certain issues with their caseworker due to the trust and sense of reliability that developed during the initial stages of casework. Others find that due to the poor relations they have with other professionals in their network, their caseworker is the most suitable person to come back to for support. Problems in the network are often caused when social workers leave their post before relationships with young people have had a chance to be built. This is usually due to constant restructuring of social service teams and poor working conditions. It is also the case that many foster carers and social workers have had insufficient training in the issues that impact on separated children and therefore sometimes find it difficult to support them. In many London boroughs, there are no longer any specialist social service teams working with separated children.

Once casework is complete, caseworkers tend to classify cases as 'inactive' rather than close them completely. This open connection allows young people to access help when they need it, preserving a sense of security and continuity that is important for the psychological recovery of war-affected children and young people. Young refugees may encounter practical issues that they need advice on at future stages, particularly in times of transition, for instance when they turn eighteen and receive different levels of support from social services. When he turned eighteen, one young person was given only one weeks' notice from his social worker about being moved to another area in London far from the one that he was settled in. The young person in question did not want to move till after his exams so that he could remain within travelling distance of his college. Advocacy support from his caseworker helped to make this possible. Some young people may also require advice about immigration issues and help in finding an immigration solicitor, particularly if the leave to reside in the UK that they have been granted by the Home Office is due to expire. It is also common for young people to revisit their caseworker to discuss emotional problems that they are facing. For example, since discovering that she is HIV positive one young person has met with her caseworker on a regular basis to talk about how she feels, despite also having a network of specialist mental health support around her. Other young people come to see their caseworker to update them on how their lives are going and how they are enjoying or coping with the changes that being older bring, such as having their own flat to live in.

The ability to re-engage with their caseworkers at later stages helps to create a circular casework model that young people are free to join and return to at any stage in their recovery process. This model acknowledges that for young people to move forward they often need a base that they can return to. This is supported by attachment theory, which argues that 'when an individual (of any age) is feeling secure he is likely to explore'; however, 'a secure home base remains indispensable nonetheless for optimal functioning and mental health'.[18] The circular nature of the model also intuitively recognises that psychological recovery from trauma does not follow a linear, teleological path. When moving forwards, individuals often have to revisit their past or tackle issues that echo problems they have faced before. Where appropriate, the casework model aims to help young separated refugees through this process. This intervention is also aided by the community framework within which it sits, as will be discussed further below.

---

18 Bowlby, *supra* note 9, at 137.

3. COMMUNITY REHABILITATION

> *'I had discovered that the plainest house can crown a fantasy or daydream. An open window can be tolerated. So can an open door. But I discovered the value of four walls and a roof. Something about containment that at the same time offers escape.'*
>
> Lloyd JONES, *Mister Pip*, 2006

In the final part of this paper we will turn to the Trinity Centre, the home within which Dost, and many other projects, came to life and continue to develop. Dost's situation within the broader context of the centre allows young refugees to feel a part of a wider community, a fundamental element of rehabilitation and reintegration.

Trinity Centre has been a community centre since 1972; it is open access and hosts an array of different community groups every day of the week, allowing for inter-generational presence and regular opportunities for interaction. Located in East London, an area in which social services place a large number of separated children, the centre takes the shape of a ready-made community for newly arrived war-affected children, which, unlike Social Services or the Home Office, is physically bounded and therefore easy to conceptualise. Young refugees commonly describe Trinity as their 'home'.

Indeed, Dost's anchor in the context of the Trinity Centre bears particular relevance to Dost's client group, for whom loss of home is a potent reality of their current context. As noted by Papadopoulos, 'whenever one thinks of refugees, from a psychological perspective, the first association is to trauma, rather than to home. (…) Yet, loss of home is the only condition that refugees share, not trauma.'[19] The containment offered by a home is not usually consciously appreciated until it is lost. 'The very fact that one has an experience of a home (regardless of how good or bad, long or brief, it may be) forms part of this substratum that contributes to the foundation of being human. Ordinarily, this layer, being so basic and fundamental, is outside the reach of our awareness unless it is disturbed.'[20]

For young separated refugees, the absence of home is often compounded by other more tangible realities and pressing needs, as has been discussed above. For instance, young people feel unsettled when they arrive in the UK because they are in a new culture and environment. Whilst, as minors, war-affected children will be provided with somewhere to live by social services, (thereby responding to pressing and tangible needs), these spaces do not always foster a

---

19 *Supra* note 11, at 9.

20 Ibid., at 17.

sense of belonging. Some children feel welcome in their foster homes but many are placed in foster homes where they feel unwanted, while many children are placed in temporary bed and breakfast accommodation or semi-independent accommodation where they feel isolated. These are functional amenities but they seldom become homes.

The Trinity Centre is an open access building and as a converted church is made up of large communal spaces including a large play hall, a worship area, several classrooms and kitchen facilities, which are all available to the local community. All staff offices are easily accessible, located on the ground floor and arranged around the central space that is referred to as the Day Centre, an area that sees a multitude of groups throughout the day. As such, the centre has a capacity to embody some of the physical and psychological characteristics of a home in the UK. One young person stated: 'I grew up here (…) With different problems, there are different people to tell them to. [But] for help, you can ask anyone.' This description of the Trinity Centre's space likens it to the family that brings you up and allows you to enter the wider world around you. Another young person explained that '[i]n the UK (…) nowhere [is home]. But I feel Trinity is like family to me. When you come [to the UK], it's difficult to be away from your family, your friends, but Trinity… Dost… No one can replace your family, but there is a way.' He then went on to describe his favourite place in the centre: the classroom, the place where he felt that his life in the UK had begun. 'In this classroom, I learnt English. It was the beginning. You always have a beginning but you don't know where is the end. This class is like the beginning – I don't know where will be the end.'

This too is a fundamental facet of psychological recovery. In the words of Simone Weil, '[t]o be rooted is perhaps the most important and least recognized need of the human soul'. To have roots signifies having a beginning, a history, meaning. Roots are grounding and are what we tend to go back towards at various points in our lives. These are all concepts that the Trinity Centre can offer war-affected children in their quest to reconstruct their lives. The consistency of the space, but also the age range present through the centre's projects, from a nursery to an old men's club, suggest that there is something for everyone and anyone who wants to be a part of it. In addition to Dost, Trinity Centre's projects include adult English as a second language (ESOL) classes, Bayaan, a youth group for young Asian girls, a full-time day care nursery and a children's centre. The centre is also used by independent community groups – regular groups include Nu-Life, a group of adults with learning difficulties who make use of the centre every morning Monday to Friday, and the Punjabi Pensioners' Group, which has been meeting for the past 14 years, coming to the centre every afternoon to have tea. Sharing spaces with different groups is a necessity for such a diversely populated centre and Dost's young people are therefore able to feel part of a wider community network and to interact in a safe context with members of the community who are not their peers. The respectful relationship between old and young and the age range present within the centre encourage a sense of community that is lacking elsewhere in unaccompanied young refugees' contexts in the UK. For example, many of the young people are happy to help set up the play rooms for the younger children or to spend hours watching the older men play cards. As such, members of the community, including young refugees, do not simply use the Trinity Centre as a functional space. Many come in simply to say hello, to have a chat, to share their grief as well as their happiness or successes. By being a place where friendships are made, new skills acquired and memories born, the Trinity Centre becomes a place where young people are able to feel rooted and to create anchors for belonging.

Welcoming spaces such as the Day Centre, and the colourful (and award-winning!) garden that surrounds Trinity, also help to foster the sense that young people are always welcome. These elements make Trinity a secure base and a constant value and help keep a sense of continuity. Whilst all other factors in young refugees' lives, including such fundamental elements as housing and asylum, are so fragmented and constantly changing, having something consistently safe and welcoming is vital for rehabilitation and recovery. This also helps to keep the casework model circular, as young people do not find it difficult to come in and re-engage.

Papadopoulos also draws on this image of home: 'The containing capacity of a home is the result of the stability that it provides in terms of continuity within a physical and emotional space where intimate relationships develop (regardless of whether they are positive or negative). The fact that these experiences are held within the context of a home creates a sense of constancy and stability.'[21] He refers to a Robert Frost poem, *The death of the hired man*, where one character answers another's question 'what do you mean by home?' with the following lines:

> Home is the place where, when you have to go there,
> They have to take you in,
>
> I should have called it
> Something you somehow haven't to deserve

Papadopoulos goes on to explain why this 'awkward sounding sentence' conveys the very essence of the idea of home: 'Unquestionably, one does not have to earn

---

21 Ibid., at 17.

the right to be at home. One should not be required to achieve anything to gain the right to be at home. Home is where one is.'[22]

From the perspective of a young refugee, whilst the UK may be where one is, the right to remain in the UK is not automatic or unquestioned – far from it. Young refugees live with the constant anxiety of being sent back to the countries they fled in fear of their lives, countries that include Afghanistan, Congo and Iraq. Whilst they wait for answers, in which they have no power of decision, their need to rehabilitate and reintegrate is constantly curtailed by the question of whether they will be uprooted once more. This reality enhances the need for places with undeniable acceptance, where one can 'just be' and belong without question.

Khalid, a young Kurdish-Iraqi explained: 'My community is any good friend. It's with people. You know different people in this country. In the Trinity Centre, you know Afghani people, even European, different religions…' Indeed, Dost's services are regularly attended by young people from 27 different countries. As such, young people from Afghanistan and Iran regularly celebrate Naw Ruz (Iranian new year) with their peers from other countries, just as Ethiopian and Eritrean young people celebrate Gena (Ethiopian new year) with their friends from many other countries. As Stedman states, 'opportunities to give public expression to one's national food, music, dress and customs in contexts which celebrate and value these are of enormous therapeutic value'.[23] These opportunities, like the positive stories from the past that young people can share with their caseworkers, allow separated children to reconstruct valued parts of their country and selves. Summerfield's work with Iraqi asylum seekers in London found that 'poor social support was more closely related to depression than was a history of torture. Unquestionably, the major protective factor is the presence of a community able to provide mutual support and nurture problem solving strategies.'[24] Furthermore, the internal and external connections that are made when such activities take place in the community activate psychosocial healing and help stem feelings of cultural bereavement.

Anthias argues that 'belonging is about experiences of being part of the social fabric and should not be thought of in exclusively ethnic terms'.[25] This is pertinent in the context of a community centre such as Trinity that itself has a social fabric, which is in turn reflective of the social fabric of the area it sits in

---

22 Ibid., at 38.

23 Stedman, *supra* note 7, at 6.

24 Summerfield, *supra* note 17, at 233.

25 F. Anthias, 'Belongings in a globalising and unequal world: rethinking translocations', in N. Yuval-David, K. Kannabiran, U.M. Vieten (eds.), *The situated politics of belonging*, Sage, London, 2006, at 21.

(Newham). As such, young refugees gradually feel a part of the community by virtue of having contributed to the make-up of the centre. As a centre that embodies a range of ages, ethnicities, people and projects, it is not by virtue of being young asylum seekers, refugees or war-affected children that young people are accepted as a part of the centre. Rather, it is despite these labels and regardless of them. This again references the idea of home as a place of unconditional belonging. Anthias further suggests that 'to belong is to be accepted as part of a community, to feel safe within it and to have a stake in the future of such a community of membership'.[26] As such, membership of the Trinity Centre is a choice and so the acceptance of the space is an empowering reality. Actively engaging with Dost and the Trinity Centre illustrates a choice by these young people to rebuild their lives and to become active participants in their communities.

4. CONCLUSION

It has been the aim of this paper to contribute to thinking around the importance of positive relationships as a fundamental element of effective healing processes. War affects the different overlapping spheres in a person's life, which integrated models of support must therefore recognise and reflect. Dost has learnt from experience that connections between social, practical and internal realities as well as present, past and future worlds must be made in order to provide the best support for separated children in exile. This understanding has formed the long-term, holistic, community-based service that Dost is today. The containment of the Dost team, Trinity's management and wider support structures enable caseworkers to alleviate a child or young person's distress and build positive healing relationships. Analogous to the concept of the Russian doll, Dost's community setting provides both a physically safe space and a sustainable community for young people and workers. This environment promotes supportive attachments and creates a secure base, thus fostering a sense of belonging. In the words of Holmes, this allows young people and their workers alike to 'endure rough seas… [and] be sure of a safe haven'.[27]

---

26 Ibid.

27 J. Holmes, *John Bowlby and attachment theory*, Routledge, London and New York, 1993, at 70.

RELEASE AND REINTEGRATION OF CHILD SOLDIERS: ONE PART OF A BIGGER PUZZLE

Lucia WITHERS

1. OVERVIEW OF CHILDREN'S INVOLVEMENT IN ARMED CONFLICT

Since the early 1990s, when the issue of child soldiers first became a feature of international human rights, humanitarian, peace and security agendas, significant measures aimed at ending children's involvement in armed conflict have been taken. A framework of international law and policy to protect children from military exploitation has been established; close to two thirds of states are parties to the core human rights treaty prohibiting children's involvement in armed conflict;[1] and some 80 states have set 18 as the minimum age at which an individual can enter their armed forces, including for training.

Progress can also be measured by the level of attention the issue now receives from key international bodies, not least the UN Security Council. A greater level of scrutiny of grave abuses against children in situations of armed conflict, including their recruitment and use as child soldiers, has been achieved through the establishment of the UN-led monitoring and reporting mechanism. This in turn, better informs the actions of the Security Council and others.

In the realm of criminal justice, successful prosecutions by the Special Court for Sierra Leone in 2007 and ongoing trials at the International Criminal Court (ICC) of individuals on such charges have underscored the gravity with which the crime is regarded internationally.

In the meantime, tens of thousands of child soldiers have been released from armies and armed groups as long-running conflicts have ended in a number of

1 As of February 2010, there were 131 State Parties to the Optional Protocol to the Convention on the Rights of the Child on the Involvement of Children in Armed Conflict.

countries, including Burundi, Côte d'Ivoire, Guinea, Liberia and Sierra Leone. Elsewhere, for example in Nepal and Sri Lanka, large-scale recruitment of children effectively ceased with the end of hostilities, although the question of the release and reintegration of those already recruited has yet to be fully resolved in both countries.

In situations where armed conflict is ongoing, efforts to release children have also yielded results. Action plans to end the recruitment of children have been agreed between the UN and parties to armed conflicts in Côte d'Ivoire, Sri Lanka, Sudan and Uganda. Negotiations are ongoing with parties elsewhere, including in the Central African Republic, Darfur, Myanmar and the Philippines. In Myanmar, three ethnic armed groups, to which access by the UN is prohibited by the Myanmar government, have unilaterally declared their commitment to preventing under-18s from joining their ranks.[2]

While the general direction is positive, if the measure for progress is a reduction in the number of children currently exposed to military exploitation or at risk from it – which is ultimately the only real measure of impact – the results remain inadequate.

In its latest Child Soldiers Global Report, the Coalition to Stop the Use of Child Soldiers ("the Coalition", at the time of writing this manuscript, yet renamed to Child Soldiers International in September 2011) found that between April 2004 and October 2007 children were actively involved in armed conflicts in 19 countries or territories;[3] nine governments had deployed children into situations of armed conflict in their armed forces during that period; and some 14 governments recruited, or permitted the recruitment, of under-18s into auxiliary forces, civilian defence groups or into militias or armed groups acting as proxies for armed forces. Dozens of armed groups in at least 24 countries had recruited, and in many cases used in hostilities, boys and girls under the age of 18.[4]

Although it is impossible to put an accurate figure on the number of affected children it is apparent that wherever armed conflict exists children are involved. In other words, international and national attention and action has not yet significantly changed the reality for many tens of thousands of children who find themselves fighting adult wars.

---

2 Karen National Union/Karen National Liberation Army; Karenni National Progressive Party/Karenni Army; and Chin National Front/Chin National Army.

3 Since the publication of the Global Report several conflicts have ended. Children are currently believed to be actively involved in hostilities in some 14 countries or territories worldwide.

4 Coalition to Stop the Use of Child Soldiers, *Child soldiers global report 2008*.

The majority of these children are associated with armed groups. Of the 56 parties in 15 different situations[5] named in the annexes to the 2008 report of the UN Secretary-General on children and armed conflict, the majority are non-state armed groups.[6] Armed groups, which in many cases have proved resistant to efforts to change their recruitment practices (appeals, engagement in dialogue, 'naming and shaming', threats of prosecutions, targeted measures etc.), represent among the greatest challenges to securing further progress in ending child soldiering.

However, the record of some governments is also not much improved. Although the number of governments that openly deploy under-18s directly in hostilities is now relatively few, a significant number are complicit in allowing children to be used by government-related paramilitaries, militias, civilian defence organisations or through their illicit support to armed opposition groups. It is notable that government armed forces still represent nine of the parties that recruit and use children in contravention of international norms listed in the Secretary-General's report. Moreover, at least ten armed groups that feature on the list currently receive, or have in the past received, the backing of governments.[7]

The Secretary-General's list does not, however, represent the full picture. There are additionally a number of parties to armed conflict that are known to recruit and use children but which have, by and large, avoided international scrutiny for these abuses. These include armed groups in India's Chhattisgarh state (Maoists/Naxalites), Pakistan (Taliban) and Thailand (National Revolutionary Front-Coordinate, BRN-C). It also includes state security forces, state-backed paramilitaries or civilian defence groups, for example in India (anti-Maoist vigilante groups/Salwa Judum and auxiliary police)[8] and the Philippines (Citizen's Armed Force Geographical Units and Civilian Volunteer Organisations).[9]

---

5 Afghanistan, Burundi, Central African Republic, Chad, Colombia, Democratic Republic of Congo, Iraq, Myanmar, Nepal, Philippines, Somalia, Sri Lanka, southern Sudan, Darfur and Uganda.

6 *Children and armed conflict: report of the Secretary-General*, UN Doc. A/63/785-S/2009/158, 26 March 2009.

7 *Children and armed conflict: report of the Secretary-General*, UN Doc. A/63/785-S/2009/158, 26 March 2009.

8 Human Rights Watch, *Dangerous duty: children and the Chhattisgarh conflict*, September 2008, see at www.hrw.org/en/node/75148/section/1.

9 *Consideration of Reports Submitted by State Parties under Article 8(1) of the Optional Protocol to the Convention on the Rights of the Child on the Involvement of Children in Armed Conflict, Initial Report of the Philippines*, UN Doc. CRC/C/OPAC/PHL/1, 7 November 2007.

Children associated with these and other fighting forces include both boys and girls. In some cases they will be very young – in the Democratic Republic of the Congo (DRC), for example, the Coalition has recent testimony from a girl who claimed to have been first recruited by an armed group at the age of seven years old. In Myanmar there are verified cases of 11-year-olds being recruited into the state armed forces.[10] In the Central African Republic, the age breakdown of 450 children released in 2007 by the armed opposition group, the Union of Democratic Forces (UFDR), was 75 per cent between the ages of 13 and 17 while some 10 per cent were between 10 and 13 years old.[11]

These and other children associated with fighting forces elsewhere will typically be employed in a variety of roles from combatants, to cooks, porters and spies or used for sexual purposes. In recent years children have increasingly been used as suicide bombers, notably in Afghanistan, Iraq and Pakistan. Palestinian children, while not formally recruited, are reported to have been used as human shields by the Israel Defence Forces in military operations against Hamas in early 2009 – a practice that is not only in contravention of international law but also of a 2005 Israeli High Court ruling on the illegality of the use of human shields.[12]

2. DDR DEVELOPMENTS AND CONCERNS

A number of major DDR programmes for children have drawn to a close in recent years, including in Afghanistan, Angola, Burundi, Liberia and Sierra Leone. Tens of thousands of children have been released through such programmes. Many thousands more have made their own way home. Currently efforts are continuing to separate children from fighting forces and to support their reintegration in conflict-affected countries that include the Central African Republic, Chad, Colombia, the DRC and Sudan.

From these and other experiences, a wealth of knowledge has been built on the identity of girls and boys in fighting forces, and their needs and priorities when returning to civilian life. The Paris Principles and Guidelines on Children Associated with Armed Forces or Armed Groups (Paris Principles) encapsulate much that has been learned and provides guidance to policy makers, practitioners and donors in the design and implementation of effective strategies and interventions to protect children from involvement in armed conflict and to

---

10 *Report of the Secretary-General on children and armed conflict in Myanmar*, UN Doc. S/2009/278, 1 June 2009.

11 *Report of the Secretary-General on children and armed conflict*: UN Doc. A/62/609-S/2007/757, December 2007.

12 *Human rights situation in Palestine and other occupied Arab territories*, Human Rights Council, Tenth Session, UN Doc. A/HRC/10/22, 20 March 2009.

secure the release and reintegration of those that find themselves caught up in it. However, implementing best practice remains a significant challenge and in many situations provision for the release and reintegration of child soldiers is still inadequate or non-existent.

2.1. RELEASING CHILDREN IN SITUATIONS OF ARMED CONFLICT – PREVENTION BETTER THAN CURE

A fundamental principle of children's DDR is that their release and reintegration should not depend on any formal peace process or be contingent on the establishment of formal DDR programmes, but rather should be prioritised at all times, including where hostilities are ongoing. This is not only a question of policy but a legal obligation on State Parties to the Optional Protocol to the Convention on the Rights of the Child on the involvement of children in armed conflict (Optional Protocol).[13]

In reality child soldiers are released from armed forces or armed groups in significant numbers only when hostilities cease or conflict ends. While efforts to demobilise children in the midst of hostilities should be actively pursued wherever possible, the obstacles are formidable, results often limited and successes short-lived.

In Sri Lanka, for example, the continued efforts since the late 1990s to bring an end to the recruitment and use of underage fighters by the Liberation Tigers of Tamil Eelam (LTTE) resulted in a series of commitments by the LTTE and led to the release of hundreds of children over the years and at times falling rates of child recruitment. However, as of the end of January 2009, over 1,400 children or persons recruited as children were recorded as having been in the LTTE ranks – due to underreporting it is likely that the actual figure was significantly higher.[14] During the final months of the conflict between January and May 2009, there was a renewed and massive wave of forced recruitment of children by the LTTE. The new recruits received minimal training and many are believed to have been among the thousands of casualties in the final weeks of the war.

Likewise in the DRC, military imperatives have repeatedly trumped commitments to end recruitment and release children. Large-scale releases of

13 The *Optional Protocol*, Article 6(3) requires State Parties to take all feasible measures to ensure that children illegally recruited or used in hostilities are demobilised or otherwise released and receive appropriate support for their reintegration.

14 *Report of the Secretary-General on children and armed conflict in Sri Lanka*, UN Doc. S/2009/325, 25 June 2009.

under-18s from government armed forces and armed groups have accompanied successive peace deals. However, each resurgence in hostilities brings with it a new wave of recruitment and re-recruitment of under-age fighters. Most recently, 'an explosion of child recruitment by non-state armed groups' was reported following the escalation in hostilities in the east of the country in late 2008, in which locally-based self-defence militia known as Mai Mai were said to account for the highest number of children in their ranks.[15]

Research by the Coalition into the persistent recruitment and re-recruitment of under-18s by Mai Mai factions in the eastern Congolese provinces of North and South Kivu reveals an entrenched cycle of enlistment and conscription of both girls and boys. The cycle is driven by chronic insecurity in the region; notions of community self-defence; local attitudes towards childhood; belief in mystical powers possessed by children; as well as precarious socio-economic conditions resulting in, among other things, a lack of access to education and employment. This recruitment/re-recruitment cycle will ultimately be brought to an end not simply by rescuing, in some cases repeatedly, under-age fighters. It also requires the environment into which girls and boys associated with Mai Mai are returned to be changed to reduce their vulnerability to recruitment. This requires a range of interconnected political, security and socio-economic measures aimed at improving stability in the region and reconciling local ethnic divisions and other tensions in order to negate the justification for community-based self-defence militia; effective implementation of national laws, in particular those protecting children; accountability for those that recruit and use under-18s; universal free access to education; and economic development that delivers meaningful opportunities for youth employment and a viable alternative to joining Mai Mai.

The Mai Mai example is transferable to many other situations in which the legal, policy and institutional frameworks that should provide protection are eroded by war (if indeed they ever existed) and where military priorities dominate – in effect child rights and protection are suspended for the duration of the conflict. However, the fact that armed conflict exists cannot be permitted to justify such a suspension. Rather, it makes it all the more urgent that effective barriers against the recruitment and re-recruitment of children are put in place and that the state's responsibility to protect and promote the rights of children is supported and enforced.

---

15 *Combined report of seven thematic special procedures on technical assistance to the Government of the Democratic Republic of Congo and urgent examination of the situation in the east of the country*, UN Doc. A/HRC/10/59, 5 March 2009.

2.2. POST-CONFLICT RELEASE AND REINTEGRATION – A LONG-TERM PROJECT

DDR programmes, even in post-conflict settings, are generally established in insecure, often highly volatile environments in which residual tensions can lead to further outbreaks of hostilities; government authority and capacities are low; the rule of law, where it exists at all, is weak; economies are shattered; and communities fragmented. DDR programmes cannot resolve these problems but must contend with them and be seen as part of a broader integrated approach to reconstruction – political, economic and social – without which the prospects for sustainable reintegration of former members of armed forces and armed groups, children and adults alike, are poor.

The Paris Principles describe child reintegration as '(...) *the process through which children transition into civil society and enter meaningful roles and identities as civilians who are accepted by their families and communities in a context of local and national reconciliation*'. According to the Principles, sustainable reintegration is achieved '(...) *when the political, legal, economic and social conditions needed for children to maintain life, livelihood and dignity have been secured. This process aims to ensure that children can access their rights, including formal and non-formal education, family unity, dignified livelihoods and safety from harm.*'[16] By definition, achieving this goal is a long-term exercise that must be closely coordinated with and linked to other peacebuilding, reconstruction and reconciliation processes. The rights of former child soldiers, or indeed any child, cannot be fully realised in a context characterised by on-going insecurity, poverty, discrimination and injustice.

The UN's Integrated DDR Standards recommends that child reintegration should extend over a period of five years or more in order to give children a viable long-term alternative to military life.[17] Typically, though, funding for national DDR programmes has been provided only for immediate post-conflict demobilisation and reinsertion into communities – normally a one-year period. The longer-term support necessary to enable former child soldiers (and other ex-combatants) to take on meaningful productive roles in their societies is rarely available.

While longer-term funding is called for, in conflict-damaged countries the rehabilitation and reintegration needs of conflicted-affected children will inevitably continue beyond the life-span of and funding windows available for

16 *The Principles and Guidelines on Children Associated with Armed Forces or Armed Groups (Paris Principles)*, February 2007.

17 UN Integrated DDR Standards, Section 5.30: Children and DDR, Sub-section 3.4: Reintegration.

even the best designed and funded DDR programmes. DDR processes should therefore also be conceived as linked to longer-term recovery and development programmes. This requires institutional mechanisms to create a linkage between bodies (and funders) responsible for short- and medium-term assistance to ex-combatants and those that provide longer-term assistance to communities and broader economic development.[18]

The relationship between failed development, failed reintegration and the resulting exploitation of children formerly associated with armed forces or groups is all too obvious in a country such as Sierra Leone where gruelling conditions are experienced by an estimated 10,000 children employed in artisanal diamond mining. The miners represent some of Sierra Leone's most vulnerable children, among whom are former child soldiers and other war-affected youth. According to a recent study by the Harvard Law School, some of the former child soldiers working in the mines specifically attributed their situation to the failure of DDR programmes, because, amongst other factors, the skills training received had not resulted in jobs.[19] More generally, the slow pace of reconstruction in Sierra Leone means that there are few viable alternatives for many war-affected youth and without state regulation of the mines and measures to address the socio-economic needs of children in them, they are exposed to daily hazards to their development, health and general well-being.

Unfortunately the situation in Sierra Leone is far from unique. A recent UN technical assistance mission to Liberia found that *'[m]any of the assessment mission's interlocutors were of the view that the reintegration programme* [which officially closed in April 2009 having demobilised some 101,500 former combatants] *had been a "quick fix" that neither transformed the violent disposition of most of the former combatants nor provided them with sustainable livelihoods'.*[20]

While the Liberian DDR programme suffered many difficulties and was considered to have been particularly poor in serving the needs of women and girls, it is also clear that there is no fast track to effective reintegration. It is also evident that the success of reintegration programmes is intricately linked to achieving progress in the political, social and economic reconstruction of war-torn countries.

---

18 For further discussion of this issue see: Leontine Specker, *The R-phase of DDR processes: an overview of key lessons learned and practical experiences*, Netherlands Institute of International Relations "Clingendael", September 2008.

19 The International Human Rights Clinic, Harvard Law School, *Digging in the dirt: child miners in Sierra Leone's diamond industry*, 2009.

20 *Special report of the Secretary-General on the United Missions in Liberia*, UN Doc. S/2009/299, 10 June 2009.

2.3. IMPROVING ACCESS TO REINTEGRATION SUPPORT

In both Liberia and Sierra Leone, the rates of participation of child soldiers in formal DDR processes did not match the numbers believed to be associated with armed forces or armed groups – a pattern which is repeated elsewhere. For example, in the DRC an estimated 30,000 children were officially demobilised by 2007 under the projects supported by the World Bank and Multi-country Demobilisation Program. Another approximately 11,000 children are reported to have left the armed forces or armed groups independently.[21] In November 2008, the UN reported that in the absence of a functioning national disarmament, demobilisation and reintegration programme children continue to withdraw from armed groups, sometimes on their own and sometimes as a result of successful advocacy and interventions by child protection partners.[22]

The figures for girls are particularly poor with average levels of participation of between eight and 15 per cent of the estimated numbers of girls associated with armed forces or groups in any given situation. In Liberia, some 2,700 girls were among 11,780 children demobilised through the formal DDR process that ended in November 2004.[23] Although high in comparison with other DDR programmes, as many as 8,000 girls did not take part. In the DRC, only 3,000 girls, or about 15 per cent of the total girls estimated to have been involved in the conflict, had been officially demobilised by May 2006 as the first national DDR programme was drawing to a close.[24]

Participation rates in official DDR programmes for both boys and girls could be improved, including through better designed criteria for eligibility and more effective outreach. However, formal DDR processes are high profile exercises which are not necessarily best suited to the needs of a population that in many cases chooses to keep a low profile. The design of and funding for reintegration programmes must therefore also take into account the fact that a significant number of children, by choice or design, will never hold formal discharge papers but will make their own way back to their communities. The challenge of providing assistance to these and other conflict-affected children and youth is considerable but necessary if those who need it are to benefit from rehabilitation and reintegration support.

21 UNICEF, *Report of the National Workshop on Children's DDR*, Goma, 12–14 April 2007.

22 *Report of the Secretary-General on the situation of children and armed conflict in the Democratic Republic of the Congo,* UN Doc. S/2008/693, November 2008.

23 UNICEF, *Evaluation of the Disarmament and Demobilisation Programme for Children Associated with Fighting Forces in Liberia*, 2005.

24 Coalition to Stop the Use of Child Soldiers, *Child soldiers global report 2008*, see at www.childsoldiersglobalreport.org/.

2.4. INVISIBLE CHILDREN

The fact that many children may make their own way home should not, however, justify the absence of programmes specifically designed for them. Although it is well established that children are likely to be associated with armed forces or armed groups where there is armed conflict, the conceptualisation of fighting forces as primarily comprising adult male combatants continues to result in DDR programmes that make no or inadequate provision for children.

For example, the August 2005 Helsinki Memorandum of Understanding between the Government of Indonesia and the Free Aceh Movement (GAM) provided for the demobilisation of 3,000 adult GAM combatants. Although under-18s had been used by both GAM and the government armed forces, including as informants or guards, for logistical and support and, less frequently by GAM, as combatants, there was no provision for the release and reintegration of under-18s. In Indonesia, both the government and GAM were unwilling to acknowledge that children had been involved in the decades-long Aceh independence war and were therefore reported to have been resistant to including provisions for under-18s in DDR arrangements.

A state of denial is not uncommon, but it is one that must be challenged because it means that children do not receive protection against recruitment or assistance for their release and reintegration either during or after the conflict. The record in Asia is particularly poor. In Thailand, for example, despite a growing body of evidence that under-18s are being widely recruited by the National Revolutionary Front-Coordinate (BRN-C), an ill-defined organisation believed to be leading the ethno-nationalist insurgency in the far south of the country, the Thai Government has so far refused to acknowledge, at least publicly, that the problem exists. As a result, no practical measures have been taken towards protecting children against recruitment or securing the release of those already associated with BRN-C.[25]

Similarly in India, no official programmes have been established to assist the release and reintegration of children despite well documented evidence of their involvement in internal armed conflict there.[26] In Myanmar, government claims that it has put in place procedures for the rehabilitation and reintegration of

---

25 See the Coalition to Stop the Use of Child Soldiers, *Briefing paper: child recruitment and use in Southern Thailand, December 2008* at www.child-soldiers.org/document/get?id=1553 and International Crisis Group, *Recruiting militants in Southern Thailand*, 22 June 2009 at www.crisisgroup.org/~/media/Files/asia/south-east-asia/thailand/170_recruiting_militants_in_southern_thailand.ashx.

26 See for example, Human Rights Watch, *Dangerous duty: children and the Chhattisgarh conflict*, September 2008, www.hrw.org/en/node/75148/section/1.

under-age recruits in the national army cannot be verified and, in any case, the number of under-18s it claims to have released represents only a fraction of those believed to be in its armed forces. In these and other situations, the question is not about the quality of reintegration support, but rather the need to engage governments to persuade them that such measures must be taken at all.

2.5. WORKING WITH COMMUNITIES

Where programmes for the release and reintegration of children do exist, child protection agencies such as Save the Children have consistently found that programming is most effective where inclusive of other conflict-affected children. Save the Children, among others, has argued that this approach avoids stigmatisation of children and reduces the likelihood of reprisals by parties to the armed conflict and peer or community resentment against returning children where they appear to be rewarded for their actions during conflict or provided with support that other equally vulnerable children cannot access.[27]

The Coalition's own work and that of others also highlights the need to consider the family and community context to which children are returning. This can be particularly pertinent in relation to girls. Escape from entrenched gender discrimination and violence, including rape and other forms of sexual violence within the home or broader community, can be a motive for joining fighting forces. While protecting them from military exploitation, simply reinserting girls (or indeed any other child) back into a potentially abusive environment exposes them to other, in some cases equally serious risks.

The risks can be further exacerbated by community attitudes to returning girl soldiers, who are consistently among those likely to experience particular difficulties in successfully reintegrating. The Coalition's research on Mai Mai, for example, indicates that while returning boys are generally treated by their communities as 'heroes', returning girls are treated with suspicion because they are perceived to have been sexually promiscuous while with the Mai Mai.[28] Preliminary research in Nepal suggests a similar phenomenon in which girls formerly associated with the Maoists have faced stigmatisation in some rural communities, and there are reports that some may now be working in dance bars, massage parlours or performing other forms of sex work in order to make a living.

---

27 Save the Children, *Stolen futures: the reintegration of children affected by armed conflict. Submission to the ten-year review of the 1996 Machel study on the impact of armed conflict on children*, 2007, www.child-soldiers.org/document/get?id=1261.

28 Forthcoming report by the Coalition to Stop the Use of Child Soldiers.

Girl mothers and their children are among the most vulnerable groups, with studies showing that they often face community judgment, stigmatisation and social distancing on their return from fighting forces – especially when their 'bush husbands' continue to be part of their lives. Understanding and responding to the complex reasons for parental and community rejection of these girls and the potentially unique set of needs of their children, who are often conceived as a result of rape, are clearly a necessary part of achieving their successful reintegration. It is not surprising therefore that studies indicate that girl mothers require gender-specific interventions coupled with longer reintegration periods and consistent follow-up.[29]

It is also increasingly apparent that mobilisation and preparation of communities is a key component of reintegration, in particular although not exclusively for more vulnerable categories of returnees such as girl mothers. Indeed, building or rebuilding familial and community relationships, sometimes referred to as the 'soft side' of DDR, may in some cases be as important as providing direct support to individual returnees.

Research into community attitudes towards returnees in several countries shows them to be complex and subject to change over time. A wide range of different factors can influence the response of a community to returnees. Among these factors can be the profile of the individual child – members of communities in northern and eastern Uganda from which children had been forcibly recruited by the Lord's Resistance Army (LRA), interviewed by the Coalition in 2008, singled out orphans, child mothers with babies born in the LRA, and children with physical injuries as those for whom acceptance was more difficult. The extent to which returning children contribute economically can also be a factor – in conditions of poverty and where basic services are lacking returnees can be perceived as an unwelcome burden, particularly if they suffer injuries or other conditions that prevent them from carrying out domestic or wage-earning work. Perceptions that returnees have violated community norms are also frequently an obstacle to the reintegration of girls who have been, or are perceived to have been, involved in sexual relations, albeit often forced while members of fighting forces.

Some studies also indicate that negativity and hostility by communities towards returnee children is influenced by their real or presumed role as perpetrators of human rights abuses and other forms of violence. International principles state

29 S. McKay, M. Robinson, M. Gonsalves and M. Worthen, *Girls formerly associated with fighting forces and their children: returned and neglected* (2006), available at: www.child-soldiers.org/psycho-social/english; *Returning home: children's perspectives on reintegration: a case study of children abducted by the Lord's Resistance Army in Teso, eastern Uganda*, unpublished paper by the Coalition to Stop the Use of Child Soldiers, February 2008.

that children who commit crimes while associated with armed forces or groups should be treated primarily as victims. However, convincing receiving communities (which in some cases will have been victims of the alleged crimes) that this should be the case is not always possible. A study by War Child in north Equateur in eastern DRC, for example, found that communities did not regard returning children as victims of war but rather as perpetrators of violence who were considered dangerous and represented a threat to the community.[30] Community consultations carried out by the Coalition in northern Uganda similarly found high levels of mistrust of under-age LRA returnees, who were considered as negative influences on other children in the community and capable of violence.[31]

Such findings suggest that overcoming community resistance to reintegrating returning child soldiers requires the question of accountability and reconciliation to be confronted. Careful consideration as to how transitional justice processes might enhance the reintegration prospects for child soldiers is needed while factoring into the debate the rights of victims of human rights abuses to justice and reparations.

3. CONCLUSION

Release and reintegration of children is clearly not a stand-alone activity, but is intricately connected to a wide range of other factors – conflict dynamics, economic development, legal reform, institution building etc. – all of which contribute to influencing the extent to which effective reintegration is achieved. Nor is reintegration a short-term activity. While returning a child to their community may be achieved relatively swiftly, their acceptance by that community and their ability to take on a meaningful role in it (both of which may also be connected) is a longer process.

The connections between release and reintegration on the one hand and the broader security, political and economic environment on the other must be factored into the design of DDR programmes. While DDR programmes cannot be expected to resolve all the problems that returning children are likely to face, many of them can be anticipated and linkages made between the shorter-term release and reintegration activities and longer-term measures aimed at addressing systemic problems that prevent children from enjoying their basic human rights

30 War Child, *Don't tell us where we belong*, October/November 2005.

31 Unpublished survey by the Coalition to Stop the Use of Child Soldiers, *Uganda: an uncertain welcome. Summary of discussions with communities and children on the situation of abducted children returning from the Lord's Resistance Army*, March 2009.

and make them vulnerable to military exploitation and other human rights abuses. Addressing the broader environment is not only essential to successful long-term reintegration, but also for preventing future recruitment and re-recruitment in situations where hostilities are continuing.

While achieving the release and reintegration of children should remain a priority, the importance of prevention cannot be overstated. It is clear from the examples of Sri Lanka, the DRC and elsewhere that there are considerable obstacles to securing release in the midst of hostilities. It is also commonplace for children to be re-recruited once released. Given that prevention rather than rescue ultimately represents the best protection for children against harm, greater attention and resources for this long-term work are required.

NO RETURN HOME

The (Non-)Reintegration of Youth Ex-Combatants in Sierra Leone as a Challenge to the Contextualisation of DDR and Transitional Justice

Martien SCHOTSMANS*

1. RESEARCH QUESTION AND METHODOLOGY

In 2003, while working with the Truth and Reconciliation Commission (hereafter the TRC or the Commission), I once had an interview with a former child soldier, together with one of the Commission's psychosocial councillors. A 24-year-old adult at the time we met, the boy had been abducted by the Revolutionary United Front (RUF) around the age of twelve or thirteen and stayed with them for about ten years. Through his bravery and "good" behaviour he rapidly climbed up to the level of "captain" and later "colonel", which included him being allowed the use of a truck (meaning he did not have to walk) and the command of a "Small Boys Unit" (SBU).[1] During the interview, he explained why and how he was feared by the others, how he had all the food and money he wanted, how he could order his boys to pass him any looted item he preferred, the crimes and abuses they committed when attacking villages, how he was given the oversight of some mining activity, what sophisticated materials they had at their disposal during combat, how he escaped when captured by another armed group, etc. The whole interview sounded like someone describing the role he played in a "Rambo" film. He seemed very proud of his acts and the status he

* The author wishes to acknowledge the funding of the Aftralaw research project by the Belgian Government, Belgian Science Policy Office (BELSPO). She also wants to thank Prof. Eva Brems and the editors of the volume for their valuable constructive comments on the chapter as well as all interviewees and those who shared documents and other information.

1 Trial Chamber judgment 2 March 2009, *Special Court, Prosecutor v. Issa Hassan Sesay, Morris Kallon and Augustine Gbao,* Case No. SCSL-04-15-T., par. 1621. for more information regarding the RUF practice of establishing specific combat units comprised of young boys. Confirmed in this regard by the Appeals Chamber on 26 October 2009. SCSL-04-15-A, par. 931–933.

acquired. His main problem was with his current status in the community where he had decided to settle down after demobilisation (instead of returning home). He seemed to feel somehow relieved about the fact that people were not aware of his acts during the war (though they knew he had been a child combatant) and he had even become an appreciated solo singer in the church choir. On the other hand, he may have had some feelings of guilt, since he wanted to come out and apologise publicly for what he had done. But his (former combatant) friends discouraged him from doing so. Coming out and laying down his old status would lose him old friends. In addition, he would run the risk of being rejected by his new community and losing his new status as well. This prevented him from showing up for the TRC's reconciliation hearing.

This chapter will focus on issues relating to the social reintegration of those children and youth who – in reality or in the eyes of the community – were not mere victims of the conflict. The question is why a number of them have not returned home since the end of the war. The chapter suggests a partial answer can be found in the extent to which the DDR[2] programmes and transitional justice mechanisms applied in Sierra Leone after the conflict took into consideration traditional justice values and the broader cultural context.

In policy development and academic writing on DDR[3] and transitional justice,[4] much attention has recently been devoted to the importance of "localising" or "contextualising" approaches, instead of adopting one-size-fits-all solutions. In this regard, the importance of considering the use of traditional practices for the reintegration of ex-combatants or for justice and reconciliation purposes is emphasised, following some positive experiences in Mozambique, Angola, Sierra Leone, Liberia and Uganda.

However, if traditional ceremonies are singled out for support while ignoring the broader traditional context, i.e. the societal view of such rituals as part of a coherent system or even world view, new problems occur. Even if the tendency to extrapolate them to become a "formula" that can be applied to any situation[5] is resisted, such singling out of particular elements of a local system[6] involves a

---

2 Disarmament, Demobilisation and Reintegration.

3 Roger Duthie, *Transitional Justice and Social Reintegration*, International Centre for Transitional Justice, paper prepared for the Stockholm Initiative on Disarmament Demobilisation Reintegration (SIDDR), Working Group 3: Reintegration and Peace Building meeting, April 4–5, 2005 at 14–16. Gwinyayi Albert Dzinesa, 'A Participatory Approach to DDR: Empowering Local Institutions and Abilities', Accord, (2006) Issue 3 *Conflict Trends* at 40–41. Joseph n. Sany, 'Reintegration of ex-combatants: the Liberia case', Accord, (2006) Issue 1 *Conflict Trends*, at 38.

4 United Nations, 'The Rule of Law and transitional justice in conflict and post-conflict societies', Report of the Secretary General, 23 August 2004, S/2004/616, par. 7; Luc Huyse and Marc Salter (eds.), *Traditional Justice after Violent Conflict. Learning from African experiences*, 2008, IDEA, Stockholm, Sweden, at 3–6.

5 Naomi Roth-Arriaza and Javier Mariezcurrena, *Transitional Justice in the Twenty-First Century. Beyond truth versus justice*, Cambridge University Press, UK, 2006, at 12 and 333.

6 Or the risk of "oversimplification", see: Lieselotte Viaene and Eva Brems, 'Transitional Justice and Cultural Context: Learning from the Universality Debate', (2010) *Netherlands Quarterly of Human Rights*, Vol. 28 (3), at 24.

double risk: on the one hand, the risk of neglecting aspects of the conflict which are not covered by the traditional mechanisms (such as the responsibility of traditional leaders), on the other hand the risk of overlooking the fact that such rituals or ceremonies are part of a process of societal confirmation, which may involve conservative power relations or harmful practices (such as FGM). These risks will be further examined here.

After a brief overview of the conflict and peace background and the role of children and youth during the war, the chapter describes how some youth ex-combatants have preferred to stay in the larger towns, in spite of – or due to the limitations of – DDR programmes. The main section tries to find some explanations of this phenomenon. It does so by analysing the lack of youth accountability in the transitional justice process, as well as the lack of accountability of elders for their role before and during the conflict, and their current role, ending with the dilemma of reintegrating youth into a traditional context.

The chapter is based on three types of information. Firstly, an analysis of existing academic and grey literature was carried out. Secondly, 52 semi-structured interviews were conducted in April 2009 in Sierra Leone, more particularly in Freetown, Makeni, Bo and Moyamba district, with key stakeholders including international donors and organisations, state actors, national NGOs and civil society organisations, traditional authorities, Sierra Leonean academics and beneficiaries of the Fambul Tok project in Moyamba district. This material was analysed in conjunction with related documents, as well as the results of more in-depth field research conducted by other authors. Finally, my experience as the head of the Legal and Reconciliation Unit of the Truth and Reconciliation Commission for Sierra Leone in 2003 contributed to the information and analysis.

2. CONFLICT AND PEACE BACKGROUND[7]

Sierra Leone experienced an extremely violent armed conflict from 1991 to 2002. During this time, many war crimes and crimes against humanity were committed by all the armed factions involved, to varying degrees: the Revolutionary United Front (RUF); the Armed Forces Revolutionary Council (AFRC), a group of young military personnel who overthrew the government in 1997 and allied with the RUF; the Civil Defence Forces (CDF), civilian self-defence groups inspired by traditional hunting societies[8], coordinated and supported by the government; and the SLA (Sierra Leone Army). Abduction,

7 Truth and Reconciliation Commission, *Witness to truth*, (hereafter: *TRC-report*) Vol. 2, Executive Summary and findings, at 1 – 113 and Historical antecedents to the conflict, Vol. 3A, at 3–35.

8 Marianne Ferme, *The underneath of things. Violence, history and the everyday in Sierra Leone*, University of California Press, 2001, at 223.

forcible recruitment and the use of children as combatants were just some of the many crimes committed by all armed groups involved in the conflict.

The Lomé peace agreement, signed on 7 July 1999,[9] provided for disarmament, power sharing, new elections, a blanket amnesty[10] and a Truth and Reconciliation Commission. The UN representative added a last-minute disclaimer for international crimes to the amnesty agreement.[11] However, violence resumed in 2000, after which President Kabbah requested the UN to set up a Special Court. This was accepted.[12] The war was officially declared to be over on 18 January 2002.

Although diamonds and other alluvial mining resources played an important role in the conflict, they did not cause it, in contrast to popular belief in the West. The TRC identified poor governance, large-scale corruption, regional discrimination and polarisation, centralisation of power in the capital, youth alienation, unemployment and poverty as the causes of the conflict, in addition to weak institutions, a lack of government oversight and the manipulation of state and civil society institutions by the government in power.[13]

3. CHILDREN[14] AND YOUTH[15] IN THE SIERRA LEONE CONFLICT

Images of Sierra Leonean children carrying AK-47s[16] have travelled around the world. All armed groups enlisted children, including the army, but the RUF and

9 *Peace Agreement between the government of Sierra Leone and the Revolutionary United Front of Sierra Leone, 7 July 1999*, transmitted to the Security Council on 12 July 1999 (S/1999/777).

10 Lomé Peace Accord: Article IX provided for a blanket amnesty for "anything done by them in pursuit of their objectives as members of" any armed faction.

11 Priscilla Hayner, *Negotiating the peace in Sierra Leone: confronting the justice challenge, Centre for Humanitarian Dialogue and International Centre for Transitional Justice*, CfHD-report, December 2007, at 10–18.

12 *Security Council Resolution* 1315 (2000), 14 August 2000 (2000)S/RES/1315 followed by the signature of the '*Agreement between the United Nations and the government of Sierra Leone on the establishment of a Special Court for Sierra Leone*' on 16 January 2002.

13 *TRC report*, Vol. 2, at 29 onwards.

14 This refers to children under the age of eighteen. *Convention on the Rights of the Child*, 2 September 1990, Art. 1.

15 This is not an official legal category, but refers to young persons between the age of 15 and 24. *United Nations Integrated Disarmament, Demobilisation and Reintegration Standards*, 2006, section 5.20 Youth and DDR, Introduction, at 2. Government policy in Sierra Leone considers everyone between 18 and 35 years a youth. *TRC report*, Vol. 3 B, at 343. Popular understanding in Sierra Leone refers to any unmarried man as a youth. This chapter starts from the UN definition.

16 Avtomat Kalashnikova model 1947 (AK-47 assault rifle).

the AFRC were the main recruiters.[17] The Special Court for Sierra Leone, mandated to prosecute the crime of "[c]onscripting or enlisting children under the age of 15 years into armed forces or groups or using them to participate actively in hostilities",[18] found evidence in this respect against each of the armed factions, even though not all individuals standing trial have been convicted.[19] The Truth and Reconciliation Commission[20] found that most armed factions used a strategy of abduction and forcible recruitment of children. Children were compelled to consume drugs and were submitted to all kinds of mistreatment.[21] Not all of them were used as combatants: many had to perform household tasks, to carry looted items, or to serve as spies, smugglers, diamond miners or "bush wives".[22]

The idea that most of these children were forcibly recruited and are to be seen as victims rather than perpetrators and therefore should not be held criminally accountable has become part of an "emerging standard" at the international level.[23] But the reality is much more nuanced.

Whereas many children – especially the very young ones – were indeed forcibly conscripted to either of the armed factions in Sierra Leone, others decided to join on a voluntary basis. This might have been inspired by feelings of revenge after the killing of a relative, the prospect of having food and clothes, the

---

17 Eric G. Berman and Melissa T. Labonte, 'Sierra Leone', in William Durch, *Twenty-first century peace-keeping operations*, US Institute of Peace Press, 2006, at 188. *TRC-report*, Vol. 3B, at 289.

18 Art. 4 c of the Statute of the Special Court for Sierra Leone. The age limit for protection against recruitment (voluntary or forced) is 15 years in the UN Convention on the Rights of the Child (art. 38). The optional Protocol against the involvement of children in armed conflict raised the age limit to 18 years for protection against forcible recruitment and 16 years for voluntary recruitment. The Convention was ratified by Sierra Leone on 18 June 1990. The optional Protocol only dates from 25 May 2000 and was ratified by Sierra Leone on 15 May 2002. See at www.sc-sl.org.

19 RUF case: Trial Chamber judgment 2 March 2009, *Prosecutor v. Issa Hassan Sesay, Morris Kallon and Augustine Gbao*, Case No. SCSL 04-15-T, par. 1614–1748 and 2221–2237. Confirmed in this regard by the Appeals Chamber on 26 October 2009.
AFRC case: Trial Chamber Judgement, 20 June 2007, *Prosecutor v. Alex Tamba Brima, Brima Bazzy Kamara and Santigie Borbor Kanu*, Case No. SCSL-2004-16-T, par. 727–738 and 1244–1278. Confirmed by the Appeals Chamber Judgment, 22 February 2008.
CDF case: Appeals Chamber Judgement of 28 May 2008, *Prosecutor v. Moinina Fofana and Allieu Kondewa*, Case No. SCSL-04-14-A, par. 115–154. There were no final convictions for such charges in the CDF trial of Moinina Fofana and Allieu Kondewa, not because of the absence of such crimes within the CDF movement (which were considered established – see judgment of the Trial Chamber, 2 August 2007, par. 688–689), but because of the lack of personal criminal liability on the part of the accused persons in this regard.

20 *TRC-report*, Vol. 2, at 94–100.

21 Ibid.

22 Berman and Labonte, *supra* note 18 at 189.

23 UNICEF, *Draft Key Principles for Children and Transitional Justice: Involvement of Children and Consideration of Children's Rights in Truth, Justice and Reconciliation processes.* Outcome of Children and Transitional Justice Conference 27–29 April 2009, at 3. See at www.unicef-irc.org.

idea of being more secure with an armed group amidst the chaos of conflict, or simply the hope for some excitement or glamour.[24] The TRC report states that youth had been excluded from any meaningful political participation since the 1960s and that many were unemployed. To them, the war came as *"a welcome opportunity through which to amass wealth and transform their status"*[25] and *"[w]ar empowered them"*.[26] Of course the sense of the term "voluntary" can be argued, given the child's limited capacity for making mature decisions.[27] Often it means that the child saw no better alternative, while the lack of alternatives was not his or her responsibility.

In addition, the conflict in Sierra Leone lasted for 11 years. This means that some children spent many years with the armed forces. As a consequence, some forcibly recruited children "grew up" in the armed group and adopted its ideas and practices. The TRC report states that children were not only victims, but became perpetrators of the most horrendous crimes, after having been *"conditioned to accept violence as a norm"*, where *"perpetrating violence became a way of survival"*.[28] Peters and Richards state that *"[a]bductees cooperated with the movement to save their lives, but some found the movement's analysis of the breakdown in Sierra Leonean society meaningful and accepted guerrilla training willingly"*.[29] Or, as one of their interviewees stated: *"Soon the AK47 brings food, money, a warm bath and instant adult respect"*.[30]

Whether forcibly recruited or not, children are easy to manipulate. The combination of extended separation from their families and home communities, indoctrination by the leaders of the armed groups, forced consumption of drug and alcohol substances, harsh living conditions and the violence used against them turned many children into atrocious killers and abusers. The horrendous amputations and other mutilations, which became the international label of the Sierra Leonean conflict, were often performed by children under the command of their leaders. In addition, abducted children were often forced to commit crimes in their home communities (and scarified), in order to prevent them from trying to escape.[31]

---

24 P.W. Singer, *Children at war*, University of California Press, California, 2006, at 57–69.

25 *TRC report*, Vol. 2, at 95.

26 *TRC report*, Vol. 3B, at 352.

27 *Supra* note 24 at 62. For this reason 'enlistment' of a child under fifteen is a crime regardless of the child's consent. *Prosecutor v. Alex Tamba Brima, Brima Bazzy Kamara and Santigie Borbor Kanu*, Case No. SCSL-2004-16-T (hereafter: AFRC case) Trial Chamber Judgement, 20 June 2007, par. 735. Also confirmed by the *ICC. Prosecutor v. Thomas Lubanga Dyilo*, Case No. ICC-01/04-01/06 (hereafter: Lubanga case), Pre Trial Chamber I, Decision on the confirmation of charges, 29 January 2007, par. 247.

28 *TRC report*, Vol. 2, at 96.

29 Krijn Peters, Paul Richards, '"Why we fight": Voices of youth ex-combatants in Sierra Leone', (1998) 2 *Africa*, Vol. 68, at 184.

30 *Supra* note 29 at 187.

31 *Supra* note 29 at 186–187.

The idea that these children and youth are victims of crimes themselves or at least of the context leading to the armed conflict will not be challenged here. Nevertheless, many of them are conscious of what they did during the war and may have feelings of guilt, remorse and shame for what they did, or regret the loss of status acquired during the conflict, like the boy cited above.

For all these reasons, communities feared the return of these children and youth after the conflict, while the children in turn feared revenge attacks or at least rejection.[32]

4. THE REINTEGRATION OF CHILDREN AND YOUTH IN SIERRA LEONE

4.1. DISARMAMENT, DEMOBILISATION AND REINTEGRATION

The United Nations has addressed the problem of children in armed conflict in several resolutions, calling upon member states to take specific consideration of the problems of children in all DDR processes.[33] In these resolutions the UN adopted DDR standards[34] with specific provisions regarding children and youth.[35]

Although most of these resolutions and the standards were adopted after the conflict in Sierra Leone, some principles and ideas had already been applied. The Lomé Peace Agreement[36] was the first ever peace agreement that recognised the existence of child soldiers and the need to take measures to address the specific needs of children in the DDR process.[37] This recognition was important, since before the Lomé Agreement child soldiers were often forgotten in demobilisation processes, if their existence was not simply ignored by the armed groups.

---

32 *Supra* note 17 at 190.

33 UN Resolutions 1261 (S/Res/1999), 1314 (S/Res/2000), 1379 (S/Res/2001), 1460 (S/Res/2003) and 1539 (S/Res/2004) 1612 (S/Res/2005).

34 United Nations, *Integrated Disarmament, Demobilisation and Reintegration Standard*, 2006, sections 5.20 and 5.30 (hereafter: IDDRS). See at www.unddr.org.

35 In addition, UNICEF has developed the *Cape Town Principles and Best Practices on the Prevention of Recruitment of Children into the Armed Forces and on Demobilization and Social Reintegration of Child Soldiers in Africa*, adopted in 1997 and adapted in 2007 to become the Paris Commitments and the Paris Principles (*hereafter: The Paris Principles*). See at www.unicef.org.

36 Lomé Peace Accord, Article XXX.

37 *Supra* note 24 at 184. For a historical and comparative overview of the inclusion of child soldiers in peace agreements, as well as the various UN resolutions in this regard, see: Stephen Kabera Karanja, 'Child Soldiers in Peace Agreements: The Peace and Justice Dilemma', (2008) *Global Jurist*, Volume 8, Issue 3 (Advances), Article 9, at 3–7.

Like most recent demobilisation programmes, the DDR programme in Sierra Leone had three components:[38] disarmament (removing weapons from the hands of the combatants), demobilisation (formal discharge of combatants from the armed groups, often by offering them temporary resettlement or passage through a demobilisation camp, also to prevent re-recruitment) and reintegration (the process of economic and social integration into society).

In Sierra Leone the DDR programme was elaborated by the government and implemented through the National Commission for Disarmament, Demobilisation and Reintegration (NCDDR), backed by UNAMSIL, the UN peacekeeping mission.[39] NCDDR stated that 75,490 combatants were demobilised after the conflict, of whom 6,845 were child soldiers (including 506 girls).[40]

For children, reintegration is the most crucial phase of the DDR process.[41] The reintegration process – the focus of this chapter – was coordinated by UNICEF, working with international and national NGOs, and comprised "… family reunification, mobilizing and enabling the child's existing care system, medical screening and health care, schooling and/or vocational training, psychosocial support, and social and community-based reintegration".[42]

Since UNICEF[43] and DDR standards[44] only consider persons below the age of eighteen at the time of demobilisation as children, many youths were treated as adults, regardless of their age at the time of recruitment.[45] Thus, they did not receive any specialised support, although their needs may even be more important.[46]

In addition, Williamson thinks that some children who were below eighteen insisted that they were adults, since that would provide them with monetary advantages children would not receive.[47] Finally, it has also been widely acknowledged that girls were practically excluded from the DDR process.[48]

38 See: IDDRS, *supra* note 15. Glossary: terms and definitions.

39 UN Security Council Resolution of 13 July 1998/(S/RES/1181 (1998) to establish UNOMSIL, *United Nations Observer Mission in Sierra Leone* and resolution of 22 October 1999 (S/RES/1270(1999) to establish UNAMSIL, a much larger mission including thousands of military personnel Berman and Labonte, Sierra Leone, at 184–192.

40 NCDDR, *Executive Secretariat Report, 3 February 2004,* at 3–4. Available at www.daco-sl.org.

41 Elisabeth Shauer, 'The psychological impact of child-soldiering', (2009), 24 February, at 33. ICC-01/04-01/06-1729-Anx1 25-02-2009 32/54 RHT. Available at www.icc.org.

42 IDDRS, Glossary: terms and definitions: *Child reintegration.*

43 *The Paris Principles*, 2.0 and 2.1.

44 IDDRS, Glossary: terms and definitions: *Child.*

45 The TRC found that boys between the age of 10 and 14 were disproportionately targeted for forced recruitment. *TRC-report*, Vol. 3B. at 289.

46 Singer, *supra* note 24 at 185.

47 John Williamson, 'The disarmament, demobilization and reintegration of child soldiers: social and psychological transformation in Sierra Leone', (2006) 3 *Intervention*, Vol. 4, at 188.

48 *TRC-report*, Vol. 3B, at 325–327. The TRC estimated that 30 percent of all child soldiers were girls, while they only represented 8 percent in the DDR process. Ibid. at 186.

Although no exact numbers are available on those children and youth who did not benefit from specific reintegration measures adjusted to their needs, the elements above make it probable that they must amount to several hundreds.

4.2. NO RETURN HOME

Since 98 percent of all officially demobilised children were reunited with their families,[49] UNICEF staff consider the reintegration of children to be successful to a large extent and think the main reason for this success was *"the involvement of communities in developing the reintegration programme for children"*.[50]

However, the reintegration was not successful for all children and youth. Williamson recognises that some children migrated to other areas to find livelihood opportunities or to avoid hostility, stigma and discrimination in their home community.[51] Regarding adults (including youths), much more criticism was expressed in respect of the reintegration phase of the DDR programme,[52] in spite of the relatively successful outcome of the disarmament and demobilisation phases.[53]

Humphreys and Weinstein[54] – not limiting their research to children or youth – found that most former CDF combatants had returned to their home communities (75 percent). In contrast, only 34 percent of former RUF combatants had returned home, while most chose to live in new communities (in 2003). As the TRC noted, many youth who had joined the RUF were from the rural areas.[55]

Young ex-combatants who have still not returned home, or came back after initial return, stay in Freetown, Makeni, Bo and other towns. Some have engaged in economic activities, such as motor-bike taxis or trade, while others are

---

49 *Supra* note 47 at 192, quoting UNICEF statistics.

50 Interview with UNICEF staff, Bo, April 2009.

51 *Supra* note 46 at 185.

52 Macartan Humphreys and Jeremy M. Weinstein, 'Demobilization and reintegration', (2007) 4 *Journal of Conflict Resolution*, Volume 51, at 531–567 even found that participation in the DDR process was not a significant factor for successful social reintegration. On economic reintegration: Krijn Peters, 'Reintegration support for young ex-combatants: a right or a privilege?', (2007) *International Migration*, Vol. 45 (5), at 35–57.

53 UNAMSIL, *Fact Sheet 1: Disarmament, Demobilisation and Reintegration*, December 2005, at www.un.org/Depts/dpko/missions/unamsil. A 2004 NCDDR report states that most ex-combatants have returned home, but that there are issues of unemployment with those who decided to stay in towns such as Bo, Makeni, Freetown, Kenema and Koidu. NCDDR *Executive Secretariat Report, 3 February 2004*, at 3–4.

54 Macartan Humphreys and Jeremy M. Weinstein, *What the fighters say, A Survey of Ex-Combatants in Sierra Leone, June-August 2003,* Centre on Globalization and Sustainable Development, Columbia University, New York, USA, Working Paper No. 20, August 2004, in partnership with the Post-conflict Reintegration Initiative for Development and Empowerment (PRIDE), at 39–45.

55 *TRC-report*, Vol. 3B. at 351.

unemployed or have engaged in illegal activities. Some young men have married local girls or have settled down with their former "bush wives". Some have gone back to their home communities but only intermittently.[56]

The question is whether there is a need for more reintegration of ex-combatants into their home communities: as the unity of the country is promoted ("we are one country"), every Sierra Leonean can reside wherever he wants.

Since the end of the war, former ex-combatant youth have merged with non-ex-combatant youth, many of whom have also left the rural areas to settle in towns. Whereas 66 percent of all Sierra Leoneans still live in rural areas, up to 58 percent of those less than 29 years old live in urban areas.[57] For many youths, the lack of social and economic opportunities in these rural areas is the main reason to settle in the towns. In this regard, the problems of youth ex-combatants do not seem to be different from those of youths in general.

However, ex-combatants have specific reasons for not returning home. Several interviewees in Sierra Leone mentioned – in addition to the lack of economic opportunities[58] – a fear of revenge or rejection, conflict with the elders and a general lack of recognition of the needs and aspirations of youth.[59]

These youths may not be the majority of all children and youth formerly associated with an armed faction, but they are particularly vulnerable to mobilisation into new conflicts, as established by Human Rights Watch.[60] As one interlocutor indicated: "*Reintegration and reconciliation will be complete only when someone comes and looks for people to fight in Guinea and no one shows up.*"

4.3. FEAR FOR RETRIBUTION AND REJECTION

Many ex-combatants, mainly those belonging to what Humphreys and Weinstein call "*abusive military factions*",[61] still fear revenge form their home communities, regardless of their individual behaviour during the war. There is no clear answer to the question whether and to what extent revenge killings have actually taken place. Although several interviewees during my research claimed there had not been any killings, others explicitly referred to initial revenge killings by secret

---

56 Interviews with UNIPSIL, UNFPA, PRIDE, Campaign for Good Governance, GTZ, academics. Bo District Human Rights Coalition, Bo Peace and Reconciliation Movement.

57 International Crisis Group, *Sierra Leone: a new era of reform, 31 July 2008*, at 23, quoting official statistics.

58 This chapter will not address the economic problems of youth, although recognised as crucial.

59 Ibid.

60 'Youth, Poverty and Blood. The lethal Legacy of West-Africa's regional Warriors', (2005) March *Human Rights Watch*, at 48 onwards.

61 Humphreys and Weinstein, *supra* note 52 at 533.

society members. There is no doubt that secret societies hold the power to punish those who transgress societal norms.[62] Fanthorpe mentions that the "*fighters' fearless transgression of secret society laws as they entered village sacred bushes*" is still an issue in rural areas.[63] Interviewees[64] claim people would be welcomed back by their family and the community elders, and then taken to be washed in the river and killed by secret society members, some of whom might be their own relatives. Others would have been burnt alive. Some managed to escape but were severely injured. This would have been the case in the south-east of the country, mainly in Kono, Kailahun, Pujehun and Moyamba.[65] These practices occurred in the immediate aftermath of the conflict, before the return to civilian rule. They only ended with the official government policy to "*forgive and forget*".[66]

Whether or not there is currently still a risk of revenge, the perception is a reality among some ex-combatants. Various researchers mention this fear of retribution as a motive for continued displacement.[67]

Rejection, on the contrary, is not just a matter of perception but a reality, both in home communities and in new communities where ex-combatants decided to settle.

Boersch-Supan's[68] findings show that superficial reintegration of (adult) ex-combatants into communities hides patterns of discrimination against them in the fields of employment, social interaction, gossip and labelling. She explains that the fear is mutual: ex-combatants fear retribution, while the population fears living with those who committed crimes in their community. The more a community has suffered, the less it will be ready to accept "its perpetrators" living with them, whereas former fighters who committed atrocities elsewhere might be more easily accepted. She concludes that "*peace partly rests on the limited freedom of movement and choice of residence for ex-combatants*", meaning that moving to another place – in other words not returning home – has become one of the coping strategies.

---

62 Manifesto '99, *Traditional methods of conflict management/resolution of possible complementary value to the proposed Sierra Leone Truth and Reconciliation Commission*, July 2002, at 21.

63 Richard Fanthorpe, 'Sierra Leone: The Influence of the Secret Societies, with special reference to Female Genital Mutilation', (2007) August, *Writenet Independent Analysis*, at 12.

64 Interview with Ministry of Social Welfare and Inter Religious Council, Freetown.

65 Johanna Boersch-Supan, 'What the Communities say: the crossroads between reintegration and reconciliation. What can be learned from the Sierra Leonean experience?', (2009) January, *Crise*, 63, at 30; refers to a small number of former fighters who were killed upon return.

66 Statement on the formal recognition of Paramount chiefs, by president Kabbah at Kenema, Bo, Makeni and Port Loko, from 26th – 30th January 2003; www.sierra-leone.org (last visited on 2 April 2009), section 6.17.

67 Simon Arthy, *Ex-combatant reintegration. Key issues for policy makers and practitioners, based on lessons from Sierra Leone*, at 20. Submitted to the UK Government's Department for International Development in August 2003, on file with author. Boersch-Supan, *supra* note 65 at 30.

68 Boersch-Supan, at 23–24, 29–30, 34, 37.

5. WHY THEY DO NOT RETURN HOME

The following section of the chapter will examine the reasons for not returning home in more detail. As we will explain, many of these reasons are linked to the cultural context of Sierra Leone, i.e. traditional values in responding to transgression of societal norms, traditional power balances and the challenges to them, and issues of social status in a traditional society.

5.1. LACK OF YOUTH ACCOUNTABILITY

While (some) children and youth undoubtedly committed crimes during the war, and while according to traditional values, children – especially those above fifteen who are considered youths – are responsible for what they do, no official accountability mechanism has been established.

Researchers looking into the problems between ex-combatants and the communities they live in have identified this lack of accountability as a motive for rejection.

Humphreys and Weinstein[69] note the fear of rejection of abductees of all armed factions by their home communities, because of the crimes they had been forced to commit there.[70]

Ginifer[71] too states that the latent hostility of communities towards ex-combatants after DDR remained a problem. Fear of violence or revenge was identified as a cause, alongside the perceived privileges given to ex-combatants as well as the attitude of some ex-combatants in refusing to acknowledge any wrong-doing.

The fact that ex-combatants are still fearful of revenge and experience rejection, while people in the community do not trust ex-combatants and discriminate against them, shows that there still is a lot of anger and frustration underneath the surface of "peaceful coexistence". Boersch-Supan[72] interprets the labelling of and discrimination against ex-combatants as a form of subtle punishment of the perpetrators by the community, inspired by the lack of an alternative, while the fact that ex-combatants accept this discrimination would be a subtle act of repentance and apology. In other words, there seems to be a lack of accountability by youths regarding their war-related behaviour.

---

69 Macartan Humphreys and Jeremy M. Weinstein, at note 52 at 542.

70 Also: *TRC report*, Vol. 3B, at 263 and 275.

71 Jeremy Ginifer, 'Reintegration of ex-combatants', in Mark Malan et al., (2003) March, *Sierra Leone. Building the road to recovery*, Monograph no. 80, at 48.

72 Boersch-Supan, *supra* note 65 at 34–39 and 45.

5.1.1. *Criminal prosecutions*

Amnesty provisions in the Lomé peace agreement, in combination with the limitation of the Special Court's[73] mandate to those who bear the greatest responsibility,[74] imply that youth ex-combatants were not held accountable for criminal acts committed during the civil war.

The question whether to prosecute children or youths who were below the age of eighteen at the time of committing a crime led to lengthy debates when the mandate of the Court was discussed. The international community was strongly opposed, while their Sierra Leonean counterparts were strongly in favour of prosecution:

> The Government of Sierra Leone and representatives of Sierra Leone civil society clearly wish to see a process of judicial accountability for child combatants presumed responsible for the crimes falling within the jurisdiction of the Court. It was said that the people of Sierra Leone would not look kindly upon a court which failed to bring to justice children who committed crimes of that nature and spared them the judicial process of accountability. The international non-governmental organizations responsible for childcare and rehabilitation programmes, together with some of their national counterparts, however, were unanimous in their objection to any kind of judicial accountability for children below 18 years of age for fear that such a process would place at risk the entire rehabilitation programme so painstakingly achieved.[75]

Finally, the Court was given jurisdiction to prosecute former child combatants who were between the age of 15 and 18 years at the time of the alleged commission of a crime, while alternative sanctions were provided.[76] By way of compromise, art. 15.5 of the Statute adds: "*In the prosecution of juvenile offenders, the Prosecutor shall ensure that the child rehabilitation programme is not placed at risk and that, where appropriate, resort should be had to alternative truth and reconciliation mechanisms, to the extent of their availability.*"

Nevertheless, the Prosecutor of the Court declared very early on that he would not prosecute anyone under the age of 18 years.[77] Indeed, he stated that

73 The Court has tried and convicted eight persons (three from the RUF, two from the CFD and three from the AFRC) for war crimes and crimes against humanity. Charles Taylor, the former president of Liberia, is currently standing trial for his involvement in the Sierra Leonean conflict. For more details see the website of the Special Court at www.sc-sl.org. Also: International Centre for Transitional Justice, *From the Taylor trial to a lasting legacy: putting the Special Court model to the test*, 2009.

74 Art. 1 of the Statute of the Special Court for Sierra Leone. See at www.sc-sl.org.

75 *Report of the Secretary-General on the establishment of a Special Court for Sierra Leone*, UN Doc. S/2000/915 (4 October 2000), par. 35.

76 *Supra* note 75, Art. 7.

77 Special Court for Sierra Leone, Public Affairs Office, Press Release, 2 November 2002, *Special Court Prosecutor Says He Will Not Prosecute Children* at www.sc-sl.org.

"although the children of Sierra Leone may be among those who have committed the worst crimes, they are to be regarded first and foremost as victims".

In the end, no children, nor any (adult) youths, were prosecuted by the Special Court.

At the domestic level hardly any prosecutions have taken place, although prosecuting those not benefiting from the amnesty, such as persons who committed crimes after the signing of the agreement, was possible.[78] The only notable exception seems to have been the prosecution of some members of the RUF and the West Side Boys.[79]

5.1.2. *Truth and Reconciliation Commission*

The Truth and Reconciliation Commission has extensively examined the situation of children and youth during the conflict and made findings on the crimes from which they had suffered.[80] The Commission, although confirming that children and youth had also become perpetrators of horrendous crimes,[81] did not make recommendations regarding any alternative accountability mechanism.

Many youths participated in the Commission's public and closed hearings.[82] Some also participated in reconciliation ceremonies, where they apologised for what they did during the war and asked traditional and religious leaders to be accepted again by the community, often lying down on the floor in the traditional way, followed by the performance of traditional rituals such as the pouring of libation or sharing of a kolanut.

5.1.3. *Traditional Practices*

UNICEF's approach towards the reintegration of children consisted in establishing contact with the child's community, which was consulted on what needed to be done. Sending children back to school, providing them with skills training or helping them to set up small businesses was only part of the formula.[83] Ultimately, acceptance by the community seemed to be conditioned

---

78 International Center for Transitional Justice, *supra* note 73 at 16; Priscilla Hayner, *supra* note 11 at 25.

79 The 'West Side Boys' were a splinter group of the African Forces Revolutionary Council and were responsible for the kidnapping of UN peacekeepers in 2000, amongst many other crimes. Ten RUF and seven WSBs were convicted in April 2006 of conspiracy of murder. Jeneba F. Kamara, 'The Arbitrary Violation of Fair Trial Protection in Sierra Leone', (2007) 20 January, *SLCMP*. See at www.slcmp.org.

80 *TRC report*, Vol. 3B, Chapter 4 on Children, at 233–339 and Chapter 5 on Youth, at 343–360.

81 *TRC report*, Vol. 2, at 95.

82 Children under eighteen were automatically heard in closed session.

83 Children below fifteen would rather go to school, while those over fifteen were offered skills training and start-up kits. *TRC report*, Vol. 3B, at 325.

by traditional cleansing.[84] Both boys and girls underwent cleansing ceremonies, regardless of their role during the conflict.[85]

Cleansing ceremonies in Sierra Leone differ from chiefdom to chiefdom and village to village. An example of the cleansing of a girl in Kono district mentioned by UNICEF staff comprised the washing of her feet and the drinking of the water by community leaders, symbolising her purification, acceptance by the community and presentation to the ancestors, to whom sacrifices of animals or kola nuts would be made.

Zack-Williams[86] describes another ritual of cleansing, where the boy or girl, after asking for forgiveness, would be taken to the sacred bush and stripped of the clothes that were symbolic of his or her former lifestyle, which would then be burned. In addition, sacrifices to the ancestors would be made to appease the angered spirit of the person killed that had caused the child's confused mental health state.

Stark[87] explains how abducted girls would return home and experience various kinds of rejection, stigmatisation and provocation, inspired by the fear of family and community members being affected by the spiritual contamination of the girl. The cleansing rituals would comprise physical care (caressing, massaging, wrapping herbs on the body), talking and telling stories, washing the girls in the river, destroying old clothes and dressing them in new ones, followed by a return to the village and a presentation of the "new" girls to the elders and the community. This would be followed by celebrating and sharing a meal. The author considers this as both a symbolic act to welcome home the "children" of the community ("community reconciliation") and an act of cleansing them from bad things that had happened to them in the bush or from bad spirits that had inhabited them ("spiritual transformation"). The common meal shared by the community after the cleansing symbolised their reintegration into the community. Girls participating in such cleansing ceremonies claimed improved self-perception and behaviour as well as improved perception and treatment by the community and more good fortune for themselves and the community.

Adult programmes organised by NCDDR did not specifically provide for traditional cleansing, although traditional mechanisms and structures were called upon to increase reintegration, alongside wider sensitisation campaigns

---

84 Honwana has described similar cleansing rituals for child soldiers in Mozambique and Angola. Alcinda Manuel Honwana, 'Healing for Peace: Traditional Healers and Post-War Reconstruction in Southern Mozambique', (1997) 3 *Peace and conflict: journal of peace psychology*, at 293–305.

85 *Supra* note 50.

86 Tunde B. Zack-Williams, 'Child Soldiers in Sierra Leone and the Problems of Demobilisation, Rehabilitation and Reintegration into Society: Some Lessons for Social Workers in War-torn Societies', (2006) March, *Social Work Education*, Vol. 25, No. 2, at 126–127.

87 Lindsay Stark, 'Cleansing the wounds of war: an examination of traditional healing, psychosocial health and reintegration in Sierra Leone', (2006) *Intervention*, Vol. 4, No. 3, at 210.

and activities.[88] Ginifer states that where cleansing ceremonies were performed a "considerable impact in terms of community relations" was noticed.[89]

Unfortunately, no figures are available on the number of child or youth ex-combatants who underwent cleansing or the number of communities where it took place. Since cleansing requires some costly rituals to be performed, no cleansing has been performed in communities that were not reached by reintegration or reconciliation projects if they were too poor to bear the cost.[90]

5.1.4. *Traditional Values*

Even though part of the population would like to see more criminal prosecutions, mainly of the mid-level perpetrators who are seen in the community,[91] most accept the fact that there will be no prosecution of children or youth who committed crimes (which of course was not the case for all ex-combatants) for various reasons.[92] Interviewees said there is no need for lengthy retributive justice trials to elaborate on all the details about what happened during the conflict.[93] However, people would like ex-combatants to acknowledge their wrongdoing and to offer apologies, which can then be accepted by the victims and the community. Thus, non-criminal accountability and apologies are necessary steps in the reconciliation process.[94]

The dire need for such accountability and reconciliation explains the success of traditional cleansing ceremonies. Williamson[95] refers to research in which two groups of young RUF ex-combatants with an average age of fifteen are compared.

88 Jeremy Ginifer, at note 72 at 45.

89 Ibid. at 47. This is acknowledged in the so-called *Machel Review Report*: *United Nations, Report of the Special Representative of the Secretary-General for Children and Armed Conflict*, 13 August 2007, A/62/228, par. 97, referring to Sierra Leone.

90 Philip Cook and Cheryl Heykoop, 'Child Participation in the Sierra Leone Truth and Reconciliation Commission: Considering the broader cultural context', Innocenti Working Papers 2009, Florence, UNICEF Innocenti Research Centre.

91 BBC World Service Trust, International Centre for Transitional Justice, *Search for Common Ground, Peace, Justice and Reconciliation in Sierra Leone: a survey of knowledge and attitudes towards transitional institutions in post-conflict Sierra Leone*, August 2008, at 54–55. The survey, conducted in 2007, shows high rates of positive answers to the question whether the commanders of armed factions should be prosecuted (87 percent), while rates are much lower regarding the need for prosecution of rank-and-file perpetrators (29 percent).

92 Beth K. Dougherty, 'Right-sizing international criminal justice: the hybrid experiment at the Special Court for Sierra Leone', (2004) *International Affairs*, 80–2, at 327. Also: Hayner, *supra* note 11 at 12.
The Trial Phase of the Special Court for Sierra Leone, November 2005, at 38, find at www.ibanet.org/Committees/WCC_SCSL.aspx.

93 Confirmed by Tim Kelsall, 'Truth, Lies, Ritual: Preliminary Reflections on the Truth and Reconciliation Commission in Sierra Leone', (2005) *Human Rights Quarterly* 27 at 389–390.

94 Confirmed by Boersch-Supan at note 65 at 24 and 42.

95 Williamson, *supra* note 46 at 201–202. Theresa Betancourt and Shawna Pochan, Marie de la Soudière, 'Psychosocial adjustment and social reintegration of child ex-soldiers

The first group had passed through an Interim Care Centre and undergone traditional cleansing while the second was composed of children and youth who had returned home directly. The reintegration of both was compared in 2002 and 2004. The research found no significant difference regarding participation in traditional cleansing ceremonies. However, those who had participated in such cleansing had "*significantly higher scores for family acceptance, pro-social behaviour and confidence, than those who had not.*" This research confirms UNICEF's and others' findings on the importance of traditional cleansing, regardless of DDR participation.[96]

Traditionally, however, cleansing as such is not an accountability mechanism. Research by the Sierra Leonean organisation Manifesto '99 notes that the objective of traditional purification is to cleanse the perpetrator of a crime of his sin (the transgression of societal norms), to protect him from "*the wrath of God or the ancestors*" and to accept him back as a member of the community.[97] Cleansing normally follows acknowledgement of wrong-doing (voluntary or following social and spiritual pressures through swearing or oath taking), apologies, restitution and some kind of compensation to the victim and the community, depending on the nature of the crime, as well as a commitment not to repeat such behaviour in the future.[98]

Although organised for the prime purpose of reintegration and therefore rather a modern adaptation of traditional cleansing,[99] the various types of cleansing performed on ex-combatant children and youth certainly had a component of reacceptance and reconciliation according to traditional values. According to UNICEF staff, an acknowledgement of wrong-doing and a request for apologies sometimes preceded the cleansing of children, although no details would be made public.[100] Not all, however, comprised elements of acknowledgement and

in Sierra Leone', *Wave II Follow-Up Analysis*, at 11. The research is available at www.usaid.gov/our_work/humanitarian_assistance/the_funds/.

96 John Williamson identified nine elements that contributed to the successful reintegration of children: community sensitisation; formal disarmament and demobilisation; a period of transition in an Interim Care Centre; family tracing, mediation and reunification; traditional cleansing and healing ceremonies and religious support; school or skills training; access to health care; individual supportive counselling and an effective collaborative approach. *Id.* at 203.

97 Manifesto '99, *supra* note 62 at 23.

98 Ibid., at 4. Also at 23: '*Depending on the ethnic group purification is usually required when any of the following crimes is committed: incest, rape, defilement of the `Bush', murder, shedding of blood and arson*'.

99 A former TRC coordinator confirmed that two types of cleansing were practised for reintegration purposes: a public, modern and more collective type on the one hand, and a more traditional one in the sacred bush for those who had previously undergone traditional initiation (who were the exceptions, as will be explained below).

100 *Supra* note 50.

apology.[101] In addition, restitution or compensation were absent from all such ceremonies.

Traditional practices can apparently be applied with some flexibility, especially in post-war circumstances, but the question remains whether such adjusted practices fulfil the tradition-based values of justice and reconciliation. In communities where problems of discrimination against and rejection of ex-combatants still occur, a lack of traditional accountability might well be the issue, although more research on the topic is necessary.

5.1.5. Current Tradition-Based Projects

Considering the identified need for more tradition-based accountability, some Sierra Leonean organisations have started projects in this regard. The Forum of Conscience, to name but one, is conducting a project for tradition-based justice, called Fambul Tok.[102] The project[103] explicitly uses traditional justice methods, although adjusting them to some extent. The methodology involves several steps, including sensitisation, mediation between victim and offender, acknowledgment of wrong-doing, the offering and acceptance of apologies and finally a reconciliation ceremony spread over two days: a bonfire in the evening reuniting and reconciling victims, perpetrators and the community; the next day traditional ceremonies to appease the ancestors and achieve spiritual reconciliation.[104] Afterwards, a peace tree is identified under which future conflicts can be resolved and follow-up is provided by Fambul Tok staff. In Moyamba district, Fambul Tok mainly focused on former CDF ex-combatants, young men who had committed abuses when they were still holding power after the end of the war and were still living in the same community. According to my interviewees, the project brought a restoration of relationships and good neighbourliness and allowed them to work together and to conceive common projects. For instance, while young ex-combatants had challenged the chief's authority by boycotting his call to participate in road maintenance, they would now organise it together and engage in community farming.

But why would young ex-combatants be challenging the chief's authority? This leads us to another aspect of the accountability problem.

---

101 Zack-Williams, *supra* note 86 at 126–127; Stark, *supra* note 87 at 210.

102 *Krio for Family Talk*, referring to the traditional method of conflict resolution through palaver.

103 Interviews with Forum of Conscience in Freetown and Moyamba. Focus group discussion with the population of Yondu section, Kagboro Chiefdom and Sennehun Section, Kombura Chiefdom, both in Moyamba district, who had benefited from the programme. Also see: Fambul Tok, *Community healing in Sierra Leone.* Our first year *Forum of Conscience and Catalysts for Peace,* 2008. For an analyses and more detailed description, see: Elisabeth Hoffman, 'Reconciliation in Sierra Leone. Local processes yield global lessons', (2008) *The Fletcher forum of world affairs*, Vol. 32.2, at 129–141.

104 Reparations were equally lacking in this project, considering the general level of poverty.

5.2. LACK OF TRADITIONAL LEADERS' ACCOUNTABILITY

Traditional justice mechanisms, as used before the conflict in Sierra Leone, did not deal with the accountability of chiefs to the members of their community. Although it has been established that traditional leaders had some share of responsibility for the conflict, no effective accountability mechanism exists to deal with this issue.

5.2.1. Role of Traditional Leaders with Regard to the War

The Truth and Reconciliation Commission clearly identified the responsibility of traditional leaders with regard to the conflict. Indeed, traditional elders, often the only source of authority in rural areas, had a tendency to abuse their powers in order to repress any challenges by youth.[105] Such challenges could be inspired by an absence of decision making power, of access to land[106] or of other economic resources, and the related absence of the possibility of marriage (the combination of the practices of polygamy and dowry[107] reduced the availability of young girls for marriage with poor youth, leading in turn to risks of adultery, which were countered by the high fines that traditional leaders imposed on youth;[108] those unable to pay these fines often had no other choice than to leave the community).[109] All these factors led to alienation and frustration amongst youth, which in its turn created a pool of disgruntled young men easily mobilised by either of the armed groups.

The International Crisis Group even notes that the conflict in Sierra Leone was also a "*rural rebellion against chiefs and customary law*".[110] This frustration and disgruntlement also explains a number of atrocities committed to humiliate

---

105 *TRC report*, Vol. 3A, at 8. More detailed examples of chieftaincy disputes and abuse of power per district can be found in the same volume, at 28–35. Also Vol. 3B, at 241 and 347.

106 Population growth and land scarcity resulted in younger sons in the family being allocated either remote or less productive parcels of land or none at all. David Keen and Greedy Elites, 'Dwindling Resources, Alienated Youths. The Anatomy of Protracted Violence in Sierra Leone', (2003) 2 *Internationale Politik und Gesellschaft*, at 79.

107 Ferme adds the costs of the initiation of the girl into the women's society, as well as the marriage licence that had to be paid to the chief. Marianne C. Ferme, *The Underneath of things. Violence, history and the Everyday in Sierra Leone*, University of California Press, 2001, 99.

108 Steven Archibald and Paul Richards, 'Converts to Human Rights? Popular debate about war and justice in rural central Sierra Leone', (2002) 3 *Africa: Journal of the International African Institute*, Vol.72, at 344.

109 Richard Fanthorpe, 'On the limits of liberal peace: chiefs and democratic decentralization in post-war Sierra Leone', (2005) *African Affairs*, 105/418, at 30–31. Ryann Elizabeth Manning, 'Challenging generations. Youth and Elders in Rural and Peri-Urban Sierra Leone', November 2008, at 4. On file with author.

110 International Crisis Group, 'Sierra Leone: A New Era of Reform?', (2008) *Crisis Group Africa Report* 143, 31 July, at 22.

elders, traditional chiefs or other "big men".[111] Many paramount chiefs felt insecure during the conflict and fled to Freetown or to displacement camps.[112] This caused an important loss of status and authority, since they left "their" people alone and were not able to protect them. In addition, the physical absence of the traditional leaders from their communities paved the way for the rise of and usurpation of authority by "the boys" of the Civil Defence Forces (CDF), even after the end of the war.[113]

5.2.2. Traditional Leaders after the War

Since many chiefs had been killed or died of natural causes during the war,[114] the Sierra Leonean government launched a programme to restore traditional chieftaincy.[115] Regardless of the past, traditional leaders are still widely accepted today in Sierra Leone.[116] For instance, people today still go to the chiefs to find solutions for many day-to-day problems.[117] They consider them to be the protectors of customary property, traditional values, secret societies[118] and local interests. Indeed, people seem to have more faith in traditional leaders than in elected politicians and bureaucrats.

Nevertheless, traditional chiefs can no longer behave like autocrats. The war and the related displacement and exposure to other values and institutions made people more aware of their rights. Even if they still accept the institution of the chief, people are therefore less willing to accept abuses of any kind.[119] Where traditional leaders do not accept this, their authority will be challenged: youths may boycott community decisions for which their collaboration is required, for instance by refusing to provide communal labour to maintain the roads or market-places or to pay taxes. Youth organisations play an important role in this regard,[120] as do the parallel power structures created by the government's decentralisation policy.[121]

---

111 *TRC report*, Vol. 3A, at 8 and 37. Vol 3B, at 352. Although Fanthorpe, *supra* note 109 at 31 sees little evidence that traditional leaders were targeted more than other authority figures.

112 Archibald and Richards, *supra* note 108 at 344.

113 For example see: ibid., at 348–349. Also Fanthorpe, *supra* note 109 at 40–41.

114 *Interview Forum of Conscience, The Hague.*

115 *Paramount Chiefs Restoration Programme.* Referred to by Fanthorpe, *supra* note 109 at 31 and Archibald and Richards, *supra* note 108 at 347.

116 Fanthorpe, *supra* note 109 at 44.

117 Owen Alterman et al., 'The Law People See. The status of dispute resolution in the provinces of Sierra Leone in 2002', (2002) *National Forum for Human Rights, Freetown*, at 22 onwards. On file with author.

118 Fanthorpe, *supra* note 109.

119 Keen, *supra* note 106 at 99. Manning, *supra* note 109 at 19–21. Fanthorpe, *supra* note 109 at 41.

120 Boersch-Supan, *supra* note 65 at 30 and 43.

121 Fanthorpe, *supra* note 109 at 27–49.

The question remains whether the checks and balances imposed on traditional authorities by government, modern society, youth organisations and others will be sufficient to erase the need to deal with the role traditional leaders played in the past and to prevent future abuses.

5.2.3. Lack of Accountability of Traditional Leaders

What is striking is that hardly any examples are known or cited of traditional chiefs actually having apologised for past abuses.

The Truth and Reconciliation Commission (TRC) referred to this in its report. The Commission stated that it had been "*surprised by the number of complaints about the violations committed by many of the Chiefs during the conflict, for which they neither as a group nor individually expressed any remorse or offered an explanation to their communities. In reality, while the Commission had to rely on the Chiefs as leaders of their communities and had to work closely with them, the Commission was cognizant of the fact that many chiefs have been discredited by their failure to explain the roles they played during the war... However, the Commission has recommended that the role of the Chiefs and the manner in which they have been manipulated by successive governments must be placed on the national agenda for discussion, as it has a huge potential for further conflict in the future.*"[122] Such a national debate did not take place, although then president Kabbah did refer to such abuses in a public speech.[123]

Apparently, people do not easily point to the issue of pre-war abuses by traditional leaders as a cause of the conflict. Even specific reconciliation projects do not very often bring up this issue, while on the other hand the responsibility of the youth for committing crimes and abuses is often mentioned.[124]

During the interviews I conducted in April 2009, only one occasion of apologies by the elders of the community was mentioned, more particularly for previously misusing community funds.[125]

Perhaps one of the reasons for this is that the abuses of power by traditional leaders were not exclusive to them: corruption, patronage and nepotism were widespread in Sierra Leone, so how could the chiefs not be affected?[126] Traditional chiefs had been manipulated by both the colonial rulers and the independent Sierra Leonean government, giving them too much power on the one hand, undermining their legitimacy and downwards accountability on the other.[127]

---

122 *TRC report*, Vol. 3B, at 438.

123 'Statement of President Kabbah', (2006) *Awarness Times*, 30 January, point 6.4.

124 *Interview Fambul Tok project, Freetown.*

125 *Interview Bo Peace and Reconciliation Movement.*

126 Fanthorpe, *supra* note 109 at 39.

127 *TRC report*, Vol. 3A, at 30–31.

In the past, traditional justice not only did not provide a mechanism for holding the chiefs themselves accountable – since they were the legislators as well as the judges and implementers of rules – but rather became a tool for abuse, with the consequences described above.

Thus, traditional justice in its usual setting – dominated by male chiefs and elders – cannot provide the answer.

But perhaps the war has created *"a window for human rights"*, as Archibald and Richards argue.[128]

Indeed, projects such as Fambul Tok are using the setting of traditional conflict resolution – the African palaver – and the traditional values of mediation and restoration of relationships, meanwhile adding new elements. Whereas conflict resolution belongs to the traditional role of the elders, Fambul Tok actively involves young people (and women) in the preliminary phases of sensitisation and mediation. Even more importantly, the project opens a space for dialogue that goes beyond traditional practices. Traditionally, for example, a young man cannot ask an older man to apologise, but at the bonfire ceremony this becomes possible and actually happened, when a traditional leader apologised for stealing food during the war.

Such adjustments are not perfect and further research on their practical impact is necessary, though they have been accepted.

5.3. REINTEGRATING INTO A TRADITIONAL CONTEXT

The lack of social empowerment of youths was identified as one of the root causes of the war and a reason for many young fighters to take up arms and challenge the establishment. Indeed, participating in the conflict did provide some young combatants with status and respect, while most experienced violence and a harsh existence in the bush.[129] Returning home empty-handed – without schooling, social skills or a source of income, habituated to drug abuse and violence – left them with nothing but the hope of being accepted again. For those who returned, traditional cleansing was an important step forward, although it involved submitting themselves to the same leaders and structures they had been challenging. But was that enough to acquire the social status they had been aspiring to? In rural Sierra Leone, social status can still only be acquired by becoming a member of a secret society.

---

128 Archibald and Richards, *supra* note 108 at 345.

129 *TRC report*, Vol. 3B, at 360.

As mentioned earlier, people in Sierra Leone still attach importance to traditional values and respect traditional authorities. Sierra Leone is particularly known for its secret societies or sodalities, which are gendered organisations of co-initiates.[130] Not the existence as such of these societies is a secret, nor even membership of a society, but rather members share a number of secrets that they cannot make public to non-initiates.[131] Manifesto '99, based on research conducted in 2001, considers secret societies to be "*dominant and important, as they are sources of non-formal education, social and behavioural control as well as social cohesion and integration*".[132] In addition, they serve as a check on the power of the paramount chief and provide an alternative method of justice.[133]

Traditionally, at least in rural areas, initiation into a secret society was an automatic "rite of passage" to adulthood. It is performed separately for boys and girls in their early adolescence and can last for several months.[134] Ferme explains that initiation is a violent, painful experience for both men (who are put through an ordeal, being scared and scarified[135]) and women (who undergo a clitoridectomy) through which "*the urgency of protecting secrets and bodily boundaries is inscribed in the initiate's flesh*".[136]

Not undergoing traditional initiation has important social consequences: indeed, a person who is not a member of a secret society will not have any status in the community, he or she will not be involved in the societies' meetings, where important decisions are taken, and will not have any authority to make proposals or take decisions regarding the community. The person will not be considered a valuable member of the community. Even persons with academic titles or economic power will not be allowed to attend decision making meetings or be elected to political positions without being a member and having the support of a secret society.[137] Access to land can be denied to them.[138]

Unlike for men, membership of a secret society for women does not confer any political power in society. However, it is important for being considered a good candidate for marriage, since women's traditional roles are taught during the initiation, on the one hand, and it provides a woman with authority in the women's community, on the other.[139]

---

130 The main secret societies are Poro and Wonde for men, Sande and Bondo for women, but others exist as well, sometimes in parallel. See: Manifeso '99 for several examples.

131 Several interviewees spoke freely about their membership, past experience or so-called secrets.

132 Manifesto '99, *supra* note 62 at 8.

133 Ibid. Also: Joe A.D. Alie, *A new history of Sierra Leone*, McMillan Publishers, London, 1990, 18.

134 Ibid. at 24–25.

135 Male circumcision was often performed at an earlier age, especially among Muslims, or even for health reasons.

136 Ferme, *supra* note 8 at 179–180.

137 *Interview academics, Freetown*. Fanthorpe, *supra* at note 64 at 7.

138 Ibid. at 12.

139 *Supra* note 137.

The war has distorted these practices, since young boys and girls were abducted or recruited before they were initiated. Some armed groups performed rituals copying traditional initiation (including scarification[140]), but these are not acknowledged as such. Young men returning home after the war consider themselves to be adults and often feel too old to submit themselves to the sometimes humiliating initiation practices.[141] Young women may have become reluctant to undergo female genital mutilation, which is normally a procedure applied to girls before they have sexual intercourse. Since most of the abducted girls have been raped or given in marriage within the armed groups and many have had children, practising FGM seems to be in contradiction to its original meaning (i.e. purifying the girl's body[142] and making her ready for marriage, with the underlying purpose of controlling the girl's sexuality).[143]

Of course, one might wonder whether being a member of a secret society is still as important nowadays, with changing values and norms and external influences on people's lives. Initiation of both boys and girls is still taking place on a large scale in Sierra Leone, although interviewees say the process has been shortened and has lost much of its educational aspect.[144] In particular, FGM is still being practised on up to 90 percent of all girls and women,[145] although voices are being raised to require the girl's consent, which she can only provide once she is above eighteen.[146]

Initiation is said to be no longer forced on children nowadays, although social pressure is still considerable.[147] Not being a member of a secret society will not exclude a person from having a meaningful life and from being respected for his economic position. But such a person will not have any social status within his home community and will be denied access to family land.[148] He will not be able to hold a position of authority or to be elected (for instance as a member of a district council or a local court, let alone at national level), since he will not benefit from the support of a secret society, support that would be automatic were he a member of one.[149]

---

140 Ferme, *supra* note 8 at 248.

141 Fanthorpe, *supra* note 63 at 14. Also acknowledged in the Paris Principles, 7.46.

142 Ibid. at 17.

143 Interview with academics, Freetown.

144 Interview with UNICEF, Pride, Centre for Democracy and Human Rights, Makeni, former TRC-coordinator.

145 Dyan Mazurana and Susan McKay, 'Girls in Fighting Forces in Northern Uganda, Sierra Leone, and Mozambique: Policy and Program Recommendations', June 2003, at 37 (note 25). Available at www.unddr.org.

146 Ibid. at 17.

147 Fanthorpe, *supra* note 63 at 14 and 20.

148 Ibid. at 12.

149 Interviews with academic, Freetown, and Paramount Chief, Makeni. Fanthorpe, *supra* note 63 at 7.

Young men returning home without being initiated into a secret society, even if they have been circumcised and even if they undergo a cleansing ritual or another tradition-based justice process, will therefore never be able to gain status in the community. This can be illustrated by the fact that a few months after tradition-based reconciliation ceremonies organised by the Fambul Tok project in Kailahun district, several hundred young men who had participated were initiated into a secret society.[150] Such initiation is considered evidence of ultimate acceptance and trust, since it involves the sharing of secrets and decision making power.[151] The same applies to women, whose initiation, however, inevitably passed through FGM.[152]

Non-initiates will not be rejected or attacked in a physical way and they may interact with other members of the community on a daily basis, but they will be excluded from a part of community life. This reality, in particular for young people who had gained a certain status in an armed movement or who joined the conflict to fight for more rights, might be difficult to accept. Such persons, if they are not initiated – and even after modernised, tradition-based cleansing – may prefer to live in town, where they can gain status through economic (if not criminal) activities.

This clearly illustrates the dilemma of taking into consideration the cultural context: support for cleansing and other tradition-based practices can have a positive impact on the reintegration of children and youth.[153] The way cleansing has been promoted in Sierra Leone illustrates the idea that traditional practices can be supported so long as they do not cause harm or violate international standards.[154] Meanwhile, the larger traditional context, including harmful practices or otherwise constraining social norms, is not considered.

The question is whether traditional practices can be modernised and if they can, whether they will still have the same impact. Beyond the mere practices, the question is also to what extent reverting to them will strengthen what Zack-Williams has called the "gerontocracy", in disregard of the youths' own aspirations and interests.[155]

---

150 Interview Forum of Conscience, The Hague.

151 In the same sense: Laura Stovel, 'Long road home. Building Reconciliation and Trust in Post-War Sierra Leone', (2010) 2 *Series on Transitional Justice*, Intersentia, Antwerp, at 179.

152 Mazurana, *supra* note 145 at 25.

153 Alie, *supra* note 133 at 145.

154 Paris Principles, 7.53: *"Appropriate cultural practices, as long as they are not harmful to children, can be essential to a child's reintegration and should be supported."* Also principle 7.61: *"Strategies should enable girls' acceptance through steps such as conducting traditional rituals, making reparations, providing health care and livelihoods support, and developing links with women's groups."*

155 Zack-Williams, *supra* note 86 at 127. Also: Alie, *supra* note 133 at 144.

6. CONCLUSION

Sierra Leone is still a very traditional, though slowly changing society. The ambiguous feelings of young ex-combatants willing to return home but no longer wanting to accept the "gerontocracy" of the elder generation illustrates this transition. The way rural communities deal with the violent past of young ex-combatants is symptomatic: in order to be accepted by the community youths will have to acknowledge their misdeeds and submit themselves to the traditional way of dealing with transgression against and conformity with societal rules. By doing this, they risk confirming or even reaffirming the very conservative structures they were challenging. Elders and traditional chiefs, on the other hand, seek to restore their authority. Being the custodians of traditional values, they rarely acknowledge their responsibility for the past. However, in order to maintain part of their power, they have no choice but to adjust their behaviour and attitude to external influences, such as human rights promotion, the presence of NGOs and the government's decentralisation policy.

The official transitional justice mechanisms have not been able to provide an answer to these dilemmas. The Special Court applied the international views on criminal accountability. The Truth and Reconciliation Commission identified the responsibility of both youth and elders in its report. Reconciliation ceremonies at the end of the hearings, however, applied traditional practices of dispute settlement, whereby those who committed crimes asked the traditional and religious leaders for forgiveness. Regarding the responsibility of traditional leaders, which came up as an important issue only near the end of the Commission's mandate, it could only make recommendations for further analysis and debate.

The DDR process and particularly the social reintegration of children (and some youth) allowed and encouraged traditional cleansing as part of the welcoming back ceremony, with some success, meanwhile turning a blind eye to the link with initiation practices.

Ongoing though limited initiatives by NGOs try to provide tradition-based modernised answers to the identified need for more communication and dialogue concerning the past, particularly between youth and elders.

International actors too face the dilemma of taking account of the cultural context: support for cleansing and other tradition-based mechanisms can have a positive impact on the reintegration of children and youth and has the advantage of providing culturally embedded and therefore easily understandable and acceptable solutions. The consensus of international actors nowadays seems to be that traditional mechanisms can be supported, insofar as they do not cause harm or violate international standards.

But what are the risks of isolating these practices from the larger cultural context, including harmful practices or otherwise constraining societal norms? Can traditional practices be modernised and if they can, will they still have the same impact? And to what extent will reverting to such mechanisms strengthen the same traditional structures that were identified as causes of the conflict, in disregard of the youths' own aspirations and interests?

Contextualising DDR and transitional justice faces the challenge of addressing the inherent problems linked to the traditional, conservative nature of this context, some of which this chapter has tried to identify.

SUPPORT TO THE EDUCATION AND LIVELIHOODS OF WAR-AFFECTED CHILDREN AND YOUTH IN NORTHERN UGANDA

Ann Lorschiedter and Femke Bannink-Mbazzi

1. THE WAR IN NORTHERN UGANDA

At the beginning of the last century, 80 to 90 percent of war casualties worldwide were military personnel and 10 to 20 percent were civilian and unarmed. By the end of the century, these figures were reversed.[1] Today, in northern Uganda and elsewhere, armed conflicts and civil wars have blurred the distinction between "combatants" and "civilians", and "civilian" itself is a diffuse and broad category of non-combatants who are living in the midst of conflict. Frontlines are not easily defined and non-combatants are often targets of harassment and deadly violence.

In northern Uganda, more than two million people were displaced from their homes as a result of the conflict between the northern Ugandan Lord's Resistance Army (LRA), led by rebel leader Joseph Kony, and the Government of Uganda, headed by General Yoweri Museveni.[2] From 1986 to 2006, the rhythm of the war in northern Uganda has been an uneven one, with sometimes long periods of lull in the fighting and rather peaceful times during which people could lead an almost "normal" life, working in their gardens and travelling rather safely on the roads. In 2005, however, nearly 90% of the population in Gulu, Kitgum and Pader Districts, those most affected by violence, had relocated into camps for internally displaced people. The IDP Camps have often been described as a

1 T. Allen and J. Seaton, 'Introduction', in T. Allen and J. Seaton (eds.), *The Media of Conflict: War reporting and representations of ethnic violence*, London and New York, 1999, 1–8; M. Kaldor, 'The structure of conflict', in L. Wohlgemut, S. Gibson, S. Klasen, and E. Rothschild (eds.), *Common security and civil society in Africa*, Uppsala, 1999, 126; C. Nordstrom, 'The backyard front', in C. Nordstrom and J.A. Martin (eds.), *The paths to domination, resistance and terror*, Berkeley, 1999, 155 and 170.

2 International Crisis Group, *Northern Uganda: Understanding and Solving the Conflict*, Nairobi/Brussels, 2004. www.unhcr.org/refworld/docid/407e70554.html [accessed 12 July 2009].

scenario of extremely poor, even inhuman living conditions, dominated by military restrictions and impoverishment, where all aspects of life were severely affected, resulting in generally high vulnerability and dependency on support from outside.[3] In the pre-displacement setting, every family lived in its own compound, and in the evenings family members gathered by the fireplace to share supper and for traditional teaching. The displacement characterised by overcrowded camps and lack of security resulted in destruction of the social fabric, with people living in a "state of fear and anxiety".[4] Youth could hardly access educational facilities and had almost no means of generating an income, which led to self-destructive practices such as drinking alcohol, unprotected sex and early marriage.

Although the war in northern Uganda has often been perceived as a local, northern Ugandan conflict and in many cases as a "primitive" or "barbaric" war, it has instead been part of a complex regional war in which the neighbouring countries Sudan and Congo were involved and which was – and still is – threatening security beyond northern Uganda. At present (autumn 2010), the LRA remains active after having shifted to southern Sudan, north-eastern Congo and the Central African Republic, conducting forced massive recruitment exercises, causing tens of thousands to flee their homes and leaving hundreds dead,[5] and it is as yet uncertain whether the future will eventually bring lasting peace to the people in the region.[6]

1.1. "CHILD SOLDIERS" IN THE LRA

1.1.1. Conscription of Minors into the LRA and DDR

In most cases, and especially since the 1990s when the LRA experienced a decrease in local support, children and youth in the LRA were abducted and did

---

3 C.O. Akumu, I. Amony and G. Otim, *Suffering in silence: A study of sexual and gender based violence (SGBV) in Pabbo Camp, Gulu District, Northern Uganda*, 2005, www.reliefweb.int/library/documents/2005/unicef-uga-15jun.pdf [accessed 19 July 2009]; J.N. Corbin, 'Returning home: Resettlement experiences of formerly abducted children in northern Uganda', (2008) *Disasters* (Online Early Articles), 316–335; E. Stites, D. Mazurana and K. Karlson, *Movement on the margins: Livelihoods and Security in Kitgum District, Northern Uganda*. Boston, 2006.

4 Retired Bishop Baker Ochola quoted in *IRIN News*: www.irinnews.org/InDepthMain.aspx?InDepthId=23&ReportId=65810.

5 Beyond Juba, *The Uganda Conflict Timeline*, 2009, www.beyondjuba.org/conflict_timeline.php [accessed 8 October 2010].

6 United Nations Security Council, *Northern Uganda/LRA Historical Chronology*, 2009, www.securitycouncilreport.org/site/c.glKWLeMTIsG/b.2880391/ [accessed 5 August 2009]; M. Schomerus, *Perilous border: Sudanese communities affected by conflict on the Sudan-Uganda border,* Conciliation Resources, London, 2007, www.c-r.org/our-work/uganda/documents/Perilous-Border.pdf [accessed 3 August 2009].

not join the rebel army as volunteers as was the case in other wars in Africa and elsewhere. Such volunteers have various motives in joining armed forces, most often linked to the war itself, poverty, education, employment and/or family.[7] Their reasons for joining armed forces voluntarily distinguish this group from abductees and must first be identified and addressed before they can be supported in their process of reintegration.[8] Unlike in other countries where children and youth were included in large-scale DDR (Demobilisation, Disarmament and Reintegration) programmes, past programming in northern Uganda focused mainly on the reintegration aspect.

1.1.2. Statistics on Abduction

According to a report from the *enough!* project in February 2008, the insurgency in northern Uganda "has resulted in arguably the highest number of child abductions in the world";[9] however, the report did not indicate specific figures. Some estimates of the number of LRA abductions appear to be higher than previously suggested, and the whereabouts of most of those abductees who have not yet returned from captivity remains unknown. By triangulating data from different sources on the number of former abductees, the Berkeley Report estimates that the LRA had abducted 24,000 to 38,000 children and 28,000 to 37,000 adults as of April 2006. The authors of the study, however, observed gaps in the data collection and insufficient information management in reception centres, and a lack of information on returnees who never passed through such a centre.[10] The Survey of War Affected Youth estimates that 66,000 children and youth were abducted, that more than 10,000 people were killed and that many thousands more mutilated during the conflict.[11] An exact number of children, youth and adults who have been abducted over the 20-year period will most likely never be available, owing to the lack of reliable statistics.

The age of those who were abducted by the rebels, as well as the length of time they spent in captivity, varied considerably. The involvement of children in the war has been "sometimes exaggerated": research shows that between 1997 and 2001, less

---

7 D.M. Rosen, *Armies of the Young: Child Soldiers in War and Terrorism*, Rutgers University Press, New Brunswick, 2005.

8 R. Brett, 'Adolescents volunteering for armed forces or armed groups', (2003) 85 *Affaires courantes et commentaries – Current issues and comments*, 852 and 859.

9 J. Prendergast and L. Rogoff, 'R2P, the ICC and Stopping Atrocities in the Real World', (2008) 13 *Enough Strategy paper*, at 2, www.responsibilitytoprotect.org/files/ENOUGH%20 Report.pdf [accessed 2 July 2009].

10 P. N. Pham, P. Vinck, and E. Stover, *Abducted: The Lord's Resistance Army and Forced Conscription in Northern Uganda*. Berkeley-Tulane Initiative on Vulnerable Populations, Human Rights Centre, University of California, Berkeley and Payson Centre for International Development, Tulane University, 2007, www2.reliefweb.int/rw/RWB.NSF/retrieveattachment s?openagent&shortid=EVOD-76JJG5&file=Full_Report.pdf [accessed 5 July 2009].

11 J. Annan, C. Blattman and R. Horton, *The State of Youth and Youth Protection in Northern Uganda: Findings from the Survey of War Affected Youth*, Kampala, UNICEF Uganda, 2006.

than one third of those abducted were children.[12] Also, not children but youths older than 12 years were usually a main target for the LRA's abductions, on average staying in captivity for more than one year. Among those who were abducted for more than two weeks, 25 percent reported having been forced to kill civilians or soldiers. 80 percent of the abductees eventually managed to escape from the LRA, with the remaining number released by the LRA or captured by the UPDF.[13]

1.1.3. Mystification of "Child Soldiers"

Ugandan and international media usually portrayed the conflict in northern Uganda as the barbaric war of one fanatical religious rebel leader with no clear political agenda, massacring people from his own "tribe". Often, media reports and research echoed this limited view and mystification also in relation to one category of its victims, namely children and youth who were forcefully abducted by the LRA rebels.

Not only but also regarding northern Uganda, "child soldiers" are often described as children heavily armed with a machine gun or a machete and turned into reckless little monsters and killing machines. Such portrayals, along with the most sensational interviews of children who had been abducted, forced to kill and commit other atrocities, are contributing to a myth of child soldiering in which the children and youth are seen as victims and perpetrators at the same time, as "time bombs" and "emotional cripples" who are totally disconnected from their family and community, deeply traumatised due to rape, forced marriage and childbirth, killings and lootings, and unable ever to live a normal life again but instead posing an ongoing security threat in their communities even after the war – they are seen as the "lost children". Although thousands of the children and youth abducted by the LRA have indeed undergone many of the events listed above, local realities often show that many of them have a strong resilience which helps them to redefine their lives after captivity and to find a place in their society.[14]

1.1.4. The Quantification of Trauma

"Trauma" is a widely used term for describing the impact of the war on the population in northern Uganda, especially in relation to former abductees.

12 T. Allen and M. Schomerus, *A Hard Homecoming: lessons Learnt From the Reception Centre Process on Effective Interventions for "Former Abductees" in Northern Uganda. An Independent Study*, Washington, DC., 2006, VI, http://pdf.usaid.gov/pdf_docs/PNADI241.pdf [accessed 8 August 2009].

13 C. Blattmann and J. Annan, 'Child combatants in northern Uganda: Reintegration myths and realities', in R. Muggah (ed.), *Security and Post-Conflict Reconstruction: Dealing with Fighters in the Aftermath of War*, Routledge, 2008, 103–126.

14 Ibid.

Symptoms of post-traumatic stress disorder (PTSD) among former abductees in northern Uganda have been investigated in several studies, for example in order to associate them with openness to reconciliation and feelings of revenge, using the Child Posttraumatic Stress Disorder Reaction Index and indicating a PTSD score.[15] Other research on PTSD was carried out by asking children to recall atrocities and horrible events.[16] Most of such studies undertaken on PTSD have shown high prevalence rates of symptoms of PTSD and depression among the returnees.[17]

On academic grounds, discussions have been held as to whether it is ethically right to carry out research on "child soldiers" with a focus on quantifying trauma through diagnosis of PTSD. Critics do not question the existence of trauma but raise concerns about a pathologisation and stigmatisation by imposing "Western" categories, and limiting the conceptualisation of the support that may be required, especially when such research is not deeply embedded in the social, economic, cultural and political realities of the informants.[18]

1.1.5. The Reintegration of Former "Child Soldiers" in the Context of Northern Uganda

A large proportion of the existing research on the reintegration of returnees in northern Uganda is written within a framework of human rights, child protection, advocacy, peace and human development, often drawing on interviews with returnees and/or others close to them (family members, social workers, local leaders, teachers etc.).[19] Other studies have a focus on mental health – in which often special emphasis is put on PTSD,[20] or on the relevance of counselling in particular and psychosocial support in general – and some refer

---

15 C.P. Bayer, F. Klasen and H. Adam, 'Association of Trauma and PTSD Symptoms with Openness to Reconciliation and Feelings of Revenge Among Former Ugandan and Congolese Child Soldiers', (2007) 298 *The Journal of the American Medical Association*, 555–559, http://jama.ama-assn.org/cgi/reprint/298/5/555 [accessed 17 August 2009]; F. Glöckner, *PTSD and Collective Identity in Former Ugandan Child Soldiers,* University of Konstanz, 2007, http://nbn-resolving.de/urn:nbn:de:bsz:352-opus-33085 [accessed 30 July 2009].

16 I. Derluyn, E. Broekaert, G. Schuyten and E. de Temmerman, 'Post-traumatic stress in former Ugandan child soldiers', (2004) *The Lancet* 363, 861–863, www.essex.ac.uk/armedcon/story_id/000178.pdf [accessed 15 June 2009].

17 P.N. Pham, P. Vinck and E. Stover, 'Returning home: forced conscription, reintegration, and mental health status of former abductees of the Lord's Resistance Army in northern Uganda', (2009) 9 *BMC Psychiatry,* at 23, www.pubmedcentral.nih.gov/picrender.fcgi?artid=2693494&blobtype=pdf [accessed 18 July 2009].

18 S. McKay and M.G. Wessels, 'Post-traumatic stress in former Ugandan child soldiers', (2004) *The Lancet* 363, 1646.

19 M.G. Wessels, *The Recruitment and Use of Girls in Armed Forces and Groups in Angola: Implications for Ethic Research and Reintegration*, Pittsburgh, 2007, at 2.

20 S. Koesler, C. Wöhrmann, B. Zwissler, A. Pfeiffer, V. Ertl and J. Kissler, 'Does remembering cause forgetting in chronically stressed people? A Study of Ugandan Civil War Refugees with and Without PTSD', (2010) 218 (2) *Journal of Psychology*, 71–79.

to reintegration from a local standpoint, often backed up by Acholi traditional and cultural aspects of healing.

Emphasis is also put on gender-based aspects of reintegration, putting in the spotlight the specific situation of girls and young women as "sex slaves" or forced "wives" of rebels or rebel commanders, highlighting an additional hardship of the "child mothers", girls or young women who gave birth in the "bush". These "child mothers" and their "children born in captivity" have increasingly been targets of special attention, with programmes specifically tailored for supporting them.[21] Concerns about ethical sensitivity in conducting research with female returnees have been raised,[22] and it is also suggested that discussions about these young women were "bedevilled with misconceptions".[23]

Media reports are increasingly to be found on the homepages of most of the larger newspapers, journals and television channels dealing with reintegration. Still, new publications on the phenomenon of abduction and on the reintegration of returnees in northern Uganda continue to be released and research projects to be designed, both for academic and programmatic purposes.

At the same time, there is a growing need to consider vulnerable youth, and not only children, in Acholiland when designing interventions targeting peace and reconciliation in northern Uganda in general, and successful reintegration in particular.[24]

---

21 E. Mbengue and I. Desiree, *Effective reintegration of female child soldiers: reality or rhetoric? Case study of Northern Uganda,* Pretoria, 2007, repository.up.ac.za/dspace/bitstream/.../mbengue%20eleke_id_1.pdf [accessed 2 July 2009]; K. Carlson and D. Mazurana, *Forced marriage within the Lord's Resistance Army, Uganda*, Medford, 2008.

22 Wessels, *supra* note 19.

23 Allen and Schomerus, *supra* note 12.

24 Annan et al., *supra* note 12; Women's Commission for Refugee Women and Children, *Listening to Youth: The Experiences of Young People in Northern Uganda. Contribution to Machel 10-Year Strategic Review,* New York, 2007, www.unhcr.org/refworld/docid/48aa83150.html [accessed 1 August 2009]; E. Baines, E. Stover and M. Wierda, *War-Affected Children and Youth in Northern Uganda: Toward a Brighter Future. An Assessment Report*, Chicago, 2007, www.macfound.org/atf/cf/%7BB0386CE3-8B29-4162-8098-E466FB856794%7D/UGANDA_REPORT.PDF [accessed 22 July 2009];
J. Annan, C. Blattman, K. Carlson and D. Mazurana, *The State of Female Youth and in Northern Uganda: Findings from the Survey of War Affected Youth, Phase II.* Kampala, UNICEF Uganda, 2008; Women's Commission for Refugee Women and Children, *Youth and Sustainable Livelihoods: Linking Vocational Training Programs to Market Opportunities in Northern Uganda*, Colombia University, 2008, www.womenscommission.org/pdf/ug_ysl_rep.pdf [accessed 5 July 2009]; F. Bannink-Mbazzi and A. Lorschiedter, 'Psychosocial support to vulnerable youth in vocational schools in northern Uganda', (2009) 7 *Intervention* 2, 130–137.

1.2. EFFORTS TO ESTABLISH PEACE IN NORTHERN UGANDA

In 2000, the Ugandan Parliament passed a comprehensive Amnesty Act "for Ugandans involved in acts of a war-like nature in various parts of the country". The Amnesty Act has been successful in providing "a way out" for those who were able to leave the LRA and be referred to a reception centre – the majority are former abductees – but the capacity of the Amnesty Commission to implement not only the reintegration of returnees but also reconciliation and justice at the local level was limited.[25]

While there has been no official end to the conflict yet, the majority of the displaced population in northern Uganda has started to move out of the IDP camps (in the Acholi sub-region, the original camp population at the end of 2005 was estimated to be 1,110,140 people, of whom in September 2009 17 percent remained in an IDP camp, while 17 percent had moved to a transit site and almost ¾ of the population had gone to their "villages of origin").[26] The situation in the neighbouring countries, however, is less calm, with the LRA still being active and at times causing massive havoc.

2. SUPPORTING WAR-AFFECTED CHILDREN AND YOUTH THROUGH EDUCATION AND GAINING LIVELIHOOD

2.1. VULNERABILITY IN THE RETURN AND RESETTLEMENT SETTING

In order to support youth in the process of return, specifically to improve their self-reliance and coping mechanisms, educational institutions need to be re-established and self-reliance can be promoted by skills training and income generating activities. With more than half of Uganda's population under the age of 15, education and economic skills are of paramount importance to the country's future.

Despite Uganda's introduction of a Universal Primary Education (UPE) programme in 1997 which waived school fees for primary students, education levels remain low; of the more than 2 million UPE pioneer students in 1997 less than 100,000 had continued through to completion of the senior level in 2008. Only eight percent of Ugandan males and six percent of females have completed

---

25 Allen and Schomerus, *supra* note 12, VII.

26 UNOCHA, *Update on IDP movement, September 2009*, IASC Working Group, Kampala, 2009, 1.

a primary-level education, and less than one percent have completed a secondary level education.[27]

The war in northern Uganda, resulting in a generally increased vulnerability, has adversely impacted on access to education, the quality of education and the possibilities of pursuing economic activities in IDP Camps for youth. Despite the efforts of donors, humanitarian agencies, religious and cultural institutions and the Government, key educational indicators remain below the national averages in most of the conflict-affected districts with few exceptions, and certainly below the internationally recommended standards. The expansion in enrolment has not been matched by supply in terms of teacher recruitment and provision of facilities. Generally, the school infrastructure is relatively better in IDP camps compared to areas of origin as many were destroyed during the conflict. Literacy and numeracy rates in northern Uganda are only 54 percent, while 23 percent of children in northern districts aged 7 to 18 years reported having never been to school, attendance is irregular, and retention and completion rates are low, especially for girls. The situation for secondary school-aged children and youth is even worse.[28]

Youth are often affected by early drop-out before completion of their Primary Leaving Exams (due to financial constraints, early pregnancy, death of the parents/guardians, and/or abduction, among others, see Table 1 below),[29] or, after completion of primary school, do not have the means to continue with their education at secondary school level. During the displacement, the most pressing needs of the population were mainly identified by NGOs and donors in order to determine the required funding and support. The focus of the interventions was usually emergency relief rather than development cooperation. Areas such as post-primary and non-formal education were not among the priorities.

From the onset of the movement from IDP camps into transit sites and return areas, the population highlighted the need to re-establish basic services such as schools as the most pressing need in the return process.[30] Lack of such services outside the IDP Camps decreased the chance of many youth to access secondary education, and instead increased protection concerns in relation to children and youth: many children opted to remain in the camps in order to attend classes, while their parents were occupied with work in the gardens and re-establishing

---

27 Ministry of Education and Sports, *The Education and Sports Sector Annual Performance Reports (ESSAPR) 2008*, Kampala, Uganda, 2009, www.education.go.ug/ESAPR.htm [accessed 22 June 2009].

28 Ministry of Education and Sports, *The Northern Uganda Education Assessment*, Kampala, Uganda, 2006, www.education.go.ug/Final%20Needs%20Assessment%20Report.doc [accessed 18 July 2009].

29 The statistics refer to the evaluation of a project of AVSI that was implemented under the Northern Uganda Rehabilitation Programme (NUREP), and are part of AVSI's final report to NUREP.

30 UNDP, *Returning to uncertainty? Addressing vulnerabilities in northern Uganda*, Kampala, Uganda, 2007, www.fafo.no/nyhet/return2uncertanity.pdf [accessed 22 June 2009].

their new homes elsewhere. Although some of these children were left on their own in the IDP camps without the supervision and care of older family members, many were taken care of by elder siblings, often youth.

Table 1. Reasons for dropping out of school: results of an assessment among 144 youth beneficiaries of an AVSI project in Kitgum District

Reasons	Number	%
Financial constraints	79	54.9
Pregnancy	21	14.6
Death of parent(s)	12	8.3
Abduction	8	5.6
Lack of family support	6	4.2
Responsibilities at home	5	3.5
Never attended school	2	1.4
Dropped out due to displacement	1	0.7
Insecurity	1	0.7
Sickness	1	0.7
Sickness/disability of the parents	1	0.7
Other	7	4.9
	144	100.0

Since the beginning of the return process, a shift from emergency relief in the education sector, through which mainly temporary structures and materials were put up for children in the IDP camps, to development projects in the areas of return focused on quality, and age-appropriate education has started. The provision of educational services, participation in psychosocial programmes, vocational training and support through income generating activities can support the successful reintegration of former abductees and provide essential support to other war-affected youth, by helping to restore hope for the future with opportunity.[31]

As for the returnees, once out of captivity many suggest a reintegration agenda sensitive to their economic wellbeing and social relations in the context of their culture and tradition, proposing psychosocial activities, vocational and

31 A. Veal and A. Stavrou, *Violence, Reconciliation and Identity: The Reintegration of Lord's Resistance Army Child Abductees in Northern Uganda*, Monograph No. 92, Institute for Security Studies, Pretoria, 2003, www.iss.co.za/pubs/Monographs/No92/Chap3.html [accessed 17 August 2009]; Annan et al., *supra* note 12; Women's Commission for Refugee Women and Children, *Youth and Sustainable Livelihoods: Linking Vocational Training Programs to Market Opportunities in Northern Uganda*, Colombia University, 2008, www.womenscommission.org/pdf/ug_ysl_rep.pdf [accessed 5 July 2009]; Annan et al., *supra* note 24, second reference.

entrepreneurial skills training, provision of credit facilities, and an education system that recognises their background and needs.[32]

Vocational training is "at the crossroads of economic recovery, education and rehabilitation and reintegration, and can be a key component of development, a method for upgrading the labour force and a factor in the holistic development of youth",[33] therefore one of the educational methods that can provide skills for livelihoods and employment. However, there is a need to diversify the skills for training, as over the years large numbers of tailors, masons and carpenters have been produced who encounter challenges in finding employment or self-employment opportunities.[34]

Access to education and support for improved livelihoods for many war-affected youth in northern Uganda cannot be the only means of empowering them to overcome their challenges; but they can be supported to gain self-confidence and to redefine their roles as independent and important members of their communities.[35] The following paragraphs outline the experiences of the AVSI Foundation (formerly called Associazione Volontari per il Servizio Internazionale) in supporting vulnerable youth through education and gaining a livelihood.

2.2. AVSI'S PROGRAMMING

AVSI, an international non-governmental organisation (NGO), was founded in 1972 in Italy. In Uganda, AVSI started implementing projects in northern Uganda in 1984. Throughout the conflict in northern Uganda, AVSI has implemented projects in the sectors of education, health, HIV/AIDS, disability, food security and livelihoods, protection, and water and sanitation. Over the years, AVSI's programmes have always been a mixture of emergency relief and developmental projects, aiming to provide immediate relief for persons in the IDP camps combined with structural support to the existing health and education systems such as hospitals, health centres and (displaced) schools.

32 K.A. P'Olak, 'Coping with Life in Rebel Captivity and the Challenge of Reintegrating Formerly Abducted Boys in Northern Uganda', (2007) 20 *Journal of Refugee Studies* 4, 641–661, http://jrs.oxfordjournals.org/cgi/content/abstract/20/4/641 [accessed 13 August 2009].

33 Women's Commission for Refugee Women and Children, *supra* note 31.

34 Northern Uganda Youth Development Centre, *Consultative Mission Report: Synopsis/Executive Summary*, Kampala, 2006, www.thecommonwealth.org/Shared_ASP_Files/UploadedFiles/2CB1DFF2-ACEA-454E-9E5C-5A54CC1E2BE6_ConsultativeMissionReport4-10Oct06NorthernUgandaYouthDevelopmentCentre.pdf [accessed 19 June 2009]; Women's Commission for Refugee Women and Children, *supra* note 31.

35 F. Bannink-Mbazzi, A. Lorschiedter, A.H. Amony and F. Opok, 'Persons living with physical disabilities in the return process in Northern Uganda', (2009) 20 *Journal for Disability and International Development* 2, 4–9.

Following the above outlined recommendations and experience in emergency relief and development cooperation in northern Uganda, AVSI developed a holistic approach to respond to the needs of the returning children and youth. AVSI's psychosocial and education programmes for war-affected children and youth, which started in 1998, have benefited over 60,000 children and youth to date.[36] The support to returning children, youth and their communities ranges from cooperation with district authorities, economic support, for example through income generating activities, community dialogue, rehabilitation and construction of school facilities, provision of teaching and learning aids and other materials, training of teachers and school administrators to improve the quality of teaching and management of school affairs, services aimed at health and HIV/AIDS, water and sanitation interventions, support to children and youth with special needs, and support to formal and non-formal vocational training, including provision of start-up tools and sponsorship for individual students, business skills training and industrial training for students, as well as psychosocial support programmes which include individual and group counselling, and follow-up of those who participated in counselling sessions. In all these activities educating the youth, starting from their potential, is central to the package provided.

For AVSI, education is not limited to accessing the educational system and acquiring a diploma, but is seen as an overall good to realise ones' potential through experience, not only in the classroom but also in society in various settings and in various roles. To achieve this, educational activities are not only focused on quantity such as the provision of materials, school structures and numbers of teachers, but also on quality, including teacher training, in class- and community-based follow-up and comprehensive packages for vulnerable children and youth and their families, including not only fees but also health care, psychosocial counselling and livelihood activities. All project activities are implemented in close collaboration with the youth, local partner organisations and schools, and local leaders.

2.2.1. Identification of Beneficiaries

The beneficiaries of AVSI's support for education are among the most vulnerable children and youth who would otherwise fall through the educational "system", and livelihood activities target youth who are not enrolled in formal or non-formal programmes.

Vulnerability for AVSI is a combination of factors that cannot be reduced to categories (i.e. people living with HIV/AIDS, formerly abducted children/youth, people with disabilities, child mothers etc.) but instead are determined by the

---

36 AVSI, *The Psychosocial Support Program of AVSI in Uganda, a case study 1999–2005*, AVSI Uganda, Kampala, 2005.

living situation of each individual. The selection of beneficiaries is therefore based on an assessment of the overall wellbeing of the person based on indicators of health, economic and psychosocial wellbeing.

The children and youth are usually referred by local authorities and leaders from the community. After receiving referrals, AVSI conducts assessments in partnership with local leaders. The assessments are done at the home of each potential beneficiary, and family and other community members are interviewed as well. This door-to-door approach greatly contributes to a thorough verification of whether a person who has been referred by local leaders is really vulnerable or not.

The assessment includes data collection of personal and household information, education, livelihood, health and motivation. It does not focus only on challenges and deficits, but rather evaluates the available resources and opportunities, looking at both strengths and weaknesses.

2.2.2. Supporting Pre-Primary, Primary and Secondary Education

AVSI's education programs endeavours to improve the capacity of local communities and families to provide sustainable and high quality care for the identified vulnerable children and youth. In 2008, 3,000 children were supported in pre-primary institutions in northern Uganda. AVSI supports early childhood development centres (pre-primary) through the provision of school materials, playground equipment, training of early childhood development caregivers, and community sensitisations.

On an annual basis, over 7,500 vulnerable children and youth received scholarships for primary and secondary education, including school fees, school materials, health care, psychosocial support and livelihood activities based on the individual needs of each child and his/her family and community. Targeted interventions to improve school structures, such as rehabilitation work and the provision of teaching materials, as well as water and sanitation facilities, are also provided to schools in AVSI's area of operation.

A cross-cutting theme in AVSI's educational work is disability.[37] Alongside the medical rehabilitation support to children and youth with special needs, AVSI supports annexes for blind children in primary schools and a primary school for the deaf in northern Uganda with special needs materials, training of staff, student sponsorships, and community sensitisation to improve access and quality education for children with visual and hearing impairment. AVSI also aims to improve access for children and youth with other disabilities by creating ramps and installing disabled-friendly latrines and other devices in schools.

---

[37] Bannink-Mbazzi et al., *supra* note 24, 4–9.

2.2.3. Supporting Vocational Training

After assessment, a selection of the most vulnerable and motivated youth is made by a team including AVSI staff and local leaders. It is followed by a discussion with the youth and his/her family members, and with local leaders, clarifying the modalities of the support for vocational training.

Support to vocational training is always combined with a short period of industrial training and training in business skills. Depending on the most urgent needs, the schools where the youth follow their courses receive support such as tools for instruction, textbooks and furniture. In case of rehabilitation works needed at the schools, construction activities are carried out by the students during their practical lessons. Instructors are invited to undertake training in quality education, psychosocial support, HIV/AIDS awareness, and the code of conduct. Early in 2008, counsellors were sent for initial assessment to the schools to assess psychosocial needs of youths and teachers within the schools.

In 2008, 184 students were supported in five different (mainly non-formal) training courses (47 percent females and 53 percent males). The average age of the students was 19.4 years, and their households comprised 4 persons on average. Half of the students completed primary education (51 percent), while 22 percent attended at least one year of secondary school. Over 60 percent had lost both parents, 12 percent had been abducted by the LRA, 9.8 percent headed a household, 9.8 percent were young mothers, 14.1 percent of the youth were handicapped, while other vulnerabilities included youth at risk of abuse and staying with elderly or sick guardians.

Psychosocial counselling was offered to all students in the vocational training schools, aimed at enhancing the coping mechanisms of the youth and focusing on interventions that could assist the students in addressing their problems on the individual as well as on the school and community levels. Students with severe psychiatric symptoms, including hallucinations and suicidal tendencies, were referred to a health centre or hospital with psychiatric staff and medical supplies.

Follow-up of youth who have completed vocational training in Kitgum shows that the majority of the youth have an increased household income after their training, applying knowledge gained through business skills training even if they do not work in the field of their vocational training. Also, many of the youth are reporting an improved psychosocial wellbeing due to the important role they are playing after the training as providers and helpers in their families and communities.

2.2.4. Training for Teachers and Other School Stakeholders, and Community Sensitisation

Annually AVSI trains about 2,000 teachers in quality education, life skills to prevent HIV/AIDS, and psychosocial support in various schools throughout Uganda using training modules developed by field practitioners.[38] The quality education training reflects on the meaning of education in order to appreciate the fact that education should form persons able to deal with all the challenges of life, developing their potential, values and attitudes and taking up their commitments and responsibilities. Through a positive educational approach the person is encouraged to understand different dynamics and factors in the educational process and promote growth. The training requires constructive and active participation, focusing on a critical reflection on their professional and personal experience.

The life skills training concentrates on basic behavioural change in the context of HIV/AIDS prevention. Respect for one's life, and therefore for one's body and health, are promoted and behavioural change processes are addressed. The training module incorporates information about HIV/AIDS transmission, but also emphasises the needs of a person and the meaning of love, freedom and sex.

The psychosocial support training covers topics such as the developmental growth of youth, trauma, the recovery process, and listening and basic counselling skills.[39] The training is not aimed at training teachers and instructors to become counsellors, but to develop their skills to identify and refer children and youth with psychosocial problems. The teachers and instructors are encouraged to practise the acquired skills in class, and also involve the family and community of the students in the education and support. The trained instructors support the counselling activities through assisting the counsellors in identifying the general problems of the students, but also refer students who might benefit from individual counselling.

An evaluation of the training of teachers in psychosocial support showed that teachers and instructors who have undergone the training feel empowered to better understand the individual problems of students and feel able to respond appropriately in difficult situations with students in the school but also outside. Many of the teachers and instructors felt the training also improved their

---

38 AVSI's Training Manuals on Quality Education titled *Basic Training on the Risk of Education*, on life skills titled *The Value of Life*, and on psychosocial support titled *Handbook for Teachers* and *Training Manual for Teachers* can be downloaded from www.avsi.org under "pubblicazioni".

39 AVSI's *Training Manual for Teachers* and the *Handbook for Teachers* were included in the technical kit of the Interagency Network for Education in Emergencies (INEE) and also published on the network's website: www.ineesite.org. The manual is currently under revision to respond to the changed needs in northern Uganda, focusing on return and resettlement.

understanding of the general developmental growth of youth, something they were never trained in as many of the instructors are not formally trained teachers but craftsmen who instruct in a certain vocation.

A male teacher who participated in one of the training courses said afterwards:

> Before the training, I used to be a very strict teacher. I would use sticks time and again for whatever mistake the students would make. I realized that the students would run away whenever they saw me around, and I was wondering why they were doing this. After the training, I stopped using sticks. Today, the students like me. They are very interested in my lessons, and they admire my teaching. I have learnt to be more tolerant with the students when they don't perform up to my expectation, and I always try to understand why a particular student is not performing well, and which are the underlying problems that prevent him or her from doing well in class. I take time talking to them about their problems. This has made my relationship to the students much more positive.

AVSI also offered training for Boards of Governors (BoG) and Parent-Teacher Association (PTA) members in 26 secondary and vocational schools in order to improve the management of the schools' affairs and to clarify the different roles of the two bodies. Training was therefore organised for 122 BoG members on policy issues and management skills and 34 PTA members were trained in their roles and responsibilities.

In 2009, AVSI organised community sensitisations on the value and importance of education in all sub-counties where partner schools were located. During quarterly coordination meetings that were held at sub-county level to share information with local leaders and partners on the implementation of the activities, which were also meant to obtain inputs for activities that were still to be carried out, AVSI was requested to sensitise parents on the value and importance of education, and to go on to parish level in order to reach as many community members as possible. Subsequently, 50 parishes were covered and the sensitisations were attended by a total of 6,687 community members. In order to increase the coverage of the sensitisations and to go in depth into issues concerning the importance and value of education, 35 radio talk shows were organised, facilitated by district and local leaders, teachers and students of the partner schools.

2.2.5. Supporting Livelihoods

From 2007 to 2009, AVSI provided income generating activities (IGA) addressing vulnerable youth in Kitgum District. 24 groups of youth with a total of 554 members have been supported in eight sub-counties in Kitgum District, in addition to 286 vocational students who completed their studies in four vocational schools.

The results of this intervention show that IGA can contribute towards improving the economic wellbeing of the beneficiaries in terms of assets owned and the types of economic activity they are involved in. Engaging in IGA can also help vulnerable persons in becoming productive and active members of society, and can improve social consideration and family support. Improvements can as well be registered in the overall health situation and in school attendance. According to their self-evaluation, the beneficiaries appreciated the psychosocial effects of IGA more than the economic effects; this could also be a consequence of the fact that the economic wellbeing of the beneficiaries is hindered by the increasing number of dependants as the income capacity of the person rises.

The objectives of AVSI's IGA interventions are to improve the quality of life of the most disadvantaged people, to enable beneficiaries to increase their household income from a sustainable livelihood, to create self-employment through engagement in productive activities, and to increase resilience among the most vulnerable people.

2.2.5.1. Group Dynamics Training

After assessment and identification of the beneficiaries of the IGA support, the youth underwent training in group dynamics since group cohesion and peer support are the prerequisites for a well-functioning group structure. This training aims at strengthening the structure and internal dynamics of the either already existing group or of the group-to-be, and at building positive dynamics and structures, especially in the newly created groups. The training in group dynamics also focuses on basic skills in the leadership and management of a group, communication habits, and mechanisms of decision making.

2.2.5.2. Business Skills Training

Through learning the basics of business planning and business notions it is possible to handle any kind of business with a low requirement in technical skills. After the group dynamics training, the group members and vocational students attending the last year of their vocational studies and on the verge of entering the job market have been trained on how to identify, select, plan and start a feasible and viable IGA. The aims of this training were to raise awareness about possible sources of start-up capital, to enable existing entrepreneurs to identify problems and constraints that affect the growth and development of their IGAs, to devise a way forward to address the problems, and to deepen the participants' understanding of the value of saving, of how to save and where to save.

One of the main challenges faced by graduates from the vocational training courses is the transition from school to work. The business skills training equips the youth with additional skills such as customer care, saving and business management that help them to create and maintain a business and that are necessary for them to overcome the transitional challenge from school into the labour market. During the training, information on the importance of saving, the use of savings and the use of saving and credit facilities was provided (referral to the existing facilities, information on informal saving and credit systems such as revolving loans, village saving and loan associations). The training in business skills is particularly important in meeting Ministry of Education and Sports directives to introduce entrepreneurial skills training into the curriculum of vocational skills.

The follow-up indicates that almost all youth who attended the training are practising gainful economic activities, and that they have added advantages over the youth that did not undergo the training in business skills to supplement their vocation. Most of them are involved in small-scale businesses ranging from baking, carpentry workshops, nursery bed management (selling of seedlings) to construction. Their monthly income ranges from 150 EUR to 200 EUR, depending on the location and the types of industry in which they were trained. The follow-up also indicates that many of the graduates of catering courses have been able to get gainful employment in restaurants within the nearby town council.

2.2.5.3. Improved psychosocial wellbeing

The IGAs contribute to improving the economic wellbeing of the beneficiaries in terms of assets owned and the types of economic activity they are involved in. Engaging in income generating activities can help vulnerable youth in becoming productive and active members of society, improving social consideration and family support.

The area that registers improvement both according to the increase of specific indicators and in the perception of the beneficiaries is the psychosocial situation. The percentage of vulnerable youth feeling that the family is very caring almost doubles and the percentage of those that do not feel care reduces from 30 to 10 percent (Graph 1). According to the leader of a youth group, members are now able to pay for the school fees of their children and for medical treatment.

Graph 1. Care for vulnerable youth from family members 2008 and 2009

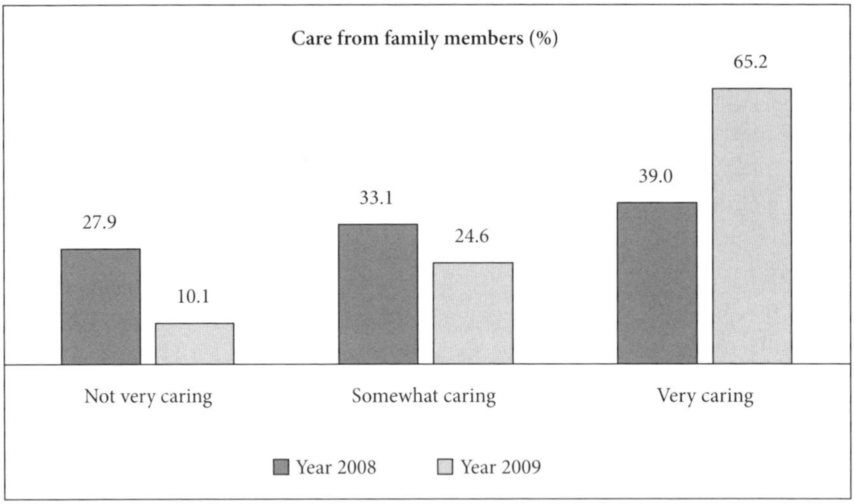

Also the perception of community support changes dramatically. The percentage of cases where community members said things to insult or hurt the beneficiary or his/her children in the previous year dropped from 33 to 12 percent, the percentage of cases where community members have been physically aggressive towards the beneficiary or his/her children dropped from 11 to 6 percent and that of community members not allowing their children to play with those of the beneficiaries has halved.

At the same time, the overall perception of the psychosocial situation and overall sense of belonging to the community increased considerably.

2.2.5.4. Group businesses leading to micro-enterprises opportunities

After the training courses, groups and the vocational students have been helped in business selection according to the viability of the business, market demand and group capacity. Start-up capital ranging from 200 to 500 EUR, depending on the business proposed, were delivered to each group. With the support and the constant follow-up and advice provided by AVSI staff and local leaders, all the groups have been able to start profitable business activities.

Amongst the micro-enterprises started up have been the retail selling of agricultural and non-agricultural products, food processing, petty business, a depot for selling sodas, and agricultural production.

Spontaneously, most of the groups have concurrently started a saving scheme whereby members can borrow from the group to start individual businesses or meet the household's basic needs. For instance, most of the members from two sub-counties are involved in petty business such as selling cassava, small fish and making small cakes, and are gaining profits both from the group and from the individual IGA.

Some of the groups have used the profits gained from one business to start other activities, showing good risk-differentiation capacity: one group is concurrently running a grinding mill business and selling crops.

Most of the vocational students (229 total: 142 male, 87 female) have instead been provided with start-up kits to enable them to employ the skills learned in the courses attended and enter the job market directly as service providers. A female beneficiary of IGA support to youth groups said:

> In our group, we have love for the others, and we are giving moral support to each other. For example, sometimes I am selling on behalf of other group members who may be having problems. The training on business skills has helped me to develope qualities that I did not have before, such as courage to face customers, people I have never met before. Our business in the group is going on very well, and our capital has already increased. Even on household level, my life has improved a lot. I am now eating twice a day instead of only having one meal, and I manage to save money which allows me to buy things which I couldn't afford to buy before. I can now even help my family members when they are having problems. Other community members who used to look down at me are now showing me respect. My life has really changed and I am sure I will not be the same hopeless person like before.

3. CONCLUSION

Returnees from the LRA have usually been classified into categories, e.g. depending on the length of life in captivity and experiences had during the time in the "bush". This categorisation can facilitate programming that tends to leave out many other vulnerable people who may have a similar or even greater need to be supported.

Acknowledging that although many former LRA abductees have suffered a wide range of abuses during their time in captivity, the war in northern Uganda has affected many if not most children and youth in the region through displacement, loss of family members, witnessing horrific events, and a lack of access to basic services such as health and education,[40] the emphasis on child soldiers – moreover, with a focus on children only – can seem disproportionate

[40] C. Dolan, *Which children count? The politics of children's rights in northern Uganda*. Conciliation Resources, London, 2002, www.c-r.org/our-work/accord/northern-uganda/which-children-count.php [accessed 11 August 2009]; M. Boas and A. Hatloy, *The Northern Uganda IDP Profiling Study*, Department of Disaster Preparedness and Refugees of the Office of the Prime Minister and United Nations Development Programme, Kampala, 2005, Vol. 1.; P.N. Pham, P. Vinck, M. Wierda, E. Stover and A. di Giovanni, *Forgotten Voices: A Population-Based Study of Attitudes about Peace and Justice in Northern Uganda*, International Centre for Transitional Justice and Human Rights Centre, University of

to the effort required for restoring "normal life" in Uganda. Research on reintegration usually concludes that humanitarian services at all levels should strengthen the capacity of families to care for the psychosocial, educational and material needs of returnees at all levels.[41] More specifically, practitioners are called upon to develop programmes not just for former "child soldiers", but rather for all vulnerable children and youth, with support for building livelihoods by focusing on alternative age-appropriate and accelerated education and economic development, taking into consideration individual differences. The importance of economic recovery has been highlighted in several studies, which recommend that aid agencies should be complementing internal motivation by supporting an environment conducive to recovery and rehabilitation rather than providing humanitarian support that may weaken internal structures and worsen vulnerabilities.[42]

The holistic approach of AVSI described in this article is based on each person's needs, abilities and strengths, with a broad focus on war-affected children and youth in northern Uganda, combining educational, psychosocial and livelihood activities.

California, Berkeley, 2005, http://repositories.cdlib.org/hrc/reports/2005_07Forgotten-Voices [accessed 8 July 2009].

41 L. Castelli, E. Locatelli and M. Canavera, *Psycho-Social Support for War-Affected Children in Northern Uganda: Lessons Learnt.* Coalition to Stop the Use of Child Soldiers, London, 2005, at 5, www.child-soldiers.org/resources/psychosocial [accessed 10 July 2009]; Corbin, *supra* note 3, at 316.

42 R. Locke, 'Community-driven economic development in Northern Uganda', (2006) 36, *Humanitarian Exchange Magazine*, www.odihpn.org/report.asp?id=2859 [accessed 10 July 2009] [accessed 17 August 2009]; USAID, *Field Report No. 2 – Economic Strengthening for Vulnerable Children: Principles of Program Design and Technical Recommendations for Effective Field Interventions*, 2008, www.aed.org/.../Principles-of-Program-Design-Economic-Strengthening-for-Vulnerable-Children-Youth.pdf [accessed 28 July 2009]; The SEEP Network, *Minimum Standards for Economic Recovery after Crisis, Washington*, 2009, http://communities.seepnetwork.org/sites/hamed/files/Econ_Recovery_Standards.pdf [accessed 17 July 2009].

TRANSITIONAL JUSTICE IMPLICATIONS FOR THE USE OF CHILD SOLDIERS IN ERITREA

Daniel R. Mekonnen

1. INTRODUCTION

The issue of child soldiers in Eritrea is a central element of the grave human rights crisis in the country. It is not at all comparable to other African experiences. There are disturbing developments that need to be curbed before these trends reach a critical level of crisis, particularly in the event of an intrastate or interstate conflict, which could erupt in the country at any time. Reportedly, thousands of Eritrean child soldiers continue to be conscripted by the Eritrean government into the regular army. This has grave implications both for the international legal obligations of the Eritrean government and for the individual criminal responsibility of some senior government officials. Seen against its protracted history of human rights violations and virulent conflicts, Eritrea is a typical forthcoming model of transitional justice. The issue of child soldiers is not only one of the most dominant factors in the ongoing debate on human rights violations in Eritrea but also central to shaping future transitional justice options for Eritrea.

By addressing the pervasiveness of underage military conscription in Eritrea and the legal and political questions surrounding this issue, the paper explores possible and relevant answers to the following central question: what strategies are helpful for addressing the challenges of underage military conscription in Eritrea in the context of future transitional justice options for the country? In so doing, it offers practical recommendations for improvement in the future. The paper focuses on the excesses of the current authoritarianism that would be confronted in the post-authoritarian era and the need to identify such excesses in the context of transitional justice. To provide context, the paper will first present a brief historical background on the Eritrean post-independence era, focusing mainly on the increasing tendencies towards authoritarianism of the Eritrean government that finally led to the drastic post-2001 political crisis.

At the outset, it should be noted that the issue of child soldiers in Eritrea is to be seen in the context of excessive militarisation that has prevailed in the country, particularly since June 1998. The practice has effectively turned the country into one of the most militarised states in the world. Once conscripted into the army, adult members of society, including many underage children, serve without any formal pay and salary for a number of years. This has caused a societal disaster in terms of the enjoyment of fundamental citizen rights. Children's rights are pervasively abused in this context. One of the core recommendations made in this paper is that rehabilitation and reintegration programmes for Eritrean child soldiers are dependent on the willingness of the Eritrean government to facilitate transition to a democratic order.

2. CONTEXTUAL BACKGROUND

Eritrea has a protracted history of human rights violations and virulent conflicts, starting from the advent of Italian colonialism in 1890 up to the current authoritarianism of the People's Front for Democracy and Justice (PFDJ), the only "legitimate" political party, which has ruled the country since independence in 1991. PFDJ is the successor to the Eritrean People's Liberation Front (EPLF), a liberation movement which won Eritrea's *de facto* independence from Ethiopia in 1991. In 1993, after an overwhelming national referendum, Eritrea's sovereign independence was formally recognised by the United Nations (UN) and the rest of the international community.[1] The early years of independence were relatively promising, during which time and among other things the EPLF transformed itself into a provisional government (but not a government of national unity); changed its name to PFDJ; promised to transit the country into a democratic system of governance by 1997, when the first "democratic" constitution of the country had to be adopted; and pledged to facilitate general elections, which are commonly seen as the litmus test for any democratisation process. However, as noted by Kjetil Tronvoll, the post-independence experience of Eritrea has become a cause for despondency in that oppression and massive human rights abuses persist in Eritrea today, sadly committed by the same liberation struggle heroes who fought for human rights.[2]

Eritrea's peaceful years in its post-independence era were very short-lived. Between 1998 and 2000 Eritrea fought a devastating two-year border conflict

1 UN Department Of Public Information, *The United Nations and the Independence of Eritrea*, UN, New York, 1996, at 19.

2 K. Tronvoll, *The Lasting Struggle for Freedom in Eritrea: Human Rights and Political Development, 1991 – 2009*, The Oslo Centre for Peace and Human Rights, Oslo, 2009, at 76. See also generally G. Kibreab, *Eritrea: A Dream Differed*, James Currey, Oxford, 2010.

with Ethiopia. The conflict ended officially on 18 June 2000 with the ratification of the Agreement on Cessation of Hostilities between Eritrea and Ethiopia. The truce finally led to the Algiers Peace Agreement, which was signed by the two countries on 12 December 2000. A boundary commission established pursuant to the Algiers Peace Agreement resolved the border conflict in April 2002 through a final and binding decision which delimitated the common border between the two countries. Due to Ethiopia's intransigence in genuinely implementing the decision of the boundary commission[3] and Eritrea's diplomatic and political ineptitude, the contested border remained undemarcated on the ground. As a result, a situation of "no war, no peace" persists between the two countries. Yet, in a strict legal sense there is no legitimate state of emergency in Eritrea.

Ever since the outbreak of the new war with Ethiopia, the Eritrean government has used the conflict obstinately as a pretext to rule the country under an undeclared state of emergency by refusing to implement the 1997 constitution, which was drafted and ratified with full support from the government. In effect, the country has been ruled without a democratic constitution since independence in 1991, almost for two decades. Undoubtedly, the stalemate with Ethiopia occupies a central space in the current political crisis in Eritrea. Using fabricated excuses of "war and threats of war", the Eritrean government postponed previously scheduled general elections and consequently the long-awaited political transition to democracy was helplessly frustrated. A combination of the reluctance of the government to facilitate democratic transition and the consequences of the recent war precipitated economic, social and political crises unprecedented since the country's independence in 1991. This has led to severe disagreement among senior government officials. The disagreement manifested itself overtly in early 2001 when a group of high-ranking government officials initiated a reform movement aimed at facilitating a democratic transition. The movement was violently crushed in September 2001 by the state president and his close aides when the majority of the initiators of the reform movement and their supporters or sympathisers were arbitrarily arrested. Since then, the country has seen an unprecedented political crisis and a disturbing record of human rights violations, including excessive levels of militarisation.

As has been stated in several instances by this author,[4] there are some unique characteristic features which make the case of Eritrea a typically desolate story.

---

3 Ethiopia has particularly refused to hand over the flashpoint of the conflict, the village of Badame, to Eritrea in accordance with the decision of the boundary commission.

4 See, for example, D.R Mekonnen, 'The Abolition of Female Circumcision in Eritrea: Inadequacies of New Legislation', (2007) 7 2 *African Human Rights Law Journal* 389, at 406–407; D.R. Mekonnen and J.L. Pretorius, 'Prosecuting the Main Perpetrators of International Crimes in Eritrea: Possibilities under International Law', (2008) 33 2 *Journal for*

Conventional features of a free and democratic government are barely visible in Eritrea. With no working constitution, functioning parliament, independent judiciary, free press, bureaucratic accountability or even an officially published national budget, Eritrea offers a bizarre example of "statehood" in the modern history of nation-states. Virtually all countries in the world have an enforceable national covenant/constitution. In the absence of written constitutions, countries may have an established constitutional framework by which fundamental rights and freedoms are guaranteed. Most countries also have functioning parliaments. They conduct regular and periodic elections, irrespective of whether they are free or fair in real terms. They allow private media outlets, even if regulations become so restrictive that they give zero freedom to the press. They also have seemingly independent judiciaries. In Eritrea, the government adopted a constitution in 1997, but has never implemented it. From 1993 there was a nominal parliament but it ceased functioning in February 2002. The Eritrean judiciary is the most emasculated public institution in the country. Private media was completely banned in 2001. Only government-owned media outlets remain, and their allegiance has always been to the ruling elite rather than the truth. Worst of all, since it gained independence the country has never seen free and fair elections.

Social and development indicators from independent sources rank Eritrea miserably. The 2009 Global Hunger Index reveals that together with Burundi, Chad, the Democratic Republic of Congo, Ethiopia and Sierra Leone, Eritrea has the highest levels of poverty and food insecurity in the world. In terms of undernourishment, Eritrea is second from the bottom, having 68 percent of its total population undernourished.[5] The country receives critical grades on the Basic Capabilities Index, denoting serious difficulties in every dimension of social development.[6] Despite its small population of around four million (out of which more than one million are said to be outside the country), Eritrea's alarming record of human rights violations has caused it to be ranked as the second largest source of refugees in the world (in absolute numbers). By the end of 2008, Eritrea had produced 62,700 new asylum seekers around the world. The simplest arithmetic model translates this into 5,225 refugees per month. In this regard, Eritrea was headed only by Zimbabwe, which had 118,500 new claims in 2008. Even failed or chaotic states such as Somalia and Iraq, which have larger populations than Eritrea, were eclipsed by Eritrea in relation to refugee outflow.[7] A 2007 report by

Juridical Science 76, at 79; D.R Mekonnen, *Transitional Justice: Framing a Model for Eritrea*, VDM Publishing, Saarbrucken, 2009, at 2–3.

5 Deutsche Welthungerhilfe, International Food Policy Research Institute (IFPRI) and Concern Worldwide *Global Hunger Index*, IFPRI, Washington DC, 2009, at 5 and 12.

6 Social Watch, *Annual Report: Rights is the Answer*, Social Watch, Montevideo, 2008, at 30.

7 UNHCR, *Global Trends: Refugees, Asylum Seekers, Returnees, Internally Displaced and Stateless Persons*, 2009, at 16.

the International Monetary Fund (IMF) reveals that Eritrea's inflation was the second highest in the world, the first being that of Zimbabwe at that time.[8]

In their 2009 annual reports, the Bonn International Centre for Conversion (BICC) and the International Institute for Strategic Studies (IISS) have ranked Eritrea as the first and the second most militarised country in the world, respectively.[9] BICC particularly states that Eritrea spends "more than 20 percent of its GDP on its armed forces compared with a mere 3.7 percent on public health".[10] Other sources indicate that Eritrea allocates about 25 percent of its budget for military use, the highest in the world.[11] Currently, Eritrea has an estimated army of 400,000,[12] which means a minimum of 10 percent of the total population, a figure which is exceedingly high given Eritrea's miniature economic size. In press freedom, Reporters Without Borders ranks Eritrea as the worst country in the world, exceeding notorious authoritarian states such as Burma, North Korea and Turkmenistan.[13] Eritrea holds this infamous record for the third consecutive year.

Basically, the country is at present in a deep economic, social and political crisis. Individuals who do not subscribe to state ideology or followers of religious beliefs not officially sanctioned by the government are systematically targeted and severely punished by the security and military apparatus. As a result, human rights violations are rampant; violation is the norm and protection the exception. Some conservative estimates suggest that between 20,000[14] and 40,000[15] people are in detention without trial or any contact with the outside in more than 300 formal and informal prison centres all over the country. Most of these sites are administered by army generals, who are not accountable to either the police or the ordinary courts. Internally, the country has been transformed into an open-

---

8 IMF, *World Economic and Financial Surveys*, IMF, Washington DC, 2007, at 225.

9 BICC, *Global Militarisation Index*, 2009; IISS *The Military Balance: The Annual Assessment of Global Military Capabilities and Defence Economies*, 2009.

10 BICC, 'The Trend towards a Build-up of Conventional Arms Continues despite Nuclear Disarmament Initiatives', available at www.bicc.de/index.php/press/press-2009/press-release-annual-report-2008–2009 (accessed 10 October 2009).

11 Christian Solidarity Worldwide (CSW) and Human Rights Concern–Eritrea (HRC–E), *Stakeholder Report on the Human Rights Situation in Eritrea*, Submitted to the Universal Periodic Review of the UN Human Rights Council, April 2009, at 7.

12 A24 MEDIA, 'Eritrea: A Nation Held Hostage', available at www.a24media.com/index.php/component/content/article/90-films/743-eritrea-a-nation-held-hostage (accessed 11 October 2009).

13 Reporters Without Borders, *Annual Worldwide Press Freedom Index*, 2009. According to Freedom House, Eritrea is fourth from the bottom (together with Cuba and Libya). It is preceded only by Burma, North Korea and Turkmenistan. See Freedom House, *Freedom of the Press: Table of Global Press Freedom Rankings*, 2009.

14 Mekonnen, 2009, *supra* note 4, at 120–121.

15 Human Rights Watch, *Service for Life: State Repression and Indefinite Conscription in Eritrea*, Human Rights Watch, Washington DC, 2009, at 19, citing Christian Solidarity Worldwide. Tronvoll, citing Eritrean refugees and exiled civil society organisations, writes that estimates of political prisoners vary between 10,000 and 30,000. Tronvoll, *supra* note 2, at 76.

air prison where all fundamental rights and freedoms are completely muzzled by nightmarish, Kafkaesque, pervasive and abusive practices. Externally, it has become a pariah state and a major destabilising actor in the Horn of Africa region, causing the UN Security Council to impose stringent sanctions in December 2009 against the country's political and military leadership.[16]

Making things worse, the stalemate with Ethiopia is in a very fragile state and as a result a full-scale armed conflict may erupt at any time. The Eritrean government has used this pretext effectively as a "justification" to govern the country under an undeclared state of emergency in terms of which every adult member of society, including underage children, is forcefully conscripted into the army for an indefinite period of time. Moreover, there are several armed Eritrean groups which have vowed to overthrow the government violently and this means that intrastate conflict or civil war may erupt in the country at any time. In practice, some of the armed opposition groups are actively involved in military operations[17] targeting government troops, the latest of such operations having taken place on New Year's Day in 2010.[18]

3. EXCESSIVE MILITARISATION AS A MAJOR SOCIETAL EVIL[19]

Apart from the economic and political crises discussed above, excessive militarisation is also a major societal evil in Eritrea. A National Military Service Programme (NMSP), which started as a seemingly "popular" national development policy in the early 1990s, has transformed the country into a completely militarised state. In effect, the NMSP has become a major political tool to suppress popular defiance, especially after the severe political crisis[20]

---

16 UN Security Council Resolution 1907 (2009), UN Doc/ S/RES/1907 (2009), 23 December 2009.

17 These are evident, for example, from the periodic military communiqués of the Democratic Movement for the Liberation of Eritrean Kumana (DMLEK), the Red Sea Afar Democratic Organization (RSADO) and the Eritrean National Salvation Front (ENSF).

18 See Gedab News, 'Clarifying Contradictions On The New Year Day Battle', 7 January 2010; Awate Team, 'Interview With Jabir Ahmed, Military Commander of ENSF', 9 January 2010.

19 This section relies heavily on Mekonnen, 2009, note 4 above, at 83–87. See also generally T.R. Hepner and D. O'Kane, 'Introduction' in D. O'Kane and T.R. Hepner (eds.), *Biopolitics, Militarism and Development: Eritrea in the Twenty-First Century*, Berghahn Books, Oxford & New York, 2009; N. Hirt, '"Dreams Don't Come True in Eritrea": Anomie and Family Disintegration due to the Structural Militarization of Society', GIGA Working Papers, 119/2010, January 2010.

20 For further discussion on this, see generally M. Plaut, 'The Birth of the Eritrean Reform Movement', (2002) 29 *Review of African Political Economy* 119–124; D. Connell, *Conversations with Eritrean Political Prisoners*, Africa World Press, New Jersey, 2004; D.R Mekonnen, 'The Reply of the Eritrean Government to ACHPR's Landmark Ruling on Eritrea: A Critical Appraisal', (2006) 31(2) *Journal for Juridical Science* 26–56.

that erupted in September 2001. It is in this aspect that the issue of child soldiers has become a serious cause for concern.

Out of the many government policies which have caused immense suffering and vulnerability to a large number of Eritreans, the NMSP stands out as the most devastating example of the post-independence era. The NMSP was officially launched in 1991 by Proclamation No. 11/1991, the "First" National Service Proclamation of Eritrea. According to this proclamation, every adult member of Eritrean society is required to complete an 18-month NMSP, which includes a harsh military training period of six months in the notorious Sawa Military Training Camp. Lately, other military training camps have been established in different parts of the country, such as Kiloma and Wia, which are known for their harsh climates. The military camps are deliberately located in unfriendly and remote geographical locations with the sole objective of isolating the conscripts. The military training is accompanied by crude and aggressive programmes of indoctrination, intended to weaken critical thinking and defiance among the youth.

Although not the outcome of a democratic process, the NMSP was initially welcomed with substantial popular support. Its initial purported objective was nation-building and reconstruction. In recent years, especially during and after the 1998–2000 border conflict with Ethiopia, it became a major instrument for repressing political dissent. The initial law[21] exempted certain categories of people, such as married women, mothers and newly-weds, from the requirement of national military service. For no clear reason, however, the exemption was withdrawn in 1995 by an amending law.[22] Another law, Proclamation No. 82/1995,[23] extended the age limit of forty years to include people up to fifty years of age. This indicates the arbitrariness of the policy and its implementation.

From 1994 until June 2009,[24] the government implemented twenty-two rounds of the NMSP.[25] Each round recruited tens of thousands of participants. One source, for example, indicates that 18,000 youths were conscripted in the twentieth round to remain under conscription for an unknown period of time.[26]

21 Article 5(4)–5(9) of the First National Service Proclamation.

22 Article 2 of Proclamation No 71/1995 (A Proclamation to Amend the 'First' National Service Proclamation).

23 Articles 3 and 6 of the 'Second' National Service Proclamation. See also article 13(2) on the duration of the NMSP. This law repeals the two previous proclamations on national service.

24 See Shabait.Com News, 'Participants of 22nd Round National Service Graduate', 28 June 2009.

25 This author is a member of the fourth round of the NMSP, implemented between December 1995 and June 1996.

26 See ኣሰና.ነት 'ተቐያያሪ ሜላ ንሓደ ፍሹል ፖሊሲ' (ASENA.NET 'Ever-Changing Ploy for a Failed Policy'), available at http://asena-online.com/index.php?option=com_content&task=view&id=226&Itemid=103 (accessed 8 July 2007).

Forceful conscription was intensified after the 1998–2000 border conflict with Ethiopia, in spite of the fact that the conflict officially came to an end in June 2000. Nearly ten years after that and irrespective of the 18-month limit stipulated by law, the programme continues with effectively no end to the abusive practices it involves. The government justifies its continuation as a necessary reaction to the threat of a renewed war with Ethiopia. There are, however, no democratic safeguards against abuse and moreover no state of emergency was promulgated in the country after the end of the 1998–2000 border conflict with Ethiopia. In 2002, to disguise the abusive continuation of the NMSP, the government proclaimed a purported "national development plan" called the Warsay-Ykealo Development Campaign (WYDC).[27] This programme was devised to frustrate the long-awaited demobilisation programme of soldiers, who were conscripted in large numbers during the 1998–2000 border conflict with Ethiopia. Strictly regulated by military rule and discipline, the WYDC was dubbed by a famous liberation struggle hero "a campaign of slavery"[28] and is believed to have kept under constant yoke of tyranny hundreds of thousands of youths. Gaim Kibreab also describes the NMSP and WYDC as typical examples of forced labour, as defined by relevant international conventions.[29]

The NMSP and WYDC are manifestly abusive and their only purpose is the continuity of a militarised system of governance aimed at the subjugation of the entire Eritrean population, particularly the most productive segment, which is seen by the government as potentially prone to defiance. The stated concern of Amnesty International in this regard is one of the most credible accounts of the harsh realities of the NMSP. The concern of Amnesty International is based on the fact that the NMSP has become a major cause of arbitrary detentions and that torture is used as standard military punishment.[30] Similarly, Human Rights Watch also describes the NMSP as an exceptional state repression which has left Eritrea's youth under no option but free "service for life".[31] The government uses the programme as a common pretext to arrest real or perceived opponents at any time and any place. Army commanders have full discretion to implement any type of punishment, including extra-judicial execution, against NMSP or

---

27 Mekonnen, *supra* note 4, at 84.

28 A. Gebremariam (translated by T.G ZEWDE), 'The Warsay/Yikaalo Campaign: A Campaign of Slavery', available at http://news.asmarino.com/Articles/2002/09/TesfagiorgisZewde-1.asp (2002).

29 G. Kibreab, 'Forced Labour in Eritrea' (2009) 47 *Journal of Modern African Studies* 41, at 64 and 67. See also S.M. Weldehaimanot, 'From Prisoners to Refugees: The Right to Leave and its Ramifications in Eritrea', (2011) 18 *East African Journal of Peace and Human Rights*.

30 Amnesty International,*'You Have No Right to Ask': Government Resists Scrutiny on Human Rights*, AI Index: AFR 64/003/2004 May 2004.

31 Human Rights Watch, *supra* note 15.

WYDC conscripts. According to eyewitness accounts,[32] brutal methods of punishment which lead to amputation of arms and other forms of permanent bodily injury are common among conscripts who demonstrate the slightest sign of defiance against the draconian policies of the government.[33]

Virtually all foot soldiers of the regular army are conscripts of the NMSP and WYDC. There are various estimates of the total number of Eritrean soldiers. In October 2001, a senior official of the National Commission for Demobilisation and Reintegration indicated that "by mid-2000, Eritrea [had] 300, 000 army personnel, more than any other time in the history of the liberation struggle".[34] This number is believed to have increased exponentially in the years that followed, during which time the government has aggressively continued to conscript new batches of tens of thousands of youths every six months. According to the report[35] of the Eritrean government to the Committee on the Elimination of Discrimination Against Women (CEDAW), women constitute, in an aggregated form, 45.27 percent of the total number of army members, including those in the "civilian" police force. This is close to half of the total personnel of the national army. The vulnerability of women army members is proportional to their numbers. There are reports that women have been sexually abused, raped and tortured by army commanders in the infamous Sawa Military Training Camp and elsewhere. Sara Rich Dorman, for example, quotes two foreign newspapers that interviewed women who claim to have been raped in the military training camp.[36]

Frustrated by the abusive practices in the NMSP and WYDC, Eritreans have fled to neighbouring countries in unprecedented numbers. All border posts in the country are heavily guarded by security personnel and a special force, called the border surveillance units. Citizens between the NMSP age margins are strictly

---

32 Informal Interview with Dr. Yosief Fessehaye, 8 March 2007. Dr. Fessehaye is a medical doctor who served in the Glas Military Hospital in Eritrea.

33 Human Rights Watch, *2006 World Report: Eritrea*, http://hrw.org/english/docs/2006/01/18/eritre12307.htm (accessed 18 January 2006). Human Rights Watch indicates that Eritreans fleeing conscription are granted asylum elsewhere "on the grounds that national service is used as a measure of political repression and that anyone forcibly returned to Eritrea is likely to be tortured". See also Human Rights Watch, *supra* note 15.

34 A. Mehreteab, 'Renewed Demobilization in Eritrea', (2001) 21 *Bonn International Centre for Conversion Bulletin*, at 1.

35 *Combined Initial, Second and Third Periodic Report of the Eritrean Government to the Committee on the Elimination of Discrimination Against Women*, UN Doc CEDAW/C/ERI/1–3/2004, 34.

36 S.R. Dorman, 'Past the Kalashnikov: Youth and the State in Eritrea' in J. ABBINK and I. Van Kessel (eds.), *Vanguard or Vandals? Youth, Politics and Conflict in Africa*, Brill Academic Publishers, Leiden, 2004, 189–204. See also C.M. Bailliet, 'Examining Sexual Violence in the Military within the Context of Eritrean Asylum Claims Presented in Norway' (2007) 19 *International Journal of Refugee Law* 471–510.

forbidden to leave the country regardless of whether they have fulfilled the NMSP or not. The border surveillance units are authorised to shoot anyone who is caught crossing the borders of the country. Therefore, many people make use of "illegal" methods to flee the country. They pay exorbitantly prohibitive prices to smugglers. In their attempts to escape, many face violations such as killings, and in the case of women, the violations include rape and sexual violence. Most of the escapees experience harsh conditions in refugee camps in neighbouring and other countries, where their right to freedom of movement is severely curtailed. The gravest restriction on the right to freedom of movement inside Eritrea by itself has unavoidable wider repercussions.[37] Several other fundamental rights have also been flagrantly violated, causing immense suffering to hundreds of thousands of Eritreans.

4. THE PLIGHT OF ERITREAN CHILDREN

At present, Eritrean high school students, including underage children, are forced to enrol in military camps for "formal education". Among them is the notorious Sawa Military Training Camp, where students are disciplined under strict martial rule. The abusive NMSP, which starts formally at the age of eighteen and ends nowhere, continues as one of the most pervasive methods of state repression. The numerous abhorrent violations of human rights perpetrated under the NMSP include rape and other sexual violence against female conscripts. In recent years, military commanders have taken effective control of all senior academic institutions.

The pervasiveness of child soldier conscription is nowhere more clearly revealed than in the twenty-first round of recruitment of the NMSP that took place between 20 August 2007 and 8 February 2008. In this round, there were 9,938 forced conscripts. From these, 3,516 were underage children, constituting 35.37 percent of the total number of conscripts in the twenty-first round. There were 1,911 male underage conscripts and 1,599 female underage conscripts. All in all, there were 4,324 female conscripts, constituting 43 percent of the total number of conscripts.[38] In the twenty-second round of the NMSP, which concluded in June 2009, official government sources indicated that 40 percent of the conscripts were female. Further details in the form of disaggregated data are not readily

---

37 In this regard, see generally Weldehaimanot, *supra* note 29.

38 ኣሰና.ነት 'ሜጀር ጀነራል ተኽላይ ሃብተስላሴ ናብ ቤት ጽሕፈት ፕረዚደንት ዝለኣኾ ውሽጣዊ ጸብጻብ' (ASENA.NEt 'Internal Report of Major-General Teklay Habteselassie to the Office of the President'), available at http://asena.delina.org/images/presidentteklay.pdf (accessed 4 February 2009). This is a leaked report by the commander of the Sawa Training Camp to the state president, Isaias Afwerki. The report illustrates that as compared to previous rounds, the majority of conscripts in the twenty-first round are very young. This is particularly mentioned on page 4 of the report.

available on this particular round and the total number of conscripts is also not yet known. Nonetheless, in a speech at the graduation ceremony, the state president indicated that the majority of participants in the twenty-second round were born in the post-independence era, implying that at the time of conscription all such recruits were underage children.[39]

The fact that there are currently no hostilities in Eritrea (in the form of interstate or intrastate conflict) could be seen as a distinct advantage compared to other African experiences.[40] Nonetheless, the government has a deplorable record of conscription of underage children into the armed forces. Reports indicate that abusive practices in the army, such as brutal methods of punishment and extra-judicial execution, are rampant. In the case of female conscripts, rape and sexual violence are common. Underage children are not immune from this. The injustice suffered by Redwan (last name unknown) illustrates this more clearly. The story of Redwan goes as follows:

> Former detainees at the underground prison in Tesseney witnessed the execution of Redwan, who was 15 years old at the time of his death. Redwan, who was shocked when soldiers came to round up young students from classrooms for military service, escaped from them and tried to go to Sudan to avoid conscription at a young age. He was caught by the border guards and put into a prison in Tesseney. He found the harsh prison conditions unbearable, and one day, when he (with others) was taken outside to relieve himself, he tried to escape barefoot by running as fast as possible. However, the prison guards shot at him, and Redwan fell down and died instantly.[41]

According to the Global March Against Child Labour, the use of child soldiers in the war of independence against Ethiopia is widely acknowledged.[42] Children as young as 14 years of age also reportedly participated in the 1998–2000 border conflict with Ethiopia.[43] Since the end of the war, the government has never implemented any programme particularly aimed at the rehabilitation and reintegration of child soldiers. To the contrary, the government has continued to conscript underage children into the army even after the end of the 1998–2000 border conflict with Ethiopia. As stated earlier, a number of armed Eritrean

39 Shabait.Com News, *supra* note 24.

40 However, it is important to note that on New Year's Day in 2010 there was a significant battle between Eritrean government troops and some armed opposition groups. The Eritrean government, however, reported that the attack was launched by Ethiopian troops. For further details, see the sources cited in *supra* note 18.

41 CSW and HRC–E, *supra* note 11, at 9.

42 Global March Against Child Labour, *Report on the Worst Forms of Child Labour*, September 2004. See also Coalition to Stop the Use of Child Soldiers, *Global Report on Child Soldiers*, 12 June 2001.

43 The Protection Project, *Human Rights Reports of Africa: Eritrea*, 2007; Human Rights Watch, *World Report*, 2002; Coalition to Stop the Use of Child Soldiers, 'Ethiopia/Eritrea: Child Soldiers Should be Demobilized', 10 July 2000.

groups are engaged in sporadic attacks against government troops. Furthermore, given the fragile and tense stalemate with Ethiopia, there is a high probability of the eruption of violent conflict in Eritrea at any time. Should any form of pervasive armed conflict begin, it is evident that the large number of underage conscripts in the army will be the most immediate victims. As long as the pervasive practice of underage conscription continues unabated, the social, political and human rights ramifications will remain intact. It is important to assess the practice in terms of Eritrea's international obligations. The next section will do this.

5. ERITREA'S AMBIVALENCE TO ITS INTERNATIONAL OBLIGATIONS AND NATIONAL COMMITMENTS

In terms of Eritrea's international obligations, the continued practice of conscription of underage children is a cause for serious concern. Eritrea acceded to the Convention on the Rights of the Child (CRC) on 3 August 1994. The Convention entered into force on 2 September 1994. On 16 February 2005, Eritrea acceded to two Optional Protocols to the CRC, namely the protocol on the involvement of children in armed conflict and the protocol on the sale of children, child prostitution and child pornography. The protocols entered into force on 15 March 2005. According to article 2 of the Optional Protocol on the involvement of children in armed conflict, Eritrea has an obligation to ensure that persons who have not attained the age of 18 years are not compulsorily recruited into the armed forces. Contrary to this, the government continues to violate the minimum age of recruitment by enlisting underage children forcefully into the army.

In all of the relevant Eritrean laws the starting age for NMSP is 18 years.[44] In practice, however, the government conscripts underage children on a regular basis. This is mainly due to the reluctance of the Eritrean government to respect the legal limit provided by law. Eritrea's legal framework is characteristically marked by a lack of implementable constitutional law or principles that guarantee fundamental rights and freedoms, including the rights of children. The 1997 Eritrean Constitution, which has never been implemented since its "ratification", recognises national service as one of the core obligations of citizens. However, it does not give details as to when the service starts and where it ends. In principle, the constitution contains a detailed bill of rights that guarantees fundamental rights and freedoms in a fairly adequate fashion. However, the constitution

[44] See Articles 2 and 8 of Proclamation No. 11/1991 and Article 8 of Proclamation No. 82/1995.

remains unimplemented, making Eritrea the only country in Africa, perhaps also in the world, without an operational constitution.[45]

In theory, the 1997 Eritrean Constitution obliges the Eritrean National Assembly (the parliament) to enact laws that should contribute towards eliminating any inequalities existing in Eritrean society.[46] Eritrea had a transitional national assembly, which was convened for the last time in February 2002. Since then, the transitional parliament has been replaced by an unelected tripartite body composed of the cabinet of ministers, regional administrators and army commanders, who are accountable only to the state president. In effect, since 2002 the country has not had a functioning parliament that could have enacted the laws envisaged by the constitution. Eritrea has also never seen free and fair general elections since its independence in 1991. For obvious reasons, this has complicated the issue of human rights, including children's rights.

Moreover, Eritrea does not have an independent and impartial judiciary that could have played a central role in improving the dire situation of human rights in the country. When it comes to the promotion of human rights in general and children's rights in particular, the Eritrean judiciary is the most ineffective government organ. Since the unceremonious dismissal of the President of the High Court of Eritrea (the highest court in the country) in 2001, the judiciary has been effectively emasculated by the executive branch. Even before 2001, judicial independence was not the hallmark of Eritrean legal culture. In the current debate, there is little that can be gleaned as a positive experience from the Eritrean judiciary. With no working constitution, functioning parliament, independent judiciary, free press, national human rights institution (ombudsman), bureaucratic accountability or even an officially published national budget, Eritrea acutely lacks the legislative, administrative and institutional mechanisms required to promote fundamental rights, including those of children.

Apart from underage military conscription, sexual exploitation and child trafficking are also some of the emerging critical challenges in Eritrea. The aftermath of the 1998–2000 border conflict with Ethiopia has increased the number of vulnerable social groups, such as women, children and destitutes living on the streets.[47] In recent years, a growing number of HIV/AIDS victims

---

45 On the fate of the 1997 Eritrean Constitution, see T. Medhanie, 'Constitution-Making, Legitimacy and Regional Integration: An Approach to Eritrea's Predicament and Relations with Ethiopia', Development, Innovation and International Political Economy Research (DIIPER), Working Paper No 9, 2008; S.M. Weldehaimanot, 'The Status and Fate of the Eritrean Constitution' (2008) 8 2 *African Human Rights Law Journal* 108–137.

46 Article 14(3) of the 1997 Eritrean Constitution.

47 The Protection Project, *supra* note 43.

have been noticed in the country with a minimum number of 24,000 orphaned children, as reported in 2002.[48] Although the Eritrean government has never released the correct epidemiological facts on the HIV/AIDS epidemic, experts[49] indicate that the total number of seropositive individuals is estimated to be close to 200,000. In a population of less than four million people, the prevalence rate is not low.

In the African continent, where 80 percent of all countries have reported internal trafficking, children are normally trafficked to meet the demand for cheap exploitative labour and prostitution.[50] Eritrea is no exception in this regard. For the year 2000, the International Labour Organisation (ILO) estimated that there were 183,000 economically active children in Eritrea, girls constituting 90,000. Of the total number, 38.4 percent were children between the ages of 10 and 14.[51] Moreover, according to the 2009 *Trafficking in Persons Report*, Eritrea has a tier 3 placement, which is the gravest rank in the report. The report describes Eritrea as a source country for men, women, and children trafficked for the purposes of forced labour and commercial sexual exploitation.[52]

Child prostitution is another emerging challenge. Data on commercial sex workers in the country collected in 1999 by the Eritrean Ministry of Labour and Human Welfare revealed that five percent of commercial sex workers surveyed were children between the ages of 14 and 17 years. It was reported that a "majority of the children entered the trade at an early age, with most of them starting off as street children and bar maids".[53] In addition, the more than 4,000 members of the UN peacekeeping forces who were stationed along the common border between Eritrea and Ethiopia were accused of purchasing sex from vulnerable

---

48 Ibid.

49 Presentation by Mr Kidane Girmay in Eritrean [Paltalk] Room for Strong and United Opposition, 30 January 2008; Informal Phone Interview with Mr. Yosief Berhe, 15 October 2008. See also generally D.R. Mekonnen, "Mandatory Premarital HIV-Testing as a Challenge to Human Rights: A Case Study of Eritrea" (2010) 5(1) *Interdisciplinary Journal of Human Rights Law* 1–23.

50 J. Fowler, 'UNICEF: Human Trafficking in Africa Fuelled by War, Economic Hardship, and Lack of Birth Registration', *Associated Press*, 23 April 2004.

51 Global March, *supra* note 42. See also International Labour Office, Bureau of Statistics, Economically Active Population 1950–2010, STAT Working Paper, 1997. The Global March Against Child Labour further reports: "It is common for rural children who do not attend classes to work on family farms, fetching firewood and water, and herding livestock among other activities. In urban areas, some children work as street vendors of cigarette, newspapers, or chewing gum. Children also work as childminders, traders, and domestic accountants and in small-scale manufacturing."

52 US Department of State, *Trafficking in Persons Report: Eritrea*, 2009, at 50 and 129–130.

53 Global March, *supra* note 42. See also End Child Prostitution, Pornography, and Trafficking (ECPAT), *International Online Database*, November 2002, citing the *Ministry of Labour and Human Welfare Survey 1999*, available at www.ecpat.net/eng/ecpat_inter/projects/monitoring/online_database/index.asp (accessed 21 July 2007).

Eritrean children and women.[54] Quoting international databases, the Protection Project asserts that displaced children fleeing conflict between Eritrea and Ethiopia have ended up in prostitution in Djibouti.[55]

Another case-study of child trafficking in Eritrea bears extraordinary characteristics. It involves the alleged participation of the Eritrean government in the trafficking of child jockeys to the Gulf States.[56] Conventionally, human trafficking is referred to as one of the "illicit markets" that pit governments against agile, stateless and resourceful networks of criminal syndicates empowered by globalisation.[57] In the Eritrean child jockey scandal, however, the government had reportedly played the role of trafficker, making the Eritrean experience typically unique from other scenarios. According to the allegations, the Eritrean government has organised the trafficking of child jockeys from the areas surrounding Tessenei in western Eritrea via Sudanese rebel groups operating in Eritrea under false Eritrean diplomatic passports.[58]

6. CRITICAL CHALLENGES AND THE WAY FORWARD

Disillusioned by the never-ending NMSP, and its concomitant, the WYDC, and traumatised by the abuses perpetrated within the army, tens of thousands of youths (including underage children) have recently fled the country in an unprecedented manner. Yet, there is lack of reliable data on these victims, apart from anecdotal accounts compiled by NGOs and rights groups. Their plight as victims remains little known. Despite the grotesque reality on the ground, little is known by the rest of the world about what is really happening in Eritrea. Several factors account for this, some of which include the lack of an aggressive advocacy and campaign strategy as well as shortage of reliable data on the total number of victims of human rights violations in the country. In a country where talking about human rights violations is "tantamount to treason",[59] research

54 J. Reilly, 'Soldiers Accused of Eritrean Sex Offenses Offered STD Test', *Sunday Independent* (Ireland), 29 June 2003.

55 ECPAT, *International Online Database*, *supra* note 53.

56 Awate Team, 'Eritrean Regime now Trafficking Children', available at www.awate.com/portal/content/view/4597/3/ (accessed 24 August 2007).

57 M. Naím, 'The Five Wars of Globalization', *Foreign Policy Magazine*, January/February 2003.

58 Awate Team, note 56 above. Similarly, Anti-Slavery International indicates that there was evidence of children being trafficked to the Gulf from Eritrea as early 1997. See Anti-Slavery International, 'Trafficking in Women, Forced Labour and Domestic Work in the Context of the Middle East and Gulf Region', Working Paper Series, 2006, available at www.antislavery.org/homepage/resources/PDF/traffic%20women%20forced%20labour%20domestic%202006.pdf (accessed 27 January 2009).

59 Human Rights Watch, *supra* note 15, at 25; Tronvoll, 2009, *supra* note 2, at 16.

work on this particular issue is completely unthinkable inside Eritrea. There is also another major challenge among many former conscripts of the NMSP, including underage children, who have left the country under inexplicable ordeals. Many of them do not consider themselves victims in the real sense of the term. Deeply influenced by excessive indoctrination and owing also to the pervasive political narrative and propaganda machination of the ruling elite, on the contrary many victims consider themselves "traitors", even after having left the country through unfathomable tribulations. As a result, many of them shy away from sharing their untold experiences, because they still suffer either from a misplaced sense of guilt and shame or a deeply traumatised past or a combination of both and other factors. This poses immense challenges in the struggle against impunity in Eritrea.

In most reports compiled by rights groups, the human rights crisis in Eritrea has generally been described as grave. Reports also indicate that victims of human rights violations are estimated in the thousands. No report has thus far provided a probable, even if not exact, figure for the total number of victims of human rights violations in general and the total number of child soldiers in particular. This is an integral part of the main challenges to the legal discourse and academic literature on Eritrea, which is characterised by a dearth of information in academic writing and publication.[60] This is particularly true in relation to the post-independence era. A lot of work needs to be done in this area in order to narrow the gap and lay a solid foundation for further actions and strategies. The availability of reliable figures is crucially important in order to address current challenges and recommend future strategies. Clearly, an objective as broad as this one may require extensive resource allocation and prolonged research time. However, there are important preliminary tasks that can be accomplished in the form of short-term research projects. One such important task is a start to work on a systematic documentation of the stories of victims of human rights violations, who are scattered in several countries.

A very important aspect of the ongoing struggle against impunity in Eritrea should be the establishment of a comprehensive, evidence-based body of knowledge of victim empowerment. As the immediate neighbours of Eritrea, Ethiopia and Sudan host a large of number of Eritrean refuges who have fled the country recently. In Europe and North America there are also tens of thousands of newly arrived Eritrean refugees, a majority of whom are former

60 T.R French, 'Legal Literature of Eritrea: A Bibliographic Essay', (1999) 24 *North Carolina Journal of International Law and Commercial Arbitration*, at 430. As a result, many legal research works in Eritrea tend to rely primarily on internet sources and grey literature. See also Mekonnen, *supra* note 4, at 13–14.

conscripts of the NMSP. Extensive research work is required in those countries in order to establish reliable data on the situation of child soldiers in Eritrea. Eritrea has one of the largest diaspora communities (proportional to its total population) in the world. In recent years, the number has increased exponentially. Anecdotal accounts indicate that more than one million Eritreans live outside the country, stretching from Africa to all other continents. These communities host large numbers of victims of human rights violations, including former child soldiers who never had the opportunity of healing from emotional and psychological trauma. Eritrean diaspora communities also host a number of perpetrators of human rights violations who are living peacefully and comfortably in the same communities as victims. The perpetrators live without any legal consequences, creating further anxiety and discomfort to victims of human rights violations who, in some instances, were victimised by the same perpetrators. These are some of the critical challenges in addressing the overall human rights situation in Eritrea and the issue of child soldiers in particular. The following recommendations are essential for addressing the challenge.

Efforts aimed at alleviating the challenges of abusive practices in Eritrea depend, in the first place, on the willingness of the Eritrean government to acknowledge these problems. However, the government is far from doing so. First and foremost, the Eritrean government needs to be amenable to a peaceful political transition in the country. It is also important that respect for the human rights and fundamental freedoms of all Eritreans, including children's rights, be restored immediately. At the same time, a halt has to be called to the indefinite NMSP and its concomitant, the WYDC. In particular, the Eritrean government is required to end the practice of conscripting underage children into the army. Furthermore, those who have already been conscripted need to be reintegrated and rehabilitated into society. Compensation has to be provided for the wrongs victims have suffered as a result of the abusive practice. Investigations must be conducted with regard to all abuses with a view to uncovering the misdeeds of the past in full and establishing as complete a picture as possible of the history of injustices in the country. This is a very important factor in facilitating a smooth political transition to democracy. In order to halt future violations, the independence and impartiality of the judiciary has to be strengthened and courts should be endowed with adequate powers to adjudicate on human rights violations. The required financial and technical assistance in this regard may be sought from the international community and be implemented via the training of judges, prosecutors and lawyers, with particular emphasis on international human rights law, international humanitarian law and international criminal law.

Some child soldiers who have been conscripted into the army may have already attained the age of majority while in the army. However, the need for trauma counselling, psychological care and effective support mechanisms for the rehabilitation and reintegration of such soldiers is a crucial factor at any stage of conscription. The missed opportunities (such as education and career development) child soldiers may have lost during conscription must be remedied by effective government programmes of rehabilitation and reintegration.

In several countries where the issue of child soldiers is a topical subject there is some space for independent research and non-governmental initiatives aimed at alleviating the suffering of children. In the Eritrean experience, the scenario is different. The government has isolated the country from external exposure and any independent initiative aimed at addressing the dire human rights situation in the country is impossible. There has to be adequate space for the engagement of NGOs, civil society and other actors that could make major contributions towards alleviating the plight of children. The international community is also expected to play a major role in this regard. In the face of the human rights violations and the continued practice of underage military conscription, the application of international coercive pressure is duly expected from the UN Security Council. In December 2009, the UN Security Council has imposed targeted sanctions against the political and military leadership of Eritrea on account of Eritrea's belligerent actions in Djibouti and Somalia. Nonetheless, the Security Council is yet to announce the list of names that are subject to these measures. The timely publication of the list may have its own role in coercing Eritrean government officials to open the required political space in Eritrea. On the other hand, the level of inhumanity prevailing inside Eritrea requires the same degree of international indignation and firm resolve as has been displayed by the UN Security Council in relation to Eritrea's belligerence in the Horn of Africa.

As noted earlier, the continued practice of underage conscription is to be seen in the context of gross human rights violations in Eritrea and Eritrea's hostile role in the entire Horn of Africa region. All of these transgressions meet the threshold of international crimes as established by the Statute of the International Criminal Court (ICC) and other relevant bodies of international law.[61] In light of the gravity of the crimes perpetrated by the Eritrean government and the failure of the latter to combat impunity, the international community is duty bound to intervene by referring the matter to the ICC Prosecutor via Security Council referral, pursuant to article 13(b) of the ICC Statute. In the meantime, the international community is also expected to implement interim punitive

[61] For further discussions on the international crimes perpetrated since Eritrea's independence, see generally Mekonnen and Pretorius, *supra* note 4.

measures such as travel bans and asset freezes against targeted individuals deemed most responsible for the perpetration of international crimes and destabilisation of international peace and order, as has already been done by Resolution 1907 (2009) of the UN Security Council. This is one of the most effective ways to alleviate the suffering of the Eritrean people, as well as to tackle the challenge of underage conscription in Eritrea.

In addition to the measures that can be adopted by the UN Security Council, Simon Weldehaimanot proposes the following considerations which he believes are important to influence political development in Eritrea. Building on the continued practice of the Eritrean government, which defies conventional understanding of the rule of the law, Weldehaimanot describes the current political situation in Eritrea as one befitting a form of illegal continuance of a transitional government in power (which, according to Weldehaimanot, is one form of coup d'état). Based on this assumption, he argues that in accordance with the Constitutive Act of the African Union (AU), the Charter on Democracy of the AU and the Peace and Security Council (PSC) Protocol of the AU, the Chairperson of the AU Commission in conjunction with the PSC of the AU can call on the Eritrean government to allow the establishment of constitutional order within a period of not more than six months. Failing such calls, the relevant organs of the AU may take punitive measures, such as sanctions, against the Eritrean government.[62]

7. CONCLUDING REMARKS

The Eritrean government has continued the forcible conscription of thousands of underage children into the regular army. Although not comparable to other African experiences, seen against the background of the human rights violations in the country the issue of child soldiers is a major reason for concern. The practice has to stop before it reaches critical levels of crisis. This is particularly true in light of the high possibility of intrastate or interstate conflict that could erupt in the country at any time.

Since its independence in 1991, Eritrea has seen serious violations of international human rights and humanitarian law, which are committed in contravention of Eritrea's legal obligations emanating from international treaties and customary international law. The issue of child soldiers is to been seen in this context. The government is doing nothing to reverse the sad state of affairs in Eritrea. To end the culture of impunity, the following considerations are essential.

62 S.A. Weldehaimanot, 'African Law of Coups and the Situation in Eritrea: A Test for the African Union's Commitment to Democracy', (2010) 54(2) *Journal of African Law* 256.

First and foremost, the Eritrean government has to be amenable to a peaceful political transition in the country. Respect for the human rights and fundamental freedoms of all Eritreans has to be restored immediately. There is a need for the government to halt the indefinite NMSP, and its concomitant, the WYDC, as well as the practice of underage conscription. Compensation needs to be offered to the wrongs suffered by victims of underage conscription. In this regard, nationwide and effective programmes of rehabilitation and reintegration are deemed important. The required assistance in this regard may be sought from the international community and can be implemented via different modalities, such as training, capacity building, funding and other opportunities. Investigations have to be conducted with regard to all abuses relating to child soldiers and guarantees of non-repetition should also be given in this regard. In order to halt future violations, the independence and impartiality of the judiciary must be strengthened and courts should be endowed with adequate powers to adjudicate on human rights violations. Pending the implementation of these recommendations and the likelihood of their frustration by the Eritrean government, punitive international measures, including prosecutorial approaches by regional and international judicial bodies, have to be pursued to the maximum possible extent.

In the last twelve years, the Eritrean government has used the border conflict with Ethiopia as a pretext for suppressing human rights and continuing its practice of underage conscription. It is imperative that the Eritrea-Ethiopia border stalemate be resolved immediately in order to improve the human rights situation and underage conscription in Eritrea. In this regard, the international community should impose punitive measures on the party which is frustrating the full implementation of the peace process, including the resumption of political dialogue between the leaders of the two governments. Ethiopia's refusal to cooperate in the demarcation of the common border is an abhorrent violation of the country's international obligations. Equally, Eritrea's rejection of any type of political dialogue and unwillingness to facilitate normalisation, as well as its refusal to cooperate with regional and international actors, are completely unacceptable. This sends a message that the simple delimitation and demarcation of the border will not bring a lasting solution in the region. The international community may put some pressure and encourage the parties to engage in a comprehensive peace plan which seeks solutions to the causes of the war and not only to its consequences. The international community, via the UN Security Council, may also utilise its Chapter VII powers against any party which fails to abide by international law. As a regional organization, the AU can also play a role in this regard, particularly via its newly established PSC. Only then can there be a lasting peace in the region. The resolution of the border stalemate may have a stabilising effect in other conflicts of the region, thereby ending the continued practice of underage conscription in Eritrea.

CHILDREN IN TWENTIETH CENTURY EUROPE AFFECTED BY WAR: HISTORICAL EXPERIENCES IN GIVING THEM REFUGE

Frank CAESTECKER

1. INTRODUCTION

Children have been affected by war throughout history. This article will analyse how children in Europe have been a privileged category in qualifying for a refuge protecting them against violence throughout the twentieth century. We focus on three cases during what some have called the long Second World War (1936–45): Basque children during the Spanish civil war, German-Jewish children persecuted by the Nazis in the late 1930s and children in France in the early 1940s. These three groups of children were considered particularly deserving and protection was granted to them. The reasons why these children were singled out for protection will be covered as well as the concrete modalities of assistance to them. Refugee policy at that time was a public-private mix and from the outset civil society was strongly involved in the decision to grant protection to the children. This contribution pays considerable attention to the input of civil society into the rescue schemes. The long-term consequences of these humanitarian programmes directed at children will also be discussed. The rehabilitation and reintegration of the war-affected children can be fully assessed through the evaluation of the rescue operations by all stakeholders, including of course the children.

2. WAR-AFFECTED CHILDREN FROM SPAIN: OFFERING ASYLUM IN AN EXTREMELY POLITICALLY POLARISED SITUATION (1937–39)

General Franco led a revolt in Spanish Morocco against the democratically elected Popular Front, a coalition of left-wing parties. The Italian fascist government supported this rebellion, thereby enabling it to spread quickly to the Spanish mainland. Burgos joined the insurgents and the rebels moved up to the north of Spain. In the Basque country the rebels met with fierce resistance and battles began by mid-August 1936. The violence of this war was extreme, not only due to the fact that it was a civil war, but also due to foreign involvement. Germany and Italy sent considerable quantities of arms and equipment to the fascist rebels – Germany even gave air support – while the Soviet Union gave military aid to the Republican side. German air support (the Condor legion) added to the high number of casualties and the extreme violence. Not only military objectives were the target: the civilian population was not spared at all.[1] The symbol of this total war was the bombing of Guernica on 26 April 1937. In all, half a million people died in the civil war.[2]

2.1. DECISION-MAKING PROCESS LEADING TO REFUGE FOR WAR-AFFECTED BASQUE CHILDREN (1937)

The democratic countries of Western Europe, although sympathetic to the legitimate government, decided on a policy of non-intervention in order to limit the internationalisation of the war. Within civil society in these countries a broad, mostly leftist movement demanded more active support for the Republic. This movement focussed, among others things, on the rescue of children from the war zone by offering them hospitality abroad. This rescue operation for war-affected children not only served humanitarian needs but also had political objectives. The children would import a strong image of francoist violence into democratic countries in Western Europe and increase the pressure for more direct involvement. The Spanish government was opposed to sending children to safety abroad. Helping the war-affected children could be done within Spain itself or at most in the French-Spanish border region. The International Red Cross and the International Union for Saving the Children agreed with the Spanish authorities and stated emphatically that it was in the best interests of the children themselves to stay in Spain.[3]

The Spanish Republican opposition to sending the children abroad was grounded in their perception that this rescue operation harboured the danger of denationalisation. Other public relations operations were considered more

---

1 J.M. Sole and J. Villarroya, *Espana en llamas: La guerra Civil desdes el Aire*, Madrid, 2003.

2 E. Temine, *La Guerre d'Espagne commence*, Scorpion, Brussels, 1986, 105.

3 J. Carballes Alonso, *1937, los ninos vascos evacuados a Francia y Belgica: historia y memoria de un exodo infantil, 1936–1940,* Associacion de Ninos Evacuados, Bilbao, 1998, 37; F. Caestecker and S. Eloy, 'De opvang van Spaanse minderjarige oorlogsvluchtelingen in België', in H. Pauwels (ed.), *Los Ninos,* EPO, Berchem, 2007, 199–204; D. Legaretta, *The Guernica generation: Basque refugee children of the Spanish Civil War,* University of Nevada Press, Nevada, 1984.

effective for conquering public opinion.[4] The authorities in the democracies of Western Europe were also rather opposed as dangers loomed over such a humanitarian operation. First of all, helping children to flee the war zone might be contrary to the policy of non-intervention as it could favour the Republicans. Secondly, although the operation was only meant to be temporary – until the violence waned – it might become more permanent as reuniting the children with their parents could prove difficult. That some children might even prefer to stay in the country of asylum was considered a problem as they would become adults who would add to competition in the labour market. At the time, western Europe was slowly recovering from the depression and had armed itself with legislation to protect domestic labour against competition from foreigners. Circumventing immigration control was not regarded favourably.[5]

Already in January 1937, the regional authorities of the Basque country, notwithstanding the position of the Spanish federal government, had devised plans to evacuate children abroad if the Basque region became a war zone. All political groups represented in the Basque Parliament obtained a quota according to their regional electoral strength. Each party could register 'their' children up to the age of twelve years for evacuation in case of war. The Catholic Basque nationalists – the Partido Nacionalista Vasco (PNV) – thereby received half the quota, the other half going to parties of the left, including the Communists, who received about 10 per cent.[6]

By 1937, in several West European countries the popular pressure to develop concrete solidarity with war-struck Spain and in particular to rescue children from the war had forced even recalcitrant organisations such as the Red Cross to mount rescue operations. Many Swiss, Belgian, French, Dutch and British families expressed their solidarity with the Spanish people by offering Spanish children a safe sanctuary in their homes.[7]

The whole movement was put to the test when after the bombing of Guernica on 26 April 1937 Basque President Aguirre sent out an urgent request across the world for asylum for women, children and the elderly. Several countries agreed to take in Basque children. This was mostly on condition that the maintenance of these children should be entirely financed by the solidarity groups (and/or the

---

4 H. Garcia, *Mentiras necesarias. La batalla por la opinion britanica durante la guerre civil*, Bibliotheca nueva, Madrid, 2008;
R. Stradling, *Your children will be next: bombing and propaganda in the Spanish Civil War 1936–1939*, University of Wales Press, Cardiff, 2008.

5 A. Schmidlin, *Eine andere Schweiz: Helferinnen, Kriegskinder und humanitäre Politik, 1933–1942,* Chronos, Zurich, 1999, 110; J. van Tol-Kamerman, 'Aanhangers van Franco tijdens de Spaanse burgeroorlog', in H. Hermans (ed.), *Een Nederlandse blik op de Spaanse burgeroorlog*, Instituto Cervantes, Utrecht, 2006, 57–62; Caestecker and Eloy, *supra* note 3 at 201.

6 D. Legaretta, *The Guernica generation*, University of Nevada Press, Nevada, 1984, at 38.

7 Schmidlin, ibid. at 61–65; Caestecker and Eloy, *supra* note 3 at 204.

Basque government) and that the children would be repatriated once the war was over. Although the move to bring children was actuated largely by political motives, the authorities insisted on neutralising it politically. The principle of non-intervention required that the rescue operation be an apolitical, merely humanitarian operation. This also had practical repercussions: children of all political groups had to be represented and these children could not be used in political demonstrations.

The Belgian authorities agreed to aid organisations taking in 5,000 children, while the British accepted 4,000. The Danish authorities agreed on 100 children for the Socialist aid organisation and the Swiss 245 for the Catholic and Socialist aid organisation.[8] The Soviet authorities agreed to take in about 4,000 children. France was an obvious destination due to its proximity. Most of the children – about 20,000 – stayed in France, sometimes at the charge of Dutch and Swedish aid organisations. In the latter countries the authorities had not agreed to take in children, although numerous families had expressed their willingness to host them.[9] The Dutch (and Swedish) aid for children was then organised in France. The children of communist families went mostly to the Soviet Union, while the other children were divided among solidarity groups of different political leanings. In total, 32,000 children left the Basque country in the spring of 1937.[10]

The division of the children into political groups led to the occurrence of some problems. Children whose parents were affiliated with leftist groups easily found a place to stay, as their allies abroad had been mobilising for months to host them. Finding a place for children from the largest political party in the Basque country, the PNV, turned out to be more difficult. The leaders of the Spanish Catholic Church fully supported Franco's coup. The Basque bishop Mateo Mugica, who supported the Basque nationalists, one of the Republican forces in the Basque country, was forced to leave for Rome in October 1936, due to the staunch support of Franco by his superiors. The lack of hospitality for the PNV children caused Bishop Mugica to call upon the Catholic hierarchy in each of the West European countries which had accepted children to provide a Catholic initiative for them. He wrote to the archbishops, stating that to date nearly all the children had 'found a hospitality which will not transmit the love of Jesus Christ, but will rather damage their beliefs… I know that these groups, which are hostile to the Church, will try to make use of this occasion to inoculate the poison of these godless principles into these pure souls'. In France, Britain, Switzerland

8 Legaretta, *supra* note 6 at 174.

9 J. J. Flinterman, 'De CPN en de solidariteitsbeweging met de Spaanse republiek in Nederland (1936–1939)', (1937) *Cahiers over de geschiedenis van de CPN*, 10.

10 J. Carballes Alonso, '*1937, los ninos vascos evacuados a Francia y Belgica*', Asociación de Niños Evacuados el 37, Bilbao, 1998.

and Belgium, Catholic Church groups, although mostly not pro-Republic, provided for the PNV children.[11]

The departure from the Basque country was a traumatic experience for all of the children. Being separated from their parents and shipped as cargo to a foreign land where they did not know anybody and did not understand the language was a traumatic experience. The sense of being cargo was expressed by the number which they were given in the Basque registration process and which became their identification abroad. As Legarreta writes, it was far more convenient for the administrators of the evacuation operation in the receiving country to use a number rather than the complex double Basque names, from both the father and mother, which the children had been given at baptism. Many of the children felt a personal sense of loss when they became numbers instead of persons. They were stripped of their identity.[12]

2.2. HOUSING AND CARE OF THE BASQUE CHILDREN

In 1937 the Basque government agreed with the Spanish federal authorities that asylum abroad could cause the alienation of the children. The Basque government advocated that the children be supervised by Basque teachers in the refugee camps in order to counter the danger of denationalisation. Private reception of the children in foster families was opposed: the children should remain in a Basque environment.

The Spanish and Basque demand that the children be housed collectively under the guardianship of their teachers was met in Britain and Denmark. The 4,000 children who sailed to Britain were accompanied by 219 female teachers and their aides, together with 15 priests. These adults stayed with the children and were all housed in camps during their stay. This was also the case in Denmark for a much smaller group. In both countries, offers of private accommodation were generally refused. But the demand from Spain was not always met. For 9,000 children in French custody, only a third stayed in camps and all others were privately housed, while in Belgium most of the 5,000 children were housed privately.

That the housing was mostly private in Belgium and France was not necessarily a deliberate choice by the aid committees, but was mainly due to their financial situation. Offers of foster families were plentiful, but appeals for financial support for children in a camp, whether in Belgium, Spain or France, were less

11 Legaretta, *supra* note 6 at 71 and 174; Carballes and Caestecker *supra* note 3 at 206.

12 Legaretta, ibid.

forthcoming. As these organisations had few independent means, they were dependent on private support. For example, of the 1,265 children sponsored by the Catholic Committee in Belgium three quarters were sent to foster families and the remainder to Catholic institutions that took in groups of children.[13]

The choice of foster families had the advantage of providing a home-like atmosphere. The intimate atmosphere of family life could be positive, but this care model could also entail hardship. Most families had volunteered to take in one child. In particular, there was a very high demand for orphans and very young girls, while boys from eight years old and older had a hard time in finding parents willing to take them in. This preference for 'easy' and single children caused difficulties for the aid organisations and the children alike. For example, 60 per cent of the Basque children allocated to Belgium in 1937 did not leave on their own, but were accompanied by siblings. When it turned out that most foster families wanted only one child, these children, on top of the traumatic experience of being separated from their parents, were also separated upon arrival from their siblings. This was a traumatic experience in particular for the oldest children as they had taken responsibility upon themselves, after the parents had sent them out, for keeping together at all costs.[14] This experience was not limited to those countries where foster families had custody of the children. In Britain a number of children also experienced this separation as there were separate camps for boys and girls. This was in particular the case for the PNV children, who were taken into care by Catholic organisations that insisted on keeping the sexes apart.[15]

Not all foster families had genuinely altruistic motives. Some foster parents had clearly political purposes: the lot of the Spanish Republic rather than the interests of the child was their reason for taking in a child. Others had agreed to take in Spanish children even for sexual or economic exploitation. More common were childless couples who hoped by taken in a Spanish child finally to fulfil their long postponed dream of having a child. They in particular asked for orphans, whom they wanted to adopt. These foster parents did not underwrite the temporary status of the children's stay in Belgium. All aid organisations had insisted that the children would only remain in Belgium for a short period of time, i.e., until the war was over. The Catholic organisations had even stipulated that the foster families would provide for the child only for a period of six months. However,

13 H. Hellemans, *De schimmen met een ster*, Antwerpen, Manteau, 2007; J. De Maeyer and P. Wynants, *De Vincentianen in België 1842–1992*, Leuven, Kadoc, 1992, 108; Legaretta, *supra* note 6 at 141.

14 H. Pauwels, *Los Ninos*, EPO, Berchem, 2007, 142; Carballes, *supra* note 6 at 162–72.

15 T. Kushner and K. Knox, *Refugees in an age of genocide. Global, national and local perspectives during the twentieth century*, Frank Cass, London, 2001, 119.

some foster families did not intend to provide shelter to a child only for the dangerous period of the war. Keeping the child was their ambition. Some of them cut their child off from their siblings and sometimes even prohibited them from contacting their parents. The dispersal of the children throughout the country made it difficult for the aid committees and the Basque teachers and priests to keep track of them all and it was particularly difficult if the foster family deliberately severed any contact with them.[16]

The manner in which they were taken care of in the host country coloured the experience of the children. Those in Britain and Denmark were all received in camps, boarding schools, orphanages, hostels… with Basque schoolteachers as their guardians, thus not severing their link to the Basque country. In this way they were not alienated from the country of origin: teaching was conducted in Spanish and they followed the Spanish curriculum.[17] Their experience was a collective one, while in Belgium and France it was much more individual. In both these countries children were mostly housed on their own in private homes and their isolation expressed itself at times in an absolute rejection of the foster parents.[18]

We know little of how the aid organisations, the foster families and the Basque teachers coped with the traumas of the children. In one of the camps in Britain the children were very frightened when airplanes appeared and some urinated spontaneously. The camp authorities did not know how to handle these neurotic symptoms. Moments of crisis also seem to have been handled in a rather naïve manner. For example, in Britain the response of the camp leadership when the devastating news of Franco's forces taking Bilbao became known to the children was to provide extra delicacies, including chocolate and ice cream, so as to help the children recover their normal high spirits. Most of the children came from Bilbao and being unaware of the whereabouts of their parents, started to cry in their anguish and the wailing lasted the whole day. Some older boys even escaped the camp to return to Spain to help their parents.[19]

16 T. Eeckhout, 'De hulp aan Republikeins Spanje uitgaande van de BWP afdeling Gent-Eeklo, meer specifiek de opvang der Spaanse kinderen', (1897) 18 12 *Belgisch Tijdschrift voor Nieuwste Geschiedenis*, at 255 and 259; Legaretta, *supra* note 6 at 149.

17 Kushner and Knox, *supra* note 15 at 119; L. Rünitz, *Af hensyn til konsekvenserne, Danmark og flygtningesporgsmalet 1933–1939*, Syddansk Universitetsforlag, Odense, 2005, 117.

18 L. de Castresana, *El otro arbol de Guernica*, Prenza Espagnola, Madrid, 1968, 91–94; I. Schepens, *Ninos de la patria. De opvang van Baskische kinderen in België tijdens de Spaanse burgeroorlog*, VRT (Flemish Radio and Television), Brussels, 2000 (documentary).

19 *The Daily Dispatch*, quoted in Kushner and Knox, *supra* note 15 at 116; Legaretta, *supra* note 6 at 114.

2.3. REPATRIATION: THE NORMALISATION OF SPAIN AT STAKE

By the end of October 1937 the war was over in the north of Spain and the Franco regime wanted a normalisation of the 'liberated' Basque country, including the return of the children whom 'the reds had stolen'. The Franco regime prodded the Basque parents to reclaim their children.[20] The Catholic Church assisted fully in this repatriation campaign. Pope Pius XI, as well as his Papal Nuncio, lent financial and moral support to the repatriation effort. The children sponsored by the Catholic organisations in Belgium and Switzerland became a test group. While in France and Britain the Catholic aid organisation could not, or did not want to, decide unilaterally to repatriate the children, the Catholic hierarchy in Belgium, which had had a very strong hold over this campaign, had already decided to make them return in August 1937. In Switzerland, repatriation had started even earlier. In April 1937 children had already been returned from Switzerland, but the numbers involved in Belgium were much greater.[21] Although Catholic foster parents in Belgium had agreed to take these children for six months, those responsible for their reception were eager to have them returned as early as possible. The last batch of Basque children arrived in Belgium on 12 August 1937; shortly thereafter, an emissary of the Cardinal left for Spain. He brought along a list of children they sponsored so that the parents could quickly reclaim them. From September 1937 onwards, small batches of children reclaimed by their parents arrived in Spain from Belgium. By November 1937 the campaign had lost much of its credibility. The Basque government in exile underlined that parents in Basque country were under considerable pressure to reclaim their children, but more important was their accusation that some reclamation letters were fraudulent. An emissary of the Spanish Catholic Church and the Franco regime had brought to Belgium a list of 900 names of children whom the parents were allegedly reclaiming. The list contained many inaccuracies, but the most glaring was that it included the children of the Basque secretary of the Catholic Committee in Belgium. As she was in Belgium with her children, the falsification was obvious. The incident was widely publicised by the Basque Government-in-exile and from then on the Belgian Cardinal required validation of each reclamation request by the Belgian consul. The repatriation process became much slower. Due to adverse living conditions it turned out that not all Basque parents wanted their expatriated children back so quickly.[22]

20 F. Blanco Moral, 'Los "ninos e la Guerra": expatriacion y repatriacion', (2004) 2 *Rastro de la Historia*; Carballes *supra* note 1 at 131.

21 Schmidlin, *supra* note 5 at 113.

22 Legaretta, *supra* note 6 at 154, 206–14 and 226; Caestecker and Eloy, *supra* note 3 at 211–14.

In February 1938, the pluralistic British aid organisation – the Basque Children's Committee – voted on the repatriation of the children from Britain. The vote was tied: political, but also financial reasons were put forward for returning the children to their homes. Funds were dwindling as many sponsors were not ready to make a lasting commitment. The Chair, the Duchess of Atholl, cast the deciding vote, which she used in favour of 'sending back the children to those parents known to be in Insurgent Spain and at liberty... with the assurance someone accompany the children to bring back any not reunited with their parents'.[23] In France, a repatriation procedure along the lines of Belgium was established in May 1938, but only in 1939, so that only after the defeat of the Spanish Republic was repatriation started on a mass scale. In Belgium, the repatriation of children sponsored by the non-Catholic aid organisations also started only after the civil war was over.[24]

Not all children returned. The British started to repatriate children in early 1938 and by September 1939, when Britain was itself at war, 2,726 children had been repatriated. But 1,155 were still in Britain because it turned out to be impossible, according to the Basque Children's Committee, to restore them to their parents. Most of the parents of the children remaining in Britain were dead, in prison, in refugee camps abroad or missing. When Britain entered the war the position of the Basque children became more precarious. The British authorities insisted upon repatriating all children except for those whose parents were in exile in France. The Basque Children's Committee, short of funding, agreed to do so, but only after an independent check on the parents' ability to support the child.[25] The Basque camps were gradually closed down and British official policy changed in 1939, allowing the older children to enrol in British state schools. Those aged over 14 were given the option to remain in Britain indefinitely. At the end of 1943, 411 of the evacuees, about 11 per cent of the children who had arrived in 1937, were still living in Britain and would remain there.[26]

In Belgium, the rate of return was partly dependent on the aid organisation and its commitment to repatriation. As mentioned above, the Belgian Catholic Committee, in close collaboration with the Franco regime, had already started to repatriate children reclaimed by their parents in the autumn of 1937 and in 1939 this repatriation effort was finalised by the return of orphans to a Falange-organised orphanage. Only 6 per cent of the 1,265 Basque children sponsored by the Belgian Catholic Committee were still in Belgium in 1940.[27] The Belgian Red Cross, which took over repatriation only in the spring of 1939, thus a year

---

23 Kushner and Knox, *supra* note 15 at 122; Legaretta, ibid. at 128 and 214.

24 Carballes, *supra* note 6 401–25.

25 Legaretta, *supra* note 6 at 222.

26 Kushner and Knox, *supra* note 15 at 123; Legaretta, ibid. at 134.

27 Legaretta, ibid. at 223.

and a half after the Catholic organisation, still had 15 per cent of its Basque children in Belgium in 1940. Among the socialist and communist aid organisations the return rate was probably even lower.[28]

The share of children repatriated was to a certain extent dependent on the length of stay in the country of asylum and the manner in which they were received. Individual care in private homes was more likely to diminish the return rate than if they were housed in refugee camps as ties of affection between children and the foster family could be detrimental to the natural families in Spain or in exile in France. The foster parents' insistence on keeping the child influenced the return rate. Parents in Spain or in exile in France sometimes agreed that the foster family could keep custody of their child after the end of the war. The difficult living conditions of the parents, the possibility of enabling a child to finish its education abroad and other reasons were evoked to explain why they should not be repatriated just yet. This agreement between natural and foster families led in some cases to a permanent settlement of the child. Age and gender were other factors influencing the return rate. The return rate of very young children in particular was lower than that of older children. A case in point is the few children sponsored by the Belgian Catholic Committee who did not return at all. They were mostly girls who had arrived as a very young age and had been placed in the custody of childless couples.[29] There were at times real struggles between the natural and foster parents. Although the natural parents had the law behind them, the foster family could dispose of a whole arsenal of

---

28 The figures mentioned in the literature are not reliable. CARBALLES is the best effort to date, but to assess the success of the repatriation campaign in the Belgian case he uses Spanish repatriation lists. These contain children repatriated in 1939 who only arrived in Belgium after the defeat of the Republic, but he attributes them to the 1937 flight. In January 1939 the defeated Spanish government called upon the world to give asylum to child refugees who had fled to France. Spanish child refugees left for Mexico, the Soviet Union and Belgium. The Belgian government agreed to take in Spanish children as some local aid organisations were ready to support them. Only pro-Republican organisations, such as the Office International pour l'Enfance (OIE), founded in 1936 to coordinate assistance to children in Republican Spain during the civil war, and leftist organisations were still eager for such help. These organisations enabled Belgian foster families to give 1,500 Spanish children a (temporary) home. Their parents were mostly in refugee camps in France. In the summer of 1939 these children started to be repatriated as many parents, under strong French pressure, had decided to return home. A number of children were reunited with their parents in exile in France, but this was dependent on the agreement of the French authorities, who were rather reluctant to accept the children if none of the parents had a stable position. Only very exceptionally were parents given the opportunity to join their children in Belgium. Most of the children returned to Spain, but exact figures are not available. Certainly more than 10 per cent up to at most 55 per cent of the 645 children in foster families for whom the pro-Republican organisation OIE had mediated had not (yet) returned by April 1940. T. RODRIGUEZ, *De opvang van Spaanse minderjarige vluchtelingen in 1939 door de Belgische afdeling van l'office international pour l'enfance,* UGent, Gent, 2008 (unpublished master thesis in contemporary history); L. STEIN, *Beyond death and exile: the Spanish Republicans in France, 1939–1955,* Cambridge, 1979.

29 LEGARETTA, *supra* note 27 at 287.

arguments. Peace, a higher economic standard and the so-called betrayal of the natural parents by sending their child off were strong arguments in this fight for the soul of the child. A few foster parents did not give up easily. Some foster parents who had been forced by the aid organisation to surrender the child to their parents in Spain travelled to Spain to convince the natural parents in person to return the child. Ten years after the arrival of the children litigation was still going on between natural and foster parents.[30]

3. A PROACTIVE REFUGEE POLICY FOR JEWS PERSECUTED IN NAZI GERMANY: ONLY FOR CHILDREN (1938–39)

The persecution of Jews in Nazi Germany also resulted in a rescue operation for children.[31] Not until the events of the year 1938 did the need arise for such a rescue operation. The radicalisation of anti-Semitic policy in Nazi Germany started in Austria immediately after the Anschluss in March 1938. The Nazi anti-Jewish legislation of 1938 that had taken several years to be introduced in Germany itself was implemented overnight in Austria. Anti-Semitic atrocities were also largely tolerated, if not promoted, by the new rulers in Austria. In Germany itself this radical policy took off on Kristallnacht in November 1938 when state-organised violence against the Jewish population was stepped up. Kristallnacht brought awareness in Jewish circles in Germany and abroad that Jews no longer had a future in Nazi Germany. This rescue operation to bring Jewish children in safety to Western Europe epitomised the hopeless situation for Jews in Germany. Terrorised parents realised that their children's only hope of survival was in 'the arms of strangers'.[32]

30 F. Caestecker, 'La acogida en Bélgica de niños refugiados de guerra españoles a partir de 1937', unpublished manuscript; P. Marqués, *Les enfants espagnols réfugiés en France (1936–1939)*, Auto Edition, Paris, 1993, 139.

31 Seeing that the National Socialist racial categorisations (Jew and Aryan) are not at all transparent and self-evident categories, the term 'Jews' refers to this racial category. Without quotation marks, Jew refers to a person who considers him or herself a member of a religious, ethnic or a sociological community.

32 We refer to the Academy Award-winning documentary *In the arms of strangers: stories of the Kindertransports* by D. Oppenheimer and M.J. Harris (2000). See also K. Kwiet, 'Gehen oder Bleiben? Die deutschen Juden am Wendepunkt', in W.H. Pehle (ed.), *Der Judenpogrom 1938. Von der "Reichskristallnacht" zum Völkermord,* Frankfurt/Main, 1988, 132–45; A. Margaliot, 'The problem of the rescue of German Jewry during the years 1933–1939. The Reason for the delay in their emigration from the Third Reich', in I. Gutman, and E. Zuroff (eds.), *Rescue attempts during the Holocaust,* Jerusalem, 1977, 247–65.

3.1. DECISION-MAKING PROCESS LEADING TO REFUGE FOR GERMAN JEWISH CHILDREN

Jewish refugee organisations convinced various Western European governments to give their agreement to the rescue operation by referring to the precedent of the protection afforded to children during the Spanish civil war. Also for 'Jewish' children only temporary asylum was necessary: the children would only be in transit in these European countries and would move on to a final destination, mostly overseas. Between December 1938 and the outbreak of World War II in September 1939 Switzerland, Sweden and France took in a few hundred children each and Belgium and Denmark a thousand apiece; the Dutch record was more generous with the Netherlands accepting 2,000 children. Great Britain received the largest number of children, about 10,000, 80 per cent of them Jewish.[33] Similar to the Basque children's rescue operation, these schemes were private initiatives and the number of children they could protect depended to a large extent on the response of the public.

However other factors played a role too, as the British example shows. Neville Chamberlain, the British Prime Minister, had, after the devastating experience of the Munich agreements, effectively given up all hope of moderating Nazi policy. He realised that the Jews in Germany had to flee and for him the only solution for the refugees was emigration to the United States. Palestine was no solution as an increase in Jewish immigration would be politically unacceptable for the resident Arab population. On the contrary, Chamberlain pursued a restrictive immigration policy for Palestine. He was also convinced that the United States could only be persuaded to open its doors if it realised that there was no European solution to the problem. These political and humanitarian considerations explain the British gesture in agreeing to rescue children as long as their (temporary) stay was financially backed by Jewish finance. That gesture was mainly meant to distract public attention from restrictive immigration policies in Palestine and to placate public feeling. At the same time, the presence

---

[33] We do not refer in this article to the Zionist-organised Hechaluz and Aliyah children as their story has other dimensions to it. The French record is unclear. L. Rünitz, *Af hensyn til konsekvenserne, Danmark og flygtningesporgsmalet 1933–1939*, Syddansk Universitetsforlag, Odense, 2005, 341; F. Caestecker, 'Onverbiddelijk, maar ook clement. Het Belgische immigratiebeleid en de joodse vlucht uit nazi-Duitsland, maart 1938-augustus 1939', (2004) 13/14 *Bijdragen tot de eigentijdse geschiedenis*, at 126; Adler-Rudel, *Jüdische Selbsthilfe unter dem Naziregime, 1933–1939*, Mohr, Tübingen, 1974, 217; R. Göpfert, *Der jüdische Kindertransport. Von Deutschland nach England 1938/39*, Frankfurt, 1999; W. Benz, C. Curio and A. Hammel (eds.), *Die Kindertransporte 1938/39. Rettung und Integration*, Frankfurt/Main, 2003; C. Curio, *Verfolgung, Flucht, Rettung. Die Kindertransporte nach Großbritannien 1938–39*, Metropol, Berlin, 2006; C. Curio, 'Were unaccompanied child refugees a privileged class of refugees in the liberal states of Europe?', in F. Caestecker and B. Moore (eds.), *Refugees from Nazi Germany and the liberal European states*, Berghahn Books, New York/Oxford, 169–89.

of the children in Britain waiting for a final country of asylum could be used as leverage for greater American hospitality.[34] The British willingness to accept children was a self-conscious effort and part of a proactive refugee policy. As Great Britain had no common land frontiers with Germany, the enormous pressure on Jews in Germany had hardly translated itself in an unregulated migration over the British borders. Great Britain, with its sea borders, had succeeded in effectively selecting the immigration of the persecuted through visas, a mechanism of external control.

Such a policy was much more difficult to implement in continental Europe with its green borders with Nazi Germany. In continental Europe a large number of refugees had arrived uninvited. Since 1933, 'Jews' fleeing Nazi Germany had been tolerated temporarily in the countries bordering Nazi Germany, as Jewish aid organisations had assisted these refugees financially. Thanks to this financial support the very oversupplied labour market during the depression was hardly affected by the influx. The assistance of the Jewish aid organisations in finding the refugees a final place of abode, mostly overseas, also helped in reducing the inconvenience of the inflow. From the spring of 1938 – the *Anschluss* – onwards, the inflow of 'Jewish' refugees increased considerably. 'Jews' were pushed out of Germany en masse and stripped of their belongings. This refugee flow was no longer a largely spontaneous flight. Groups of refugees literally dumped by the Nazi authorities arrived at the borders and in the neighbouring countries. This explicit involvement of the Nazi authorities prevented the refugees from taking any of their belongings with them. The Jewish organisations still undertook the management of the refugee influx. By the winter of 1938, the authorities in continental Europe suspended the private-public mix of refugee policy. They no longer tolerated the 'Jewish' refugees and no longer considered collaboration with Jewish aid organisations to be in their interest. The large numbers of destitute refugees arriving in the countries bordering Nazi Germany caused fear in governmental circles that the private aid organisations would no longer be able to meet their financial needs. If the Jewish refugee organisations were forced to withdraw their financial responsibility for the refugees, this would result in rising welfare expenditure and increased competition on the labour market. Even foreign policy considerations, which had been an element since 1933, played a role in this new policy as by their mere presence the refugees were a critique of Nazi Germany. The growing popularity of anti-Semitic and xenophobic positions was also responsible for this change of policy. The authorities considered the refugees increasingly a threat to their national interest. By the winter of 1938 hardly any frontline states still lived up to their nations' humanitarian self-image: 'Jewish' refugees were refused access to the country in the consulates and

---

34 L. London, *Whitehall and the Jews, 1933–1948: British immigration policy and the Holocaust*, Cambridge UP, Cambridge, 2000, 111–12.

at the border, but even refugees who had succeeded in circumventing the border guards and those who had overstayed their visas were deported to Germany. The authorities repeated time and again that they were willing to accept 'Jewish' refugees, but only if they could select those whom they would protect. The proposal to accept a selected group of unaccompanied children, all organised by Jewish organisations and hosted by foster parents, fitted in perfectly with this conception. Their agreement to this scheme also enabled the authorities to point out that they were not blind to the suffering of the refugees in Germany. A well-organised rescue operation could legitimise the brutal treatment of the unorganised, 'wild' flight of refugees. The authorities condoned this privately initiated rescue scheme for children to distract public attention from worsening conditions for Jewish refugees from Nazi Germany.[35]

Initially the Swiss and Danish authorities demanded absolute certainty about the prompt final emigration of these children and this in line with their very restrictive admission policy, but given the large popular support for the initiative within both countries, they finally agreed on a quota without any guarantees of departure at short notice. Similar to other European continental countries, the quota could be replenished when children left for overseas.[36] In Britain, all children whose maintenance could be guaranteed received permission to enter, but they were required to re-emigrate before they were eighteen or upon completion of training, which the aid organisation promised to provide.[37] Although it does not seem that any West European authorities exerted pressure directly on the refugee committees to force the children to leave for a final destination, the refugee committees themselves were eager to find a country of settlement overseas as a way of alleviating their expenses. For continental European countries, departure to a final destination was a prerequisite for enabling more 'Jewish' children to leave Nazi Germany.

Notwithstanding the lenient policy towards final emigration, control over the immigration of children in need of protection was the cornerstone of this rescue operation. This became obvious when children who had not been selected by the aid organisations were sent by their parents alone over the border, hoping that the border authorities would treat them more favourably than they did adults.

35 Caestecker and Moore, *supra* note 33.

36 H. Kocher, *'Rationierte Menschlichkeit'. Schweizerischer Protestantismus im Spannungsfeld von Flüchtlingsnot und öfffentlicher Flüchtlingspolitik der Schweiz 1933–1948,* Zürich, 1996, 153; L. Rünitz, *Af hensyn til konsekvenserne, Danmark og flygtningesporgsmalet 1933–1939,* Syddansk Universitetsforlag, Odense, 2005, 341.

37 R. Stent, 'Jewish Refugee Organisations', in W. Mosse (ed.), *Second change: two centuries of German-speaking Jew in the United Kingdom,* JCB Mohr, Tübingen, 1991, 590; London, *supra* note 34 at 91 and 113; A.J. Sherman, *Island refuge: Britain and refugees from the Third Reich, 1933–1939,* University of California Press, Berkeley, 1973.

Children who arrived at the Dutch borders without entry papers were treated relatively generously, as long as they did not arrive in groups. They were deducted from the official quota of two thousand. In January 1939 there were already 500 child refugees in the Netherlands whose illegal immigration had been legalised. Groups of children were generally returned to Germany, as the Dutch authorities were afraid of encouraging organised German dumping practices by accepting them. Fears that Germans would 'exploit' a 'too humanitarian' policy with regard to illegal Jewish refugees were also evident in the Belgian case. When seven unaccompanied and undocumented children arrived at the Belgian-German checkpoint in Lontzen-Herbesthal in early January 1939, the Belgian border police received an order from the alien police that undocumented children should not be treated differently from adults without papers; thus they were refused entry. This drastic policy was legitimised not only as opposition to the German expulsion policy, but also through a more anti-Semitic reasoning expressed by Belgian policy makers. The refugee children were regarded as the vanguard of a Jewish invasion. This expulsion of children by the border guards quickly became public knowledge. A local newspaper published an account that was taken up by the national papers and caused a public outcry. Nevertheless, the practice was maintained, except for children under the age of three years. Those toddlers were to be passed on to the refugee committees as part of their quota. The authorities raised the quota from 250 to 750; other unaccompanied children who succeeded by different means in entering Belgium without the border patrols noticing them were also to form part of the quota.[38] The expulsion of unaccompanied children was not limited to Belgium. The Swiss and from March 1939 onwards also the Dutch authorities not only rejected children at the borders, but children were also expelled after they had already managed to enter the country. The strict measures for illegal immigrants in continental Europe became applicable to all, adults as well as children.[39]

In continental Europe protection for unaccompanied 'Jewish' children in danger was no longer self-evident even if they arrived at the border or in the country itself. The protection of these children became dependent on previous authorisation in order to limit the numbers and to assure a firm commitment by the private Jewish aid organisation. Even in Britain, with its impressive record of admission, the selection criteria of the aid organisations show that not all children in danger were equally suitable for the child transports. Initially urgent need for protection was the selection criterion when the 'Jewish' children in Germany and Austria were screened, but this became increasingly meaningless as all 'Jewish' children were in danger. Teenage boys, prone to detention and

---

[38] Caestecker, *supra* note 33, 121–26.

[39] C. Berghuis, *Joodse vluchtelingen in Nederland,1938–1940*, Kok, Kampen, 1990; Curio, *supra* note 33, 178.

anti-Semitic violence and considered by their parents as old and mature enough to go abroad by themselves, applied in large numbers for places on the child transports, but foster homes and even private guarantors preferred very young children, especially girls, whom Jewish parents in Germany were particularly reluctant to send abroad alone.[40] 'Supply' and 'demand' were not easily matched and increasingly the selection procedure was bent towards the demand side. As Claudio Curio has shown for the British case, from March 1939 at the latest onwards, all candidates underwent a thorough examination regarding their suitability as immigrants. The selection criteria to which the children had to conform had to do with their potential to adapt socially and psychologically. In Britain, foster families were not restricted to the small Jewish community; gentile families also offered to host a Jewish child. The demands of would-be foster families played a role in the selection procedure. Potential foster parents and private guarantors could even choose a child from the aid organisation's card index. The ideal candidates were little girls, preferably blond. The potential to fit in without trouble was measured by means of school and kindergarten reports, information about social background and physical appearance. Children of 'Aryan' appearance had better chances of being selected than 'Jewish-looking' ones. Overall, the potential of these child refugees to become invisible was considered the greatest asset. For the refugee aid organisations and the authorities alike, their public presence had to remain unnoticed so it would not be contested. The most desired children were children without family attachments, so that the foster families could raise them as their own children. Most children, however, left their parents in Germany. Although the child transports offered a way out, it was not rare for parents and children alike to intend a family reunion in exile. Children sometimes took the responsibility upon themselves to enable their parents to join them. The children's loyalty to their parents at times caused tension with their foster families.[41]

3.2. HOUSING AND CARE FOR GERMAN JEWISH CHILD REFUGEES

Discussion about the best form of accommodation for unaccompanied 'Jewish' children was determined by political and economic arguments rather than by the best interests of the children. In the Netherlands, despite thousands of offers from Dutch families that were prepared to take in a refugee child after the November pogrom and the evident financial advantages for the aid organisation, the Dutch

---

40 Curio, *supra* note 33, 70–72.

41 Curio, *supra* note 33; B. Leverton and S. Lowensohn, *I came alone: the stories of the kindertransports*, Sussex, 1990; B. Turner, *... and the policeman smiled: 10,000 children escape from Nazi Germany*, Bloomsbury Books, London, 1990.

authorities were determined not to tolerate any private accommodation for children except with relatives. It was feared that otherwise these children would assimilate and that this would endanger their departure from the Netherlands. The children were mainly housed in orphanages and other similar institutions all over the country. It was not until August 1939 that government permission was given for children up to the age of 14 to be placed with families.[42] In Belgium, the refugee aid committee preferred foster families, for evident financial reasons. The Belgian authorities did not oppose this private initiative. Too few offers came in, especially for boys, with the result that boarding houses became necessary.[43]

In Great Britain the aim was to spread the children across the country to avoid clusters and to make them 'invisible'. The best means of achieving this was accommodation in private – and not necessarily Jewish – foster homes. Both foster parents and aid organisations expected the children to be socially and psychologically adjustable and able to keep a low profile, preconditions for a fast and complete assimilation into the host family and society. This implied in most cases the loss of the children's identity as Jews, and as Germans or Austrians. The aid organisation explicitly neglected religious, cultural and language bonds. Many children were accommodated in Christian homes, thus isolating them from Jewish life and religion. There were quite a few cases of attempted Christian conversion, a fact that aroused worry and anger among the orthodox Jewish community in Britain, which went so far as to attack the Refugee Children's Movement as a 'Child Estranging Movement'.[44] Even in their school careers the refugee children were expected to have no high ambitions; a low profile had to be kept, which implied that competition with locals for scarce highly skilled jobs had to be prevented.[45]

4. FLIGHT TO AND HOLIDAY IN SWITZERLAND (1940–42)

In 1940 a broad range of Swiss civil society organisations, in agreement with the Swiss authorities, started a humanitarian operation for children in war-torn

42 At the time of the German occupation in May 1940, of the 1,350 children in the Netherlands about 450 were in private homes.
C. Berghuis, *Joodse vluchtelingen in Nederland,* Kampen, 1990, 41, 68 and 83; Curio, *supra* note 33.

43 S. Collignon, 'Les homes Bernheim et Speyer (1938–1940): Témoignages d'enfants réfugiés d'Allemagne et d'Autriche', (2005) 6 *Bijdragen tot de eigentijdse herinnering.*

44 D. Kranzler, *Holocaust hero: the untold story and vignettes of Solomon Schonfeld*, KTAV, Jersey City, 2004.

45 C. Curio, '"Unsichtbare Kinder", Auswahl- und Eingliederungsstrategien der Hilfsorganisationen in Die Kindertransporte 1938/39', in W. Benz, C. Curio and A. Hammel, *Die Kindertransporte 1938/39. Rettung und Integration*, Frankfurt/Main, 2003.

Europe. They focussed on aid for children because children were the innocent victims par excellence of the war. Any humanitarian operation on their behalf aroused great sympathy among the Swiss population, while being able to meet the demand of the Swiss authorities to be neutral. The campaign to offer children a three-month holiday with Swiss families had a tremendous appeal. Between November 1940 and December 1941, 7,124 children, mostly from France, were sent to Switzerland for a holiday. The federal authorities, in line with their concept of neutrality, wanted also to offer such holidays to children from Italy and Germany. However, transport problems and little or no interest in this initiative from the Axis powers resulted in the operation being largely limited to neighbouring France.

This operation had, due to the insistence of the Swiss federal authorities, an anti-Semitic tinge to it. Due to the denaturalisation operation planned by the Vichy government, the Swiss authorities worried that Jewish children who came on a three-month holiday would be stuck in Switzerland or even worse, that the children themselves, supported by their Swiss foster parents, would be unwilling to return. This induced the Swiss authorities to decide that all those who were 'non-Aryans', including old stock French, would be excluded from the humanitarian operation. The decision was also legitimised by the (anti-Semitic) authorities by referring to the danger of rising anti-Semitism if the percentage of 'Jews' within the Swiss population were to rise further.[46]

In 1941, the federal authorities saw a need to polish the Swiss image as a neutral country. That image had been tarnished among the allies by the close German-Swiss economic cooperation in the early war years. Swiss public relations were to be improved by giving neutrality a more positive connotation. The federal authorities used the humanitarian operation for children to silence criticism from abroad. Domestic criticism, mainly of the very restrictive Swiss refugee policy, would also be silenced.

The federal authorities assured close control over the operation by putting it under the leadership of the Swiss Red Cross and appointing representatives of the federal authorities to key positions. The authorities took care that their interventions remained hidden. The image to be transmitted was that the Swiss people provided this aid as an expression of their neutral solidarity. As Antonia Schmidlin (1999: 331) states, the advantage was that the authorities ran the

---

[46] Schmidlin, *supra* note 5 at 137 and 364. This article refers only to the French situation. Whether the 2,025 children from Belgium who were sent to Switzerland for a three-month holiday were only of Belgian nationality and whether 'non Aryan' origin excluded them has not yet been subject of research. S. Machler, 'Kampf gegen das Chaos. Die antisemitische Bevölkerungspolitik der eidgenössischen Fremdenpolizei und Polizeiabteilung 1917–1954', in O. Fussli, *Antisemitismus in der Schweiz 1848–1960*, Zürich, 1998, 357–421.

operation while the population paid for it. Thanks to the authorities, the operation could be enlarged in 1942 and 18,616 mainly French children, selected in line with the anti-Semitic criteria of 1940, were received for three months in Switzerland.[47] The Swiss press denounced the anti-Semitic selection criteria and in order not to harm the Swiss image the head of the alien police, Heinrich Rothmund, agreed to accept some token Jewish children. The Swiss Jewish foster families (and their community leaders) were under strong pressure to make the children return after their three-month holiday. For each of these Jewish children the explicit agreement of the Vichy and German authorities was requested. From October 1941 onwards, notwithstanding the fact that Jews were prohibited from leaving the German Empire, a small batch of Jewish children were still able to enjoy a holiday in Switzerland. The German authorities granted very few authorisations and even reprimanded the Vichy government for being too generous. They cancelled the whole operation in November 1942.

In the meantime the Swiss Red Cross had demanded a more proactive refugee policy for children, but the Swiss authorities declined. The child aid organisation of the Swiss Red Cross had proposed saving Jewish children by admitting 500 of them permanently and 1,000 temporarily until they could re-emigrate to the United States. Both proposals were rejected by the Bundesrat in September 1942.[48]

Only illegal emigration remained open for Jewish children, but if caught at the Swiss border these children were returned. In the summer of 1942 the Swiss authorities drastically tightened their measures against unauthorised immigrants on Swiss territory, all of whom, unaccompanied children included, had to be repatriated. However, in contrast to the anti-refugee measures in 1938, which the Swiss public had hardly noticed, in 1942 these measures were exposed publicly and strong protests followed. The protests led to the Swiss alien police decreeing that certain groups of particularly vulnerable unauthorised immigrants would be excepted from expulsion. This applied to children below the age of 16 as well as parents with children under 16.[49] The decision to privilege these cases of hardship was a token gesture. A proactive policy was never implemented. In early 1943 some agents of the Swiss aid organisations were involved in the illegal smuggling of 'Jewish' children from France into Switzerland. The federal

---

47 Among those 472 children from Belgium and 457 from Serbia, but in March 1942 these transports had to be stopped by decision of the German occupation authorities of those countries. In October 1942 further transports from occupied France were cancelled and the occupation of Vichy France in November 1942 stopped transports from that region too. A. Schmidlin, *Eine andere Schweiz*, 236–40.

48 Unabhängige Expertenkommission Schweiz-Zweiter Weltkrieg, *Die Schweiz und die Flüchtlinge zur Zeit des Nationalsozialismus*, Bern, 1999, 135.

49 Ibid. at 117.

authorities and the Swiss Red Cross were enraged and the latter fired all those involved.[50]

5. THE LONG-TERM CONSEQUENCES OF THE CHILD RESCUE OPERATIONS

These humanitarian programmes directed at children can be evaluated half a century later. The historical dimension enables researchers to make a thorough evaluation of the rescue schemes. Those who had been protected as children can look back on how the experience shaped their lives. This experience has definitely had a strong impact on them. A number of them have written their memoirs and many joined organisations to commemorate the humanitarian operations such as the Kindertransport Association (KTA) and the Associacion de Ninos Evacuados el 37.

It is, however, striking that very few social scientists have embarked on developing such a long-term perspective. Historians, although mostly induced by the commemorative organisations and the public interest they evoked, have mainly focussed on the rescue operation itself and the political actors involved. The commemorative organisations, on the other hand, have in their publications put the children and the foster families at centre stage. However, these publications, as well as the coverage in the media of their historical experience, are characterised by a rather uncritical attitude towards the humanitarian operations, an attitude partly attributable to the positive experiences most of the persons who later joined such organisations had enjoyed as children in exile.

The experience of the Basque (and other Spanish) children has only recently become the subject of historical analysis in Spain, part of the belated coping with the legacy of the Spanish civil war made possible by the peaceful change of regime in that country. Only at the beginning of the twenty-first century did the Spanish authorities acknowledge those who had fled as children to Western Europe as part of the painful twentieth century Spanish history. In the countries of asylum interest in these humanitarian operations arose a few decades earlier, together with the refugee crisis in Western Europe. Most scholarly interest focused, however, on the experience of the German Jewish children as part of the Holocaust boom in historical writing.

It is mainly from this Jewish experience that some conclusions can be drawn about the long-term consequences. Psychological analysis shows that very young

50 The secretary of the children section of the Swiss Red Cross, Hugo Remund, passed this information to the German Red Cross in Berlin, but it does not seem that it was passed on to the German authorities in France. Schmidlin, *supra* note 5 at 313.

children in particular had great difficulty in understanding why they had to leave alone. This divorce from the parents was understood as a punishment, with concomitant feelings of fear and guilt. The long-term psychological results of being separated from their parents in these adverse conditions led to depression and a permanent fear of being deserted. That Jews and in particular orthodox Jews were already in an outsider position made it easier for them to cope with these conditions, with which Orthodox children had fewer problems than did other children. Those children who had joined family members after the war, mostly in Israel or the US, were also able to cope better with their childhood experience. Being reunited with family members and in countries with greater tolerance of people from an immigrant background and a greater empathy with the Holocaust experience had positive psychological results.[51]

6. CONCLUSION

Being the apolitical victims of war and persecution makes children the focus par excellence for any humanitarian operation. The three schemes outlined in this historical overview were private initiatives which thrived because the public responded generously. The willingness to join one of the child rescue operations was related to their age-specific features, which enabled them to count on more political and public support than the rescue of adults. An important advantage of the child protection scheme was the invisibility of the child refugees, so that their presence was not noticed and thus not contested. Even if they ultimately settled in the host country they were soon entirely assimilated, since they came without their families and at an age when environmental influences were at their most powerful. Giving refuge to children was a suitable way to meet humanitarian commitments, while the risks associated with the admission of refugees were minimised. The admission of children could also be presented as a purely humanitarian operation without any political connotation. Still, the political ramifications of these initiatives were fully realised by the participants. The Basque programme was strongly politicised as it was interwoven with the political fight over the legitimacy of the Republican and Franco regimes. In the case of the rescue operation for 'Jewish' children from Nazi Germany, there was an intimate interrelation between tightening regulations for 'Jewish' refugees in continental Europe and opening the border for a selected category of children. The admission of these children was utilised to cushion the inhumanity of

---

51 V. Hamilton, *A retrospective study of child refugees from Nazi Germany*, Department of Psychology, University Reading, 1985;
H. Keilson, *Sequentielle Traumatisierung bei Kindern. Deskriptiv-klinische und quantifizierend-statistische Follow-up-Untersuchung zum Schicksal der jüdischen Kriegswaisen in den Niederlanden*, Stuttgart, 1979.

policies towards those fleeing persecution in Nazi Germany. Domestic and international public opinion could be distracted away from humanitarian shortcomings, and this with the least possible risk. During the war years the Swiss humanitarian policy towards children in France deliberately excluded Jewish children, the most vulnerable group. Excluding the most needy children as a selection criterion had already become obvious in the other child rescue schemes, but at that time it was the choices of the foster families which determined that it was not always the most needy children that were helped. The Swiss operation had in addition a political dimension which made it even more reprehensible. The interests of the children were not always a priority in rescue operations because of the political interests involved.

That the neediest children were largely excluded from the Swiss operation reveals that 'doing good' can at times disguise highly egoistical and uncaring actions. The manner in which the children were received is also indicative of the less than altruistic values motivating the programmes. That the Basque children in Belgium and France were hosted by foster families – contrary to the wishes of the Basque government – was largely due to the limited financial support for a less personal and less visible kind of aid. This individualised care could be beneficial, but implied heavy pressure on each of the children. In particular, the foster families' unsatisfied wish for children collided with the interests of the parents and thus also with the children's interests. On the other hand, the reception of German Jewish children into institutions, as decided by the Dutch authorities, was not motivated by the best interests of the children. The Dutch authorities opted for a collective and isolated housing of the children in order to prevent their assimilation, which would only jeopardise their interest in the children's departure. Still, that the children could move on and that public support for the rescue operations could be generous was in the interests of children in danger too. Given the limited means available, it enabled more children in grave peril to be rescued.

The historical experience shows that humanitarian gestures, on the part of the authorities as well as of the public, may be largely motivated by self-interest, a self-interest which can harm the children involved. Children are very vulnerable and humanitarian action in their support should offer enough guarantees that the child's interest figures centre stage.

PART III

EXPLORING RESOURCES THROUGH EMPIRICAL RESEARCH

LIFE IN REBEL CAPTIVITY AND ITS CHALLENGES FOR THE PSYCHOSOCIAL REHABILITATION AND REINTEGRATION OF FORMER CHILD SOLDIERS: THE CASE OF NORTHERN UGANDA

Sofie VINDEVOGEL, Kathleen COPPENS, Ilse DERLUYN, Gerrit LOOTS and Eric BROEKAERT

1. INTRODUCTION

1.1. CHILD SOLDIERING IN NORTHERN UGANDA

In northern Uganda, a civil war has been waging for more than two decades between the rebel faction Lord's Resistance Army (LRA) and the Ugandan Government. Although, the roots of this conflict reach back to the colonial era and the conflict has known many episodes; an intensification occurred when Yoweri Museveni, president of Uganda, seized power in 1986 and Joseph Kony, leader of the LRA, set up his guerrilla campaign.[1]

The battlefield of this conflict is situated in the northern districts of the country, where the Acholi population resides. The LRA adopted various civilian-targeting strategies from a political and operational aim, resulting in numerous civilian casualties.[2] Attacks on villages, the maiming of civilians, ambushes, massacres and other atrocities were countless during this emergency.[3] It is estimated that over a million and a half had to flee their homes and reside in

1 T. ALLEN, *Trial justice. The International Criminal Court and the Lord's Resistance Army*, Zed Books, London/New York, 2006; H. BEHREND, *Alice Lakwena & the Holy Spirits. War in Northern Uganda 1985–97. Eastern African Studies*, Fountain Publishers, Kampala, 1999; HUMAN RIGHTS WATCH, *The Christmas massacres. LRA attacks on civilians in Northern Congo*, New York, Human Rights Watch, 2009.

2 INTERNATIONAL CRISIS GROUP, *Northern Uganda: understanding and solving the conflict*, International Crisis Group, Nairobi/Brussels, 2004.

3 ALLEN, *supra* note 1.

internally displaced persons camps[4] and that thousands of children sought protection as night commuters in town each night.[5] Furthermore, the conflict limited their access to security, food, employment, education and health services.[6]

One of its adopted strategies, mainly targeting children, is the violent abduction and forced recruitment of minors to serve as child soldiers. It is estimated that so far about 25,000 children have been forcibly involved as child soldiers in the LRA.[7] These children are used to empower the LRA by filling its ranks and are thereby actively engaged in the battle against the government and people of Uganda.[8]

In captivity, abducted children live in harsh circumstances, are exposed to several potentially traumatising events and are made perpetrators of atrocities against their own people.[9] There can be no doubt that these experiences affect the child's well-being and development.[10] Research has found that they are psychologically distressing,[11] resulting in high rates of post-traumatic stress symptoms among former child soldiers.[12] These in turn pose serious threats to the long-term rehabilitation and reintegration of the former child soldiers.[13] In order to obtain a clear view of and foresee an adequate response to these

---

4 E. Baines, E. Stover and M. Wierda, *War-affected children and youth in Northern Uganda: toward a brighter future. An assessment Report*, MacArthur Foundation, Chicago, 2006; C. Blattman and J. Annan, 'Child combatants in northern Uganda: reintegration myths and realities', in R. Muggah (ed.), *Security and Post-Conflict Reconstruction: Dealing with Fighters in the Aftermath of War*, Routledge, 2008, 103–126.

5 Coalition to Stop the Use of Child Soldiers, *Returning home. Children's perspectives on reintegration. A case-study of children abducted by the Lord's Resistance Army in Teso, eastern Uganda*, Coalition to Stop the Use of Child Soldiers, London, 2008; T.M. Thomsen and R. Bjerngaard, 'Beyond night commuting – psychosocial needs among war affected children in Uganda', (2008) 60 2 *Nordic Psychology*, 87–100.

6 Baines et al., supra note 4; J.N. Corbin, 'Returning home: resettlement of formerly abducted children in Northern Uganda', (2008) 32 2 *Disasters*, 316–335.

7 Coalition to Stop the Use of Child Soldiers, *supra* note 5; Human Rights Watch, *Abducted and abused: renewed conflict in Northern Uganda*, Human Rights Watch, New York, 2006.

8 International Crisis Group, *supra* note 2.

9 I. Derluyn, E. Broekaert, G. Schuyten and E. De Temmerman, 'Post-traumatic stress in former Ugandan child soldiers', (2004) 363 9412 *Lancet*, 861–863; K. Amone-P'Olak, 'Coping with life in rebel captivity and the challenge of reintegrating formerly abducted boys in Northern Uganda', (2007) 20 4 *Journal of Refugee Studies*, 641–661; Blattman et al., *supra* note 4; R.N. Pham, P. Vinck and E. Stover, 'The Lord's Resistance Army and Forced Conscription in Northern Uganda', (2008) 30 *Human Rights Quarterly*, 404–411.

10 Coalition to Stop the Use of Child Soldiers, *supra* note 5.

11 Amone-P'Olak, *supra* note 9.

12 Derluyn et al., *supra* note 9.

13 M. Wessells, *Child soldiers: from violence to protection*, Harvard University Press, Cambridge, 2006; R. Williams, 'The psychosocial consequences for children of mass violence, terrorism and disasters', (2007) 19 3 *International Review of Psychiatry*, 263–277.

challenges, a thorough understanding of what these children have gone through and of the impact of this trauma is indispensable.[14]

Although the 'cessation of hostilities agreement' in 2006 led to the LRA taking refuge outside Uganda and a decrease in its recruitment of children, many children remain in captivity and cases of recruitment by the LRA continue to be reported in the Democratic Republic of Congo, Sudan and Central African Republic.[15] While warfare in northern Uganda has been in cessation since 2006, the LRA thus seems to be continuing a reign of terror in the neighbouring countries.

1.2. RECEPTION CENTRES

In order to address the challenges of child soldiering for the rehabilitation and reintegration of returnees, various reception centres were established during the emergency in northern Uganda for the reception, rehabilitation and reintegration of returned former child soldiers. A special reception unit was considered necessary, as often these children appeared to have been traumatised by their experiences and traces of their relatives were erased by the warfare. Such units provided rehabilitation and reintegration activities, mainly addressing the physical, psychological and social needs of returnees.[16] To a lesser extent, educational and economic resources were offered in order to strengthen the position of the former child soldier in society. The children stayed approximately 2 to 6 weeks in this centre before being handed over to the care of relatives.[17]

Findings on the total number of returned former child soldiers vary owing to incomplete registration; in addition, it is estimated that only about half of the returnees passed through such a reception centre.[18] Research on reintegration through reception centres suggests that this process has yielded limited success in northern Uganda, finding that many former child soldiers are not residing in their home community/camp or are overrepresented in juvenile crime units.[19] This raises questions concerning the role of reception centres in the psychosocial rehabilitation and reintegration of former child soldiers. This research is therefore shaped by inquiries into the need for and additional value of reception centres for former child soldiers, comparing indicators of the psychological and

14 Blattman et al., *supra* note 4.

15 Coalition to Stop the Use of Child Soldiers, *supra* note 5; Human Rights Watch, *supra* note 1.

16 K. Hill and H. Langholtz, 'Rehabilitation programs for African child soldiers', (2003) 15 3 *Peace Review,* 279–285; Blattman et al., *supra* note 4; Corbin, *supra* note 6.

17 Pham et al., *supra* note 9.

18 Blattman et al., *supra* note 4.

19 G. Akello, A. Richters and R. Reis, 'Reintegration of former child soldiers in northern Uganda: coming to terms with children's agency and accountability', (2006) 4 3 *Intervention,* 229–243.

social well-being of returnees who benefited from support, especially from reception centres, and those who did not.

Although most of the reception centres were closed down after the emergency and former child soldiers currently return only sporadically in northern Uganda, lessons can be learned from these experiences for developing adequate resources for the rehabilitation and reintegration of former child soldiers in neighbouring countries, where this need remains pressing.[20]

1.3. THEORETICAL FRAMEWORK

The framework of this research is based on a social-ecological model of development, which considers the child's development in the context of interrelated settings and relationships.[21] The chapter will focus on the psychosocial well-being of former child soldiers from a perspective in which this individual level is interrelated with various social layers:

1. Micro-level: the level of the individual victim, e.g. emotional difficulties, physical injuries, etc.[22]
2. Meso-level: the level of the immediate environment, e.g. disruption of families, stigmatisation, lack of (mental) health care, etc.[23]
3. Macro-level: the level of the society in which the victim lives, e.g. feuding between ethnic groups, a climate of distrust, etc.[24]

Even years after the formal cessation of the war, smouldering remains and post-conflict threats cause profound and persistent problems on these different levels,

---

20 Human Rights Watch, *supra* note 15.

21 U. Bronfenbrenner, *The ecology of human development,* Harvard University Press, Cambridge, 1979; D. Summerfield, *The impact of war and atrocity on civilian populations: basic principles for NGO interventions and a critique of psychosocial trauma projects*, Overseas Development Institute, London, 1996.

22 A.M. Sibai, N.S. Shaar and S. El Yassir, 'Impairments, disabilities and needs assessment among non-fatal war injuries in South Lebanon, Grapes of Wrath, 1996', (2000) 54 1 *Journal of Epidemiology and Community Health,*35–39; E. Karam and M.B. Ghosn, 'Psychosocial consequences of war among civilian populations', (2003) 16 *Current Opinion in Psychiatry,* 413–419; Derluyn et al., *supra* note 9; E. Zinsstag, 'Sexual violence against women in armed conflicts: standard responses and new ideas', (2005) 5 1 *Social Policy & Society,* 137–148.

23 L. Shanks and M. J. Schull, 'Rape in war: the humanitarian response', (2000) 163 9 *Journal de l'Association Médicale Canadienne,* 1152–1156; R. Beneduce, L. Jourdan, T. Raeymaekers and K. Vlassenroot, 'Violence with a purpose: exploring the functions and meaning of violence in the Democratic Republic of Congo', (2006) 4 1 *Intervention,* 32–46.

24 Ibid.; M.B. Lykes, C.M. Beristain and M.L.C. Perez-Arminan, 'Political violence, impunity, and emotional climate in Maya communities', (2007) 63 2 *Journal of Social Issues,* 369–385; K.M.D. Rauchfuss and B.A. Schmolze, 'Justice heals: the Impact of impunity and the fight against it on the recovery of severe human rights violations, survivors', (2008) 18 1 *Torture,* 38–50.

possibly jeopardising the individual recovery process in this transitional stage.[25] A solid approach towards the rehabilitation and reintegration of former child soldiers should therefore address the recovery process on the different social levels:

1. Micro-level: initiatives oriented towards the individual victim, e.g. psychosocial counselling, educational support, vocational skills training, etc.[26]
2. Meso-level: initiatives oriented towards the networks of victims, e.g. reunification programmes, peace building groups, food distribution, etc.[27]
3. Macro-level: initiatives oriented towards the society, e.g. sensitisation campaigns, a peace, recovery and development plan, etc.[28]

This social-ecological model provides the framework within which the research question is studied, meaning that the value of reception centres for former child soldiers will be evaluated at each of the different social-ecological levels.

1.4. RESEARCH QUESTIONS

So far, the greater part of the research conducted in this field is qualitative and largely case-based, and there is an underrepresentation of quantitative data grounding these findings.[29] Moreover, follow-up and monitoring of former child soldiers is limited, which makes it difficult to evaluate the work of relief initiatives and draw evidence-based conclusions.[30] Most existing evaluations are based on the perceptions of beneficiaries and their networks.[31] Even if evidence-based data

25 Beneduce et al., *supra* note 23.

26 J.R. Annan, A.P. Amuge and T. Angwaro, 'Counseling for peace in the midst of war: counselors from northern Uganda share their views', (2003) 25 4 *International Journal for the Advancement of Counseling*, 235–245; Shanks and Schull, *supra* note 23.

27 R. Williams, D.A. Alexander, D. Bolsover and F.K. Bakker, 'Children, resilience and disasters: recent evidence that should influence a model of psychosocial care', (2008) 21 *Current Opinions in Psychiatry*, 338–344.

28 Bolton et al., 'Group interpersonal psychotherapy for depression in rural Uganda. A randomized controlled trial', (2003) 289 23 *JAMA-Journal of the American Medical Association*, 3117–3124; T. Allen, '*Trial justice. The International Criminal Court and the Lord's Resistance Army*', London/New York, Zed Books, 2006; Oxfam International, *From emergency to recovery. Rescuing northern Uganda's transition*, Oxfam briefing paper, 2008, www.oxfam.org/files/bp118-uganda-from-emergency-to-recovery.pdf.

29 Blattman and Annan, *supra* note 4; Coalition to Stop the Use of Child Soldiers, *supra* note 5; Corbin, *supra* note 6.

30 T. Allen and M. Schomerus, *A hard homecoming: lessons learned from the reception centre process in Northern Uganda. An independent study commissioned by USAID & UNICEF*, Management Systems International, Washington, 2006.

31 Ibid.; Amone-P'Olak, *supra* note 9.

are available for evaluation, many initiatives lack the opportunity to integrate these in their programmes.[32]

This research therefore addresses the need for a better understanding of the prevalence of potentially traumatic experiences among former child soldiers and the challenges this poses for their rehabilitation and reintegration when they return from captivity. Information on the profiles of these children could assist reception centres in adapting their programmes to the characteristics and needs of these returnees and therefore in facilitating the recovery process that these children face.

Quantitative data, collected by a reception centre in northern Uganda at the moment of arrival at the centre (intake) and after some months following reintegration (follow-up), will be analysed in order to explore the events that affected former child soldiers during captivity, the prevalence of some symptoms of distress at intake and follow-up and some social indicators of reintegration. The aim of this research is to address the need for and additional value of reception centres for the rehabilitation and reintegration of former child soldiers, as well as to broach some challenges and thresholds for reception centres in attaining their goals.

2. METHODOLOGY

2.1. PARTICIPANTS

Cooperation was established with a former reception centre in northern Uganda, Rachele Rehabilitation Centre, which operated from 2003 until 2006 in Lira and received more than 2,000 returnees. The returnees were handed over mainly by the Child Protection Unit of the Ugandan government's army (UPDF), but could also apply on their own initiative or on referral by the community. For the greater part, the returnees arrived immediately or soon after their return from the LRA. If the reception centre was full, it referred returnees to one of its partner organisations in northern Uganda. Although it was mainly oriented towards minors, the databases include a small proportion of former child soldiers who had reached the age of 18 at the moment of registration. A more detailed profile of the returnees will be presented in this study.

After its closure, the centre turned into a school and the organisation engaged in sponsoring former child soldiers in their education by providing a school package, paying school fees, etc. The paper-based databases they compiled during

32 E. Baines, E. Stover and M. Wierda, *War-affected children and youth in Northern Uganda: toward a brighter future. An assessment Report*, MacArthur foundation, Chicago, 2006; N. Boothby, 'Political violence and development: an ecological approach to children in war zones', (2008) 17 3 *Child and Adolescent Psychiatric Clinics of North America*, 497–514.

these years were made available for research and were digitalised. One database consists of intake information on 1,877 returned formerly abducted children who were registered and received at the centre. The other database contains information on 1,028 former child soldiers who all went through the reception centre and either did or did not benefit from additional support of a reception centre at the moment of monitoring in the community. The databases were not aggregated as they do not necessarily cover the same sample.

2.2. MEASURES

The first study was carried out using the intake database of Rachele Rehabilitation Centre. Soon after the arrival of a returnee at the centre, an intake form was completed by the social workers, registering socio-demographic background information on the returnee and their life story while in LRA captivity. Consequently, this database contains information on the demographic status of the returnee, their relatives and place of origin, the abduction, living conditions in the bush, exposure to traumatic events, involvement in atrocities, and the return and route to the reception centre.

The second study was conducted using the database of Rachele Rehabilitation Centre gathered during monitoring visits to communities. After a period of 6 to 12 months after reunification, social workers visited communities or camps where former child soldiers were reunified. They announced their visit through the local radio and summoned former child soldiers, whether they had passed through the reception centre or not. A brief assessment of the well-being of formerly abducted children was conducted, registering different life areas. This database therefore contains some basic socio-demographic information and indicators of the psychological, physical, social and economic well-being of the child. With respect to the focus of this research on the psychosocial aspect, data on the economic status were not included in the analysis.

2.3. ANALYSIS

The database was analysed using SPSS Statistics 17. Descriptive statistics were used to present the socio-demographic characteristics of the samples, as well as the prevalence of the measured experiences and indicators of well-being. In order to examine plausible differences between subgroups (itemised by gender, age category, beneficiary from support, beneficiary from reception centre, etc.), comparative analysis was conducted using χ^2 for ordinal and nominal variables and Independent Sample t-tests or One Way Analysis of Variance for interval and ratio variables. Due to missing values, denominators may vary according to the analysis executed.

3. RESULTS

3.1. INTAKE

3.1.1. Socio-Demographic Characteristics

Information on the socio-demographic characteristics of the former child soldiers who passed through Rachele Rehabilitation Centre after their return from captivity, shows that 64.5% of the cases in the sample (n = 1211) were male and 35.5% (n = 666) were female. The returnees had an average age of 14.52 years (SD = 3.01) at the moment of arrival at the centre. With respect to gender, girls tended to be significantly older (mean: 15.36 years, SD = 3.71, $t_{(984.790)} = 8.16$, $p < 0.01$) than boys (mean: 14.05 years, SD = 2.43) at the moment of return from captivity. Most returnees (n = 1668, 94.3%) were previously attending school, and 89.3% of them (n = 1578) were at the primary level at the moment of their abduction. A significantly higher proportion of girls (n = 86, 86.0%, $\chi^2_{(1)} = 128.15$, $p < 0.01$) than boys (n = 14, 14.0%) were not going to school. The returnees originated from various districts in the northern part of Uganda, mainly Lira (n = 557, 29.7%), Pader (n = 419, 22.3%), Kitgum (n = 308, 16.4%), Gulu (n = 212, 11.3%) and Katakwi (n = 205, 10.9%). Yet 82.2% (n = 1390) had their family displaced due to the conflict and residing in an IDP camp. More than one quarter of these returnees (n = 508, 27.3%) had lost their father and 12.6% (n = 234) had lost their mother. A minority of 6.8% of this subsample (n = 127) were orphaned.

3.1.2. Abduction

Most returnees have been abducted at a young age (mean: 13.4 years, SD = 2.59), as 75.0% were about or less than 15 years old. The abduction mainly took place in the homes of the children (n = 1290, 74.6%) and was as likely to take place during the day (n = 838, 46.5%) as at night (n = 966, 53.5%). The abductions were conducted violently, especially for boys, of whom 73.6% (n = 854) were reported to have been tied up ($\chi^2_{(1)} = 194.56$, $p < 0.01$) and 55.2% (n = 637) to have been beaten ($\chi^2_{(1)} = 16.36$, $p < 0.01$) at the time of abduction. Not only the abductees were victimised, as 60.4% of the sample (n = 591) witnessed atrocities against others taking place at the time of the abduction, mostly killing (n = 304, 43.8%), looting (n = 162, 23.3%) and torturing (n = 154, 22.2%).

3.1.3. Life in Captivity

The returnees of this sample spent on average more than 1.5 years (mean: 560.30 days, SD = 824.92) in captivity. Although one quarter of the sample (25.0%) spent less than three months, almost half of them (n = 769, 41.9%)

spent more than one year and one in ten (n = 167, 9.1%) spent more than five years in captivity. The length of the abduction varied significantly according to gender ($t_{(764.304)} = 11.45$, $p < 0.01$) and age ($F_{(1)} = 790.76$, $p < 0.01$), with adult females having spent the longest time in captivity ($F_{(2)} = 419.63$, $p < 0.01$), on average eight years.

Table 1. Potentially traumatising experiences in captivity

Type of trauma	Total sample (n = 1877[a]) n(%)	Sex			Age			
		Boys n(%)	*Girls* n(%)	χ^2/t	*≤ 12* n(%)	*13–18* n(%)	*≥ 19* n(%)	χ^2/F
Living conditions								
Walk long distances	1780(98.8)	1158(99.2)	622(98.0)	5.55*	449(98.5)	1197(98.8)	132(100)	2.00
Hunger/thirst	1629(96.3)	1074(97.3)	555(94.5)	8.11**	405(96.6)	1110(96.4)	112(93.3)	3.54
Torture/beating	1629(91.8)	1072(92.9)	557(89.7)	5.47*	398(89.0)	1112(92.7)	117(92.1)	5.94
Carry heavy loads	1583(88.9)	1028(89.5)	555(87.8)	1.24	388(87.6)	1083(90.0)	111(84.7)	4.44
Military training	1072(61.2)	809(71.2)	263(42.7)	136.19**	238(54.5)	736(62.1)	96(75.0)	18.96**
Taken to Sudan	453(26.0)	226(19.9)	227(37.2)	61.62**	52(11.9)	309(26.3)	90(70.9)	178.83**
To be wounded	364(21.2)	238(21.4)	126(20.8)	0.08	67(15.6)	263(22.6)	34(28.1)	12.88**
Assignment to a man	343(16.8)	0(0.0)	343(56.0)	8.79**	13(12.3)	238(57.6)	92(92.9)	137.14**
Witnessed atrocities								
Cumulative number	2.09(1.10)[b]	2.09(1.08)[b]	2.10(1.14)[b]	0.30	1.88(1.07)[b]	2.13(1.09)[b]	2.54(1.10)[b]	20.56**
Captives die from hunger/thirst	326(89.1)	160(87.9)	166(90.2)	0.50	44(83.0)	217(88.2)	63(96.9)	6.26*
Killing of people	1489(85.4)	969(85.7)	520(84.8)	0.22	355(82.0)	1011(85.6)	121(94.5)	12.61**
Other captives compulsorily killing	1315(76.4)	855(76.6)	460(76.0)	0.07	308(71.5)	898(77.3)	107(84.9)	11.39**
Captives getting wounded/killed on the battlefield	621(65.4)	435(71.9)	186(54.1)	30.83**	135(56.7)	442(68.5)	43(66.2)	10.72**
Participated atrocities								
Cumulative number	1.99(1.64)[b]	2.10(1.61)[b]	1.78(1.68)[b]	-3.82**	1.40(1.37)[b]	2.14(1.66)[b]	2.56(1.83)[b]	43.46**
Looting	1166(66.6)	787(69.3)	379(61.5)	10.95**	220(50.7)	848(71.3)	96(76.2)	66.45**
Killing	820(46.9)	575(50.6)	245(40.0)	17.98**	177(40.0)	572(48.6)	69(54.3)	12.75**
Abducting	671(38.8)	469(41.7)	202(33.3)	11.58**	105(24.2)	508(43.3)	57(46.7)	51.73**
Fighting	461(26.6)	319(28.4)	142(23.4)	5.06*	53(12.5)	347(29.6)	60(46.5)	74.87**
Destructing	410(24.0)	264(23.8)	146(24.4)	0.06	66(15.4)	294(25.5)	49(40.5)	36.86**

* $p \leq 0.05$, ** $p \leq 0.01$, [b] Mean (standard deviation)

During their abduction, these children lived in harsh circumstances and were thereby exposed to numerous potentially traumatising events (Table 1). Nearly all returned child soldiers declared that they had suffered from physical exploitation, such as being forced to walk long distances, suffering from hunger or thirst, torture and sexual abuse. Moreover, these former child soldiers often witnessed atrocities against other abductees, soldiers or civilians. The greater part of this sample saw someone being killed, with the majority witnessing other captives being forced to participate. A considerable proportion of the former child soldiers further declared that they had been forced to perpetrate atrocities themselves, of which most targeted civilians. Many former child soldiers were sent to villages in order to participate in looting, the abduction of children and the destruction of civilian property. Moreover, almost half of the sample admitted to having actually killed someone. Child soldiers were also engaged in battles against other armed factions, in which a quarter of this sample had participated.

On their arrival at the centre, the returnees were asked to indicate their worst experience in LRA captivity. Analysis indicates that the witnessing of atrocities against others was perceived by almost a quarter of this sample (n = 401, 23.4%) as their worst experience. This is followed by physical suffering caused by torture (n = 327, 19.1%) and walking long distances while carrying heavy loads (n = 260, 15.2%). The killing of people was for almost a sixth of the returnees (n = 241, 14.1%) the hardest experience. Sexual abuse was reported by 5.30% (n = 91) of the returnees to have been the worst experience.

3.1.4. Return

The greater part of the returnees (n = 1427, 81.9%) managed to escape from the LRA on their own initiative, mainly when under attack (n = 343, 19.7%), at night (n = 293, 16.8%) or during marching (n = 257, 14.8%). About one tenth of the returnees (n = 193, 11.1%) were released by the LRA, generally when left behind because they were seriously injured or their commander decided to surrender. A minority of this sample (n = 122, 7.0%) were rescued by another armed force. When they returned from captivity, the former child soldiers mostly reported to soldiers (n = 1337, 80.3%), in most cases UPDF soldiers, whose barracks were spread throughout the country and who established a Child Protection Unit to receive the returnees. Others (n = 228, 13.7%) reported to civilians they met on their way back home or in their home town or village. On average, half of the returnees (50%) were referred, mainly by the army (n = 1250, 64.2%), or reached the centre on their own initiative (n = 670, 34.4%) within one week (mean: 8 days) of their return.

3.1.5. Stay in the Centre

An assessment of some symptoms of distress was registered by social workers on the arrival of former child soldiers at the centre. On average, the children presented with approximately 5.79 (SD = 2.9) symptoms. An overview of the most recurrent symptoms is provided in Table 2.

Table 2. Symptoms on arrival in the reception centre

Symptoms	Prevalence
PHYSICAL	
Unhealthy	1185(70.1%)
Weak and malnourished	945(56.0%)
Skin disease	193(30.9%)
Wounds	362(21.2%)
– Bullet wounds	162(44.8%)
– Bomb splinter wounds	156(43.1%)
– Both	44(12.2%)
Diarrhoea	223(13.2%)
PSYCHOLOGICAL	
Fear	1083(64.0%)
Low self-esteem	822(48.7%)
Withdrawn	685(40.5%)
Nightmares	656(38.8%)
Lack of concentration	641(37.9%)
Emotional	460(27.2%)
Sensitive	337(19.9%)
Mistrust	385(22.8%)
Bitterness	326(19.3%)
Daydreaming	301(17.8%)
Restlessness	266(15.7%)

Analysis found that the majority of the former child soldiers in this sample were physically in a bad condition when they returned from captivity. Not only were they weak and unhealthy, some of them also suffered from serious injuries due to the living conditions and the role they fulfilled within the LRA. With regard to their psychological well-being, analysis shows that the returnees displayed a range of symptoms, of which the most frequently reported were fear, low self-esteem, being withdrawn and nightmares.

On average, the children stayed about 7.5 weeks (mean: 52.05 days, SD = 48.27) in the centre. A quarter of the study population stayed for less than or about one month, and another quarter stayed for more than 3 months. During their stay in the centre, the social workers explicitly indicated that extra care, supplementary to what was usually offered, was required for 165 children or 8% of this study population. In 60.6% of the cases this referred to psychological needs, in 13.3% to physical/medical needs, and in 26.1% of the cases to both kinds of need. After this period, nearly all returnees could be reunified with their parents (n = 680, 87.3%) or extended family (n = 63, 8.1%), but a minority of 4.7% (n = 36) were referred to another organisation for further medical or psychological care.

3.2. FOLLOW-UP

3.2.1. Socio-Demographic Characteristics

This follow-up sample of monitored children was composed of 721 (70.1%) males and 307 (29.9%) females, with an average age of 15.54 years (SD = 2.73). Compared to the children included in the intake database, this sample contains significantly fewer females ($\chi^2(1) = 15.48$, $p < 0.01$) and more older children ($t(2852.52) = 14.86$, $p < 0.01$). These children also originated from significantly different districts ($\chi^2(14) = 1118.05$, $p < 0.01$), mainly Pader (n = 375, 36.5%), Amuru (n = 250, 24.4%) and Lira (n = 234, 22.8%).

One in two children (n = 498, 48.4%) stated that they had received support. Half of them (n = 266, 53.6%) had received the amnesty package and 13.3% (n = 66) had benefited from additional support of a reception centre. Furthermore, a proportion of former child soldiers also stated that they had benefited from the donation of support for income generating activities by NGOs (n = 165, 33.2%) and food items by the UN World Food Programme (n = 101, 20.3%). Further analysis of the follow-up data will be itemised in terms of whether they have received support and whether this support came from a reception centre (Table 3).

3.2.2. Personal Status

Table 3. Indicators of psychosocial well-being at follow-up

Variable	Total sample (n=1028) n(%)	Receiving support?			Kind of follow-up support?		
		Yes n(%)	*No* n(%)	χ^2	*Reception Centre* n(%)	*Other* n(%)	χ^2
1. PERSONAL							
1.1 Psychological							
Hypersensitive	607(60.3)	295(60.3)	309(60.5)	0.00	40(63.5)	254(59.9)	0.29
Sleeping disorders							
- Nightmares	378(37.1)	198(40.1)	177(34.2)	3.69	29(46.0)	169(39.4)	1.00
- Sleepiness	174(17.4)	73(15.0)	100(19.7)	3.81	11(18.0)	62(14.6)	0.48
- Lack of sleep	126(12.3)	66(13.4)	59(11.5)	0.88	10(15.9)	56(13.1)	0.35
Fear	374(36.8)	182(37.0)	189(36.5)	0.02	26(41.3)	156(36.5)	0.52
Vigilance	193(19.3)	89(18.4)	103(20.2)	0.54	17(27.4)	72(17.1)	3.82*
Fighting	155(15.7)	89(18.7)	65(12.9)	6.01*	10(15.9)	79(19.1)	0.38
Suicidal	99(9.9)	57(11.8)	42(8.2)	3.43	10(16.1)	47(11.2)	1.28
Withdrawn	79(7.9)	32(6.6)	45(8.8)	1.67	4(6.8)	28(6.6)	0.00
1.2 Physical							
Chest pain	552(53.7)	269(54.0)	280(53.6)	0.01	44(66.7%)	225(52.3)	4.74*
Wounds	136(13.4)	76(15.5)	59(11.4)	3.68	17(25.8%)	59(14.0%)	5.97*
2. SOCIAL							
2.1 Relationships							
Play with friends	999(97.7)	478(96.8)	514(98.7)	4.11*	64(97.0)	412(96.7)	0.01
Feel accepted by friends	981(95.9)	488(98.4)	486(93.5)	15.54**	66(100)	420(98.1)	1.25
Treated well in community	972(95.1)	480(97.2)	486(93.3)	8.32**	65(98.5)	413(96.9)	0.48
Insulted by others	514(50.0)	268(53.8)	241(46.2)	5.96*	33(50.0)	234(54.4)	0.44
2.2 Occupation							
Attending school	741(72.2)	336(67.5)	398(76.2)	9.72**	28(42.4)	306(71.2)	21.48**
Other activities				5.87			1.87
- Domestic help	151(67.1)	25(20.7)	10(9.6)		9(27.3)	16(18.2)	
- IGA	35(15.6)	74(61.2)	77(74.0)		20(60.6)	54(61.4)	
Married	34(15.5)	18(14.9)	16(15.4)	0.01	4(12.1)	14(15.9)	0.27

* $p \leq 0.05$, ** $p \leq 0.01$

As illustrated in Table 3, analysis of the children's well-being found that a considerable proportion of these former child soldiers continuously experienced symptoms of psychological and physical impediment at the moment of monitoring in the community. The most common psychological complaints were hypersensitivity, fear and sleeping disorders. For most psychological symptoms, no significant differences were found between those returnees who received support and those who did not, except for involvement in fights, with those who received support being more likely than the others to report fighting. Yet, no difference based on support from a reception centre was found for fighting. However, such a difference could be identified for vigilance, with a bigger proportion of those who benefited from a reception centre reporting a heightened alertness. Physical suffering was mostly reported as being due to chest pain or unhealed wounds. With regard to these symptoms, analysis found that children who benefited from a reception centre were still suffering significantly more from these physical injuries than other supported children.

3.2.3. Social Status

Analysis indicates that nearly all children reported positively on the social variables measured, such as playing with friends, feeling accepted by friends and being treated well in the community. However, half stated that they had often been insulted by others, most frequently as "child or wife of Kony", "rebel" or "killer". Comparing these variables between those returnees who received support and those who did not, some significant differences were found. The former child soldiers who received support were reported as playing less with their friends and as being insulted more by others, yet a higher proportion felt accepted by their friends and treated well in the community. Further social variables indicate that the majority were attending school, mostly at primary level (n = 531, 93.1%), proportionally more than returnees who did not benefit from any kind of support. Analysing the kind of support received, it was found that considerably fewer of the children who benefited from a reception centre returned to school after captivity, compared to children who received a different form of support. Those who did not attend school were reported as providing domestic help, such as farming (n = 143, 63.6%), or as carrying out income-generating activities, such as running a small shop (n = 12, 5.4%). Notably, one in six former child soldiers were engaged in marriage at the moment of monitoring in the community.

4. DISCUSSION

Based on the results of this study, as highlighted above, the need for reception centres for returned child soldiers will be discussed from the perspective of intake data, with some reflections on the thresholds for such centres from the perspective of follow-up data. This evaluation is grounded in an ecological model of development.

4.1. THE NEED FOR AND ADDITIONAL VALUE OF RECEPTION CENTRES

This research reveals the vastness of potentially traumatising experiences lived through by former child soldiers during LRA captivity. Not only the precarious living conditions, but also their exposure to and forced participation in numerous atrocities poses serious threats to their well-being and development.[33] A considerable proportion of these former child soldiers returned with clear symptoms of psychological distress, such as fear, low self-esteem and withdrawal. Many of them also appeared to be physically unhealthy and injured.

Moreover, the long duration of their abduction and absence from society as well as their extensive involvement in civilian-targeting actions by the LRA, both illustrated in this research, make their role in society dubious.[34] Besides, due to the prolonged nature of the warfare and the massive displacement of people in northern Uganda, linkages to a supportive network may be erased, possibly hindering the reintegration of the returned child.

These findings underline the need for a quickly available safety net by which the highlighted needs can be met. The network of reception centres in northern Uganda forms such a facility, by providing support for basic needs, offering counselling and medical care, tracking down relatives, providing reinsertion activities/support and reunifying the former child soldiers. From this perspective, reception centres for formerly abducted children are a vital link in the rehabilitation and reintegration processes faced by returnees.

Nevertheless, evaluating the challenges of civilian wars from an ecological perspective, some remarks can be made with respect to the role of reception centres on the micro-, meso- and macro-levels of recovery.

4.2. REFLECTIONS ON RECEPTION CENTRES

4.2.1. *On the Micro-Level*

The majority of monitored children did not report the measured complaints about their psychological and social well-being, which leads one to suspect that most former child soldiers recovered well from their experiences in the LRA. However, the findings from this research have demonstrated the persistent presence of some personal symptoms of distress, reported by a minority of the sample. Research suggests that this minority mainly consists of children who

33 Amone-P'Olak, *supra* note 9; Coalition to Stop the Use of Child Soldiers, *supra* note 5.

34 Blattman and Annan, *supra* note 4; Coalition to Stop the Use of Child Soldiers, ibid.

experienced the most severe violence and who returned to the least supportive environments.[35]

Compared to earlier, similar research on the psychological impact of abduction and the reintegration status of formerly abducted children,[36] where symptoms of distress were present in approximately a sixth of the former child soldiers, the rates of psychological symptoms at the moment of monitoring in the community were considerably higher in our research. Fear tended to be a prominent reported symptom, both at the moment of return from captivity (63.6% of the sample) and at the moment of monitoring in the community (36.8% of the sample). In the literature, fear is mostly attributed to dreaded reprisals by the LRA, human rights violations by soldiers or civilians and retribution from the community.[37] Although the number who reported fear declined drastically between these two moments, it was still disturbing more than a third of the former child soldiers who benefited from a reception centre.

This finding may bring forward some reflections about the additional value of reception centres for the psychological well-being of the child. Research on reception centres in northern Uganda stated that the "psycho" in "psychosocial" was severely underrepresented in the work reception centres were carrying out and was generally reduced to teaching on how to behave appropriately.[38] Hence, decisions on the state of the child and its readiness for reunion were more likely to be based on social behaviour than on psychological well-being,[39] which may explain why the prevalence of some symptoms remained relatively high among former child soldiers who benefited from reception centres. However, there may also be a reporting bias because these children became more aware of their well-being and psychosocial symptoms during their stay at the reception centre.

Moreover, the finding that non-benefiting former child soldiers are doing as well as their supported peers also points to the importance of other personal and social factors that stimulate recovery from potentially traumatic experiences. These resources need to be more acknowledged, as they may play a significant role in rehabilitation and reintegration.[40]

---

35 Amone-P'Olak, *supra* note 9; Blattman and Annan, ibid.

36 J. Annan, *Self-appraisal, social support and connectedness as protective factors for youth associated with fighting forces in Northern Uganda*, Unpublished dissertation, Indiana University.

37 Allen and Schomerus, *supra* note 30.

38 Ibid.

39 Ibid.

40 M. Olff, W. Langeland and B.P.R. Gersons, 'The psychobiology of PTSD: coping with trauma', (2005) 30 *Psychoneuroendocrinology*, 974–982; Amone-P'Olak, *supra* note 9; Corbin, *supra* note 6.

4.2.2. *On the Meso-Level*

Reception centres can be regarded as a gradual transit zone from life in captivity to life in the community.[41] However, our research indicates that this transit did not seem to have happened as gradually as might be desirable.

First of all, research indicates that segregated centres tend to induce a unidirectional responsibility. It is argued that the centres stimulate minimal involvement by the child's social network and thereby unintentionally spread the message that the relatives are relieved of the responsibility to take care of the returned child.[42] The network therefore entrusts their child to the care of professionals, which means that they are hardly associated with the rehabilitation and reintegration of their child during its stay in the reception centre.

Moreover, this research reveals thresholds that may have reduced the involvement of the social network. One of the agreements among reception centres was initially that the child needed to be taken to its district of origin as quickly as possible.[43] Yet children who were received at the Rachele Rehabilitation Centre originated from various districts in the north and stayed for an average of almost two months. As mobility was often limited, this may have impeded opportunities for relatives to restore a relationship with their child and therefore may have hindered the reintegration process.

Furthermore, research reports that the follow-up of the former child soldiers was mostly out of necessity reduced to a minimum, equating reintegration efforts with the organisation of a reunion ceremony with the relatives and the donation of a reinsertion package to the child.[44] This may have implied an abrupt termination of professional support at a time when the family and community were unprepared to take it over. This lends support to a revision of the reintegration and follow-up activities of organisations targeting formerly abducted children.

4.2.3. *On the Macro-Level*

Insight into the experiences of former child soldiers in the LRA indicates that the majority were forcibly involved in atrocities against their own people, often their own neighbours, family or friends. This might have put former child soldiers in the dubious role of direct victim of violations by the LRA yet forced perpetrator of violations against civilians, making their status at return

41 Hill and Langholtz, *supra* note 16; T. Allen, *War and Justice in Northern Uganda: an assessment of the International Criminal Court's intervention*, Crisis States Research Centre, Development Studies Institute, London School of Economics, London, 2005.

42 Allen and Schomerus, *supra* note 30.

43 Ibid.

44 Ibid.

precarious.[45] Other research underlines that not all former child soldiers, not even those who were initially coerced by abduction, stayed within the LRA by force alone.[46] This may explain why the use of child soldiers may yield a social impact long after the cessation of warfare.

Earlier research raised the problem of negative attitudes towards returned former child soldiers, e.g. distrust, stigmatisation and social disruption.[47] Moreover, warfare engenders a climate of bitterness and condemnation in society.[48] This study indicates that at the time of follow-up, half of the former child soldiers had experienced insults by others owing to their former involvement in the LRA. This proportion is twice the amount found in earlier research, where only 25% reported negative attitudes in their social environment.[49]

The finding that significantly more of those who benefited from support suffer from this social phenomenon could indicate that this support was a source of controversy in society, as it might have been perceived as a reward for perpetrated violence.[50] Research stated that the initial focus of relief organisations, especially reception centres, on former child soldiers left many victimised civilians with a lack of acknowledgement of what was done to them – not infrequently by these former LRA combatants.[51]

Nevertheless, it is noteworthy that nearly all former child soldiers felt accepted by their social network. These relatively high rates of acceptance are also found in several other studies.[52] Although a higher proportion of benefiting former child soldiers stated that they played less with friends and experienced more insults than other former child soldiers, they seemed to feel better accepted than those who did not receive any professional support. This may indicate that these factors do not influence the subjective perception of their social status or deter their reintegration,[53] yet it needs to be taken into account that they may create new daily stressors, threatening or delaying rehabilitation and reintegration.[54]

45 Derluyn et al., *supra* note 9.

46 M. Wessells, 'Child soldiers, peace education, and post conflict reconstruction for peace', (2005) 44 4 *Theory into Practice,* 363–639; Akello et al., *supra* note 19; Allen and Schomerus, *supra* note 30.

47 Coalition to Stop the Use of Child Soldiers, *supra* note 5; Akello et al., *supra* note 19; Corbin, *supra* note 6.

48 International Crisis Group, *supra* note 2.

49 Allen and Schomerus, *supra* note 30.

50 Ibid.; Blattman and Annan, *supra* note 4.

51 Ibid.

52 Ibid.

53 Ibid.

54 Akello et al., *supra* note 19; Amone-P'Olak, *supra* note 9.

5. RECOMMENDATIONS

In order to address the aforementioned limitations and pitfalls of reception centres for formerly abducted children, and thereby possibly enhance their efficacy in rehabilitation and reintegration, some recommendations can be formulated based on the results of this study. These recommendations can be situated at the micro-, meso- and macro-levels. Research made clear that the conflict in northern Uganda generated tremendous devastation, not only for the directly victimised child soldiers but also through social disruption. Subsequent symptoms, such as fear and stigmatisation, are perceptible even long after the cessation of warfare and need to be tackled on these different levels. Reception centres should therefore pay attention to both individual and social healing.

5.1. ON THE MICRO-LEVEL

The finding that the majority of formerly abducted children, even those who did not benefit from a reception centre, did not report psychological symptoms, prompts the necessity of recognising the importance of other resources on the individual and social level that might help former child soldiers to recover from their trauma. Such resources can be individual resilience, coping strategies and supportive networks. However, a more elaborated psychological approach towards the significant minority who are in need of more specialised mental health care needs to be available and further expanded in the programme that reception centres offer to formerly abducted children. Building the capacity of counsellors in mental health and increasing the availability of such professionals should be promoted. Ideally, both should be combined in an integrated, subsidiary approach whereby individual and social resources form the priority and can be reinforced by more specialised professional mental health care.

5.2. ON THE MESO-LEVEL

Organisations providing rehabilitation and reintegration services, such as reception centres, should create a more gradual transitional phase between the stay at the centre and the return to the community/camp. Such a gradual transition promotes a shared responsibility between the professionals and the relatives of the child. Earlier research on former Ugandan child soldiers found that parents can play a supportive role in the rehabilitation of a child from post-traumatic stress[55] and in the reintegration of the child into the broader society.[56]

55 Derluyn et al., *supra* note 9.

56 Corbin, *supra* note 6.

This resource should be revalued by professional caregivers. Shared responsibility can be promoted by involving the social network of the returned child, from the moment of return onwards, and investing in building their capacity, in order to be able to support the child adequately when it returns home. Furthermore, the assistance of the professionals has to remain available when needed for the child's network to call on when found necessary. Moreover, the aftercare offered should be oriented towards the social network that is supporting the child rather than towards the individual former child solder.[57] Hence, the responsibility and capacity of the network is stimulated and this might enhance the sustainability of the support.

5.3. ON THE MACRO-LEVEL

As stigmatisation happens to be a frequently occurring social reaction towards former child soldiers, sensitising and awareness-raising initiatives covering the position, experiences and needs of these children remain necessary for stimulating a context of reconciliation.[58] At the same time, a cautious approach is recommended so as not to overemphasise the victimisation of former child soldiers or to ignore the way all civilians were affected by the war. Hence, it is more often recommended that the focus of follow-up care be shifted from the individual former child soldier who passed through a reception centre, to the community's living situation, addressing all vulnerable people.[59] Such an integrated approach allocates additional support based on needs (vulnerability) rather than on status (ex-combatant).[60] This shift may defuse the counterproductive effect of targeting formerly abducted children and thereby reduce envy and resentment towards formerly abducted children who are supported by organisations.

6. LIMITATIONS

While the findings of this research may yield some tendencies in traumatic exposure of former child soldiers and the challenges it brings forth with regard to their rehabilitation and reintegration, the limitations of the study design call for caution in interpretation.

Some limitations relate to the procedure of data collection. The context in which the Rachele Rehabilitation Centre operated was one of high rebel activity

57 Ibid.

58 Coalition to Stop the Use of Child Soldiers, *supra* note 5.

59 Allen and Schomerus, *supra* note 30; Amone-P'Olak, *supra* note 9.

60 Blattman and Annan, *supra* note 4.

and insecurity. As former child soldiers could sometimes return in large numbers, the preconditions for accurate registration on arrival were often precarious. Moreover, follow-up outreach activities were restricted for security reasons and because of immobility. The actual data collection could therefore deviate from the prescribed protocol, meaning that registration was postponed or even cancelled. As a result, the circumstances in which the data were collected vary and the databases lack some missing data due to unregistered, illegible or lost information. For example, the elapsed time between return from captivity and follow-up may vary significantly for those children who were not registered at the reception centre.

Limitations can also be attributed to the nature of the registered data. The intake forms sought retrospective data, which implies that returnees were asked to recall historical facts. Moreover, the reliability of self-reported measures of these facts is questionable. Additionally, information on the pre-war status of the returnees is lacking, which makes interpretation of the influence of their experiences as a child soldier difficult. Furthermore, information from a control group of non-abducted children is lacking, and an estimation of their war experiences and its consequences for their well-being remains unknown. For example, the date of and age at abduction may rather be an estimation, especially if the abduction occurred years ago.

Other limitations can be ascribed to the fact that non-standardised instruments and protocols were used to collect the data on the psychosocial well-being and recovery process of the returnees. The instruments were designed by employees of the Rachele Rehabilitation Centre and other reception centres in northern Uganda. Although a workshop on the use of these instruments was organised for the social workers, assessment was mainly based on an individual appraisal. Though this may enhance the cultural validity of the data, it may bring into question the validity of the construct. For example, differences may have arisen between the conceptualisation of the psychological construct "fear" in the questionnaire and the measurement made by the social worker.

These limitations generate restraints on the generalisation of the research findings and should be taken into account when interpreting this study.

PSYCHOSOCIAL CARE IN REHABILITATION CENTRES FOR FORMER CHILD SOLDIERS IN NORTHERN UGANDA*

Kathleen COPPENS, Sofie VINDEVOGEL, Ilse DERLUYN, Gerrit LOOTS and Eric BROEKAERT

1. INTRODUCTION

This chapter aims to outline an overview of psychosocial caretaking activities organised by rehabilitation centres (RCs) for former child soldiers in northern Uganda. The conflict in northern Uganda is sometimes referred to as 'one of the most forgotten conflicts in the world' or 'one of the worst violations of children's rights anywhere in the world'.[61] For over 20 years this country has suffered from a cruel and bloody war between the government army (Ugandan People's Defence Force, UPDF) and the Lord's Resistance Army (LRA), a rebel group under the command of Joseph Kony.[62] The LRA had a tremendous impact on daily life as it concentrated its terror on the civilian population by looting and attacking villages, burning houses, and, worst of all, by mutilating, killing and

* The authors wish to express their thanks to all the children and staff members who participated in the research. Without their help this research would not have been possible. Special thanks also to Lieve Milissen and her family for providing a safe and warm place to start and finish this study. This research was conducted by two researchers from the Centre for Children in Vulnerable Situations and supported by Sponsoring Children Uganda (SCU), with financial support of the Department of Peace Building (FOD Foreign Affairs).

61 AMNESTY INTERNATIONAL, *Breaking God's commands': The destruction of childhood by the Lord's Resistance Army,* 1997. Consulted on www.amnesty.org/en/library/info/AFR59/001/1997; RELIEF WEB, *Northern Uganda briefing paper: May 2006,* 2006, see at www.reliefweb.int/library/documents/2006/ocha-uga-31may.pdf.

62 H. BEHREND, *Alice Lakwena & the Holy Spirits. War in Northern Uganda 1985–97,* Eastern African Studies, Fountain Publishers, Kampala, 1999; F. GOLOOBA-MUTEBI, 'Collapse, War and Reconstruction in Uganda: An Analytic Narrative on State-Making', (2008) 2 *Crisis States Working Papers Series* 27; S. TANGELDER, *Spelen met Vuur: Kindsoldaten en hun Strijdtoneel,* Haasbeek, Amsterdam, 1999.

abducting children and adults.[63] It is estimated that over the course of the conflict, Kony and his army were responsible for the deaths of about one million people, while nearly two million people were forced to live in camps for internally displaced persons (IDP) for several years.[64]

The abduction or use of children for the purpose of forced conscription and sexual exploitation is even today an important problem, as it is estimated that between 250,000 and 300,000 children are deployed as child soldiers in 17 conflicts worldwide.[65] Northern Uganda had its share, with estimations ranging from 24,000[66] to 38,000 children[67] to as many as 66,000 children and young adults between 14 and 30 years old.[68] Even more striking, Annan et al.[69] found that more than one third of male youths and one fifth of female youths questioned in their study reported being abducted. Once abducted by the LRA, children were confronted with very difficult living conditions and without doubt life became a true struggle for survival. It started at the moment of abduction, when many children were tied, beaten and/or given heavy loads to carry.[70] Most of them were forced to walk long distances without proper

63 Human Rights Watch, *Stolen Children: Abduction and Recruitment in Northern Uganda*, Human Rights Watch, New York, 2003; A.C. Blattman and J. Annan, *The Consequences of Child Soldiering*, 2007, see www.hicn.org.; E. De temmerman, *En Toen Moest Ik Mijn Broer Doodbijten*, Houtekiet, Antwerpen, 2007; Human Rights Watch, *The Scars of Death. Children Abducted by the Lord's Resistance Army in Uganda*, Human Rights Watch, New York, 1997, see www.hrw.org.

64 Blattman and Annan, ibid.; M. Mailer, M.-L. Tusinguare Jorgensen and S. Carvalho, *From Emergency to Recovery: Rescuing Northern Uganda's transition*, Oxfam Briefing Paper, Oxfam International, 2008; D. Paul, *Fulfilling the Forgotten Promise: The Protection of Civilians in Northern Uganda*, InterAction, 2006, see http://internal-displacement.org; Relief Web, *supra* note 1.

65 Coalitation to Stop the Use of Child Soldiers, *Child Soldiers Global Report 2008*, 2008, see www.child-soldiers.org/library/global-reports; G. Machel, *Promotion and Protection of the Rights of Children: Impact of Armed Conflict on Children*, United Nations Department for Policy Coordination and Sustainable Development (DPCSD), 1996; G. Machel, *The impact of armed conflict on children. A critical review of progress made and obstacles encountered in increasing protection for war-affected children*, Unicef-Unifem, London, 2001.

66 Coalition to Stop the Use of Child Soldiers, ibid.; Z. Lomo and L. Hovil, *Behind the Violence: the War in Northern Uganda*, 2004, see www.iss.co.za/pubs/Monographs/No99/Contents.html; Relief Web, *supra* note 1.

67 P. Pham, P. Vinck and E. Stover, *Abducted: The Lord's Resistance Army and Forced Conscription in Northern Uganda*, Human Rights Center Reports, University of California, Berkeley, 2007.

68 J. Annan, C. Blattman, K. Carlson and D. Mazurana, *The state of female youth in Northern Uganda: Findings from the survey of war-affected youth (SWAY). Phase II*, 2008, see www.sway-uganda.org; K. Carlson and D. Mazurana, *Forced Marriage within the Lord's Resistance Army, Uganda*, Feinstein International Centre, 2008, see http://wikis.uit.tufts.edu; World Bank, World Development Report 2007: Development and the next generation, 2007, www-wds.worldbank.org/external/default/WDSContentServer/WDSP/IB/2006/09/13/00011274220060913111024/Rendered/INDEX/359990WDR0Complete.txt.

69 Annan et al., *supra* note 8.

70 Blattman and Annan, *supra* note 3.

food or drinkable water. Some children received (short) military training; others were sent to fight without any preparation.[71] However, not all children became soldiers; some were used as spies, others as guards or cooks for example.[72] Abducted girls were often given as wives to commanders; others were required to perform household-like duties or were used as babysitters or even – perhaps contrary to what might be expected – as soldiers.[73, 74] Apart from these harsh living conditions, they were isolated from others, beaten frequently for no reason and forced to commit atrocities such as killing innocent people (often family members or other people they knew). When they did not follow the orders given, they were seriously beaten or killed.[75] How then could child soldiers return from the LRA and what happened to them afterwards?

There were different pathways through which abducted children came back home.[76] In spite of knowing they could be killed when they got caught,[77] some children tried to escape;[78] others were rescued by the UPDF during an attack on the LRA,[79] released (e.g. when a commander wanted to surrender) or left behind to die (e.g. because they were wounded).[80] In Uganda, most of the returning

71 Human Rights Watch, *Abducted and Abused: Renewed Conflict in Northern Uganda*, Human Rights Watch, New York, 2003; S. Vindevogel, K. Coppens, I. Derluyn, E. Broekaert and G. Loots, 'Forced conscription of children during armed conflict: Experiences of former child soldiers in Northern Uganda', (2011) 35 7 *Child Abuse and Neglect*, 551-563.

72 T. Allen and M. Schomerus, *A Hard Homecoming: Lessons Learnt From the Reception Centre Process in Northern Uganda. An Independent Study*, Management Systems International Corporate Offices, Washington, 2006, see www.childsoldiers.org; Human Rights Watch, *supra* note 3; J. Guyot, *Suffer the Children: the Psychosocial Rehabilitation of Child Soldiers as a Function of Peace-Building*, 2007, see www.child-soldiers.org/psycho-social/Linked_Guyot_2007.pdf; Human Rights Watch, *supra* note 3.

73 E. De Temmerman, *Rachele Rehabilitation Centre: Rehabilitation and reintegration of war affected children in Northern Uganda*, Internal evaluation report (unpublished) 2006.

74 M. Wessells, *Child Soldiers: From Violence to Protection*, Harvard University Press, Cambridge, 2006.

75 Amnesty International, *supra* note 1; Human Rights Watch, *supra* note 11; Coalition to Stop the Use of Child Soldiers, *supra* note 6; De Temmerman, *supra* note 13 and 3; B. Mergersberg, *Crossing boundaries: Experiences of returning "child soldiers"*, 2005; see www.child-soldiers.org/regions/country?id=222; Uganda Coalition to Stop the Use of Child Soldiers, *Time to Implement: National and international legal instruments related to the recruitment and use of children in armed forces and groups*, 2007, see www.child-soldiers.org/regions/country?id=222; Vindevogel et al., *supra* note 11.

76 K. Hill and H. Langholtz, 'Rehabilitation programs for African child soldiers', (2003) 15 3 *Peace Review*, 279–285.

77 Lomo and Hovil, *supra* note 6.

78 Amnesty International, *supra* note 1; Human Rights Watch, *supra* note 3; P.W. Singer, *Children at War*, University of California Press, Berkeley, 2006.

79 Human Rights Watch, ibid.

80 Allen and Schomerus, *supra* note 12; De Temmerman, *supra* note 13 and 3; Human Rights Watch, ibid.; Wessells, *supra* note 14.

child soldiers were brought to a UPDF military barrack.[81] Here, the child stayed in the Child Protection Unit (CPU), normally for only 48 hours,[82] although research revealed that children stayed on average for two weeks and were often not treated properly (e.g. over-interrogating to find out more about the LRA; abuse; lack of care[83]). However, as more and more children returned, two major problems arose. First, tracing the families of the children turned out to be a complex process constrained by many problems: some children had been abducted for such a long time or at such a young age that they did not remember the names of their parents or home,[84] while some families had moved to an IDP camp during the period of the child's captivity.[85] Second, many children returning from the LRA had many prevailing needs,[86] both physical needs, such as bullet and other wounds, malnourishment, scabies and diarrhoea; and mental problems, such as anxiety, restlessness, low self-esteem, nightmares and aggressive behaviour.[87] All these problems hampered the children's reintegration and daily functioning.[88] For none of these difficulties did the UPDF have the capacity or financial means to help the former child soldiers. The communities to which the children were returning were also in need, and, in most cases, not capable of coping with the extra burden of rehabilitating them.[89]

1.1. FORMAL SUPPORT INITIATIVES FOR FORMER CHILD SOLDIERS

This initial period led to the setting up of a variety of support initiatives for former child soldiers in northern Uganda, of which we here will focus on psychosocial care services. Although defining the term 'psychosocial' is not that easy,[90] we here take the IASC guidelines[91] on psychosocial support as our starting point:

---

81 Amnesty International, *supra* note 1; Human Rights Watch, *supra* note 11; Human Rights Watch, *supra* note 4; Tangelder, *supra* note 2.

82 Paul, *supra* note 4.

83 Allen and Schomerus, *supra* note 12; Paul, ibid.

84 De Temmerman, *supra* note 13.

85 Human Rights Watch Children's Project, *Children in combat*, Human Rights Watch, New York, 1996.

86 De Temmerman, *supra* note 13 and 3; Vindevogel et al., *supra* note 11.

87 Vindevogel et al., ibid.; Pham et al., *supra* note 7; Tangelder, *supra* note 2.

88 M. Wessells, 'Child Soldiers', (1997) 53 6 *The Bulletin of the Atomic Scientists*, 32–39.

89 A. Veale and A. Stavrou, *Violence, reconciliation and identity: The reintegration of Lord's Resistance Army child abductees in Northern Uganda,* Institute for Security Studies, 2003, Monograph '92; Wessells, *supra* note 14.

90 Inter-Agency Standing Committee, *IASC Guidelines on mental health and psychosocial support in emergency settings*, IASC, Geneva, 2007; Singer, *supra* note 18.

91 Ibid.

> Any type of local or outside support that aims to protect or promote psychosocial well-being and/or prevent or treat mental disorder.

After some publications on the appalling situation of Ugandan child soldiers,[92] several volunteers, humanitarian aid agencies and non-governmental organisations (NGOs) started targeting them as a special group of beneficiaries. Their efforts were directed at promoting the rehabilitation of the children and their reintegration into the community. In particular, inpatient (residential) care by means of rehabilitation centres (RCs) was established,[93] the kind of support we also will focus on in this paper. However, readers should be aware that inpatient care was not the only available option,[94] as some children also could benefit from day care (semi-residential) and outpatient (ambulant) support programmes (e.g. individual and/or group counselling, educational support, income generating activities, vocational training). Besides these (psychosocial) activities, other support aimed at people's basic needs was also provided, such as the distribution of food packages. However, many children were left without further support.[95]

1.1.1. Inpatient Support

The establishment of RCs is an important part of formal, UN-led and internationally endorsed 'DDR' (Disarmament, Demobilisation and Reintegration) programmes.[96] Disarmament refers to reducing the number of combatants and collecting their weapons in order to demilitarise the environment. The demobilisation component encloses an interim stage between the army and returning to the community. It is here that RCs for child and/or adult combatants have their place. Reintegration consists of a long-term process in which not only the former combatants need to return home and be 're-'integrated, but also the communities themselves and family bonds must be strengthened and supported.[97] In other words, DDR programmes are set up to

---

92 Human Rights Watch, *supra* note 3; Amnesty International, *supra* note 1; E. De Temmerman, *De meisjes van Aboke: Kindsoldaten in Noord-Oeganda,* De Kern, 2000 (published in English as *'Aboke Girls: Children Abducted in Northern Uganda'*, Fountain Publisher, Kampala, 2001).

93 Human Rights Watch, ibid.

94 K. Coppens, S. Vindevogel, G. Loots and I. Derluyn (in preparation), *Child soldiers in Northern Uganda: Their experiences, stories and recovery process* (working title); B. Kalksma-Van Lith, D. De Graaff, E. Jansveld and A. De Jager, *State of the art: Psychosocial interventions with children in war-affected areas,* 2007, War Child International Holland.

95 Allen and Schomerus, *supra* note 12; J. Annan, C. Blattman and R. Horton, *The state of youth and youth protection in Northern Uganda: Findings from the survey of war affected youth (SWAY – study 1),* 2006, see www.sway-uganda.org; Hill and Langholtz, *supra* note 16; Pham et al., *supra* note 7.

96 Singer, *supra* note 18.

97 S. Meek and M. Malan, 'Identifying lessons from DDR experiences in Africa', (2004) *ISS Monograph* 106; Singer, ibid.; Wessells, *supra* note 14.

try to end a conflict and bridge the gap between living as a soldier and returning to the community. However, there are many variations in DDR programmes, depending on the country and the nature of the conflict,[98] as DDR programmes should be developed in concert with larger programmes for national recovery.[99]

1.1.2. Rehabilitation Centres in Northern Uganda

World Vision was the first to open a rehabilitation centre in northern Uganda, operating in Gulu from 1995. Gulu Support the Children Organization (GUSCO) started up in 1994, an initiative taken by a small group of concerned mothers and other local civilians, and opened its rehabilitation centre in 1997 with the support of an external NGO. In the following years, other centres were established in Apac, Gulu, Lira, Katakwi, Kitgum, Pader and Soroti.[100] Overall, it is estimated that 43 per cent[101] or about 25,000 of abducted children[102] passed through a RC in Northern Uganda.

RCs were particularly responsible for addressing the most urgent needs of children returning from the LRA and aimed to facilitate their rehabilitation and social reintegration.[103] All centres provided the following support: medical/physical care (e.g. food, treatment of wounds, other diseases and STDs); psychological support; education or skills training (e.g. tailoring); recreational activities (e.g. dancing, music, sport); and family tracing and reintegration.[104] As soon as the child had recovered and a family member had been found, the child was reunited with his/her family.[105] Most of the reunited children received a so-called reunification package containing goods such as

---

98 A. Abatneh, *Disarmament, Demobilization, Rehabilitation and Reintegration of Rwandan Child Soldiers,* Master Thesis in Sociology, University of South Africa, 2006; I. Specht, *Experiences of girl-combatants in Liberia. Programme on crisis response and reconstruction.* International Labour Office Geneva, *2006,* see www.ilo.org/crisis; L. Specker, *The R-Phase of DDR processes: An overview of key lessons learned and practical experiences,* Netherlands Institute of International Relations 'Clingendael', Conflict Research Unit, 2008, www.clingendael.nl/cru; B. Verhey, *Child Soldiers Preventing, Demobilizing and Reintegrating,* 2001, see at www.worldbank.org/afr/wps/wp23.pdf; Wessells, *supra* note 14.

99 Meek and Malan, *supra* note 37.

100 Allen and Schomerus, *supra* note 12; Pham et al., *supra* note 7; Tangelder, *supra* note 2; Veale and Stavrou, *supra* note 29.

101 Allen and Schomerus, ibid.; Annan et al., *supra* note 35.

102 Pham et al., *supra* note 7.

103 Veale and Stavrou, *supra* note 29.

104 Allen and Schomerus, *supra* note 12; Human Rights Watch, *supra* note 3; Coalition to Stop the Use of Child Soldiers, *supra* note 5; J.N. Corbin, 'Returning home: resettlement of formerly abducted children in Northern Uganda', (2008) 32 2 *Disasters*, 316–335; Veale and Stavrou, *supra* note 29.

105 Corbin, ibid.; Veale and Stavrou, *supra* note 29.

food and a mattress.[106] Another activity included was community advocacy or sensitising the community to the plight of former abducted children (FAC). Community volunteers were supposed to conduct follow-ups once children had been reunited.[107] However, the RCs did not accomplish this goal and especially after the end of the conflict, more efforts were made to follow up the children.[108]

The setting up of rehabilitation centres has thus been a very important way of trying to tackle the needs of larger groups of FAC. However, there is little research studying the way the RCs undertook their activities,[109] and certainly not in northern Uganda.[110] One exception is Allen and Schomerus's study,[111] for which they visited rehabilitation centres in northern Uganda and assessed the services offered to FAC. However, it provides little information towards an overall description of the psychosocial support offered by RCs. We would therefore like to elaborate on this aspect in more depth, also paying attention to the problems practitioners were encountering and what preconditions needed to be fulfilled – according to the practitioners – in order to promote the successful rehabilitation and reintegration of former abducted children.

2. METHOD

2.1. PARTICIPANTS

The main purpose of this paper is to develop an inventory of the psychosocial caretaking activities organised by RCs for former child soldiers in northern Uganda. Abducted children were brought to these centres by the Ugandan military. However, according to Dolan[112] it remains unclear how many children were recruited by the UPDF to take part in the fighting. Our analysis is therefore based solely on the experiences of staff members working with children and/or adults abducted by the LRA.

For this research we visited all RCs that were operating in four districts (Gulu, Lira, Kitgum and Pader) in northern Uganda during the war period (1987–2006), aiming to interview at least two persons from each centre, preferably

106 Allen and Schomerus, *supra* note 12; Paul, *supra* note 4.

107 Ibid. note 43.

108 Ibid. note 46.

109 Hill and Langholtz, *supra* note 16.

110 Allen and Schomerus, *supra* note 12; Veale and Stavrou, *supra* note 29.

111 Ibid.

112 C. Dolan, *Which children count? The politics of children's rights in Northern Uganda*, ACCORD, 2002, see at www.c-r.org/our-work/accord/northern-uganda/which-children-count.php#text2.

one social worker (someone working closely with the children) and one director or programme manager (someone involved with the planning of the activities and other organisational aspects). In total, seven different RCs were visited, where eight social workers and nine staff members with a coordinating function were interviewed (Table 1). Some centres originally had several divisions scattered around northern Uganda. By the time we conducted our research, very few or no child soldiers were returning from the LRA, so most organisations remained with only one branch operational (except for CPA, Caritas and WV). All centres were closed one by one after the ending of the conflict in 2006.

Table 1. Overview of the rehabilitation centres visited

NAME CENTRE	TARGET GROUP			INTERVIEWEES
	Children	Child mothers	Adults	
Caritas - Pader, since 2000 (closed July 2007) - Lira, since 2004* (closed January 2007)	X	X	X	2 Social workers (Pader) Director (Lira)
Christian Counseling Fellowship (CCF) - Pader, since 2002 (closed 2007)	X	X	X (although very little)	Social worker Field Coordinator
Concerned Parents Association (CPA) - Kitgum, since 2003 - Lira, since June 2003 (closed February 2004) – transit centre	X (Lira)	X (Kitgum & Lira)	X (Kitgum & Lira)	Programme Officer– former Social worker (Kitgum) Executive Director (Lira)
Gulu Support the Children Organization (GUSCO) - Gulu, since 1997 (closed 2007)	X	X		Social worker Centre Administrator Former Programme Coordinator
Kitgum Concerned Women's Association (KICWA) - Kitgum, since 1998 (closed mid-2006)	X	X		Programme Manager Programme Assistant
Rachele Rehabilitation Centre (RRC) - Lira, since October 2003 (closed October 2006)	X	X	X	2 Social workers Programme Director

NAME CENTRE	TARGET GROUP			INTERVIEWEES
	Children	Child mothers	Adults	
World Vision (WV) - Gulu, since 1995 (closed 2007) – As the number of retuning youths was too big, a separate centre for adult males was opened in 2002 and for child mothers in 2004. - Pader**	X	X	X	Social worker Management Coordinator

Note on the terms used: Children (< 18 years old); Adults (18 years old and above); Child mothers are girls and women returning from the LRA with children. We say RCs are 'closed' although local staff do not see it as a real closure since Joseph Kony (LRA) has failed to sign the peace agreement and the conflict is therefore not officially ended.

* All staff members of the psychosocial programme in Pader were out for the week so interviews were done via e-mail; in Lira only the Director was available but he was not familiar with the practical work methods. Therefore we might miss some information concerning the working of Caritas.

** World Vision also had a small branch in Pader. For lack of time we were not able to visit this division. In Gulu we were told they used similar working methods in all their branches.

Overall, these RCs have been responsible for the rehabilitation and reintegration of thousands of FAC, although their capacity differed markedly, with numbers ranging from about 60 (CPA, Lira) to as many as 400 (GUSCO) or 600 (WV, Gulu). Furthermore, although we nearly always talk about abducted *children*, many RCs also rehabilitated *adults,* using, overall, the same methods and activities, leading some adults to complain that they were treated like children.[113]

2.2. DATA COLLECTION AND ANALYSIS

The data collection was undertaken in November and December 2008 by the first two authors in four northern Ugandan districts: Gulu, Lira, Kitgum and Pader. These were chosen because they were among the most conflict-affected districts[114] and because the RCs/NGOs that were operational during the war were still active in this region at the time of our research. In each RC, semi-structured interviews were conducted, built up around certain themes to obtain focused information on their way of working:[115] general information about the organisation (e.g. location, departments, work area); organisational aspects in

113 Allen and Schomerus, *supra* note 12.

114 Ibid.

115 S. Kvale, *InterViews. An Introduction to Qualitative Research Interviewing,* Sage Publications, London, 1996; J.A. Smith, 'Semi-structured interviewing and qualitative analysis', in J. Smith, R. Harre and L. Van Langenhore (eds.), *Rethinking methods in psychology,* Sage

the past and at present (e.g. staff, networking, values, history, financial resources, infrastructure); what programmes or activities were and are still implemented; how the programmes were evaluated; and lessons learned from working with FAC (dos and don'ts, preconditions for successfully rehabilitating and reintegrating FAC). On average, all interviews took between two to three hours. In every organisation we also requested brochures, annual reports and other material that could be useful for our research.

All interviews were conducted in English. Although English was for both interviewers and interviewees not their mother tongue, we did not encounter serious language problems. All interviews were recorded and transcribed literally.

The procedure for analysing our interviews was based on Giorgi and Giorgi,[116] Kvale,[117] and Smith and Osborn.[118] First, all interviews were fully read to gain an overview of the information available. Afterwards, the transcripts were analysed using MAXqda2.[119] All information was coded according to the themes discussed in the semi-structured interviews and other subthemes were identified. Then themes and subthemes were compared and summarised across all RCs. The extra information gathered from brochures and annual reports was used to elaborate and check the information from the interviews, mostly when inconsistencies between the answers of different respondents were encountered.

3. RESULTS

In this section, we describe some of our results concerning the psychosocial support provided to returning child soldiers by different RCs in northern Uganda. First we discuss their working methods, then we summarise what can be learned from the experiences of staff members working with the children. We elaborate our own descriptions with quotations from our interviewees. To guarantee their anonymity, we refer to the organisation they belong to by way of letters.

Publications, London, 1996, 9–26; J. Smith, *Qualitative psychology: A practical guide to research methods,* Sage Publications, London, 2003.

116 A.P. Giorgi and B.M. Giorgi, 'Phenomenology', in J. Smith ibid., 25–50; A.P. Giorgi and B.M. Giorgi, 'The descriptive phenomenological psychological method', in P.M. Camic, J.E. Rhodes and L. Yardley (eds.), *Qualitative research in psychology: Expanding perspectives in methodology and design,* American Psychological Association, Washington, 2003, 243–274.

117 Kvale, *supra* note 55.

118 J.A. Smith and M. Osborn, 'Interpretative phenomenological analysis', in J.A. Smith, *supra* note 55, 51–80.

119 MAXqda2, *Handleiding MAXqda2,* VERBI Software, Berlijn, 2004.

3.1. THE PROCESS OF REHABILITATION IN A REHABILITATION CENTRE: AN OVERVIEW

Although we focus mainly on psychosocial caretaking activities in the rehabilitation centres, for clarity we firstly summarise rehabilitation centres' other activities.

All staff members described the terrible condition of newly arriving FAC. Physically, socially and psychologically, they were very vulnerable:

> They return when they are so traumatised because of the experiences they have gone through… others have serious wounds. Some come in very alarming condition, they are sick, come with swollen legs, … (C).

Fulfilling their *basic needs* and giving *medical treatment* was therefore one of the first priorities:

> We provide them with clean water and food to restore their normal weight… they are obviously malnourished, and with other specific requirements like clothes, soap, a mattress, … (E); and also medical treatment (C).

However, their social and psychological needs were also tackled from the start.

> Some being severely traumatised and in need of special care and counselling (A).

In order to gain the children's trust and make them feel at ease at the centre, they were welcomed by staff members and the other children:

> This is the first healing process (D).

This *welcoming* could be done with a song, something to eat or drink or with joined prayers. Furthermore, it was explained to the children why they were in the centre and that their safety would be guaranteed. It was also stressed that their time in the centre would be short and that they would go home soon:

> [This] gives them the assurance that all is well and that they should feel at home (D).

In all centres, staff expressed the need for children to leave their past life in the bush behind and to focus on the future and life in the community. All centres therefore performed a ritual, named '*the burning of the clothes*':

> They are supposed to forget about the bush (A), this is a new chapter in your life… there is hope for the future and you can reconstruct your life (D).

During this small ceremony, either performed only with the new returnees (e.g. in KICWA) or with all children staying at the centre (e.g. in RRC, GUSCO,

World Vision), all things from the bush (such as clothes, charms and gumboots) were burnt.

> We wanted to destroy the evidence because we saw that it reminds them of being there (B).

This ceremony was also organised for hygienic reasons and because many of these objects had been stolen from people in the community. Only in CCF was the burning not conducted in the presence of the children. Here, the clothes were collected by the matron and burned afterwards, without children even being aware of it.

In all RCs children were given some responsibilities through involvement in *household work:*

> Most of the activities planned would be home-like activities as a step towards rehabilitating (A).

They needed to clean their sleeping place and the compound; others assisted the cook(s) in preparing the food. Involving them in these household activities had several reasons, but mainly because it helped children to learn how to conduct these tasks and get ready for daily life in the community, and secondly because as children had been indoctrinated by the LRA and therefore feared staying at the centre, it helped to overcome their fear by involving them in the preparation of the food and making sure children and staff ate the same food together:

> They need to know these things… to easily resettle in the community (G).
> They have fear… they were indoctrinated from captivity, that if you come back into the community they will kill or poison you (E).

In World Vision, children were further encouraged to behave responsibly by involving them in the daily running of the centre. For example, a head boy and girl, a head cook who had the responsibility to choose those who were to cook, a health prefect ('to see that the compound, bathroom… are really clean') and dorm captains ('if somebody is not feeling all right at night, that [dorm captain] has to report to the matron') were all elected by the other children.

Other activities organised included *health education*, lessons given by the centre's nurse on diseases such as HIV/AIDS and how to take care of one's own body and health, and *catch-up classes*. In all centres except for Caritas and CPA, these lessons, although very basic, were organised in order to help children get used to class routine and to teach them to concentrate again:

> [They] develop skills of listening, concentrating… instil some degree of discipline into them… and share with others in the class (F).

English (learning how to read and write) and mathematics classes were given everywhere, in RRC also social studies and agriculture classes. The frequency of the lessons varied from once (e.g. KICWA) to two or three times a week (e.g. CCF, RRC and WV). Sometimes, children were divided into groups according to their previous level of education. According to staff, the importance of these classes cannot be underestimated as they played an important role in the recovery of the children:

> The classes helped to keep their minds busy in a positive, constructive way and prevented them from pondering about the past… [they] played an important role in their emotional and psychological recovery (F).

In general, child mothers and older children were least likely to return to school after their stay at the centre. Therefore, they could learn an *income generating activity* (IGA) or follow *vocational training* in, for example, baking bread, tailoring or hairdressing:

> [so] that they can start some small-scale business and make their living out of that (B).

After the training, a start-up kit with basic material, such as a sewing machine, was given to enable them to start up a business. In RRC and GUSCO these courses were given while children were at the centre. In all other centres such training was given or sponsored after the children had returned home.

3.1.1. Psychosocial Support

Apart from the abovementioned activities, most of the time spent at the centre was dedicated to psychosocial caretaking activities (Table 2). The wide definition of 'psychosocial support' we use was acknowledged in the accounts of staff members:

> When you are doing psychosocial support programmes, you need to integrate counselling, education and structured activities like games, dances… that can promote communication (D).
> Music and singing are very very important, even games that they play, is also counselling (C).

All psychosocial activities were used to see how children were coping with what they had been through:

> They are tools in assessing the level of trauma in these children… and to help them (E).

In all centres, *counselling* was considered an important tool in helping children to overcome their trauma from the bush and prepare them for living in the community:

> Group counselling helped children develop life skills and deal with the society around them… Life skills like assertiveness, problem-solving, decision-making, creativity, critical thinking, communication and empathy needed to be restored (F).

As can be seen in Table 2, different kinds of counselling were conducted. However, the frequency of counselling sessions varied in time. All centres planned to give individual counselling but the number of returnees turned out to be too large while the number of staff was too small to conduct frequent individual counselling sessions with all children. As such, group counselling was taken as a starting point and therefore much more prevalent. Furthermore, '[the group counselling] helped to identify those ones who need close attention' (C). When child-specific problems were noticed during group counselling, individual sessions were conducted with that particular child.

In GUSCO, RRC and WV the group of returnees was split up into a 'high-' and a 'low-risk' group. It was mainly the 'high-risk' group that received the individual counselling as they were judged to be more in need compared to the 'low-risk' group:

> The "low-risk" groups are mainly involved in structural activities such as dancing, sport and games. The "high-risk" categories are the ones that are followed by the social workers for more detailed counselling (D).

The social workers decided on the grouping of the children by talking to them and observing their behaviour:

> The entry point in supporting a child, you first develop a good rapport, good interpersonal relationship with the child… you let the child tell you the abduction story, experience in captivity… In the process when talking to a child, you get to know whether this is a "high-risk"…or "low-risk" category. Normally if you don't address issues of "high-risk" category, that's when the psychological reactions begin to show in the community (D).

The criteria for assignment to 'low-' and 'high-risk' groups are described in the following account:

> There are those who are extremely aggressive…who are really very tough and very difficult, they would hardly speak nor smiling. That's the "high risk"…you need to give more time to those. …Then there are those who are just normal, they just talk normally and they are just easy to approach (G).

Further, in CPA, for some group counselling sessions, children were divided in separate groups according to similarity in problems. In this way it was easier for children to open up, as all children in the group were familiar with the problems they were having:

> If you mix them up with other people who don't have that particular problem, they might shy up talking about it openly.

In other centres and depending on the themes discussed, children were also grouped according to age or sex (e.g. RRC, KICWA, GUSCO). For example, when talking about reproductive health or family planning the younger ones did not need to be there:

> There are times when we have separate sex talks... when we have talking about reproductive health. In our culture you cannot talk about certain things in the presence of both boys and girls... So we put boys separately from girls and the male staff talks to boys when the female staff talks to girls (D).

However, apart for some counselling purposes, children were hardly ever divided in groups according to age or gender and RCs tried to mix them as much as possible. A clear indication as to why this was done is given in the following account:

> We think... they should start living together. They should stop the life in the bush. When you were a commander, that privilege is no longer here. You are a child, we treat you equally... You do everything that a child does from here (E).

For the individual counselling sessions children were allocated to a particular counsellor:

> One social worker always follows one particular person (C).

This allocation was done rather arbitrarily (e.g. RRC, Caritas, CPA-Lira, WV) or on a county basis (e.g. KICWA, GUSCO). The reason for this latter choice was mainly pragmatic as family reunion and follow-up turned out to be easier this way. In other centres, children were free to choose their own counsellor (e.g. CCF, CPA-Kitgum). However, in all centres, children could talk to any staff member or counsellor as they felt the need:

> Sometimes the formerly abducted decides on who he or she wants to talk to about his or her problems. But also, as social workers, sometimes you see that maybe this person has to be helped, so you also talk to the person (C).

When there was no 'match' between the child and the counsellor (s)he was allocated to (i.e. the child did not or could not open up to that counsellor) or when gender-specific problems needed to be tackled, children could also turn to another counsellor.

Other psychosocial activities deemed as essential parts of the rehabilitation centres' programmes were *recreational activities*, such as traditional dances, sports and games, as

> [t]raditional dance and music [were] an important part of the counselling (F).

At times even more prominent was the significance attached to *religion*, *praying* and *religious education*:

> Prayers were considered an important source of comfort (F).

Especially in the Christian-based organisations, the importance of religion can be seen in the amount of time dedicated to it on a weekly basis. In these organisations, every morning, evening and during weekends there was time for prayers:

> Children were given the liberty to go for prayer to the churches of their denomination although every morning all the children would go to the church in [the] mission for morning devotion (A).
> They pray a lot and that's the tool they use for helping children (G).

In the other RCs, praying was also important, but religious activities were mainly conducted during the weekend, especially on Sunday mornings when priests were invited for a mass at the centre (e.g. RRC and GUSCO, which both organised Catholic and Protestant masses), or children were brought to the community to go to church (e.g. in CCF, Caritas, KICWA, Caritas).

Table 2. Overview of the psychosocial support provided during the rehabilitation process in a rehabilitation centre (RC)

Name of Activity	Description	Aim	Used by
Group counselling, drawing	Sometimes children are free to draw whatever they want, at other times they receive a more specific assignment, like 'Draw what is disturbing you/what happened in the bush/what dreams you have for the future.' Afterwards, the drawings are discussed, in group or during individual counselling	It is used as an indirect way of learning what is disturbing the children. Especially for newly arrived children who are not able to talk yet, drawing is often quite effective. It is also used as a first step to individual counselling, in which drawings can be discussed in more detail: 'They draw pictures of things that the rebels always do… in most cases you'll find that they begin telling you [about it]… You find out their feelings about what happened' (C). 'It was another way of exposure' (F).	All RCs
Group counselling, debate	Children discuss on themes like 'How do you react when they call you a rebel?' Depending on the centre, topics were chosen by children or given by social workers, sometimes by both. Other themes often discussed are: life at home before abduction, life in captivity, escape story. Sometimes children are divided in two groups and need to defend different positions.	During debate communication skills and skills such as critical thinking and problem solving are practised: 'It might be like "an educated girl is better than an uneducated" or "conflict can either be through war or resolution, which one is better? War or peaceful?"…There would be proposers and opposers… We [the social workers] listen to them, to guide the discussion' (G). 'You find a reasoning, why, what they think' (E).	All RCs
Group counselling, role play or drama	In small groups, children re-enact their experiences as child soldiers. Other topics were family reunion, life in the IDP camps or the village, and traditional marriage. Most of the time the social workers give them an assignment and after preparation, the children perform their drama in front of the others. In most centres this is followed by a debriefing session because it often evokes intensive reactions: 'Debriefing after the drama was crucial so as not to reinforce the experiences' (F).	It is a useful technique for children who are not able to talk about their experiences. After using this approach some of them opened up: 'We ask them to reason again, what they have learned. What important lessons they have picked from it and how they can now… go ahead…what positive things they have seen' (E). '[They] play in front of the rest. Sometimes even time to laughter when they are dramatising because it's like it's funny but it's painful…Those were ways of making them come out of their trauma. …After the play we [the social workers] would discuss again with them' (B).	All RCs

Name of Activity	Description	Aim	Used by
Group counselling, news analysis	Some children receive the assignment to listen to the radio and tell the other children what they have learned. Afterwards these items are analysed and discussed in group. Children can choose what themes or facts they want to discuss in order to increase their participation level.	Making children familiar with everything that has happened in the world (in Uganda, but also in other countries) during their time in captivity: 'Isolation and information management were some of the techniques used by the LRA to persuade, manipulate and control its members' (F).	Only F
Individual counselling	The child and the social worker (s)he was allocated to sit together and start a casual conversation to learn more about the life story of the child. Building up rapport is important. Sometimes drawing or a technique called 'the life line' is used as a way to start talking. It is also used as one of the ways to prepare children for reunion, sometimes together with other family members: 'There is no particular topic that is always given. It all depends on the kind of problem you see the client is undergoing or what the client has told you about his/her problem' (C).	Children are given the chance to talk about their past and what disturbs them, at their own pace. For some children it is less intimidating to talk with someone without the presence of others. It is used as a way of tackling problems specific to the individual. 'You will have the person open up, then there is a lot of probing to get to know information… not only information that is talked of by the client, but you also have to observe the feelings of the person. So, we keep on exploring together with the client. So it takes some time' (C).	All RCs
Story telling	Children tell each other stories and share their experiences, e.g. about life in captivity or how they are coping. Sometimes they will make up stories to stimulate their creativity.	In this way children learn about what others do to make them feel better (or to heal) and were also made to realise that other children underwent the same experiences while in captivity: '[It] helped others even to heal or to feel better… You also ask that child questions on "How were you able to cope with this?" ' (F).	A, C, F (*)
Guest speakers	People from outside the centre, such as local leaders, are invited to come to the centre. They can talk about life in the IDP camps, for example, so that children who had been abducted for a long time, will be prepared for returning home and learn about what they can expect. Discussions between guest(s) and children are possible.	To make children familiar with different opinions and people. It also extended their knowledge because they could learn new things, certainly when a foreigner visited the centre. Moreover, it improved their communication skills and critical thinking: 'The guest speakers talk about what is expected from the children when they return to the community but also what they should expect in the community. It's not the same community they left, that they are going back to. Things have changed' (C).	A, C, F (**)

Name of Activity	Description	Aim	Used by
Radio	Children are brought to a radio station and talk, live on the radio, about their experiences with the LRA. The children staying behind in the centre listen to the programme. Sometimes other guests (such as community members) are invited in order to make a discussion between the guest(s) and the children possible.	Radio talks are used in order to convince commanders still in the bush to surrender and prove to children in captivity that they will not be killed by community members when they escape (as the LRA made them to believe). It also serves as a sensitisation strategy, to inform the community about the plight of the abducted children and a way of letting parents know their children have returned: 'Major reasons were: first, to sensitise the community about the plight of FAC; secondly, we wanted to use these children to indirectly talk to fellow children they left in captivity or even the commanders, they appealed to them to come home, take advantage of the amnesty which was granted; and then thirdly, through participation, their community members or relatives or parents got to know their children were back' (F). 'They would go and make an appeal, calling those ones still in captivity to come back' (G).	D, F, G
Video shows	Informative videos (e.g. on HIV or a documentary on past experiences) or entertainment videos (e.g. comedies) are shown.	Informative videos are used to teach children new things; the entertainment videos are recreational, for fun. Afterwards there was a discussion of the films: 'We also had a film to counsel them and a film [on] Jesus's suffering' (B). 'Children from outside come and join and sit together, that breaks the barrier [with the community]' (D).	A, B, D, E, F
Recreational activities: sports & games	Children are free to play sports like football and netball or games like Ludo (local games). Sometimes children from the community are invited to come to play together or football competitions are organised as a way of involving the community.	These activities produce stress release: they give them the opportunity to be children again and create a context in which social interaction is enforced and where they can learn social skills (stimulate openness). When involving the community, it is a good way of promoting integration and reducing the level of stigmatisation. It is an important tool for assessing the level of trauma. Once this goes down, the child will be more social and will start to play: 'In these activities one is regaining their self-esteem' (D). 'Promote healing and openness with children' (E). 'We find out how they [the children] are relating, interacting' (E).	All RCs

Name of Activity	Description	Aim	Used by
Recreational activities: music & dance	Children are free to dance and play/make music, at other times they receive classes in traditional dance. Some centres invite community members to participate. It is often performed in front of visitors as a welcome.	It is supposed to reduce the level of stress. Dancing is important in Ugandan culture as it provides an identity and creates a feeling of togetherness. It is an important tool for assessing the level of trauma; once this goes down, you see children participating more: 'It's very very important…in most cases they act on what has been taking place on them… So it's the process of kind of getting out of such kind of problems. We believe in the saying "forgive and forget, that is not true, but you forgive and remember, but your remembering has to be in a good way"' (C). 'We find out how they [the children] are relating, interacting' (E). 'They create a feeling of togetherness and happiness and are a way of setting free people' (F). 'In these activities one is regaining their self-esteem' (D).	All RCs
Religious education – prayers	In Catholic-based RCs, praying is conducted every morning and/or evening and on Sunday. In other centres children can go to a church on Sunday or a priest is invited to come to the centre.	Praying provides emotional support, encourages healing and enables children to keep faith in the future: 'We need to be very open to the belief system of the child' (D). 'And even during devotion, some of them open up' (B). 'Prayers were considered an important source of comfort' (F). 'Religion plays a very pertinent part, role in rehabilitating these children or in changing their mind… It's from the religious teaching that good attributes are always sealing them' (E).	All RCs
Visit something	Visiting the university, schools or important places in the district.	Intention to teach children something and orient them to the future, e.g. when they see the other children in school or at the university, it stimulates them to study and focus on their education: 'We realised that the system of outing was also somehow helpful to them… we took them just to the school and see and they took interest and they are there…[this boy] is now in S3' (G).	D, G

Notes:
* In the other RCs it was not seen as a separate activity, but as part of the group counselling (debate).
** In the other RCs guests were welcomed and could participate during debates, but they were not specifically invited to do this.

3.1.2. Leaving the Rehabilitation Centre

While the psychological and physical healing at the centre continued, efforts were made to *trace* the *family* of the children. In order to make this possible, information about the child (such as name, age, names of parents and place of living before abduction) was registered as soon as they arrived at the centre. When children were evaluated as 'recovered' (i.e. when cured physically and mentally, no longer showing any symptoms and interacting freely with other children and staff), children were seen as ready to leave the centre and to be reunited with their family. In all centres the *mean duration* of children staying there took from two or three weeks (e.g. CPA Lira as mainly 'transit' centre) to two (e.g., Caritas, GUSCO, KICWA, RRC) or three months (e.g. CCF, WV). However, this period was not static as the time children needed to recover varied greatly. Especially pregnant women/girls or children who were seriously injured or sick could stay longer.

Before children were reunited, *family (and community) visits* were organised in order to prepare them for the return of their child and to determine their readiness to receive the child:

> We tell them the life experiences of these children. How they may behave one time if they go back home… Some can be still having queer behaviour (B).
> To brief them on what the child has gone through and what they should expect (C).

But also the child was prepared for his/her reunion:

> We would talk to the child that very soon we are going to take you back to the family. And life in the family is abc, you'll meet these challenges and you'll need this kind of support from the family… So that is how you should go about it when you meet those kinds of challenges (B).

At the time of reunion the child received a *reunification or resettlement package*, mostly consisting of household goods and sometimes money:

> We provide them saucepans, food items which include sugar, beans, cooking oil, … mattress, blanket, plates, cups… those are the packages that we have to make sure they go back with to the community (C).

The child also received an *amnesty certificate* from the government in which it was declared the child would never be prosecuted for what (s)he did while in the LRA.

Caritas, CPA, KICWA and GUSCO supported *traditional cleansing ceremonies* (e.g. slaughtering a goat or 'Moyo Tipu') (mainly) financially, since they acknowledged the importance of these rituals within Ugandan culture. The rituals were performed within the community at the return of the child:

> Such rituals are very powerful, even [more than] the counselling we were doing... providing this child recovery. It's not harmful... it's a way of the community showing that "we accept you back" (D).

All centres tried to *follow up the children* in order to evaluate their physical, social and psychological functioning and their reintegration within the community. However, many practical constraints (such as insecurity, lack of staff and funding, difficulties in tracing the child) made follow-up at that time nearly impossible. Follow-ups were therefore mainly performed after the war ended, although quite differently. To illustrate, we give three examples. In CPA, follow-ups were first conducted by social workers and later handed over to Parent Support Groups to conduct follow-ups every two months – up to date. In Caritas, children were followed up by staff (with the support of Community Resource Persons – trained catechists and other devoted community members) two weeks after reunion, then after one month and a last time after three months. In GUSCO, children were followed up by social workers every three months during the first year. There are thus clear differences in the persons responsible for conducting the follow-ups, their frequency and the duration of the follow-up period.

3.2. AFTER CLOSING DOWN THE CENTRE

Nearly all RCs closed in 2006 or 2007, and no longer exist as such, although they are still prepared to receive new returning child soldiers. As a result, all started to conduct outreach activities in the communities, while the provision of psychosocial support became less prominent in their programmes. However, there are some exceptions (e.g. CPA, WV), as some organisations followed up the FAC they rehabilitated for a long time (e.g. GUSCO, CPA) or have been working on community building through cleansing ceremonies or traditional dances (e.g. Caritas). Especially CPA puts great effort into psychosocial activities, as they still provide counselling services in the community through Parent Support Groups. Overall, the centres currently concentrate on educational support through paying school fees (e.g. RRC, CCF, Caritas) or providing school packages (e.g. GUSCO, KICWA, RRC), and on income-generating activities and vocational training (e.g. WV, GUSCO, CCF, Caritas, RRC). Child protection (e.g. GUSCO, CCF), peacebuilding (e.g. CPA), and advocacy and awareness campaigns (e.g. GUSCO, CCF, KICWA, Caritas) are some other programmes frequently implemented. Sensitisation initiatives are less common at the moment as stigmatisation is said to be less of a problem:

> I don't deny the fact that it is there, ... but it's not common (C).

Furthermore, all centres have enlarged their scope of action. While in the past they focused exclusively on FAC, they have now included 'war-affected' and especially 'the most vulnerable children' (e.g. child-headed households, orphans and child mothers). Others are explicitly tackling the community by taking families as their central focus (e.g. Caritas).

3.3. LESSONS LEARNED

The second aim of this paper is to gain more insight into the lessons that can be drawn from the experiences of staff members of RCs in northern Uganda, focusing on the problems staff experienced, the good things to do when working with FAC and what better to avoid, necessary conditions for providing successful inpatient support, and, based on their own experience, how staff would handle a new emergency situation.

3.3.1. Problems Encountered

The problem mentioned most by all staff members was the shortage of financial resources RCs had at their disposal (table 3), having important implications for both the structural and organisational levels and the day-to-day working of the centre. Secondly, because of the high workload, because they were constantly confronted with the horrible stories of the children, because of a lack of training options for staff and of psychological support for social workers, many became traumatised themselves or were burnt out. Also, staff felt they were not sufficiently qualified to handle the most traumatised children or those wanting to return to the LRA. Furthermore, the continuation of the war, together with the high level of insecurity, adversely affected their work, for example the inability to follow up reintegrated FAC. Finally, stigmatisation turned out to be quite common within the community, as several FAC were bullied or accused of being rebels. However, the RCs only addressed this problem at a later stage, mainly after the centres were closed.

Table 3. Problems encountered when rehabilitating and reintegrating former child soldiers

Problem	Leads to	Consequences for the Rehabilitation and Reintegration Process
Lack of available financial resources	– Too little logistical and structural support – Availability of (trained) staff, especially social workers, was limited – Psychological support to social workers and other staff and opportunities to take some time off were all absent – Training options were very few – Sensitisation of family and community was rarely undertaken (but more frequently near the closure of the centres)	– Not enough means to provide educational/economic support (IGA, vocational, livelihood) to all rehabilitated children Lack of proper buildings, dormitories, … – High workload (even more in combination with the large number of children residing at the centre) – No or less frequent follow-up of children – Traumatised staff or burn-out, so even fewer staff available – Difficulties in handling the most traumatised children or those wanting to return to the LRA (cf. Stockholm Syndrome) – Stigmatisation of FAC
Insecurity situation and long term war	– Dangerous to travel without being escorted by the UPDF – People were forced to move to IDP camps – Civilians and children fear becoming victims of the LRA; FAC fear re-abduction – children lie about their names or the name of their village – Collapse of the northern Uganda economy and poverty – Eroded traditional cultural values (e.g. respect for elders and the importance of family bonds)	– Difficult to conduct family visits and follow-up and to tackle stigmatisation – Tracing family members became more difficult – use of radio or family networks instead – Tracing of family members was complicated – (Extended) families are less eager to take care of (orphaned) FAC as they already have such limited means for their own children. They often need to be persuaded to take responsibility for their family members

3.3.2. *Good and Bad Practices*

When working in a RC one should be aware that in the end, all children must return home. All RCs therefore found it important to involve the family even when children were still staying in the centre (Table 4). Inviting parents to come to the centre and providing family counselling to prepare both family and child for its return was a strategy used by all RCs. Other activities, such as football competitions or traditional dances, were also organised in which both children staying at the centre and community members were involved (e.g. Caritas, GUSCO), to promote interaction between children and communities, sensitise communities and families and reduce stigmatisation.

Table 4. Some good and bad practices when rehabilitating and reintegrating FAC

Good Practices	Bad Practices
– Involving family and community members (e.g. family counselling, inviting them to join activities at the centre) – Implementing culturally appropriate activities (e.g. traditional dances) – Sensitising family and community to the plight of FAC and making sure they know their responsibilities – Providing support to FAC and other vulnerable children – Provision of educational support, IGA or vocational training to earn an income – Community-based support	– Promise children things you cannot fulfil. Building up rapport with the children is difficult and when promises cannot be met, they lose trust – Staff/social workers getting too much involved in their job → risk of becoming traumatised – Life in the RCs not resembling life in the community or camp – Provision of reunification packages only to FAC – Not following up FAC

Although staff made tremendous efforts, these efforts sometimes also had negative consequences. Staff realised that certain of their actions promoted stigmatisation rather than reducing it, such as the provision of reunification packages and other support, as, for example, sometimes brothers or sisters of a former child soldier could not go to school, leading to many conflicts and jealousy within families and communities:

> There are some people within the community that see that the packages that are given, they are kind of reward for the atrocities done by the FAC (C).

Furthermore, as described above, too few follow-ups were conducted during the war, which was probably one of the reasons why the problem of stigmatisation became so widespread.

In several RCs (e.g. CPA, GUSCO, KICWA) staff talked about the difficulties children had in adapting to life in the community after staying at the centre for a couple of weeks or months. In the RCs, children had a place to stay, received three meals a day, and had an entire programme. When returning home, they had to sleep on the ground, received only one meal a day and were required to work much harder. Life therefore looked completely different for FAC once they were home. Not surprisingly, many of them found it hard to adjust to life at home and some even asked to return to the centre.

> There are cases that always come back to the centre (B).
> 'They think life should continue [as] in the centre… The weakness of the centre-based is sometimes that you create an artificial situation and the level is slightly higher than the level of general lifestyle that exists in the communities' (D).

KICWA tried to overcome this gap through, for example, using not stone buildings but grass-thatched houses to sleep in:

> It's just a traditional setting that they will find definitely in the community. So that's why… we don't have a very modern structure, we are not very institutional, … because it's also part of the rehabilitation process for these children.

In all centres the problem was also tackled by preparing and explaining to children how they would be living in the community and by keeping the time children stayed at the centre as short as possible.

4. DISCUSSION

In this section, we want to take a more critical stance in looking at the results presented above. As in the previous part of our paper, quotations from staff members are used to elaborate our findings. To conclude, some critical remarks and limitations concerning our own research will be outlined.

4.1. MAIN GOALS OF INPATIENT CARE

To understand how the abovementioned programmes were developed and why certain activities were chosen, it is important to know more about the underlying ideas guiding the rehabilitation and reintegration of FAC. This first part of our discussion will therefore be build up around the main goals staff strived to accomplish during the stay of FAC at their centres. The two overall and most central goals stated in all RCs are 'fostering the healing of children' (B), physically, socially and mentally; and preparing them for living in the community or getting them used to community life:

> We prepare them… we tell them "This is exactly what might happen to you and as we have discussed, go and put it into practice" (G).

Furthermore, the following goals were also outlined: building up rapport and trust – 'build up confidence in these children' (D); and 'interact among another' (E):

> [They] interact freely with the children in the centre and outside the centre (D).

In the following paragraphs these goals are linked with the activities the RCs organised, as described in the section on results.

First, one of the central tasks for children staying at a RC was to *recover* from the trauma they had gone through, physically, socially and psychologically. All activities in the centre were considered as being helpful in achieving this goal, not only counselling and religious activities, but even recreational activities, welcoming children and the ritual of the burning of clothes. However, it is generally admitted that the childrens' stay at the centre was only the start of a long-term process:

> Rehabilitation itself is a process; we cannot claim that once a child stays at a centre, the child is fully rehabilitated. We just start the process and we expected to continue while the child is in the community. So to some extent, they get rehabilitated, but it … has to continue in the community (D).

This also means that reintegration is a communal process and 'parents need to take up their responsibilities' (E), which is one of the reasons why frequent follow-up of the children is so important to further guiding this process.[120] However, other authors suggest that the time in the centre is too short to make the positive modelling by the staff effective and long-lasting.[121]

Second, all centres wanted to reorientate children and reaccustom them to *daily life in the community* by inducing responsible and culturally approved behaviour. Boothby and colleagues[122] talk about 'establishing appropriate codes of conduct' and Veale and Stavrou[123] about 'facilitating social reintegration'. Contrary to the tasks they were forced to conduct while in the bush, such as looting or killing

---

120 T.S. Betancourt, 'Child soldiers: Reintegration, pathways to recovery, and reflections from the field', (2008) 29 2 *Journal of Developmental & Behavioral Pediatrics*, 138–141; Wessells, *supra* note 14.

121 N. Boothby, J. Crawford and J. Halperin, *Mozambique Child Soldier Life Outcome Study: Lessons Learned in Rehabilitation and Reintegration Efforts*, Colombia University and Save the Children Uganda, 2006, see at http//www.forcedmigration.org.

122 Ibid.

123 Veale and Stavrou, *supra* note 29.

people, children now learned about the different roles they could fulfil within the community. They were given 'normal' responsibilities such as involvement in household tasks (cooking, cleaning). Moreover, the educational and vocational support these centres provided was another way to prepare FAC for living in the community. Apart from this practical support, children were also prepared during counselling sessions, for example when discussing themes such as how to react when civilians call you a rebel. One of the guiding principles of RCs, namely to treat children in their district of origin, was oriented towards the goal of getting children used to common local cultural practices and traditions, and to help to strengthen family bonds, as family members could visit their children while they were still at the centre.

Third, as most of the children were very suspicious at their arrival, *building up rapport and confidence* was another important goal during the first days and weeks children were at the centre. Creating a safe and structured environment was seen as a good way of creating predictability, gaining their trust and promoting their rehabilitation:

> This creates a healing environment that promotes recovery at a faster rate (A).

From morning till evening, a variety of activities were organised (timetables were used to promote the transparency and predictability of the daily/weekly routine) in order to create this structured environment and to help children in making the transition from living with the rebels to a 'normal' life in the community:

> We establish a routine in the life of the child... they must be busy throughout the day (D).

Creating this structured environment was also a precondition for making counselling possible. It is evident that children who are very suspicious will not easily open up.[124] Furthermore, briefing and explaining to children what they can expect from their stay demystified the role of RCs even further:

> You need to brief these new arrivals on what is normally being done in the centre so that they don't feel like it is a strange thing or they are not safe (G).

124 De Temmerman, *supra* note 3.

Predictability and structure are indeed recognised as important preconditions when working with traumatised children[125] as it can improve their engagement and participation level.[126]

Fourth, as many children had been abducted for a long time and had therefore lost many years of their childhood, another reason for treating them by means of inpatient support was to give them time to *interact with each other* and *to behave like other children*:

> Just to interact among themselves without any activity. So that they know about each other, share also their experiences. Because in captivity, they don't have time to share those experiences (C).

Staff believed that by involving children in (age-appropriate) recreational activities, such as games, sports, dance and music, the level of trauma could be reduced and they could open up. Play activities were also considered to help children to build up self-esteem and to tell their story:[127]

> Recreational activities that can promote healing and openness with children and this can be games, sport and traditional dances. ... The aspect of dance in the community here is quite paramount... It plays a big role in building a person, in providing an identity to a person (E).

4.2. IMPORTANT LESSONS TO TAKE INTO CONSIDERATION WHEN DEVELOPING REHABILITATION AND REINTEGRATION PROGRAMMES FOR FAC

To conclude this paper, we summarise the most important aspects or preconditions deemed essential according to staff members of RCs for promoting the successful rehabilitation and reintegration of FAC (see Table 5).

---

125 B.D. Perry and I. Azad, 'Posttraumatic stress disorders in children and adolescents', (1999) 11 4 *Current Opinion in Pediatrics*, 310–316.

126 L. Hanney and K. Kozlowska, 'Clinical practice and family therapy history – healing traumatized children: Creating illustrated storybooks in family therapy', (2002) 41 1 *Family Process*, 37–66.

127 J. Donnelly, 'Art therapy with families', in A. Gilroy and D. Waller (eds.), *Art therapy: A handbook,* Open University Press, Philadelphia, 1992, 125–139; J. Lantz and K.A. Alford, 'Art in existential psychotherapy with couples and families', (1995) 17 3 *Contemporary Family Therapy*, 331–342; K. Kozlowska and L. Hanney, 'An art therapy group for children traumatized by parental violence and separation', (2001) 6 *Clinical Child Psychology & Psychiatry*, 49–78.

Table 5. Preconditions for the successful rehabilitation and reintegration of FAC

Rehabilitation	Reintegration
– Availability of sufficient financial and structural means (e.g. medical equipment, trained staff, psychological support to staff, …). – Building up rapport with the child so that (s)he can start to trust you – importance of debriefing and explaining. – Provide support that is culturally specific and meaningful to the children, e.g. using music and dance. – Provide children with educational support, IGA or vocational training. – Do not keep children at the centre for too long. They must be sent home as soon as possible because 'it's at home the further healing can take place. Rehabilitation is only the first step of this process' (D). – Involve parents and community members and make them realise they have to take up their role as caregivers. – Being supported by the government, UPDF, the community, …	– Do not focus all the support on FAC, but pay attention to the needs of other vulnerable and war-affected children. – Provide educational support, livelihoods, IGA or vocational training to vulnerable or war-affected children, not only to FAC. – Sensitise the community to the plight of FAC so that people understand their children were *forced* to kill people and commit other atrocities (e.g. using radio programmes, video shows, drama, community debates, …) and start with it as early as possible. – Organise activities that involve FAC and other community members in order to bring people together again and rebuild trust in each other. – Support provided by different organisations should be better coordinated and built on the resources or structures (for providing support) already available in the community. – Everything that is done must be in the best interests of the child and one must show respect for the child. – Pay attention to culturally specific ways of healing, e.g. traditional healing ceremonies.

One of the most essential and often stated aspects that needs to be taken into account when developing rehabilitation and reintegration programmes for FAC, are *culturally relevant practices and beliefs,* especially if the children believe in them. In Uganda, this can be seen in the need to treat children as much as possible in the way they will be treated in the general community, thus corresponding to the local culture. It is also reflected in the importance attached to traditional healing or cleansing rituals. Although there were some differences between the RCs, most of them provided (financial) support for performing these rituals at the return of the child:

> Rituals are performed as ways of acceptance into the community (D).

When developing programmes, it is important to be aware of and familiar with local beliefs as they can either promote or constrain the healing of the children. Furthermore, all staff agreed that when a new emergency situation occurred, traditional practices would definitely need to be there and they would even include them more frequently than they had been doing in the past:

> The counselling aspect… I would try to uplift it a lot more from the western to cultural (E).

In all centres the importance of *explaining and debriefing children* on every activity was mentioned, merely because most children had been 'brainwashed' by the LRA, as they were told they would be killed by RCs' staff or by community members. This debriefing was especially important during the 'burning clothes' ceremony and after role plays.

It's evident that sufficient financial *means* are essential for good programming, both for the children and the staff. The literature on trauma notes that working with traumatised children can have a profound effect on *health care providers* as they may suffer from mental health problems, such as compassion fatigue.[128] Organisations should therefore not limit funding for the provision of support to staff. If there are not enough staff (emotionally) available, children will not be supported properly and may suffer even more. Furthermore, enough funds should be made available to provide *educational support, livelihoods, IGA or vocational training,* as these are seen as one of the most important strategies for reintegrating FAC successfully, because they orientate children to the future or provide them with a way of gaining an income and living independently.[129]

128 A. Dyregrov and J.T. Mitchell, 'Work with traumatized children – Psychological effects and coping strategies', (1992) 5 1 *Journal of Traumatic Stress*, 5–17; T. Woodard Meyers and T.A. Comille, 'The trauma of working with traumatized children', in C.R. Figley (ed.), *Treating compassion fatigue,* Psychosocial Stress Series, Routledge, US, 2002, 39–56.

129 Wessells, *supra* note 14.

Moreover, education and skills training – based on good and rational choices[130] – were the types of support most appreciated by Ugandan youth.[131] However, making good choices in what kind of vocational training is provided turns out to be very important (see also[132]). In Uganda many women were given training in tailoring. However, other studies found it was difficult for Ugandan youth to earn an income from skills learned in this form of vocational training.[133] These authors therefore suggest that the focus should be more on agriculture and herding, as these were traditionally the way Ugandan people earned an income. Apart from these forms of support, sufficient financial means must also be made available to address the underlying and often unmet mental health needs of FAC and other community members.[134]

The rehabilitation and reintegration of FAC are seen as a community-based process in which *cooperation* is very important. Good cooperation between the RCs and the different stakeholders (e.g. UPDF, local leaders, communities, other aid organisations) is therefore indispensable. Apparently, this was not always the case in the past. At certain moments, RCs were rather working alongside each other instead of together, so some children could benefit several times from support, while others never received any. Sometimes there was even competition between RCs to receive the highest number of children and thus extract more funding.

Cooperation with the community is also crucial as children need to return to the communities. By preparing families of FAC and the surrounding community for the return of the child, and by organising several sensitisation and advocacy meetings, the reintegration of FAC can be promoted and thus reduce the level of stigmatisation.[135] Furthermore, it is important to start as soon as possible with sensitisation initiatives and follow up FAC thoroughly, so that if problems occur, they can be handled straight away.[136] Another way to limit the level of stigmatisation is by not restricting support only to FAC. It is important to provide services based on the needs of people rather than, as has been the case in the past, taking the abduction status as a precondition for receiving aid.[137]

---

130 Meek and Malan, *supra* note 37; Veale and Stavrou, *supra* note 29.

131 Veale and Stavrou, ibid.

132 Meek and Malan, *supra* note 37.

133 Annan et al., *supra* note 8.

134 Betancourt, *supra* note 60.

135 Meek and Malan, *supra* note 37.

136 Coalition to Stop the Use of Child Soldiers, *supra* note 5; S. Skarbek-Borowska and G.W. Skarbek-Borowski, 'Child Soldiers', in R.E. Antosia and J.D. Cahill (eds.), *Handbook of Bioterrorism and Disaster Medicine*, Springer, US, 2006, 401–404.

137 Annan et al., *supra* note 8; Betancourt, *supra* note 60.

Lastly, we want to stress that this description of the RCs' activities may create the impression that everything was strictly organised and planned. However, as the RCs operated during times of high insecurity, this was clearly not the case. Sometimes new children arrived in large numbers and staff needed to help them immediately, so that other activities could not be performed as there were too few staff members available. The things described in this article are therefore not always 'real' descriptions of how these centres actually worked, but rather, 'ideal' ways of working staff strived for. However, we must clearly state that our interviewees expressed a lot of sympathy with and respect for the children and although they had few means and difficult working conditions, they were trying the best they could to help FAC.

4.3. LIMITATIONS OF OUR RESEARCH

The study is limited as it was sometimes difficult to find staff who worked in the centre during the war, because of the high level of staff turnover, leading on the other hand also to the fact that we could interview staff members that had worked in different organisations. Further, our interviews could have been constrained by some language barriers and interviewees' time constraints, although all participants were very open to participating and to sharing information. Last, in this paper we have focused on the perceptions of staff exclusively and the perspective of the beneficiaries is therefore lacking.

LESSONS LEARNT FROM THE REHABILITATION AND REINTEGRATION OF GIRL MOTHERS IN NORTHERN UGANDA: A CASE-STUDY FROM GULU DISTRICT

Sarah Kamya and Charles N. Bwana

1. INTRODUCTION

There is a widespread consensus on the critical importance of addressing the protection and promotion of the rights of the girl child. However, girls still bear the worst human rights abuses, during and after armed conflict,[1] which have mental, emotional, spiritual, physical and material repercussions. These violations include abduction, forced removal from families, forced recruitment of children into fighting forces and a wide range of physical and sexual violations, including rape, enforced pregnancy, forced prostitution, forced marriage and forced child-bearing. This is especially true for girls who return from captivity with children who are considered particularly vulnerable.[2] The result has been untold suffering and trauma. This has implications for the delivery of psychosocial support services for the girls as stipulated in Article 39 of the Convention on the Rights of the Child (CRC).[3]

The northern part of Uganda has been beset by conflict for the last 22 years as a result of the insurgency mainly of the Lord's Resistance Army (LRA), one of Africa's most notorious and brutal wars. The conflict in northern Uganda has been devastating and has had an adverse impact on people's lives; many people, especially women and girls, have been abducted, raped, tortured and even killed.

1 D. Mazurana and K. Karlson, 'From Combat to Community: Women and Girls of Sierra Leone,' in W.W.P.P. Commission (ed.), *Washington DC: Women Waging Peace Policy Commission*, 2006.

2 UNICEF, *The state of the World's Children 2006: Excluded and Invisible*, New York, 2006.

3 UN Convention on the Rights of the Child (CRC), see at www.unicef.org.uk/crc?utm_source=google&utm_medium=cpc&utm_campaign=General_DM_OtherCRC&utm_term=uncrc%201989.

Due to the conflict in northern Uganda, up to 2 million people (80%) have been displaced and forced to live in neglected internally displaced persons camps; these have been displaced within districts of Gulu, Kitgum, Pader, Lira, Apac, Soroti, Kaberamaido and Adjumani.[4] Displacement has led to the erosion of the Acholi culture, destruction of individuals, families and communities, reinforcement of feelings of economic and political marginalisation, and loss of property (ibid.). Although not as numerous as boys, girls have been abducted in large numbers by the Lord's Resistance Army (LRA), which has been waging war against the Government of Uganda since 1987. Of an estimated 38,000 children abducted by the LRA since the beginning of the conflict, 7,500 are girls and 1,000 are "girl mothers" who conceived children while in captivity.[5]

This paper discusses the lessons learnt from the reintegration and rehabilitation of girl mothers in northern Uganda. The lessons are reflected through the achievements of and challenges faced by the stakeholders and the experiences of the girl mothers in accessing psychosocial support services and reintegrating into the community.

2. METHODS

The study was carried out in Gulu District, one of the districts which have been adversely affected by war in northern Uganda. Gulu District has traditionally been widely acknowledged as the regional capital of the northern region. The study was cross-sectional in nature and essentially used qualitative research methods. The study population consisted of returnee girl mothers, practitioners (social workers), key informants and parents/ guardians. These were purposely selected to ensure that we interviewed people who had adequate knowledge and played a critical role in the rehabilitation and reintegration of girl mothers in northern Uganda.

During August 2007, we conducted twenty in-depth interviews in Gulu District with girl mothers aged 15 to 18 years from reception centres such as GUSCO and World Vision, a Women's Development centre that was involved in training girls in different skills such as numeracy, tailoring and home management, and from schools such as Laroo Boarding School, which was training children affected by war.

---

4 Z. Lomo and L. Hovil, *Behind the Violence: The War in Northern Uganda*, Institute for Security Studies, 2004.

5 Bureau of Democracy, Human Rights and Labor, *Country Reports on Human Rights Practices 2005*, 8 March 2005. See at www.state.gov/g/drl/rls/hrrpt/2005/.

Secondly, three focus group discussions were conducted to obtain information about the rehabilitation and reintegration experiences of the girls. Two of these focus group discussions were conducted with girl mothers (aged 15 to 18 years), each consisting of eight participants; one of these was held in Awer IDP-camp (camp for Internally Displaced Persons), 13 km from Gulu municipality, while another was held in Gulu municipality. One focus group of ten parents and guardians, both males and females of between 30 to 45 years of age was conducted to obtain information about their views relating to the rehabilitation and reintegration of their daughters.

Thirdly, semi-structured interviews were held with ten key informants such as Government and NGO officials, practitioners and opinion leaders. The Government officials included the District Disaster Committee chairman, who was in charge of coordinating emergencies such as children returning from captivity, and one male head teacher. On the other hand, the NGO officials included three male programme managers (32–37 years old) from organisations such as World Vision, GUSCO (Gulu Support the Children Organisation) and CPA (Concerned Parents Association), and one female programme coordinator from the Mother to Daughter Project, who were involved in psychosocial support of girl mothers. The study also included two female social workers (25–30 years old) from World Vision and GUSCO reception centres, who worked as counsellors at the same time. Two male community leaders, comprising a County Chief (35 years old) and a camp leader (36 years old) from Awer IDP-camp, were also subjected to key informant interviews. These played a large role in protecting the rights of children, ensuring the safety and welfare of the returnee children and other children affected by the LRA war.

In order to obtain information from the girls, we ensured that the girls were participating of their own free will and that their rights were fully respected in the research process. This was achieved by reading out the consent form before the beginning of the interviews. Furthermore, we carefully explained to the children the aim and methods, as well as the intended and possible outcomes of the research. Furthermore, it is important to note that interviews with girls were carried out by female researchers to avoid any bias in the data obtained and to ensure that the girls were comfortable. Interviews with other respondents were conducted by both male and female researchers.

3. FINDINGS

This section presents and interprets results and discusses the lessons learnt from the rehabilitation and reintegration of formerly abducted girl mothers.

It is important to note that during the war, the girls were subjected to violations of their rights. The results from the focus group discussions revealed that most girls were abducted between 1998–2004, at the tender age of 8 to 16 years. Being abducted at such an age made them vulnerable and this exposed them to more violations, such as sexual violation through forced marriage, forced pregnancy and forced child-bearing. Consequently, the majority of the girls experienced unwanted/forced pregnancies through forced sex and delivered between one to three children at the young age of 14 to 17 years.

3.1. REHABILITATION AND REINTEGRATION SERVICES

The findings revealed that the girls who reported to the reception centres commonly displayed physical and psychological problems. The physical problems included ill health, with about 30% of the girl mothers suffering from the consequences of early delivery of children such as abdominal pains, sexually transmitted diseases such as HIV/AIDS, swollen legs due to walking long distances, chest pain, broken limbs or dislocated jaws (children with disabilities). One of the social workers working in the Gulu Support The Children's Organisation (GUSCO) reported that the children of the girl mothers looked malnourished and generally unhealthy. Furthermore, she indicated that some girl mothers had behavioural problems, such as fighting and stealing, while others were experiencing lack of sleep, nightmares, hallucinations, fear, aggressiveness, feelings of revenge, bed wetting and overeating. These problems justified psychosocial support for the girl mothers to ensure their recovery. As a consequence, most of the reception centres emphasised the needs of "girl mothers" as a special group. The reception centres provided these girl mothers mainly with basic requirements, such as clothing and food, medical services, counselling services, and class therapy through which the girl mothers were equipped with writing and numeracy skills. This method of rehabilitation also helped the girl mothers to get used to a school environment in case they were to go back to school when they returned to their communities. The girl mothers who returned from captivity with mental problems were referred to the psychiatric department at Gulu Independent Hospital. In addition, child resilience programmes were put in place at some of these reception centres to help the girl mothers to recover from trauma.

The study also found out that, while at the reception centres, the girl mothers were also prepared by the counsellors and other staff to go back to their communities. The preparations mainly included family tracing, family reunification, traditional rituals, apprenticeship and skills training. Although some parents were identified and informed about their daughters, they refused to go to the centres to meet them, especially when they learnt that they had come back with children born in captivity. Findings from interviews with the Government and NGO officials indicated that reunification of the girl mothers with their families was difficult compared to that of the boys. This was attributed to the negative attitude of the parents towards the girls. One of the programme co-ordinators of the Young Mothers project reported that the boys were more easily accepted by the parents than the girls, mainly because the latter had children. Such negative attitudes can be attributed to the parents' fear and shame of being associated with formerly abducted children, who were expected to have committed atrocities during the war, and with those who came back with children. On the other hand, such attitudes raise questions about the nature of the counselling obtained by the families and the parents' perceptions of counselling.

3.2. CHALLENGES OF SERVICE PROVIDERS

In providing rehabilitation and reintegration services, the Government and NGO officials faced several challenges, including those discussed below.

First, most organisations faced a problem of duplication of services. They have focused on tailoring as a form of skills training, and, consequently, the majority of girls from different organisations have been trained as tailors. This has implications for the job market in Gulu and other districts in northern Uganda. Tailoring was the norm at the reception centres and vocational institutes. Yet the organisations could have encouraged the girls to go for other skills. In addition to the reception centres, there are several vocational institutes in Gulu town which also equipped girls with tailoring skills. Duplication of services can be attributed to donor support, in terms of which the NGOs have to follow the principles of the donors. If the donors were interested in offering skills training in tailoring then the organisations had to focus on equipping the girls with tailoring skills.

Secondly, one of the Government officials expressed the view that some of the skills which were provided at the centres, such as tailoring, catering and hairdressing, could not match with opportunities in the rural economy. Having observed this anomaly, he even considered retraining the abductees. This implies that returnees should have been equipped with skills which were relevant to their needs and suited to their environment. The organisations should have exposed the girls and other children to skills which were applicable to both the rural and urban areas. Today, many people, including the young women, have gone back to their villages, but the above-mentioned skills are not relevant unless they have had some training in livelihood strategies.

Thirdly, the Government and NGO personnel reported that they were constrained by inadequate resources in terms of funds and manpower. In its efforts to provide rehabilitation and reintegration services, the Government had very few staff (community development assistants) from the local government to oversee all the IDP-camps in an entire sub-county. Furthermore, there were very limited funds for reintegration interventions. The NGOs were also constrained by having few members of staff on the ground to handle the increasing number of children returning from captivity. This also had implications for funding to ensure the provision of adequate psychosocial support services at the centres.

Fourthly, one of the greatest challenges for the service providers was to establish what worked best for the rehabilitation of the girls and other returnee children, whether Western-based approaches or traditional approaches. During the semi-structured interviews, some Government and NGO officials indicated that traditional methods of rehabilitation were better, because once one goes through the traditional cleansing rituals, that person is allowed to put the past behind him. Traditional methods, such as burning clothes, thus symbolise forgetting about the past and starting a new life. This contradicts with Western approaches to rehabilitation, which generally emphasise recalling of the experiences one went through and encouraging the clients or victims to talk about their experiences. The service providers in the NGOs and Government combined the two approaches. However, it is not clear which approach works better in the rehabilitation of returnee girl mothers.

Lastly, the social workers/counsellors who worked with returnee children at the World Vision and GUSCO reception centres reported that some girl mothers had behavioural problems, such as fighting and stealing other people's property, while other girls had mental problems and suicidal tendencies. Behavioural problems were not limited to the reception centre environment; the girls also experienced them when they returned to the community. For example, when some of the girls went back to the community, they still thought about killing other people. This is illustrated by one key informant who reported that there was a certain returnee girl who went to dig with her mother and sister. As soon as the mother left them behind in the garden, the girl chopped her sister into pieces. This shows that handling such cases is a great challenge for the service providers.

3.3. REINTEGRATION CHALLENGES OF GIRL MOTHERS

The girl mothers had the opportunity to access psychosocial support, especially from reception centres. The reception centres were set up to provide first a safe area for the girl mothers and other returnees where they could adjust to the transition from the LRA to the IDP-camps. Secondly, they were set up to provide space for people returning from the LRA.[6] At the reception centres, there was

6 T. Allen and M. Schomerus, *A Hard Homing Lesson Learnt from the Reception Centre process in Northern Uganda, An independent Study*, Management Systems International, 2006.

security and cover from any attacks of rebels. However, when most girls left the reception centres they moved to a different or changed environment, "the community", in which they faced huge reintegration challenges. These are discussed below.

One of the programme coordinators said that when the girl mothers moved from the centres to the community, namely camps, camp life and settlement proved to be incompatible. Movement from the reception centres to the community raised questions such as "reintegration into what kind of community"? For example, Barth,[7]who studied female fighters in Eritrea, and Veale and Stavrou[8] who studied former LRA abductees, asked the question "reintegration into what?", meaning that reintegration was not possible where the community no longer existed or was disjointed or dissimilar to what it was before they left.

Camp life did not provide the girl mothers a typical community life, which is characterised by settings based on clanships and family structures and in which individuals are accustomed to residing in dispersed rural homesteads. The girl mothers therefore found it very difficult to settle in the camps after being released from the reception centres. Most of them reported that they would rather live in town than in camps. This was attributed to the poor conditions of camp life. For example, there was limited space in the huts where their families and relatives lived, the huts were congested, the latrines were not in a good location, some lacked clean water and sanitation facilities and there was very limited space for the children to play. In comparison, life in the reception centres was far better because they had better shelter, availability of food and other basic requirements and could talk to staff such as counsellors and nurses about their concerns.

The girl mothers experienced identity problems. Some girls reported that while in the bush, they were referred to as wives or adults, but when they joined their families upon return from captivity, the parents/guardians treated them as children. This new identity created a degree of confusion on return and perhaps explains what their parents regarded as their "strange" behaviours. The girls expressed unhappiness and felt belittled about the way their parents treated them. The parents would send them on small errands such as buying paraffin from a shop like small children. This reaction shows that girls became socialised into military and bush life to the extent that they acquired new roles, identities and status such as wives and had domestic workers or even escorts while in

---

7 E.F. Barth, *Peace as Disappointment: The Reintegration of Female Soldiers in Post-Conflict Societies*, PRIO Report, 2002, see at www.prio.no/Research-and-Publications/Publication/?oid=54806.

8 A. Veal and A. Stavrou, 'Reception, Reintegration and Reconciliation', (2003) 92 *Monograph*, November 2003; The Reintegration of Lord's Resistance Army Child Abductees in Northern Uganda, www.theirc.org/news/latest/the-difficult-path-from-war.html.

captivity. The girls expected to sustain this status even after they returned to their communities, but this proved to be difficult because, culturally, the parents, relatives and members of the community considered them to be children, despite the fact that they were mothers and have grown bigger.

Another major problem that girl mothers faced upon return was a lack of identity for their children. The girl mothers came back with children born in captivity as a consequence of sexual violence. The girls confessed that, although they were welcomed back by their families, their babies were poorly accepted. If the father is unknown, the stigma is greater.[9] Stavrou[10] observed that even worse than sexual abuse is girls returning with babies. The girl mothers said that they were anxious about their children who were born in captivity. This was because the parents questioned the identity of the children born in captivity. One of the counsellors working with girls in one of the reception centres reported that the parents asked whether the children were Ugandans or Sudanese. The parents were concerned about the identity of these children because their lack of identity represents an additional dishonour for the family. On the other hand, some girls expressed helplessness, especially when they asked where they were going to put the children and what the Government could do with their children. The identity of children was complicated by some girls who produced children from more than one man. For example, one of the girls indicated that she had children with three different men. A lack of identity for the children would lead to insecurity for the girl mothers in their own homes.

While some girls were "physically" accepted into living with their families or relatives, the families refused to support them and their children, explaining that the children "were an extra charge" to the family. Furthermore, they could not afford to look after them because they were impoverished by the war.

Therefore, due to poverty, girl mothers find it difficult to look after their children in terms of feeding, clothing and a means to provide them with education and take them to hospital for medical treatment. The focus group discussions revealed that, although the girls indicated that they were forced into becoming wives while in the bush, some said that they would prefer to go back to their bush husbands instead of being impoverished while living in the community. This is a clear indication that the girl mothers could not live on their own as single parents. Nonetheless, some of them remained single because they wanted their "bush" children to be treated fairly, but were often trapped in difficult dilemma: on the one hand, if they chose marriage, their children would be rejected and stigmatised; on the other hand, if they remained single, they

---

9 S. McKay, *Girl Mothers and Fighting Forces And their Children in Northern Uganda and Sierra Leone/Liberia: Action Research to Assess and Improve their Situation*, 2006, see at www.uwyo.edu/girlmothersparsupport/docs/Veale.pdf.

10 Veal and Stavrou, *supra* note 8.

would face difficulties in raising children on their own and with little economic and social support.[11]

Findings from individual interviews with the girls indicate that some of them felt like committing suicide or killing their children because they could not look after them. This indicates that in reality children born in captivity were a heavy burden to their girl mothers. Although some returnee boy soldiers were also living in poverty, they were not so much affected as the girl mothers because they had no extra responsibility with children to look after.

At the time of the study a major problem mentioned by most respondents was that economic opportunities in the IDP-camps and the urban municipalities were very limited, because the technical skills learned at the reception centres were not adequate for securing a livelihood or did not match with the rural living environment. This is a clear gap that needs to be addressed to ensure proper rehabilitation of the girls.

On their return from the centres, most girls and key informants reported that they faced a lot of stigmatisation in the community. The study found out that the girl mothers were not readily accepted by their own relatives and family members. They reported that they were living in constant agony because of their experiences as they faced rejection, abuse and resentment from their immediate families and their own relatives. They were also stigmatised by being labelled names by people in the community such as *wun anyira olum* (wives of the rebels) and their children were also perceived as "enemies" and referred to as *lutino alum-lum* (child of the rebels). One the girls reported in a focus group discussion:

> Within the villages, even our own parents and relatives fear to associate with us. There is the problem of acceptance of our children we came with from the bush. They say if this child was millet, I would have burnt (killed) it.

Such rejection made the girls feel like misfits in the community and this sometimes induced them to run away from their families and relatives to go and live on their own. Most of the girl mothers said that they felt more comfortable staying on their own rather than living with their relatives. They confessed that although living on their own was difficult, it was better than living with people who did not love them nor their children. Consequently, the girl mothers rented houses in the peri-urban areas of Gulu town, leading to female-headed households in post-conflict situations. This is why as heads of households the

---

11 The Justice and Reconciliation Project, *Field Notes (2006) Young Mothers, Marriage, and Reintegration in Northern Uganda: Considerations for the Juba Peace Talks*, Liu Institute for Global Issues and the Gulu, Kitgum and Pader District NGO Forums Field Notes, 2, September 2006.

girls have to struggle to provide the basic needs of their children, as one girl mother put it in one of the focus group discussions:

> At the beginning life was hard as I did not know what to do. First I stayed with a friend near Gulu town. Our neighbour employed me as a bar maid and with the little money I saved I was able to rent a room. I used to leave my child with our neighbours whenever I would go to work. But the money I get is not enough for us so I sometimes go back to the reception centre run by Gulu Support the Children Organisation (GUSCO) to get some food items and clothes. Sometimes I also get additional income from customers who ask for my 'services'.

In society, the family plays a central role in protecting and nurturing children, and this is also reflected in a wide range of international conventions and policy statements. However, due to war, the family has been destabilised and disrupted. While the family in periods of peace plays a protective and mediating role for war-affected children,[12] many children in war-affected areas have not had this opportunity, because of the death of their parents or separation from their parents. The study findings indicate that upon return, half of the girl mothers found either one or both parents dead. Those who lost both parents had to live with relatives. Some relatives, such as uncles, said that they were already burdened by their families and therefore found it difficult to support the girls with their children. This lack of parentage increased their vulnerability as they had nobody to fall back on. Moreover, most girls expressed a strong desire to go back to school, but this was not possible due to the loss of parents, lack of parental support and poverty. In addition, the fact that most of them were in primary school at the time of their abduction made it difficult for them to find formal employment. Hence, most of the girl mothers were involved in petty business as a form of survival. Nor did the nature of communities they were living in, mostly in or near camps of displaced people, favour other occupations such as agriculture. Many girls have therefore resorted to fending for themselves in urban centres or marrying someone for financial support. These circumstances have predisposed them to prostitution as a survival strategy.

As already mentioned, the study found that most of the girl mothers were experiencing psychological problems, such as fear, lack of sleep, nightmares, stomach-aches and constant headaches. The feelings of fear among the girl mothers were related to possible rebel attacks and re-abduction, and unsupportive family relations. This fear led many girl mothers to relocate to places which they felt were safer. The girl mothers suffered visions of attacks by rebels; as one girl mother put it in one of the focus group discussions:

---

12 A. Ager, 'What is a family? The nature and functions of a family in time of conflict', in E. Boothby, A. Strang and M. Wessells (eds.), *World Turned Upside Down; Social Ecological Approaches to Children in War Zones*, Kumarian Press Inc, US, 2006.

> At night, I get bad visions and dreams whenever I try to sleep. I always dream that I am being guarded by soldiers. The other night I dreamt when the rebels had come for me and my son. And this makes me have sleepless nights. I am scared.

One of the programme coordinators reported that one of the significant prevailing psychosocial problems among children was the high suicide rate. He indicated that some children committed suicide as soon as they came back from captivity, whereas others committed suicide after some time when they felt that they could not take it any more. These findings concur with those of MacMullin and Loughry[13] (2004) and Feingold,[14] who said that girls are more anxious and/or depressed than boys after traumatic experiences. Furthermore, the study found that there was a tendency for girl mothers to have low esteem. This confirms the observations of Dodge and Raundalen[15] (1987) that such ill feelings tend to reduce prospects for their successful reintegration into the community. All the above challenges indicate that the reintegration of girl mothers is quite difficult. One programme coordinator of a Young Mothers project reported that it was easier to reintegrate boys than girls, mainly because girls had more problems, such as experiences of rape, having children and community rejection.

It is important to note that the reintegration of girl mothers has been difficult to realise so far because the tendency of the government and other stakeholders has been to look at the reintegration process from a micro perspective (individual girl mothers) and to give limited attention to the meso perspective (community). Assistance such as the provision of skills training and reinsertion packages to the girl mothers, while desirable, has not been enough to facilitate the process of reintegration. This is because the reintegration process must promote positive interactions between the post-conflict community members. The community must be involved in the construction of these post-conflict interactions. It must try to recognise and accept its new post-conflict identity. Secondly, the war in northern Uganda has altered the pre-war community arrangements and therefore reinsertion packages alone have not been (or may not be) able to effect the kind of post-conflict environment which recombines and reunites people's lives, at both the individual and group levels, into a social group which they regard as their community.

---

13 C. MacMullin and M. Loughry, 'Investigating Psychosocial Adjustment of Former Child Soldiers in Sierra Leone and Uganda', (2004) 17 4 *Journal of Refugee Studies*, 460–472.

14 A. Feingold, 'Gender Differences in Personality: A Meta-Analysis', (1994) 116 3 *Psychological Bulletin*.

15 C.P. Dodge and M. Raundalen (eds.), *War, Violence and Children in Uganda*, Norwegian University Press, Oslo, 1987.

4. RECOMMENDATIONS

Out of the above mentioned findings, we would like to suggest some recommendations towards rehabilitation and reintegration processes for girl mothers returning from captivity.

At first, we suggest that community structures should be strengthened to support the psychosocial healing process of the girl mothers and their reintegration into the community. Furthermore, activities undertaken by communities should be set up in the best interests of girl mothers and of other vulnerable children. This involves, amongst other themes, that people in the community should be continuously sensitised about children's rights, in order to ensure the protection of the children living in the community and to eliminate stigmatisation of former child soldiers.

Secondly, there is a need to pay particular attention to the children of girl mothers, as they should be protected from stigma, discrimination, abandonment and infanticide by the girl mothers. This can be achieved through sensitisation of the girl mothers and their parents. Furthermore, the girl mothers should be empowered through livelihood strategies to enable them to meet the basic requirements of their children, such as food, clothing, education and medical treatment.

Thirdly, the psychosocial support for the girl mothers should not stop at the reception centres, but should be extended to the community. This requires consistent follow-up of the girl mothers while in the community to eliminate outstanding problems such as stigmatisation, poverty, recurrence of psychological problems and limited economic opportunities, so as to ensure their effective reintegration.

Fourthly, some of the technical skills learnt at the reception centres could not match with rural economic opportunities. There is therefore a need to develop a critical understanding of the situation to which abductees are returning. Returnees need to be equipped with skills which are relevant and applicable to their surroundings. This will ensure realistic opportunities to use their newly acquired skills and set up relevant income-generating projects that are adequate for securing a livelihood.

Fifthly, girl mothers should be given the opportunity to receive education, as many of them see this as a chance to regain control of their lives, support themselves and their children, become independent, and be reintegrated into civil society. This applies not only to formal education but also to informal education. It can be achieved by opening childcare centres where they can leave their young ones as they attend school.

Sixthly, the Western-based psychosocial support services should be carefully tailored to fit the local conditions of the girl mothers and other vulnerable children. This can be achieved by integrating cultural beliefs and traditions that enhance human dignity with the provision of psychosocial support and reintegration services to girl mothers and other returnees. This will enhance their recovery from traumatic experiences and their settlement in the community. It will also enhance social cohesion and sustain an acceptable moral fabric.[16]

Lastly, the stakeholders should promote the involvement of the family in the rehabilitation and reintegration interventions provided to girl mothers, as this is a key resource in all domains, such as the provision of care and protection, fostering basic skills, and transmission of local knowledge and values. If the families are impaired by conflict, they should be given support in recovering capacity in this area.[17]

5. CONCLUSION

As a conclusion, despite the presence of protective legal instruments and children's rights conventions, such as the UNCRC (1989), the human rights of girl mothers in conflict and post-conflict situations continue to be violated. Those who reported to the reception centres benefited from psychosocial support services, such as medical treatment, provision of basic requirements and counselling, and reintegration services, such as family tracing and reunification, a reinsertion package and capital to start businesses. In their efforts to provide rehabilitation and reintegration services, the service providers from both Government and NGOs faced several challenges. The service providers need to use a multidisciplinary and holistic approach, addressing all life domains, in order to ensure the effective rehabilitation and reintegration of the girls. The girl mothers reported that they felt better when they received psychosocial support, but once they moved to the communities they were overwhelmed by a range of challenges, such as poverty, stigmatisation, lack of identity for their children, just to mention a few. The findings indicate that children tend to recover at the centres; however, some degenerate once they go back to the community, "a changed environment". Our findings highlight an urgent need for the protection of the rights of girl mothers and to ensure their empowerment through the establishment of comprehensive community strategies by stakeholders that can help them cope with the changing environment so that they lead better lives.

16 Ministry of Gender, Labour and Social Development, *The Uganda National Culture Policy: A Culturally Vibrant, Cohesive, Progressive Nation*, 2006, 20–21.

17 Ager, *supra* note 12.

COMMUNITY-BASED APPROACHES TO THE REINTEGRATION OF SELF-DEMOBILISED CHILD SOLDIERS: THE CASE OF THE DEMOCRATIC REPUBLIC OF CONGO

Mulanda JUMA

1. INTRODUCTION

While the demobilisation of child soldiers from armed forces and armed groups has received widespread attention since the United Nations (UN) multiplied efforts aimed at ending the use of children in hostilities, the critical question of the reintegration of self-demobilised child soldiers has often been taken for granted, instead of being critically studied. In this regard, it is of paramount importance to stress that demobilisation does not necessarily signify reintegration. In fact, for the past six years in the Democratic Republic of Congo (DRC) more child soldiers have self-demobilised without really being reintegrated. Current estimates put their number at about 11,000. Despite their significant number, the substantial means available to the government and the UN, and the fact that child soldiers' reintegration is considered a human right issue, the question of how to reintegrate self-demobilised child soldiers has been left out of the Disarmament, Demobilisation and Reintegration (DDR) process. The sole support for these children often comes from poor communities (families and local organisations), who find it difficult to access locally available resources and hammer out a solution to this important problem. Many researchers and authors have paid attention to the issue of children in the DDR process but thus far have not examined the question of self-demobilised child soldiers.[1] This paper proposes community-based reintegration approaches to mobilising resources and to addressing the immediate and long-term psychosocial needs of the children.

1 The concept of 'self-demobilised child soldiers' refers to children associated with armed forces and armed groups who voluntarily return to civilian life through unofficial means. In other words, they do not go through the Disarmament, Demobilisation and Reintegration (DDR) process.

To explore this issue, data were collected using variety of techniques, including documentary analysis of the literature on the question of child soldiers and email questionnaires sent to practitioners from local non-governmental organisations (NGO) working with child soldiers in the eastern DRC. The paper is also based on the author's experience as a peace trainer working with the NGOs. Additionally, data has been gathered through the author's observation of the life experience of self-demobilised child soldiers in the Kivu provinces.

This paper is divided into three sections. The first section reviews the context and the support provided to self-demobilised child soldiers. The second section presents evidence from the ground on the psychosocial effects of armed conflict on self-demobilised child soldiers in the DRC. The final and most important section proposes three concrete community-based approaches to address their psychosocial needs for reintegration in terms of (1) the need to focus on promoting human dignity, (2) raising awareness in communities about the need to address psychosocial problems and assist local communities to mobilise and utilise locally available resources, and (3) training selected persons from among community members in basic stress management and trauma healing.

2. REASONS BEHIND SELF-DEMOBILISATION

Growing attention has been given to the specificity of children in combat, most notably by international legislation, firstly from the Cape Town recommendations, then from the 2007 Paris Principles, which gained the endorsement of over 60 countries, and finally also through the UN Optional Protocol to the Convention on the Rights of the Child, which came into force on 12 February 2002 and has been ratified by well over 100 countries.[2] The UN treaty bans the use of children in hostilities. In line with the treaty, during the Red Hand Day Campaign Ceremony the UN Secretary-General, Ban Ki-moon, was quoted saying:

> We must not rest, until all children who have been recruited or used in violation of international law have been released, and until all children feel safe in their homes, schools and communities, without fear that they will be forced into war.[3]

This call clearly indicates that child soldiers should not only be released, but also should not and cannot be re-recruited or subjected to arbitrary arrest and detention after their release. However, some self-demobilised child soldiers have faced abuse by the government police force since their release. Human Rights Watch

---

2 Coalition to Stop the Use of Child Soldiers, *Child Soldiers Global Report 2008*, www.childsoldiersglobalreport.org/files/country_pdfs/FINAL_2008_Global_Report.pdf (accessed 2 April 2009).

3 Human Rights Watch, *UN Secretary Pledges to 'Stamp Out' Use of Child Soldiers*, 2009, www.un.org/apps/news/story.asp?NewsID=29891&Cr=child+soldiers&Cr1 (accessed 24 July 2009).

demonstrates that in Goma (North Kivu) alone in the first half of 2008, government officials jailed dozens of children for alleged past involvement with armed groups.[4]

However, the DRC still finds itself in a cycle of release and re-recruitment, due to ongoing conflicts. While on the one hand fighting forces bow to the international pressure to release children, they continue to recruit them and trample on international standards. Ostensibly, considering sanctions for those violating international humanitarian law and international human rights law has only little bearing on some fighting forces, from both the government and the armed groups.

Another response to the widespread recruitment of child soldiers in the Great Lakes of Africa region came with the Multi-country Demobilization and Reintegration Programme (MDRP), Africa's largest DDR collaboration, spearheaded by the World Bank. It involves over forty agencies and seven countries, including the DRC. MDRP supports the release and reintegration of former child soldiers. In addition, the decision by the International Criminal Court (ICC) to bring to book Thomas Lubanga,[5] accused of using child soldiers, has sent a strong message to political leaders that the use of child soldiers in combat is a war crime and would have serious consequences. The ICC has also indicted Germain Katanga[6] and Mathieu Ngudjolo Chui[7] on multiple counts, including the use of children in hostilities. On similar counts, an arrest warrant was issued by the ICC against Bosco Ntaganda.[8] His prosecution was delayed by the government, which – somehow ironically – seems to choose 'peace' before human rights. Interestingly, the end of active combat in early 2009 between the government armed forces (*Forces Armées de la République Démocratique du Congo*, FARDC) and Bosco Ntaganda's *Conseil National pour la Défense du Peuple* (CNDP) pushed more children into self-demobilisation.

Following various peace agreements, such as the 2008 Goma peace accord between the government and armed groups from North and South Kivu provinces, in which the parties agreed to release all children associated with their armed forces and groups, the government has recommitted itself since mid-2008 to taking further action to remove all children from within its ranks. To achieve

---

4 Human Rights Watch, *Submission to the Committee on the Rights of the Child for the Periodic Review of the Democratic Republic of Congo*, 2008, www.hrw.org/sites/default/files/related_material/hrw.drc.crc.0808.pdf (accessed 12 July 2009).

5 Thomas Lubanga is the President of the Union of Congolese Patriots (UPC), a militia group purporting to further the interests of the Hema ethnic group in the Ituri region of north-eastern DRC. Lubanga's trial is the first at the ICC. He is also the first to be tried by the ICC on charges concerning the recruitment, enlisting and use of child soldiers.

6 Germain Katanga is a senior member of the Ituri Patriotic Resistance Forces (FRPI), a Ngiti-based group in Ituri.

7 Mathieu Ngudjolo is the senior member of the Nationalist and Integrationist Front (FNI), a Lendu-based militia in Ituri.

8 Bosco Ntaganda was made a General in the Congolese army (FARDC) in January 2009. He is wanted on an arrest warrant by the ICC for the war crime of enlisting and using child soldiers in combat. He is also accused of commanding troops that massacred 150 civilians, mostly women and children, in Kiwanja, North Kivu, in November 2008.

this, it launched a 'zero tolerance' campaign. Subsequently, despite being a slow process, the release of child soldiers has continued both officially and unofficially.

However, several challenges and limitations of DDR processes push many children to opt for self-demobilisation. Human Rights Watch observes that demobilisation efforts often fail to reintegrate former child soldiers into their communities because programmes supporting reintegration are too brief and located too far from children's home villages.[9]

Many children simply opt to demobilise themselves because they are unable to reach demobilisation centres or they find the process too demanding. In many cases they have to wait for a long time before receiving their promised gratuities. Hence some are discouraged from joining the DDR programme. More often than not, girls are rendered invisible or marginalised, and excluded from the distribution of resources, such as reintegration packages.[10]

For many children, the protection of their self-identity is another issue. Many do not want to make their participation in armed groups widely known for fear of putting themselves and their families in danger. For the same reason some avoid going through the formal DDR process to avoid providing information that they think might be later used against them:

> If children talk openly about their experiences, others may recognise them, remember the damaging things they had done, and seek revenge.[11]

Furthermore, Human Rights Watch notes that 'over a period of a year, thousands of child soldiers escaped, were abandoned, or left the FARDC and armed groups without being officially demobilised.'[12] Among other reasons, they fear stigmatisation and social rejection.

3. PSYCHOSOCIAL EFFECTS OF WAR ON SELF-DEMOBILISED CHILD SOLDIERS IN THE DRC

In the DRC, particularly in North and South Kivu provinces, the impact of war on self-demobilised child soldiers is evident.[13] Evidence from practitioners

---

9 Human Rights Watch, *supra* note 4.

10 Female combatants in Sierra Leone and Mozambique were excluded from demobilisation and reintegration benefits regardless of their roles in combat in various armed groups.

11 G. M. Wessells, 'Review: Children, Armed Conflict, and Peace', (1998) 355 *Journal of Peace Research*, 635–646.

12 Human Rights Watch, *AU Summit: Protect the Vulnerable and Stress Accountability – Deficit in Justice and Civilian Protection in Somalia, DRC, Zimbabwe, Sudan and Guinea*, 2009, www.hrw.org/en/news/2009/01/22/au-summit-protect-vulnerable-and-stress-accountability (accessed 10 July 2009).

13 Examples of this abound within local NGOs, such as the Organisation des Femmes et Enfants pour le Développement (OFED), Association des Jeunes pour le Développement Intégré de

shows that self-demobilised children may present, amongst others, the following characteristics: pride, a kind of 'superiority complex' over civilians or those who did not join the fighting forces, disrespect and chronic depression. Some feel guilty about the atrocities they committed against their own community members, while others seek revenge and are easily provoked. They sometimes use violence as a means of dealing with conflict, while others revert to substance abuse as a way of compensating for lack of education, a livelihood and other basic needs. Consequently, they are prone to re-recruitment by armed groups that promise them a better life and education and/or a higher position at a certain point in government. Other children – particularly girls who served as sex slaves or wives in armed groups – may suffer from an excessive desire for sex. In one of the workshops I conducted on the reintegration of child soldiers in the Great Lakes region in June 2009, this issue was raised among over thirty practitioners from Angola, Burundi, DRC, Liberia, Sierra Leone, Rwanda and Uganda, where no satisfactory response was given. This is a strong indication of knowledge limitation in psychosocial assistance among local actors. The exposure to sex, rape and other forms of sexual violence is likely to have resulted in self-demobilised children being HIV-positive, although most children who were tested in community health centres were said to be HIV-negative. This leads local organisation workers to question whether the test performed is effective or not.

Rejection by communities is considered to be one of the major problems that self-demobilised child soldiers face. It is caused by the acts committed by these children or by their armed group, but also results from the weakening of community solidarity due to tribal and family rivalries caused by armed conflict. The result of rejection is that self-demobilised children lack the social bonds necessary for feeling part of their community again, which is essential to their psychosocial well-being. This is one of the reasons why they find it difficult to integrate with other children in their communities. For example, this is evident in primary schools in I'amba-Makobola village in South Kivu, where self-demobilised child soldiers find it difficult to live in the community. In this village, following the massacre allegedly carried out by the Goma-based Congolese Rally for Democracy (RCD) rebels, which claimed over 550 people – mostly women and children – among the Fuleru, Bavira and Bembe tribes from 30 December 2008 to 1 January 2009, a number of children joined the Mai-Mai militias in revenge. It turned out that some of them committed atrocities not only against other tribes but within their own tribes, leading to rivalries between families. Consequently, they are rejected by their communities and are not able to make friends among

Kalundu (AJEDI-KA) – Uvira, Association des Volontaires pour l'Encadrement des Vulnérables et Enfants Non Accompagnés (AVEVENA) – Uvira, Laissez l'Afrique Vivre (LAV) – Bukavu and Comité d'Aide aux Jeunes en Difficulté (CAJED) – Goma and Jesuit Refugee Service-Uvira.

non-combatant children. Not long ago, reintegration efforts were initiated by the village Chief Juma Lubambo M'sambya III and other local organisations.

4. PSYCHOSOCIAL REINTEGRATION OF SELF-DEMOBILISED CHILD SOLDIERS IN THE DRC

The importance of the psychosocial rehabilitation of child soldiers has been extensively recognised. The study by Bayer, Klasen and Adam, for example, shows that child soldiers returning to their community still suffer from high levels of post-traumatic stress disorder (PTSD).[14] Specht concurs that child soldiers need special attention because some are seriously traumatised, lack parental support and missed out on education opportunities.[15] On the other hand, Humphreys and Weinstein[16] observe that many former child soldiers become integrated civilians in their communities and function at par with others, both socially and economically.

According to Amnesty International, by 2004 over 40,000 child soldiers were estimated to be serving with the government armed forces and non-state armed groups in the DRC alone.[17] Between 2003 and 2006, some 30,000 of them were removed from the ranks of both the regular armed forces and various armed groups, as in the case of the Mai-Mai militia, due to the efforts of international workers.[18] As mentioned, most child soldiers reintegrate into their communities through formal DDR processes. However, there is also a large number of self-demobilised child soldiers, who also need to be reintegrated into their local communities. It is estimated that there are at least 11,000 self-demobilised child soldiers,[19] and that their number is even on rise, although exact numbers remain unknown, since DDR actors do not identify them. Human Rights Watch reports that between January and July 2008, over 500 children left armed groups, but most by unofficial means.[20]

---

14 C. P. Bayer, F. Klasen and H. Adam, 'Association of Trauma and PTSD Symptoms with Openness to Reconciliation and Feelings of Revenge Among Former Ugandan and Congolese Child Soldiers', (2007) 298 5 *JAMA-Journal of American Medical Association*, 555–556.

15 L. Specht, 'Jobs for rebels and soldiers', in E. Date-Bah (ed.), *Jobs After War: A Critical Challenge in the Peace and Reconstruction Puzzle,* International Labour Office, Geneva, 2003, 73–109.

16 M. Humphreys and J.M. Weinstein, 'Handling and Manhandling Civilians in Civil War', (2006) 100 3 *American Political Science Review*, 429–447.

17 Amnesty International, *No End to War on Women and Children: North Kivu, Democratic Republic of Congo,* Amnesty International Publications, London, 2008.

18 United Nations Security Council, *Report of the Secretary-General on Children and Armed Conflict in the Democratic Republic of Congo*, S/2007/391, 2008.

19 Coalition to Stop the Use of Child Soldiers, *'Child Soldiers Global Report 2008'*, www.childsoldiersglobalreport.org/files/country_pdfs/FINAL_2008_Global_Report.pdf (accessed 2 April 2009).

20 Human Rights Watch, *supra* note 4.

Those demobilised through the formal DDR processes receive attention, whereas this substantial group of self-demobilised children does not receive any reintegration support from national and international actors. The result is that their rights are not protected and they have to fend for themselves in reintegrating socially and psychologically. As a matter of fact, while some reintegrate successfully into their families and communities, others are unfortunately left with no choice but rejoin armed groups or gangs to earn a living and/or create social bonds.

The problem of reintegrating self-demobilised child soldiers is thus left to local communities, although without any training or support. For example, in eastern DRC, through solidarity, various local NGOs are accompanying these children through their reintegration process without the needed toolkits in terms of psychosocial capacity and economic resources. They carry out the following activities: child identification; host and transit family identification; family reunification; medical assistance; educational support; life skills training; and legal assistance.

4.1. CHILD IDENTIFICATION

Self-demobilised child identification is not an easy task, as the children are scattered in local communities. First and foremost, the identification is carried out in local communities by members of local organisations. The process of identification is more difficult in towns than in small rural villages, as in villages almost everyone knows each other, which is not the case in towns. Additionally, in villages local traditional, religious and other leaders, in the name of solidarity, facilitate those who want to help self-demobilised children to reach them, provided they are consulted and involved. An example is the abovementioned local Chief of I'amba-Makobola village, Mr Juma Lubambo. Although in small number, other children are identified when they come to seek help (e.g. when in need of food and shelter) from the organisations. Others are identified through a survey. According to one local NGO worker, from a survey conducted by local organisations in Fizi and Uvira territories in South Kivu in 2007 some 528 self-demobilised girls were identified. It was found that the girls were receiving no assistance and that most of them had come back with babies and without partners.

4.2. HOST AND TRANSIT FAMILY IDENTIFICATION

The concepts of host and transit family are used interchangeably among local organisations to mean the same thing: once a child is identified, a family in the village or town, depending on the location and needs of the child, is identified to take care of the child on a temporary basis. While in this family, the child receives psychosocial support and basic literacy courses to learn how to read and write in what are called '*Centre-Jours*' (daily centres). In these centres, not only self-demobilised children are cared for, but also other children in vulnerable situations, such as orphans and unaccompanied children. These families provide the children with their basic needs, such as food, shelter and accommodation.

4.3. FAMILY REUNIFICATION

A second form of support includes family reunification, as this is found to be the best option for many self-demobilised children. For those whose families are identified, they are often unified with their families. Generally, children are easily accepted back into their families, because they fought for a good cause: against enemies or aggressors. However, in some cases they are not welcomed back because they are considered to be traitors, especially those who served in rebel groups supported by neighbouring countries (e.g. Rwanda), such as the RCD, and those who served in Mai-Mai militias. Some are not accepted back for fear that families might become targets for the government law enforcement agencies, in particular the police. They fear being arbitrarily arrested, jailed or tortured. Once this happens, they would be asked to pay ransoms over and over again. Thus the best way seems to be to keep a distance from their children. For girl children, especially those who return pregnant or with children and are abandoned by their partners, families are often not willing to welcome them back. Generally, reconciliation processes take place when needed. As a result, some children rejoin their families and receive the necessary social support, which helps them fare better than those who are rejected. For others, once welcomed they become family breadwinners. Hence, they are under constant pressure to find livelihoods.

4.4. MEDICAL ASSISTANCE, STRESS MANAGEMENT AND TRAUMA HEALING

Self-demobilised child soldiers receive medical care for various reasons, such as sexually transmitted diseases, HIV/AIDS, malaria or tuberculosis. Secondly, children may suffer from severe psychological trauma. A typical example that comes to mind is that of a self-demobilised child who served as bodyguard of the Congolese Army Chief Commander at the beginning of the second war in 1998. This child fought in Bukavu in August of the same year, where the Army Commander was serving at the time. He and others were taken hostage by Rwandan soldiers and transported to Kavumu Airport, about 50 km from Bukavu, for execution. Not only did he witness the killing of his colleagues but also he was shot in his right arm and bled almost to death. He heard Rwandan soldiers saying that he was dead before they left. After they were gone, he stood up and went to a nearby medical clinic in Katana, where he received basic medical treatment for the wound. No psychological counselling was given to him. Afterwards, he left the army unofficially and resumed civilian life. From time to time, he claims to have nightmares and also his wound starts bleeding, revealing the feeling that his arm is almost falling off. He is being assisted by one of the local organisations in Uvira; however, the costs of treating the medical problems caused by the wound are too high to be provided by the local organisation.

Some self-demobilised child soldiers go through basic stress and trauma counselling sessions, although owing to a lack of know-how these services are not available to all the children requiring them. Generally, these services are provided by workers of local organisations who attended short training courses on stress management and trauma healing. Psychological support is also provided though what is mostly known as '*nyumba ya mahombi*' (prayer home). These Christian homes, which are not only popular but also a major means of healing all kinds of sickness in local communities, are used to cast out evil spirits through intensive and prolonged prayers.

4.5. EDUCATION

Some self-demobilised children have the opportunity to pursue their education in primary schools, and some receive school kits. However, in many cases, they sell them or give them away, despite follow-up. These educational opportunities are not provided to all children, owing to a lack of resources and an overwhelming number of children wanting to return to school. Depending on their age and choices, some children receive support for various kinds of life skills training, such as repairing bicycles, auto-mechanics, driving, agriculture and fishing. In some cases, similar training is given to those who live in town and rural areas, such as auto-mechanics. After training, they are also assisted in getting such things as a driver's license or toolkits for agriculture, with limited external support.

4.6. LEGAL ASSISTANCE

From time to time, former children associated with armed groups are arrested and detained by the police, particularly those who left armed groups through unofficial means. In a few cases, legal assistance is offered to self-demobilised child soldiers, for example to children unlawfully arrested and detained by the police so that they can be released. In some cases, it is difficult to provide such assistance because children are jailed far from their villages and far from the reach of local organisations.

5. CHALLENGES AND LESSONS LEARNED FROM THE REINTEGRATION OF SELF-DEMOBILISED CHILD SOLDIERS

Activities to reintegrate self-demobilised child soldiers present challenges, but they also bring forth positive and negative lessons. These will be explored in detail in the following section.

5.1. CHALLENGES

The reintegration of self-demobilised child soldiers faces five major challenges. First, local organisations and families lack needed funding to ensure the effective reintegration of the children. This is partially due to a failure to mobilise and utilise effectively locally available resources, such as land, to mount projects that can generate income. They also fail to resort to traditional means of dealing with psychological problems. For example, they are not using traditional mechanisms to deal with stress and trauma despite their availability and accessibility. This is to a greater extent due to reliance on foreign help to run their projects rather than effectively exploring locally available resources.

Moreover, families are seriously impoverished to the extent that rather than children being assisted by them, families pin their hope on self-demobilised children for help. This puts more strain on the children and may push them back into military work whenever an opportunity is offered or into substance abuse as a way of dealing with stress. In some cases, children join one of the mushrooming bandit groups to earn a living. It is therefore essential to empower families as first and foremost duty-bearers to be able to assist self-demobilised children to reintegrate back into communities. With no adequate means, despite the existence of local resources, local organisations are less able to empower families.

Second, there is a great lack of support from the government and international organisations. It stems from the above situation that there is still a gap between the national and international call to demobilisation and the assistance provided to ensure the effective reintegration of self-demobilised child soldiers. Local NGOs that take initiatives to help these children are often faced with negative responses whenever they seek support from international organisations. The governmental support to these children simply does not exist. Often the response is that '*the problem of these children is so complex, their number is small compared to adult combatants going through DDR processes, and they do not represent a threat to peace and security*', which shows a lack of commitment on the part of the government and international organisations to the reintegration of self-demobilised child soldiers even though it is widely recognised that long-term reintegration requires not only internal but also external support.[21]

Third, there is a lack of skills in stress management and trauma healing. Especially local organisations in eastern DRC lack the basic know-how in both Western stress management and trauma healing mechanisms for dealing with the psychological needs of self-demobilised child soldiers, as well as in traditional healing mechanisms. Yet they need to deal with children's stress and trauma resulting from violence in a much more effective way. This lack of capacity means that local organisations' workers fail to understand and respond effectively to children's needs. It also prevents them from exploring locally available resources. Moreover, educational curricula from primary school to university also do not include stress management or trauma healing components, and have never been revised to respond to post-conflict demands. Further, this lack of knowledge and adequate response finds an explanation in both African and Christian traditions and beliefs, which generally maintain that those suffering from distress and trauma are 'possessed by the devil'. The lack of awareness of the necessity for children to learn coping mechanisms in this area could well be an additional reason. It leaves them powerless when faced with stress.

Fourth, ongoing conflicts pose a great challenge to those working with self-demobilised child soldiers. This is partly due to the fact that many children are lured back into armed groups, which wreak havoc in villages and towns. Bryden, cited in Edmonds, Mills and McNamee, maintains that:

> Where the social and economic reintegration of ex-combatants has not been adequately provided for, and where they are left with no legitimate means to support themselves, the risk of sexual violence against women and other human rights abuses increase significantly.[22]

In Bukavu, for example, many small gangs exist and cause insecurity, especially at night: breaking into houses, robbing on the street and killing and sexually molesting women. Some self-demobilised child soldiers also take part in these activities, including some who were once assisted by local community organisations to reintegrate into their communities. One explanation could be that the reconciliation between the child and his or her family fails and the child decides to leave the family and seek alternative means of living. Where

---

21 I. Nubler, 'Human Resources Development and Utilization in Demobilisation and Reintegration Programmes', in K. Kingma (ed.), *Demobilization in Sub-Saharan Africa: The Development and Security Impacts*, MacMillan Press, 2000, 45–77.

22 M. Edmonds, G. Mills and T. McNamee, 'Disarmament, Demobilization and Reintegration and Local Ownership in the Great Lakes: The Experience of Rwanda, Burundi, and the Democratic Republic of Congo', (2009) 21 *African Security*, 29–58.

reconciliation is said to have been successful or a child has been accepted by his or her family and/or transit family, it could also result from the reappearance of trauma which was not addressed in the process.

Fifth, the lack of capacity in the area of restorative justice and peer mediation is very evident, meaning that those working with self-demobilised children are not able to empower them with the knowledge and skills to deal constructively with conflict with other children when encountered. Where restorative justice is not used, retributive justice or punishment becomes an important alternative. The challenge is that this justice can induce children to run away from their communities in order to avoid punishment.

5.2. LESSONS LEARNED

A number of important lessons can be drawn from the above discussions. First, trauma healing and reconciliation are inseparable in the journey from violence to peace. You can be fully healed, but if you have not reconciled your differences, you leave the door open for the event to happen again. Similarly, you cannot move towards reconciliation if you are not fully healed. Both healing and reconciliation are essential for self-demobilised child soldiers to live in peace. Additionally, restorative justice and other forms of peaceful conflict resolution are critical to children's reintegration. It is essential for children to learn how to handle their conflicts peacefully and to find ways of addressing their past in a more constructive way. Thus equipping children with conflict resolution skills will go a long way not only towards addressing conflicts, but also towards preventing them from reviving poisonous war memories.

Second, there is a direct link between the labour market and psychosocial reintegration. The failure to carry out an analysis of the labour market before conducting life skills training for children resulted in some skills not being useful for children. Consequently, they could not find jobs and thus became frustrated, which is not helpful for psychosocial reintegration. For example, some self-demobilised child soldiers had the opportunity to learn auto-mechanics, but at the end of the training their skills became irrelevant since they could not find job opportunities simply because there were no cars to fix. This shows that no labour market study was done before conducting the training. Thus, in order to run the training in the best interests of self-demobilised children and to prevent stress arising from a lack of job opportunities, it is essential to provide them with skills that match the requirements of the conflict-affected labour market in the geographical area where reintegration is taking place.[23]

23 M.E. Juma, *Linking Disarmament, Demobilization and Reintegration to the Labour Market: A Case Study of the Democratic Republic of Congo*, Masters of Commerce Dissertation, Durban, University of KwaZulu-Natal, 2005.

Third, life skills training, such as in conflict resolution and stress management strategies, is highly effective in reintegration and reconciliation. It creates a space where self-demobilised child soldiers from various armed groups, including former enemies, can come together. It also accords an opportunity to self-demobilised child soldiers and the community to work together. Hence, it facilitates the exchange, and acceptance as well as mutual development. As a strategy for tackling social exclusion, it can be effective in empowering women, children and youth, and in providing an avenue for sharing experiences and promoting reconciliation.[24] Moreover, training is an important tool for peace processes, political stabilisation and national reconciliation.[25]

Fourth, gender continues to receive less attention, despite worldwide efforts to mainstream it. Regardless of the special needs of self-demobilised girl child soldiers, for example those who return to communities with babies, and their significant number, no specific measures are being taken to assist them to reintegrate. This means that more should be done to create gender awareness among local actors, particularly those working in the reintegration process, so that they take girls' special needs into account. As Neimanis puts it:

> Gender mainstreaming approach does not necessarily make the need for specific policies, programmes or projects on gender equality absolute. The level of intervention will depend on the specific needs and priorities revealed by a gender-sensitive situation assessment.[26]

6. APPROACHES TO THE REINTEGRATION OF SELF-DEMOBILISED CHILD SOLDIERS AND THE ROLE OF THE COMMUNITY

Psychosocial effects are always situated in a wider set of interacting effects regarding poverty, education, health, security and other basic human rights and needs. The above analysis of the activities of local communities in assisting self-demobilised children to reintegrate has provided useful approaches and important insights. They also present numerous challenges and limitations. In the following section, I turn to additional approaches that would be valuable in facilitating their reintegration. These approaches can help to address the challenges encountered by local communities in assisting self-demobilised child

24 M. Ducci, *Guideline for Employment and Skills Training in Conflict-affected Countries*, International Labour Organisation, Geneva, 1998.

25 P. Barcia and E. Date-Bah, 'Skills Training Challenges in Post-conflict Contexts', in E. Date-Bah (ed.), *Jobs after War: a Critical Challenge in the Peace and Reconciliation Puzzle*, International Labour Organization, Geneva, 2003, 211–224.

26 A. Neimanis, *Gender Mainstreaming in Practice, A Handbook*, United Nations Development Programme RBEC, Bratislava, 2002, 1-148, at 7.

soldiers' reintegration and to enhance their work. Their value comes from the fact that they exploit resources which are within the reach of local communities. By addressing challenges faced by local communities, they can make communities' efforts more sustainable for meeting both the short- and long-term psychosocial needs of self-demobilised child soldiers. As rightly put by the IAWG-DDR (Inter Agency Working Group on DDR) in the Integrated Disarmament, Demobilisation and Reintegration Standards (IDDRS), 'the more children are supported within and through their new reintegration environment, the more reintegration is likely to succeed.'[27]

In exploring these approaches, importance is accorded to the emotional needs of self-demobilised child soldiers as well as to their physical needs, such as for food.

6.1. PROMOTING THE DIGNITY OF SELF-DEMOBILISED CHILD SOLDIERS

Human dignity is at the core of all human rights. 'To speak of dignity of the human person is to speak of the worth or value of the concrete existing human being.'[28]

As such, every person – and thus every male and female self-demobilised child soldier – has inalienable and transcendent human dignity. Respect for the dignity of the human person should therefore be considered as the foundation for every effort to transform society, to make peace and to promote human rights and the reintegration of self-demobilised child soldiers.

Human dignity helps to glue many varied forms of intervention, for example restorative justice, accountability, decent work, psychological care and humanitarian assistance. It is a significant criterion and a good starting point from which to ground various strategies, both psychological and social, for the reintegration of self-demobilised child soldiers. Because of the active participation of Congolese children in armed conflict either through voluntary or forced recruitment, their human dignity is denied, undermined and obscured. Hence it is essential to protect and promote it as this contributes to a better world.[29]

Kelman[30] specifies two helpful components of human dignity that can lead to action in the reintegration process: identity and community. He argues that to

---

27 IAWG-DDR, *supra* note 22.

28 J.C. Dwyer, 'The dignity of the person', in J.C. Dwyer (ed.), *The New Dictionary of Catholic Social Thoughts*, The Liturgical Press, Collegeville, 1994, 724–736.

29 K. Bayertz, *Human Dignity: Philosophical Origin and Scientific Erosion of an Idea in Sanctity of Life and Human Dignity*, Kluwer Academy Publishers, Boston, 1996.

30 C.H. Kelman, 'The Conditions, Criteria, and Dialectics of Human Dignity: A Transnational Perspective', (1997) 21 3 *International Studies Quarterly*, 529–553.

accord an identity to a person is to see the person as an individual, independent and distinguishable from the rest of other persons. It means to regard the person as an individual who is capable of making choices, an individual who is entitled to live his own life and pursue his own goals. However, to view a person as a community is to perceive him or her as a part of the whole where people care for each other.

Community leaders (traditional leaders, religious leaders, parents, teachers, women, youth, caregivers and other community members) can accord identity and community, and thus maximise the human dignity of self-demobilised child soldiers, by carrying out a number of activities: (1) creating opportunities for self-demobilised child soldiers to participate in local structures, such as schools, cultural, traditional and religious events, and in traditional conflict resolution processes and restorative justice systems, such as *lùbùnga* (cf. *infra*); (2) civilians and police working together to protect former child soldiers from re-recruitment by armed forces and groups, by forming community policing forums involving police officers, community leaders and self-demobilised child soldiers, that can address community security issues and prevent arbitrary arrests and imprisonment; (3) raising awareness to refer to self-demobilised children by their names rather than as 'combatants'; and (4) ensuring access to benefits available in the community, such as land, food, shelter, clothing, healthcare, education, market places and sports, which will prevent marginalisation and ensure the creation of an environment where children can easily exercise their rights and fulfil their duties as well.

6.2. RAISING AWARENESS AND ASSISTING THE COMMUNITY TO MOBILISE LOCAL RESOURCES

Local communities affected by armed conflicts have a wealth of knowledge and first-hand experience of resources that can be used to deal with the psychosocial needs of their community members including self-demobilised child soldiers. However, it is essential to raise awareness among local organisations of the existence of such resources and how to access them because they look outside for help. Awareness should focus on a number of things, such as the challenges faced in the reintegration of self-demobilised child soldiers and the strategies for addressing them, tapping into locally available resources. Moreover, raising awareness must be appropriate to the targeted population, thus 'it is necessary to communicate in a manner that is compatible with the local culture'.[31]

Often efforts at grassroots level are affected by decisions made at higher levels of society, the more so in societies affected by armed conflicts like the DRC. It is therefore necessary to make the middle-range and top-level of leadership aware that addressing the needs of self-demobilised child soldiers is not only important

[31] World Health Organization, *International Consultation to Review Community-Based Rehabilitation (CBR)*, World Health Organization Publication, Geneva, 2003.

to the local community but also to the peace and security of the nation. Thus addressing the needs of this group, along with those of other members of the community, will benefit the larger community and the entire country.

Creating awareness requires advocates[32] from the community. They should approach different target groups in the community. Often a good starting point is traditional leaders and other local community leaders, such as religious leaders, teachers, women, youth and caregivers. It is also important to involve local government leaders. Each of them should be approached with a different strategy. Whatever the strategy, however, demonstrating the problem and the importance of addressing it is critical. To get involved in finding a solution to their problem, leaders and people must feel strongly about the need for a solution. Peace, understanding, security, solidarity, education, job creation, well-being and other community needs are motivations for action. The role of the various community leaders is to identify available resources, mobilise them and facilitate access to them. This role can be supported by several strategies, which we will now discuss in more detail.

6.2.1. Traditional Healing Mechanisms

Communities must be made aware that the psychosocial needs of self-demobilised child soldiers should not be treated in isolation. In order to cleanse self-demobilised child soldiers of the trauma of past atrocities and human rights violations, it is important that communities take into account multiple layers and complementary approaches. The trauma healing journey can therefore be seen as a process of cleansing, empowerment and reconnection with the social fabric that must be embarked on both individually and collectively to ensure that their reintegration is sustainable. Next to this, we should consider the relevance of spirituality, such as ritual purification ceremonies conducted by community healers to cast out evil spirits and to encourage acceptance of child soldiers into local communities, in healing, reconciliation and reintegration processes.[33] We see it as essential for local actors to tap into this important traditional knowledge and resource, which is available without much cost in almost every community, in order to address issues of stress and trauma. The use of traditional means does not preclude referring children to non-traditional means, such as clinics and hospitals, when such mechanisms show their limitations.

---

32 Advocates make use of communication and media, outreach and mobilisation, lobbying and negotiation, and organisation and leadership strategies to influence and educate the public and decision-makers.

33 S. Meek and M. Malan, *Identifying Lessons from Disarmament, Demobilisation and Reintegration Experiences in Africa*, Institute for Security Studies, Pretoria, 2004, 106.

6.2.2. *Transformation of Relationships*

Efforts that aim to transform people and their relationships use an array of processes that address trauma, eliminate conflict and do justice. In the absence of a national mechanism for dealing with the legacy of the past, unlike the case of post-apartheid South Africa with its Truth and Reconciliation Commission, other traditional mechanisms can fill the gap. Means of mending broken relationships between self-demobilised child soldiers and other community members are available locally. For example, in South Kivu there is a traditional restorative justice mechanism widely known as *Lùbùnga,* comparable with the South African traditional restorative processes known as *Kgotla* or *Inkundla.*[34] *Lùbùnga* is used to resolve conflict between people and to restore broken relationships under the leadership of traditional or community leaders. Accuser and defendant meet together in a roundabout house dedicated to conflict resolution and community well-being, along with other members of the community. Under the mediation of a community leader, they each share their side of the story. Solutions are proposed by the parties and the mediator announces a mutually beneficial solution that takes into account the needs of the parties and of the community. Often, the 'Chief' and village elders consult wise women in the village before deciding on the matter, especially on issues of great importance to the community. The *Lùbùnga* process is guided by *Ujamaa*[35]or *Ubuntu*[36] principles: unconditional acceptance, tolerance, respect, human dignity, compassion, hospitality and stewardship. This community-led process offers an opportunity to the individual and his or her family to seek reconciliation in a non-violent way. It is restorative in that it encourages acknowledgement of the hurt and guilt, requires a public apology and requests reparation. At the end of the process, a white chicken is slaughtered to mark the end of conflict and a new beginning of reconciliation and trust. As Sofield, Hammett and Juliano noted:

> The quality of trust is an enigma in any community or in any relationship. Yet it is an enigma that must be grappled with if relationships are to develop.[37]

Lùbùnga provides an opportunity to those who are psychologically wounded to start the journey of healing the wounds and bad memories. Among other advantages, it offers a safe space that allows individual survivors to look back at

---

34 Kgotla or Inkundla: A South African indigenous people's forum.

35 Ujamaa: An indigenous perspective articulated among Swahili-speaking Africans popularised by Mwalimu Julius Kambarage Nyerere, then President of the United Republic of Tanzania, articulating a sense of community.

36 Ubuntu: An indigenous perspective articulated among South African Bantu people that underlies traditional African thinking generally, premised upon a collective sense of being and responsibility.

37 L. Sofield, R. Hammett and C. Juliano, *Building Community: Christian, Caring, Vital,* Ave Maria Press, Indiana, 1998, 2-15, at 5.

what happened to them or their loved ones. People share their stories, such as sexual abuse. Wise men and women listen with passion and interest. In the process, survivors put themselves on the road from war to peace. Self-demobilised child soldiers thus can find in *Lùbùnga* a participatory process that addresses their issues of justice, human rights abuses, sexual violence and other forms of dispute. Because the aim is to restore relationships, it is thus a good tool for transitional justice.

6.2.3. Support Groups

The formation of support groups is one way of mobilising support locally. Groups can be organised around self-help activities, such as soccer teams, and around development projects, such as farming groups. Local community leaders and other members of local communities can set up self-help groups by identifying self-demobilised child soldiers and other children and youth affected by war, and forming groups. In so doing, gender should be taken into account. Support groups offer a unique opportunity for addressing the needs of all children together. They give various advantages, such as preventing the marginalisation and stigmatisation of self-demobilised child soldiers and promoting solidarity and opportunities for job creation. Community members can share their knowledge with support groups and provide them with guidance and other moral support. The local private sector as well as the government could also provide financial and other forms of assistance, thereby helping to prevent children from joining armed groups or become internally displaced in search of livelihoods.

6.2.4. Creation of Job Opportunities

Social and economic aspects of reintegration are inextricably linked. Annan and Patel allude to the fact that 'one's social role is often related to economic input and lack of income and can increase levels of distress, while psychological problems can interfere with one's ability to engage in economic opportunities'.[38]

Thus, a job should not be regarded simply in economic terms, since in post-conflict societies, especially for the reintegration of self-demobilised child soldiers, it is also a psychosocial factor.

Notwithstanding this view, not every type of job is necessary for reconciliation and community healing. In his study on linking DDR to the labour market in

[38] J. Annan and C.A. Patel, *Critical Issues and Lessons in Social Reintegration: Balancing Justice, Psychological Well Being and Community Reconciliation*, Paper Presented at the International Conference on Disarmament, Demobilization and Reintegration (CIDDR), Cartagena, 2009, 1-25, at 17.

the DRC, Juma[39] found that some strategies of job creation, such as micro-credit programmes targeting individuals in isolation and employment in the army and police, do not facilitate social reintegration as they create unhealthy competition. They should be used with caution in conflict-affected communities. In the case of the army, apart from not being appropriate for child soldiers the merger of former enemies in the same camps without an effort at reconciliation brings frustration and is less effective in bringing reconciliation.

Community-based labour-intensive public works and employment in agriculture and fishing are job strategies with a high rate of effectiveness in facilitating reconciliation. On the other hand, they may also have some factors that hamper reconciliation, for example in cases where there is unequal distribution of land. Three essential job opportunities are explored in the following sections: labour-intensive public works programmes; agriculture and fishing; and education and training.

6.2.5. Labour-Intensive Public Works Programmes

Government can provide jobs through public works programmes (PWPs) to self-demobilised child soldiers and other community members. It should be noted that this is one of the best ways of getting help for self-demobilised child soldiers from international organisations. Such support is necessary to make the work and reintegration more sustainable. Currently, there is a massive ongoing reconstruction programme in the DRC called '*Cinq Chantiers*',[40] offering potential job opportunities in various areas, including infrastructure development such as roads, schools, hospitals and lodging. PWPs could also offer an opportunity to facilitate reintegration and reconciliation because they help to bring self-demobilised child soldiers and communities into working together. Experience from South Africa has shown that PWPs contribute to conflict resolution and sustainable peace.[41] However, it is essential to provide self-demobilised child soldiers with a broad range of skills to enable them to use the opportunities arising from PWPs.

---

39 M.E. Juma, *Linking Disarmament, Demobilization and Reintegration to the Labour Market: A Case Study of the Democratic Republic of Congo*, Masters of Commerce Dissertation, Durban, University of KwaZulu-Natal, 2005.

40 Cinq Chantiers is DRC President Joseph Kabila's programme for reconstruction covering the following areas: health and education, infrastructure, lodging, water and electricity, and employment.

41 KwaZulu-Natal Department of Transport, Zibambele: Labour-based Construction and Maintenance Programme, 2005, www.kzntransport.gov.za/programmes/zibambele/labour_based_construct (accessed 22 June 2005).

6.2.6. *Agriculture and Fishing*

Like PWPs, employment in agriculture and fishing is not an option for all children. Such jobs are good for grown-up self-demobilised child soldiers, their host families and parents. While job opportunities in countries emerging from armed conflict are usually very limited in the public and private sectors, agriculture and fishing offer more scope.[42] One of the major problems faced in agriculture in the aftermath of armed conflict is access to land, possibly leading to conflicts between ex-combatants and local community members. However, where well managed, access to land can become a source of income and reconciliation. Thus agriculture and fishing are highly effective in providing opportunities, not only for livelihoods but also as a degree of acceptance of self-demobilised child soldiers and other combatants.

6.2.7. *Education and Training*

Self-demobilised child soldiers should have the opportunity to attend school and other community training opportunities. The former Secretary-General of the United Nations, Kofi Annan said: 'Education is quite simply, peace-building by another name...'[43]

And Rousseau stated: 'Education is a fundamental factor in social integration and a mark of personal achievement as well as an instrument of economic progress'.[44]

Education imparts knowledge and understanding to those that receive it. However, the aim of education is not the compilation of ever more facts, but an existential knowledge, a competence for orientation, as well as the ability to apply knowledge in action. Education becomes convincing when it brings life and teaching together as a unity and when it unites body and soul, in other words develops a person as a whole – spiritually, intellectually and physically. It becomes convincing as a way of life where one lives in practice what he or she wants to pass on.

Self-demobilised child soldiers' education should not only focus on the mind, but also on the heart. Thus, it should not only provide skills but also abilities, such as the importance of dialogue and communication, of justice, peace and solidarity, of critical thinking and analysis, and of positive values. The change of curriculum in schools in the DRC is thus important to adapting it to the new

---

42 Nubler, *supra* note 21.

43 United Nations Institute for Disarmament Research, *Disarmament Forum 3-Education for Disarmament*, United Nations Institute for Disarmament Research, Geneva, 2001, 1-18, at 1.

44 R.W. Rousseau, *Human Dignity and the Common Good: The Great Papal Social Encyclicals from Leo XIII to John Paul II*, Greenwood Press, Westport Conn, 2002, 3-286, at 268.

demands of the post-conflict society. This will benefit not only self-demobilised children but also other non-combatants' children.

Although education and training do not create jobs directly, they can overcome constraints on the supply side of labour. Ducci argues that employment promotion along with skills training are among the effective means of reintegration of conflict-affected people.[45] Nubler concurs that 'most education and training for ex-combatants aims at facilitating economic and social reintegration.'[46]

He further points out that training plays a double role: to provide skills to those who have none and to enhance and refresh the skills of those who have some. By building and enhancing capacity, training helps to remove barriers to social, economic and political opportunities, and shapes the attitudes, values, norms and behaviour of ex-combatants. Thus education and training can be highly effective in reintegration and reconciliation.

Training can also create a space where former enemies come together, facilitating exchange and providing opportunities for mutual development. It is thus an important tool for peace processes, political stabilisation and community reconciliation. It can also be used as a tool for tackling the social exclusion of some self-demobilised child soldiers and empowering them. Care should be given to mainstream all social groups in the training process to prevent tension in local communities.

6.3. PROVISION OF BASIC STRESS MANAGEMENT AND TRAUMA HEALING TRAINING

Finally, communities should be trained in stress management and trauma healing skills, equipping them to be able to assist self-demobilised child soldiers. For the training, it is important to target individuals selected from among community leaders, teachers, women, youth, self-demobilised child soldiers and other children in the community. The purpose is to equip them with tools to assist affected people, particularly self-demobilised child soldiers, in attaining a stable life and integrated functioning. Training should also aim at enabling communities to empower self-demobilised child soldiers and other members of the community to journey from brokenness to wholeness and to move from conflict to peace. This training needs to cover different aspects, which will be elaborated below.

45 Ducci, *supra* note 24.

46 Nubler, *supra* note 21, at 60.

6.3.1. *Understanding Stress and Trauma*

Often people in the community assume that responses to traumatic events (e.g. seeing or hearing things that are not there, being easily shocked or jumpy) are caused by demon or spirit possession, and then they avoid survivors. It is important that in dealing with self-demobilised child soldiers, communities learn that not every such response is demon possession. Equally, they should not use avoidance as an appropriate solution to the problem, even in extreme cases where a child may feel as though he or she is losing his or her mind.

By being able to define stress and traumatic stress, communities can better help children. They should understand that stress is a response to a situation that is understood to be demanding or challenging. It is a natural response that can assist people in completing their task or meeting their demands or expectations. It can serve as a motivator and provide positive energy, or it can become overwhelming and result in negative energy. It should be made clear that stress is positive or negative depending on the individual's response to a specific situation.

Contrary to stress, trauma is a word used for any event that causes major distress to a person. Trauma may be physical, such as a wound, or it may be emotional, such as grieving for a death. Traumatic stress is an acute response to a traumatic event in which psychological balance is disrupted. When this happens, individuals are unable to think, feel or behave in normal ways. The usual coping skills fail and there is evidence of humans not being able to function well. It changes the mind-set of a person, who then experiences pain, loss, grief, despair, anger, bitterness, hopelessness, apathy and feelings of revenge. Since most common problems affecting child soldiers arise from post-traumatic stress disorder (PTSD),[47] it is important for communities to understand it so that they can hammer out solutions. Post-traumatic stress is complex but natural and adaptive. It should not be labelled pathological (i.e., needing counselling or therapy) unless it is prolonged, blocked, excessive, or interferes with regular functioning to a major extent.

6.3.2. *Causes and Effects of Stress and Trauma*

Communities should be able to identify the causes and effects of stress and trauma and distinguish between them. It is obvious that the traumatic

[47] K. Johnson, J. Asher, S. Rosborough, A. Raja, R. Panjabi, C. Beadling, L. Lawry and K. Johnson, 'Association of Combatant Status and Sexual Violence with Health and Mental Health Outcomes in Post-conflict Liberia', (2008) 30 6 *JAMA-Journal of the American Medical Association*, 676–690.

experiences of self-demobilised child soldiers are generally caused by war. However, limiting the causes only to war may limit the way people identify the effects of trauma experienced by individual self-demobilised child soldiers and thus how they address the problem. Every self-demobilised child soldier has his or her own story to tell. Although, they are affected differently, and not all of them are traumatised, each child's story contains more causes and each cause more effects. These are often hidden from sight by tough behaviour and attitudes,[48] and also obscured by culture and tradition. Communities should learn that the emotional wounds are as dangerous as the physical wounds. If ignored, the wounds of the heart may result in loss of life. Angi and colleagues demonstrate more effects and call for care in identifying them by maintaining that:

> [s]ome people express their distress though somatic complaints. This discomfort manifests itself through headaches, stomach aches, back aches, heart problems, faintness, hotness or coldness, and so on. People go to the doctor for help with these symptoms. It is important not to minimise these complaints. It is necessary to distinguish between pain caused as a result of injuries sustained in the traumatic event, and illnesses that are a result of the emotional distress of the trauma.[49]

6.3.3. Solutions to Stress and Trauma

Solutions to stress and trauma should be understood by communities. First, they should know that reactions to traumatic stress are a normal response to an abnormal event. The process is normal and over time, symptoms will reduce and can be healed, but if ignored, they may get worse. Although individuals will not be exactly the same as they were before the wound, traumatic stress can be treated. These wounds of the heart cause people a lot of pain. Such an understanding will go a long way in helping communities not to isolate self-demobilised child soldiers, as is often the case, but to stay close to them and seek means of helping them through support from family and friends, counselling (individual or group) and spiritual comfort. In cases where the problem is prolonged, they can help the child to seek psychiatric support, in addition to other traditional solutions such as church deliverance and traditional cleansing ceremonies.

A countless number of practices exist traditionally, but many people use them without knowing that they have some bearing on psychological well-being. For example, when women and girls in rural areas go to the river, they often spend a

---

48 K. Angi, G. Nygaard, M. Lundberg, P. Mossegard, T.G. Skoglund, E. Ekelund and E. Berggren, *Community-Based Psychological Services in Humanitarian Action: A Facilitator's Guide*, Norwegian Church Aid, Oslo, 2005.

49 Ibid.

long time sharing their inner family stories on every aspect of life, much longer than they do in most homes and other settings. Since every story needs a listener, this is where, in many cases, women and girls find good listeners for their joyful and painful stories. However, for the most part women do not know how important such encounters and social bonds are in stress management and trauma healing. These common practices must be given a meaning and be encouraged though education and awareness campaigns.

Care should be taken with facilitators and trainers. As Agordzo argues: 'The success of any training is largely dependent on the quality of trainers.'[50] By the same token, Juma maintains that teachers in post-conflict societies need to be role models, otherwise they may end up causing more damage to the society.[51] It is therefore important for trainers to understand the context, to have the relevant knowledge and use appropriate methodology in facilitating the psychosocial learning.

Once teachers, leaders, youth, women, parents, caregivers, host families and other members of the community are empowered with psychosocial skills, they must use them to help self-demobilised child soldiers in their daily activities and other activities that involve them. The participation of local communities in the reintegration of self-demobilised child soldiers will increase the potential effectiveness of approaches to the reintegration of self-demobilised child soldiers. Communities must identify and mobilise locally available resources and make use of them, taking into account the cultural context and the needs of other war-affected groups. This is critical both in the reintegration of self-demobilised child soldiers and other members of the community and for the future growth of their communities. It is also critical in building local ownership of the reintegration process and sustainable peace and development.

7. CONCLUSION

The psychosocial reintegration of self-demobilised child soldiers into their families and local communities is a crucial process for their long-term well-being. The main objective of this paper has been to examine additional means of improving local communities' interventions, using community-based approaches to the reintegration of self-demobilised child soldiers. To do so, the paper has

---

50 B.K. Agordzo, 'Filling the 'Security Gap' in Post-Conflict Situations: Could Formed Police Units Make a Difference?', (2009) 2 16 *International Peacekeeping*, 287–294.

51 M.E. Juma, *Education and Human Security in Post-conflict Societies in Africa*, Paper presented at the Third Annual CUEA Philosophy Conference on Philosophy of Education at the Catholic University of Eastern Africa, Nairobi, 2008.

explored the ongoing activities of local communities to facilitate these children's psychosocial reintegration.

Based mainly on field experience and to some extent literature review, the paper explored the reasons for self-demobilisation and the effects of armed conflicts on self-demobilised child soldiers in the DRC. It examined the strategies used by local communities, in particular local organisations, in assisting the children to reintegrate psychologically and socially, as well as the challenges encountered and lessons learned from the process.

Three community-based approaches were proposed to address the challenges and enhance the work of local communities: promoting the dignity of self-demobilised child soldiers; raising awareness in communities about the need to address psychosocial problems and assisting the community to identify, mobilise and utilise available resources for healing and reconciliation; and, thirdly, providing basic stress management and trauma healing training to community members. Awareness and capacity building are particularly important in influencing the participation of communities and building local ownership of the process.

The participation of community members was found to be critical in the process. It is essential in mobilising local resources and facilitating psychosocial reintegration of self-demobilised child soldiers. It also means that these children are given special attention to protect their dignity at the same time that attention is paid to the larger community to improve life condition and facilitate reintegration.

PSYCHOSOCIAL ADJUSTMENT AND MENTAL HEALTH SERVICES IN POST-CONFLICT SIERRA LEONE

Experiences of CAAFAG and War-Affected Youth, Families and Service Providers

Theresa BETANCOURT, Sandra ZAEH, A'Nova ETTIEN and Laura KHAN

1. INTRODUCTION

From 1991 to 2002, Sierra Leone endured a brutal civil war which left approximately 50,000 people dead, 20,000 brutally mutilated and three quarters of the country's population displaced.[1] The marginalisation and political exclusion of youth were considered to be two major contributing factors to the war.[2] Many young people were forcibly abducted by the Revolutionary United Front (RUF), the rebel group central to the conflict, whereas others joined willingly. Youth were also involved in the ranks of the civilian defence forces and factions of the Sierra Leone army.[3] Although official estimates indicate that some 5,000 to 10,000 children were involved in the different warring factions,[4] other sources report estimates as high as 48,000.[5] This range in estimates is due in part to difficulties in tracking children involved in combat given the continual

---

1 M. MEREDITH, *The Fate of Africa*, Free Press, London, 2006.

2 TRUTH and RECONCILIATION COMMISSION, *Chapter Five: Youth. The final report of the Truth and Reconciliation Commission of Sierra Leone*, 2007 (accessed 8 February 8 2009 at http://trcsierraleone.org/drwebsite/publish/v3b-c5.shtml).

3 M. WESSELS and J. DAVIDSON, *Recruitment and reintegration of former youth soldiers in Sierra Leone: Challenges of reconciliation & post-accord peace building*, in MCEVOY-LEVY (ed.), *Troublemakers or peacemakers? Youth and post-accord peace building*, 2006, University of Notre Dame Press, Notre Dame, 27–47.

4 COALITION TO STOP THE USE OF CHILD SOLDIERS, *Child soldiers: Global report 2008*, Coalition to Stop the Use of Child Soldiers, London, 2008.

5 S. MCKAY and D. MAZURANA, *Where are the girls? Girls in fighting forces in Northern Uganda, Sierra Leone, and Mozambique: Their lives during and after war*, International Center for Human Rights and Democratic Development, Montreal, 2004.

displacement of persons, lack of infrastructure, and the fact that combat groups kept no records. The National Committee for Disarmament, Demobilization and Reintegration (NCDDR) estimates that nearly 7,000 children were formally demobilised. At the conclusion of the war, many youth and child combatants underwent a formal disarmament, demobilisation and reintegration (DDR) process, where various international and local non-governmental organisations (NGOs) provided psychosocial services including family reunification, counselling, education and job skills training.[6] Many other youth and child combatants self-reintegrated without formal services, and are therefore not captured by DDR statistics.

Today, years after the war's conclusion, many of the issues which spurred the conflict in Sierra Leone remain unaddressed or unresolved.[7] The country ranks at the bottom of the Human Development Index with up to 70 percent of youth classified as underemployed or unemployed.[8] Evidence has suggested that war-affected children and youth are at increased risk of mental health problems, including depression, post-traumatic stress disorder, anxiety and aggression.[9] In addition, recent research has indicated that children associated with armed forces and armed groups (CAAFAG) demonstrate higher rates of mental health problems compared to matched controls.[10] Formal mental health services alone are insufficient to address this risk. Sierra Leonean youth, families and communities have demonstrated significant strength and resilience, a source of "untapped potential"[11] that might provide a basis for sustainable interventions to assist war-affected youth. However, these strengths have not been adequately harnessed and efforts to develop social services for war-affected youth and

---

6 J. Williamson, 'The disarmament, demobilization and reintegration of child soldiers: Social and psychological transformation in Sierra Leone', (2006) 4 3 *Intervention*, 185–205.

7 Truth and Reconciliation Commission, *Chapter Five: Youth. The final report of the Truth and Reconciliation Commission of Sierra Leone,* 2007 (accessed 8 February 2009 at http://trcsierraleone.org/drwebsite/publish/v3b-c5.shtml).

8 Republic of Sierra Leone and United Nations Sierra Leone, *Priority plan for peacebuilding fund Sierra Leone,* 2008 (accessed February 8, 2009 at: www.unpbf.org/docs/PBF-Sierra-Leone-Priority-Plan.pdf).

9 C.P. Bayer, F. Klasen and H. Adam, 'Association of trauma and PTSD symptoms with openness to reconciliation and feelings of revenge among former Ugandan and Congolese child soldiers', (2007) 298 5 *JAMA-Journal of the American Medical Association,* 555–559; B.A. Kohrt, M.J.D. Jordans, W.A. Tol, R.A. Speckman, S.M. Maharjan, C.M. Worthman and I.H. Komproe, 'Comparison of mental health between former child soldiers and children never conscripted by armed groups in Nepal', (2008) 300 6 *JAMA-Journal of the American Medical Association,* 691–702; M. Wessells, 'Supporting the mental health and psychosocial well-being of former child soldiers', (2009) 48 6 *Journal of the American Academy of Child and Adolescent Psychiatry,* 587–590.

10 Kohrt et al., *supra* note 9.

11 Women's Commission for Refugee Women and Children, *Untapped Potential: Adolescents affected by armed conflict,* Women's Commission for Refugee Women and Children, New York, 2000.

families in the post-conflict environment have been weak. The current lack of organised services and the numerous daily stressors facing impoverished youth in the post-conflict environment may further exacerbate the risks they face, making healthy psychosocial adjustment and the successful reintegration of CAAFAG extremely challenging.[12]

According to the WHO Mental Health Atlas, more than 62 percent of countries have Child and Adolescent Mental Health (CAMH) programmes.[13] Nearly 78 percent of European countries and 81 percent of nations in the Americas region have such programmes, compared with only 37 percent of countries in Africa. In the accompanying Atlas on Child and Adolescent Mental Health[14] Sierra Leone is listed as having "no information available" on child and adolescent mental health and mental health services. The Atlas lists the most important reason for the dearth of information as "lack of services" along with "absence of an identifiable national focal point for child and adolescent mental health services" and "fragmentation in the service systems responding to the needs of children with mental disorders". The quality of the programmes that do exist to serve children and youth is highly variable and regions affected by armed conflict are even less likely to have CAMH programmes.

Clearly, the lack of organised mental health and psychosocial services for children, youth and families in the post-conflict setting is not unique to Sierra Leone, but the country's situation provides an opportunity to analyse priority settings and post-conflict investments in addressing the needs and rights of war-affected youth. It is important to consider this challenge within the context of the troubled history and current hardships in the country. Nonetheless, the country's inability to provide sustainable services for young people whose healthy development has been severely undermined by the war and its aftermath poses significant threats to human capital. Such threats include decreased productivity, violence, and destabilisation of integral institutions, such as the educational system.[15] While some research has explored the burden of mental health problems among war-affected youth in general and in former CAAFAG within post-conflict Sierra Leone,[16] very little information exists about either

12 K. Miller, P. Omidian, A. Rasmussen, A. Yaqubi and H. Daudzai, 'Daily stressors, war experiences, and mental health in Afghanistan', (2008) 45 4 *Transcultural Psychiatry*, 611–638.

13 WHO, *Mental Health Atlas 2005*, World Health Organization, Geneva, 2005.

14 WHO, *Atlas: Child and Adolescent Mental Health Resources: Global Concerns, Implications for the Future*, World Health Organization, Geneva, 2005.

15 M. Belfer, 'Child and adolescent mental health disorders: the magnitude of the problem across the globe', (2008) 49 *Journal of Child Psychology and Psychiatry*, 226–236.

16 T.S. Betancourt, I.I. Borisova, R.B. Brennan, T.P. Williams, T.H. Whitfield, M. de la Soudière, J. Williamson and S.E. Gilman, 'Sierra Leone's former child soldiers: A follow-up study of psychosocial adjustment and community reintegration', (2010) 81 4 *Child Development*, 1077-1095; T.S. Betancourt, R.T. Brennan, J. Rubin-Smith, G.M.

current or planned systems to address the needs of this war-affected generation. To support maximum health and functioning of the country's youth, Betancourt et al.[17] have suggested that research is needed to understand how systems of mental health and psychosocial support, both formal and informal, function in Sierra Leone's resource-poor post-conflict setting.

In this paper, we aim to investigate the current state of mental health and psychosocial support available to war-affected youth and families in Sierra Leone, using data from key informant and focus group interviews with war-affected youth and adults, and key informant interviews with individuals involved in the provision and leadership of mental health service infrastructure. We paint a picture of the services that currently exist in various parts of the country and consider how, if at all, those services contribute to an integrated, systemic effort to meet the mental health needs of youth.

By more closely examining the existing mental health system in Sierra Leone, our qualitative research provides insight into how war-affected youth are currently coping with mental health problems, how the current system of mental health care and psychosocial support is structured, and what kinds of services must be further developed and implemented to provide higher quality and sustainable care for all children, youth and families. Furthermore, we highlight successful and recommended strategies that can be used in similar post-conflict settings to provide more sustainable systems of care during the transition from humanitarian relief to post-conflict development and beyond.

2. BACKGROUND

2.1. THE IMPACT OF WAR ON THE MENTAL HEALTH OF YOUTH

Research in the past two decades has indicated higher levels of psychopathology among children affected by war and armed conflict.[18] For example, a recent study conducted in the Gaza strip of 229 adolescents who were exposed to

---

Fitzmaurice and S.E. Gilman, 'Sierra Leone's former child soldiers: a longitudinal study of risk, protective factors, and mental health', (2010) 49 6 *Journal of the American Academy of Child and Adolescent Psychiatry*, 606–615.

17 T.S. Betancourt, I. Borisova, J.E. Rubin-Smith, T. Gingerich, T. Williams and J. Agnew-Blais, *Psychosocial adjustment and social reintegration of children associated with armed forces and armed groups: The state of the field and future directions*, Psychology Beyond Borders, Austin, 2008, 1–101.

18 J. Barenbaum, V. Ruchkin and M. Schwab-Stone, 'The psychological aspects of children exposed to war: practice and policy initiatives', (2004) 45 *Journal of Child Psychology and Psychiatry*, 41–62.

continual violence found that 68.9 percent of individuals had developed post-traumatic stress disorder (PTSD), 40 percent had moderate or severe depression, and nearly 94.9 percent had severe anxiety.[19] There has been conflicting evidence, however, concerning the duration of mental health disorders from war. Some studies suggest mental health difficulties such as PTSD persist over time,[20] while others find more short-term traumatic reactions.[21] Of note, however, are cases of acute short-term trauma in the wake of violent conflict that can evolve into long-term distress when exacerbated by loss of family support or financial and other material deprivation, which can often negatively affect a child's developmental trajectory.[22]

Children associated with armed forces and armed groups (CAAFAG) can be particularly at risk of mental health disorders due to a wide range of experiences spanning the conflict and post-conflict period, including separation from loved ones, prolonged abuse, and in some cases, active participation in violence.[23] Bayer, Klasen, & Adam[24] found that more than one third of child soldiers in rehabilitation camps in Uganda and the Democratic Republic of Congo exhibited clinical symptoms of PTSD. Derluyn and colleagues[25] found that 97 percent of 71 former child combatants in northern Uganda exhibited symptoms of PTSD. Of additional concern is the finding that mental health issues in former combatants may persist over an extended period of time. Evidence from 293 former child soldiers in El Salvador showed that even 10 years after the conclusion of the war, nearly 60 percent of interviewees reported that they always or often remembered encounters they had lived through during the war, almost 40 percent admitted to being tired and depressed often, and 37 percent reported problems with emotion regulation such as becoming easily annoyed.[26]

---

19 S. Elbedour, A.J. Onwuegbuzie, J. Ghannam, J.A. Whitcome and F. Abu Hein, 'Post-traumatic stress disorder, depression, and anxiety among Gaza Strip adolescents in the wake of the second Uprising (Intifada)', (2007) 31 7 *Child Abuse and Neglect*, 719–729.

20 W.H. Sack, C. Him and D. Dickason, 'Twelve-year follow-up study of Khmer youths who suffered massive war trauma as children', (1999) 38 9 *Journal of the American Academy of Child and Adolescent Psychiatry*, 1173–1179; A. Dyregrov, R. Gjestad and M. Raundalen, 'Children exposed to warfare: a longitudinal study', (2002) 15 1 *Journal of Traumatic Stress*, 59–68.

21 S. Weine and D.F. Becker, 'Adolescent survivors of "ethnic cleansing": Observations', (1995) 34 9 *Journal of the American Academy of Child and Adolescent Psychiatry*, 1153.

22 Miller et al., *supra* note 12.

23 C. Blattman and J. Annan, 'The consequences of child soldiering', *Review of Economics and Statistics*, forthcoming.

24 Bayer et al., *supra* note 9.

25 I. Derluyn, E. Broekaert, G. Schuyten and E. De Temmerman, 'Post-traumatic stress in former Ugandan child soldiers', (2004) 363 9412 *Lancet*, 861–863.

26 M.L. Santacruz and R.E. Arana, 'Experiences and psychosocial impact of the El Salvador civil war on child soldiers', (2002) 22 *Biomedica*, 283–397.

In Sierra Leone, Betancourt et al.[27] conducted longitudinal work examining psychosocial adjustment and social reintegration in a large sample (over 500) war-affected youth, including those served by ICCs, a community sample, and a sample recruited as self-reintegrated from the Makeni region. Data collection began at the conclusion of the conflict in 2002 with follow-up assessments conducted two years later in 2004 and again in 2008. The average burden of psychosocial distress was similar between baseline and both waves of follow-up. However, for individuals involved in killing others or experiencing rape, there was a negative impact on psychosocial adjustment over time, with increased risk for problems such as hostility and anxiety. When including a group of comparison youth in the analysis, there were comparably high rates of depression, anxiety, and hostility among both the general population of war-affected children and children associated with armed forces and armed groups. This finding highlights the prevalence of psychosocial distress experienced by youth throughout the country, and the need for broad and inclusive approaches to mental health and psychosocial services as opposed to solely targeting select groups such as former CAAFAG.[28] This also speaks to the importance of and direction for the development of a truly comprehensive and holistic health system in the country, which cannot exclude mental health as a priority.

2.2. A SOCIAL ECOLOGICAL APPROACH TO RISK AND RESILIENCE

War affects the lives of youth across all levels of their social ecology, from individual experiences and events, to implications for family and community functioning, to the larger socio-cultural environment.[29] Resilience – in this case in the face of the traumatic effects of war – is defined by Masten and Coatsworth as "overcoming adversity" to achieve "good developmental outcomes". Resilience is not based solely on the individual characteristics of a child, but is founded on a complex ecology of risk exposure and protective processes.[30] Personal traits, strong connections to family and community, and socioeconomic and cultural context are factors that may contribute to a child's resilience in the face of trauma. It must be recognised that conflict tears at the social fabric that normally supports healthy child development and mental health. In this manner, war sets off a cascade of secondary stressors which may have just as much or even greater

27 Betancourt et al., *supra* note 16.

28 Ibid.

29 T.S. Betancourt and K.T. Khan, 'The mental health of children affected by armed conflict: Protective processes and pathways to resilience', (2008) 20 3 *International Review of Psychiatry*, 317–328.

30 A.S. Masten and J.D. Coatsworth, 'The development of competence in favorable and unfavorable environments', (1998) 53 2 *American Psychologist*, 205–220.

influence in determining subsequent psychosocial adjustment as war experiences themselves. For instance, in a study of 320 adult men and women in Afghanistan, Miller et al.[31] found that the influence of daily stressors – including inability to work, financial instability, and lack of safety – were more highly predictive of depression and impaired functioning than war-related violence. Specific to CAAFAG, Betancourt et al.[32] observed that post-conflict experiences of stigma explained a significant proportion of variance in post-conflict mental health outcomes. We observed that post-conflict experiences of discrimination largely explained the relationship between past involvement in wounding/killing others and subsequent increases in hostility. Stigma similarly mediated the relationship between surviving rape and depression. These findings suggest that variance in the distress levels reported by war-affected youth may be greatly shaped post-conflict stressors as well as different war experience.[33] This evidence highlights the importance of emphasising a holistic or community-based approach to mental health treatment to help alleviate or assist families in managing such stressors.[34]

2.3. SERVICE PLANNING AND IMPLEMENTATION: MOVING BEYOND THE "FALSE DICHOTOMY" BETWEEN CLINICAL SERVICES AND BROAD-BASED PSYCHOSOCIAL RESPONSES

There is a tendency in the field of mental health to categorise approaches dichotomously as either clinical service or psychosocial service provision. In fact, mental health approaches should not be "either/or", but rather should incorporate appropriate biomedical approaches with culturally relevant psychosocial and local approaches. Clinically-oriented services often seek to identify individuals suffering from the most severe mental health disorders and

31 Miller et al., *supra* note 14.

32 T.S. Betancourt, J. Agnew-Blaise, S.E. Gilman, D.R. Williams and B.H. Ellis, 'Past horrors, present struggles: The role of stigma in the association between war experiences and psychosocial adjustment among former child soldiers', (2010) 70 1 *Social Science and Medicine*, 17-26.

33 D. Silove, 'The psychosocial effects of torture, mass human rights violations, and refugee trauma: toward an integrated conceptual framework', (1999) 187 4 *Journal of Nervous and Mental Diseases*, 200–207; K.E. Miller, M. Kulkarni and H. Kushner, 'Beyond trauma-focused psychiatric epidemiology: bridging research and practice with war-affected populations', (2006) 76 4 *American Journal of Orthopsychiatry*, 409–422; K.E. Miller, S.M. Weine, A. Ramic, N. Brkic, Z.D. Bjedic, A. Smajkic, E. Boskailo and G. Worthington, 'The relative contribution of war experiences and exile-related stressors to levels of psychological distress among Bosnian refugees', (2002) 15 5 *Journal of Traumatic Stress*, 377–387.

34 Miller et al., *supra* note 12.

offer treatment specifically to reduce targeted symptoms and impairment.[35] Identification of clinical issues of priority is usually organised according to existing diagnostic classification systems such as the International Classification of Diseases (ICD-10) or the Diagnostic and Statistical Manual of the American Psychiatric Association (DSM-IV).[36] However, these standard classification systems have been widely criticised for their failure to take cultural perspectives into account,[37] and for their neglect of many developmental issues for children.[38] Furthermore, DSM-IV and ICD-10 take an individualistic approach to diagnosis and treatment that, combined with the absence of cultural perspectives, turns intervention planning towards programmes likely to be unsuitable for the assessment and treatment of those who have suffered larger-scale social traumas. Miller et al.[39] have also suggested that the biomedical focus on PTSD in war-affected populations fails to consider local idioms of distress and neglects local mental health concerns and priorities. Relying solely on biomedical approaches to address mental health concerns in war-affected communities is insufficient for adequate understanding of the true depth and breadth of needs.

Many mental health issues require a more holistic and often psychosocial approach.[40] The term "psychosocial" suggests a relationship between psychological and social effects. Psychological effects impact on "emotion, behaviour, thoughts, memory, learning ability, perceptions, and understanding", while social effects refer to "altered relationships due to death, separation, estrangement and other losses, family and community breakdown, damage to social values and customary practices, and the destruction of social facilities and services".[41] Psychosocial interventions may be particularly important in war-affected communities because daily stressors may modify the relationship between past war exposure and mental health.[42] Such interventions tend to focus on the entire affected population by attempting to restore the structure and

---

35 T.S. Betancourt and T. Williams, 'Building an evidence base on mental health interventions for children affected by armed conflict', (2008) 6 1 *Intervention*, 39–56.

36 K.E. Miller and L.M. Rasco, 'An ecological framework for addressing the mental health needs of refugee communities', in K.E. Miller and L.M. Rasco (eds.), *The mental health of refugees: Ecological approaches to healing and adaptation*, Lawrence Erlbaum Associates, New Jersey, 2004, 1–64.

37 K.M. Munir and W.R. Beardslee, 'A developmental and psychobiologic framework for understanding the role of culture in child and adolescent psychiatry', (2001) 10 *Child and Adolescent Psychiatric Clinics of North America*, 667–677; J.K. Bass, P.A. Bolton and L.K. Murray, 'Do not forget culture when studying mental health', (2007) 370 9591 *Lancet*, 918–919.

38 Belfer, *supra* note 15.

39 Miller et al., *supra* note 33.

40 WHO, *The World Health Report 2001: Mental Health: New Understanding, New Hope*. World Health Organization, Geneva, 2001.

41 Betancourt et al., *supra* note 17.

42 Miller et al., *supra* notes 12 and 33.

cohesiveness of the individual's previous environment[43] and often include reconnecting strong family and community ties, educational opportunities, skills training, spiritual support, community empowerment, or even economic initiatives such as providing low-interest loans for individuals to start small businesses.[44]

Guidelines for minimum standards of mental health and psychosocial support in conflict settings were released in 2007 by the Inter-Agency Standing Committee (IASC), a body created by the UN as a coordination agency for major humanitarian actors such as UN agencies, the Red Cross and NGOs. The guidelines emphasise the importance of incorporating both clinical and psychosocial approaches into emergency settings. The IASC's 25 action points suggest a holistic view of mental health and outline a continuum from basic services to more specialised services for those who need them.[45] The action points consider the psychosocial and clinical needs of war-affected individuals in terms of a pyramid. Individuals at the bottom of the pyramid are those who may have experienced grief and loss of family members, but who demonstrate resilience and function well[46] despite the disruption of war. These individuals can thrive once fundamental security and services, such as food, shelter, and basic health care, are re-established. War-affected individuals in the middle level of the pyramid are those who are resilient but face the risk of deteriorating if they do not receive support through services at the family and community level. Individuals at the top of the pyramid are those who exhibit difficulty coping with daily life due to more persistent mental health problems. They are in need of more extensive long-term and specialised services focused on their specific needs.[47] The research featured in this paper supports a holistic, integrated approach to the mental health of war-affected youth and communities as suggested by the IASC pyramid.

43 Betancourt et al., *supra* note 17.

44 Miller et al., *supra* note 12; Betancourt et al., *supra* note 32.

45 Inter-Agency Standing Committee, *IASC Guidelines on Mental Health and Psychosocial Support in Emergency Settings*, IASC, Geneva, 2007.

46 M. Wessells, *Trauma, culture, and community: Getting beyond dichotomies,* Coalition to Stop the Use of Child Soldiers, 2007 (accessed on-line on April 18, 2009 at: www.child-soldiers.org/psycho-social/Getting_beyond_dochotomies_2007.pdf).

47 T.S. Betancourt and W. Tol, 'Mental Health Interventions for Children Affected by War: An Ecological Perspective', in S. Muntasser (ed.), *Children and War,* Springer, 2008.

3. METHODS

3.1. SAMPLE

As part of a longitudinal study,[48] maximum variation sampling was used to conduct key informant and focus group interviews with war-affected children, youth and adults in Sierra Leone in 2004 and 2008. Interviews were conducted with 31 CAAFAG and their caregivers (n = 12), 10 focus groups were conducted with 90 youth and 17 focus groups were conducted with 120 caregivers and community members in Kono, Kenema, Bombali and Bo districts. Data was collected concerning the post-conflict psychosocial adjustment and social reintegration of war-affected youth, with particular attention to CAAFAG. In particular, we sought to examine the formal and informal sources of support available to war-affected youth in the post-conflict environment. Most recently, in June, July and August of 2008, a series of in-depth key informant interviews were conducted with 42 individuals involved in the provision and leadership of mental health services in Kono (Eastern Region), Makeni (Northern Region), Kamikwe (Northern Region) and Freetown (Western Area). Interviewees included individuals from the biomedical mental health system as well as traditional healers, spiritual leaders and representatives of local and international NGOs, the Ministry of Health and Sanitation and the Ministry of Social Welfare, Gender and Children's Affairs.

Interviews were conducted in English or Krio as appropriate. A semi-structured interview protocol was followed for all key informant and focus group interviews. Data was collected concerning the psychosocial adjustment and reintegration of former CAAFAG. Questions were also asked about the mental health and psychosocial services currently in place for youth and families as well as community resources that young people might turn to for assistance with mental health related problems. During interviews with policy and programmatic staff, additional questions were asked pertaining to the challenges faced in providing social services, and successes within the mental health system since the conclusion of the war. All interviews were audio-taped and subsequently transcribed.

3.2. DATA ANALYSIS

The interview transcripts were analysed with a grounded theory methodology in three stages to allow salient themes to emerge from the data itself without a

48 Betancourt et al., *supra* notes 16 and 17.

preconceived schema.[49] Data analysis followed multiple steps. First, transcripts were coded using an open coding technique. Data management and analysis was assisted by the use of the NVivo qualitative analysis software (QSR International). Themes and codes were drawn inductively from the data. Codes identified in initial interviews were compared to themes from later interviews to ensure reliability in the creation of codes. After developing initial coding categories, codes were saturated with examples from the data. This process included the creation of sub-categories within codes, to better capture similarities and differences between interviewee responses. Next, the analysis also included axial coding, which allowed the researcher to make connections between various codes and consider relationships emerging from the data. Axial coding helped to capture the "bigger picture" among codes and sub-categories. In this third step of the process, the researcher considered how the analysed data related to the research questions driving the analysis, re-examining the data for verification of findings. Throughout the stages of the data analysis process, triangulation was performed by comparing quotes across different participants.

4. RESULTS: SITUATIONAL ANALYSIS AND SYSTEMS ASSESSMENT

Several risk and protective factors have been observed that influence the psychosocial adjustment and reintegration of CAAFAG, including both war-related and post-conflict experiences.[50] Even six years after the war's conclusion, some CAAFAG continued to face stigma and marginalisation.[51] These factors interacted with daily stressors such as unemployment and limited access to education, contributing to issues in the mental health and psychosocial well-being of some war-affected youth. Sadly, there are few social and mental health services for this population. Since the services that do exist are heavily concentrated in urban areas and are not integrated into communities or health and education systems, they are unable to address the full spectrum of needs or target services to those who need them most. Many voluntary community-based child protection efforts, facing problems with sustainability of staff and funding, have ceased their operations.

---

49 A. Strauss and J. Corbin, *Basics of Qualitative Research* (2nd ed.), SAGE Publications, London, 1998.

50 Betancourt et al., *supra* note 29.

51 Betancourt et al., *supra* note 32.

4.1. SITUATIONAL ANALYSIS

4.1.1. Past Trauma Versus Present-Day Stressors

War-affected children and youth in Sierra Leone face the double burden of past traumatic war experiences and current daily stressors. Interviews indicated that some youth struggled with persistent psychological trauma related to activities which occurred during the war. Children described recurring nightmares, sadness, and thoughts concerning violent activities they witnessed or participated in during the war:[52]

> When I remember the war I become worried. I think about the way [my sister] was raped and killed. (Female adolescent focus group participant, Bombali)

> Whenever I think of my father and mother I feel sad and resort to things I'm not supposed to do ... Even among friends I become violent and get annoyed over trivial issues. (Male, adolescent interviewee, Bo)

The struggles of such youth do not go unnoticed in the community, though their suffering is not always met with sympathy. Because so many community members experienced violence at the hands of rebel groups, the psychological suffering of CAAFAG is sometimes seen as secondary to the suffering of those who witnessed or suffered abuses at the hands of the RUF rebels. As one man from Kenema explained in a focus group, "I know of a man who witnessed the killing of a whole family, mother, father and children, that man has never been okay since then. The things that some people witnessed frustrates them to date." The caregiver of a former CAAFAG in Bo noted that "With the return of those children, people were disgruntled about them because according to the popular opinion these children have destroyed our lives, houses and property. Therefore these ex-child combatants were called different names. There was total rejection of them, some people even disowned their own children."

In fact, in the case of CAAFAG some community members directly attributed the actions of young people during the war to their subsequent mental health problems. Interviewees also describe the symptoms of those in their communities who have "gone mad" and are unable to function in society; these individuals are largely left to their own devices:

> There is one mad man who, since the day he was disarmed, he just isn't himself. He goes about begging for his living. (Male focus group participant, Kenema)

52 Betancourt et al., *supra* note 16.

> … [the war]… is now affecting them, some have gone mad, they are just roaming about the street. (Female ex-CAAFAG, focus group participant, Kono)

> Those who killed their families are the ones living on the street and those with good families are the ones going to school and some of them are learning. It is like a lizard that eats its own mother, so most of the crazy ones you now see around are because of the bad things they did. (NGO worker)

The last comment suggests a clear understanding of the direct link between past actions as a combatant and current problems. It also refers to the highly destructive impact of RUF strategies, which commonly included forcing young people to commit atrocities against their own family members.[53] At the very least, perpetrating violence against their families compromised the ability of youths to return to surviving family members after the war. In some cases, young people were without living family because of their own actions. This situation is a double challenge to the mental wellness of young people, as these youth must live with the knowledge of their past actions and continue without the support of family (found to be a critical factor in the reintegration process).

Family support and acceptance not only brought a young person back into the family itself, but was also an important factor in helping them negotiate a return to the larger community. In the context of such support, several youths interviewed described how their behaviour and attitudes had improved with time. One girl from Moyamba who had been abducted into the RUF said: "My problem was, if I am hurt, I'll take a cutlass [machete] … to damage people, but now I don't do that." In an interview with her mother, the woman agreed, saying: "When [my daughter] came back, she had bad character[istic]s in her, like she was stubborn and rebellious, but now she is totally different." In a discussion of the ways in which young people reintegrate, one male focus group participant indicated his perception of the critical factors: "It depends on the way your family takes care and encourages you – some really don't have people to encourage them to do something. If you have relatives who correct you when you do wrong them, things would be better for people." Further evidence of the importance of family support and guidance is examined below in the discussion of resilience in war-affected youth.

The impact of everyday stressors was also highlighted as contributing to mental health problems among these youths. "The economic issues of the day – the way people are coping – some people don't cope… I think this impacts mental health

---

53 M. Wessells and J. Davidson, 'Recruitment and reintegration of former youth soldiers in Sierra Leone: Challenges of reconciliation & post-accord peace building', in S. McEvoy-Levy (ed.), *Troublemakers or peacemakers? Youth and post-accord peace building*, University of Notre Dame Press, 2006, 27–47.

on a daily basis", stated a male NGO worker in Kono. Economic pressure, and the lack of resources and opportunities, prevails throughout Sierra Leone. "Think about the unemployment situation for youth", said a male NGO worker in Makeni. "Youth do not have work to engage in. And youth that do not have jobs are not educated." This lack of opportunity for employment or educational progress makes even regular day-to-day activities stressful. A female NGO worker in Makeni said: "Lots of our youth are going through lots of stress, just to make ends meet." Young people themselves expressed a similar sentiment, as a female adolescent in Kono explained: "…everything is limited right now so poverty is everywhere. To even eat food these days you have to be well off."

CAAFAG were identified as having "similar needs" (and thus facing similar challenges) to their peers who were not directly involved in the conflict, which is unsurprising in a setting where the war swept broadly over the population and many basic services and opportunities have yet to be restored. However, many interviewees also suggested that in addition to these basic needs, CAAFAG were still feeling the impact of a difficult reintegration process due to their experiences during the war. "There are some who were on hard drugs and they are getting the effects now. There are some that had medical problems that [are] bothering them to date. There [are] the war wounded. They carry those scars to date", said an older adolescent male from Kenema. A female former CAAFAG from Makeni reiterated such experiences: "Some of them wanted to go back to school but no one was there to help pay the fees. When you eventually approach someone for help, they call you a rebel and don't help. But in actual fact you didn't choose to become a rebel. You were forced to go and live with them and now everybody blames you."

CAAFAG may be subject to particular stress related to being treated differently to other youth either in school or the public domain, within foster families, or by their own families after years of separation. "Some of them were living with friends, distant relations", noted a female NGO worker in Makeni, "and we all know the economic situation in this country. We don't have that – you know – love or commitment like you would do for your own biological child… It is really difficult – getting them educated formally, prepare them for white collar jobs – it is not possible." Other young people described abject experiences of neglect and abuse:

> Things are difficult for me, the caretaker that I am with is not treating me well, he always tells me of my attitude … of that of a rebel … it makes me think of my mother and father who up till now [I have] not seen … I feel sad and resort to doing things I'm not supposed to do. (Older male ex-RUF, Bo)

> I will never trust my mother. She does not like me. All she wants from me is for me to do everything, even sleep around so I could give her things. (Female ex-CAAFAG, Makeni)

Young people in this situation fall in the middle of the IASC pyramid; they cannot be expected to thrive with the provision of merely basic services and opportunities, but it is highly likely that interventions to improve resources at the family and community levels would be very effective.

4.1.2. Factors Contributing to Resilience in the Face of Trauma

In spite of significant past trauma and present daily stressors, some former CAAFAG show a remarkable capacity for resilience. Family and community support was one of the most significant factors contributing to resilience described by war-affected youth in Sierra Leone. Young people often spoke of the importance of having an understanding person to confide in:

> I have a sister who is my friend. Whenever I think of my past during the war, I normally call her to attention and she will come and sit by me, then I will start to explain to her how I suffer in the war with the fighter[s], she normally [encourages] me saying that the war is over, that I should forget about everything. In addition, I will say to her I have just explained to get it off my mind. (Female ex-CAAFAG, Kono)

> My grandmother stopped them [from calling me names]. She told people that what happened was not my fault as I was captured. She [also] reported [the matter] to the Chief. [Now] I feel fine. (Female ex-CAAFAG, Kono)

These quotes provide good examples of the ways in which advocacy and simple listening and support from an understanding person can assist in the healing of traumatic war experiences.

Family support was also important in helping young people relearn positive social behaviour and navigate challenging situations. A mother of a former female CAAFAG in Moyamba described her difficulty with her daughter's return, but said that she and other family remained supportive and patient: "If she takes an object to hit somebody if I tell her to stop she will not listen to me and she was always quarrelling with people, but with counselling I was able to make her reason with me that those habits are wrong… When my family saw her return after all those years they cried with her and [were] very happy for her. They encouraged her to leave her bad ways and live a normal life so they really helped to counsel her." Family and community thus help young people to reintegrate, and to find opportunities for advancement. For example, caregivers and family members may counsel returning CAAFAG on how to get along with the wider community, as one father of a returning male adolescent former RUF described: "While we were at home, we used to play and laugh, but I used to tell him not to be hot-tempered to people. If you do, people will say you are a rebel because you are coming from rebel zone whether you are a rebel or not. I told him to be calm and that is what he does. He has never had a problem with any person."

Families often provide more than emotional support and counselling to youth who are at an age when they must begin to participate actively in their own growth and development, whether it is education or finding a livelihood. One younger adolescent female from Kenema described the support her aunt provided for her: "For example my aunt gives me money to do petty trading so that I can use the profit to take care of my needs. Sometimes I buy palm oil and sell it, then keep the profit to pay my school fees, that is how I paid my fees when I was in Form Two."

Not all young youth received help and support from their families and communities, and even among those who did, stigma and discrimination were commonly reported by CAAFAG upon their return home. Most war-affected youth who experienced such treatment reported that it affected them negatively:

> For me, I did not meet the neighbours. I [lived] in our community but when they knew about our ordeal, they didn't mix with us and point[ed] fingers at us rebels so it was difficult to mingle with them. (Female ex-CAAFAG, Kono)

> ... Even up to now I am feeling the effect. I do not have any man because as soon as somebody shows interest in me people tell the person that I am a witch and a bad one at that. I have a child and the father has abandoned me because of this same problem. (Female ex-CAAFAG, Makeni)

In some cases, however, resilient young people explained that this stigma led them to push themselves in a positive way: "I wanted to prove people wrong because they thought anybody who had been with the fighting forces did it voluntarily and they start pointing fingers at you", said an older adolescent female in Kenema. Similarly, some young people's reflections on their war experiences gave them a sense of purpose for the future, like this older adolescent female also from Kenema: "... during the war for instance I saw that the field of medicine was very essential because most of the time people got sick or wounded, especially women and children suffered the most during such problems. So I thought if I do medicine I will be helpful to other people." With the right support, this self-efficacy and agency in Sierra Leonean youth can be mobilised and enhanced.

4.1.3. The Status of Systems of Psychosocial Support and Mental Health Services in Sierra Leone

Immediately following the war, community-based psychosocial services emphasising the general needs of children and youth were somewhat available in post-conflict Sierra Leone, but with limited accessibility. Psychosocial services were primarily provided by international and local NGOs in Freetown and throughout the provinces. "There are a number of NGOs providing psychosocial services in the country", reported a female NGO worker in Freetown. A male NGO worker in Makeni explained: "The NGOs are the major players as they are the ones doing all of the capacity building and have done most of the work to address psychosocial needs." Psychosocial services for children and youth focused on the provision of education and life skills training, indoor and outdoor recreational games, cultural activities and interactive drama. NGOs also offered material support for young people. "We provided educational support by paying school fees until 2004, in addition to providing skills training with informal education. This included things like learning how to handle your own business and knowing how to write your name", said a male NGO worker from Makeni. Another male NGO worker said that some services were similar at his NGO employer in Kono: "We provided basic primary education for children and youth. This included all of the scholastic materials – like pens." This sort of service is an important step in the IASC model, as the restoration of basic services and opportunities will help all war-affected children thrive, and may be sufficient for some. However, for those at the middle and upper levels of the IASC pyramid, educational services alone are not sufficient to assist them with the myriad of stressors they face in the aftermath of the war.

For those youth requiring a higher level of mental health care, clinical psychiatric services are available at Kissy Mental Hospital, the only mental health institution in the country. When interviewed in 2008, the team was described as comprising three individuals: the country's sole psychiatrist and two trained psychiatric mental health nurses. The doctor remains the only practising psychiatrist in the country, and runs a private clinic in Freetown in addition to serving as the government consulting psychiatrist for Kissy Mental Hospital. He prescribes psychiatric medications for patients in the hospital and within his private practice. Kissy Mental Hospital is Sierra Leone's referral hospital for patients with psychiatric mental illness. Founded in 1900, Kissy Mental is one of the oldest mental health hospitals in West Africa. It was renovated in 2006 by the Islamic Bank to repair damage caused during the war. While the hospital has the capacity to hold 400 in-patients, it was only operationally capable of serving a maximum of 150 patients in 2008 due to its lack of sufficient staff.

When asked about mental health or mental health services, interviewees from various NGOs and government ministries frequently referred to the psychiatrist's role in the provision of mental health services throughout Sierra Leone. "[He] is *very much* the mental health system in this country. He is the only psychiatrist, the head of the psychiatric hospital (Kissy Mental), and is the head of the mental health unit at the Ministry of Health", explained a female NGO worker in Freetown. (Note: Words or phrases emphasised by interviewees appear in italics)

A male employee at the Ministry of Health and Sanitation said: "If you want to know *anything* about mental health in this country, you must go to [him]. This has been his thing for a *very very long time* and he has very little help from elsewhere in terms of professional support." A male NGO worker in Kono summed it up in simple terms: "In the whole country, we have only one trained psychiatrist … He has a lot on his head." What is striking about Sierra Leone is the lack of community-based mental health services in the provinces given the burden of trauma experienced by these communities and the support needed to ensure the healthy reintegration of war-affected youth in general, and ex-CAAFAG in particular.

While few NGOs provided psychosocial counselling at the community level for children and youth, the Community Association for Psychosocial Services (CAPS) was one example of a local organisation providing free individual, group and family counselling. CAPS was started by Sierra Leoneans in Kono and Kailahun as the international NGO Center for Victims of Torture (CVT) phased out its counselling services in those regions. The organisation employed twelve Sierra Leonean counsellors trained by CVT on a voluntary basis as the organisation lacked adequate funding. CAPS offered individual, group and family counselling in addition to holding community education sessions regarding topics such as stigma and the impact of torture.

The director of CAPS described how the programme worked actively within the community to perform outreach and education, and to identify cases for intervention: "We first went out into the community to sensitise the displaced community about the war that took place – how people suffered and how people have been affected by the experiences they went through. During the sensitisation, we spoke about the symptoms, how people manifested those symptoms, but since people were not aware of what actually they were going through, it would have been difficult for them to identify those symptoms as something affecting them."

The director also explained that a variety of therapeutic techniques are used to help war-affected youth, depending on the nature of the problem. These techniques included art therapy and family counselling. He related that art therapy techniques can be effective in helping children cope with post-war trauma, describing one memorable case of a child he worked with: "... what was most disturbing was the nightmares – the persistent dreams, about the mother and the father and the way they were killed. He was very disturbed, so I asked him to draw the nightmare as it comes to him and try to explain the drawings stage by stage... as we went through the sessions, he said that the nightmares had been reduced – there weren't too many nightmares anymore."

In addition to individual therapies, the director of CAPS spoke of the importance of family and community involvement in psychosocial services, but noted the need for proceeding carefully given the sensitivity of war-related trauma: "Now if what the client is going through is related to the family, then we can ask the consent of the client whether the counsellor can do family mediation or you can have family counselling and if the client agrees, then they can go together, but they have to work on how best the client will feel comfortable. Which method to apply so that the client will not carry more problems for himself or herself in the absence of the counsellor." As he explained, it takes a great deal of sensitivity to work within complex family and community dynamics.

4.1.4. Child Welfare Committees

In addition to hospital-based psychiatric services and community-based counselling in pockets where certain NGOs operate, the child protection community in Sierra Leone has important contributions to make to the package of psychosocial supports available for war-affected youth. In fact, the child welfare committees were "born out of the reintegration of both former child combatants and separated children" (NGO worker, Makeni) after the war. Child welfare committees were initiated at the conclusion of the war by the Ministry of Social Welfare, with funding from UNICEF and implementation support from various international NGOs throughout the country. These committees included individuals from "different walks of life" such as teachers, social workers and health personnel. Interviewees stated that the purpose of child welfare committees was to "serve and mediate situations with children", aid in the "reintegration" of children within the community, "monitor child rights violations", and serve in child protection issues, including neglect and abandonment.

However, by 2008 many of these child welfare committees were no longer in existence or had been rendered ineffective by lack of staff and funding. "Right after the war, there were child welfare committees existing in each and every part of the country. But now, the structures are there, but they are not very effective", explained a male NGO worker in Freetown. Another male NGO worker in

Makeni said he knew that "in the past, child welfare committees were very active" but that he was "unsure if these organisations even still existed."

Some interviewees believed that the disintegration of child welfare committees was linked to a lack of funding. A female employee from the Ministry of Social Welfare stated that some child welfare committees received funding for logistical support, but others did not. "Those [child welfare committees] that were supported financially – they kept up. Those that didn't get anything, they fell apart." A younger Sierra Leonean male employed at an international NGO in Makeni suggested it was unfair to evaluate how well child welfare committees were functioning because "there is no means for them" and "they don't have funding". Many NGO workers expressed frustration at the inconsistent and short-sighted funding that often ends up being inadequate to address the challenges they seek to resolve. One male NGO worker in Kono summed it up: "Donors don't normally go for long term projects. But problems can be very long term."

4.1.5. The "Informal" Services System: The Extended Family

The extended family plays a critical role in the reintegration and rehabilitation of war-affected youth. As we previously discussed, family can be essential in promoting or detracting from children's resilience and reintegration. The concept of "family" is not only limited to blood relations, but can include adoptive, foster and community relationships. As the Sierra Leonean psychiatrist explained: "The extended family system is for everyone in Sierra Leone – all over, even Freetown. It is much stronger in small communities. Freetown is a bit anonymous, you know – different people from different communities all clustered here. While the communities, they know one another and they know everybody." This strong community bond was helpful to many ex-CAAFAGs in the reunification process, as in the case of this younger adolescent female from Kenema: "We got news that our [father] was in Kenema; however, we did not find him there so we were fostered by a man we call grandpa, as we all come from the same village."

In Sierra Leone, the extended family and community can operate as a sort of safe network, and there are many stories of war-affected young people being supported and reintegrated through this network. A mother in Pujehun described the experience of her daughter and the support she received from the community upon return home: "There was a section chief who was my husband's friend, he was good to her… [When she relocated with us] she did not have any problems, because when they took her to Samalin, the chief was present so she was never mocked about being with the fighting forces." As the psychiatrist explained: "*Everyone* in the community will help you if you have a mental health problem. You just say 'I have a problem' and the whole church will come – *the whole church*. The whole mosque, the whole community. The whole society comes to help."

The rallying drive of community support is described by one younger female adolescent, an ex-CAAFAG, who linked the community to the family unit: "The people in this village are living like a family and have love for each other." A younger adolescent female from Kenema described a mentor from an NGO as her "father, because he has helped me through school and he assists with anything we ask of him, he also advise[s] us all the time."

It should be noted that not all interviewees reported such full support in their communities as seen in previous examples, and many reported that such support can fail in the case of mental health needs or severe mental illness. A social worker we interviewed spoke of the benefit of family and community support, but made it clear that this support was far from universal:

> [The mentally ill] live in the street. Relatives take them to the hospital and once they've dumped them, they don't go to visit them – they don't care. I was living just by the mental hospital and I had relatives there…anyone who was my relative, I provided for them. I provided them food, washed their clothing, helped them with their needs. There was one who was a graduate of college – he was a BSc with honours and was working at the bank. But he went mad. And he was smoking [cannabis] – so he went mad. He was going naked in the street and they took him to the mental hospital. They gave him both traditional and western treatment. When he was finished, they took him to job for about three years in a bank before he went to America. He got his Master's [degree] there and now he's doing great, he got married and no one even knows that he was mad. Some people just turn their backs on these people and it is pathetic. And they are not treated well – even in the hospital. I mean years back, the government [gave] food and provision and everything. (Social worker and former NGO employee, Makeni)

The failure of the family/community network in the case of mental illness may spring from a variety of causes, including a lack of understanding of mental health issues, stigma surrounding mental illness, and the ever-present lack of resources.

4.1.6. Traditional and Spiritual Healing

Traditional healers play an important role in the provision of mental health services for youth and children, most notably in Sierra Leone's provinces.[54] One male health care professional based in Freetown explained that there were upwards of 800 traditional healers providing mental health services in the

54 L. Stark, N. Boothby and A. Ager, 'Children and fighting forces: 10 years on from Cape Town', (2009) 33 4 *Disasters*, 522–547.

provinces: "Traditional healers are the *first* and *foremost* point of contact for the *majority* of African patients." He explained that there are various kinds of traditional healers who perform different types of services such as "diviners" who "strictly use prayer to cure patients – usually prayers from the Koran", "pure herbalists" who "solely use herbal medication to cure patients", "diviners cum herbalists" who "combine prayer and herbs", and "sorcerers" who "perform ritual killings" to expunge demons. He described the services provided by traditional healers as "group psychotherapy, including group singing and group dancing". He added that traditional healers also perform "sacrifices and exorcism".

Sierra Leoneans often attribute mental disorders to external forces and many interviewees believed traditional healers to be the most – or even the only – successful providers of care. In the local psychiatrist's words: "The cultural belief here is that mental health problems come from the evil environment that has witchcraft, sorcerers, evil spirits and black magic. And the only people that can get that spell out of you are the traditional healers." A Sierra Leonean traditional healer based in a village close to Freetown explained: "I can cure things that the English doctor cannot see." Traditional and biomedical approaches are perceived as being in opposition, but this does not have to be the case. An employee at the Fatima Nurses' Institute in Makeni advocated for the integration of traditional and medical systems: "…as you know, this is Africa. We have our own separate beliefs. Is that not so? And it is strongly believed that some of the causes [of] mental problems in Africa [are] quite different from Europe. Is that not so? So we thought that there might be some ways of dealing with these people, treating this people – so it is very important to incorporate these traditional healers – even in hospitals."

Traditional healers can play a key role in helping war-affected youth reintegrate into their communities, by providing support through cleansing ceremonies and other rituals that promote reintegration and acceptance. One adolescent male from Kono described how traditional healing processes combined with family support allowed him to recover normalcy and acceptance in his community after returning from his period as a rebel: "People feared me at first when I returned. But I approached my parents about this, and they appealed to the community for my acceptance. My parents also offered prayers and sacrifices for the drugs and other bad things I did whilst on the side of the rebels. I knew of sacrifices and cleansing ceremonies before going to war. They are a sort of communication with God for blessings and forgiveness." Many other interviewees also spoke of these ceremonies being a part of their healing and reintegration process.

In addition to traditional healers, some Sierra Leoneans described seeking Christian spiritual assistance for coping with mental illness. An excellent example of Christian spiritual healing for mental illness came from the City of Rest in Freetown, an organisation that uses prayer and biblically-based individual counselling to provide care for drug abusers and the mentally ill. The pastor, who founded the organisation in 1996, explained: "There is *no* sickness, *no* disease that God cannot heal." He was firm in his belief that it is the responsibility of the church to take in the mentally ill. "If they can't come into the church and we push our doors against them, where do you want them to go?", he asked. His question was phrased rhetorically, but is relevant given the status of mental health services in Sierra Leone. There are very few options for those in need.

4.2. SYSTEMS ASSESSMENT

4.2.1. The State of Mental Health Services

Discussions concerning the state of mental health services in Sierra Leone suggested a general lack of services and funding for youth throughout the country; an urban/rural divide in the provision of services; minimal integration and coordination between services; and questions about the approaches of the NGOs working in Sierra Leone. While NGOs were praised for their provision of needed psychosocial services, interviewees questioned the "donor driven" priorities of NGOs, including this NGO worker from Kono: "Most of the programming of NGOs, is it reflective of what is needed in the community? Or is it driven by what money you can get from where?" Many NGO workers are honest about the need to obtain funding where they can find it. Individuals involved in the provision and leadership of mental health services throughout the country were frank about the limited capacity of the biomedical mental health system to provide for youth. The system was described as "collapsing" and "inadequate" to meet observed need. A female NGO worker stated: "The mental health care system is very limited to almost non-existent." A male health care professional who worked in Freetown estimated that "the mental health system of Sierra Leone is about 30 percent effective." Even when mental health services are available, they are often limited in scope. "There are very few mental health services offered here. The things that do exist are for deformity or handicap, but for things like mental capacity, they no longer exist", reported a female NGO worker in Kono. A number of quotes like these underlined the degree to which services which had been in place at the height of the conflict relief were largely unsustained over the long term, despite the indication of remaining unmet needs.

The major exception to the absence of mental health services is Kissy Mental Hospital, but it remains a centralised organisation at which services are only available in Freetown, with few or no specialised services offered at the community level or in the provinces. Many families have also had to provide supplemental payment for both office visits and medication, which poses a number of barriers, particularly for very poor families. Many interviewees emphasised this urban/rural divide in mental health services for youth, such as a female NGO worker in Freetown who explained: "All I know is that we have one mental hospital… and for the rest of the country, there are no hospitals working on mental health. There are no services there." While there are health centres located throughout Sierra Leone, mental health is not integrated into the services provided at these locations. "We have a mental health hospital in Freetown – but that is it. We have government hospitals all over the country… but there are no wards for psychiatric patients", explained a male NGO worker in Makeni. Another male NGO worker observed: "All the services are centred in the city here, Freetown. So people do not have *access* to the services that the government is providing through [the psychiatrist]. That alone is a setback." As a result, only families who were "very dedicated" and had enough financial support were capable of sending mentally ill family members to Kissy and to outpatient services in Freetown.

Interviewees spoke of the need for decentralisation of mental health services. "We need to move from a *big psychiatric hospital* to more community-based care. I believe in trying to integrate mental health services at the primary health care level", stated a female NGO worker in Freetown. The local psychiatrist agreed: "The next step is decentralization – to go into different communities and look at different institutions." A female government employee in Freetown's stated: "We should work towards having one psychiatrist per major district."

Along with a deficiency in the overall availability of services, the interviewees observed a lack of integration between the few services currently in place. While biomedical, psychosocial and community mental health services exist at varying degrees of functionality and effectiveness, there has been minimal integration and coordination of services. More specifically, the "formal" biomedical mental health system, provided by the psychiatrist in Freetown, largely failed to interact with the "informal" mental health system provided by traditional healers, religious institutions and support from families. A male health care provider based in Freetown says this about the interaction between biomedical services and traditional healers: "*We do not work together. There is no way you can stop them* [patients]. They shuttle from us to them and from them to us." Another says: "There is stigma from Western healers, and jealousy – they think if traditional healers come on board, they will take their patients away."

Interviewees did not generally discuss any kind of relationship between the clinical mental health services offered in Freetown and community-level psychosocial services offered by NGOs such as CAPS and child welfare committees. The lack of connection between "mental health" and "psychosocial" services is probably influenced by the previously described dualistic thinking about the two concepts. In 2008, this duality was also mimicked by the structure of Sierra Leone's government. Clinical mental health in Sierra Leone was the responsibility of the Ministry of Health and the psychosocial welfare of children and youth was the responsibility of the Ministry of Social Welfare, Gender and Children's Affairs and the Ministry of Youth and Sport, respectively.

4.2.2. Challenges to Mental Health Services Implementation

Interviewees identified many barriers to the provision of mental health and psychosocial services to children and youth, including funding challenges, a shortage of health care professionals specialising in mental health, and the lack of prioritisation of mental health by government.

4.2.3. Funding

Interviewees often cited inadequate funding for government services as a barrier to service provision, similar to the previous discussion of the child welfare committees. Representatives of the Ministry of Social Welfare described its budget as "*really* a meagre sum, a small sum". A male employed at the Ministry of Health and Sanitation in Freetown explained that basic health care needs received few resources in Sierra Leone's budget: "What is allocated to health from the government budget is still not at the level of what is required to support *minimum* health services." A male NGO worker in Makeni said that mental health services are essentially omitted during considerations of what minimum necessary services are: "If you talk to Dr Nahim, he will tell you that the resources which are being provided by the Ministry are so negligible that there isn't much he can do for mental health."

Funding difficulties also impacted on international and local NGOs. While explaining why certain NGOs no longer existed or had scaled back their services, interviewees frequently said that "they ran out of funding" or had "funding problems". According to a male NGO worker from Kono: "Our biggest challenge is funding – money is the umbrella, when you have money you can have better logistics." Another NGO worker from Makeni agreed: "We used to have a programme which provided psychosocial services for street children. But the funds ran out and it was difficult to get any more funding."

4.2.4. Human Resources

A shortage of mental health care personnel and human resources was considered the second major barrier to the provision of services. "There really aren't enough counsellors in Sierra Leone – the number is few", explained a male NGO worker in Kono. A female NGO worker in Freetown concurred: "We don't have the trained and qualified personnel to handle the mental needs of youth." While many interviewees asserted their opinion that the country's sole psychiatrist had "done a lot" for the country and was "a very good doctor", it was also acknowledged that he alone "could not meet the caseload of the country" (male NGO worker, Freetown). The reason for this burden was expressed quite simply by a male employed at the Ministry of Health and Sanitation in Freetown: "[He] has very little help from elsewhere in terms of professional support because we don't have it."

Individuals attributed the dearth of human resources for providing mental health services to the "newness" of the discipline, inadequate training opportunities, and the challenges of the job itself. "If you look at their training and curriculum, many Sierra Leoneans have never had any training in communication skills, let alone opportunities to learn how to counsel", said a female NGO worker in Freetown. "The Ministry of Health made provision for sponsorship of individuals willing to train in psychiatry, but we haven't had a lot of enthusiasm and we didn't have anyone apply", a male employee from the Ministry of Health and Sanitation in Freetown explained. A male health professional in Freetown admitted: "It is a difficult job to do, and difficult to work with the patients. Also, the study is very, very difficult"; and one from Makeni stated bluntly that "[p]sychiatry is not a money-making area".

4.2.5. Government Prioritisation

Finally, many service providers criticised the government for its failure to prioritise mental health. The psychiatrist asserted that "[m]ental health is underfunded, neglected, and not on the priority list for anything". This perspective was supported by NGO workers. "The government does not pay attention to mental health", said a male NGO worker in Freetown. Another man who worked at a NGO in Kono agreed, saying: "The political will to make mental health an issue is not there."

Representatives of the Ministry of Health and Sanitation explained that the government's priorities tended to focus on reproductive health given the country's difficulties with maternal, new-born and child health. While it is undoubtedly true that reproductive health is a critical consideration in Sierra Leone's development (it has some of the highest rates of maternal and infant mortality anywhere), some individuals working for NGOs in the field felt that the prioritisation of these issues completely eliminated attention to other important issues. A female NGO worker in Freetown commented that Sierra

Leone's high maternal mortality and infant mortality rates were "used as an argument not to pay attention to mental health at all".

5. LIMITATIONS OF STUDY AND OPPORTUNITIES FOR FURTHER INVESTIGATION

We provide here some insight into the mental health issues facing individuals, communities and systems in Sierra Leone from the perspective of community children, youth and their caretakers as well as those involved in the provision of services and policy and programmatic leadership. As interviewees were purposively sampled, the opinions in this paper may or may not be representative of all individuals working in the provision of mental health services within Sierra Leone as a whole. It is important to note that interviewees were selected from discrete regions within Sierra Leone and may not provide or have access to services which are representative of the services available throughout the country. Finally, there is the potential for bias induced by the interviewer within this study. Focus groups and key informant interviews with CAAFAG were conducted by local trained interviewers, but the policy and programmatic stakeholder interviewees were interviewed by a graduate student from Harvard University. Several asked the student if she knew of funding opportunities for their organisation through Harvard. This knowledge may have caused mental health providers to overemphasise funding challenges or barriers to care.

Future work should consider the availability of mental health and psychosocial services from the perspective of youth, potentially utilising geographic mapping of the services which currently exist countrywide. Additionally, this study has touched on a number of topics that merit further exploration. One such topic is the role of child welfare committees in communities, with specific consideration of communities where the committees have been sustained versus those where they have deteriorated. Another important area of study would be a more thorough examination of the mental health services provided by traditional healers and the types of mental health disorder they see. A qualitative investigation of how "clinical mental health" services versus "psychosocial support" are defined by service providers would also be of great benefit in clarifying a direction for progress, whether for systems-level interventions or for holistically developing the national health system.

6. CONCLUSIONS/RECOMMENDATIONS

6.1. THE IMPORTANCE OF A SUSTAINABLE MENTAL HEALTH RESPONSE

In Sierra Leone, the impact of the war, including exposure to violence, has affected everyone, resulting in threats to the healthy development of all young people. The trauma of war experiences is compounded by daily stressors such as an undeveloped economy, lack of education and employment opportunities, and low financial resources for government ministries and programmes. In many cases impoverished youth and families face difficulty in accessing even basic healthcare and adequate nutrition and shelter. In such an environment, mental health concerns and psychosocial support receive little if any attention.

However, our qualitative evidence suggests there is tremendous resilience and strength among war-affected families and communities. These groups provide emotional and financial support to youth throughout their times of need. Groups like CAPS in Kono provide free services on a small budget in the face of significant obstacles. Nonetheless, the resilience of war-affected youth, families and communities should never provide an excuse for not developing and implementing more robust services for those in need. Mental illness and psychosocial needs are an area of major concern for these youth and their families, particularly as they begin to come of age and assume adult roles. If Sierra Leone does not address the recovery and social reintegration of a generation, it may be unable to maximise goals for its economic and social agenda. By considering the current mental health system available to youth in Sierra Leone and the barriers they face to accessing services, we can start to conceptualise ways to improve the mental health response to meet the continuing needs of youth in post-conflict environments. Given the difficult past they have endured and the current daily struggles they face, it is critical to enhance the services available to youth and to ensure they can take advantage of the opportunities the future will bring.

While efforts have been made in domestic and international legislation to mediate the challenges facing youth in Sierra Leone, including the IASC guidelines and the Sierra Leone Child Rights Act, these regulations fail to address the current crises facing many war-affected youth. Counsellors, ministers and NGO workers have all identified reasons for the continuing inadequacy of the mental health services in Sierra Leone, as well as ways in which current untapped resources might contribute to a more efficacious and inclusive approach to mental health in the future. Such resources include the agency of youth, the vast network of traditional healers and the family and community support that can be mobilised through sensitisation and community-based interventions like the Child Welfare Committees. Those Committees can be taken as exemplary structures, and their failure speaks to the need for long-term sustainability of funding, staffing and programming to serve youth facing mental health and psychosocial challenges. Community-based counselling services, such as those provided by CAPS, risk the same fate.

6.2. KNOWLEDGE FROM CURRENT SERVICE MODELS

Betancourt and Tol[55] highlight the importance of three kinds of intervention which are critical for comprehensive service provision for war-affected children and youth: prevention, treatment and maintenance. Prevention efforts, or interventions which consider risk and protective factors to prevent mental health disorders or psychosocial distress, can be identified on several levels. At the individual level, interventions might focus on enhancing an individual's capability to cope, developing problem-solving skills, and strengthening personal self-esteem.[56] On the family level, it is important for children and youth to have strong social networks with loving relationships for primary prevention. In the case of children associated with armed forces and armed groups in Sierra Leone, family reunification and community reintegration services were critical as well as widespread sensitisation campaigns aimed at reducing stigma and enhancing the community acceptance of CAAFAG.[57]

Treatment, described by Betancourt and Tol[58] as "the identification and treatment of mental health disorders and psychosocial distress" (similar to the clinical interventions discussed above) can also occur on individual, group and community levels. Appropriate treatment approaches require culturally sensitive diagnoses as a foundation for the development of the treatment plan. In more highly resourced countries, an evidence base has been established to respond to the mental health needs of children and adolescents, and a number of evidence-based mental health interventions have been tested. For instance, for the treatment of depression or anxiety disorders, cognitive-based therapies (CBT) may be utilised. For conduct problems, varieties of multisystemic therapy (MST) may be used, which can influence the various social factors in an individual's life and address risk factors.[59] However, very little research has examined the

55 T.S. Betancourt and W. Tol, *supra* note 47.

56 Ibid.

57 Ibid.

58 Ibid.

59 V.R. Weersing and D.A. Brent, 'Cognitive behavioral therapy for depression in youth', (2006) 15 4 *Child and Adolescent Psychiatric Clinics of North America*, 939–957; S. Henggeler and T. Lee, 'Multisystemic Treatment of Serious Clinical Problems', in A.E.

cultural appropriateness and transportability of these intervention models to assist children in war-affected low-resource settings.[60] In addition, these interventions require both financial and human resources and are often too costly for use in low-resource settings like Sierra Leone. Additionally, mental health interventions that are standard in developed nations may require additional adaptation and validation for cultural differences, which is time- and resource-intensive but a major topic for a research agenda to advance the field.

Finally, maintenance interventions, which work to reduce the likelihood of relapse once treatment has been provided, are critical given the long recovery process and the often chronic nature of many mental health issues, such as the rampant drug use problems among Sierra Leonean youth in the post-conflict period. Few studies have been conducted regarding maintenance interventions. In fact, in the case of war-affected children and ex-CAAFAGs, very few resources generally exist to establish sustainable systems of care that offer ongoing support and monitoring for those requiring additional services following prevention or treatment-focused interventions. No doubt in part because of the lack of resources, most post-conflict interventions tend to be short term and crisis-focused. However, as the literature and research to date show, war-related trauma is by no means short term, and sustained interventions are of critical importance.

To create the most appropriate prevention, treatment, and maintenance services within Sierra Leone, there must be an understanding of how individuals cope with mental health problems and the host of non-formal resources from individual coping to family and community supports as well as additional sources of strength found in religious faith and traditional healing approaches that should be built on in the development of systems of care. The mental health and psychosocial needs of war-affected youth occur along a continuum and providers should work together to address and link services for broad-based or general support as well as more specialised needs. The WHO[61] recommends collaboration with non-health-focused governmental groups, NGOs, and village and community healthcare workers to ensure that individuals with mental health disorders receive the services they need and are able to reintegrate within their community. Traditional healers, also working at the community level, have been shown to provide an important element of mental health care, especially in post-conflict settings where they may be an integral part of the reintegration of

---

Kazdin and R.J. Weisz (eds.), *Evidence-based psychotherapies for children and adolescents*, The Guilford Press: New York, 2003, 301–322.

60 T. S. Betancourt and T. Williams, *supra* note 32.

61 WHO, *Integrating mental health into primary care. A Global Perspective.* World Health Organization, Geneva, 2008.

youth.[62] Traditional healers are potentially very effective partners in the provision of mental health services due to their acceptance and accessibility within communities, along with community confidence in their ability to manage mental health difficulties, their role in reducing stigma through purification and exorcism ceremonies, and their cost-effectiveness.[63] Given the qualitative evidence concerning cultural beliefs regarding the influence of external forces on mental health, it is particularly important for traditional healers and spiritual leaders to be included in any psychosocial response. In attempting to create patient- and family-centred mental health services for youth it is essential for Sierra Leone's stakeholders to expand its mental health workforce by training more primary health care workers in mental health issues and supporting them in their work. Another option might involve including community health care workers (CHWs) in the mental health response as the use of CHWs has been shown to increase the uptake of services by communities and increase outreach to vulnerable groups.[64]

6.3. MULTI-SECTORAL, INTEGRATED APPROACHES TO SERVICE DELIVERY

A multi-sectoral response to addressing the psychosocial and mental health needs of youth is also essential to Sierra Leone's efforts to create a continuum of services. It is important for individuals involved in the clinical mental health system to work closely with international and local NGOs to help inform psychosocial service provision. This integration should be mimicked in the structure of government, with greater coordination between the Ministry of Health and Sanitation and the Ministry of Social Welfare, Gender and Children's Affairs as well as the Ministry of Education, Youth and Sport. Given the large burden of daily stressors discussed by interviewees within the post-war context and the potential impact these stressors make on mental health, psychosocial services for youth must be expanded along with greater opportunities for education and employment. Because NGOs will eventually phase out the services they provide, it is essential that from the inception of their programmes they consider sustainability through local capacity-building and partnership. Government ministries that provide services for youth and children, such as the Ministry of Education, must also coordinate more effectively with other agencies

62 K. Amone-P'Olak, 'Mental states of adolescents exposed to war in Uganda: finding appropriate methods of rehabilitation', (2006) 16 2 *Torture*, 93–107; Stark et al., *supra* note 54.

63 R.F. Mollica, B.L. Cardozo, H.J. Osofsky, B. Raphael, A. Ager and P. Salama, 'Mental health in complex emergencies', (2004) 364 9450 *The Lancet*, 2058–2067.

64 J.S. Mukherjee and E. Eustache, 'Community health care workers as a cornerstone for integrating HIV and primary healthcare', (2007) 19 *AIDS Care*, S73-S82.

to provide psychosocial support and mental health services, including co-locating such services into existing systems of care such as schools and paediatric programmes.[65]

Additionally, the barriers discussed by interviewees – inadequacy of funding, lack of mental health personnel, stigma, and low prioritisation of mental health by government – must be addressed. The nature of these barriers and potential strategies for addressing them have been examined in a number of important policy articles on global mental health.[66] Given the many tasks facing Sierra Leone's current government, including President Koroma's chief interest in addressing energy needs (particularly access to electricity), agriculture and self-sufficiency in food production, and infrastructure development, it is difficult to know whether greater political will or attention to the mental health of children and youth will be delivered to overcome these barriers. The planned establishment of a Youth Commission for Sierra Leone may present one platform for advocating for holistic and integrated approaches to the needs of this war-affected generation, but as of the writing of this article this important policy development was not yet actualised. However, there are many promising factors for the long-term recovery and development of Sierra Leone. Not least is the mostly untapped potential found in the people of Sierra Leone, who show great resilience and strength. With the investment of support and political will, this human capacity could well prove to be Sierra Leone's greatest resource. Such support and political will is apparent in some programmes, such as First Lady Sia Koroma's women's health initiative and the Flaxis Project to build civic pride and responsibility in young people through a variety of school-based and community activities.

Groups looking to promote the use of sustainable community structures to address the mental health concerns of youth and issues of child protection must learn from the mistakes made in the unsuccessful maintenance of entities such as Child Welfare Committees. As discussed, Child Welfare Committees were given inconsistent financial and logistical support, making it difficult for them to continue functioning. For groups like these to be "revived", they must be supported with logistics, supervision, technical and management skills, and strategic support for dealing with cases requiring referral and continuity in an

---

65 K. Allden, L. Jones, I. Weissbecker, M. Wessells, P. Bolton, T.S. Betancourt, Z. Hijazi, A. Galappatti, R. Yamout, P. Patel and A. Sumathipala, *Mental Health and Psychosocial Support in Crisis and Conflict: Report of the Mental Health Working Group,* 2009.

66 WHO, *Atlas: Child and Adolescent Mental Health Resources: Global Concerns, Implications for the Future*, World Health Organization, Geneva, 2005; B. Saraceno, M. van Ommeren, R. Batniji, A. Cohen, O. Gureje, J. Mahoney, D. Sridhar and C. Underhill, 'Barriers to improvement of mental health services in low-income and middle-income countries', (2007) 370 *The Lancet*, 1164–1174; S. Saxena, G. Thornicroft, M. Knapp and H. Whiteford, 'Resources for mental health: scarcity, inequity, and inefficiency', (2007) 370 9590 *The Lancet*, 878–889.

environment which is sorely lacking in accessible, affordable and appropriate services that match the level of need. Most important is the consideration of providing professional development and remuneration to individuals working in child welfare committees. While this sort of approach has been criticised as "unsustainable" by some groups, major global health organisations such as Partners In Health have observed important patient benefits, staff retention and health system improvements by ensuring high quality training and appropriate remuneration of community health workers in impoverished areas. This approach is an excellent way to support effective systems and simultaneously build local capacity for sustainable long-term services.

While it is impossible for Sierra Leone to change what took place in the immediate post-conflict period, it is certainly not too late to take positive and effective action to promote the recovery and development of its young people. Our research illustrates that it is possible to support positive outcomes for young people, often in ways that support the overall development of the country (i.e. access to educational and work opportunities). Above all, Sierra Leone should look towards ways of developing the untapped potential inherent in the country's youth, families and communities. One important part of this process would be to support intervention studies, based on existing evidence and modified to the needs and resources in this context, for Sierra Leonean war-affected youth and communities.

6.4. THINKING BEYOND SIERRA LEONE

Sadly, the world will continue to witness children, youth and families affected by war. International and domestic responses to the issue must consider the importance of mental health and psychosocial needs, particularly those that arise in the transition from humanitarian relief to post-conflict development. Sierra Leone provides an example of a country with numerous cultural and family resources to support healthy reintegration which have not been adequately harnessed to develop a more robust system of monitoring and support for its war-affected generation. Many young people continue to fall between the cracks. This experience should be weighed in the future development of policies and interventions targeting war-affected youth and communities. Early interventions should be constructed with an eye towards promoting the long-term recovery of war-affected communities, building on the profound capacity for resilience and strength shown by so many in spite of extremely adverse circumstances. Attention should be given to certain critical elements that predict successful reintegration such as galvanising protective processes in youth, families and communities and monitoring situations where family and community relations go awry (manifested in persistent stigma, abuse or neglect). Although the period of immediate reintegration is important in the psychosocial adjustment of CAAFAG, robust support is also required over the long term to sustain healthy functioning, link those needing additional support to appropriate services and engage with problems that may arise. Although indigenous strengths will probably serve most children well, additional professional services, training and resources must also be set aside to navigate skilfully more serious problems such as breached family placements, abuse and neglect, emotional and behavioural problems (including substance abuse) and persistent community stigma. Increased access to opportunities for education, job skills training and health care are also essential not only for CAAFAG, but for *all* war-affected youth. Appropriate systems should be put in place to monitor reintegrated youth and to provide ongoing psychosocial support and clinical services where needed to those who have particular difficulty resettling. Such ancillary services are an essential part of ensuring the success of efforts invested in returning children home after the war. In summary, it is critical that humanitarian relief models include, from the beginning, a capacity to recognise and maximise local resources and local capacity and that they transition to more sustainable support for war-affected youth over time. Incorporating lessons learned in Sierra Leone may ensure better immediate and long-term outcomes for war-affected youth, families and communities in other nations.

THE FIT BETWEEN MENTAL HEALTH NEEDS AND PROGRAMMING RESPONSES FOR WAR-AFFECTED CHILDREN IN NORTHERN UGANDA*

James OKELLO, Ilse DERLUYN, Seggane MUSISI and Eric BROEKAERT

1. INTRODUCTION

The challenges of reintegration in post-conflict settings have been a focus of attention in Uganda, which experienced over 20 years of armed conflict between the government of Uganda and the rebel Lord's Resistance Army (LRA) that ended only five years ago. War-affected children in Uganda include not only those who were abducted by rebel forces, but all those children and adolescents who suffered – amongst other difficult experiences – internal displacement, loss of livelihood and caregivers, and disruption of infrastructure and services during the prolonged armed conflict.[1] Several studies have highlighted the important interaction between exposure to possible traumatising experiences, available social and professional support and children's mental health in conflict settings.[2] Simultaneously, a large number of interventions have been created in these conflict settings to tackle the possible impact of traumatising experiences on the mental health of war-affected young people.

This paper will focus on the fit between children's mental health needs on the one hand and the programming responses for children in (post-)conflict settings on the other hand by providing, firstly, an overview of child- and adolescent-traumatising experiences and their outcomes; secondly, discussing the

* Acknowledgements go to the German Embassy in Uganda through their support to the Psychotraumatology Division, Department of Mental Health, Gulu University. We extend our gratitude to An Verelst and Prof. Ekkehard Doering for their assistance with the literature search, creative ideas and helpful comments on earlier drafts.

1 G. MACHEL, *The impact of war on children*, Hurst & Company, London, 2001.

2 C.C. HENRICH and G. SHAHAR, 'Social support buffers the effects of terrorism on adolescent depression: findings from Sderot, Israel', (2008) 47 *Journal of the American Academy of Child and Adolescent Psychiatry*, 1073–1076.

interventions that have been used with war-affected children and adolescents to improve their mental health; and, lastly, discussing practice implications for the fit between mental health needs and feasible programming responses.

2. TRAUMATISING EXPERIENCES AND MENTAL HEALTH NEEDS OF WAR-AFFECTED CHILDREN IN NORTHERN UGANDA

A mental health disorder can be defined as 'the presence of psychological distress; impairment in psychological, social, or occupational functioning; or, any disorder that is associated with an increased risk of suffering death, pain disability or loss of freedom'.[3] Mental health problems among war-affected children have been well documented in Uganda.[4] Most of these studies have focused on post-traumatic stress disorder (PTSD),[5] although the prevalence rates of PTSD in these studies vary considerably, ranging from 97[6] to 27%.[7]

Other mental health problems have also been documented, including depression,[8] generalised anxiety disorders and substance abuse.[9]

Adolescents who experience more war-related traumatic experiences are at greater risk of a range of negative mental health problems, including internalising (e.g. post-traumatic stress disorder, anxiety disorders, depression)[10] and

---

3 M. Boyd and M. Nihart, *Psychiatric Nursing: Contemporary Practice*. Philadelphia, Lippincott, 1998.

4 K. Amone-P'Olak, N. Garnefski and V. Kraaij, 'Adolescents caught between fires: Cognitive emotion regulation in response to war experiences in Northern Uganda', (2007) 30 *Journal of Adolescence*, 655–669; C.P. Bayer, F. Klasen and H. Adam, 'Association of trauma and PTSD symptoms with openness to reconciliation and feelings of revenge among former Ugandan and Congolese child soldiers', (2007) 298 *JAMA-Journal of the American Medical Association*, 555–559: J. Okello, T.S. Onen and S. Musisi, 'Psychiatric disorders among war-abducted and non-abducted adolescents in Gulu district, Uganda: A comparative study', (2007) 10 *African Journal of Psychiatry*, 225–231.

5 Ibid.; I. Derluyn, E. Broekaert, G. Schuyten and E. De Temmerman, 'Posttraumatic stress in former Ugandan child soldiers', (2004) 363 *Lancet*, 861–863.

6 Derluyn et al., ibid.

7 Okello et al., *supra* note 4.

8 P. Bolton, J. Bass, T.S. Betancourt, L. Speelman, G. Onyango, K. Clougherty et al., 'Interventions for depression symptoms among war-affected adolescents in northern Uganda: A randomized controlled trial', (2007) 298 5 *JAMA-Journal of the American Medical Association*, 519–527.

9 Okello et al., *supra* note 4.

10 Derluyn et al., *supra* note 5; K. Johnson, J. Asher, S. Rosborough, A. Raja, R. Panjabi, C. Beadling et al., 'Association of combatant status and sexual violence with health and mental health outcomes in post conflict Liberia' (2008) 300 *JAMA-Journal of the American Medical Association*, 676–690.

externalising (e.g. risk behaviours) problems.[11] Traumatic experiences are a necessary but not a sufficient condition for the development of PTSD, as only a minority of those exposed to trauma develop clinically significant PTSD and there seem to be few linear causal relationships between trauma exposure and the development of disorders, including PTSD,[12] suggesting that other factors, such as different child-, family- and community-related factors, the availability and protection of family systems and perceived social support and attachment, play a moderating role in this relationship.[13]

Despite several studies documenting psychological symptoms among war-affected children and adolescents,[14] there is some indication that the majority of these children are able to adjust following reintegration or return from captivity.[15] Studies supportive of this view suggest that while symptoms of PTSD and depression persist years after their reintegration, many of these young people become integrated civilians and function at par with others in their community, both socially and economically.[16]

---

11 A. Al-Krenawi, J.R. Graham and Y. Kanat-Maymon, 'Analysis of trauma exposure, symptomatology and functioning in Jewish Israeli and Palestinian adolescents' (2009) 195 *British Journal of Psychiatry,* 427–432; J. Garbarino and K. Kostelny, 'The Effects of Political Violence on Palestinian Children's Behavior Problems: A Risk Accumulation Model', (1996) 67 *Child Development,* 33–45; S. Quota, R.L. Punamaki, T. Miller and E. El Sarraj, 'Does War Beget Child Aggression? Military Violence, Gender, Age and Aggressive behaviour in Two Palestinian Samples', (2008) 34 *Aggressive Behaviour,* 231–244; T. Sibai, R.A. Tohme, H.A. Beydoun, N. Kanaan and A.M. Sibai, 'Violent behavior among adolescents in post-war Lebanon: the role of personal factors and correlation with other problem behaviors', (2008) 31 1 *Journal of Public Health,* 39–46.

12 J. C. Markowitz, B. Milrod, K. Bleiberg and R.D. Marshall, 'Interpersonal Factors in Understanding and Treating Posttraumatic Stress Disorder', (2009) 152 *Journal of Psychiatric Practice,* 133–140.

13 J.S. Brook, D.W. Brook and M. Whiteman, 'Growing up in a Violent Society: Longitudinal Predictors of Violence in Colombian Adolescents' (2007) 40 *American Journal of Community Psychology,* 82–95; F. Declercq and V. Palmans, 'Two subjective factors as moderators between critical incidents and the occurrence of post traumatic stress disorders: "Adult attachment" and "perception of social support"', (2006) 79 *Psychology and Psychotherapy: Theory, Research and Practice,* 323–337; M. Dieperink, J. Leskela, P. Thuras and B. Engdahl, 'Attachment style classification and posttraumatic stress disorder in former prisoners of war', (2001) 71 3 *American Journal of Orthopsychiatry,* 374–378; Garbarino and Kostelny, *supra* note 11; M. Shamai and S. Kimhi, 'Teenagers Response to Threat of War and Terror: Gender and the Role of Social Systems', (2007) 43 4 *Community Mental Health Journal,* 359–374; S. Quota, R.L. Punamaki, T. Miller and E. El Sarraj, 'Predictors of psychological distress and positive resources among Palestinian adolescents: Trauma, child, and mothering characteristics', (2007) 31 7 *Child Abuse & Neglect,* 699–717.

14 Bayer et al., *supra* note 4; Derluyn et al., *supra* note 5; Johnson et al., *supra* note 10.

15 Amone-P'Olak et al., *supra* note 4.

16 T.S. Betancourt, 'Child Soldiers: Reintegration, Pathways to Recovery and Perspectives from the Field', (2008) 29 2 *Journal of Developmental & Behavioral Pediatrics,* 138–141.

3. PROGRAMMING RESPONSES

Interventions in northern Uganda directed towards war-affected children and adolescents typically include either basic mental health literacy or specific mental health or psychosocial interventions.[17] In post-conflict settings, the provision of specific interventions addressing mental health problems may not be feasible given that the most important considerations are those of basic mental health literacy,[18] focusing mainly on psycho-education about mental health symptoms children may experience and aiming at normalising children's reaction to stress, as well as to provide an opportunity for health care providers to suggest to the children ways of managing these symptoms and of coping with them.[19] The Ministry of Health, through its division of mental health, and other stakeholders in trauma work in northern Uganda have specifically focused on training general health workers and the public to recognise common mental illnesses and on designing Information, Education and Communication (IEC) materials specific to the needs of war-affected persons.[20]

Specific mental health or psychosocial interventions can generally be classified into four types: individual-based, school-based, family-based and community-based.[21]

Individual-based mental health and psychosocial interventions in northern Uganda include, amongst others, trauma counselling, skills and vocational training, group psychotherapy and provision of material support.[22] Studies of specific individual-based interventions are few, and the evidence regarding the efficacy of individual-based interventions varies depending on the population and the context studied. MacMullin and Loughry[23] found that psychosocial interventions provided by agencies in northern Uganda improved the psychosocial adjustment of former child soldiers compared to those who returned directly home after captivity. However, they found that important differences still existed among the different agencies, suggesting that significant

---

17 C. Crowley, 'The mental health needs of refugee children: A review of literature and implications for nurse practitioners', (2009) 21 *Journal of the American Academy of Nurse Practitioners*, 322–331.

18 Ibid.

19 Ibid.; J. Okello and B. Alipanga, *The Fit between Mental health and Programming Responses for War Affected Children in Northern Uganda*, Proceeds from the 2nd Peter Alderman Foundation workshop Eastern Africa Psycho-trauma Training Workshop, Kampala, Uganda, July 2009.

20 Ibid.

21 Crowley, *supra* note 17.

22 C. MacMullin and M. Loughry, *An investigation into the psychosocial adjustment of formerly abducted child soldiers in northern Uganda*. Kampala, Uganda: The International Rescue Committee, 2002.

23 Ibid.

contextual and cultural factors should be considered when measuring post-conflict adaptation. Secondly, Neuner and colleagues[24] found that exposure-based therapy might be safe and effective in treating children with war-related PTSD in post-conflict settings in developing countries.

Family-based approaches, such as family tracing, have also been studied as a way to ameliorate the mental health status of war-affected children. Qualitative research has shown that many war-affected children in northern Uganda primarily depend on their own families for support and guidance and may be reluctant to seek help from outside the family.[25] In a survey of war-affected youths in northern Uganda, Annan and Blattman[26] provide evidence of the integral role of the family in the reintegration of former child soldiers and in former child soldiers' long-term mental health: high family connectedness and social support predicted lower levels of emotional distress and better social functioning. Family-based interventions have therefore been thought to be effective.[27]

School-based interventions, often concretised into the training of teachers to recognise mental health problems among school-going children,[28] have been proposed as an effective way to reach war-affected children and adolescents.[29] Not only do schools provide a place for learning, but they also facilitate the development of peer relationships and a sense of identity.[30] Moreover, schools can play an essential role in the successful integration or reintegration of war-affected adolescents into their community, and can serve as a strong foundation not only for educational but also for social and emotional development.[31] The

24 F. Neuner, M. Schauer, C. Klaschik, U. Karunakara and T. Elbert, 'A comparison of narrative exposure therapy, supportive counselling and psychoeducation for treating posttraumatic stress disorder in an Afrikcan refugee settlement', (2004) 72 4 *Journal of Consulting and Clinical Psychology*, 579-587.

25 J. Annan, M. Briere and F. Aryemo, 'From "rebel" to "returnee". Daily life and reintegration for young soldiers in northern Uganda', (2009) 24 *Journal of Adolescent Research*, 639–667.

26 Annan et al., 'The psychological resilience of youth in northern Uganda: Survey of War Affected Youth, Research Brief 2', available at www.sway-uganda.org/SWAY.RB2.pdf (accessed 6 February 2008).

27 Crowley, *supra* note 17; Annan, ibid.; T.S. Betancourt and K.T. Khan, 'The mental health of children affected by armed conflict: Protective processes and pathways to resilience', (2008) 20 3 *International Review of Psychiatry*, 317–328.

28 J. Okello and B. Alipanga, *Training Programs to Improve Mental Health Services in Northern Uganda: Issues and Challenges*, Proceeds from the 2nd PCAF Eastern Africa Psycho-trauma Training Workshop, Kampala-Uganda, July 2009.

29 Okello and Alipanga, *supra* note 19.

30 Ibid.

31 Okello and Alipanga, *supra* note 28; P.I. Ibeziako, O. Olayinka and T.B. Tolulope, 'Assessment of need for a school-based mental health programme in Nigeria: Perspectives of school administrators', (2008) 20 3 *International Review of Psychiatry*, 271–280.

role of schools as a setting in which to intervene and effect improvements in mental health outcomes for war-affected children are therefore promising.

Finally, *community-based interventions*, including, amongst others, group psychotherapy, community education, cleansing ceremonies and community capacity building, have been suggested as a fourth type of intervention. Community-based approaches in northern Uganda have shown some evidence of effectiveness in reducing symptoms of mental ill health. For example, Bolton and colleagues[32] have demonstrated in a randomised-controlled trial of 314 adolescents aged 14–17 years in two camps for internally displaced persons in northern Uganda that a therapy-based intervention (i.e. group interpersonal psychotherapy) was effective in reducing depression symptoms in war-affected adolescent girls (not in boys) compared to an activity-based intervention (i.e. creative play). However, neither group interpersonal psychotherapy nor creative play was effective in improving anxiety symptoms, conduct problems or general functioning among boys or girls.

4. DISCUSSION

Several significant observations can be made about current interventions and mental health approaches in the war- and post-war region of northern Uganda.

Firstly, as shown in the above mentioned typology of interventions in war-affected regions, we clearly can state that there is often a tendency to overlook issues of trauma in recovery efforts and that interventions and resources also seemed to be mainly concentrated on selected categories of youth, such as former child soldiers.

Secondly, most programmes focus solely on (severe) mental health problems and tend to overlook the broader range of psychosocial problems with which northern Ugandan war-affected children and adolescents are confronted, although most children in (post-)conflict settings do not show severe mental health problems but suffer from a broader range of psychosocial problems. This means that children suffering from this broader range of psychosocial problems often do not find appropriate support for dealing with them.

Thirdly, in the immediate aftermath of war, short-term humanitarian responses are usually phased out during the transition to the post-conflict and the reconstruction phases. However, the needs of war-affected children do not follow

32 Bolton et al., *supra* note 8.

a similar phasing-out process, particularly when they have been poorly addressed at the outset.[33]

In post-conflict phases, many adolescents and their families are also still confronted with feelings of loss of control over current circumstances, as well as feelings of distrust towards others.

Fourthly, there is clear evidence of the major impact of the disruption to family and other social structures on adolescents' mental health in (post-)conflict settings.[34] However, mental health interventions addressing and/or including family and other social structures remain rather limited, overlooking important possibilities for strengthening families and communities in their ability to support children's and adolescents' mental health and psychosocial functioning.

Similarly, there is little knowledge of how schools and their academic programmes can best contribute to children's mental health,[35] although they seem to be an excellent context for engaging with children and adolescents. However, defining what works for school mental health is a daunting challenge in view of the general lack of school mental health programmes, policies and services in post-conflict settings.[36] In an effort to explore the role of school in post-conflict settings, there is need to determine the feasibility of utilising schools to promote or address the mental health of school-going children from the perspectives of those who must deliver the services: school teachers and administrators.[37] A recent review of the perspectives of high school teachers revealed that most thought the best way mental health specialists could help was to ensure that teachers were trained in basic mental health skills, such as recognition of mental health problems and adequate referral of students with mental health problems to further specialised interventions.[38] Moreover, context-specific factors unique to the developing world that dictate how mental health services for children and adolescents can be provided need to be taken into account. For example – and in contrast with school settings in the developed world – currently almost no mental health services are provided by schools in developing countries.[39] In Uganda too, the burden of mental health problems

---

33 Okello and Alipanga, *supra* note 28.

34 Ibid.

35 E. Haruri, *The relationship between mental health academic performance of school children in Gulu municipality Gulu,* University Dissertation, Gulu University, Gulu, Uganda.

36 Okello and Alipanga, *supra* note 19.

37 Okello and Alipanga, *supra* note 28.

38 Crowley, *supra* note 19; Okello and Alipanga, *supra* note 19.

39 Okello and Alipanga, *supra* note 28 P. Graham and J. Orley, 'WHO and the mental health of children', (1998) 19 3 *World Health Forum*, 268–272; O.O. Omigbodun, 'Mental health services for children in Nigeria. Where should the focus be?', (2004) 4 1 *Archives of Ibadan Medicine*, 12.

among school-going children has been documented, but specific school-based interventions to address them do not exist.[40]

This lack of school-based interventions is also due to the fact that in northern Uganda most interventions for war-affected children are provided within institutional settings – and often only within rehabilitation centres for former child soldiers. However, these programmes addressing mental health in institutional settings have been seriously criticised because the successes registered there, if any, are seldom translated into actual changes of behaviour when the children are reintegrated into their homes or communities.[41]

The heterogeneous nature of children in these institutions means that it is imperative that individualised approaches are used to address their mental health or psychosocial problems. Such approaches are, however, often not possible because the institutions lack specialised and trained staff members. Furthermore, the post-conflict setting in northern Uganda presents special challenges in the lack of basic mental health literacy, child-specific mental health services, specialised mental health staff for children and adolescents and evidence-based mental health treatment programmes for children and adolescents. These deficiencies therefore raise major obstacles to developing an adequate approach towards children and youngsters with severe mental health problems.[42]

Lastly, although there is a significant need to provide evidence-based culturally appropriate psychosocial and mental health interventions to war-affected children, few such services exist, raising questions about the cultural validity of the services provided,[43] all the more so because many of these interventions are offered by international organisations and executed by non-local workers.

In relation to this last remark, the above-mentioned findings about interventions' efficacy and effectiveness also need to be considered in light of significant measurement problems, imposing Western concepts and practices on non-

[40] Amone-P'Olak et al., *supra* note 4; J. Nalugya, 'Dissertation: A study of Depression amongst adolescent in secondary schools in Mukono district, Uganda', 2004.

[41] C. Savino, 'A Report on Displaced Children and Orphan Fund Programs in Gulu and Kitgum', (2000) *USAID's Displaced Children's and Orphan's Fund*, 1–9.

[42] Okello and Alipanga, *supra* note 19; T.S. Betancourt, L. Speelman, G. Onyango and P. Bolton, 'A Qualitative Study of Mental Health Problems among Children Displaced by War in Northern Uganda', (2009) 46 2 *Transcultural Psychiatry*, 238–256.

[43] Okello and Alipanga, *supra* note 4; Betancourt, *supra* note 16 and 25; T.S. Betancourt, 'The psychosocial impact of armed conflict on children: Rethinking traditional paradigms in research and intervention', (2001) 10 4 *Child and Adolescent Psychiatric Clinics of North America*, 797–814; D. Summerfield, 'The invention of post-traumatic stress disorder and the social usefulness of a psychiatric category', (2001) 322 *British Journal of Medicine*, 95–98.

Western societies and on non-Western responses to trauma.[44] Moreover, most studies have focused on the impact of interventions on specific mental health problems and often solely on their impact on post-traumatic stress symptoms, while a broader range of mental health and psychosocial issues, such as general functioning, and the role of other factors in children's mental health, such as openness to reconciliation, feelings of revenge[45] and cognitive emotional processing of trauma,[46] have seldom been included or evaluated.

5. IMPLICATIONS

As children continue to be victims of war, psychosocial interventions adapted to children's specific needs using a public health approach are increasingly important and relevant for post-conflict settings. Conscious efforts are needed to improve child and adolescent mental health services and mental health literacy among conflict-affected populations. Because schools provide the most feasible way of accessing children, there is need to work with and provide specialised training for teachers, parents and general health workers in recognition of common mental health problems among children and adolescents affected by armed conflict. An integrated model of trauma intervention must not only reflect Western psychotherapeutic interventions, but also embrace the mores of the culture within which the intervention is offered.[47] The primary focus of any model should include empowerment of indigenous populations to teach trauma intervention principles within their communities, operationalise programmes supportive of the ongoing trauma intervention as they define it, and accomplish this without dependence on international funding. We recommend that a mental health policy specifically adapted to the needs of children and adolescents affected by armed conflict is developed within each (post-) conflict setting.

---

44 Summerfield, ibid.

45 Amone-P'Olak et al., *supra* note 4.

46 Ibid.

47 M.G. Wessells, *Child soldiers: From violence to protection*, Harvard University Press, Cambridge (Mass.), 2009.

PART IV

LOOKING BACK, REACHING FORWARD

WAR-AFFECTED CHILDREN, INTERNATIONAL CRISIS OF MEANING, AND THE LIMITS OF REHABILITATION PROGRAMMES

Vanessa Pupavac

1. WAR-AFFECTED CHILDREN AND INTERNATIONAL PSYCHOSOCIAL PROGRAMMES

'Child psychology is a luxury which only a small section of the world's parents can afford', the childhood researchers Elizabeth Newson and John Newson argued back in the 1970s.[1] Yet the early 1990s witnessed an explosion of international trauma and other psychosocial therapeutic programmes. Their astonishing rise followed Western expanding therapeutic programmes and diagnosis of Post-Traumatic Stress Disorder (PTSD) which was formally recognised as a condition by the American Psychiatric Association in 1980.[2] Why did global policy-makers make therapeutic programmes previously considered a luxury a humanitarian priority for war-affected populations? Therapeutic programmes were offered by international organisations in developing countries suffering acute health needs evidenced in high infant mortality rates and low life expectancy rates. The PTSD advocacy literature had previously argued that therapeutic interventions were needed in western societies because they lacked the traditional communal support relations, which remained in the developing world. International imperatives to provide psychosocial programmes to war-affected populations was not therefore a self-evident communal priority given so many other urgent basic needs.

---

1 J. Newson and E. Newson, 'Cultural aspects of childrearing in the English-speaking world', in M. Richards (ed.), *The Integration of a Child into a Social World*, Cambridge, Cambridge University Press, 1974, 56. Also quoted in S. Kraemer, 'Promoting Resilience: Changing Concepts of Parenting and Child Care', (1999) 3 *International Journal of Child and Family Welfare* 274.

2 American Psychiatric Association (ASP), *Diagnostic and Statistical Manual of Mental Disorders*, Washington, DC, American Psychiatric Association, 1980.

International psychosocial interventions became promoted as a policy priority because of how the causes of violent conflict and war had become psychologised and increasingly sought in communal relations and norms.[3] We may contrast Clausewitzian approaches seeing war as the continuation of politics, that is, conflicting political causes and interests[4] to psychosocial approaches seeing war as the continuation of unhealthy psychology. Social psychology commonly approaches social problems as cycles of intergenerational dysfunctionalism, tracing back social pathology to primary socialisation. Essentially, social psychology believes that the construction of culture and personality is key to both comprehending and addressing social problems. So psychosocial approaches are concerned with children's development and socialisation as part of promoting social function. Underlying international psychosocial approaches is the cycles of violence thesis: war is seen as deriving from cultures or cycles of violence and the solution as breaking vicious cycles by changing cultural attitudes and instilling non-violent conflict resolution skills.[5] The new psychosocial model located the origins of ethnic conflict in the 'powerful reservoir of traumatic memory'.[6] Trauma, international reports contended, drove victims to perpetuate the violence they had experienced.

International psychosocial approaches sought to rehabilitate war-affected children as part of conflict management and peacebuilding. It was feared that children growing up in what were described as 'Kalashnikov cultures' had been socialised into accepting violence as normal and that they were more likely to become future perpetrators of violence.[7] 1990s' UN briefings were filled with statements concerned that, 'the world has only just begun to realise that left untreated, the psychological wounds of war can be most damaging, as children grow up unable to function normally, often driven to perpetuate the violence

3 V. Pupavac, 'Pathologizing Populations and Colonizing Minds: International Psychosocial Programs in Kosovo', (2002) 27 *Alternatives* 489–511; V. PUPAVAC, 'War on the couch: the emotionology of the new international security paradigm', (2004) 7(2) *European Journal of Social Theory* 149–170.

4 C. Clausewitz, *On War*, Harmondsworth, Penguin, 1968.

5 Commission On Global Governance, *Our Global Neighbourhood: The Report of the Commission on Global Governance,* Oxford and New York, Oxford University Press, 1995; M. Mackmoud, 'Children in war', (1994) 2 March/April *World Health* 21–23; Save The Children, *Prospects for Africa's Children*, London, Headway, Hodder & Stoughton, 1992; Unesco, *Action Programme to promote a culture of peace*, UNESCO Executive Board 141 EX/16, 1993; Unesco, *Round table on An Agenda for Peace: A Challenge for UNESCO,* Paris, UNESCO, 1993; Unicef, *Country Programme Report on Lebanon/Country Recommendation*, E/ICEF/P/L.28, 1992; Unicef, *Anti-war Agenda,* 1996 (also available at www.unicef.org/sowc96pk/antiwar1.htm).

6 Norwegian Ministry of Foreign Affairs, *Evaluation of Norwegian Support to Psycho-Social Projects in Bosnia-Herzegovina and the Caucasus: Final Evaluation Report,* Oslo, Royal Ministry of Foreign Affairs, March 1999, 18.

7 Commission On Global Governance, *Our Global Neighbourhood: The Report of the Commission on Global Governance,* Oxford and New York, Oxford University Press, 1995, 16–17 and 49; Save The Children, *Prospects for Africa's Children,* London, Headway, Hodder & Stoughton, 1992, 10.

they have experienced'.[8] The heightened fears over war's impact on children's development are illustrated in the following extract from UNICEF's country report on Lebanon, one of the first countries where the new psychosocial peace programmes were introduced:

> For an entire generation of Lebanese children, war has been the only reality they have ever known. This generation of children's attitudes towards society, interpersonal relations and basic value systems and their outlook on life have all been profoundly affected by the violence and destruction that has been a constant part of their daily existence. The war has, in fact, rendered virtually all young Lebanese 'children in especially difficult circumstances.[9]

The report is dramatic about war's harm to the attitudes of the whole child population, a matter that only a few years before, the organisation did not even document. In the 1990s UNICEF's estimates of the numbers of children traumatised by war around the world escalated into millions, correlating with the size of populations affected by war, with around 1.5 million children in 1993 in former Yugoslavia alone.[10] Belief in the need for the psychological rehabilitation of societies at war led UNICEF to define new policy areas: 'best practice in the context of psychosocial counselling; how to demobilize and detraumatize child soldiers; how to deal with the conditions of social breakdown in the "failed state".[11]

In 1993 UNICEF started to address the issue of war-traumatised children in all its programmes in countries affected by war. The UNICEF Evaluation and Research Office, the Programme Division and the Office of Emergency Programmes undertook a joint review of psychosocial programmes for children in situations of armed conflict. Concern for war-traumatised children became an integral part of UNICEF's emergency operations and was incorporated into new editions of its emergency manual.[12] UNICEF produced literature such as *Survivors: Rehabilitation of Children in Armed Conflict* or *Children in War* (1993) addressing the issue of war-traumatised children.

International psychosocial programmes aimed to break the perceived cycles of violence and change the culture of societies that have been at war towards peace. UNICEF and UNESCO's Joint Committee on Education called for priority to be given to psychosocial trauma counselling and education for peace.[13]

---

8 UNICEF, *News in Brief*, London, UNICEF, March/April 1994.

9 UNICEF, *Country Programme Report on Lebanon/Country Recommendation*, E/ICEF/P/L.28, 1992.

10 UNICEF, *News in Brief*, London, UNICEF, March/April 1994b, 1; UNICEF, *I dream of Peace, Background Information Material*, New York, UNICEF, 1993, 2.

11 M. BLACK, *Children First: The Story of UNICEF, Past and Present*, Oxford, Oxford University Press, 1996, 272.

12 UNICEF, *Emergency Operations*, E/ICEF/1994/11, dated 31 March 1994.

13 UNESCO, *Round table on An Agenda for Peace: A Challenge for UNESCO*, Paris, UNESCO, 1993.

In 1994 UNESCO set up its Culture for Peace Programmes based on the idea that a whole society needs to be re-programmed out of a culture of violence. There have been many international projects based on the cycle of violence thesis since the early 1990s aiming to provide therapy for war victims, counter aggressive feelings or 'hyper-arousal'[14] and instil non-violent conflict resolution skills in both children and adults. UNICEF's Anti-war Agenda initiative summarises this approach: 'Disputes may be inevitable, but violence is not. To prevent continued cycles of conflict, education must seek to promote peace and tolerance, not fuel hatred and suspicion'.[15]

Numerous pamphlets, guides or reports came out on psychosocial work with children in the 1990s.[16] The new priority was evident in both donor funding and NGO work. Traditional relief and development NGOs shifted the focus of their work to include psychosocial programmes. UNICEF's own Children in Extremely Difficult Circumstances (CEDC) programme, originally set up in response to anxiety about the effects of structural adjustment programmes, began to prioritise psychosocial intervention. Education programmes took more interest in children's emotional development.[17] Indicative of the rising therapeutic concerns was how UNESCO's former director-general referred to the 'rehabilitation' of a country after war, rather than its reconstruct.[18] Moreover the international development goal of well-being is informed by social psychological perspectives. I now want to consider how international policy understands complex emergencies related to cycles of trauma and violence, before going onto to consider the limitations of psychosocial rehabilitations against an international crisis of meaning and purpose over the future.

2. CYCLES OF TRAUMA AND VIOLENCE?

A complex emergency is commonly defined by international organisations as:

> a humanitarian crisis in a country, region or society where there is total or considerable breakdown of authority resulting from internal or external conflict and

---

14 Unicef, *I dream of Peace, Background Information Material*, New York, UNICEF, 1993, 3.

15 Unicef, *Anti-war Agenda*, 1996 (also available at www.unicef.org/sowc96pk/antiwar1.htm).

16 IFRC, *Psycho-social Assistance for Children Affected by Armed Conflict*, Geneva, IFRC, 1999; Save the Children, *Promoting Psychosocial Well-Being Among Children Affected by Armed Conflict and Displacement: Principles and Approaches*, Washington, DC, Save The Children, 1997; Unicef, *Survivors: Rehabilitation of Children in Armed Conflict*, New York, UNICEF, 1992.

17 Unesco, *EFA 2000 Bulletin*, April-June 1993, 11, 2; Unicef, *Emergency Operations*, E/ICEF/1994/11, dated 31 March 1994, 11.

18 Unesco, *Round table on An Agenda for Peace: A Challenge for UNESCO*, Paris, UNESCO, 1993.

> which requires an international response that goes beyond the mandate or capacity of any single and/or ongoing UN country progress.[19]

The concept sees the causes of disasters and conflicts as multi-causal, allowing diverse radical or conservative interpretations by different actors.[20] The concept merges emergency, development and political analysis and is influenced by social psychological theories. The concept encompasses internal and external causes, but its policy application effectively marginalizes external causality emphasised in earlier international politics, or transforms it into imperatives for external intervention. Importance is given to mobilising the international community of those states deemed responsible, along with international organisations and non-governmental actors.[21] Global strategies tend to focus on populations' cultural norms, and internal social and political inequalities, rather than the international political economy. At the same time evolving global governance is underpinned by implicit international hierarchies between powerful states and developing countries.

Complex emergencies are conceptualised as cycles of poverty, trauma and violence in which populations become pathologised as corrosive communities, and traumatised victims are deemed at risk of psychosocial dysfunction and therefore potential future perpetrators.[22] Under global management strategies, communities require governance to break intergenerational cycles of poverty, trauma and violence. International psychosocial programmes are particularly concerned about the rehabilitation of child soldiers, paralleling the cycles of abuse model popular in the family violence literature.

Children literally embody future society so it is unsurprising that societies anxious about the future should be anxious about children's development, especially the recovery of children who have been affected by war. The Second World War experience promoted pioneering studies in child development such as Anna Freud and Dorothy Burlingham's *War and Children* (1943).[23] One of the early studies commissioned by the newly established World Health Organisation was John Bowlby's *Maternal Care and Mental Health* (1951)[24] on Europe's homeless children after the Second World War. Bowlby's research on war-

---

19 IASC (Inter-agency Standing Committee), *Working Paper on the Definition of Complex Emergencies*, Geneva, IASC Secretariat, 1994 (also available at www.humanitarianinfo.org/iasc/).

20 M. Duffield, *Development, Security and Unending War*, Cambridge, Polity, 2007.

21 ICISS, *The Responsibility to Protect: Report of the International Commission on Intervention and State Sovereignty*, Ottawa, International Development Research Centre, 2001.

22 V. Pupavac, 'Pathologizing Populations and Colonizing Minds: International Psychosocial Programs in Kosovo', (2002) 27 *Alternatives* 489–511.

23 A. Freud and D.T. Burlingham, *War and Children*, Westport, Connecticut, Greenwood Press, 1943.

24 J. Bowlby, *Maternal Care and Mental Health: a report prepared on behalf of the World Health Organization as a contribution to the United Nations programme for the welfare of homeless children*, Geneva, World Health Organization, 1951.

affected children informed his understanding of child development and his elaboration of attachment theory. Bowlby and other influential figures such as John Dewey, saw healthy childhood experiences as important to foster the healthy personalities needed for healthy democracies.[25] Thus if children's development was adversely affected, it could damage their future functionality as citizens and peacebuilding. Questions over children's development are being addressed beyond welfare organisations by the security community. Thus NATO held a workshop in the early 2000's on the *Importance of Psychosocial Wellbeing of Children in the Postwar Period for Social Reconstruction and Stability of Terrorist & War Affected Regions.*[26]

The phenomenon of child soldiers explicitly violates modern norms of childhood and childhood development, as embodied in the UN Convention on the Rights of the Child 1989.[27] International advocacy has focused on codifying and enforcing international law to prevent children becoming soldiers in the first place. The UN Convention requires states to 'take all feasible measures to ensure that persons who have not attained the age of fifteen years do not take a direct part in hostilities' (Article 38(2)), while the Optional Protocol on children involved in armed conflict to the Convention refers to eighteen years.[28] Its Preamble states it is 'Disturbed by the harmful and widespread impact of armed conflict on children and the long-term consequences it has for durable peace, security and development'. The UN Convention requires states to protect (Article 38) and rehabilitate children affected by armed conflict (Article 39):

> States Parties shall take all appropriate measures to promote physical and psychological recovery and social reintegration of a child victim of: any form of neglect, exploitation, or abuse; torture or any other form of cruel, inhuman or degrading treatment or punishment; or armed conflicts. Such recovery and reintegration shall take place in an environment which fosters the health, self-respect and dignity of the child (Article 39).

The Optional Protocol to the Convention specifically requires states to provide programmes for the "psychological recovery and social reintegration" of former child soldiers, where necessary (Article 6). Children's rights advocates treat

---

[25] J. Dewey, *Democracy and Education: an introduction to the philosophy of education*, New York, Macmillan, 1916.

[26] Nato, *NATO Advanced Research Workshop on the Importance of Psychosocial Wellbeing of Children in the Postwar Period for Social Reconstruction and Stability of Terrorist & War Affected Regions*, Ljubljana, NATO, 2003.

[27] Un Convention on the Rights of the Child 1989, General Assembly resolution A/RES/44/25, www2.ohchr.org/english/law/crc.htm.

[28] Un Optional Protocol to the Convention on the Rights of the Child on the Involvement of Children in Armed Conflict, General Assembly resolution A/RES/54/263, 2000 (also available at www2.ohchr.org/english/law/crc-conflict.htm).

armed combat as a form of child abuse.[29] There is not just policy concern for children's welfare, but also concern over 'children as weapons of war'.[30] It is feared children make more abusive, inhumane soldiers because their immature physical, psychological and moral development leads them to be more easily manipulated by militaries. In the words of Goodwin-Gill and Cohen's influential study on this subject, child soldiers 'feel little fear and revulsion for the massacres which they carry out with greater enthusiasm and brutality than adults'.[31] The consequences of entire generations growing up with violent conflict for their developing identity and value system are feared, especially when children have been involved in killings[32]:

> Unfortunately, ensuring the successful reintegration of former child combatants is rife with complexities. Children who have known only violence are likely to resort to violence when solving personal problems. Those who have been forced to commit atrocities sometimes return to their homes only to be shunned and stigmatized by their own communities.[33]

Much of the advocacy literature has highlighted the forced recruitment of child soldiers rather than voluntary recruitment. The latter has tended to be addressed by targeting recruiting groups, rather than the conditions that make taking up arms attractive. Since legal approaches have struggled to eradicate child soldiers, increasing emphasis has been put on punitive measures, encompassing sanctions, prosecutions and military enforcement. However as child soldiers are prohibited under international law, then parties become reluctant to admit under-eighteens' existence in their ranks, inhibiting recognition of their entitlements or provision of official rehabilitation programmes to address their problems. Tensions over national peace-building processes create problems for rehabilitating and reintegrating former child soldiers.[34] Child soldiers may be viewed as perpetrators, not just victims, and questions of amnesty or prosecution are contested.[35] Moreover the international advocacy sector has promoted legal

---

29 P. Onyango, 'The impact of armed conflict on children', (1998) 7 (4) *Child Abuse Review* 220.

30 J. Becker, 'Children as weapons of war', (2004) *Human Rights Watch World Report 2004*, New York, HRW, (also available at www.hrw.org/wr2k4/11.htm).

31 G. Goodwin-Gill and I. Cohn, *Child Soldiers: The Role of Children in Armed Conflicts*, Oxford, Clarendon Press, 1994, 26.

32 P. Onyango, 'The impact of armed conflict on children', (1998) 7 (4) *Child Abuse Review* 219–229.

33 M. Odeh and C. Sullivan, *Recent Developments in International Rehabilitation of Child Soldiers*, Youth Advocate Program International Resource Paper, Washington, YAPI, undated, 2 (also available at www.yapi.org/rpchildsoldierrehab.pdf).

34 F. Faulkner, 'Kindergarten Killers: Morality, Murder and the Child Soldier Problem', (2001) 22 (4) *Third World Quarterly* 491–501.

35 A. Veale and A. Stavrou, 'Former Lord's Resistance Army Child Soldier Abductees: Explorations of Identity in Reintegration and Reconciliation', (2007) 13 (3) *Peace and Conflict: Journal of Peace Psychology* 273–292.

approaches wanting to eradicate cultures of impunity and establish the International Criminal Court or other tribunals to prosecute war crimes and crimes against humanity. Should former child soldiers be granted amnesty or would this be interpreted as maintaining a culture of impunity? International children's organisations have been against the prosecution of former child soldiers, but their opposition is in tension with their broader support for prosecutions and other punitive responses which influence attitudes towards former soldiers, including former child soldiers (many of whom will obviously have become adults). So while legal compromises are worked out at the international level, individual former child soldiers and their communities have to mediate tensions over the implementation on the ground.[36]

3. CONTENTIONS OVER PSYCHOSOCIAL TRAUMA MODELS

Earlier war and disaster studies appeared more optimistic about populations' responses, including children's. Emile Durkheim's classic sociological study *On Suicide* was interested in how war conditions were not necessarily associated with increased civilian psychosis because they could temporarily strengthen group bonds and increase intra-group social responsibility.[37] Sociological studies emphasised communal meaning in conflict and disasters, not only their scale. Post-Second World War US and international disaster studies were influenced by social optimism about the future as well as Second World War reports of populations' stoical responses to wartime aerial bombardment against earlier predictions of mass civilian panic.[38] The Blitz spirit, or courage and resolve under aerial bombardment, encapsulated optimistic postwar expectations of ordinary people's communal, altruistic, stoical responses to disasters.

Sociological studies documented spontaneous creation of therapeutic communities.[39] Leading postwar US disaster expert Charles Fritz was struck how

---

36 F. Faulkner, 'Kindergarten Killers: Morality, Murder and the Child Soldier Problem', (2001) 22 (4) *Third World Quarterly* 491–501.

37 E. Durkheim, *On Suicide*, London, Penguin, 2006.

38 C. Fritz, *Disasters and Mental Health*, Disaster Research Center, University of Delaware, 1996, 48–50 (also available at http://dspace.udel.edu:8080/dspace/bitstream/19716/1325/1/HC%2010.pdf).

39 A. Barton, *Communities in Disaster*, New York, Ward Lock Educational, 1969; C. Fritz, *Disasters and Mental Health*, Disaster Research Center, University of Delaware, 1996, 48–50 (also available at http://dspace.udel.edu:8080/dspace/bitstream/19716/1325/1/HC%2010.pdf); G. Kreps, 'Sociological Inquiry and Disaster Research', (1984) 10 *Annual Review of Sociology* 309–330; S. Saunders and G. Kreps, 'The Life History of the Emergent Organization in Times of Disaster', (1987) 23 *Journal of Applied Behavioral Science* 443–462.

large-scale disasters produced 'mentally healthy conditions'.[40] His 1961 study *Disasters and Mental Health* argued that 'disaster-struck communities and societies naturally develop therapies that quickly and effectively overcome the losses, traumas, and privations of disaster – without the intervention of mental health care professionals'.[41] Fritz contested 'overworked metaphors of pathology', although he warned of different responses if 'outside forces or authorities intervene in spontaneous community processes of adjusting to the disaster'.[42] Against negative predictions, the study suggested panic and hysteria were rare, people exhibited self-control and concern for welfare of others, and reports of looting were typically exaggerated.[43] Fritz questioned disaster approaches extrapolating from 'routine crises or small-scale accidents to later-scale disasters' arguing their enormity shook up cultural norms and everyday behaviours.[44] Significantly, disaster-affected communities might cross existing social, racial, minority divisions[45] and 'most of the behavioural pathologies of everyday life fail to increase or actually decline in disaster'.[46]

In recent decades, ecological accounts displaced sociological accounts in international disaster management literature. They are more pessimistic about the responses of disaster affected-communities. Ecological accounts or agent specific approaches focus on the scale and causes of disasters, and communities' vulnerabilities to external risks, as opposed to their capacity to recover and progress from disasters. They argue technological disasters involving human error foster 'corrosive communities' rather than therapeutic communities, because disputes over culpability divide communities.[47] Disasters attributed to human agency have expanded, as have concepts of disasters and toxic disasters.[48] Historically human-created disasters, including Hiroshima, did not necessarily cause community corrosion.[49] However contemporary policies presume therapeutic governance of disaster and war-affected 'corrosive' communities is required, whereas earlier sociological accounts presumed spontaneous creation of 'therapeutic communities'.

Psychosocial programmes to address war-affected countries became extremely popular with aid agencies in the 1990s. However criticisms were raised

---

40 C. Fritz, *Disasters and Mental Health*, Disaster Research Center, University of Delaware, 1996, 9 (also available at http://dspace.udel.edu:8080/dspace/bitstream/19716/1325/1/HC%2010.pdf).

41 Ibid., 25.

42 Ibid., 27–28.

43 Ibid., 18.

44 Ibid., 23.

45 Ibid., 40–42.

46 Ibid., 27.

47 K. Erikson, *A New Species Of Trouble*, London, W.W. Norton & Company, 1994.

48 F. Furedi, *Disaster and Contemporary Consciousness*, London, Terrorism Research Net, 2005 (also available at www.terrorismresearchnet/finalreports/Furedi/FurediReportFull.pdf).

49 C. Fritz, *Disasters and Mental Health*, Disaster Research Center, University of Delaware, 1996 (also available at http://dspace.udel.edu:8080/dspace/bitstream/19716/1325/1/HC%2010.pdf).

over the efficacy of Western PTSD models presuming universal trauma responses and treating distressful experiences as triggering traumatic symptoms causing dysfunctionalism, requiring preventive or rehabilitative interventions.[50] The uncritical use of diagnostic checklists for PTSD was challenged. Normal distress symptoms should not be confused with mental conditions requiring treatment. Some distress symptoms are adaptive, not dysfunctional, for example, hyper-alertness in dangerous situations. Distress symptoms may be epiphenomenal, that is, they are of secondary importance 'not what survivors are attending to or consider important: most of them remain active and effective in the face of continuing hardship and threat'.[51] The appearance of mental conditions requiring specific psychological interventions remains particular, not universal. People may respond to adversity by becoming more resilient. There are manifold personal, political and social factors, as well as military circumstances, which mediate traumatic war experiences and influence how individuals or communities cope. These include the resilience of populations used to adversity, political engagement or identification with the war aims, community support and purposeful activity.

Many criticisms were taken on board. Indeed although many international psychosocial programmes in the 1990s assumed mass war trauma, aid agencies' own assessments or evaluations did not necessarily support such assumptions.[52] New inter-agency guidance was developed seeking more sensitive interventions, which build on local social networks and existing coping ways. Guidelines now instruct aid agencies not to assume that 'everyone in an emergency is traumatised, or that people who appear resilient need no support'.[53] Guidelines distinguish those individuals suffering severe mental disorders from ordinary distress responses and instruct: 'Do not provide one-off, single-session psychological debriefing for people in the general population as an early intervention after exposure to conflict or natural disaster'.[54] Advice

---

50 P. Bracken, *Trauma: Culture, Meaning and Philosophy*, London, Whurr, 2002; P. Bracken and C. Petty (eds.), *Rethinking the Trauma of War*, London, Free Association Books, 1998; D. Summerfield, 'A Critique of Seven Assumptions Behind Psychological Trauma Programmes in War-Affected Areas', (1999) 48 *Social Science and Medicine* 1449–1462; D. Summerfield, 'The Invention of Post-Traumatic Stress Disorder and the Social Usefulness of a Psychiatric Study', (2001) 322 *British Medical Journal* 95–98.

51 D. Summerfield, 'Childhood, War, Refugeedom and Trauma: Three Core Questions for Mental Health Professionals' (September 2000) 37 (3) *Transcultural Psychiatry* 232.

52 For example: IFRC, *Psycho-social Assistance for Children Affected by Armed Conflict*, Geneva, IFRC, 1999; Norwegian Ministry of Foreign Affairs, *Evaluation of Norwegian Support to Psycho-Social Projects in Bosnia-Herzegovina and the Caucasus: Final Evaluation Report*, Oslo, Royal Ministry of Foreign Affairs, March 1999; Oxfam, *Health Report*, Skopje, Oxfam, April 1999; P. Wiles et al., *Independent Evaluation of Expenditure of DEC Kosovo Appeal Funds. Phases I and II, Volume II. ODI with association with Valid International*, London, ODI, April 1999–January 2000.

53 IASC, *IASC Guidelines on Mental Health and Psychosocial Support in Emergency Settings*, Geneva, IASC, 2007, 11.

54 Ibid., 12.

has become more self-conscious of how aid interventions may overpower locals.[55] Guidance recommends aid practices which integrate supporting people's dignity, safety and well-being through paying attention to how matters such as camp design, as opposed to treating the psychosocial as discreet interventions. Guidelines instruct 'Do not assume that methods from abroad are necessarily better or impose them on local people in ways that marginalise local supportive practices and beliefs'.[56] But it is also warned, 'Do not assume that all local cultural practices are helpful or that all local people are supportive of particular practices'.[57]

The new guidance illustrates how there have been moves in global therapeutic work to shift policy thinking from vulnerability to resilience, building on individuals or communities' strengths. The new emphasis on resilience followed the 9/11 terrorist attacks. The changed emphasis may be novel in the dominant therapeutic models, but actually continues common assumptions in international development thinking, which assumes the ability of poor populations to be physically resilient and have physical coping strategies in the midst of material scarcity.[58] These ideas continued to inform international poverty strategies in the 1990s, notwithstanding psychosocial models questioning their psychological capacity. Yet if we examine official policies on resilience they often share many of the assumptions of the vulnerability approaches that individuals or communities are at psychosocial risk and in need of psychosocial management, albeit with modified language. Resilience tends to be abstracted from experience and treated as something needing to be taught, as opposed to arising through adversity and related to meaning in people's lives. The older concepts of stoicism and courage involved frameworks of meanings and moral qualities as Charles Moran's *Anatomy of Courage* outlines. Conversely the international political paradigms of vulnerability or resilience implicitly treat war-affected populations as morally dysfunctional.

4. CONTENTIONS OVER REHABILITATION MODELS

International approaches towards war-affected children and child soldiers have been dominated by legal or psychosocial approaches, that is, explanatory models

---

55 IASC, *IASC Guidelines on Mental Health and Psychosocial Support in Emergency Settings*, Geneva, IASC, 2007; IASC, *Mental Health and Psychosocial Support:Checklist for Field Use*, Geneva, IASC, 2008.

56 IASC, *Mental Health and Psychosocial Support:Checklist for Field Use*, Geneva, IASC, 2008, 12.

57 IASC, *IASC Guidelines on Mental Health and Psychosocial Support in Emergency Settings*, Geneva, IASC, 2007, 12.

58 M. Duffield, *Development, Security and Unending War*, Cambridge, Polity, 2007.

and solutions based on methodological individualism. This emphasis is evident from the ICRC's international legal initiatives in the 1970s, UNICEF's CEDC programme in the 1980s and the 1989 UN Convention on the Rights of the Child, through studies such as Goodwin Gill and Cohn's 1994 study[59], and Graca Machel's 1996 study[60] to more recent studies. This emphasis persists even though the Optional Protocol on children in armed conflict states 'the necessity of taking into consideration the economic, social and political root causes of the involvement of children in armed conflict'. Again this emphasis persists despite studies discussing a spectrum of causes for children's participation in armed conflict. Nevertheless specific proposals are focused around interventions to change the norms of individuals or groups. So while development is highlighted, there is something ritualistic about its invocation. Contemporary development models essentially repeat the methodological individualism and psychosocial approaches to improve individual capabilities and sense of well-being, rather than material transformation[61], as I will discuss below.

The phenomenon of child soldiers cannot be resolved as a problem of psychosocial dysfunction or social pathology. To what extent are children in armed combat abused children or 'child labourers'?[62] Where many children in developing countries have to take on adult responsibilities, including labour, in peacetime conditions, it is unsurprising that children are found taking on adult responsibilities including (para)military activities in conflict conditions. Child soldiers are banned under international law based on universalist arguments, but non-mechanised family labour, and therefore child labour, is perpetuated under sustainable development models based on cultural relativist ideas. Effectively global governance is universalizing post-industrial childhood and children's rights norms, but not universalizing the development conditions which underpin those norms.[63] If the peacetime material conditions do not secure a safe childhood, wartime conditions are hardly likely to. The use of child soldiers is only common in societies where infant mortality is high and where child labour remains the norm and a necessity in predominantly non-industrial, non-mechanised agricultural economies. Child labour is a function of non-industrial or semi-industrial social conditions in peacetime and child soldiering becomes a function of such social conditions in wartime. Unless peacetime child

---

59 G. Goodwin-Gill and I. Cohn, *Child Soldiers: The Role of Children in Armed Conflicts*, Oxford, Clarendon Press, 1994.

60 G. Machel, *Impact of Armed Conflict on Children*, New York, UN, 1996 (also available at www.unicef.org/graca/).

61 V. Pupavac, 'Children's Human Rights Advocacy', in M. Goodhart (ed.), *Human Rights: Politics and Practice*, Oxford, Oxford University Press, 2009, 219–238.

62 P. Onyango, 'The impact of armed conflict on children', (1998) 7 (4) *Child Abuse Review* 220.

63 V. Pupavac, 'Children's Human Rights Advocacy', in M. Goodhart (ed.), *Human Rights: Politics and Practice*, Oxford, Oxford University Press, 2009, 219–238.

deaths become rare through significant material development, then the use of child soldiers will not become rare.

The international psychosocial models, positing trauma as leading to social dysfunction and violence, provided an over-socialised account of individual and collective behaviour, yet divorced from material conditions that involve struggles over resources. Local political war economies involve conflicts over profitable routes into the international political economies[64], while the worst armed conflicts and killings, notably the Rwandan genocide and the DR Congo, involved significant regional power shifts including from Francophone to Anglo-American power. The experience of violence does not simply lead people to become violent, more violent or indifferent to violence. The cycle of violence model from the family violence literature is premised on contentious retrospective studies (sometimes relying on explanations involving self-justifications!), which elevate past experience of violence or trauma over a multitude of other factors that lead to abuse.[65] Difficult to sustain in the context of interpersonal behaviour, the trauma and violence model becomes harder to sustain when applied to social or political conflicts such as civil wars.[66] Individuals in violent conflict continue to make moral and political judgements about what violence they consider legitimate and illegitimate. Even in civil war, there are limits to social disintegration. Writing on the problem of social order, the sociologist Dennis Wrong observes:

> Societies never fall apart to the extent of literally lapsing into a war of all against all. Nation-states may fragment […] into several hostile groups controlling different localities […] But underneath these processes social order survives at least at a micro-sociological level – the level of families, small groups, and networks of interacting individuals cooperating in the pursuit of common goals.[67]

The very possibility of being able to mobilise people to fight involves some social responsibilities, however crude.[68] Armies cannot rely on coercion alone, even where they use forced mobilisation, including child soldiers. Wartime health indicators are not always worse than peacetime, indicating how local political

64 M. Duffield, *Global Governance and the New Wars,* London, Zed Books, 2001.

65 M.D. Pagelow, *Family Violence*, Westport CT, Praeger Publishers, 1984; R. McNally, *Remembering Trauma*, Cambridge, Mass., Belknap Press of Harvard University Press, 2003; A. Young, *The Harmony of Illusions: inventing post-traumatic stress disorder,* Princeton, N.J., Princeton University Press, 1995.

66 D. Summerfield, 'Childhood, War, Refugeedom and Trauma": Three Core Questions for Mental Health Professionals', (September 2000) 37 (3) *Transcultural Psychiatry* 417–433.

67 D. Wrong, *The Problem of Order: What Unites and Divides Society,* Cambridge, Mass., Harvard University Press, 1994, 243.

68 M. Duffield, *Global Governance and the New Wars,* London, Zed Books, 2001; M. Duffield, *Development, Security and Unending War,* Cambridge, Polity, 2007.

war economies involve relations of obligation while political mobilisation imperatives may lead to expanding welfare provision to encompass otherwise marginal groups.[69] Controversially, the attribution of violent conflict to 'traumatised nationalism' in international aid echoes interwar Western racial psychology with its descriptions of the damaged personality or 'pathological state of mind' of the colonial subject.[70]

Today's policy pessimism over post-conflict communities and war-affected children contrasts with earlier social optimism over children's recovery from war or domestic brutality. Earlier portrayals of child soldiers were as national heroes in anticolonial struggles. Children's participation in armed conflict was therefore not necessarily seen as harmful to themselves or their society, but as liberating and building the nation. Images of child soldiers in the era of national movements liked to show children in educative activities such as listening to an instructor and holding slates or books. Such images fitted with optimistic cultural depictions of children globally in a century believing in social progress and political potential. From Mark Twain's *The Adventures of Huckleberry Finn* to Maxim Gorky's *My Childhood* to JG Ballard's *Empire of the Sun*[71] we see protagonists transcending the brutality and violence of their childhood and affirming the human spirit and the hope to resurrect lives or forge a progressive politics. In Gorky's words, 'Life is always surprising us – not by its rich, seething layer of bestial refuse – but by the bright, healthy creative human powers of goodness that are for ever forcing their way up through it'.[72] Gorky, Twain[73] or Ballard's confidence in children's moral resilience was shared globally in a politically and socially more optimistic period but seems naïve today. Contemporary policy expectations seem closer to William Goldings' anti-humanist *Lord of the Flies.*

The loss of policy confidence in children's moral resilience is bound up with the erosion of belief in national movements and national development projects. We may note how township children were represented in the anti-Apartheid struggle as heroes. Conversely post-Apartheid disappointments have revised how children in the townships are represented.[74] Nevertheless national and international practitioners working with former child soldiers tend to report positive changes through intervention. However fears are expressed over young people's futures and that their revived hopes will be dashed and their reintegration undermined by the limited prospects their societies can offer them.

---

69 Ibid.

70 F. Furedi, *Colonial Wars and the Politics of Third World Nationalism*, London, I.B. Tauris, 1994.

71 J.G. Ballard, *Empire of the Sun*, London, Flamingo, 1984.

72 M. Gorky, *My Childhood*, Harmondsworth, Penguin, 1996.

73 M. Twain, *The Adventures of Huckleberry Finn*, Harmondsworth, Puffin, 1983.

74 S. Jensen, *Gangs, Politics and Dignity in Cape Town*, Chicago, Chicago University Press, 2008.

International psychosocial approaches have been largely focused on addressing the past to address the future. I want to look at problems over the future into which young people are being rehabilitated and reintegrated. In considering the question of the recovery, rehabilitation, and reintegration of children, the question of what future world children are being integrated is crucial. The rest of the chapter considers the problem of that loss of wider global social and political purpose and its implications for children.

5. PSYCHOLOGICAL CRISIS OF MEANINGLESSNESS

It has long been recognised that psychological well-being is influenced by people's sense of purpose.[75] The political philosopher Charles Taylor has specifically written against psychological models, which neglect human meanings.[76] Some studies do explore the importance of social or political meaning in children's experience of war.[77] Controversially we need to ask to what extent international rehabilitation approaches replace the sense of meaning and belonging child soldiers might have had in military participation, not withstanding its harshness, cruelties and dangers?[78] International child rehabilitation programmes take place against a broader international crisis of vision and purpose. Moral uncertainty and psychological fragility have been treated as an inherent tendency of modernity experienced by individuals released from the bonds of traditional society.[79] Modern society has found it difficult to create stable sources of meaning, marked by contested frameworks of meaning, and the threat of meaninglessness. Recovering meaning today involves different problems from societies in transition from feudalism or under the previous more politicised modern conditions. If people felt torn by contested ideological meanings at critical points in the twentieth century, the twenty-first century problem is rather of meaninglessness. A sense of meaninglessness is hardly unique to contemporary society, but was commonly confined to a small privileged minority in society. The difficulty of finding meaning and purpose is a more general problem, especially across Western societies today, whose

75 V. Frankl, *Man's Search for Meaning*, New York, Simon and Schuster, 1984.

76 C. Taylor, *Human Agency and Language: Philosophical Papers I*, Cambridge, Cambridge University Press, 1985.

77 R.J. Apfel and S. Bennett (eds.), *Minefields in Their Hearts: The Mental Health of Children in War and Communal Violence*, New Haven, Yale University Press, 1996; P. Bracken and C. Petty (eds.), *Rethinking the Trauma of War*, London, Free Association Books, 1998; E. Cairns, *Children and Political Violence*, London and Cambridge, Blackwell, 1996; A. Raviv, L. Oppenheimer and D. Bar-Tal (eds.), *How Children Understand War and Peace*, San Francisco, Jossey-Bass, *1999*.

78 R. Rosenblatt, *Children of War*, New York, Anchor Press/Doubleday, 1983.

79 E. Fromm, *Escape from freedom?*, New York, Holt, Rinehart and Winston, 1941.

perspectives, as major donor countries, have influenced international humanitarian and development responses.

The Post-Cold War world has not created sources of meaning comparable to the competing Cold War ideological frameworks, as Zaki Laidi's *A World Without Meaning* perceptively analyses.[80] Cold War rivalry required the Western and Soviet powers to elaborate comprehensive visions of modernisation to win the hearts and minds of the newly independent developing countries and politically secure them to their blocs. The Cold War struggle to demonstrate the superiority of one's own way of life against the competing international models enhanced nationalism and domestic sources of meaning. Potentially any area of life could become significant under international competition: from scientific advancements, artistic and sporting achievements, space exploration to architecture and educational attainment. The Cold War period was therefore filled with meaning as the competing powers projected grand visions internationally to secure international influence.[81] Their promises of a better life raised people's expectations internationally, and orientated proponents and opponents alike. Tangible, but uneven, material social progress in the postwar period made aspirations seem graspable and fostered political struggle where blocked.

The Berlin Wall's collapse was initially greeted euphorically as the West's victory over political alternatives[82], but the celebratory mood was short-lived. The era of TINA ('there is no alternative'), to borrow Margaret Thatcher's phrase, was quickly marked by pessimism. The Cold War politics had given Western societies a sense of purpose, invigorated progressive politics and checked cultural tendencies towards disenchantment, trivialisation and meaninglessness already evident, which have now come to the fore.[83] Societies were disorientated by the demise of rival grand transformative visions. Older nationalisms weakened lacking the invigorating international dimension felt during the Cold War. Narrower, more narcissistic ethnic nationalisms surfaced out of national life's fragmentation, embodying the pettiness of small differences rather than the universal internationalist dimension associated with past national self-determination struggles.[84] The Cold War divisions were removed, but international inequalities were reinforced.

Previous sources of international meaning were destabilised, but the Western powers immediately found it difficult to project a global vision and have continued to do so. The American dream no longer holds the international enchantment it did historically and has been compromised as belief in the United States as an exceptional moral progressive power has dissipated. An

80 Z. Laidi, *A World Without Meaning*, London, Routledge, 1998.

81 Z. Laidi, *A World Without Meaning*, London, Routledge, 1998.

82 F. Fukuyama, *The End of History and the Last Man*, New York, Free Press, 1992.

83 P. Hammond, *Media, War and Postmodernity*, London, Routledge, 2007.

84 Z. Laidi, *A World Without Meaning*, London, Routledge, 1998.

alternative European dream, embodied in the European Union, remains a technocratic bureaucratic project distant from ordinary people.[85] The economic rise of the BRICs of Brazil, Russia, India and China has re-invigorated belief in economic advancement, but has not so far translated into new sources of international political meaning. Political leaders represent globalisation and integration into the global economy fatalistically as an inevitable process to be adapted to without meaning or enchantment.[86] Wealth-creation and international development have gone their separate ways. So OPEC countries like Saudi Arabia have followed a wealth-creation and charity model, rather than universal political, social and economic material transformation. Meanwhile South Africa's powerful movement for universal political, social and economic material transformation fragmented following the compromises with the old Apartheid regime. Solutions to social problems in South Africa, as elsewhere, are essentially seen in terms of individual improvement and empowerment within the existing capitalist world economy.[87]

The erosion of communal sources of meaning has encouraged contemporary problems to be understood from the perspective of individual or group psychology. In the decline of external references and collective consciousness, contemporary culture increasingly takes the self and the self's subjective feelings as the reference point.[88] On both sides of the Atlantic policy-makers see emotional engagement as the way to overcome current disconnection with the public[89], whether the social inclusion policies, the 'journalism of attachment'[90] or 'politics of attachment' mooted in the 1990s[91] or the 'happiness' agenda, informed by positive psychology, of the new Millennium.[92] Consequently, engaging citizens more emotionally is seen as vital to revitalise citizenship and participation in public affairs. There has been a converging demand for social or political problems to be approached 'in a feeling-based way'.[93]

Indicative of the psychosocial turn is the adoption of social exclusion as an approach to address social problems, which incorporates concerns over the

---

85 Z. Laidi, *A World Without Meaning*, London, Routledge, 1998; L. McClaren, *Identity, Interests and Attitudes to European Integration*, Basingstoke, Palgrave Macmillan, 2006.

86 Z. Laidi, *A World Without Meaning*, London, Routledge, 1998.

87 S. Jensen, *Gangs, Politics and Dignity in Cape Town*, Chicago, Chicago University Press, 2008.

88 J. Nolan, *The Therapeutic State*, New York, New York University, 1998.

89 F. Furedi, *Therapy Culture*, London, Routledge, 2001; J. Nolan, *The Therapeutic State*, New York, New York University, 1998.

90 M. Bell, 'TV News: How Far Should We Go?', (1997) 8(1) *British Journalism Review* 7–16.

91 S. Kraemer and J. Roberts, *The Politics of Attachment: Towards a Secure Society*, London, Free Association Books, 1996.

92 R. Layard, *Happiness: Lessons from a New Science*, London, Penguin, 2005.

93 A. Samuels, *Politics on the Couch: Citizenship and the Internal Life*, London, Profile Books, 2001, 3.

psychological experience of exclusion or self-exclusion.[94] Western social policy strategies treat emotional self-esteem as the cause of and solution to the spectrum of social problems from teenage pregnancy to unemployment and poverty. In other words, addressing the psychology of teenage girls, the psychology of the unemployed, the psychology of the poor, the psychology of ethnic minorities comes to the fore. So diagnosis and prescriptions to overcome social problems becomes focused on individual or group psychology. Emotional well-being is given central policy relevance, but too often comes to be treated by psychosocial management strategies as an independent variable, shorn of actual social experience and meaning.[95] What progressive future does a social inclusion policy seek to include citizens into? What vision of society does a social cohesion agenda seek to cohere citizens around? If poverty is tackled as a problem of hope, what does hope mean without a social vision for the future? Interventions tend to neglect the relation between emotion and meaning, despite the growing body of studies linking psychological problems with meaning. Strikingly the social exclusion, social cohesion or diversity and multiculturalism approaches are all concerned about incorporating groups or individuals into mainstream society and culture, yet there is a hollowness at the core, epitomised by the difficulties to cohere a sense of a shared national identity.

The philosopher-psychiatrist Patrick Bracken's *Trauma: Culture, Meaning and Philosophy* (2002)[96] has written insightfully on how common psychological problems in contemporary society relate to cultural ontological insecurity, bringing together philosophical and sociological writing of the last decades on existential anxiety over meaninglessness. It has long been observed that every age and society has its particular character type and characteristic pathologies.[97] In this vein Bracken has perceptively explored Post-Traumatic Stress Disorder as a disorder of meaning and 'an extreme form of the contemporary crisis of meaning'.[98] Bracken argues that since past frameworks giving people's lives purpose and coherence have weakened, individuals experience more anxiety over the direction of their lives. Bracken is not alone in noting how 'conditions that are supplied by contemporary culture are not conducive to the formation of

94 R. Levitas, *The Inclusive Society? Social Exclusion and New Labour*, Basingstoke, Macmillan, 1998.

95 J. Nolan, *The Therapeutic State*, New York, New York University, 1998; F. Furedi, *Therapy Culture*, London, Routledge, 2001; J. Nolan, *The Therapeutic State*, New York, New York University, 1998.

96 P. Bracken, *Trauma: Culture, Meaning and Philosophy*, London, Whurr, 2002.

97 C. Lasch, *The Culture of Narcissism: American life in an age of diminishing expectations*, New York, Norton, 1979; V. Frankl, *Man's Search for Meaning*, New York, Simon and Schuster, 1984; S. Frosh, *Identity Crisis: Modernity, Psychoanalysis and the Self*, Basingstoke, Macmillan, 1991.

98 P. Bracken, *Trauma: Culture, Meaning and Philosophy*, London, Whurr, 2002.

a deep and integrated sense of secure being'.[99] Diverse disciplines have proclaimed the death of public man, the death of the hero, the death of character, and the death of the subject, and along with the decline of community and social solidarity.[100] Popular professional models and individuals themselves are attracted towards self-identities based on diagnosis or wounded attachments to a traumatic past, which the recent resilience models do not essentially change.[101] The cultural phenomenon of individuals seeking refuge from social meaninglessness in diagnosis reveals problems with the notion of psychological rehabilitation today. Indicatively contemporary professional rehabilitation models are sceptical about recovery, and tend to suggest that individuals are ever vulnerable to relapse and potentially in need of professional support. The significance of global ontological insecurities for psychological vulnerability and the recovery of meaning for individual and communal resilience needs to be addressed.[102]

6. REHABILITATING CHILDREN TO THE STRUGGLE FOR SURVIVAL?

Social pessimism and disorientation with the decline of progressive politics has led to a preoccupation with children, but the contemporary crisis of meaning, following Bracken[103], inhibits the ends of reintegration. Global governance today lacks earlier ambitious visions. Instead of children being reintegrated into a socially inspiring and meaningful vision of the future, children are being reconciled to lowered expectations of social and material prospects. International concern for children's psychosocial development and rehabilitation has risen against the context of the demise of development of the South. Global development strategies have abandoned the aspiration for universal prosperity, and become orientated around selective basic needs poverty and expect populations to provide for their own survival. Substantial material transformation for the majority of the world's population is now off the agenda,

---

99 S. Frosh, *Identity Crisis: Modernity, Psychoanalysis and the Self*, Basingstoke, Macmillan, 1991, 63.

100 J. Heartfield, *Death of the Subject Explained*, Leicester, Perpetuity Press, 2002.

101 P. Bracken, *Trauma: Culture, Meaning and Philosophy*, London, Whurr, 2002; W. Brown, *States of Injury: Power and Freedom in Late Modernity?*, Princeton, Princeton University Press, 1995; F. Furedi, *Therapy Culture*, London, Routledge, 2001; J. Nolan, *The Therapeutic State*, New York, New York University, 1998; I; Shaw and L. Woodward, 'The Medicalisation of Unhappiness? The management of mental distress in primary care', in I. Shaw and K. Kaupinnen (eds.), *Constructions of Health and Illness: European Perspectives*, Aldershot, Ashgate Press, 2003, 125–138.

102 B. Durodie, 'The limitations of risk management in dealing with disaster and building social resilience', (March 2005) 8 (1) *Politik* 14–21; B. Durodie, 'Fear and terror in a post-political age', (2007) 42 (3) *Government and Opposition* 427–450.

103 P. Bracken, *Trauma: Culture, Meaning and Philosophy*, London, Whurr, 2002.

although radical psychosocial or normative transformation is promoted and indeed has become the main meaning of development, as I will discuss below.

Yet the psychosocial norms envisaged under global strategies appear out of step with the lives envisaged for populations in developing societies. Sebastian Kraemer, a leading child psychiatrist at the Tavistock Clinic, who has argued for therapeutic approaches in politics, implicitly casts doubt on the efficacy of international psychosocial programmes promoting post-industrial western norms of child development for populations having to survive in difficult, insecure social conditions. Kraemer argues: 'Resilience based on secure attachment is essentially generous and open minded, and is of little value in an unjust or oppressive society'.[104] Are children being rehabilitated to conditions in which they are able to thrive or only may merely hope to survive? Global policies for the rehabilitation and reintegration of children have encompassed education, including livelihoods training. Research by Janaka Jayawickrama of Northumbria University, who has worked as a community mental health practitioner, has found children in refugee camps in Africa and Asia dreaming of becoming doctors, actresses or journalists, influenced by the internationals they have encountered.[105] So kindling children's expectations of life beyond camp is very possible. Typically former boy soldiers are given help with becoming farmers and former girl soldiers are given help with training as seamstresses, following sustainable development approaches. However there are questions over whether the former child soldiers are content with returning to the life of peasant farming. There are also questions over whether the microenterprises, such as making clothes, are viable in village communities organised around peasant farming, which cannot afford new clothes. For Jayawickrama, the tragedy is how the peace envisaged for these children does not offer them the potential of realising their dreams. Even more tragically some of children he encountered might not even reach adulthood, given the poor mortality rates in the local and refugee populations. Unsurprisingly some officials and practitioners have observed young people, whose mental health had been improving in refugee camps, through programmes, becoming depressed on return to their villages. It is feared that young people, who have been successfully reintegrated into education, will become disillusioned when they leave education and their high aspirations to become lawyers or other professionals or creative workers are brought to a halt by the economic and social realities of their societies.

The rise of interest in the rehabilitation of children from the mid-1980s and especially the 1990s, parallels the growing influence of social psychology on

---

104 S. Kraemer, 'Promoting Resilience: Changing Concepts of Parenting and Child Care', (1999) 3 *International Journal of Child and Family Welfare* 273.

105 J. Jayawickrama, *Community Mental Health and Wellbeing: Case Studies from Sri Lanka, Sudan and Malawi*, University of Northumbria, Unpublished research, 2009.

global development strategies. International development policy since the 1990s has put new emphasis on individual and cultural functionality, and empowerment of the poor takes on the meaning of promoting capability to function.[106] Not only are the means of achieving development and global justice changing, but the nature of injustice and the goal of justice have been transformed into the social psychological notions of well-being and ill-being. The global social justice paradigm which developed in the 1990s became concerned with facilitating a sense of well-being by tackling feelings of injustice, exclusion and low self-esteem through empowerment and participatory programmes. These perspectives are evident in the much hailed World Bank *Voices of the Poor* report which defines well-being and ill-being thus:

> *Wellbeing and illbeing are states of mind and being. Wellbeing has a psychological and spiritual dimension as a mental state of harmony, happiness and peace of mind. Illbeing included mental distress, breakdown, depression and madness, often described by participants to be impacts of poverty* (italics in original).[107]

The psychologising of social problems is evident in the report's definition of poverty which encompass 'vulnerability, powerlessness, the shame of dependency, and social isolation'.[108] The emphasis on the psychology of post-conflict societies and the psychology of the poor groups denotes a deprioritising of material transformation in tackling social grievances, and dovetails with the way that injustice is being redefined psychologically under the prevailing Western social exclusion model of justice and order (see Levitas, 1998, for extensive discussion).[109] In this reinterpretation, welfare has become primarily about psychic transformation and improving interpersonal relations. The concept of exclusion, as leading sociologist and third way thinker Anthony Giddens explains, 'is not about gradations of inequality, but mechanisms that act to detach groups of people from the social mainstream'.[110] Highlighting the low self-esteem of the marginalized, the social exclusion model implies radical therapeutic interventions to improve capability and overcome feelings of deprivation and alienation. Thus Giddens proposes that 'counselling, for example, might be more helpful than direct economic support'.[111] Similarly

---

106 Unesco, *Research and Policy SHS/SRP contribution to the Document on Poverty for the 152nd session of the Executive Board*, Geneva, UNESCO, 1997 (also available at www.unesco.org/most/povsrp.htm).

107 D. Narayan, R. Chambers, M. K. Shah and P. Petesch, *Voices of the Poor: Crying Out for Change*, Oxford, Oxford University Press for the World Bank, 2000, 21.

108 D. Narayan, R. Patel, K. Schafft, A. Radenmacher and S. Koch-Schulte, *Voices of the Poor: Can Anyone Hear Us?*, Oxford, Oxford University Press for the World Bank, 2000, 274.

109 R. Levitas, *The Inclusive Society? Social Exclusion and New Labour*, Basingstoke, Macmillan, 1998.

110 A. Giddens, *The Third Way: The Renewal of Social Democracy*, Cambridge, Polity Press, 1999.

111 Ibid., 117.

tying incapability to the psychology of marginalized groups, a 1990s' UNESCO and UNICEF project states how it contributes to poverty eradication:

> by reducing within this group prevailing feelings of social discrimination, low self-esteem, absence of control, isolation, and vulnerability, and in instilling them the understanding that they have the right to participate [...] and that change can be possible through participation.[112]

Retreating from material transformation, the new international social justice paradigm essentially seeks to reach out to the marginalized and prevent individuals becoming alienated and dysfunctional through empowerment and participatory development programmes. The underlying aim of these programmes is to modify the personality, intimate relationships and communal networks and cultural attitudes of populations. Global policy demands not only 'modernisation without development'[113], that is, the transformation of traditional cultural norms without material advancement, but treats well-being as divorced from material circumstances. As such social justice becomes increasingly about manipulating a sense of well-being in which feelings of social injustice, alienation and lack of well-being are treated as a form of psychological dysfunctionalism requiring therapeutic management. The goal of well-being effectively involves the promotion of a contented emotional state amidst the struggle for survival and continuing poverty. In other words cultivating well-being involves cultivating happiness with the status quo, and social transformation is being relocated to self-understanding and interpersonal communication. This effectively makes international development a requirement that individuals transform themselves and increase their capability to function in the face of indefinite poverty. Oppression is thus re-conceptualized as deriving from interpersonal relations, thereby making victims of global processes culpable for their circumstances. Empowerment is conceptualized therapeutically as improving the psychosocial capability of individuals and communities to cope with risks from the perspectives of risk-adverse western societies, which today pathologize human relations as inherently prone to abuse. Ultimately, the significance of the model is to challenge the moral personality of individuals, along with the moral economy of the household.

There is a serious gap between young people's aspirations, and the norms and the future being offered to them under global strategies. Normative psychosocial approaches have developed against global material conditions perpetuating

---

112 UNESCO, *Research and Policy SHS/SRP contribution to the Document on Poverty for the 152nd session of the Executive Board*, Geneva, UNESCO, 1997 (also available at www.unesco.org/most/povsrp.htm).

113 F. FUREDI, *Population and Development: A Critical Introduction*, Basingstoke, Palgrave Macmillan, 1997.

scarcity and survival as way of life with the conflicts it entails. Are liberal post-industrial personalities best able to cope with harsh, unforgiving insecure material conditions where you have to be tough to survive? Kraemer suggests cultivating emotional empathy may be dysfunctional and undermine survival strategies in insecure communities:

> if life is primarily a struggle for survival, where there are few or no trusted neighbours, and where it is better not to think about other people's states of mind. If you have to steal from others to survive, for example, it is a hindrance to be bothered about their feelings.[114]

As Durkheim observed in his sociological studies 'to will a morality other than that implied by the nature of society is to deny the latter'.[115] A gulf exists between the post-industrial childhood development ideal being globalised through international psychosocial programmes and the actual experience of childhood for most children in war-affected developing countries, yet material means of bridging that gap have been abandoned.

The disciplining aspects of empowerment and participatory development programmes are mystified by the disavowed therapeutic language of self-reflection, facilitation, mediation, and self-esteem. However, a significant body of literature has developed over the last two decades criticising global empowerment and participation approaches as representing a new oppressive burden on the marginal: denoting people taking responsibility for their own welfare in the absence of state services.[116] Earlier participatory development practice had been criticised for having naïve romantic views of community, alongside its growing managerialism. In contrast, cutting edge gender and children's rights thinking emphasises 'the myth of community': the problematic nature of community relations and how presumptions of communal solidarity mask conflicting interests, inequalities and abuse within communities. Yet even while the myth of community is deconstructed, a myth of harmonious rural subsistence is maintained as an ideal to be realized through harnessing *authentic* voices and local knowledge. In its search for empowering authentic community and selfhood, future global development practice is set to put informal relations under greater scrutiny.

One avenue for a few individual former child soldiers is to have been trained to become youth advocates. These youth advocates have been taken up by

---

114 S. Kraemer, 'Promoting Resilience: Changing Concepts of Parenting and Child Care', (1999) 3 *International Journal of Child and Family Welfare* 287.

115 R. Levitas, *The Inclusive Society? Social Exclusion and New Labour*, Basingstoke, Macmillan, 1998, 185.

116 R. Abrahamsen, Disciplining Democracy: Development Discourse and Good Governance in Africa, London, Zed Books, 2000; B. Cook and U. Kothari (eds.), *Participation: The New Tyranny?*, London and New York, Zed Books, 2001; M. Duffield, *Development, Security and Unending War?*, Cambridge, Polity, 2007.

international organisations and increasingly are brought along to address international meetings, such as the launch of an international report. In this vein, former child soldier youth advocates addressed the Security Council on 29 April 2009 related to the UN Secretary-General Ban Ki-moon new report on children in armed conflict. The youth advocates echoed Secretary-General, the Special Representative of the Secretary-General for Children in Armed Conflict, Radhika Coomaraswamy, and UNICEF Executive Director Ann M. Veneman in being focusing on normative approaches emphasising prosecutions of or sanctions against groups involved in the recruitment and abuse of child soldiers.[117] There is something rather self-affirmatory about international bodies and the children's NGOs sector listening to their views from youth voices whom they have trained. The young people's managed presence and voices feel uncomfortably like a stage army as they echo and legitimise this official report or others.

International empowerment discourse has echoes of the nineteenth century self-help ethos, along with nineteenth century reformers' preoccupations with the demoralization of the working class.[118] Indeed present policy in its individualisation of social problems has been criticised as a retreat from universal welfare towards a moralistic project focused on the attitudes and behaviour of the marginalised rather than their material needs.[119] However, the parallels between past discussions of demoralization and contemporary concern for empowerment tend to be overlooked because today's debates are not conducted within a moral framework deploying moral precepts, but within a social psychological paradigm deploying therapeutic concepts of empowerment and self-actualisation. So while nineteenth century policy was concerned with overcoming moral deprivation, contemporary empowerment or inclusion programmes concern psychological deprivation. While poverty is treated as a lack of capability to function, that lack is increasingly imagined in psychological and social terms. Endless doubts are expressed about the ability of individuals to relate to each other successfully without life-long relationship training and support.

7. CONCLUSION

The psychosocial models of cycles of trauma and violence reflect social pessimism about humanity as responsible and progressive beings and the possibilities of social transformation and transcendence of the past. Other eras

117 Unicef, *UN Security Council addresses latest report on children in armed conflict. Press release*, 2009 (also available at www.unicef.org/protection/index_49537.html).

118 G. Stedman-Jones, *Outcast London*, Oxford, Oxford University Press, 1971.

119 R. Levitas, *The Inclusive Society? Social Exclusion and New Labour*, Basingstoke, Macmillan, 1998.

were more optimistic about the spontaneous recovery of children without professional intervention when society believed it was forging a better world for children in the peace. Psychosocial rehabilitation programmes for war-affected children, just as social exclusion or social cohesion approaches domestically, face the fundamental question of what children are being integrated or rehabilitated into. The rise and expansion of psychosocial approaches both domestically within Western donor countries and globally has occurred against the context of a crisis of international meaning.[120] However psychosocial approaches cannot substitute for social meaning.

Ruth Levitas concludes her study of Britain New Labour's social inclusion agenda of a decade ago, with the following observation:

> While we should use the concept of social exclusion to pursue as much equality as possible, we should remember that the political framework within which it operates is one which itself excludes the possibility of an equal society. If we or future generations are to have any hope of living in a society which is built around our needs as persons, and which would make possible [fulfilling, unalienated] relationships, the question of alternatives to capitalism must be reopened. It may be countered that capitalism is the only game in town and there is not an alternative; but mankind must sometimes set itself questions which it cannot immediately solve.[121]

Without meaningful alternative progressive political and social visions then psychosocial rehabilitation means rehabilitating children to the present international social inequalities and global governance. For any hope of progressive politics, there is a need to re-affirm humanism and its faith in ordinary humanity. In so far as psychosocial approaches embody anti-humanist sentiments and mistrust ordinary people, they represent an obstacle to redeveloping a progressive politics and overcoming fundamental conflicting social interests.

---

120 Z. Laidi, *A World Without Meaning*, London, Routledge, 1998.

121 R. Levitas, *The Inclusive Society? Social Exclusion and New Labour*, Basingstoke, Macmillan, 1998, 188–189.

EXPLORING THE CONTEXT FOR ADOLESCENT MENTAL HEALTH AND PSYCHOSOCIAL ASSISTANCE IN THE EASTERN DEMOCRATIC REPUBLIC OF THE CONGO

Cindy MELS, Ilse DERLUYN, Eric BROEKAERT
and Koen VLASSENROOT

1. INTRODUCTION

Although clashes between social groups are as old as mankind, the characteristics of warfare and how it is conceptualised have changed through history. During recent decades, a shift has become clear from wars between states to conflicts within states, which appear to be characterised by a mixture of political, economic, military and social forces in competition for power and scarce resources, thereby violently targeting civilians who now compromise up to 90 per cent of war casualties.[1] The case of the Democratic Republic of the Congo, the focus of this paper, is a striking example of such contemporary prolonged conflict, frequently referred to as a 'Complex Political Emergency' (CPE).[2]

Following these changed dynamics and conceptualisations, the international community has simultaneously been confronted with the limitations of its traditional humanitarian principles and approaches.[3] Subsequent to past failures when intervening in CPEs, new ideas of development relief and conflict sensitivity have arisen, introducing 'community-based' as the new buzzword in

---

1 D. PEDERSEN, 'Political violence, ethnic conflict, and contemporary wars: broad implications for health and social well-being', (2002) 55 *Social Science & Medicine*, 175–190; J. BARENBAUM, V. RUCHKIN and M. SCHWAB-STONE, 'The psychosocial aspects of children exposed to war: practice and policy initiatives', (2004) 45 1 *Journal of Child Psychology & Psychiatry*, 41–62.

2 J. GOODHAND and D. HUME, 'From wars to complex political emergencies: understanding conflict and peace-building in the new world disorder', (1999) 20 1 *Third World Quarterly*, 13–26.

3 A. BELLAMY, 'Power, rules and argument: new approaches to humanitarian intervention', (2003) 57 3 *Australian Journal of International Affairs*, 499–512; D. RIEFF, 'Humanitarianism in crisis', (2002) 81 6 *Foreign Affairs*, 111–121.

the intervention field.[4] While these new trends have stimulated humanitarian agencies to broaden their scope into maximising contextual conditions for sustainable peace and development, they have equally been criticised for entailing unintended consequences, reproducing structural inequalities and providing simplified and unsustainable solutions.[5]

Within this 'new aid paradigm', the mental health of war-affected societies has gained attention, as psychological problems in civilians, resulting from their massive exposure to violence, have been increasingly recognized as threats to the development and long-term security of society.[6] Firstly, psychologically and socially well-functioning people and societies are considered an essential prerequisite for the rehabilitation and rebuilding of political, social and economic institutions.[7] Secondly, as is confirmed in recent findings on the association of post-traumatic stress symptoms on the one hand with feelings of revenge and negative attitudes towards reconciliation on the other, mental health problems could undermine peace-building processes and may eventually lead to renewed or sustained violence.[8] However, critical voices have related the humanitarian interest in psychosocial work to their search for legitimacy in consequence of growing criticism, inducing a new form of international governance.[9]

Beyond the question of legitimacy, how best to address mental health in CPEs has been the subject of much debate and controversy among academics, practitioners and international agencies. This discussion has determined the present humanitarian framework for the understanding of mental health and psychosocial wellbeing in war-affected situations, and subsequent humanitarian assistance.[10] In the following section, we will briefly outline the debate on mental health interventions in the humanitarian field, its path to consensus and its confined evidence base.

---

4 Goodhand and Hume, *supra* note 2; Bellamy, *supra* note 3.

5 S. Autesserre, 'Hobbes and the Congo: frames, local violence, and international intervention', (2009) 63 2 *International Organization*, 249–280; K. Vlassenroot and T. Raeymaekers, *Conflict and social transformation in Eastern DR Congo*, Academia Press, Gent, 2004.

6 D. Winter and M. Cava, 'The psycho-ecology of armed conflict', (2006) 62 1 *Journal of Social Issues*, 19–40.

7 N. Boothby, 'Political violence and development: an ecologic approach to children in war zones', (2008) 17 *Child and Adolescent Psychiatric Clinics of North America*, 497–514.

8 C. Bayer, F. Klasen and H. Adam, 'Association of trauma and PTSD symptoms with openness to reconciliation and feelings of revenge among former Ugandan and Congolese child soldiers', (2007) 298 (5) *Journal of the American Medical Association*, 555–559.

9 V. Pupavac, 'Therapeutic governance: psycho-social intervention and trauma risk management', (2001) 25 4 *Disasters*, 358–372.

10 H. Kienzler, 'Debating war-trauma and post-traumatic stress disorder (PTSD) in an interdisciplinary arena', (2008) 67 *Social Science & Medicine*, 218–227; D. Silove, Z. Steel and M. Psychol, 'Understanding community psychosocial needs after disasters: implications for mental health services', (2006) 52 2 *Journal of Postgraduate Medicine*, 121–125.

1.1. OUTLINING THE DEBATE ON MENTAL HEALTH INTERVENTION IN THE HUMANITARIAN FIELD

In accordance with its dominant biomedical paradigm, mental health research and clinical interventions amongst war-affected populations have traditionally focussed on the pathological consequences of exposure to violence, mainly in terms of post-traumatic stress disorder (PTSD), which is perceived as a universal intra-psychological reaction to trauma.[11] However, during the past decade several critical voices have been raised both in the humanitarian and in the academic field, questioning this leading trauma-focussed approach for varied reasons.[12] Firstly, it has been contested as being 'too narrow' and fundamentally ethnocentric, not accounting for variations in culture and context and the major impact these undeniably have on (1) the subjective interpretation of an event as stressful, (2) the expression of stress reactions, and (3) how these are interpreted.[13] Secondly, this discourse suggests clinical treatment methods in order to 'heal' the trauma, such as cognitive behavioural therapy.[14] However, clinical practices aimed at identifying high risk cases, which in turn are treated by counselling, are hardly feasible or sustainable in low-income countries, nor has their efficacy been proven.[15] In most low-income countries, the scene in which complex emergencies mostly take place, there are few mental health professionals, nor are dedicated mental health systems available in order to facilitate such specialised care.[16] In the Democratic Republic of the Congo, for example, 0.04 psychiatrists and 0.01 psychologists are available per 100,000 people.[17] Moreover, these sparse resources are heavily concentrated in urban areas.[18] Furthermore, in situations so massively affected by violence the outcome of an individual-level clinical approach in terms of number of people reached is bound to be inadequate.[19]

---

11 Kienzler, *supra* note 10.

12 K. Miller, M. Kulkarni and H. Kushner, 'Beyond trauma-focussed psychiatric epidemiology: bridging research and practice with war-affected populations', (2006) 76 4 *American Journal of Orthopsychiatry*, 409–422.

13 A. Almedon, and D. Summerfield, 'Mental well-being in settings of complex emergency: an overview' (2004) 36 *Journal of Biosocial Science*, 381–388.

14 M. Van Ommeren, J. Morris and S. Saxena, 'Social and clinical interventions after conflict or other large disaster', (2008) 35 5 *American Journal of Preventive Medicine*, 284–286; J. Morris, M. Van Ommeren, M. Belfer, S. Saxena and B. Saraceno, 'Children and the Sphere standard on mental and social aspects of health', (2007) 31 1 *Disasters*, 71–90.

15 Kienzler, *supra* note 10; A. Almedon and D. Summerfield, *supra* note 13.

16 M. Van Ommeren, S. Saxena and B. Saraceno, 'Mental and social health during and after acute emergencies: emerging consensus?', (2005) 83 *Bulletin of the World Mental Health Organization*, 71–76.

17 World Health Organization, *Mental Health Atlas*, WHO, Geneva, 2005.

18 D. McDaid, M. Knapp and S. Raja, 'Barriers in the mind: promoting an economic case for mental health in low- and middle income-countries', (2008) 7 *World Psychiatry*, 79–86.

19 Boothby, *supra* note 7.

Thirdly, the medicalised notion of a universalised mechanistic response to trauma has led to pathogenic assumptions that war-affected populations are traumatised and in need of therapeutic interventions.[20] Nonetheless, evidence shows that many individuals do not develop enduring symptoms in CPEs and continue to function normally, reducing mental health problems following life-threatening events during CPEs to normative responses that subside naturally once safety and stability have returned.[21]

Finally, despite its potential value the PTSD discourse has been accused of medicalising social problems, leaving structural causes and important social and material consequences of conflict unattended. Political violence affects every level of society (individuals, families, communities and institutions), and its effects are social, political and economic realities that shape everyday life. It is the socio-political and economic effects of war – such as impunity, disruption of community and family ties, extreme economic conditions, gender-based violence, interrupted education, etc. – that determine the context shaping psychological wellbeing and recovery, lifting it far beyond the biopsychological.[22]

1.2. TOWARDS CONSENSUS

Following their experiences in the field with the intrusive nature of the social, political and economic causes and consequences of conflict, international agencies have gradually agreed on a broad focus on mental health in CPEs, following years of debate.[23] From this perspective, armed conflict is no longer seen as massively traumatising individuals, but rather as destabilising different systems in the affected community on the micro- (e.g., family, peers), meso- (e.g., school, health care system) and macro-level (e.g., social norms, politics), challenging individual psychological development.[24] Furthermore, it is thought that this context should be analysed from a community perspective, allowing community members to identify how they are affected by their lived experiences of violence, and what their priorities are in terms of mental health and psychosocial assistance.[25]

---

20 V. Pupavac, *supra* note 9.

21 Silove, Steel and Psychol, *supra* note 10.

22 Almedon and Summerfield, *supra* note 15.

23 Van Ommeren, Morris and Saxena, 'Social and clinical interventions after conflict or other large disaster', (2008) 35 (5) *American Journal of Preventive Medicine*, 284–286.

24 T. Betancourt and K. Khan, 'The mental health of children affected by armed conflict: protective processes and pathways to resilience', (2008) 20 3 *International Review of Psychiatry*, 317–328.

25 Miller, Kulkarni and Kushner, *supra* note 12.

As such, humanitarian agencies have now largely agreed on the need for a long-term, integrated and multi-level approach, outlining participatory methods that reduce the risk of aid being harmful. This consensus has been crystallised in policy documents and guidelines, such as the Sphere Project (2004) standards and subsequently in the Inter-Agency Standing Committee Guidelines on Mental Health and Psychosocial Support in Emergencies.[26] The latter provides a broadly supported multi-sectoral, inter-agency framework for intervention. It proposes a multi-layered system of complementary supports, illustrated by a pyramid (see Figure 1), that as a whole should meet the broad mental health and psychosocial needs in society.[27]

Figure 1. IASC multi-layered supports pyramid (adapted from the IASC Guidelines on Mental Health and Psychosocial Support in Emergency Settings, 2007)

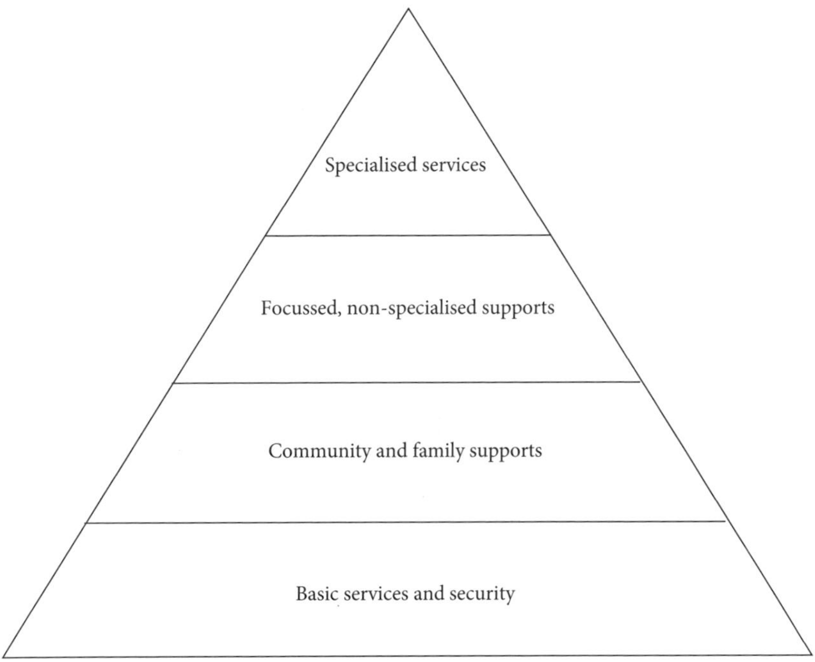

26 Inter-Agency Standing Committee, *IASC Guidelines on mental health and psychosocial support in emergency settings,* IASC, Geneva, 2007, www.who.int/mental_health/emergencies/guidelines_iasc_mental_health_psychosocial_june_2007.pdf.

27 M. Van Ommeren and M. Wessells, 'Inter-agency agreement on mental health and psychosocial support in emergency settings', (2007) 85 1 *Bulletin of the World Health Organisation*, 822–823.

Nonetheless, the recommendations on mental health and psychosocial interventions in these guidance documents are mainly based on expert opinion rather than research.[28] To date, the evidence base on 'broad' contextualised mental health needs in CPEs remains scarce and offers few tangible incentives for practitioners that could support the development of contextually appropriate, empirically sound mental health interventions. In order to implement adequately the ideas outlined in consensus documents, more evidence is required on the specific needs occurring in particular conflict-affected contexts and how they are understood: how this context is perceived by the local community, how it is altered by crisis, and which psychosocial challenges emerge from this.[29] Furthermore, additional evidence is needed to reflect on these new guidelines and to put their proposed actions into practice.[30]

In an effort to (1) move beyond the predominantly individualised approach to mental health in (post-)conflict settings and (2) add evidence on 'broad' contextualised mental health needs in CPEs, this paper will explore the locally perceived context shaping adolescent mental health in Ituri, North-Eastern DRC. Building on the experiences of local actors in youth psychosocial care, our research aimed to explore the specific post-war challenges for adolescent mental health in Iturian society. Further in this chapter, we will use these data to reflect on the IASC Guidelines on Mental Health and Psychosocial Support in Emergencies.[31]

This study formed part of a larger project investigating Eastern Congolese adolescents' mental health responses to political violence and post-war challenges.[32]

2. BACKGROUND OF THE CONFLICT

For over 15 years, the DRC has been the centre of a complex array of social, economic and politically induced conflicts involving local, national and

28 J. Morris et al., *supra* note 14.

29 Ibid., note 32.

30 Ibid., note 35.

31 Inter-Agency Standing Committee, *supra* note 26.

32 C. Mels, I. Derluyn, E. Broekaert and Y. Rosseel, 'Traumatic exposure and post-traumatic stress symptoms in adolescents in war-affected Eastern Democratic Republic of Congo', (2009) 163 6 *Archives of Pediatrics & Adolescent Medicine*, 525–530; C. Mels, I. Derluyn, E. Broekaert and Y. Rosseel, 'Community-based cross-cultural adaptation of mental health measures in emergency settings: validating the IES-R and HSCL-37A in Eastern Democratic Republic of Congo', (2010) 45 9 *Social Psychiatry & Psychiatric Epidemiology*, 899–910; C. Mels, I. Derluyn, E. Broekaert and Y. Rosseel, 'The psychological impact of forced displacement and related risk factors on Eastern Congolese adolescents affected by war', (2010) 51 10 *Child Psychology & Psychiatry*, 1096–1104.

international actors.[33] While a struggle for power on the national level was fought by different armed groups, simultaneously slumbering local ethnic disputes were stirred up in several territories, particularly in the east. These fuelled the formation of local militias, which in many cases were offered military support by neighbouring countries.[34] In 1999, following a massively disrespected ceasefire accord between the warring parties, the Security Council created MONUC (United Nations Mission in the Democratic Republic of the Congo). The Sun City accords in 2003 put a transitional government in place, paving the way for the country's first democratic elections since independence, held in 2006.[35] Although this agreement formally put an end to the war, it mainly concentrated on the national and international political levels and disregarded the local dynamics of conflict, failing to stop the violence.[36]

In this paper, we will focus on the Ituri district in Eastern DRC, where historically rooted ethnic tensions between Hema and Lendu over access to land had been mobilised by local politicians in search of a power base during the democratisation process announced at the beginning of the nineties. In parallel with a struggle for power on the national level some years later, local militias – backed up by competing foreign (Ugandan, Rwandan) forces – began to operate in Ituri in a struggle for control over the local political and economic space. By increasingly mobilising ethnic tensions in this endeavour, the Ituri conflict gradually transformed 'from a political struggle between rebel movements into a conflict between mono-ethnic militias, which became entirely targeted at civilians'.[37] Between 1999 and 2006 the conflict induced extensive human rights abuses, such as massacres, mutilation, rape, torture, house to house raids and the looting and burning down of houses, sometimes entire villages.[38] These atrocities earned Ituri the notorious name of 'the bloodiest corner in DRC', and led to the opening of the very first investigation by the International Criminal Court.[39] The crisis came to a head in 2002–2003 with a massacre in the district capital Bunia, inducing the deployment of Operation Artemis – the first-ever operation by a joint European military force

33 K. Vlassenroot and T. Raeymaekers, 'The politics of rebellion and intervention in Ituri: The emergence of a new political complex?', (2004) 103 412 *African Affairs*, 385–412.

34 S. Autesserre, 'The trouble with Congo', (2008) 87 3 *Foreign Affairs*, 94–110.

35 L. Davis and P. Hayner, 'Difficult peace, limited justice: ten years of peacemaking in the DRC', *International Centre for Transitional Justice*, New York, 2009, www.ictj.org/static/Africa/DRC/ICTJDavisHayner_DRC_DifficultPeace_pa2009.pdf.

36 S. Autesserre, *supra* note 5; Vlassenroot and Raeymaekers, *supra* note 5.

37 Ibid.

38 J. Pottier, 'Displacement and ethnic reintegration in Ituri, DRCongo: challenges ahead', (2008) 46 3 *Journal of Modern African Studies*, 427–450.

39 International Criminal Court, *Report on the activities of the court. International Criminal Court, The Hague*, 2005, www2.icc-cpi.int/NR/rdonlyres/3075AD18-33F7-4586-B221-D26D33498820/278545/ICCASP515_English.pdf.

– which was later taken over by MONUC. The violence in Ituri killed over 60,000 and caused more than 500,000 people to flee, often encountering further violence and hardship on their way.[40] Around 210,000 remain displaced in the Ituri district, with numbers fluctuating as occasional local upsurges of violence continue to create new flows of forced displacement.[41] While formally all Iturian militias were demobilised in 2007, some rebel groups currently remain active.[42] Furthermore, many of the dispersed and non-integrated militia have joined the Popular Front for Justice in Congo (FPJC), destabilising the area again in September 2008.[43] In addition, the northern border with the Haut-Uele district has recently been menaced by the Ugandan Lord's Resistance Army (LRA), brutally killing civilians and abducting children.[44]

Different ways of analysing the conflict in Ituri have been proposed. While mostly simplified as an ethnic conflict, or a struggle over natural resources for financial and economic gain, critical authors have advocated that their origins and dynamics, underlying logics and outcomes, should also be analysed historically in terms of social stratification and access to power.[45] Furthermore, these analyses emphasise that more than an economy of plunder based on mere rebel predation, the conflict in Ituri has led to the establishment of new 'complexes of power, profit and protection', in which economic and political networks have become increasingly related to ethnic identity, shaping grass-roots economic and social structures and livelihood options.[46]

The humanitarian consequences of the conflict in DRC have been devastating. While the eastern provinces remain unstable and volatile up until today, the International Rescue Committee nominated the DRC as the world's deadliest crisis since World War II. It is estimated that 5.4 million excess deaths occurred between August 1998 and April 2007, which were either directly related to violence or indirectly through social and economic disturbances caused by conflict, such as ongoing displacement, restricted humanitarian access and chronically low levels of income, education and health care.[47] According to Bell,

---

40 Human Rights Watch, *Covered in blood. Ethnically targeted violence in Northern DRC*, HRW Publications, New York, 2003, www.hrw.org/en/reports/2003/07/07/covered-blood-0.

41 Pottier, *supra* note 38.

42 L. Davis and P. Hayner, *Difficult peace, limited justice: ten years of peacemaking in the DRC*, International Centre for Transitional Justice, New York, 2009, www.ictj.org/static/Africa/DRC/ICTJDavisHayner_DRC_DifficultPeace_pa2009.pdf.

43 IRIN, *DRC: Hoping for peace in Ituri*, 2009, www.irinnews.org/Report.aspx?ReportId=82842.

44 HRW, *The Christmas massacres. LRA attacks on civilians in Northern Congo*, HRW Publications, New York, 2009, www.hrw.org/en/reports/2009/02/16/christmas-massacres-0.

45 Pottier, *supra* note 38; Vlassenroot and Raeymaekers, *supra* note 33.

46 *Supra* note 5.

47 International Rescue Committee, *Mortality in the Democratic Republic of the Congo: an ongoing crisis*, NY: International Rescue Committee, New York, 2008, www.theirc.org/resources/2007/2006-7_congomortalitysurvey.pdf.

the DRC has among the worst child survival and nutrition rates in the world: half a million children under five die each year, making it one of the top three deadliest places in the world in which to be born.[48]

Furthermore, the failing demobilisation and integration of militias into the national unified army FARDC (Forces Armées de la République Démocratique du Congo), together with underpayment and ill-discipline in FARDC, all prolong the insecurity for civilians.[49] FARDC has failed to protect civilians from attacks by armed groups, and moreover has become the region's worst perpetrator of human rights abuses.[50] In addition, sexual assault has reached endemic proportions,[51] children continue to be recruited for military service,[52] and impunity persists due to an inadequate justice system.[53] Democracy appears fragile following reports of repression and intimidation by government forces, and of journalists and political opponents being assaulted and 'neutralised'.[54]

3. METHOD

Following constructionist perspectives, we applied a community-based approach aimed at actively involving local social workers throughout different aspects of the research process. While building on existing community resources, knowledge, skills and attributes, this approach aims at enhancing local ownership and empowerment and promotes the formation of networks around a certain theme, maximising sustainability.[55] MEDAIR, an international relief organisation present in the Ituri district since 1997, was used as a starting point for snowball sampling of secondary schools and international and local community relief and development organisations active in the field of adolescent psychosocial care in Ituri. The staff members and volunteers associated with these organisations were involved in focus group

48 M. Bell, *Child Alert: Democratic Republic of Congo*, UNICEF, New York, 2006, www.unicef.org/childalert/drc/.

49 Amnesty International, *DRC: children at war, creating hope for the future*, Amnesty International, London, 2006, www.amnesty.org/en/library/info/AFR62/017/2006.

50 Pottier, *supra* note 38.

51 W. Wakabi, 'Sexual violence increasing in Democratic Republic of Congo', (2008) 371 *Lancet*, 15–16.

52 Bell, *supra* note 48.

53 Davis and Hayner, *supra* note 42.

54 Human Rights Watch, *We will crush you. The restriction of political space in the Democratic Republic of Congo*, HRW, New York Publications, 2008, www.hrw.org/en/reports/2008/11/25/we-will-crush-you-0.

55 M.J. Clark, S. Cary, G. Diemert, R. Ceballos, I. Atteberry and S. Trieu, 'Involving communities in community assessment', (2003) 20 6 *Public Health Nursing*, 456–463.

discussions or interviews, and were subsequently asked to identify which other organisations in the region were knowledgeable, until saturation was reached. This resulted in a sample entailing three secondary schools, three international and twelve local non-governmental organisations (NGOs). A total of 66 key figures in youth psychosocial care (27 females, 39 males) of varied age and background (mental health professionals, social workers and volunteers, nurses and secondary school teachers with a training in psychosocial care) participated in ten focus groups (ranging between three and eight participants) and twelve individual interviews through April and May 2007. All focus groups and interviews were led by the first author, assisted by a local psychologist, and were held in the premises of the participating organisations and schools. They were unstructured and built around the central question '*What are the consequences of the war for the community in general and for the behaviour, thinking and feeling of adolescents in particular?*'.

All interviews and focus-group discussions took place in French. They were tape-recorded and subsequently transcribed verbatim. Data were first coded into themes, which were then ordered into a coding framework, using Maxqda2 qualitative software package.[56] Subsequently, all relevant data were assigned to this framework. This resulted in qualitative data on specific symptoms observed in adolescents, which are reported elsewhere,[57] and several community trends that were perceived by local practitioners as forming a menace to the psychosocial wellbeing and further development of Congolese youngsters and to the fragile stability and peace in post-conflict Ituri.

Prior to data collection, this study was approved by the Ethics Committee of the Faculty of Psychology and Educational Sciences, Ghent University, Belgium.

4. RESULTS

In the following, we describe the themes and sub-codes arising from our data. Coding frequencies are reported merely for methodological clarity, and should be interpreted with caution as they do not necessarily reflect the strength of participants' views.[58]

---

56 U. Kuckartz, *WinMAX. Scientific text analysis for the social sciences*, User's guide, BSS Dr. Kuckartz, Berlin, 1998, www2.essex.ac.uk/cs/documentation/use/acrobat/winmaxmanual98.pdf.

57 Mels et al., *supra* note 32.

58 J. Asbury, 'Overview of focus group research', (1995) 5 *Qualitative Health Research*, 414–420.

4.1. SEPARATION AND THE BREAKDOWN OF FAMILY STRUCTURES

Despite the cessation of political violence, many children remained separated from their parents against their will for several reasons (23): 'There are different problems with different solutions. There are parents who have rejected their children, or children who turned against their parents themselves. Parents need to accept their children, no matter what happened during the war.'[59] Direct causes for separation were the death of caregivers (7) and separation whilst fleeing from violence (6). Many children remained unaware of their family's whereabouts following displacement, or they simply 'forgot' where they originated from. Also, during the war most interethnic couples were forced to separate, thereby often casting off their offspring (5). For the children who remained with one of their parents, a risk of repudiation continued to exist when the parent remarried and the new spouse's family did not accept the child.

As an indirect consequence of the war, the loss of material and economic assets and the current adverse economic situation induced separations in families that were no longer financially able to take care of their children (7). Additionally, reports were made of children being abandoned by their family (11) due to 'odd' or disobedient behaviour. In other cases, children were hindered from rejoining the family after returning from the battlefield or after being raped (this is associated with the traditional system of 'dotes', implying a loss of value for the family once a girl is pregnant or no longer a virgin).

4.2. AN INADEQUATE FRAMEWORK FOR THE SUPPORT OF YOUNGSTERS

Inadequate support and assistance to youth, especially from family (14) and school (10), was seen as most significantly threatening post-conflict rehabilitation on an individual, familial and societal level. 'Parents are supposed to support their children and send them to school. Yes, there are those children who have lost their parents, but also, there are children whose parents are unemployed, and who can't afford to send their children to school, or who don't encourage them. And thus, there is no one to support them.'[60] Furthermore, lack of guidance was instinctively associated with disobedience and aggressive behaviour in youngsters.

---

59 Focus group with local relief organisation aimed at children and mothers, 4 participants, 23 April 2007.

60 Focus group with local organisation for development and gender equality, 5 participants, 26 April 2007.

Separation and casting out from the family has been discussed above; however, even children who remained in the family were often found not to be supported or supervised properly. This was ascribed to an absence of parental authority (7) and deficient economic assets (9), resulting in an inability to pay for the child's education or the necessity to mobilise children as breadwinners.

As high importance was ascribed to education as a precondition for personal as well as community development, insufficient schooling was discerned as one of the largest menaces to society (10). However, it was perceived as being of limited importance to the government, in turn receiving inadequate funding. Consequently, school fees were high and impossible for parents suffering harsh socio-economic conditions to pay, keeping poor children out of school. Furthermore, the war has destroyed most educational infrastructure, blocking large groups of children from formal education.

International aid was seen as focussing merely on relief, frequently aiming at special target groups (5). This was found to create limited long-term opportunities and left many in need unassisted. Finally, the government was criticised for the complete lack of psychiatric services (9), leaving those with severe mental illness and in need of professional care unsupported.

4.3. CONSTRAINED FUTURE PERSPECTIVES AND OPPORTUNITIES

Insecurity (14) and a confined future perspective (6) were perceived as restraining community development and individual wellbeing. As one informant stated: '*There is a lack of future, nothing is sure. This paralyses the population. We are waiting. There is no long term project. We just live from day to day.*'[61] A sense of future and the usefulness of investment in social capital were seen as prerequisites for rehabilitation on an individual and societal level. However, it was believed that many youngsters could not see the use of going to school or learning a profession, leading many pragmatically to favour activities with short-term yet certain financial outcomes. Limited economic opportunities (10) and a dysfunctional school system (10) – due to destroyed infrastructure, the failing government and the impossibility of caregivers paying school fees – were targeted as main causes.

[61] Interview with a missionary, 19 April 2007.

4.4. CHANGING MORAL STANDARDS

Many youngsters were deemed to have lost their discipline and respect for adults (14) – traditional in Congolese culture – which was seen as a logical consequence of their large-scale participation in violent conflict. It was well argued that living an 'adult' life in the militias, backed up by weapons, had given these youngsters a sense of power, making them insusceptible to parental authority: '*Before, children had respect for the elders, but now, what's the use of respect if you can get things done by use of a weapon?*'[62] Their experiences had supposedly altered the traditional power relations within the family, creating disobedience, a lack of discipline and oppositional behaviour.

A blurring of moral standards in society became especially obvious whilst discussing the current widespread increase in rape cases (13), both in quantity and in perceived extremeness: '*Male behaviour has changed. We can notice that everywhere, even in areas where there hasn't been fighting during the war. There is a lot of sexual abuse. It's extremely traumatising and discouraging.*'[63] This trend was ascribed to impunity (6) having become an established standard during the war and to the enduring failing to re-establish a system of justice and accountability in the post-war phase.

Finally, traditional moral reference figures (4), such as church and community leaders, were criticised by some participants for their often contentious role in the conflict as promoters of an ethnic discourse. This had transformed them into facilitators of moral downfall in society during the war (or some even still today), and it had resulted in them and their institutions losing their credibility, contributing to continuing moral decay.

4.5. NEW DISTURBING SOCIAL PHENOMENA

The widespread separation (voluntary or involuntary) and casting out of children, had led to large numbers of unattended children. According to our participants, this has induced disturbing societal problems that did not exist before the war.

In the past few years, many children had resorted to the streets (12) by force, free will or fear of returning to the family (e.g., ex-combatants or raped girls fearing retribution): '*They have run away from their families, because they received beatings there, or they got rejected. Many times, that is the case in second marriages. They don't get accepted by the new spouse and her family, and they are*

62 Local organisation for the reintegration of unaccompanied and demobilised children, 3 participants, 18 April 2007.

63 Focus group with local organisation for development, 6 participants, 8 May 2007.

treated badly. So, they are better off on the streets.'[64] Participants reported on rape, stealing, disrespect and prostitution being common in this population: '*Those children aren't all orphaned. Many of them have parents, but they have rebelled against them and preferred to live on the streets. They want to be free, do what they want. They can leave at night, use drugs... and there are some among them who rape other children.'*[65]

An interrelated unsettling phenomenon was the large-scale emergence of drug and alcohol abuse (14). Many participants recognised this as a means of coping with war trauma and the current desperate situation, combined with a lack of parental authority. Others attributed this striking rise in drug use to militia practices, drugging the child combatants before going to battle, and leaving them addicted.

4.6. ATMOSPHERE OF INTERETHNIC TENSION, HATRED AND VENGEANCE

Although the participants reported a vast improvement in interethnic relations, many worried about lasting tensions (11). In spite of several interethnic and peace-building initiatives by international and local organisations, at the time of data collection segregation largely remained a fact. Ethnic apprehension was perceived as most worrying and persistent among youngsters (9), illustrated by the following quote: '*There is still a lot of mistrust and hatred among youngsters from different ethnic origins. There are many youngsters who don't want to live together with other ethnicities (...) There are also those who have lost their family in the war and want revenge.'*[66] Cited reasons for this were the fact that youngsters had never experienced the peaceful coexistence of both ethnicities, as many adults had before the war, and chiefly, that many youngsters had participated actively in the war. This created an atmosphere of hatred and vengeance, especially aimed at youths known to be ex-combatants.

64 Focus group with a local church-lead organisation aimed at street children, 8 participants, 23 April 2007.

65 Focus group with local organisation for development and gender equality, 5 participants, 26 April 2007.

66 Focus group with local organisation for development and gender equality, 5 participants, 26 April 2007.

5. DISCUSSION

Despite the high prevalence of PTSD symptoms found in adolescents in eastern DRC,[67] this study shows that rather than past traumatic exposure, adolescent psychosocial wellbeing was predominantly ascribed by local practitioners to a lack of systems of youth guidance and parenting support, limited economic and educational opportunities, changed moral standards, inadequate security, and issues of vengeance and hatred in society. While only exploratory in its nature, this study provides us with useful insights for understanding ecological issues shaping adolescent mental health beyond exposure to war violence. In our discussion of these findings, we will relate the identified adolescent mental health challenges in the post-war Ituri context to their potential individual level mental health outcomes and make suggestions for humanitarian assistance. To facilitate reflection on the IASC guidelines,[68] we will apply the concrete needs brought forward by the local practitioners in our study to its proposed multi-layered supports pyramid (see Figure 2) for mental health and psychosocial responses to emergency.

We should, however, remain aware of possible limitations to our method, such as the risk inherent to the focus group method of creating a 'group think' and thereby possibly leaving out minority opinions.[69] While this has been tackled by supplementary individual interviews, we cannot be sure of having heard all possible views and opinions. Moreover, we were unable to analyse whether responses differed according to participants' gender, age or background. Furthermore, we wish to emphasise that our results incorporate the perspective of local practitioners following their field experience with adolescent psychosocial wellbeing, each with their own history and experiences, and occupying a particular place in the social reality constituting conflict and its aftermath, which is likely to differ from adolescents' place.[70] Despite its potential value, time and language constraints prevented us from complementing these adult views with the voices of youngsters themselves. Finally, we should be aware that our findings reflect the reality of a particular time and place. Nonetheless, to a certain extent they could offer us insights applicable to similar settings.

---

67 Mels et al., *supra* note 32.

68 Inter-Agency Standing Committee, *supra* note 26.

69 Clark and Cary, *supra* note 55.

70 L. Jourdan, 'Being at war, being young: violence and youth in North Kivu', in K. Vlassenroot and T. Raeymaekers (eds.), *Conflict and social transformation in Eastern DR Congo*, Academia Press, Gent, 2004, 157–176.

Figure 2. Participants' perceived needs applied to the IASC (2007) multi-layered supports pyramid

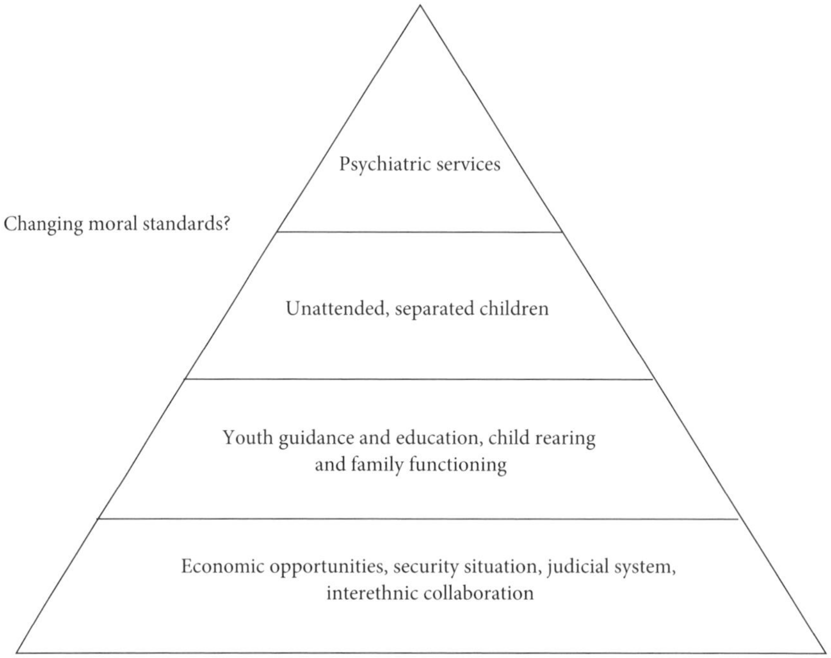

5.1. MULTI-LAYERED NEEDS FOR PSYCHOSOCIAL INTERVENTION IN ITURI

Level 1: Basic Services and Security

The stimulation of *economic opportunities* was discerned as a pressing condition for post-conflict rehabilitation in Ituri, and could enhance youth mental health through the alleviation of hopelessness, effective coping and empowerment.[71] Furthermore, it could open up alternatives for youngsters to achieve positive roles in their family and society.[72]

Rehabilitation, however, requires a prompt yet durable improvement in the *security situation*. Not only would this stimulate protective economic and social activities, it would also prevent renewed trauma.[73] A particular example of the serious lack of security and its disabling societal effects is found in the frequent

71 Boothby, *supra* note 7; M. Grgić, V. Vidović, S. Butković-Soldo, Z. Vukšić-Mihaljević, D. Degmečić and D. Laufer, 'The mental health of children upon their return home after a long displacement period', (2005) 29 2 *Collegium Antropologicum*, 537–542.

72 Jourdan, *supra* note 70.

73 Betancourt and Khan, *supra* note 24.

occurrence of rape in eastern DRC.[74] The absence of punishment and accountability for such abuses has resulted in their 'normalisation' into a 'culture of violence', which calls for the installation of an *effective and credible judicial system*.[75]

Irrespective of apparent peaceful coexistence, *interethnic collaboration and tolerance* should be continuously promoted on the community level. As traumatic exposure, PTSD symptoms, feelings of revenge and less openness to reconciliation are tightly interwoven, psychosocial programmes should address feelings of hatred, revenge and forgiveness, while peace-building – and more specifically peace education initiatives – likewise should address issues of psychological trauma.[76]

Level 2: Community and Family Support

A substantial expansion is needed in the field of *youth guidance and education*. Schooling is considered an important protective factor for mental health in war-affected children,[77] and thus demands a solid social and educational policy on the national level, contrary to the pre-war situation in DRC where such policy was either insufficient or non-existent.[78] While certain NGOs and UN agencies have made successful efforts to improve school accessibility,[79] a further democratisation of education is warranted (e.g., reducing school fees, promoting gender equality, decentralisation), and should include short-term vocational initiatives for those who have no educational background or dropped out of school due to the war, in order to offer immediate yet sustainable return.[80]

The new *challenges in child rearing and family functioning* should be seen within the new social reality created by conflict through its reorganisation of social, economic and political space.[81] These dynamics have affected local traditional forms of leadership and social interaction, including on the family level. Furthermore, the war has opened up opportunities for marginalised youth to go beyond their social role or invert it – imposing their authority on adults –

74 Wakabi, *supra* note 62.

75 R. Beneduce, L. Jourdan, T. Raeymaekers and K. Vlassenroot, 'Violence with a purpose: exploring the functions and meaning of violence in the Democratic Republic of Congo', (2006) 4 *Intervention*, 32–46; E. Rackley, 'Democratic Republic of the Congo: undoing government by predation', (2006) 30 4 *Disasters*, 417–432.

76 Bayer et al., *supra* note 8.

77 J. Barenbaum, V. Ruchkin and M. Schwab-Stone, 'The psychosocial aspects of children exposed to war: practice and policy initiatives', (2004) 45 1 *Journal of Child Psychology & Psychiatry*, 41–62.

78 Rackley, *supra* note 75.

79 Bell, *supra* note 48.

80 Betancourt and Khan, *supra* note 24.

81 Vlassenroot and Raeymaekers, *supra* note 5.

by the use of violence.[82] Psychosocial interventions that address these social transformations and related challenges in family functioning – such as the need to re-establish a balance in family relations, taking new roles for youths into account and trying to overcome conditions of economic hardship – could entail an important stimulation for youth development and recovery, as positive family relations are considered a major determinant of war-affected youths' mental health.[83]

Level 3: Focussed, Non-Specialised Support

The needs of cast-out, *unattended and separated children* that are currently living on the street, leaving them at risk of abuse and social dislocation, should be met.[84] From a social perspective, the problematisation of street children and their explicit association with negative behaviours such as rape and drug abuse could be interpreted as a power struggle between youth in search of new roles and adults in search of 'correctional' responses.[85] As such, interventions responding to the growing numbers of street children and the associated growth of drug and alcohol abuse should focus on contextual factors that result from voluntary and involuntary separation (e.g., poverty, maltreatment, etc.), yet also on the symbolic value of street life and its function as an alternative identity for youth.

Level 4: Specialised Services

Except for isolated efforts from traditional healers, severe psychiatric cases remain unattended, as no system or policy for mental health has ever been established in DRC.[86] In addition, the severely mentally ill are often overlooked by international organisations.[87] The installation of a specialised alternative for those with serious psychiatric disorders is called for, preferably in close connection with other (mental) health promoting initiatives and respecting traditional systems of healing.[88] Nonetheless, seen in the context of historical social, political and economic stratification in Ituri and other conflict settings, caution is warranted while building on local social capital (likely to be highest

82 Jourdan, *supra* note 70.
83 Barenbaum et al., *supra* note 1.
84 Boothby, *supra* note 7.
85 Jourdan, *supra* note 70.
86 World Health Organization, *supra* note 17.
87 D. Silove, Z. Steel and M. Psychol, 'Understanding community psychosocial needs after disasters: implications for mental health services', (2006) 52 2 *Journal of Postgraduate Medicine*, 121–125.
88 Pedersen, *supra* note 1.

in local elites) in order to prevent the reproduction of existing social inequalities.[89]

5.2. REFLECTIONS ON THE IASC GUIDELINES

Our findings emphasise that political violence impinges on every level of society – families, communities, values and social institutions – indirectly affecting the individual, and thereby taking mental health threats in CPEs well beyond direct exposure to violence.[90] This suggests that the locally perceived need for interventions addressing youth mental health in Ituri could best be tackled by a holistic, social ecological framework, rather than by a predominantly trauma-focussed approach. However, besides comprehensive interventions aimed at strengthening families and communities, the need for specialised mental health services for a minority with persisting psychiatric problems also featured in our analysis.[91] As such, the coordinated multi-level and multi-sectoral strategy for psychosocial intervention that is advocated in the IASC guidelines[92] to a certain extent responds to the needs articulated by the practitioners in our research. While the basic needs expressed by our informants are broad and many, climbing up the pyramid, focussed or specialised needs are few. At a glance, the framework appears to address the different areas (e.g., protection, health, human rights, education) found to influence youth mental health in Ituri, while simultaneously integrating specialised responses for the severely mentally ill.[93]

Nonetheless, our study also uncovers certain limitations to the IASC guidelines. Firstly, not all concerns addressed by our participants can be easily related to the IASC framework. More specifically, there appears to be a blind spot in addressing moral issues and altered standards in society following violent conflict (see 'changing moral standards' in Figure 2). These issues appear to be directly related to the social transformation induced by conflict.[94] Family disruption and events such as rape, unwanted pregnancy, oppositional behaviour and participation in armed forces have posed challenges to families and communities to come up with new yet acceptable roles for youngsters, new ideas on parental authority, and new moral standards on what is acceptable behaviour

89 G. Mohan, 'The disappointments of civil society: the politics of NGO intervention in northern Ghana', (2002) 21 1 *Political Geography*, 125–154; Vlassenroot and Raeymaekers, *supra* note 5.

90 H. Kienzler, 'Debating war-trauma and post-traumatic stress disorder (PTSD) in an interdisciplinary arena', (2008) 67 *Social Science & Medicine*, 218–227; Mille et al., *supra* note 12.

91 Van Ommeren et al., *supra* note 14.

92 Inter-Agency Standing Committee, *supra* note 26.

93 Van Ommeren and Wessells, *supra* note 27.

94 Vlassenroot and Raeymaekers, *supra* note 33; Beneduce et al., *supra* note 75.

for youngsters and adults. While these needs are broad and involve the whole community, the challenges arising from social transformation do not appear to be addressed by the lowest level in the IASC pyramid, comprising basic physical and security support.[95] Indeed, there is no humanitarian intervention sector on 'moral standards', nor are there any agencies specialised in such matters. Nonetheless, the need to address newly risen moral dilemmas reflecting societal changes in the aftermath of war featured strongly in our study participants' views. As long as a moral consensus on certain key issues in contemporary society does not develop, stability will remain under threat, and situations of abuse, brutality and neglect will continue to strain mental health.[96]

Secondly, despite recognising the need for a long-term vision in the design and implementation of interventions, the IASC guidelines primarily aim at delivering emergency phase 'minimum responses',[97] which are inherently short term and focussed on the initial conflict-inducing crisis. This raises questions about how well the local dynamics of conflict and its lingering effects on society are taken into consideration in the current guidelines for intervention,[98] particularly as little consideration is given to the succession to the suggested minimum response following continuing transformation on the grassroots level. Our study illustrates that the context for mental health is highly dynamic, with new challenges and support arising in the aftermath of crisis through social transformation. Intervention strategies should repeatedly assess and address these newly developing risks and opportunities for mental health in order to be truly effective in the long term.

Thirdly, our study provides evidence on how political conflict alters society, and how new challenges in different sectors continue to emerge even when political conflict has officially ended.[99] However, a major obstacle for the practical implementation of a comprehensive and integrated response, such as professed in the IASC guidelines, is its dependency on funding provided by actors utilising a seemingly irreconcilable framework. Despite calls to link relief to development in order to enable long-term, holistic approaches to challenges following complex emergencies, the institutionalised gap between relief and development remains.[100] It is up to policy makers to address such limitations, and to humanitarian agencies to provide concrete examples of how to overcome them, with respect to local social, political and economic reality.

---

95 Ibid., note 107.

96 D. Winter and M. Cava, 'The psycho-ecology of armed conflict', (2006) 62 1 *Journal of Social Issues*, 19–40.

97 Inter-Agency Standing Committee, *supra* note 6.

98 M. Van Rooyen, S. Hansh, D. Curtis and G. Burnham, 'Emerging issues and future needs in humanitarian assistance', (2001) 16 4 *Prehospital & Disaster Medicine*, 216–222.

99 T. O'Dempsey and B. Muslow, 'Globalisation, complex humanitarian emergencies and health', (2006) 100 5 *Annals of Tropical Medicine & Parasitology*, 501–515.

100 A. Ackermann, 'The idea and practice of conflict prevention', (2003) 40 3 *Journal of Peace Research*, 339–347.

In conclusion, despite its merit in broadening the scope of mental health beyond traditional individualised approaches, the Inter-Agency Standing Committee Guidelines on Mental Health and Psychosocial Support in Emergencies[101] do not entirely seem to grasp the social context determining mental health in CPEs. Most importantly, they underestimate the highly dynamic nature of societies so deeply disrupted by extreme violence and crisis, a dynamic that induces new mental health risks, yet also new potential sources for support. Moreover, they inadequately address issues of power, be it on the local level – determining personal (e.g., parent-child) and community relationships (e.g., moral standards) – or on the international level (funding strategies).

6. ACKNOWLEDGEMENTS

We would like to thank MONUC and the coordinators of MEDAIR Bunia for their logistical support, the MEDAIR staff for their cooperation, and all local NGOs, secondary schools and the participating pupils for help making this research possible.

---

101 Inter-Agency Standing Committee, *supra* note 26.

A GENDER PERSPECTIVE ON GIRLS AND YOUNG WOMEN IN ARMED CONFLICTS AND ORGANISED ARMED VIOLENCE

Some Examples from Latin America

Maria Luisa Bartolomei

'The human rights violations that occur when children are used in hostilities are not limited to children killing and being killed or injured. Girls also are used as soldiers, have been victims of rape and other sexual abuse. The human rights impacts ... are terrible and far-reaching, and ... have an impact not only on those children directly concerned but also on their families and communities, and continue long after the hostilities have ended.'

(Mary Robinson, 2000)

1. INTRODUCTION AND BACKGROUND

While many children are involved in wars today, it is equally important to account for those children who are involved in organised armed violence. In doing so we can understand the true nature of the problem of how armed children and young people are affected socially, economically and politically in the region as a whole. This chapter deals with girls and young women who are involved in armed conflicts and organized armed violence in Latin America. We will adopt a sociology of law perspective and will look at the interrelation between gender, age, class and ethnicity. Some insights are drawn from the feminist concept of intersectionality (Yuval Davis) and the concept of gender advanced by Ramazanoglu and Holland, while other ideas come from feminist child law (Bridgeman and Monk) and the dilemma of the girl child in international human rights law. Some of the questions being addressed from a gender perspective include: Why do girls join the armed forces and become members of armed opposition groups in the first place, and what roles do they play as members? And on a more general level, are there any differences between the processes of recruitment into armed conflict and juvenile gangs, which are involved in organised armed violence? Our study is based on a number of sources, including reports from international organisations (United Nations, UNICEF and UNIFEM, as well as the OAS and UNESCO) and from international and national NGOs (particularly Human Rights Watch, the Coalition to Stop the Use of Child Soldiers, Save the Children and Amnesty International).

The chapter is organised as follows: the first part introduces the background to the problem of young women and girls as child soldiers involved in armed conflict and armed violence; the second part examines to what extent girls and young women are involved as child soldiers, their entry and the roles they play in armed conflict and organised armed violence, later illustrated by examples from Colombia and El Salvador; furthermore, we look at gender mainstreaming strategies at the level of the United Nations and other international organisations, and also address the concept of gender and feminist methodology and theory; finally, the different integrated strategy approaches in the prevention and rehabilitation of children and youth are discussed.

International sources roughly calculate that over 300,000 children younger than 18 years old have been caught up in over 30 conflicts worldwide.[1] The United Nations Children's Fund (UNICEF) has defined 'child soldier' as any child under 18, either male or female, 'who is part of any kind of regular or irregular armed force or armed group in any capacity, including, but not limited to: cooks, porters, messengers, and anyone accompanying such groups other than family members. It includes girls and boys recruited for forced sexual purposes and/or forced marriage. The definition, therefore, does not only refer to a child who is carrying, or has carried, weapons.' This definition is based on the Cape Town Principles.[2] In 2002, the Optional Protocol to the Convention on the Rights of the Child on the Involvement of Children in Armed Conflict entered into force. This Optional Protocol outlaws the participation of children under 18 in hostilities, and in doing so raises the previous age of 15 set by the Convention on the Right of the Child (1989) and the 1949 Geneva Conventions and their 1977

[1] 300,000 children make up the estimated number provided by most sources, for example M. Hobson, Forgotten *Casualties of War: Girls in Armed Conflict*', The Save the Children Fund, London, 2005, 1; Unicef, *Fact sheet: Child Soldiers*, 2005, available at www.unicef.org/emerg/files/childsoldiers.pdf; International Rescue Committee, *Child Soldiers Fact Sheet*, 2007, available at www.theirc.org/resources/irc-cypd-child-soldiers-fact-sheet-august-2007.pdf. However, these numbers are always in flux as conflicts decrease or intensify.

[2] Unicef, *Fact sheet: Child Soldiers*, 2005; see also Machel Strategic Review Report, *Will You Listen? Young Voices from Conflict Zones*, 2007, available online at www.un.org/children/conflict/machel. and Spanish9971999Global World.

Additional Protocols. In addition to requiring States to raise the age for compulsory recruitment and direct participation in conflict to 18, the Optional Protocol also requires State parties to raise the minimum age for voluntary recruitment beyond the current minimum of 15.

Significantly, the estimated 300,000 child soldiers mentioned are only a fraction of the total number of children and young people who use weapons. On the top of these children at war, it is necessary to take into account children in organised armed violence, as a whole, socially, economically, politically and culturally, so as to understand the true nature of the problem.[3] The consequences of this exposure are that several categories of children become vulnerable to situations involving armed conflict. These especially include girls, refugees, internally displaced children and child-headed households. These children and young people require special support, including awareness and security. Girls, for instance, are often the victim of sexual violence and exploitation, while they are increasingly being recruited into fighting groups.[4] The phenomenon of youngsters engaged in organised armed violence is not the same as our general understanding of 'war'; at the same time, it is even further away from our general understanding of 'peace'. The level of insecurity related to this problem is making youth violence one of the top priorities on government agendas. Special measures, for instance, are being considered to repress youth gangs.[5]

The growing engagement of children and young people in organised armed violence is becoming more common in some regions of the world. This is certainly the case in Latin America, particularly Brazil, Colombia, El Salvador and Ecuador. The World Report on Violence and Health in 2002 clearly showed that over the last decade, those aged between 15 and 24 years were the most frequent victims of homicide. In some countries, even major achievements in reducing child mortality have not had an impact on average life expectancy, because these gains are cancelled out by growing rates of homicide among children and young people.[6]

3 See W. Morales, 'Girl Child Soldiers: The Other Face of Sexual Exploitation and Gender Violence', (2008) 2 1 *Air and Space Power Journal* 62–77, available at www.airpower.maxwell.af.mil/apjinternational/apj-s/2008/1tri08/moraleseng.htm; L. Dowdney, *Neither War nor Peace: International comparisons of children and youth in organised armed violence*, Editora 7 Letras, Rio de Janeiro, 2005, available at www.coav.org.br; Hobson, *supra* note 1, vi-1.

4 Hobson, *supra* note 1, 1–2; Morales, *supra* note 3.

5 M. Carranza, 'Detention or Death: Where the "Pandillero" Kids of El Salvador are Heading', in Dowdney, *supra* note 3; I. Ramirez, *Medellin: The Invisible Children of the Social and Armed Conflict*, Coalición contra la Vinculación de Niños, Niñas y Jóvenes al Conflicto Armado en Colombia, 2005, at www.coav.org.br.

6 Demoscopia S.A., *Maras and gangs, community and police in Central America*, SIDA and CABEI, 2008, available at www.sida.se/publications; Dowdney, *supra* note 3, 9.

In the present-day climate, many argue that special attention must be given to the specific needs of girls and young women. Furthermore, a deeper understanding of the acute vulnerability of girls in situations of armed conflict is required, which should allow for more gender-sensitive strategies. An agenda of disarmament, demobilisation and reintegration should give special attention to victims of sexual exploitation and the girls, including the young women who are heads of household. It is also important to remember in this context that sexual and gender-based violence and the vulnerability of girls in the context of armed conflict have gradually become a particular preoccupation and focus for a number of organisations, at both the national and international levels.[7]

2. GIRLS AND YOUNG WOMEN IN ARMED CONFLICT AND ORGANISED ARMED VIOLENCE

2.1. WHERE ARE THE GIRLS?

A number of experts who consider the question 'Where are the girls?' explain that this is very rarely brought up in discussions or in the research about children in armed conflicts and organised armed violence. Just as the use of child soldiers has been a largely invisible and unappreciated international phenomenon, limited attention has been given to girls in conflict and armed violence and their diverse experiences, as well as gender-specific human rights violations.[8]

According to McKay and Mazurana, the majority of reports, international campaigns and proposals predominantly use the generic expression 'child soldiers' or 'children', which almost always means 'boys'. Subsequently, they do not identify the degrees of difference or the consequences for boys and girls before, during and after armed conflict from a gender perspective.[9] They observe the methodological difficulties that the marginalisation of girls within peace accords pose, which includes their 'invisibility' as children in the armed groups. Systematic gathering and analysis of data is required, so as to better identify the extent of the girls' transnational involvement and experiences in these groups. A case in mind is when a debate about girls is often embedded in a paragraph or in several pages of a larger report, or in conference proceedings. This information is

---

7 S. McKay and D. Mazurana, *Girls in Militaries, Paramilitaries, and Armed Opposition Groups*, 2004, at www.waraffectedchildren.gc.ca/girls-en.asp, 1.

8 Dowdney, *supra* note 3; Y. Keairns, *The Voices of Girl Child Soldiers – Colombia*, Quaker United Nations Office, New York, 2003, available at www.themastering.com/www_edit/upload/cades/courses/051206/QUNO%20-%20Girl%20Soldiers%20Colombia.pdf.

9 McKay and Mazurana, *supra* note 7, 1.

usually minimised and can be very confusing because of uncorroborated generalisation. This often becomes self-perpetuating.[10]

There are many multiple challenges to understanding better the experiences of girls in armed conflict from a holistic and gender perspective. For instance, rarely are the views of girls situated contextually or comprehensively within particular armed conflicts, geopolitical conditions, time periods, countries or regions. Likewise, the varying character of their role expectations and their interaction with men, boys or other girls and women in the armed groups have yet to be studied and analysed in depth. The majority of data regarding child soldiers has also provided scattered and at best limited information about a girl's entrance into these various armed conflicts. Finally, no systematic investigation has been carried out on girls during the pre-conflict, conflict and post-conflict phases.[11]

Some experts also point to the absence of information about what happens after the fighting ends. What, for example, happens to the girls and their babies and what happens to the children within Disarmament, Demobilisation and Reintegration programmes for former girl soldiers?[12]

2.2. GIRLS AND YOUNG WOMEN IN ARMED CONFLICT

Of the numbers of child soldiers mentioned above some 40 per cent, that is to say 120,000 child soldiers are girls, whose plight is often unrecognized. This is because international attention has been devoted largely to boy soldiers. The girls are the less visible 'shadow armies' in conflicts around the world. Girls not only work as active fighters, but also carry out other military services, from intelligence and medical support to cleaning and cooking. Even more, a number of young girls are used as sex slaves to service the forces, or are forced into pseudo-marriages with commanders of armed groups.[13] There is a lack of statistics in many cases since leaders of irregular forces and armies do not advertise the role of child soldiers, much less young girls, for fear of being prosecuted for war crimes.[14]

---

10 McKay and Mazurana, *supra* note 7, 2; Hobson, *supra* note 1, 1.

11 McKay and Mazurana, *supra* note 7, 3; Keairns, *supra* note 8.

12 Hobson, *supra* note 1, 1–2. In the case of El Salvador, it was reported that approximately 30 per cent of the child soldiers in armed opposition groups were girls, see International Coalition, 2000a and 2000e.

13 Hobson, *supra* note 1, vi; McKay and Mazurana, *supra* note 7.

14 Morales, *supra* note 3, 4.

Girls are gradually becoming unwilling warriors or sexual partners of soldiers in conflicts throughout the world. It has been estimated that between 1990 and 2003, girls as young as 13 were part of military and paramilitary groups in 55 countries. It is reported that girls participated in armed conflict in 38 of those countries. At present, more than 120,000 girls are participating in armed conflicts worldwide. It is worth noting that some girls become soldiers voluntarily, but that in most cases they are abducted and forced to participate in combat operations. Once they become soldiers, they frequently become part of a process of sexual exploitation and abuse. As a result of sexual relations and rape by fellow soldiers, they often get sexually transmitted infections, which are common amongst men.[15]

Civil wars and armed conflicts weaken the ability of both families and communities to shield their children and this is certainly the case with very young girls, who are socially, culturally and often religiously controlled, even in peacetime. Furthermore, a large number of girl victims become orphans and refugees because of the conditions of social chaos and violence. They then become easy victims in a cycle of abuse. Global conflicts, in some way, deny them childhood, their humanity and their very lives.[16]

Even though girls are gradually receiving more attention, the child protection community, academia and other stakeholders must do their utmost to deepen knowledge concerning these girls and young women, which should lead to more effective support and programmed intervention. They should also, in turn, give priority to sexual and gender-based violence. This can be done through adopting appropriate national legislation and rigorous and systematic investigation and prosecution of violent crimes, with an emphasis on the support and well-being of victims.[17]

Although not as widespread as on other continents, Central and South America have incorporated child soldiers, particularly since the 1960s. Girl recruitment into the frontlines, either by incentive or by force, was a feature of many guerrilla and paramilitary groups, who gained membership mainly from the peasantry and indigenous groups. The *Sendero Luminoso* or Shining Path guerrilla movement in Peru, for example, had a significant young female contingent.

---

15 C. Chelala, 'Girl soldiers are casualties of war', 2007, Seattle-Pi at www.seattlepi.com/opinion/319903_girlsoldiers15.html; Coalition to Stop the Use of Child Soldiers, *Child Soldiers – Global Report 2008*, London, 2008, at www.childsoldiersglobalreport.org; Hobson, *supra* note 1, vi–3.

16 Morales, *supra* note 3, 4; Hobson, *supra* note 1.

17 H. Charlesworth and C. Chinkin, *The boundaries of international law – A feminist analysis*, Juris Publishing, Manchester, 2000, 14–15; McKay and Mazurana, *supra* note 7.

Moreover, many of the various guerrilla groups of El Salvador, Guatemala, Honduras, Nicaragua and Colombia included girl soldiers.[18]

Research findings to date indicate that the involvement of girls in the armed forces and armed opposition groups comes about as a result of the girl being born to a mother in the group or taken in as an orphan by the group. Other girls may have a parent, often the father, or husband implicated in the force/group. A number are given to the armed forces or to the armed opposition groups by a parent as a form of 'tax' or because the girl has been dishonoured in some way and made an outsider in her family and community.[19]

Many girls become members for their own safety, while many have access to food, shelter and clothing. Some girls advance their career options by joining particularly government, political or military organisations. Many are recruited in schools or from the streets. Quite a few are abducted or press-ganged and some join in response to state violence against their families and communities.[20]

In their studies, most experts agree that girls carry out a number of duties during armed conflicts. According to several reports, girls assisted as porters and cooks, or performed a variety of domestic duties as camp followers; some were used as spies to collect and provide information, as well as looting villages taken over by the armed forces/armed opposition groups. Numerous girls were required or systematically forced to provide sexual services for male soldiers. Some girls functioned as combat soldiers, often with front-line duties, particularly suicide missions and minesweeping.[21]

What is important to make clear here is that in many cases girls were performing numerous roles, so a clear separation of duties – fighter versus cook, porter versus wife – was not wholly accurate. Girls should, therefore, be looked at in the context of the force or group and the conflict itself so as to define the roles they played.[22]

2.3. GIRLS AND YOUNG WOMEN INVOLVED IN ORGANISED ARMED VIOLENCE

With the end of civil wars and conflicts, a number of young girls and boys then became targets for juvenile gangs and organised armed violence in Latin

18 Morales, *supra* note 3, 4.

19 McKay and Mazurana, *supra* note 7, 5.

20 Hobson, *supra* note 1, 11; Keairns, *supra* note 8.

21 McKay and Mazurana, *supra* note 7, 7; Hobson, *supra* note 1, 11; Keairns, *supra* note 8.

22 McKay and Mazurana, *supra* note 7, 7; Hobson, *supra* note 1, 1, 8, 11.

America.[23] In a number of cases, they were voluntary recruits drawn to a popular cause or runaways from poverty and conflict, as well as from reprisals by state security forces and paramilitaries. However, voluntary recruitment did not keep them from abuse and exploitation, nor were they free to leave.[24]

The gender roles of members of armed groups in Brazil, Colombia, El Salvador and Ecuador were not included as an explicit research variable in Dowdney's research. Consequently, the interviews showed that women were not so different to men. Many girls, for instance, had also left school directly before, or after, joining an armed group. In addition, girls were from poor communities and faced the same socio-economic difficulties as boys from those same communities. Importantly, though, in most of the armed groups examined female members were not inclined to use firearms to the same level as male members, if at all. They instead tended to rely on other weapons, such as knives. Some female gang members talked of only having guns of a lower calibre, unlike their boyfriends.[25] According to Dowdney,[26] the distinction in the use of firearms means that although girls are part of armed groups, and in some cases may be armed themselves, their direct involvement in armed violence is less than that of boys. In El Salvador in 2000, for example, for every female who died from gunshot wounds up to 35 males died from the same cause. The 'differing usage' of firearms by male and female group members may give us a clue as to why more boys than girls join armed groups. In many of the communities covered by Downey's study, notions of 'manhood' were tied to gaining respect. Some of the female respondents in Colombia said they had joined a *banda* because they were involved with a male member. In contrast, none of the boys interviewed said they had joined as a result of a female member. On the contrary, for many adolescent males joining an armed group is a way of asserting a particular vision of masculinity; participating in a strong and recognized group and using a gun means that they become more attractive to the opposite sex.

There is no doubt that more research is needed on gender roles within armed groups. The limited information that is available, in this research, barely scratches the surface in a complex set of relationships and culturally propagated gender-based behaviour. Learning more about these gender roles can significantly assist programmers and policy makers in implementing successful prevention and re-insertion models, while at the same time targeting those interventions with greater precision.[27]

---

23 Demoscopia, *supra* note 6; Dowdney, *supra* note 3.
24 Morales, *supra* note 3, 4.
25 Dowdney, *supra* note 3, 117–18 and 339.
26 Ibid., 118–119.
27 H. Covey, *Street Gangs throughout the World*, Illinois, Charles C Thomas – Publisher, 2003; Demoscopia, *supra* note 6.

3. THE CASES OF COLOMBIA AND EL SALVADOR

In the following paragraphs we will illustrate the developments sketched above through the practices of Latin America, in particular Colombia and El Salvador.

3.1. COLOMBIA

The armed conflict in Colombia has continued for over 40 years and the conflict is often accompanied by extensive human rights violations and breaches of international humanitarian law (IHL), which include abuses against children.[28] The conflict has seen thousands of civilians killed while thousands more have been subjected to enforced disappearance by the security forces or paramilitaries, or abducted by guerrilla groups. It is also calculated that 3–4 million people have been forcibly displaced as a result of the conflict. Although indigenous people make up only around 3.4 per cent of the population, they account for 7 per cent of Colombia's total displaced population.[29] Indigenous and Afro-Colombian communities have been victimised by all parties to the conflict and it has also been marked by widespread sexual violence against girls and women.[30]

This internal armed conflict has continued to have a devastating impact on civilians. Many have certainly been the victims of extrajudicial executions, enforced disappearances and intimidation, and a number have been the victims of anti-personnel mines,[31] as well as of arbitrary attacks and compulsory displacement.[32] Children, it is clear, represent a high percentage of these victims.[33] The grave violations against children have been attributed to all

28 UN High Commissioner for Human Rights, *Report on the situation of human rights in Colombia*, UN Doc. E/CN.4/2006/9; see also here the International Committee of the Red Cross (ICRC), *Colombia: Humanitarian Situation Remains of Concern*, 2006; ICRC, *Annual Report 2006, Colombia*, available at www.icrc.org.

29 More than 60 per cent of displaced people in Colombia have been forced from their homes and lands in areas of mineral, agricultural or other economic importance (Amnesty International, *The Struggle for Survival and Dignity – Human Rights Abuses Against Indigenous Peoples in Colombia*, 2010, 2, available at www.amnesty.org.

30 Ibid., 2–8; Human Rights Watch, *World Report 2010 – Colombia*, available at www.hrw.org/; Gay McDougall, *Report of the independent expert on minority issues – Mission to Colombia*, UN Doc. A/HRC/16/45/Add.1, 9–13.

31 See, for example, the Human Rights Council, 4th session, provisional agenda item 2, Report of the United Nations High Commissioner for Human Rights, above note 8; HRW, *Maiming the people: guerrilla use of antipersonnel landmines and other indiscriminate weapons in Colombia*, July 2007.

32 Displacement is one of the greatest threats facing indigenous communities. Often living in areas of intense military conflict and rich in biodiversity, minerals and oil, indigenous peoples are at particular risk of forced displacement (Amnesty International, *supra* note 29, 8–9).

33 In one case, in March 2006 army troops took up positions in a village school near Puerto Asís, Putumayo, causing 30 village families to leave their homes after FARC announced that

parties, but mainly to illegal armed groups, as they continue to recruit children and commit crimes, although there have been instances of violations by individual officials of the Colombian armed forces. Those illegal armed groups continue to recruit children and commit crimes of sexual violence against women and girls, including killing civilians, planting anti-personnel mines and carrying out abductions.[34]

All parties have claimed respect for international human rights law; however, in reality the tactics of an irregular war have eroded the distinction between combatants and civilians.[35] Moreover, defenceless indigenous peoples,[36] Afro-descendants, peasants and their families have been victims of marauding private armies, which are out to conquer and appropriate territory and resources. There have been massacres on all sides, particularly of women and children, and there are now millions of displaced Colombians, who are internal refugees or live in camps in bordering states.[37] Of these, over half are under 18 years old and can be considered children under current human rights law.[38]

3.1.1. Child Recruitment and Mistreatment

Government security forces did not, on record, recruit under 18s, but they did use captured children for intelligence-gathering, regardless of the legal prohibition.[39] Those children who were arrested by the security forces for longer than the 36-hour period under the law had to be sent into the care of the Colombian Institute of Family Welfare (*Instituto Colombiano de Bienestar Familiar*, ICBF). Children who had left the armed groups told the Ombudsman's Office that they were kept in police stations and army bases for long periods and

---

it would attack the site. In June 2006, the Representative of the UN Secretary-General on the Human Rights of Internally Displaced Persons observed that 'the armed forces had installed their headquarters in the middle of the village [of Toribo, Cauca], next to a primary school, and had erected posts in the central square of town immediately next to a playground and a church centre' (Coalition to Stop the Use of Child Soldiers, *supra* note 15, 101).

34 Coalition to Stop the Use of Child Soldiers, *supra* note 15, 101; see also UN Security Council, *Report of the Secretary-General on children and armed conflict in Colombia*, UN Doc. S/2009/434, 3 and 16; Human Rights Watch, *supra* note 30; Human Rights Watch, *Paramilitaries' Heirs – The New Force of Violence in Colombia*, 2010, available at www.hrw.org/en/reports/2010/02/03/paramilitaries-heirs-0.

35 Amnesty International, *Annual Report – Colombia*, 2011, 1–2, available at www.amnesty.org.

36 Ibid., 2.

37 More than 280,000 people were forcibly displaced in 2010, compared with 286,000 in 2009. Between 3 and 5 million people have been displaced in the last 25 years (ibid., 3).

38 Ibid., 7; see also Morales, *supra* note 3; F.E. Osorio Pérez, 'Forced Displacement among Rural Women in Colombia', (2008) 35 *Latin American Perspectives*, 29–40; UN Security Council, *supra* note 34, 17; P. Alston, *Report of the Special Rapporteur on extrajudicial, summary or arbitrary executions*, UN Doc. A/HRC/14/24, 28–30.

39 Coalition to Stop the Use of Child Soldiers, *supra* note 15, 101–102.

were forced to give information about the groups they had left.[40] Training programmes, such as those of the Air Force, allow for 16-year-old recruits, while 17-year-olds can train with the national army. Students can also join as cadets in military secondary schools.[41]

Children were recruited and used by the opposition FARC and ELN and other armed groups as well. The recruitment of children by FARC and ELN, for instance, extended to the borders of Ecuador and Venezuela.[42] Children were forcibly recruited by FARC or joined for lack of alternatives. They served mostly as soldiers, or laid explosives, transported supplies, carried messages or worked as guides. Girls generally were subjected to sexual abuse, rape and enforced abortions.[43] Children were often taken from vulnerable groups such as the Afro-Colombians and the indigenous population; they are still exposed to recruitment today.[44]

Children were 'compulsorily and voluntarily' recruited into, and used by, the two main armed opposition groups, the Revolutionary Armed Forces of Colombia – FARC (*Fuerzas Armadas Revolucionarias de Colombia)* and the National Liberation Army – ELN (*Ejército de Liberación Nacional*), and by pro-government paramilitary groups – the United Self-Defence Forces of Colombia – AUC (*Autodefensas Unidas de Colombia*). Children were used as soldiers, especially for laying mines and explosives as well as other military functions. In the case of girls, many were subjected to sexual abuse, including rape and forced abortion. Some children stayed on with these paramilitary groups after they had failed to demobilise completely.[45]

After the rise of these major guerrilla movements in the 1960s and 1970s, a growing number of girl soldiers and female cadres joined or were forced to join a growing number of guerrilla, narco-terrorist and paramilitary groups. Of the approximately 14,000 child soldiers recruited by these paramilitary and armed

40 Committee on the Rights of the Child, *Concluding Observations: Colombia (2006)*, UN Doc. CRC/C/COL/CO/3.

41 See Colegio Militar Simón Bolívar, www.colegiomilitarsimonbolivar.com/; Colegio Militar José María Córdoba, www.colmiljosemariacordoba.edu.co.

42 Coalition to Stop the Use of Child Soldiers, *supra* note 15, 101–102; Amnesty International, *supra* note 29, 6.

43 UN High Commissioner for Human Rights, *Report on the situation of human rights in Colombia*, UN Doc. E/CN.4/2005/10; Special Rapporteur on the Rights of Women of the Inter-American Commission on Human Rights, *Violence and Discrimination against Women in the armed conflict in Colombia*, Doc. OEA/Ser.L/V/II, Doc. 67 of 18 October 2006; Defensoría del Pueblo and UNICEF, *La niñez y sus derechos, Caracterización de las niñas, niños, adolescentes desvinculados de los grupos armados ilegales*, November 2006.

44 Amnesty International, *supra* note 35; UN Security Council, *supra* note 34, 4 and 5; Amnesty International, *supra* note 29, 2; Human Rights Watch, *supra* note 30.

45 Coalition to Stop the Use of Child Soldiers, *supra* note 15, 99.

opposition groups, the numbers of women and girl recruits were quite high. In the ranks of FARC and ELN, for example, women and girls represented up to 50 per cent of all forces. In 2001, a United Nations official openly condemned the use, rape and sexual abuse by commanders of more than 2,500 girl soldiers, who were primarily members of FARC. Although these paramilitaries have a propensity to have fewer women and girls in their ranks, girl soldiers attached to armed groups on all sides of the civil war were treated cruelly. Most women and girls were also often forced to use contraceptives and to undergo abortions.[46]

In 1998, ELN promised to stop child recruitment by signing the *Puerta del Cielo* agreement in Germany. Today, though, the UN High Commissioner for Human Rights still receives reports of child recruitment. Presently, for example, ELN continues to carry out child recruitment campaigns in schools in and around Cauca.[47]

Some children were still thought to be with AUC and other partially demobilised paramilitary groups, such as the peasant self-defence forces *Casanare* and the *Cacique Pipinta Front*. The Office of the Ombudsman in 2006 reported that more than 200 children in AUC's ranks had not yet been demobilised.[48] There are confirmed reports that corroborate that illegal armed groups, such as the *Autodefensas Campesinas Nueva Generación*, *Aguilas Negras* and the *Ejército Revolucionario Popular Antiterrorista de Colombia*, are recruiting children. There is also evidence that former AUC colleagues have contacted many children offering them money or forcing them into joining other illegal armed groups.[49]

3.1.2. Disarmament, Demobilisation and Reintegration (DDR)

Rules and practices governing demobilisation are not very clear. The legal position (Law 782 of 2002), for example, states that children surrendering to the armed forces should be placed in the care of the ICBF within 36 hours. Decree 128 states that only those who leave an armed opposition or paramilitary group voluntarily are allowed to benefit from the government-run DDR programme. Nevertheless, since child soldiers were required to identify themselves as members of an armed group under Law 782, those who escaped or were discharged, including those who were afraid to reveal their identity, were unable to receive assistance. In practice though, the majority of FARC and ELN child

46 Morales, *supra* note 3, 4; Amnesty International, *supra* note 29, 2.

47 Coalition to Stop the Use of Child Soldiers, *supra* note 15, 102; UN Security Council, *supra* note 34, 5; Amnesty International, *supra* note 35; Human Rights Watch, *supra* note 30.

48 Coalition to Stop the Use of Child Soldiers, *supra* note 15, 102–103.

49 Amnesty International, *supra* note 35, 5–6; UN Security Council, *supra* note 34, 5; Human Rights Watch, *supra* note 30; Human Rights Watch, *supra* note 34.

soldiers entering the DDR programme had already surrendered to the security forces or had been handed over to the ICBF. Some 3,300 former child soldiers, mostly from FARC, took part in the government's DDR programme from its inception in 1999 to 2007.[50]

In 2005, the Justice and Peace Law (JPL), Law 975, was passed. This was done within the framework of a transitional justice process, which helped to regulate the procedures for demobilising members of illegal armed groups. Within the framework of the JPL over 2,000 child victims have been identified, including 11 homicides, 20 enforced disappearances, 2 cases of sexual violence, 7 kidnappings, and 1,320 displacements. Out of the 3,284 former members of AUC who currently participate in the depositions provided for by the Law, a number have confessed to the recruitment and use of over 650 children within their ranks. The Attorney-General's Office is currently verifying 366 additional cases. However, fewer than 400 children were handed over in the collective demobilisation of AUC.[51]

Under the Justice and Peace Law (2005), the release and handover of children was a prerequisite for accessing benefits. According to the UN Colombian High Commissioner for Peace, over 390 children were handed over in the process of collective demobilisation of AUC. A total of 32,000 adults were released from AUC and some estimates by child protection agencies suggest that approximately 20 per cent of the total number of AUC combatants were under the age of 18. There is also some useful information about the number of children who were not handed over by their commanders, or who did not go through a formal process of demobilisation.[52]

As the handing over of children was an absolute requirement for accessing benefits from the JPL, it is paramount that these national authorities investigate whether the former commanders of the AUC have fulfilled this requirement. The JPL was broadly condemned for failing to comply with international law. This raised doubts as to whether many AUC members would be held accountable for these abuses and other related criminal acts.[53] The law allowed paramilitaries the opportunity not to supply information on offences they had committed, or to turn over illegally obtained possessions or release information about the criminal actions of the group during that period.[54] Despite positive advances,

50 Coalition to Stop the Use of Child Soldiers, *supra* note 15, 102.

51 UN Security Council, *supra* note 34, 12.

52 Ibid., 13–14.

53 Amnesty International *Colombia, Justice and Peace Law Will Guarantee Impunity for Human Rights Abusers*, 26 April 2005.

54 Constitutional Court of Colombia, 18 May 2006, C-370/2006; Human Rights Watch, *Smoke and mirrors: Colombia's demobilization of paramilitary groups*, August 2005.

impunity for grave violations against children, as well as obtaining secure information on convictions and proceedings, remain major challenges in Colombia today.[55]

The DDR programme has been run by the ICBF, which has been operating in partnership with a number of international and national organisations that offered direct services, care and support. At the beginning, some returning children received medical attention and selected forms of counselling at a 'transition home'. Afterwards, they were moved to specialised institutional care centres, for those up to the age of 18, for a period of 9–12 months in preparation for 'reintegration'. The programme initially predicted that children would be reunited with their families or placed in a foster home. In reality, security concerns and the risk of re-recruitment made it impossible for many child soldiers to go back to their families in areas affected by the armed conflict. Foster care, on the other hand, presented an even more telling challenge, with many families fearful of being targeted by the armed groups. The stigmatisation of child soldiers, who are commonly perceived as violent and threatening, meant too that families were hesitant about receiving former child soldiers. While efforts continued to reinforce fostering and family-based care, approximately 60 per cent of those entering the DDR programme were in institutional care by 2007.[56]

Child soldiers from FARC and ELN experienced particular difficulties. They were separated from family, friends and community support systems, and faced the extra challenge of being stigmatised by the urban population. Child soldiers released from AUC suffered greatly from psychological and behavioural troubles, especially drug addiction.[57]

The UN Committee on the Rights of the Child in June 2010 pointed out that the programme run by the ICBF had helped over 4,200 children over the past decade, but that many children had not received comprehensive reparations and adequate assistance for their physical and psychological recovery. It specially recommended that gender perspectives should be taken into account in reparation measures and it gave particular concern to the recruitment and use of Afro-Colombian and indigenous children.[58]

55 UN Security Council, *supra* note 34, 12.

56 Coalition to Stop the Use of Child Soldiers, *supra* note 15, 102; UN Security Council, *supra* note 34, 15–17.

57 Coalition to Stop the Use of Child Soldiers, *supra* note 15, 102–103; Human Rights Watch, *supra* note 34.

58 Committee on the Rights of the Child, *Concluding Observations: Colombia (2010)*, UN Doc. CRC/C/OPAC/COL/CO/1, 6–9.

The Child Soldiers report also gives details, from early 2006, of the rearming of demobilised paramilitary units; the persistence of groups not involved in the AUC demobilisation and the integration of some former paramilitary units within several criminal organisations, which are often implicated in drug trafficking. Evidence has also emerged of new armed groups and criminal organisations establishing business relations, especially over drugs, with elements of FARC and ELN. Some of these groups have reportedly functioned along similar lines to AUC, including participation in counter-insurgency operations and attempting to control territory.[59]

3.1.3. Integrated Reparation for Children

In recent years, the Colombian State has taken positive steps towards the provision of reparation for victims. The implementation of these measures is especially challenging, as it is taking place against a background of continuing violence. The JPL, for instance, established a number of provisions, including the setting up of the National Commission for Reparation and Reconciliation with an 8-year mandate. Although the Commission has a designated department for gender and population, the focus on children needs strengthening.[60]

3.2. EL SALVADOR

The Republic of El Salvador has been torn by civil war. The war had been long and difficult, with enormous costs in both human and material terms. Around 80,000 people were killed and many more wounded. On a political level, the conflict had an intensely disruptive effect on Salvadoran society, and the country has remained one of the most politically polarised in the region during the post-war period.[61] With the end of that war came a genuine hope for change in the country. One of the most remarkable and negative characteristics of the period following the signing of the peace accords in 1992 in El Salvador, however, was the increasingly high levels of violence.

A common-sense vision of 'peace' is usually projected as the opposition to war; even so, the continuation of violence and increasing crime have weakened both the experience and the reality of peace and have called into question its very significance. In 2006, for example, the average number of murders per 100,000

---

59 Coalition to Stop the Use of Child Soldiers, *supra* note 15, 100–101. See also Human Rights Watch, *supra* note 30.

60 UN Security Council, *supra* note 34, 15.

61 M. Hume, 'The Myths of Violence: Gender, Conflict, and Community in El Salvador', (2008) 35 *Latin American Perspectives* 59, 1; I.A. Luciak, 'Gender Equality in the Salvadoran Transition', (1999) 26 *Latin American Perspectives*, 43–67.

citizens was 55.3 in the country as a whole. El Salvador may project 'peace', but the reality is that it is one of the most violent nations in the world, today. This current post-war violence creates a critical 'paradox' in the efforts to achieve peace. Moreover, the dismantling of the wider structures of impunity, from the state to the family, has become an ongoing struggle in the post-war period.[62]

Mo Hume explains the violence in El Salvador and its history in terms of certain groups being marginalised. Groups such as peasants, workers, women and youth are constantly exposed to violence in their everyday lives and are isolated from the mainstream of justice and the law.[63] It is more about a dominant culture than just individually subjective, which conditions normative behaviour, Hume explains further. Thus in her view violence has been accepted as a part of everyday life in Salvadorian society and in familial relations. Her point is to look at the causes of the corrupt and oppressive forces in society that allow violence to be accepted as, in her words, a 'routine element in the history of El Salvador'. The state is therefore in her view the central protagonist, and has left the population in perpetual fear and subjection. This process is made possible, she emphasises, by exclusion.[64]

In the country today, there is a common idea that the emergence of the *maras* and *pandillas* happened at the same time as the country's civil war ended. Even if gangs had already existed before the war, they became more evident in the 1990s. The conviction that gangs came into existence only because of the war or because of the deportation of young people from Los Angeles, or were due to a criminal tendency inherent in youth, ignores several important factors in the cultural structure of violence as well as the long history of violence in the country. Even though it is clear that youth delinquency has increased post-war, it would be erroneous to state that young people were mainly responsible for the increasing levels of violence. Some studies have shown that the growth and influence of North American gangs on Salvadoran *pandillas* have not been a major determinant. More to the point is the fact that the *pandillas* began and grew because of a number of factors, which have more to do with the long history of violence in El Salvador, and the country remains one of the most politically polarized in the region in the post-war period.[65]

---

62 Ibid.; see also J.J. Dalton, 'Ola de asesinatos en El Salvador', *Diario El País*, 16 September 2009.

63 Hume, *supra* note 61, 62.

64 Ibid., 64–68; see also M. Hume, *The Politics of Violence – Gender, Conflict and Community in El Salvador*, Oxford, Wiley-Blackwell, 2009.

65 Carranza, *supra* note 5, 213–214; M. Carranza, *Detention or Death: Where the 'Pandillero' Kids of El Salvador are Heading*, 2001, available at www.coav.org.br. For instance, according to the National Civil Police statistics in 1996, only 12 per cent of the arrests carried out were of minors. Furthermore, according to the Supreme Court, in 1995 only 10 per cent of court cases corresponded to youth offenders.

According to Carranza's research, for example, young people tend to join the *pandillas* at the age of 15, some joining between the ages of 11 and 15 years (51.9 per cent) and others joining between the ages of 16 and 25 (46.1 per cent). Most of the *pandilleros* do not attend school. Figures show that 75 per cent did not attend school in 1996, increasing to 92.3 per cent in 2000. The unemployment rate for youths involved in gangs is also high. In 1996, around 75 per cent of *pandilleros* were not employed, which dropped to 66.6 per cent in 2000. In addition, the economic conditions for employed gang youths are unstable, since 45 per cent of them are only in temporary jobs.[66]

Gang membership is often connected to children who have been abandoned or who live on the street. It is also known that a large number of them live with both their parents. In 1996, they accounted for 25 per cent of all *pandilleros* interviewed, which rose to one-third of the interviewees by 2000. Around 25 per cent of them live with their mothers. In general terms, they live either with one or both parents or with a close family member. Overall, young people who are involved in *maras* and *pandillas* have not had their economic, emotional or safety needs met at home. In the majority of cases, the respondents' birth mothers and fathers were no longer together and many respondents did not live with their families. For those who had a father figure as a reference, many considered his main responsibility to be as the provider of economic support; therefore, a large part of the conflict between the respondents and their fathers involved economic issues.[67]

In 1995, the Legislative Assembly ratified the Juvenile Offender Law (*Ley del Menor Infractor*), which was a special measure addressing children in conflict with the law. Youth Courts were also created. At the same time, a clandestine paramilitary group called Black Shadow (*Sombra Negra*) emerged and was accused of murdering at least 13 *pandilleros* between 1994 and 1996.[68]

Harsh anti-gang laws and law enforcement measures (Anti-gang Laws) have been used against gangs of youths (*maras or pandillas*) in El Salvador. In 2004, the National Council for Public Security started implementing a 'safe country' plan, the so-called 'Super Heavy Hand' (*Mano Super Dura*) policy,[69] under which members of the armed forces patrolled areas with the civilian police. The Anti-gang Law ensured that belonging to a *pandilla* was a crime. The Anti-gang Law sought to harden penalties for *pandilleros*. Accordingly, punitive measures won through over prevention or rehabilitation.[70] Children were blamed for

---

66 Carranza, *supra* note 5, 216, 220.

67 Ibid.

68 Ibid., 214.

69 País Seguro: Plan de Gobierno 2004–2009, available at www.servicios.gob.sv.

70 Carranza, *supra* note 5, 230.

increasing criminal violence, although of the 300,000 suspects detained between 2000 and 2006, fewer than 6 per cent were below 18 years of age. Significantly, human rights organisations have accused the Government of the arbitrary detention of hundreds of young people under the security policy.[71] It is worth noting that some 43 per cent of under-18s were held without proof of illegal association.[72]

Conversely, young Salvadorans have not been integrated into the political system and, more importantly, there has not been progress in the establishment of political and economic openings for the youth of the country. There is a deficiency of funding for youth-related policies and small-scale projects, which seek solutions at the local level, contained in the budgets of both the Ministry of Education and the Department for Employment Creation and of Labour, as well as the Social Security Ministry. The only important changes in government policy so far have taken place in the legal system, with the creation of special Courts for Minors.[73]

The UN Committee on the Rights of the Child has called on El Salvador to abrogate its second Anti-gang Law of April 2004 and apply its Juvenile Offenders Act as the only legal binding instrument in the area of juvenile justice.[74] The authorities considered lowering the age of criminal responsibility to 12 years, with penalties ranging from therapy to custody in a juvenile detention centre.[75] In March 2005, the Inter-American Court of Human Rights asked the government of El Salvador to establish a national commission to determine the whereabouts of children who had disappeared during the 1980–91 armed conflict. It has been noted that many children had been abducted and given to families in other countries for illegal adoption.[76] In September 2005, the Ministry of Foreign Affairs referred the case of the Serrano Cruz sisters for investigation, on which the Court's decision was based.[77] In the same month, the governments of El Salvador and the US signed an agreement to establish an

---

71 Centro por la Justicia y el Derecho Internacional (CEJIL), *Políticas de seguridad salvadoreñas violan derechos humanos de la niñez y adolescencia*, March 2007, www.cejil.org.

72 Coalition to Stop the Use of Child Soldiers, *supra* note 15, 135–136; see also Covey *supra* note 27, 114–118; Comunidad Segura, *Toward a national youth policy in El Salvador*, 24 October 2006, www.comunidadesegura.org.

73 Carranza, *supra* note 5, 217.

74 Committee on the Rights of the Child, *Concluding Observations: El Salvador (2004)*, UN Doc. CRC/C/15/Add.232.

75 Ministry of Interior, *Proyecto de Reformas a la Ley Penal Juvenil*, www.gobernacion.gob.sv.

76 Inter-American Court of Human Rights, *Serrano-Cruz Sisters v. El Salvador*, Judgment of 1 March 2005, Series C, No. 120,.

77 *Written replies by the Government of El Salvador to the Committee on the Rights of the Child on implementation of the Optional Protocol*, UN Doc. CRC/C/OPAC/SLV/Q/1/Add.1, 12 May 2006.

International Law Enforcement Academy (ILEA) to train police officers, prosecutors and judges on drug enforcement and counter-terrorism practices in the region.[78]

3.2.1. Government: National Recruitment Legislation and Practice

The Constitution of El Salvador provides for compulsory military service by all nationals aged between 18 and 30 years old, in compliance with Article 215. The Armed Forces (Military and Reserves Service) Act allows Salvadorans over 16 years of age to voluntarily submit an application to perform military service.[79] This needs parental consent, but the General Staff of the Armed Forces has asked the Department 'to refrain from accepting minors among newly recruited personnel'.[80] The Committee on the Rights of the Child recommended that El Salvador explicitly prohibit, by law, the voluntary recruitment of 16- and 17-year-olds, to reflect current practice, and the recruitment of minors into armed forces. It also recommended the prohibition of direct participation by under-18s in hostilities. The government informed the Committee that legal reforms were under way to increase the minimum age of voluntary recruitment from 16 to 18 years of age.[81] The candidates for the *Capitán General Gerardo Barrios Military School* have to be aged 17–22 and must have completed a secondary education.[82] In 2005, there were four 17-year-olds attending the school: three males and one female.

3.2.2. Disarmament, Demobilisation and Reintegration (DDR)

An estimated 2,000 children served in the FMLN, while 80 per cent of all the recruits in the government armed forces had been under 18 during the armed conflict.[83] The government of El Salvador reported in 2002 that former members of the Farabundo Martí National Liberation Front (*Frente Farabundo Martí para la Liberación Nacional* – FMLN) who were 15 and 16 in January 1992 and who had not benefited from a land programme agreed between the government and

78 Gobierno de El Salvador, *El Salvador quinto país del mundo en contar con ILEA*, 21 September 2005, www.gobernacion.gob.sv.

79 *Initial Report of El Salvador to the Committee on the Rights of the Child on implementation of the Optional Protocol*, UN Doc. CRC/C/OPAC/SLV/1, 15 August 2005.

80 Ibid.

81 Committee on the Rights of the Child, *Concluding Observations: El Salvador (2006)*, UN Doc. CRC/C/OPAC/SLV/CO/1.

82 Escuela Militar, www.escmilitar.edu.sv.

83 Coalition to Stop the Use of Child Soldiers, *El Salvador: Children in the Farabundo Martí National Liberation Front (FMLN) and the Armed Forces of El Salvador (FAES)*, July 2006, available at www.child-soldiers.org.

the FMLN, had received educational and technical training.[84] According to the official statistics, 152 children had opted to return to school, while 97 had chosen technical training. Of these, only nine had successfully been incorporated into the educational system and just one had completed a course of studies. The Committee on the Rights of the Child though criticised the lack of measures as well as the programmes put into action for former child soldiers and children affected by the conflicts.[85]

4. GENDER PERSPECTIVE ON CHILDREN'S RIGHTS

4.1. THEORETICAL BACKGROUND AND FEMINIST METHODOLOGY

The theoretical perspectives in this chapter adopt the feminist concept of intersectionality (Yuval Davis) and Ramazanoglu's and Holland's concept of gender.

Intersectionality explores, as a theory and a methodological approach, the intersection of class, race, ethnicity, sexuality and gender in scientific discourse, practice and process. It is, importantly, defined in terms of the relation of ideas to social structures and hierarchies in gender and economic class, as well as sexuality and ethnicity/race. The search for the 'universal' predicament of women may homogenise women's experiences and obscure the position of those who suffer from multiple forms of discrimination, particularly in relation to race/ethnicity, class, age and sexual orientation.[86]

Yuval-Davis, for instance, presents the concept of intersectionality in two ways: one way is to look at it from the point of view of the intersections in people's lives in terms of the different positions they hold in relation to gender, sexuality, race, class, religion, nation/state, age and other social categories. The second way of looking at intersections is not so much a question of finding out what inequalities exist and for whom, but to understand the processes involved. She argues that it

---

[84] *Written replies by the Government of El Salvador to the Committee on the Rights of the Child on implementation of the Optional Protocol*, UN Doc. CRC/C/OPAC/SLV/Q/1/Add.1, 12 May 2006.

[85] Committee on the Rights of the Child, *supra* note 81.

[86] N. Yuval Davis, 'Intersectionality and Feminist Politics', (2006) 13 3 *European Journal of Women's Studies*, 193–209; E. Grabham, D. Cooper, J. Krishnadas and D. Herman (eds.) *Intersectionality and Beyond – Law, power and the politics of location*, Routledge, Cavendish, 2009; M.L. Bartolomei, 'Género, Ciudadanía y Derechos Humanos – algunas reflexiones feministas sobre la ciudadanía y el Estado Nación en América Latina', to be published by Iberoamericana in June 2011.

is important not to focus on the intersections in terms of constructing people as belonging to fixed and permanent groups, but rather to focus on social processes, practices and outcomes as they impact on social categories, social structures and individuals. This approach provides a methodological tool that challenges hegemonic approaches to the study of stratification as well as reified forms of identity politics. Intersectional analysis of social divisions has come to occupy central spaces in both sociological and other analyses of stratification, as well as in feminist and other legal, political and policy discourse on international human rights. The investigation of the specific social, political and economic processes involved in each historical instance is, at this juncture, very important.[87]

In the same mode, for others:

> … intersectionality can be used to investigate how inequalities are *produced* on the institutional scale, through structures, processes and techniques of governance. Within these frames, inequality is imagined at the level of the home, the workplace, the state, or the international "community": complex inequalities are constituted through the operation of global capital, through international relations, monetary policies, domestic social policies, the employment relationship or the family. Deployments of intersectionality help to trace the complex material effects of these processes, and, in some respects, parallel earlier models such as dual systems theory, which focused on the relationship between patriarchy and class oppression.[88]

The intersections of multiple layers of marginalisation and the interrelationship between race, ethnicity and gender, in particular, need to be examined to expose the complex system of dependence and independence between them. Concepts of gender are connected to hierarchies of race and class.[89]

Some UN bodies, such as the Committee on the Elimination of Racial Discrimination, have already identified and recognized the importance of intersectional analysis and methodology. At the institutional level, intersectionality has, to some extent, become enmeshed with the principle of mainstreaming, involving gender and human rights, within the institutions of the United Nations.[90] However, some questions do arise: can intersectional analysis, for example, illuminate the gendered, racialised and sexualised character of social structures; and how do state agencies, including the courts, constitute, understand and deploy the intersecting character of the relations of inequality?

---

87 Yuval Davis, *supra* note 86.

88 Grabham, *supra* note 86, 3.

89 Charlesworth and Chinkin, *supra* note 17, 18–19.

90 D. Buss and A. Manji (eds.), *International Law – Modern Feminist Approaches*, Oregon, Oxford and Portland, 2005.

In feminist theory and methodology, there has also been a sizeable debate about the nature and interrelationships of sex, reproduction, identity, gender and power. In this respect, some authors argue that sexuality, reproduction, subjectivity and gender are interrelated and socially or politically constituted. The term 'gender' covers how specific people experience sexuality and reproduction, masculinity and femininity and the boundaries and interstices between them. This also includes cultural categories for conceptualising what is lived and what is thought.[91] Ramazanoglu and Holland point out that 'feminist knowledge of gender should include practical social investigation of gendered lives, experiences, relationships and inequalities'.[92] As such, feminist methodology is distinctive to the extent that it is shaped by feminist theory, politics and ethics and grounded in women's and girls' experience.[93]

4.2. FEMINIST PERSPECTIVES ON CHILD LAW – THE DILEMMA OF THE 'GIRL CHILD'

Feminists have provided a critique of the understanding of law as a neutral, universally applicable set of rules. Their analysis also rests on a commitment to challenge male domination over women. A feminist constructivist approach sees gender and sexual differences as socially constructed. This approach seeks to expose the way in which discourses construct subjects differently, so as to create a space for alternative understandings to emerge. 'Gender' draws attention to aspects of social relations which are culturally conditional and without foundation in biological necessity.[94] At the same time, some feminists believe that there are similarities between the social conditions of women and children. What this means is that feminism can provide insights into the position of children in society, including in law. These incorporate being denied equal rights or lacking capacity, as well as having decisions made on their behalf or being treated as a social problem.[95]

The constructionist approach also reveals that in relation to different legal issues different legal subjects are constructed. In the first place, the 'woman of legal discourse' is created, and stands in opposition to the male norm. Secondly, the law shapes different types of women, depending upon the issue and those who are measured against the 'ideal woman'. The ideal women and the types of

91 C. Ramazanoglu and J. Holland, *Feminist Methodology – Challenges and Choices*, SAGE, London, 2006, 4–5.

92 Ibid., 5.

93 Bartolomei, *supra* note 86.

94 J. Bridgeman and D. Monk (eds.), *Feminist Perspective on Child Law*, Cavendish publishing, London, 2000, 7–9; Charlesworth and Chinkin, *supra* note 17, 1–3.

95 Bridgeman and Monk, *supra* note 94, 14.

women that are constructed by legal discourse, however, bear little relation to the real lives of women.[96] Feminist perspectives, therefore, have also been concerned with the way the law constitutes identities, such as 'masculinity' and 'femininity', and how gender is constructed and reconstructed in discourse.[97]

In this respect, different authors believe that attitudes towards children, expectations of them and understandings of their capacities are not unitary, permanent and stagnant. Rather, they are contingent, exchangeable and contested and the understanding of and meanings given to childhood are culturally and historically specific, which is to say that childhood is also socially constructed. The way in which discourses construct childhood has had an influence upon the lives of children, as they and adults change their manner and their attitude in response. This does not mean that there is a universal understanding for children. Children actively shape their own lives and have different experiences, which may depend upon, for example, their sex, race/ethnicity, class, religion or nation. A social constructionist analysis of childhood should not lose sight of the reality of children's embodied lives, identities and subjective nature.[98]

Even as the production through discourse and law and of different sex and gendered subjects has been at the centre of much feminist analysis of the law, the gender or sex of the child subject has not received the same study. In many children's and family law textbooks, which adopt a broad socio-legal approach, rarely, if at all, is there any mention of 'boys' or 'girls'; rather, the gender-neutral construction of the child remains unchallenged. In relation to many issues, the sex and gender of the child would appear to be irrelevant in the understanding of the law. The myth of the gender-neutral child makes the law blind to the specific identities of the individual boy or girl child.[99] Consequently, feminist perspectives may show the treatment of children within the law as gender-neutral, thus masking the extent to which the identity and experiences of male and female children are different.[100] Feminist analysis must explore the unspoken commitments of apparently neutral principles of international law and human rights and the ways that male perspectives are institutionalised in it.[101]

Alongside the rights of the 'girl child' must be a specific recognition of the inequality that shapes the meaning and experience of childhood. Relying on an

96 Ibid., 16.
97 Charlesworth and Chinkin, *supra* note 17, 44–45.
98 Bridgeman and Monk, *supra* note 94, 3.
99 Ibid., 16–17.
100 Ibid., 7–10.
101 Charlesworth and Chinkin, *supra* note 17, 48–52.

unspecified 'childhood' as a category for rights protection is problematic precisely because the false universality of 'childhood' masks the 'particularity' of childhood. One of the central challenges for international human rights is to find a way to balance the universality of rights guarantees with the particularity of inequality.[102] Feminist excursions into international law and human rights would also attempt to transcend gendered public/private dichotomies, incorporating and responding to women's and girls' needs and their concerns. Feminist analysis, as such, should explore the unspoken commitments of apparently neutral principles of international law and in doing so, look at the ways that the male perspective is institutionalised in it.[103]

4.3. MAINSTREAMING GENDER IN CHILDHOOD

The United Nations have responded to criticism of its marginalisation of women by bringing about policies on what is called 'gender mainstreaming'. This process links the concerns of gender into the activities that are funded or undertaken by an organisation. This, in turn, helps spread the responsibility for gender issues throughout the organisation, as well as implementing suitable guidelines and training for staff, so that they become an aspect of the everyday work of all staff.[104]

The origins of mainstreaming can be traced to the international development community in the years following the 1985 Third World Conference on Women in Nairobi. Mainstreaming was adopted in Beijing, a decade later. The Beijing Declaration and Platform for Action (the Beijing Platform), embraced at the Fourth World Conference on Women (Beijing, 1995), established gender mainstreaming as 'the global strategy for promoting gender equality'.[105]

At the UN, a broad-based and system-wide gender mainstreaming mandate was created through the adoption of Agreed Conclusions 1997/2 by the Economic and Social Council (ECOSOC).[106] The definition of gender mainstreaming has been outlined by ECOSOC. In its definition the emphasis is on ensuring that both women and men have gender equality in all areas and at all levels at the polity and in society at large.[107] The emphasis since then has been on the notion

102 D. Buss, 'How the UN stole childhood: The Christian Rights and the International Rights of the Child', in Bridgeman and Monk, *supra* note 94, 287–294.

103 Charlesworth and Chinkin, *supra* note 17, 56–59.

104 Ibid., 195–196.

105 S. Kouvo, 'The United Nations and Gender Mainstreaming: Limits and Possibilities', in Buss and Manji, *supra* note 90, 237.

106 See ECOSOC, *Agreed Conclusions 1997/2*, UN doc. A/52/3.

107 ECOSOC defined gender mainstreaming as 'the process of assessing the implications for women and men of any planned action, including legislation, policies or programmes, in all

that equality between the sexes should no longer be addressed as a separate 'women's issue', but in future should be part of all UN activities.[108] This has been the case as today nearly all important international organisations, including the World Bank, the United Nations Development Programme, the Organisation for Security and Cooperation in Europe, and others such as UNESCO, the Food and Agriculture Organisation (FAO), the World Health Organisation (WHO) and the International Labour Organisation (ILO) have adopted this policy.[109]

In addition to ECOSOC, the UN Office of the High Commissioner for Human Rights' (OHCHR) Gender Mainstreaming Strategy has provided a framework for progressing the integration of gender perspectives.[110] The objective is to show that the human rights of women, which often go unnoticed, should be better protected and promoted by the range of activities carried out by OHCHR. The focus of the Strategy, however, is not based on the need to identify new areas of activity which are designed to promote women's human rights, but to ensure that existing activity addresses them in an appropriate manner. The main strategies put forward are the implementation and evaluation of human rights in policy and initiating priorities and objectives. This involves training and awareness programmes for staff, consultants and human rights bodies, while procedures and protocols are put in place based on gender.

The OHCHR puts forward mechanisms to ensure that national governments help towards guaranteeing women's rights. They include treaty bodies and special mechanisms, through the Commission on Human Rights and the Sub-Commission on the Promotion and Protection of Human Rights. The OHCHR, as it puts it, has the objective of building a common understanding of the fundamental link between gender issues and the human rights of women and girl children. It is furthermore committed to achieving internal gender parity at the workplace.

Some authors believe that the formal agreements and statements on gender mainstreaming, with their detailed provisions and institution-wide design, stand in sharp contrast to the difficult reality of actually mainstreaming gender. Some questions are raised here: how is it possible to translate the complex ideas

areas and at all levels. It is a strategy for ensuring that the concerns and experiences of women, and men, are an integral part of the design, implementation, monitoring and evaluation of policies and programmes in all political, economic and societal spheres. This also ensures that women and men benefit equally and that inequality is not perpetuated. From the outset, the ultimate goal has been to achieve gender equality' (ibid., §4).

108 Kouvo, *supra* note 105, 238.

109 E. Hafner-Burton and M.A. Pollack, *Mainstreaming Gender in Global Governance*, EUI Working Paper RSC No. 2001/46; Yuval Davis, *supra* note 86; Buss and Manji, *supra* note 90; Charlesworth and Chinkin, *supra* note 17, 246–247.

110 ECOSOC, *supra* note 106, §4.

summarised in the term 'gender' into a policy applied across a large bureaucratic institution by various actors, with different, and possibility conflicting, understandings of what 'gender' means? Is it possible to mainstream gender without losing an understanding of gender as a complex social ordering process, not simple reducible to 'male' or 'female'? Gender is not an easily transmissible technical concept and can also be very threatening to those already holding power.[111]

According to some feminist authors, although the vocabulary of 'gender' has been adopted in international criminal law, there are few signs that its significance is appreciated. In the International Criminal Court (ICC) Statute (1998), therefore, 'gender' is defined as simply 'the two sexes, male and female, within the context of society'.[112] The authors explain that this definition was the result of lobbying by the Holy See and the Catholic and Islamic states to ensure that the term 'gender' could not be read as including homosexuality, and presents gender as primarily an issue of biology rather than one of social construction and thus has limited transformative boundaries in international law and human rights.[113]

5. INTEGRATED STRATEGIC APPROACHES FOR CHILDREN AND YOUTH

5.1. GENDER-BASED VIOLENCE AND GIRL CHILDREN

A number of feminists concur that violence against women is neither accidental nor circumstantial. To a certain extent, it is a structural problem, directly connected to the various expressions of unevenness in power between women and men in society, which can be found all around the globe. Violence both results from, and reinforces, the powerlessness of women within society at the local, national and regional level.[114]

How then is this defined? According to Radhika Coomaraswamy, the Special Representative of the UN Secretary-General for Children and Armed Conflict, there are four major reasons for gender-based violence:

> First, men's views of female sexuality and its role in the social hierarchy make women susceptible to sex-related crimes. Women in particular positions of powerlessness,

[111] Buss and Manji, *supra* note 90, 9–10; Charlesworth and Chinkin, *supra* note 17, 196.
[112] Rome Statute for the ICC, article 7(3).
[113] Charlesworth and Chinkin, *supra* note 17, 335.
[114] Ibid., 14–15.

> such as refugees, migrant workers and girl children, are especially vulnerable to sexual violence. Second, a woman's familial relationship to a man or to a group of men makes her vulnerable to types of violence that are 'animated by society's concept of a woman as the property and dependent of a male protector'. Third, violence against women may be directed towards the social group of which she is a member. For example 'to rape a woman is to humiliate her community'. This type of violence is well-illustrated in the conflicts in the former Yugoslavia and Rwanda in the 1990s. Finally, there is a strong connection between militarisation and violence against women. The more general acceptance of armed conflict to resolve international disputes also gives a legitimacy to violent responses to domestic disputes, accentuating violence against women.[115]

From another perspective, the Women Commission for Refugee Women and Children's Report in 2006, *Displaced Women and Girls at Risk*, defined gender-based violence in the following way:

> Gender-based violence – harm perpetuated against a person because of gender-based power inequities – Is aimed primarily at women and girls. In refugee settings, this violence can take the form of intimidation, physical harm, sexual abuse including rape, and unequal access to humanitarian assistance. Although no systematic data exist about the magnitude of the problem, reports by numerous international organisations over the past two decades demonstrate that sexual abuse of refugee women and girls is pervasive and present in almost all refugee settings...[116]

As societal structures collapse during conflict and during the lengthy reconstruction phase, gender-based violence often reaches an epidemic level. This is, in the main, due to the erosion of the protection of traditional structures and the breakdown of legal and judicial systems at the local and national level.[117]

The cases presented above show how in internal and external warfare, gender-based violence, or violence that specifically targets women and girls, is employed by irregular and even by regular armies systematically and intentionally, as an effective instrument of terror. It is also psychological warfare against

115 R. Comaraswamy, 'Of Kaly born: women, violence and the law in Sri Lanka', in M. Schuler (ed.), *Freedom from Violence: Women's Strategies From around the World*, UNIFEM, New York, 1992, 49–50. See also R. Comaraswamy, *Preliminary Report submitted by the Special Rapporteur on Violence against Women, its Causes and Consequences*, UN Doc. E/CN.4/1995/42.

116 Women's Commission for Refugee Women and Children, *Displaced Women and Girls At Risk: Risk Factors, Protection Solutions and Resource Tools*, New York, February 2006, 9, available at www.womenscommission.org.

117 Ibid., 8; see also UNIFEM, *UNIFEM and Transitional Justice: The Peruvian and Colombian Cases*, Bogotá, 2007, at www.unifem.org/attachments/gender_issues/women_war_peace/UNIFEMAndTransitionalJustice_ThePeruvianAndColombianCases.pdf.

communities, which involves ethnic cleansing. In this respect, as Meertens and Stoller describe about Colombia:

> In all practice of war, gender, as a principal structure of social and culture dynamics (Scott, 1987), has always been present. Men continue to be the principal actors of war, and they therefore bear the brunt of its direct consequences... Women, however, not only participate increasingly as actor in armed actions but also are a specific military object, although in historically variable fashion.
>
> ...
>
> During La Violencia, the massacre of peasant families of the other side was a common practice. In these killings, torture, rape, and mutilation of pregnant women fulfilled the symbolic role of "destroying the seed" of the hated enemy... Women were the specific object of violence in their conditions as mothers, as actual or potential procreators of the enemy, and as bearers of the identity and honor of the enemy community... Frequently these killings are perpetrated anonymously, since it is inconvenient to admit the murder of women and children... Sexual violation also continues to be a practice of war, although largely undocumented.[118]

Indeed the International Rescue Committee and United Nations human rights mechanims report the use of rape, sexual slavery, forced prostitution and 'marriage', and general violence and mutilation as typical weapons employed against female child soldiers worldwide. Clearly these tactics escalate to major human rights abuses and war crimes in some situations, but they also threaten the public health and safety of the populations where they occur. Other consequences of these actions have seen a high maternal and infant mortality rate, including subsequent suicides by young mothers and the abandonment of unwanted children.[119]

Gender-based violence is directed against girls and women from all cultures and socio-economic classes in male-dominated societies, although in saying that, it is the poor and dispossessed who are more readily targeted. Women and girls are targeted because they are the most vulnerable and powerless generally. This is especially the case in conflict-ridden peripheral and semi-peripheral countries. In life and death situations, female child soldiers are forced to barter their sexual services as a way of avoiding greater abuse and mutilation, or simply to remain alive for another day or week. Gender, age, and ethnic and class differences,

---

118 D. Meertens and R. Stoller, 'Facing Destruction, Rebuilding Life: Gender and the Internally Displaced in Colombia', (2001) 28 *Latin American Perspectives*, 132, at 133–34; see also Inter-American Commission on Human Rights, *Violence and discrimination against women in the armed conflict in Colombia*, 2006, Doc. OEA/Ser.L/V/II.Doc.67, available at www.cidh.org/countryrep/ColombiaMujeres06eng/TOC.htm.

119 Morales, *supra* note 3, 5; UN Security Council, *supra* note 34, 8–14; UNIFEM, *supra* note 117.

among others, provide sources for construction and deconstruction as well as the meaning of the 'other'.[120]

The Special Representative of the UN Secretary-General for Children and Armed Conflict on in her Recommendation 8 (110) on ending gender-based violence, gives priority to protecting children from gender-based violence. The report asks governments to legislate for the needs of child survivors and that adequate resources are placed into community-awareness campaigns, including education programmes. The weight accorded to a strategy to prevent sexual exploitation and abuse that focuses on women and girls, the report clearly outlines, must be given by what it calls 'stakeholders'. Member States are therefore asked to ensure that 'rigorous systems are in place to promptly investigate and address allegations of abuse'. This involves training and effective sanctions and support for victims.[121]

5.2. NON-GOVERNMENTAL ORGANISATIONS – THE SAVE THE CHILDREN FUND

The 2005 Report by the Save the Children Fund, *Forgotten Casualties of War: Girls in Armed Conflict*, emphasised not only the terrible abuse of girls, but also the special difficulties in correcting the consequences of human rights violations and reintegrating them into their communities. Programmes of disarmament, demobilisation and reintegration (DDR) have had less success with girl child soldiers, because females are regularly met with censure and rejection.[122]

Women and girls are caught up in a no-man's land, where they are 'trapped between recrimination from the armed group if they leave and from the community if they return home'. On the one hand, according to the report, large numbers are 'too scared to stay and too scared to leave', while on the other hand, families and communities reject them as 'unclean', 'immoral', or even as 'whores'. Many girls returning with babies found even greater resentment and isolation in their communities. Without the protection of the community or international intervention, they became a greater risk for re-recruitment by armed groups.[123]

---

120 Osorio Pérez, *supra* note 38, 34; Morales, *supra* note 3, 5; Inter-American Commission on Human Rights, *supra* note 118; UNIFEM, *Justicia Transicional desde abajo y con perspectiva de Género*, Bogotá, IFEM/Canada, 2009, www.unifemandina.org/images/stories/Documentos/Paz_y_seguridad/jt_desde_abajo%20pdf.pdf.

121 R. Coomaraswamy, *Report of the Special Representative of the Secretary-General for Children and Armed Conflict*, UN Doc. A/62/228, 13 August 2007, 35.

122 Hobson, *supra* note 1.

123 Ibid., vi, 12 and 15–16; see also Morales, *supra* note 3, 5; Keairns, *supra* note 8.

The report also highlighted the chronic under-funding of DDR programmes. As funds became scarce and dried up, only girls who could prove that they knew how to fire a gun were assisted with a meagre package, which was usually some food, water, plastic sheeting for shelter or, on occasions, a small, one-time payment and perhaps a ride home. Reintegration into society is therefore far more difficult for girls than for boys.[124]

The same report also criticised international efforts on behalf of girl soldiers. The findings emphasised a fundamental problem of gender discrimination. Girls, the report showed, 'face discrimination on a daily basis – from their fellow soldiers, commanders, fellow citizens, governments – and perhaps most shocking of all, from the international community'.[125]

In its conclusion, the report recommends that a minimum of 40 per cent of funding be used for the DDR and that girls in particular require and should receive special assistance outside the formal DDR process. It also suggests that community development is essential to the DDR programme and that 'all states should ratify, enforce, monitor and report on international treaties to protect children', especially the CRC and OPAC.[126]

In the report, girls identified a number of ways that the international community could help them, such as mediation work with the community and family, assistance in establishing and maintaining livelihoods, access to school and skills training, networks which provide emotional support, and medical tests and assistance – especially related to reproductive health and sexually transmitted diseases (STDs). It is worth noting that none of these services are currently provided for girls as part of the current reintegration process.[127]

5.3. DOWDNEY AND CHILDREN IN ORGANISED ARMED VIOLENCE

Among the measures suggested by Dowdney's study, particularly in the case of Brazil, Colombia, El Salvador and Ecuador, are community empowerment; gun control; socially and economically inclusive policies focused on impoverished urban areas; and fast-track education in vulnerable areas.

124 Hobson, *supra* note 1, 7–12; see also Morales, *supra* note 3, 5–6.
125 Hobson, *supra* note 1, 1–2.
126 Ibid.
127 Ibid., 2; see also Keairns, *supra* note 8.

It is also necessary to ensure that the security and judicial systems work, including the application of international child protection standards. The life stories of those who joined armed groups is marked by an overlapping of human rights violations, as many of them had no access to education, proper nutrition, housing, health care, personal safety, family protection or jobs.[128]

In regards to a gender perspective, he suggests that future research should address the following key questions about girls and young women in organised armed violence:

- Are girls who do join organised armed groups doing so for the same reasons as boys? If they are not, what then are their primary motives?
- What are the specific demobilisation, reintegration or rehabilitation needs of girls and young women in the types of organised armed groups being investigated in each case?
- To what extent do the actions of support or the endorsement of violent masculinity by mothers, sisters and girlfriends have on men joining these armed groups?
- Finally, how does sexual violence, i.e. the perpetration of it and the escape from it, influence the behaviour and involvement of girls, boys, men and women in these armed groups?[129]

6. CONCLUSION

This chapter has examined several questions which need further research, especially from a gender, class, ethnic and race perspective. The questions asked were predominantly about gender and organised armed groups. Why, for instance, do girls join the armed forces and become members of armed opposition groups and what roles do they play as members of these groups? And how are these roles affected by war and conflict? On a more general level, are there significant differences between recruitment into armed conflict and into juvenile gangs and who is actually involved in organised armed violence?

In the final analysis, the situation for girl soldiers is both extensive and complex, and is certainly long term. It represents an integral component of gender-based violence, with the intersection of ethnic, racial, social class categories and the marginalisation of women and girls in society. The solution will require not only sensitivity and understanding, but also a better understanding from a gender

128 Dowdney, *supra* note 3, 335–346; see also Demoscopia, *supra* note 6, 6–25.
129 Dowdney, *supra* note 3, 119.

perspective, and the consistent enforcement and financial commitment of home governments and the wider international community.

The root causes of the problem must also be addressed. Until a majority of these countries can achieve socio-economic stability and a working democracy, most solutions will remain rather tentative and extremely limited. Where intervention initiatives for war-affected children are in place, like in the case of community-based reintegration programmes, girls, it would appear, are more often than not bypassed, even though they are the ones in the greatest need of care and services. Far too often, girls are missed simply because many of them are unwilling to come forward in the first place or they are discriminated against. In terms of programme response, all of these factors represent critical challenges for the international community. Despite that, resources fall short of the scope and complexity of the situation in the case of girl soldiers.

One of the main questions highlighted is why some girls voluntarily become soldiers in spite of the obvious dangers. Many girls, as is shown, do it for the benefits provided for them by the various groups; protection from ill-treatment and escaping domestic exploitation or abuse are but one amongst many examples. The girls also, it seems, do it for the sense of power, and this is a very important point to remember. Nevertheless, all of this depends, of course, on whether the girls are recruited voluntarily or not.[130]

The 2007 Report of the Special Representative of the Secretary-General for Children and Armed Conflict points out that 'even though girls are gradually receiving more attention, including in the context of post-conflict rehabilitation and reintegration programming, the child protection community, academia and other stakeholders must strive to deepen the knowledge base on girls to inform more effective advocacy and programme interventions'.[131]

As is known, gender-based violence is directed against girls and women from all cultures and socio-economic classes, although it must be emphasised that it is the poor and displaced that are readily targeted. Women and children are targeted because they are the most vulnerable and powerless and because of the power structure in male-dominated societies. Gender, age, ethnicity, race and class differences, in particular, provide sources for the construction and deconstruction of 'subjectivities', as well as in the understanding of the dehumanisation of the 'other'. These important factors will, it is clear, be extremely useful for future research on girls and young women in armed conflict and organised armed violence in Latin America.

---

[130] Keairns, *supra* note 8.

[131] Coomaraswamy, *supra* note 121, 3.

The final question related to what happens to the girls and the young women when the fighting ends. In the case of armed conflicts, a gender approach allows us to understand that men and women do react differently to the conflict, since they have different needs, different skills and different ways of coping and surviving. Moreover, gender roles and power dynamics change during conflict. Gender roles, hierarchies, and injustices can enable and exacerbate human rights abuse in complex and varied ways. This is also the case with the situation of girls in armed conflict and organised armed violence in Colombia and El Salvador, which should be further researched from a gender perspective.

The State also has a duty to address, from an integral and gender perspective, the specific impact of armed conflict on women and girls, particularly in the areas of health, justice and education. It also has a duty to sanction, eradicate and prevent violence and discrimination against girls.[132] What is more, it is important to do away with discriminatory socio-cultural patterns based on sex, race, and ethnic background, and to take these differences and conditions of vulnerability into account in the development of public policies, such as reparation, reconciliation and reintegration programmes.[133]

In this respect, and in discussing policies of 'recovery and reintegration' in the case of child victims of armed conflicts in Colombia, the UN Committee on the Rights of the Child in 2010 showed concern about the measures for children, particularly those vulnerable groups living in poverty, indigenous and Afro-Colombian children and those affected by armed conflict or displacement.

At the same time, in the case of child soldiers and the recruitment and use of children by illegal armed groups in Colombia, the UN Committee against Torture made clear its concern about the ongoing recruitment and use of children by illegal armed groups. The Committee, though, in December 2007 complemented the efforts made by the State through the establishment of an Inter-Sectoral Commission on the unlawful recruitment of children and young people by illegal organised groups. The Committee was worried that:

> such children are not given sufficient support to ensure their physical and mental rehabilitation and recuperation, that different levels of protection are offered depending on whether the children are demobilised from guerrilla or other illegal armed groups, and that when children are taken captive by security forces, they are not always handed over to the civil authorities within the 36-hours legal deadline. The Committee is also concerned that the security forces use children for intelligence

132 UNIFEM, *supra* note 120, UNIFEM *supra* note 117.

133 Inter-American Commission on Human Rights, *supra* note 118.

> purposes, occupy schools in areas of conflict and organise 'military days' in schools throughout the country...[134]

The UN Committee on the Rights of the Child, at the time, pointed in a similar vein to issues of protection, recovery and reintegration of child soldiers in Colombia, especially where it is known that these child soldiers did not receive help or support. The Committee recommended that gender perspectives should be taken into account in reparations measures and it added particular concern about the recruitment and use of Afro-Colombian and indigenous children and what measures need to be developed in consultation with those affected communities. It also explained that the programme run by the ICBF had, up to the present, assisted over 4,200 children over a ten-year period, but that many of the children who had been victims in the armed conflict had not received comprehensive reparations and adequate assistance for their physical and psychological recovery.[135]

When it comes to the implementation of Act No. 975 of 2005 (Justice and Peace Law) and child recruitment, the UN Committee on the Rights of the Child was, in its own words, 'gravely concerned over the very low number of children, less than 400, released during the demobilisation of paramilitary groups'. Moreover, it expressed a worry that Law 975 in practice had resulted in impunity for war crimes of child recruitment. There had been 1,137 confessions of recruitment, for instance, but only 92 charges and, significantly, no convictions.[136]

What is noticeable is that the disarmament and rehabilitation of girl soldiers in Colombia has been a slow and difficult process. In this respect, there is a clear need to understand the multiple factors involved in the situation of girls in armed conflicts and organised armed violence, from a holistic and gender perspective. How, for instance, can their views be 'contextualised' and understood within particular armed conflicts, i.e., the geopolitical and social conditions that prevail or in the spheres of cultural and economic conditions? It goes without saying that the varying character of their role expectations and their interaction with males, including with other girls and women, need to be studied more and analysed further.

On the role of girls and adolescents in organised armed violence, as has been pointed out before in this chapter, there is a very little information available about the role played by women in these groups, as in the case of El Salvador. For instance, the fact that typically masculine characteristics and values, such as

---

134 Committee against Torture, *Concluding observations: Colombia (2009)*, UN Doc. CAT/C/COL/CO/4, §29.

135 Committee on the Rights of the Child, *supra* note 58, 6–9.

136 Ibid., 6.

aggression, bravery and the competent use of firearms, are held in high esteem means that women and 'traditional femininity' are undervalued within gangs. Sexual inequality, hierarchies and subordination have been highlighted in some of the data collected, particularly in the case of women's participation in El Salvador, and this something which needs further research and contextualisation from a gender perspective, as both Dowdney in 2005 and Demoscopia in 2008 have noted.

Bridgeman and Monk have also discussed the importance of participation in the process of implementing children's rights, and as they have pointed out, 'a better understanding of the nature of the harm arising from the specificities of children's lives can only be achieved if we listen to children'. They also go on to say that, 'participatory models are premised upon hearing the voices of children, involving them by empowering them and supporting them in the extent to which they wish to become involved in issues affecting them'.[137]

This approach is crucial in an integrated strategic approach for the prevention and rehabilitation of girls and young women. There is, in addition, a need to add a gender perspective to all this. Feminist knowledge of gender should therefore embrace 'practical social investigation of gendered lives, experiences, relationships and inequalities'.[138]

To this, there should be added an intersectional perspective, which maps the simultaneous articulation of different systems of oppression or discrimination that a girl and a young women experience. This process will show how there is a multiplicity of power structures in each society, i.e. contextualising gender, ethnic, race and class divisions. This is crucial in the case of Latin America, in general, and in the case of Colombia, in particular.

Two vital questions come to light here. What, for example, are the differences between an indigenous girl, a black girl and a white girl who participate in armed struggles or in organised armed violence in Latin America and does it make any difference whether they are educated or not, or that they come from a peasant community or from a middle-class background? There is the added factor of how their wishes are also met in the process of reintegration.

As Yuval-Davis explains, theoretically intersectionality, as a human rights policy methodology, is to enhance women's empowerment:

> The point of intersectional analysis is not to find "several identities under one"... This would reinscribe the fragmented, additive model of oppression and essentialize

137 BRIDGEMAN and MONK, *supra* note 94, 9.

138 RAMAZANOGLU and HOLLAND, *supra* note 91, 5.

> specific social identities. Instead, the point is to analyse the differential ways in which different social divisions are concretely enmeshed and constructed by each other and how they relate to political and subjective constructions of identities.[139]

Along with the rights of the girl, there must also be a specific recognition of the differences that shape the significance and experience of childhood. The false universality of 'childhood', therefore, masks the 'particularity of childhood' in each context and the possible solutions to achieve in the end the distinctive welfare of the girl.

---

139 Yuval Davis, *supra* note 86, 205.

ON CHILDREN'S RIGHTS AND WRONGS

The Challenges for a Rights-Based Approach to Reintegration

Yannick Weyns

At an unmatched pace children's rights have set a new standard in programs dealing with the plight of children affected by armed conflict. In particular, fieldwork shows that taking children's rights as an overarching guideline and aspiring to fully implement them are widely seen as 'best practice' in programs aimed at the reintegration of children associated with armed forces and groups in South Kivu.

However, children's rights with their concepts and categories are not just objectively given, as they are necessarily situated through their genealogy and context. The question thus arises whether they are that easily transposable on the situation in South Kivu. From this perspective, children's rights are not merely an instrument, but they rather actively define and structure how we perceive reality and act upon it. Which problems does the children's rights approach highlight? But also – and maybe more importantly – what does it neglect, leave behind?

Based on fieldwork carried out in South Kivu, this essay aims firstly at unravelling these structural silences. Drawing on narratives of spirit possession amongst former *mayi-mayi* and of children struggling to come to terms with their guilt, we will see how culture and the child soldiers' perpetrator side are systematically undervalued. This allows to shed light on the meeting between the children's rights discourse and its legal concepts on the one hand and the local context on the other, and also permits to find out to what extent they are compatible and where they get lost in translation. By doing so we can put children's rights in perspective and complement them with a culturally sensitive approach.

1. CHILDREN'S RIGHTS, A TOOL YET TO BE MASTERED

While the conflict in Eastern Congo was still smouldering, children's rights emerged as an important road map for the reconstruction of society and as an essential building block in the efforts made to reintegrate children associated with the armed forces or armed groups. The introduction of children's rights in these programs has meant a leap forward in bringing the interests of the child victims to the forefront of action. The attention has shifted away from short-term demobilisation goals towards strengthening these children's education and livelihood opportunities over the long run. Moreover, the approach has significantly contributed to raising concern about issues of discrimination, e.g. girls as the invisible victims of child recruitment. In this respect, a major success of the rights-based approach has been to redefine child soldiering in a new inclusive way whereby not only those immediately involved in the hostilities are entitled to protection and reintegration assistance of governmental and non-governmental actors.

In spite of the major achievements made by child rights advocates and aid workers alike, this is not yet the time for complacency. Children's rights have become an important tool at the disposal of the architects and executives of the reintegration programs. The efficiency of tools is, however, limited by the handling techniques and proficiency by which they are used. The introduction of children's rights has raised new questions and left many more unanswered. Amongst these figures the central question concerning the actual and potential contribution of this rights regime to the reintegration effort. How can and should we handle children's rights to the best interest of those we want to assist? It is with this question at the back of my mind that I ventured off to South Kivu, one of the provinces in Eastern Congo that have been scarred the most by Africa's first 'world war'.

In this chapter, we will first unravel the determining impact that is exerted by children's rights on the reintegration effort, ranging from offering a perspective that brings the problems facing demobilised children to light over modelling the interventions to providing a standard to evaluate the programs. Thereafter we will see that there is an implicit premise underlying the rights-based approach as it has unfolded in South Kivu, namely that the gross, if not all, of the problems of reintegration can be translated into children's rights.

This raises the important question to the specific relation between the tantamount of problems these children are experiencing on the ground and the violation of their rights. Given the fact that the children's rights regime has been designed and developed outside of the Congolese context wherein it is currently being applied, it might well be that the regime only partially manages to grasp the complex plight of the children associated with the armed groups in South

Kivu. Therefore, we will scrutinise two hurdles these children often have to overcome on their road towards a new, civilian life and are difficult to be labelled as children's rights violations. The first issue is the spirit possession former mayi-mayi combatants are haunted by once they are trying to shed their military past. Secondly, we will discuss the feelings of guilt experienced by demobilised child soldiers. It appears that these problems are either still undiscovered or unremedied by the reintegration programs. This finding will lead us to a critique of the programs as they are currently put into place, and to the recommendation of dealing with reintegration in a more culturally sensitive way.

2. ARMED CONFLICT: DETRIMENTAL TO CHILDREN'S RIGHTS, BENEFICIAL TO THE CHILDREN'S RIGHTS DISCOURSE

2.1. MAPPING THE PROLIFERATION OF CHILD SOLDIERS IN EASTERN CONGO

The protracted armed conflict which is haunting the Kivutian population since the midst of the nineties has had a detrimental impact on the enjoyment of nearly all human and children's rights. Besides the large scale violation of children's basic rights, such as survival, education and health, the most eye-catching and problematized plight the Kivutian children are faced with is their recruitment in the national army or in one of the various armed groups which are roaming around the lush Congolese hills. In this regard, the conflict in Eastern-Congo has the unfortunate and dubious honour to have the highest concentration of child soldiers of all contemporary conflicts.

From the onset of his march to the capital in 1996, Laurent-Désiré Kabila and his AFDL[1] purposefully sought to draw on the large generation of economically deprived youngsters and children. Under the pretext that he would provide them with an income or pay for their studies, as well as by the use of intimidation and force, he succeeded in his recruitment objective. Once the Mobutu regime was overthrown, many of these minors were conscripted in the new national army, the *Forces armées congolaises*, or left to a life on the streets in a city many hundreds of kilometres away from their home towns. During the second rebellion wave starting in 1998, the most important human resource of nearly all Rwandan or Ugandan backed rebel groups and the various local *mayi-mayi* movements were youngsters and minors.

In 1999, the Lusaka Cease-Fire Agreement was signed, but the conflict in the Kivu's continued largely unabated until April 2002, when the Sun City

1 *Alliance des Forces démocratiques pour la libération du Congo.*

Agreement was concluded. The implementation of this agreement, whereby all undersigning armed factions were to be integrated in the new unified army, the FARDC[2], was painstakingly slow. Only in 2004 a concerted effort gained momentum to demobilize and reintegrate children associated with the armed forces or groups. Under the auspices of the *Commission nationale de démobilisation et réintégration* (CONADER) the minors were separated from the adult combatants in *brassage*-centers, where the members of armed groups were gathered to either demobilise or be integrated in the new national army. From there on, the children were brought to transition centres to commence their further reintegration into society.

Since that time, an estimated 31,000 children have been demobilized either through the *brassage*-process or through mediation efforts of non-governmental actors.[3] At least an additional 8,000 have 'auto-demobilised', which means that they never received any assistance and stay invisible for the aid community. Often it concerns girls frightened to have their personal history of sexual abuse known by the community, youngsters having fled from their group or left behind by their commanders. Nowadays, more than 5,000 children[4] are still awaiting demobilisation, mostly in armed groups not involved in the Sun City Agreement or in non-integrated brigades of the FARDC.

Out of the 31,000 children, about half had the opportunity to go through a social and economic reintegration program.[5] Notwithstanding the clear lack of capacity of the aid-giving community in logistical and financial terms figuring in this number, we will focus our attention on those who did receive reintegration assistance. Reintegrating so many minors formerly associated with armed groups is an arduous task. To what extent did the programs succeed? And which trajectory has been laid out to achieve their goals? Both goals and means of the reintegration programs have been strongly inspired and defined by a children's rights perspective.

That the conflict in Eastern-Congo is a harsh and hostile environment for children and their rights is obvious. Enrolment in armed groups, an acute lack of food and access to schooling or basic health care all seriously infringe children's rights and hamper their development. The relationship between armed conflict and children's rights is, however, more ambiguous than it might seem at first glance.

---

2 *Forces armées de la république démocratique du Congo.*

3 United Nations, S/2007/391 para. 65.

4 These numbers exclude children amongst the FDLR rebel group, on whom there is little information. Interview with Office Director of UNICEF, Bukavu, 3-12-2008.

5 United Nations, S/2007/391.

2.2. HOT TALK: THE PROLIFERATION OF THE HUMAN RIGHTS DISCOURSE

Strolling around Bukavu, one is immediately struck by the near complete absence of publicity, disregarding the few billboards left advertising the importance of the past elections in 2006. A second, more thorough look draws the attention towards the multitude of banners across and alongside the streets. Publicity at last, it seems. But they do not promote any goods, services or firms. Nevertheless, the message they convey cannot be misunderstood. '*Femmes rassemblées pour leurs droits. Séminaire sur la violence sexuelle, du 15 à 17 octobre*' (Women united for their rights. Seminar on sexual violence, from the 15th till the 17th of Octobre); '*Hukumu la kufa, nasema hapana! Wacongomani pamoja nyuma ya haki za binadamu.*' (The death penalty, I say no! The Congolese people united behind human rights.); or '*Non contre les violations des droits de l'enfant [...] Tous nos enfants ont droit à l'éducation!*' (No to the violations of children's rights [...] All our children are entitled to education!). These are but a few examples out of the myriad of messages and rallying calls we came across. The emblems and acronyms of the United Nations, UNICEF and many local and international NGOs are printed beneath the text. Where does this strong interest in the dissemination of human rights stem from? The answer is to be found in the white jeeps with long antennas conquering the unpaved Congolese roads.

The advent of the Rwandan refugees in 1994 was the beginning of a new era for the inhabitants of the Kivu's. Not only did it transform the socio-economic crisis and ethnic tensions into an open conflict, the Kivu's came in the focal point of the international community's attention. A plethora of international organisations and NGOs arrived on the scene. With them they brought millions of dollars for their humanitarian and development effort. Also – and maybe even more importantly – they came with a vision determining how this money has to be spent and their projects have to be modelled. The nexus between human development, human security and human rights is central to this vision and underpins it.[6] As Kofi Annan, the former Secretary-General of the United Nations summarized the contemporary approach: '*[They] go hand in hand [...] We will not enjoy development without security, we will not enjoy security without development, and we will not enjoy either without respect without respect for human rights. Unless all these causes are advanced, none will succeed.*'[7] In this way, the implementation and dissemination of human rights becomes a crucial pillar in confining conflict situations and transforming them into a safe and

---

6 See *inter alia* the United Nations Commission On Human Security, *Human Security Now*, New York, United Nations Publications, 2003; United Nations Development Program, *The Human Development Report 2005*, New York, Oxford University Press, 2005.

7 United Nations, *In Larger Freedom: towards security, development and human rights for all*, A/59/2005, para. 17.

positive environment for the development of the population. The banners in the streetscape are silent witnesses of this humanitarian mission to empower people to enjoy and claim their rights.

The impact of the presence of the international community is, however, more far-reaching than solely the publicity given to the rights discourse. Local NGOs, seeking to cooperate with the international actors, have all turned human rights into their main endeavour. Sometimes explicitly, by referring to the human rights instruments in their mission statement, sometimes implicitly, by framing problems and their remedies in terms of human rights. The rights discourse is not restricted to these actors geared towards the international community, but trickles down to the entire social network. Each parish organises children's rights days in cooperation with NGOs. Through days such as these and other sensitisation and capacity-building efforts at the community level, children and adults are increasingly made aware of a new part of their identity, namely being a legal subject with human or children's rights. From this point of view, armed conflict, in spite of being prejudicial to human rights, serves as a catalyst for the proliferation of the human rights discourse. A discourse also being prominently present in the reintegration efforts made by the international community.

3. THE INTRICATE CONNECTION BETWEEN CHILDREN'S RIGHTS AND REINTEGRATION PROGRAMMES

3.1. THE CHILDREN'S RIGHTS PARADIGM

The demobilisation and reintegration of children is but one of the many domains wherein the aid agencies are active. In light of the aforementioned larger developments it therefore comes as no surprise that human and children's rights are also constitutive for the specific mode of action concerning child soldiers. All recent soft law instruments and guidelines in this respect do propagate children's rights as the blueprint of the programs. According to the Paris Principles and Guidelines[8] for example, the fundamental principle shaping reintegration efforts is '*a child rights approach – meaning that all interventions are developed within a human rights framework – [which] should underpin all interventions aimed at preventing recruitment or use, securing the release of, protecting and reintegrating children who have been associated with an armed force or armed group.*'[9] Another set of guidelines developed by the non-governmental community in the context of the West African conflicts upholds that one of the main lessons learned, consists

[8] The Paris Principles and Guidelines on Children Associated with Armed Forces or Armed Groups, hereafter: the Paris Principles.

[9] The Paris Principles, p. 8.

in the imperative importance of putting children's rights and the core principles contained in the Convention on the Rights of the Child (CRC) at work in the reintegration programs.[10] Thirdly, the Integrated Disarmament, Demobilisation and Reintegration Standards (IDDRS) of the United Nations[11] similarly propose these rights as the basis upon which all action *vis-à-vis* recruited children has to be modelled. This vision is echoed on the terrain. Staff members of UNICEF, international and local NGOs all denoted the violation of the rights of recruited children as their main concern and the progressive realisation of the CRC for these children as their main ambition. Both in the texts and on the terrain we thus discovered a manifold of testimonies to the fact that there is a tremendous commitment to children's rights and there appears to be a crucial impact of these rights on the reintegration programs. This raises the important question as to what this rights-based approach precisely entails in practice.

3.2. LAYING OUT THE BLUEPRINT: A RIGHTS-BASED SITUATION ANALYSIS

One of the main advantages of the rights-based approach according to a 1998 executive directive of UNICEF[12] is that one does not longer need to use different analytical frameworks to analyse the situation concerning for example malnutrition or education, but that they can all be integrated in one single model, whereby children's rights figure as the indicators for the situation analysis, considering that 'in the analysis of problem causes, the problems identified will most often constitute violations of children's rights.'[13] Moreover, seemingly unrelated problems find common cause in the violation of these rights. The importance of children's rights for the situation analysis does resurface in the IDDRS. In line with these standards, the basic principles of the CRC have to be applied in all different stages of the intervention, from the situation analysis and the development of programs up to their implementation and evaluation. In South Kivu, the organisations follow this 'child rights situation analysis'[14] by framing the issue in terms of the rights violations these children had to suffer prior to their enrolment in an armed group and again at the dawn of their new civilian life. In brief, the organisations provided us with the following insights in the causes for the proliferation of the phenomenon and the problems upon reintegration.

---

10 Save The Children, *Inter-Agency Guidelines for Developing Reintegration Programs for Children Affected by Armed Conflict in West Africa: Field Test Version*, Freetown, Save the Children UK, 2007.

11 United Nations, *Integrated Disarmament, Demobilisation and Reintegration Standards*, New York, United Nations Publications, New York, 2006, 772 p.

12 Unicef, 'A Human Rights Approach to UNICEF Programming for Children and Women: What it is, and Some Changes it Will Bring …', CF/EXD/1998-04.

13 Unicef, op. cit., II.2.a.

14 Ibid.

Widespread poverty, which is violating the right to an adequate standard of living and even the right to survival, is not only directly responsible for the decision of children and youngsters to join the army in an attempt to gather a living, but also impedes the enjoyment of other basic rights. Firstly, a lack of education and secondly, a lack of parental protection, as the parents are no longer capable of bearing the financial burden their children bring with them and are often necessitated to use them as an extra income earner. The infringement of these rights and the absence of protection by parents or school does render children all the more vulnerable to recruitment and nourishes their motivation to join these groups. For parents, handing over their children to an armed group might seem an attractive strategy to alleviate the pressure on their livelihood and maybe even – as they are often misleadingly told – to bring in some extra cash.

The rights based approach does not only focus on the specific rights that the children are prevented to enjoy, but also on the duty-bearers who are to address these rights violations. Often the parents are not aware of their children's rights, their own duties towards them and more specifically the illegality of child recruitment.[15] The duty-bearers, in this case the parents[16] and the state, are thus to be targeted by sensitisation programs. Moreover, as having the will to protect and having the ability thereto are far from synonymous, the rights based situation analysis also highlights the lacking capability of the duty-bearers, especially the parents and the broader community, to fulfil their responsibility towards the demobilised children and those at risk of recruitment as part of the problem. The approach therefore stresses the importance of capacity building of the duty-bearers.

3.3. CONSTRUCTING THE INTERVENTION

3.3.1. The Transit Centres

The way in which children's rights are instructive for the situation analysis, the analysis itself models in turn the actual outlook of the reintegration programs. During the demobilised children's stay in the *centres d'accueil transitoires* or transition centres, the aid agencies search and mediate with their family and community, inform the children on their rights and offer them a fixed daily life

---

15 Only 22 percent of the respondents in South Kivu were of the opinion that forced recruitment of minors should be held criminally responsible. In North-Kivu 24 percent agreed and in Ituri a mere 16 percent. P. Vinck et al., *Living with fear: a population based survey on attitudes about peace, justice and social reconstruction in eastern Democratic Republic of Congo*, University of California, Berkeley, 41.

16 Parents do not directly derive legal obligations out of the CRC and are thus not duty-bearers *sensu stricto*, but are denominated as bearing the primary responsibility for the child's development. In this way, the guidelines equally consider the parents to be duty-bearers. Save The Children (2007), loc. cit., 26.

structure. This structure helps them to overcome their trauma's, which are also tackled by listening, showing patience towards the children and organising recreational activities. Since they have been able to exert considerable power over civilians during their experience of being armed and growing up in a militarised environment, thereby inversing the normal authority relations, demobilised youngsters find it difficult to accept parental authority once again. Therefore, they are also taught to be respectful and obedient towards their parents and elder civilians.

3.3.2. Socio-Economic Aid: Livelihood Assistance

After being reinserted in their community, the youngsters receive job training in a regional centre near their home town. The dire living circumstances in South Kivu being identified as the single most important root cause for the proliferation of child recruitment gives rise to the central importance of professional training and income generating activities offered to the demobilised children and youngsters. In order to become sustainably reintegrated, it is regarded as the *conditio sine qua non* that one must be transformed from a financial burden for the family and the community into a financial – and thus social – asset. Remaining dependent would be detrimental to the social reintegration and thus constitutes an important push factor leading back to the armed groups. This implies firstly that youngsters have to be able to provide for themselves and secondly that taking care of school-going children must be accompanied by receiving material support.

Typically, the professional training programs run for a three to six month period plus an traineeship for another three months. Only youngsters who have reached the age of fifteen are eligible for job training.[17] In spite of an existing study ordered by the International Labour Office[18], which suggests a set of economic activities fitted to the opportunities in the different regions, the organisations in practice always fall back on the same set of professions. On the countryside, masonry, carpentry and tailoring are offered together with either agriculture or cattle herding. In the cities, some additional training opportunities are offered specifically tied to the urban economy. Mechanics, driving and welding are attracting young people who do not intent to go back to their parental village, but seek to build new futures in the city. Not returning to the parental home is, however, clearly regarded as a second-best solution by the aid workers, as parental protection and care are both considered to be a children's right and a children's need to develop physically and mentally. Therefore, not returning to the community is generally considered to be against the best interest of the child and deemed only appropriate for e.g. girls fearing to be ostracised by their community and near-adults.

---

17 ILO Convention 138 has set fifteen as the minimum legal age to work.

18 GOTEC, *Analyse Sectorielle du Marché local du travail pour les EAFGA, mimeo.*

Children who have not yet attained the age of fifteen are to be reintegrated in the formal education system. Considering the fact that before their recruitment and consecutive demobilisation, the parents were in most cases unable to pay the tuition fees, materials and 'motivation fee'[19], the need for directly targeting the capacity of the parents comes here more than ever in the spotlight. Many organisations active in this field pay the fees and materials for a two year period. During this time they also provide microcredits to the families, either in cash or in the form of livestock, and in second degree to the community as a whole. This must allow the family to gather the means necessary to finance the further education of their child and prevent dependency relations with the aid community to root. Therefore, once beyond this two year period the family has again to manage on its own.

3.3.3. Follow-up and Constituency Building

A second aspect of capacity building consists in the establishment of informal community networks, meant to gather the community around children's rights issues. In the 'Community Child Protection Networks', devised by Save the Children, elected members commit themselves on a voluntary basis to sensitize the broader community, identify rights-related problems and rally support for found solutions. The community approach is still in full development. Besides eleven community networks put in place by Save the Children, the local NGO ADED[20] has initiated three *vijiji vileleso* or 'model villages' around Uvira. In these villages, a social worker assists the community during a one year period helping them to get organised around children's rights and child related problems.

The networks also have the advantage of being able to follow up on reintegrated children far better and more continuously compared to the NGOs who are often based in the cities and find it difficult and cost inefficient to travel long distances in order to visit children going through or finished with the programme. Nowadays, the follow-up is mostly done by the local organisations providing professional training, who have but a partial image of the social situation and psychological resilience of the children. Moreover, many of these organisations do not perceive follow-up beyond the training period as one of their primary responsibilities. As a result, adequate feedback to the organisations on the reintegrated children is often lacking, if given at all.[21]

---

19 Since teachers do not receive any wages from the government, it is a widespread practice in Congo for the parents to pay a fee. If the fee is not paid, pupils risk to be expelled from school.

20 Appui au Développement de l'Enfant en Détresse.

21 B. Verhey, *Going Home: demobilising and reintegrating child soldiers in the Democratic Republic of the Congo*, London, Save the Children, 2003.

3.4. FROM A PROGRAMME FOR ACTION TO A STANDARD FOR EVALUATION

From this brief overview of the programs, it becomes clear that children's rights firstly serve as a grid of perception to understand the complex situation demobilised children are confronted with, and secondly have a determining impact on the concrete outlook of the interventions. As the dire livelihood situation is identified as the main culprit of rights violations, which on their turn facilitate child recruitment, youngsters receive job training and the parents of school-going children are financially supported. For lacking awareness and capacity are deemed equally responsible for the continuation of these violations and for an increased risk of re-recruitment, constituencies are built and information is disseminated.

The interviews we had with the aid organisations in South Kivu and the evaluation reports they made, brought a third important function of children's rights in the reintegration programs to light. In accordance with the different guidelines mentioned above children's rights serve as a yardstick to measure the achievements of the intervention. Firstly, children's rights are used in a procedural way. Discrimination is to be avoided and the consultation of children to be pursued. Secondly, children's rights serve as a substantive measure. In order to evaluate a program and to see whether a child has successfully been reintegrated, the organisations check whether the child is staying within a family environment, has an income or is able to go to school. As the Paris Principles state: '*Sustainable reintegration is achieved when the political, legal, economic and social conditions to maintain life, livelihood and dignity have been secured. The process aims that children can access their rights, including formal and non-formal education, dignified livelihoods and safety from harm.*'[22] These are all characteristics of the socio-economic situation wherein these children find themselves. In this way, external conditions, rather than the subjective experience of children may come to be used as the criterion for success. Indeed, these conditions are in line with children's and human rights, the responsibilities of the duty-bearers and with the operational goals the organisations have set for themselves.

4. WHO IS GUARDING THE GUARDS? THE EVALUATION EVALUATED

For the purposes of this chapter we are not concerned with evaluating the programs in accordance with the indicators used in South Kivu, although there

22 The Paris Principles, p. 8.

are serious questions regarding the effectiveness of the programs in light of their own parameters. Due to structural socio-economic conditions, such as land shortages, limited market access and the endemic poverty, youngsters are often impeded to practice the job they have been taught. In Walungu, for example, over the course of a year, more than twenty five girls have taken a course to become a tailor. This causes the market to be saturated in a condition wherein there already is a low demand for clothes given the poverty of the population. The same goes for masons and carpenters. Microcredits provided for schooling are spent on direct expenditure instead of being used as an investment, as the families are struggling with an acute lack of financial means to cover even daily living expenses.[23] This undermines the sustainability of the aid given.

The issue we are concerned with at this point is whether from the fulfilment of children's basic rights it can objectively be inferred that the children are fully reintegrated and that the programs have succeeded in this regard. Children's rights are surely objective in that they offer parameters allowing for a comparison between the rights situation before and after the intervention and between the impact of different programs in this respect. But are they also objective in the sense that they provide us with an undistorted image of what it means to be reintegrated?

The problems highlighted by the situation analysis are all positive duties of the state, the parents or the community. Education, an adequate standard of living and protection are all rights linked to a clearly identifiable duty-bearer. The cultural domain is within the legal framework conceptualized as a fundamental freedom, entailing an essentially negative duty of the state to respect this freedom. The question arises whether problems on the cultural plane are that easily translated into specific violations of this right. The fact that throughout the discussion of the situation analysis and programming we only in the margins came across the cultural dimension, might in this regard be an indication that there are aspects of the problem staying unnoticed for the children's rights gaze. In the following paragraphs, we will go into a culturally specific stumbling block the children are faced with upon reintegration, namely spirit possession. Is this problem being tackled by the reintegration programs and if so, how? Thereafter, we will discuss a second issue which is difficult to be classified under a children's rights violation and hard to reconcile with the image of childhood figuring in and structuring the CRC. Upon reintegration, child soldiers are confronted with the crimes and acts of violence they have committed. Do the programs manage to defuse this confrontation and again, if so, how?

---

23 E. Lecoutere et al., *Conflict, Food Insecurity and Fragility in Eastern D.R. Congo*, Gent: Conflict Research Group, 2008.

5. SPIRIT POSSESSION AMONGST THE MAYI-MAYI

Contrary to the conflicts in Uganda[24] and Mozambique[25], there is no general cultural experience amongst combatants of being possessed or tormented by the spirits of their victims. Throughout the fieldwork we carried out, it became clear that there is a far more contemporary and modern experience of possession haunting both adult and child combatants. This experience is intertwined with the specific practices spread amongst the different *mayi-mayi* movements. The *mayi-mayi* constitute a mosaic of armed groups, differing in command structures, alliances and politico-military goals, ranging from opportunistic self-enrichment to fully fletched nationalist political movements.[26] Their shared name however refers to their common roots and characteristics. 'Mayi-mayi' in Congolese Swahili signifies 'water-water' and it is derived from their use of magic water. This water would in combination with following a set of strict behavioural rules, such as sexual abstinence and the prohibition of looting or merely touching civilians, render the combatant immune to bullets or even make him invincible. Apart from magic water, the *mayi-mayi* also use other *dawa* (medicines) and invoke the spirits of their ancestors through fetishes, or power-objects, and rituals.

Being defunct of modern technologies of warfare, these (re)invented traditional practices applied in a modern context serve as an important 'technology of the self' wherein the group is tied together, their identity as mayi-mayi warriors is crafted and their mental state is altered.[27] As a consequence, this provides them an edge on the battlefield and contributes to their image of being fierce and fearless warriors. These practices and rituals have a strong psychological impact, for the better during combat, but for the worse during reintegration, when in combination with factors such as stress, trauma's and the continuous use of marihuana and alcohol – a bad habit they have often picked up in the armed group – this can lead to the impression of being possessed by the spirits invoked and to clinical pictures comparable with psychiatric dysfunctions.

The recourse mayi-mayi groups take to magic water and other *dawa* has an important and highly deplorable effect on the average age of children recruited

---

24 L. Victor, '"Abomination": local belief systems and international justice' in *Field Notes* 5, 1–14.

25 A. Honwana, *Child Soldiers in Africa*, Philadelphia, University of Pennsylvania Press, 2006; V. Igreja and B. Dias-Lambranca, 'Restorative justice and the role of magamba spirits in post-civil war Gorongosa, central Mozambique', in L. Huyse and M. Salter (ed.), *Traditional Justice and Reconciliation after Conflict: learning from African experiences*, Stockholm, International Institute for Democracy and Electoral Assistance, 2008.

26 K. Vlassenroot, 'Violence et Constitution des Milices dans l' Est du Congo: le Cas des Mayi-Mayi', in *L'Afrique des Grands Lacs. Annuaire 2001–2002*, Paris, L'Harmattan, 115–150.

27 K. Hoffmann, *Governing the 'Maquis': a Case Study of General Padiri's Maï-Maï movement*, 2006, Gent, Conflict Research Group.

by them. According to *mayi-mayi* belief, the *dawa* and water are during preparation not to be touched by an adult. These are considered to be impure as they already have been sexually active. Therefore, the *mayi-mayi* have an additional function for young children, some of them are as young as six at the time of their recruitment. These children are called the *kadogo-dawa*[28] and are specifically responsible for the preparation of potions and the handling of the fetishes under the supervision of the *mganga* or *docteur.*

Laurent[29] was such a *kadogo-dawa*. At the age of eleven, he was forcibly recruited by the regional *mayi-mayi* movement in Nyangezi, fairly close to Bukavu. Once demobilised at the age of fifteen, he underwent strong psychological suffering, even after being re-admitted in the educational system. Lucid periods were alternated with periods of mental absence or constant screaming and uncontrollable spasms. In his eyes and according to his family and community this suffering was triggered by the fetishes and ancestral spirits he came in contact with during that period. In the same village, we were approached by the family of Furaha[30], who joined the *mayi-mayi* at the age of fifteen. She had already been back in her village for over a year, but the feeling of being possessed by the spirits she had invoked during combat only grew stronger. Voices went through her head and time and time again she woke up at night re-experiencing the moments she was drinking blood.

Preferably, the family and the local priest told us, they would have sought recourse with the local king, the *mwami*, who is traditionally concerned with the ritual healing of his subjects. But as all of the traditional authorities were no longer present in the village, the children and their families felt as having no other option but to seek assistance with an exorcist in Bukavu through mediation of the priest. Upon return, the symptoms disappeared and the children were healed according to their family.

The catholic exorcist enjoys a very good reputation around Bukavu, but wished to stay anonymous for reasons of personal security. He was familiar with the problem of former *mayi-mayi* being possessed. Over the course of half a year, he had already treated about twenty comparable cases. In his opinion, these were only the tip of the iceberg. Indeed, one must have the will to be treated and enjoy the support of the community in order to reach him. Several other priests from different parishes in Kanyola and Bukavu and involved with former child soldiers did confirm the existence and the considerable scale on which this phenomenon was taking place.

According to the Congolese NGO workers, feelings of possession were totally or almost completely inexistent due to traditional beliefs gradually having been

28 '*Kadogo*' signifies 'little thing' in Congolese Swahili and it is the local term to refer to child soldiers.

29 The names of the children have been changed for reasons of security.

30 Ibid.

lost or because the combatants thought to be killing out of revenge. Throughout the many interviews we carried out with the aid organisations, we did not succeed in finding a single staff member being knowledgeable about the aforementioned phenomenon affecting former *mayi-mayi* combatants. There are three reasons explaining the unfamiliarity of the aid workers therewith. Firstly, during the children's stay in the transit centres, the condition of these children is easily interpreted to be caused by ordinary trauma's and to be treated likewise. Secondly, recalling the deficient follow up, it is increasingly difficult to keep track of these children once they have left the transit centres and even more so once their job training is finished. Finally, the organisations are focussed on identifying livelihood problems and rights violations. Being possessed fits neither of these. Therefore, the phenomenon is not actively been searched for and thus easily overlooked by the aid workers. However, non-identification of the problem does not imply that it is irrelevant. Indeed, as the children go through this culturally specific experience of possession to the detriment of their psychological and social lives, can they be considered as fully reintegrated, regardless of them being enrolled in a training program or school?

6. A CHILDREN'S RIGHT, A SOLDIERS PLIGHT: INNOCENCE AND GUILT

Ciri Kabanga[31], who founded an NGO to work on art projects with child soldiers, coined the issue of the dividing line between the notions of child and adult becoming blurred and problematic when it concerns child soldiers. '*But is it really possible to still perceive someone who has killed and raped, who has seen parts of reality that most of us never even do, as a child?*', he said, '*Children's horizon is supposed to be limited to their school, their family, their fantasy…*'. As Alcinda Honwana has rightly pointed out, the term child soldier contains an oxymoron.[32] Child soldiers are a combination of two opposing terms. They are nor completely children, whom we associate with terms as vulnerable, innocent and morally immature, nor entirely soldiers, thought to be adults, strong and able to make decisions about life and dead. Child soldiers are 'betwixt and between' these two identities, caught between being children or victims and actors or perpetrators.

A significant amount of child soldiers in the strict sense of the word have killed, either for due cause during combat or as sheer criminal acts. Upon demobilisation and reintegration, these children go through tremendous psychological stress and mental suffering. The symptoms fit well with the

31 His name has equally been altered given the volatile security situation in Eastern Congo.

32 A. Honwana, 'Innocents et Coupables: les enfants soldats commes acteurs tactiques' in *Politique Africaine*, 80, 58–68.

condition of Post Traumatic Stress Syndrome (PTSS), as they constantly re-experience their traumatising acts. There is however one particularity linked to these instances of PTSS, i.e. the attribution of responsibility made by the children concerned is different. Through their 'rediscovery of killing as a moral transgression'[33] they are confronted with themselves as perpetrators. Opening up the discussion on the moral and penal responsibility of child soldiers in this essay would lead us too far, but what we are concerned with here is that the children themselves live under the impression that they did not act under mere duress. In their experience, they themselves have sporadically or even often chosen to loot or to commit attacks against life and limb. These children have to learn how to deal with these feelings and with that aspect of their personal history, in order to leave the past behind and grow into an adult civilian. Some of them will pursue the strategy of trying to forget it, whilst others have to experience a catharsis whereby they go through confrontation, acceptance and being forgiven by the community.

In South Kivu, the perpetrator side of child soldiers is covered in silence amongst the aid community. Nevertheless, all who work in direct contact with demobilised children have already been approached many times by children struggling with their guilt. The way in which this undoubtedly very difficult situation is dealt with psychologically is through reassuring the children that they need not hold themselves responsible for their actions, as they were victims of the situation. '*Il est clair que ces enfants sont des victimes. Dans certains cas déplorables la situation les a pressés à commettre des crimes, mais on ne peut pas les considérer coupables.*' ('It is clear that these children are victims. In certain unfortunate cases the situation has forced them into committing crimes, but one must not consider them to be guilty') or '*Je leur dit que ce n'est pas leur faute et que personne n'a choisi d'être née comme ça.*' ('I tell them that it is not their fault and that no one has chosen to be born that way') were often heard replies. This is in line with the guidelines, where it is stated multiple times that child soldiers are 'primarily to be treated as victims' and that, according to the IDDRS: '*Child soldiers are victims of criminal policies for which adults are responsible. [...] Children shall not be prosecuted for military crimes or for criminal acts while associated with armed forces or groups.*'[34]

Whether one agrees with the foregoing perspective does not alter the fact that children's objective responsibility or fault and their subjective experience thereof are two separate issues not necessarily to be dealt with in the same fashion. In the *Manuel d'Opérations*[35], written by the CONADER in cooperation with the NGOs, there is rightfully devoted plenty of attention to traumas, the right to

[33] I. Cohn and G.S. Goodwinn-Gill, *Child Soldiers. The Role of Children in Armed Conflicts*, Oxford, Clarendon Press, 107.

[34] United Nations, loc. cit., 5.30.9.

[35] Commission Nationale de Démobilisation et Réintégration, *Manuel d'Opérations: cadre opérationnel pour enfants associés aux forces et groupes armées*, 2004, *mimeo*.

privacy, silence and education. Terms as guilt, perpetrator or fault on the contrary, do not surface even once throughout the text.

It seems as if an artificial fission is made between the child as perpetrator, which is ought to be the concern of the judicial organs of the state or other judicial mechanisms not put into place, and the child as a victim, which on its turn is the object of care of the reintegration programs. The question coming to the fore is once again whether the silence hanging around children's perpetrator side or even the structural neglect thereof is in their best interest. Can children being entangled in their past and struggling to come to terms with their actions and feelings regarding those be considered to be fully reintegrated?

'*Un vélo ne remplace pas la conscience*' (A bike does not replace conscience) was the way in which an abbot in Bukavu eloquently phrased the inability of the reintegration programs as they are currently put into place to address these feelings of guilt. According to him, the aid effort is overly focussed on providing the children economically, causing these organisations to miss out on the crux of the matter, namely the broader psychological well-being of the children, their self-esteem and civilian identity construction. This concern was corroborated by the ten year long experience of Ciri Kabanga with former child soldiers. Throughout these years, he found that the most recurring complaint of these children was their constant victimisation by the programs, being soothed, instead of being understood and acknowledged in the guilt they are confronted with.

7. REINTEGRATION – CHILDREN'S RIGHTS AS AN END OR AS A MEANS?

The answer to the question whether these minors can considered to be reintegrated depends on the definition of 'reintegration' one adheres to. The understanding of the organisations on the terrain of what it means to be reintegrated, was both informed and reflected by the specific significance given thereto by the Paris Principles. The introduction of children's rights as indicators for the situation analysis as well as for the evaluation seems to have brought along with it a subtle shift in the definition of 'reintegration'. Following the definition in the Paris Principles cited above, the successful nature of reintegration depends on livelihoods being provided for and basic rights being met.

In South Kivu, this definition has led to the delineation of the reintegration process into a specific set of well-circumscribed operational goals linked to children's rights. During their stay in the transition centres, the right to psychological recovery is tackled. Thereafter, in the second phase, the right to parental protection, an adequate livelihood and education are dealt with. Finally, constituencies are built at the community level to help organise them around these children's rights. The side effect hereof is that it does not only lead to the fragmentation of the programs, during the second phase for example there is little room for psychological support, but also to a fragmentation of the way one looks at the children concerned and the problems they are confronted with. The child as the victim of traumas, as entitled to and in need of livelihood or education.

This causes the cultural dimension of the plight faced by these children overlooked, except when it fits with the children's rights framework. Possession is unheard of for example, but discrimination of girls because of cultural ostracism after sexual abuse is very well-known and problematized. Secondly, the children's rights perspective naturally focuses on the child or victim aspect of child soldiers. Therefore, aid workers and the programs tend to make abstraction of or downplay their soldier or perpetrator side. A major achievement of the child rights approach has been to bring all children fallen victim to armed groups under the attention, instead of merely the underage soldiers in the strict sense of the word. The rights-based approach would, however, become the victim of its own success if it does not succeed in grasping the specific needs and difficulties of those who have carried weapons and used them, such as feelings of guilt, and continues to apply a homogeneous, standardised response to the diverse and heterogeneous difficulties these children are faced with, such as spirit possession amongst demobilised *mayi-mayi*.

The application of children's rights in the analysis offers a specific grid of perception, which is very powerful in capturing a particular set of causes and consequences of child recruitment, namely lack of livelihood, education and parental or state protection. The perspective offered by children's rights is therefore certainly a highly advantageous one. The danger resides however in taking it as a one-sided approach, which leaves different aspects of the problem unnoticed and thus untreated. In this regard, it is mostly cultural causes and ramifications, loss of identity and feelings of guilt which are difficult to file under a specific right being infringed or endangered. Furthermore, in these instances it is very hard, if not impossible, to pinpoint an identifiable duty-bearer to address these issues.

Not forgetting that there are many different ways in which children's rights can be used and implemented throughout the reintegration process, the way in which they are nowadays applied in South Kivu, causes the consequences of recruitment to be seen as the sum of the socio-economic causes of the problem and the occurring traumas. The causes on their turn are perceived to be unsustainable livelihoods and other rights violations, in particular the right to education and protection. The children are thought to be prevented to enjoy the latter rights primarily because of the livelihood situation of their parents. As a result, the integrative effect of introducing children's rights in the intervention, which is supposedly one of the most important advantages brought by the new approach, is washed away by the reductionist tendency to single out livelihood as the biggest common denominator of all parts of the problem encountered during reintegration and to subsequently model nearly all the interventions around the livelihood issue.

Loss and reconstruction of identity and self-esteem for example being undeniably one of the biggest challenges, we asked the aid workers to explain how this issue was being addressed in the programs. They all concurred on the importance thereof. The manner in which the issue was dealt with according to them was once again through providing livelihood and jobs or education. These can make an important contribution indeed, but identity can not and must not be reduced to economic reintegration and formal schooling, nor to a necessary and logic result of providing those. Moreover, the question arises what remains of the newly gained identity and self-esteem once it turns out that the profession one has learned and on which this identity and self-esteem are founded, can not be practiced. Given the harsh economic conditions reigning in South-Kivu, this is not a far-flung hypothesis, but a reality confronting the large majority of children 'graduating' from the training programs.

Within the entire reintegration process, the realisation of children's rights is beyond doubt an important goal. This goal is, however, but a means towards the larger, overarching goal of individual sustainable reintegration. Through confusing operational goals as an end by themselves, reintegration came to be conceived of as a process whereby rights and livelihoods are progressively provided, rather than a process whereby minors construct a new identity, build up self-esteem and are simultaneously socially and mentally des-integrated from their past militarised social networks, experiences and identity. The aforementioned real-life problems experienced by demobilised children abundantly show that apart from structural social-economic constraints, cultural realities, loss of identity and feelings of guilt are in many instances equally responsible for preventing them to wipe the slate clean and be fully engaged within the civilian world. Therefore, albeit being a necessary condition for reintegration, the provision and protection of children's rights are not a sufficient one.

So far we have seen that there are several important difficulties children are faced with upon reintegration that slip through children's rights' grid and grip. The problem at stake does not lay in the application of these rights as such, but in the closed nature of the children's rights regime as it has unfolded in South Kivu. Taking children's rights as a starting point for the situation analysis, one draws up a program wherein actors and their responsibilities are delineated by the specific rights being at stake. From the point of departure onwards one thus has a partial image of the hurdles to be overcome during the reintegration process. The analytical, top-down approach towards the situation does not contain an incentive to actively look for possession issues for example. As a result, this dimension of the problem easily remains overlooked and unaddressed. As the evaluation of the programmes is founded upon the same principles that mould the situation analysis and the programming, one remains caught in the very logic that causes the former to be biased. We thus have arrived in a situation in which children's rights constitute the diagnosis of the problem as well as the remedy and the evaluation.[36] Therefore, the children's rights regime in South Kivu forms a self-referring and self-confirming system that at the least passively excludes dimensions unrelated to children's rights, as well as alternative approaches to the solution of the problem.[37]

8. THE UNTAPPED RESERVOIR OF CULTURAL REMEDIES

Apart from identifying the root causes of recruitment and the problems upon reintegration, the rights based approach also identifies the main actors to be involved in the effort. The international community and the state on a general level and the parents, family and community on a more direct, day-to-day level are primarily perceived as responsible to fulfil their respective duties regarding the rights of the affected children. It is thought to be important to rally the support of the traditional authorities for children's rights, being eminent members of the community, in constituency building initiatives. In analogy to the causes and consequences of recruitment in reality being of a more far-reaching nature than in the analysis brought about by the particular application of children's rights we are here concerned with, the potential contribution of these actors goes far beyond the fulfilment of their duties in the strict sense of the word.

The traditional kings, or *Bami*[38], can play a pivotal role in the social and economic reintegration of children formerly associated with the armed forces or groups in the social fabric of the villages. Moreover, they are indispensable actors in traditional rituals and mediation mechanisms alleviating feelings of guilt and remedying possession. Hereafter, we will extensively discuss the key role of the traditional authorities that has yet to be unlocked.

The traditional social and economic reality is built around the *kalinzi*.[39] The *kalinzi* is a contribution in kind or in money representing a part of the harvest, to be paid directly to the *Mwami* or those higher up the social hierarchy of whom one rents the land. These on their turn will hand over a part of their revenues to the *Mwami*, as ultimately all the land belongs to him. Apart from an annual contribution, an initial payment has to be made to acquire the right to cultivate a

---

36 P. Reynolds et al., 'Refractions of Children's Rights in Development Practice: A view from anthropology – Introduction', *Childhood*, 13(3), 292.

37 Ibid.

38 '*Bami*' is the plural of '*mwami*'.

39 F. Van Acker, 'La "Pembénisation" du Haut-Kivu: Opportunisme et Droits Fonciers Revisités', in *L'Afrique des Grands Lacs. Annuaire 1998–1999*, Paris, L'Harmattan.

patch of land. The problems facing youngsters wanting to cultivate their own field is firstly that there is a historic land shortage. Secondly, the fields are often too small due to consecutive generations of sons all inheriting an equal part of their father and too infertile to produce a surplus that can be used as a tribute. The initial payment itself also demands a far too high financial burden for the youngsters to bear. In this respect, the active involvement of the *Bami* could be fruitful to have land allocated to the youngsters and lessen the initial costs and annual tributes they have to pay. The *Bami* could therefore have a crucial and even determining impact on the sustainability of the livelihoods of demobilised youngsters and their civilian counterparts.[40] Up till now, no structured efforts have been made to involve the *Bami* in the economic reintegration of the youngsters in the community.

The *Manuel d' Opérations* of the CONADER includes an interesting guideline underlining the importance of traditional rituals and practices that might contribute to the social reintegration of the children. Recalling the interventions of the exorcist in Bukavu and the family wanting to seek recourse with the traditional authorities, it becomes clear that canonical or ritual healing practices can also further the psychological recovery of the demobilised youngsters. Unfortunately, but understandably given the analysis unfolded in this chapter, this guideline is the odd one out and is not being followed up by the organisations on the ground. Only one Congolese NGO worker was able to give some examples of the rituals being practiced by the community upon return of the children, such as slaughtering a goat or dancing on the graves of the ancestors. During his six year long career he had witnessed these practices on only two occasions. The other NGO workers were unfamiliar with the practices, let alone actively searching and supporting them.

Apart from these smaller, less institutionalised practices, there are firstly ritual healing practices aimed at freeing individuals of nightmares and spirits. One of these practices consists out of wearing an amulet or *chikoko* around the neck. Secondly, there are also purification rituals traditionally to be performed by the *Bami*. Amongst the *Balega*, for example, there exists a ritual specifically designed to cleanse combatants upon return from the battlefield. The *Bashi* profess a more general purification ritual, wherein at the start of the rainy season the people and the land are purified. These rituals could contribute significantly to alleviating the feelings of guilt experienced by the former child soldiers and to increasing the acceptance of children who are supposed to have transgressed the fundamental moral codes of the community[41], such as drinking blood or attacking their own village. This brings our attention to a third set of cultural

40 P. Namegabe, 'Le Pouvoir Traditionnel au Sud-Kivu de 1998–2003: Role et Perspectives', in *L'Afrique des Grands Lacs. Annuaire 1998–1999*, Paris, L'Harmattan, 226, 234.

41 A. Honwana, *Reintegration of Youth into Society in the Aftermath of War*, www.un.org/esa/socdev/unyin/documents/namibia_honwana.pdf.

institutions. Initiation rites are not specifically targeted at the feelings of guilt and wrongdoings of the youngsters, but at their social integration in the community, which contributes to their identity construction. An example of such an institution is the Balega's *bwami initiatique*. Throughout the ceremony, youngsters receive strong moral imperatives and are given a power object they have to keep and to protect as a sign of both responsibility towards and trust from the community.[42]

Just as children's rights, traditional practices and authorities do not offer a magic and easy solution to the complex issue of reintegration. Years of intensive colonisation, dictatorship and consecutive armed conflicts have taken their toll on traditional institutions and practices. The *Bashi* and *Bavira* are in this respect less acculturated, causing their rituals still to be performed far more often than by for example the *Bazimba* and the *Bangu-Bangu*. Some *Bami* have lost their authority either because they have sold communal lands or have collaborated with the Rassemblement Congolais pour la Démocratie (RCD).[43] In other *territoires*, there are however *bami* who have been far more engaged with their communities since the armed conflict. It is in these *territoires* that there are important opportunities to involve the traditional authorities in the reintegration of children and youngsters. Finally, it is of tantamount importance that the demobilised minor himself believes in the traditional cultural framework.[44] The specific context therefore has a determining weight. For the reintegration effort to be effective, both personal and local problems and opportunities thus have to be discovered. In conclusion, the capacity-building on the community level must not only be directed towards children's rights, but just as well towards discovering cultural practices and drawing the attention of the traditional authorities to their responsibilities in this regard. Abiding by the aforementioned guideline in the *Manuel d' Opérations* one the one hand and trying to tackle the '*kalinzi*-hurdle' on the other, would in this regard already be two major steps in the right direction.

9. PUTTING CHILDREN'S RIGHTS IN PERSPECTIVE

The partial approach of the children's rights regime to reintegration does not stem from the application of children's rights as such. The failure to address

42 For further information on the efficiency of traditional mechanisms in reintegration practice, see for example A. Honwana, 'Child Soldiers: community healing and rituals in Mozambique and Angola', in C. Diaute et al. (eds.), *International Perspectives on Youth, Conflict and Development*, 2006, Oxford, Oxford University Press.

43 F. Van Acker, op. cit.; P. Namegabe, op. cit.

44 Not only the consent of the minor is important, the practices must also serve their best interest. Some traditional practices might go against their interest and thus be unfavourable to both their reintegration and their rights. In this respect, we might think of 'female genital mutilation', which is however not practiced in South Kivu.

possession or feelings of guilt on the one side and to apply and strengthen culturally specific mechanisms as part of the solution on the other originates firstly out of the closed nature of the children's rights paradigm as it is nowadays being used in South Kivu. By measuring the success of the programs in terms of the operational goals set in the situation analysis, one does not arrive at scrutinizing these goals themselves.

Unsustainable livelihoods and lacking education opportunities undoubtedly have a tremendous impact on the proliferation of child recruitment and can be detrimental to the sustainability of the reintegration. Owing to the children's rights approach, these issues are dealt with according to the priority they both deserve and need on the terrain. However, these are but part of the story, which brings us to the second reason for the structural blind spots of the interventions. By treating the realisation of these particular children's rights as the goal of reintegration, instead of as one of the means thereto, the aid giving community does not arrive at putting children's rights in perspective. This tendency to mistake ends with means is facilitated by using children's basic rights as a yardstick as mentioned above.

Many of the critiques we came across and of the additions we made to the rights-based approach currently in place are not incompatible with these rights but can be accommodated in them. Firstly, dealing with past crimes can be seen as an integral and indispensable part of the right to psychological recovery, instead of being considered as a matter external to the actual reintegration effort and to be left to national or traditional justice. Secondly, the preamble of the CRC already mentions the importance of giving due weight to traditional practices and beliefs. When it comes to these practices and actors, the reintegration programs may not let themselves be caught in merely talking the talk, as found in the *Manuel d' Opérations*, instead of walking the walk.

In order for the programs to be effective, an equal amount of effort has to be invested in building and strengthening this cultural road towards sustainable reintegration, as the effort invested in providing basic social-economic rights with easily discernable duty-bearers. In this respect, the community based approach of NGOs such as Save the Children and ADED can only be applauded, but care has to be taken that the capacity-building is not only concerned with children's rights issues. Identifying traditional coping and justice mechanisms and ensuring the involvement of the traditional authorities herein, is indispensable. The cultural dimension of difficulties towards economic reintegration through the *kalinzi* equally has to be acknowledged.

The CRC is an incredible acquisition and a catalyst for positive change in the lives of countless children. However, it does not contain ready-made solutions and can be interpreted and applied in many different ways. It is up to the aid organisations to determine in which way the invigoration of children's rights can contribute to the best of its abilities to an all-encompassing strategy to achieve sustainable reintegration for the tens of thousands of children in South Kivu entitled to it.

ABOUT THE EDITORS

Ilse Derluyn obtained her Ph.D. in pedagogical sciences at Ghent University (Belgium) and is currently affiliated as post-doctoral researcher to the Department of Orthopedagogics, Ghent University and as guest lecturer to the University of Kent – Brussels School, where she teaches courses in migration and refugee studies. Ilse is also the coordinator of the Centre for Children in Vulnerable Situations, an interuniversity centre researching the psychosocial well-being of children in vulnerable situations in the South. Her main research topics concern the psychosocial well-being of migrant and refugee children, child soldiers, unaccompanied minors, war-affected children and victims of human trafficking (www.centreforchildren.be).

Cindy Mels started her research career at the Department of Orthopedagogics of Ghent University (Belgium), working on social support for unaccompanied asylum seeking minors. Throughout her Ph.D. study on the psychosocial well-being of war-affected adolescents from the Eastern Congo, she specialized in the cross-cultural adaptation and validation of psychological screening instruments, issues of trauma and daily stressors and their effects on mental health, and community-based research aimed at promoting psychosocial assistance in low-income and war-affected areas. She currently teaches at the Universidad Católica del Uruguay (Uruguay), where she continues working on the cross-cultural adaptation of mental health instruments and the impact of community violence and daily stressors on Latin-American low-income adolescents' mental health (www.centreforchildren.be).

Stephan Parmentier studied law and sociology at the K.U.Leuven (Belgium) and sociology and conflict resolution at the University of Minnesota-Twin Cities (U.S.A.). He currently teaches sociology of crime, law, and human rights at the Faculty of Law of the K.U.Leuven and served as the head of its Department of Criminal Law and Criminology (2005–2009). He was appointed in 2010 as the secretary-general of the International Society for Criminology and also serves on the Advisory Board of the Oxford Centre for Criminology and the International Institute for Sociology of Law Board (Oñati). Stephan's research and publications relate to human rights violations and international crimes in situations of violent conflict, strategies and mechanisms for justice and peace building, and quality management in the administration of criminal justice. He carried out field research in Bosnia, Guatemala, Serbia and South Africa (www.law.kuleuven.be/linc).

Wouter Vandenhole teaches human rights and holds the UNICEF chair in children's rights at the Faculty of Law of the University of Antwerp (Belgium). Vandenhole is co-director of the Law and Development research group of the University of Antwerp Law Research School. His research focuses on economic, social and cultural rights, children's rights, and the relationship between human rights law and development. He has a particular interest in children's rights and migration, poverty and development co-operation. Wouter is a founding member of the editorial board of the journal *Human Rights & International Legal Discourse* (www.ua.ac.be/wouter.vandenhole).

ABOUT THE AUTHORS

Femke Bannink-Mbazzi studied cultural anthropology and sociology, as well as psychology at Leiden University (The Netherlands). After working in the department of migrant and refugee care in a mental health institution in the Netherlands, she moved in 2003 to Kampala, Uganda, where she has been working since. Femke currently works for the Italian NGO AVSI as a program advisor and alongside also gives guest lectures at Makerere University Institute of Psychology, Kampala, and St. Mary University Juba (South Sudan). She also provides counselling to national and international clients at an international clinic in Kampala. In 2010, she started the Ph.D. programme in educational sciences at Ghent University, Belgium.

Maria Luisa Bartolomei studied law in her native Argentina and is currently senior lecturer at the Institute for Latin American Studies at the University of Stockholm (Sweden). She previously held a position in sociology of law at the University of Lund (Sweden). Her research interests are general human rights in the third world and Latin America, human rights as they are connected to legal cultures and globalization, and indigenous children's rights in Latin America. She has extensive experience with internet courses on human rights and legal development, and has served as a consultant to NGOs dealing with children's rights in Latin America and other parts of the world, such as Save the Children.

Theresa Betancourt, Sc.D. and M.A., is assistant professor of child health and human rights in the Department of Global Health and Population at the Harvard School of Public Health (HSPH). Dr. Betancourt is a member of the François-Xavier Bagnoud Center for Health and Human Rights, where she directs the Research Program on Children and Global Adversity (RPGCA). Her central research interests focus on the developmental and psychosocial consequences of concentrated adversity on children and families, resilience and protective processes in child mental health, health and human rights, and cross-cultural mental health research. Previously, she worked as a mental health clinician in both school and community settings and consulted on global children's mental health issues for various international NGOs and United Nations agencies. In 2007, Betancourt was awarded a K01 Career Development Award from the U.S. National Institute for Mental Health to study modifiable protective processes in the mental health of refugee children and adolescents.

Eric Broekaert heads the Department of Orthopedagogics (Special Education) at Ghent University, Belgium. He has a long experience in the field of substance abuse treatment and research, both nationally and internationally. He founded the first therapeutic community ('De Kiem') in Belgium. He is the Chairman of the Orthopedagogical Observation and Treatment Centre for children with behavioural disorders, and of the European Workshop on Drug Policy Oriented Research. Broekaert is a board member of the European Scientific Association for Residential and Foster Care and of the Centre for Children in Vulnerable Situations and honorary vice-president of the European Federation of Therapeutic Communities. He is actively involved in a variety of national and international research projects concerning substance abuse treatment. He has authored numerous scientific publications, and is co-editor of The International Journal of Therapeutic Communities.

Charles N. Bwana obtained his Ph.D. in political science from the University of Bordeaux (France) and is currently the dean of the School of Social Sciences at Makerere University (Uganda). He is also a lecturer in the Department of Political Science and Public Administration, where he teaches courses in Ethics in International Relations, Foreign Policy Analysis and International Organization. Since 2005, he has been a senior researcher on a SIDA funded project on Conflict and Conflict Conciliation for Social Change and Development in Uganda. Specifically, his research has mainly been focusing on the processes of post-conflict adaptation in the post-conflict areas of the country.

Frank Caestecker obtained his Ph.D. in history at the European University Institute in Florence, entitled "Belgian Alien Policy, 1840–1940. The creation of Guest Workers, Refugees and Illegal Aliens" (Berghahn books, 2000). He teaches history at Ghent University and the University College Ghent (Belgium), and after his undergraduate studies he worked at the universities of Brussels, Warsaw, Osnabrück and Madison (Wisconsin, USA). He edited with Bob Moore the volume "Refugees from Nazi Germany and the Liberal European states, 1933–1939" (Berghahn books, 2010) and his research and publications relate to migration management since the 19th century in the North Atlantic world.

Javier Ciurlizza is director of the Latin American and Caribbean Program of the International Crisis Group in Bogota (Colombia), where he also served as the Americas director of the International Centre for Transitional Justice (ICTJ). He held previous positions as the director of the Institute on Democracy and Human Rights of the Catholic University at Lima, a special advisor to the Ministry of Foreign Affairs on extraditions in human rights cases, the executive director of the Peruvian Truth and Reconciliation Commission, the chief of cabinet of the Peruvian Ministry of Justice and the Secretary General of the Andean Commission of Jurists. Ciurlizza has a M.A. from the University of Warwick

(UK) and teaches at the Universidad Externado and Santiago de Cali, Colombia, and the Catholic University in Peru.

Radhika Coomaraswamy is currently the special representative to the United Nations secretary general for children and armed conflict and also holds the office of under-secretary-general of the United Nations. She is well known as an advocate of human rights, particularly the rights of children and women in conflict situations and her personal activism has resulted in the extensive awareness amongst members of the U.N. Security Council of the issue of sexual violence used as a weapon of war. Some of her previous positions include chairperson of the Sri Lanka Human Rights Commission, director of the International Centre for Ethnic Studies in Colombo, and United Nations special rapporteur on violence against women. Ms. Coomaraswamy received her B.A. from Yale University, her J.D. from Columbia University, an LL.M. from Harvard University and honorary Ph.D.s from Amherst College, the University of Edinburgh, the University of Essex and the K.U.Leuven. She is a member of the Global Faculty of the New York University School of Law and teaches a summer course at New College Oxford University.

Kathleen Coppens obtained her Master in psychological sciences (option Clinical Psychology) at the Free University Brussels (VUB, Belgium) in 2008. She is currently working as a doctoral researcher at the Faculty of Psychology and Educational Sciences of the same university and at the Centre for Children in Vulnerable Situations. Kathleen has been involved in research on the psychosocial support offered to former abducted children in northern Uganda, the cultural validation and adaptation of questionnaires on symptom behaviour, the development of questionnaires on coping and traumatic experiences of youth in northern Uganda, and mapping and analysing traumatic experiences and symptoms of former abducted children. Currently, she is conducting research on the resettlement processes of war-affected communities in northern Uganda, and on a longitudinal follow-up of the reintegration processes of formerly abducted youth.

Jaap E. Doek is emeritus professor of family and juvenile Law at the Free University of Amsterdam (VU, The Netherlands) and served as dean of its Law Faculty between 1988 and 1992. He has been a member of the United Nations Committee on the Rights of the Child (CRC) between 1999 and 2007 and its chairperson from 2001 on. Mr. Doek currently is the chairperson of Aflatoun – Child Savings International, since December 2006, a member of the Advisory Committee of the Innocenti Research Centre of UNICEF in Florence (Italy) and a member of the Board of Trustees of the African Child Policy Forum (Ethiopia). He also serves as an advisor/consultant involved in activities of the special representative of the secretary general of the United Nations on children and armed conflict, UNICEF and some governments States Parties to the CRC.

A'Nova Ettien received a Masters of public health degree from Boston University in 2006, with a dual concentration in Maternal & Child Health and Health Law, Bioethics & Human Rights. She has served one year with Teach for America in New Orleans, and two years as a U.S. Peace Corps Volunteer in Jamaica, where she worked with the Western Regional Health Authority's health education team. From 2008 through 2010, Ms. Ettien worked as a research coordinator under Dr. Theresa Betancourt at the Program on Children and Global Adversity at Harvard's François-Xavier Bagnoud Centre for Health and Human Rights. While with the RPCGA, she coordinated projects in Sierra Leone and Boston. She now works in the Pacific Northwest of the United States for Ecotrust, a non-profit organization devoted to creating reliable prosperity and social equity while protecting and preserving the natural environment.

Mulanda Juma is a Ph.D. candidate in politics, human rights and sustainability at the Scuola Superiore Sant'Anna (Pisa, Italy) and holds a Masters of commerce in peace studies from the University of KwaZulu-Natal (South Africa). His current doctoral research is entitled "Building local ownership of community-based reintegration of former combatants in the Congo through a rights-based approach". Juma is also regional peace advisor for Southern Africa of the Mennonite Central Committee. He served as the director of the Dag Hammarskjöld Centre for Peace, Good Governance and Human Rights, Zambia (2006–2008) and has field experience in peace-building from the Great Lakes region of Africa, Kenya, South Sudan and Colombia. His research interests are human security and a rights-based approach to community-based reintegration of war-affected populations.

Sarah Kamya is currently a lecturer and a doctoral student in the Department of Social Work and Social Administration, School of Social Science, at Makerere University, Uganda. She teaches Social Services Design and Delivery and Family Services and the Law and has a particular interest in the protection and advocacy of children's rights. She has worked with international organizations such as UNICEF, Save the Children and ILO/IPEC, NGOs and community-based organisations in preventing and eliminating the violation of children's rights. Her research focuses on the welfare of children living in difficult circumstances specifically those affected by conflict and post-conflict situations.

Laura Khan received her Master of Sc. degree from the Harvard School of Public Health in 2011 and her B.A. degree from Tufts University in 2006. She was a U.S. Peace Corps Volunteer in the Fiji Islands from 2006–2008 working with Indian women on social infrastructure creation, health promotion, and income-generating projects. After finishing her service she worked for the Research Program on Children and Global Adversity at Harvard's François-Xavier Bagnoud Centre for Health and Human Rights, and has collaborated extensively with faculty at Harvard's Centre for Population and Development Studies. Khan conducted field research for her thesis in Mumbai, India, in the summer of 2010 investigating slum-dwelling women's delivery practices, and will begin a Ph.D. programme in Demography and Social Policy in the fall of 2011.

Gerrit Loots is professor at the Faculty of Psychology and Educational Sciences of the Free University of Brussels (VUB, Belgium), and visiting professor at the Department of Special Education of Ghent University (Belgium) and the Instituto de Investigaciones en Ciencias del Compartamiento, Departamento de Psicología of the Universidad Católica Boliviana "San Pablo" at La Paz (Bolivia). He is running a research group on Interpersonal, Discursive and Narrative Studies in Psychology and Educational Sciences, and is director of the Centre for Children in Vulnerable Situations. His fields of interests and research are infant psychology, namely early parent-child interaction, the psychosocial well-being of children affected by war, migration, poverty and social exclusion; and psychotherapy, more specific postmodern family therapy. He has been practising family therapy since the 1980s in different counselling and therapeutic settings. At the moment, he is working from a narrative/collaborative perspective in the psychotherapeutic centre Hestia in Mechelen (Belgium), and he is also a guest trainer at different training institutes in family therapy.

Ann Lorschiedter studied special needs education in Halle (Germany). Between 2002 and 2009 she carried out research with former child soldiers in Uganda, looking at the long-term effects of their reintegration with a specific focus on the educational aspects. She also worked for AVSI, an Italian NGO, overseeing educational programs in Kitgum District, Northern Uganda. In Germany, she worked as a consultant for various German NGOs, among others in the area of global learning. Currently, she is coordinating the Volunteers' Abroad Program for Internationaler Bund in Fuerth (Germany).

Daniel Mekonnen studied law in Eritrea (Dip. Law and LL.B., Asmara) and South Africa (LL.M., Stellenbosch and LL.D., Free State). His work experience ranges from adult education teaching, to judgeship, human rights teaching and activism, editorship in peer-reviewed academic journals, programme management and leadership in active non-violent struggle, including in the non-profit sector. Formerly, he was a judge of the Zoba Maekel Provincial Court in Asmara, Eritrea's capital. At the time of writing, he was a post-doctoral researcher at the Human Rights Centre in Ghent University (Belgium) and a research associate at the Department of Constitutional Law and Philosophy of Law, University of the Free State.

Jessica Muir is senior practitioner at Dost (United Kingdom) and has worked with children and young people in a variety of contexts. Jessica's current role entails providing Dost's clients, who are mainly children subject to immigration control, with advice, advocacy and therapeutic support. Jessica focuses on helping Dost's clients to navigate the asylum process. She also regularly advocates on behalf of children to access their full statutory rights and entitlements to education, social services support, housing, health care and treatment. Jessica is interested in mental health, particularly in relation to war and conflict. She is studying child psychotherapy at the Tavistock Clinic and has an honorary placement at Newham Child and Family Consultation Service as an assistant child and adolescent psychotherapist.

Seggane Musisi is full Professor of Psychiatry and Head, Department of Psychiatry of Makerere University College of Health Sciences (Uganda). His research interests include trauma, HIV, psychiatry and consultation liaison psychiatry. His clinical work has focused on providing services to survivors of violence within community mental health and hospital settings. He also serves as consultant on local and international capacity building projects related to mental health and psychosocial programming that focus on populations affected by trauma (e.g., gender based violence, civil conflict, natural disasters).

Bo Viktor Nylund is a protection officer and legal practitioner with degrees in law and political science from Abo Akademi University (Finland) and Columbia University Law School (U.S.A.). Since 2008 he is pursuing a Ph.D. in international law on the issue of child soldiers and transitional justice at the Graduate Institute for International Studies in Geneva (Switzerland). He has served with the Office of the High Commissioner for Refugees in Geneva and Kenya from 1994 to 1996. Since 1998 he is working with UNICEF in the areas of child protection, corporate social responsibility, humanitarian policy, and human rights, based in Bangkok, Colombo, Khartoum, New York and Geneva.

James Okello, a Ugandan trained psychiatrist since 2005 with a special interest in trauma, is currently based in Gulu, Uganda. James' clinical work has focused on providing services to children and adolescents within community mental health and hospital settings. He was a lecturer in mental health at Gulu University between 2005 and 2010, and holds a position as director for the Children for Tomorrow clinic in war-torn northern Uganda and as consultant on capacity building projects related to mental health and psychosocial programming for populations affected by trauma. He also serves as a doctoral researcher at the Department of Orthopedagogics and the Centre for Children in Vulnerable Situations at Ghent University (Belgium), with research focusing on war trauma, attachment and risk behaviour among adolescents.

Kirrily Pells completed her Ph.D. (London) on rights-based approaches with children and young people in post-conflict situations with a case study on Rwanda. This was followed by a post-doctoral fellowship on a Mellon Sawyer-funded seminar series, "Fratricide and Fraternité: Understanding and Repairing Neighbouring Atrocity". She has been a consultant for Save the Children UK, CARE International and the UK Foreign and Commonwealth Office. Her research and publications relate to children and post-conflict, rights-based approaches and participation, genocide and trauma. She is currently a policy officer for the Young Lives international study of childhood poverty at the University of Oxford (United Kingdom).

Vanessa Pupavac has a bachelor of arts degree in Russian and Serbo-Croation and a doctorate from the University of Nottingham and completed her legal training in 1992. She is currently a lecturer in international relations at the University of Nottingham and has previously worked for the United Nations Criminal Tribunal for the Former Yugoslavia and other international organizations. Her research encompasses international human rights, children's rights, linguistic rights, humanitarian and development politics. In recent years she has been examining the international politics of trauma, that is, the influence of Western therapy culture on international aid policy and the rise of international psychosocial programmes. Her research is underpinned by an interest in contemporary subjectivity and the crisis of meaning in international politics.

Jeremy Sarkin is chairperson-rapporteur of the United Nations Working Group on Enforced or Involuntary Disappearances but writes in this volume in his private capacity. He is an extraordinary professor of law at the University of South Africa (UNISA), holding a B.A. and LL.B. from the University of Natal (Durban), an LL.M. from Harvard Law School and an LL.D. from the University of the Western Cape. He is admitted to practice as an attorney in the U.S.A. and South Africa. He served as an acting judge in 2002 and 2003 in the Cape High Court and as the national chairperson of the Human Rights Commission of South Africa between 1994 and 1998. He is a member of various journal editorial boards and his most recent books include 'Germany's Genocide of the Herero: Kaiser Wilhelm II, His General, His Settlers, His Soldiers' (2011); 'Reparations for Colonial Genocide' (2009); 'Human Rights in African Prisons' (2008) and 'Reconciliation in Divided Societies: Finding Common Ground' (2007).

Martien Schotsmans is a researcher at the Human Rights Centre at Ghent University (Belgium) regarding the role of external actors in the use of traditional justice as a transitional justice mechanism in post-conflict Sub-Sahara Africa (Aftralaw project, funded by the Belgian Science Policy Office (BELSPO) under its 'Society and Future Programme'). She holds Master's degrees in law and in criminology from the K.U.Leuven (Belgium). She has worked as a private practice lawyer in Belgium for over ten years, followed by several years of field work on the genocide trials in Rwanda, on the Hissène Habré case in Chad and on the Truth and Reconciliation Commission in Sierra Leone.

Elhum Shakerifar is a research fellow of the Department of Anthropology at Goldsmith University (United Kingdom) with extensive experience of working with young refugees and running participatory projects. She is also a filmmaker and producer, and a co-founder and director of the award-winning collective Postcode Films that works with schools, colleges, universities and community groups to facilitate film projects that promote active citizenship and social inclusion. Postcode's work was most recently screened at the London Film Festival and the Human Rights Watch Film Festival. Elhum has long been involved with the Trinity Centre, first as a photography workshop facilitator, then as a centre trustee and finally as assistant director of Dost, the centre's project working with separated children subject to immigration control.

Pietro Sullo holds an M.A. and a Ph.D. in international human rights law from the Sant'Anna School of Advanced Studies (Pisa, Italy). He is adjunct professor in history of justice and criminal law at the law faculty of the Ateneo Federico II in Naples since 2004. Sullo's main areas of interest include transitional justice, international criminal law and international human rights law. He has overseas research experience in Sudan, Morocco, Rwanda, Tanzania, Uganda, Guatemala, Cambodia and the United States and has collaborated with different international NGOs, focusing in particular on the challenge of post-genocide justice. Currently he is a legal teaching and research fellow within the Africa Projects at the Max-Planck-Institute for Comparative Public Law and International Law in Heidelberg, working on Sudan and Somalia. His duties include in-depth research on international criminal, humanitarian and human rights law and conducting workshops for senior lawyers in Sudan and Somalia within the framework of the MPI Global Knowledge Transfer Project targeting post-conflict societies.

Sofie Vindevogel, after obtaining her Masters in educational sciences – orthopedagogics at Ghent University (Belgium), started working at the Department of Orthopedagogics of Ghent University as a researcher. She was involved in research projects on supporting models for ethnic minority groups, effectiveness of youth care models and integrated drug policy. When the Centre for Children in Vulnerable Situations was established in 2008 Sofie became involved as a Ph.D. student. Her research deals with the psychosocial processes that former child soldiers go through after having been recruited in armed factions, as well as the resources that may support these processes, with a specific focus on northern Uganda.

Koen Vlassenroot is professor of political science at the University of Ghent (Belgium), where he coordinates the Conflict Research Group. He is also the Director of the Central Africa Programme of Egmont, the Royal Institute for International Relations in Brussels. He has carried out research in the Great Lakes Region for more than 10 years, with a particular focus on militia formation, land issues, transborder dynamics and rebel governance in eastern DR Congo and Northern Uganda. One of his latest books (with Tim Allen) is entitled 'The Lord's Resistance Army: Myth and Reality' (2010).

Michael Wessells is professor in the Program on Forced Migration and Health at Columbia University in New York (USA). His research has focused on the psychosocial impact of armed conflict, the effectiveness of psychosocial interventions, cultural supports in healing and peace-building, and the reintegration of children, including girl mothers, who had been associated with armed forces or armed groups. He has a special interest in action research and is currently principal investigator of a three-country, inter-agency project that aims to strengthen community-based child protection mechanisms by supporting linkages with national systems of child protection.

Yannick Weyns holds master degrees in law and social and cultural anthropology from the K.U.Leuven and in international relations and diplomacy from the University of Antwerp. He conducted research on the use of children's rights in the development of reintegration programs for children associated with armed forces or armed groups in South Kivu, Democratic Republic of the Congo. Currently he is working as a human rights officer for the United Nations Stabilization Mission in the Democratic Republic of the Congo. The views expressed by the author do not necessarily reflect those of the United Nations.

Lucia Withers is the senior advisor to the International Program at the Coalition to Stop the Use of Child Soldiers (UK) where she is responsible for leading the Coalition's research and advocacy on all issues relating to children's involvement in armed conflict and its prevention. Prior to this, she worked in the field of human rights including for over a decade at Amnesty International's International Secretariat (London) where she was the researcher for Indonesia and Timor-Leste. She has also worked as an advisor on transitional justice to United Nations peacekeeping and human rights missions in Afghanistan and Nepal and as a consultant on the issue of police reform and human rights.

Sandra Zaeh is currently a medical student at Emory University School of Medicine (Atlanta, USA), with an expected graduation in 2013, after having completed her master's degree in global health and population in 2009 at the Harvard School of Public Health and her bachelor's degree in sociology from Princeton University in 2007. For her master's degree she conducted research concerning the mental health system of Sierra Leone and she continues to be involved with global health work and aspires to pursue a career in global health and medicine.